Studia Fennica
Historica 18

The Finnish Literature Society (SKS) was founded in 1831 and has from the very beginning engaged in publishing. It nowadays publishes literature in the fields of ethnology and folkloristics, linguistics, literary research and cultural history.

The first volume of Studia Fennica series appeared in 1933. Since 1992 the series has been divided into three thematic subseries: Ethnologica, Folkloristica and Linguistica. Two additional subseries were formed in 2002, Historica and Litteraria. Subseries Anthropologica was formed in 2007.

In addition to its publishing activities the Finnish Literature Society maintains a folklore archive, a literature archive and a library.

Editorial office
Hallituskatu 1
FIN-00170 Helsinki

Fibula, Fabula, Fact

The Viking Age in Finland

Edited by Joonas Ahola & Frog with Clive Tolley

Finnish Literature Society • Helsinki

Studia Fennica Historica 18

The publication has undergone a peer review.

The open access publication of this volume has received part funding via Helsinki University Library.

A digital edition of a printed book first published in 2014 by the Finnish Literature Society.
Cover Design: Timo Numminen
EPUB: Tero Salmén

ISBN 978-952-222-603-7 (Print)
ISBN 978-952-222-764-5 (PDF)
ISBN 978-952-222-622-8 (EPUB)

ISSN 0085-6835 (Studia Fennica)
ISSN 1458-526X (Studia Fennica Historica)

DOI: http://dx.doi.org/10.21435/sfh.18

A free open access version of the book is available at http://dx.doi.org/10.21435/sfh.18 or by scanning this QR code with your mobile device.

Contents

Part II: Space

Part III: People

Afterword

Preface

The Project, Goals, Methods and Outcomes

VIKING AGE IN FINLAND

The chapters of *Fibula, Fabula, Fact – The Viking Age in Finland* are intended to provide essential foundations for approaching the important topic of the Viking Age in Finland. These chapters are oriented to provide introductions to the sources, methods and perspectives of diverse disciplines so that these resources and the history of discourse from which they emerge are accessible to specialists from other fields, specialists from outside Finland, and also to non-specialist readers and students who may be more generally interested in the topic. Rather than detailed case studies of specific aspects of the Viking Age in Finland, the contributors have sought to negotiate definitions of the Viking Age as a historical period in the cultural areas associated with modern-day Finland, and in areas associated with Finns, Karelians and other North Finnic linguistic-cultural groups more generally. Within the incredible diversity of data and disciplines represented here, attention tends to center on the identification of the Viking Age through differentiating it from earlier and later periods, and on contextualizing it geographically in an era long before the construction of modern nations with their fenced and guarded borders. Most significantly, the contributions lay emphasis on contextualizing the Viking Age within the complexities of defining cultural identities in the past through traces of cultural, linguistic or genetic features.

Fibula, Fabula and Fact in the Pursuit of the Viking Age in Finland

In the title of this volume, *Fibula, Fabula, Fact* refers to the triangulation and negotiation of '*facts*' about the Viking Age in Finland, sorting through the *fibulae* and *fabulae* of different disciplines. In addition to being a term for a particular leg-bone, a *fibula* is a variety of brooch. The type of fibula depicted on the cover of this volume is geographically associated with Finland and chronologically associated with the Viking Age. It has thereby become considered emblematic of Finland in the Viking Age. In the title, this fibula is emblematic of material or tangible evidence of the Viking Age in Finland as one of two broad categories of data discussed in this collection. On the other hand, this fibula is equally emblematic of aspects of evidence encountered in different fields that point directly or indirectly to the Viking Age in Finland. Thus, this type of fibula's geographical and chronological associations point to connections or continuities from the Viking Age and/or cultural contacts with Finland even when the specific examples are found in later or geographically remote burials. A *fabula* is a narrative or tale. The term is here used to refer simultaneously to the narratives in medieval sources, such as Old Norse saga literature, that offer early information on Finland in the Viking Age, and also to the epics and other stories in vernacular folklore that have been connected with the Viking Age. More generally, it is emblematic of aspects of intangible culture and heritage including language, which represent the other broad category of data discussed in this collection. In addition, 'fabula' also refers to all of the fabulous tales that have circulated in academic and popular writing about the Viking Age in Finland. It is therefore simultaneously emblematic of the social construction of the image of the Viking Age in Finland that remains vital and significant in the present day. Sorting through the *fibulae* and *fabulae* of different disciplines makes it possible to triangulate and negotiate *facts* about the Viking Age in Finland and their reliability.

Every field, every discipline works with particular types of source materials – 'facts' of data that can be analyzed. However, the term 'fact' is thus somewhat deceptive. It implies some type of absolute and incontrovertible truth, when it really means that something is – or should be – accepted as beyond controversy, or generally agreed to be 'true'. The reality is that 'facts' are socially constructed and negotiated. This does not mean that nothing is 'true', but rather that accepted 'facts' can be questioned, tested and contested from different perspectives and in relation to new data and new methods. Even construing data from raw information can never be divorced from interpretation: identifying a 'fact' of data is a process of interpretation and categorization, separating what is considered relevant from what is considered irrelevant – and perspectives may vary considerably over time and by discipline. The 'facts' that provide data for analysis and interpretation in different disciplines are subject to these processes, both on a case by case basis and more generally regarding the relevance and significance of different categorical types, whether these are spear-heads in archaeology or genres of folklore. Also subject to these processes are the broader 'facts' that provide fundamental backgrounds and frames of reference for discussion, such as that there was indeed a 'Viking Age', that during this period, groups of individuals travelled literally thousands of kilometers for trade, exploration and spiritual pilgrimage, and so forth. The fewer the layers of interpretation between a 'fact' and raw information, the more likely it will prove sustainable, but even something as simple as 'a fibula was found' could be a misidentification, misinterpretation or even a strategic misrepresentation. This is important to recognize because 'facts' tend to be taken for granted as eternal, when in reality they are placed in continuous dialogue both within and across disciplines and fields of inquiry.

Each type of source material presents its own potential evidence of different historical cultures and historical periods. In fields dealing with tangible evidence of cultures and physical processes, such as archaeology, potential evidence may be situated in an absolute chronology. However, this evidence is often extremely difficult to interpret in relation to cultures, cultural practices and its significance to living communities. Potential evidence from intangible aspects of culture, such as language and forms of expressive cultural practice, is often only documented long after the Viking Age. Such data can be much easier to interpret in relation to cultures, cultural practices and significance in society, but the potential information extractable from such data can often only be situated in a relative chronology and/or very broadly and according to a degree of probability. A significant problem has been that for the past several decades, disciplines have generally negotiated the 'facts' of their data internally or only across closely related disciplines. Opening discussion more widely across disciplines brings a much more extensive and various range of 'facts' into dialogue. An inevitable consequence of this increase of (sometimes inconsistent or contradictory) 'facts' in the discussion is that facts are tested, reassessed, negotiated. From this will follow a more generally, cross-disciplinarily viable and relevant understanding of the Viking Age in Finland, and of what can and cannot be said about it from the perspectives of these disciplines.

The VAF Project and Its Goals

The recent international interest in the question of the Viking Age in Finland has been frustrated by the language barrier. Any investigation faces the challenge that the lack of early written sources from territories of Finland and Karelia has resulted in enormous chronological gaps between the data addressed by different disciplines. Thus even within Finnish scholarship, the time between archaeological evidence and relevant evidence from linguistics or folklore opens like a ravine that at times has seemed impossible to bridge. The present volume is the product of the first stage of the interdisciplinary research project Viikinkiaika Suomessa – The Viking Age in Finland (VAF). The VAF formed as a cooperative group of scholars from different disciplines and institutions across Finland and also internationally with a primary concern of overcoming the problems of the plurality of data and working toward a nuanced, multidisciplinary perspective on the question. Thanks to the support of the Finnish Cultural Foundation, we brought together a wide variety of specialists in order to give concentrated attention to this topic and the methodological problems that it posed in an environment of cross-disciplinary discussion. Among our goals was precisely to make the outcomes of these negotiations internationally accessible, open to be engaged by international scholars through the publication that you presently have before you.

Rather than seeking to coordinate and build bridges between only two disciplines, this project seeks to develop dynamic holistic models through the triangulation of as many relevant fields and perspectives as possible. These models work toward a synthesis of insights, approaches and evidence offered by diverse disciplines while taking into consideration both the history of discourse surrounding the Viking Age as well as the strengths and limitations of the contributions from each field. Rather than fixating on whether specific features or details are or are not connected to the Viking Age, we seek to recontextualize details and perspectives in a broader cross-disciplinary perspective for the construction of a more comprehensive overview of the Viking Age for Finno-Karelian cultures and cultural areas of habitation. The present collection has been organized to meet the interest and need to open and explore discussion on the Viking Age in Finland. This is the first concerted effort to bring together representatives of these different disciplines and to address and negotiate these issues.

The first phase of the VAF project has concentrated on constructing a working definition of the Viking Age in Finland and an outline of the significance of this era in cross-disciplinary perspective. This has been a foundational endeavor for opening discussion across diverse disciplines and for negotiating understandings between them. The title of the project reflects its two sides: *time* and *space*. On the one hand, it is necessary to consider what precisely the 'Viking Age' refers to with regard to Finland and North Finnic cultures – for example, is it simply 800–1050 AD or, like the Iron Age, should it be considered to begin and end at different times than in Western Europe? Or is it indeed relevant at all? On the other hand, it is necessary to consider what is meant by 'Finland' centuries before the formation of national borders, and how or whether this should be regarded especially in relation to (or as distinct from) Lapland and Karelia. At the nexus of negotiations related to time and space has remained the central question of *people* – the Viking Age was not simply a historical period; it was a social phenomenon, and discussion inevitably returns to how it affected peoples' lives and cultures.

'Relevant Indicator' as a Working Tool

There is almost no direct evidence of the cultural circumstances in Finland during the Viking Age. In order to construct an overall picture, it is therefore necessary to seek and triangulate a plurality of diverse evidence and research results associated with different fields. To use the emblems and metaphors introduced above, the many *fibulae* and *fabulae* of different disciplines are all potentially relevant to understanding aspects of culture in the Viking Age in Finland. Assessing the relevance (and irrelevance) of particular *fibulae* and *fabulae* to an aspect of culture, to a cultural practice or to any other cultural phenomenon, inevitably involves interpretation. Placing different *fibulae* and *fabulae* in dialogue both tests these interpretations and offers the possibility of yielding new information and new perspectives on the relevance of particular data within and across disciplines. The challenge is sorting out which *fibulae* and *fabulae* from different disciplines should be placed in dialogue with one another. The VAF project approaches such evidence in terms of *relevant indicators* – potential indicators of different aspects of cultural reality that can be discerned from the data and findings of different disciplines.

Within individual disciplines, data indexing strategies are easily organized according to formal features. Across the past half-century in particular, different disciplines have developed rich infrastructures for indexing data of this type. These research infrastructures allow a single fibula or coin found in an archaeological excavation to be easily situated on a chronology because, with the vast number of examples, huge comparative surveys showed correlations between formal types and historical periods. These research infrastructures similarly allow such a fibula or coin to be situated in relation to an overall geographical distribution of other finds of the same type and the geographical distribution of places or regions where they were produced. Corresponding infrastructures similarly allow a remarkably detailed chronology of phonetic histories for different languages. In other words, the history of linguistic research has developed something like a 'map' of sound changes that enable the reconstruction of the probable earlier form of a particular word for any period in a language's history. Potential loan-words can then be assessed by comparing the probable phonetic and semantic histories of words in different languages, looking for a point where they might historically coincide. However, data indexing strategies according to formal criteria tend almost invariably to be discipline-specific.

Formal features do not work as a foundation for cross-disciplinary indexing because the data almost inevitably has different formal criteria. For example, archaeological data, loan-words and motifs from mythology may all reveal information about the historical assimilation of iron-working technologies. However, these three groups of data will not share any formal features and therefore cannot all be indexed for potential comparison according to common formal criteria. In order to accommodate this, the VAF project proposed *relevant indicator* as a discipline-neutral term that provides a tool for relating diverse data from a plurality of disciplines. A 'relevant indicator' is direct or indirect evidence of cultural processes, cultural practices or human activity. Although the relevant indicator may be realized through formal features, such as the appearance of a new style of fibula or a shift in stress in words of a language, the formal features are *indicators of* socio-historical processes that occurred in real-time cultural arenas. In some cases, the relationship to cultural features may be considered self-evident – e.g. a fishing-hook is a relevant indicator of fishing practices. However, correlation with other indicators related to settlements, livelihoods, the symbolism of cultural expression, and so forth can be triangulated for perspectives on the significance of fishing within the culture. A single relevant indicator may also prove significant to multiple developments simultaneously. For example, a new design used in jewelry could simultaneously be a relevant indicator of changes in metal-working technologies, cultural aesthetics, mythology in the images it portrays or belief and ritual activity through patterns of use. Correlating diverse relevant indicators according to themes and areas of cultural practices brings them into dialogue for the production of information. For example, the etymology of the Finnish word for 'hops' can be identified as a Germanic loan that was introduced into the language at some point during a long period in the Iron Age, but it cannot be situated more narrowly on the basis of phonetic evidence alone. When this etymological information is situated in relation to palaeoecological data on hops in agricultural practices in Finland, the linguistic loan can be situated in the Viking Age with a high probability. (See HÄKKINEN and ALENIUS.) The use of 'relevant indicators' as a cross-disciplinary indexing strategy is intended to help stimulate and advance the negotiation of diverse data across disciplines as well as to assist in the identification of bundles or clusters of relevant indicators that appear to be interconnected with common historical processes.

Methods of the VAF Project

Opening discussion across diverse disciplines can be a feat far more challenging than it may at first sound. Research disciplines do not exist in isolation from one another and the seminars which produced this volume highlighted again and again that every discipline involved was dependent on others in order to develop informed interpretations of their own data. However, tensions and difficulties arise because representatives of different disciplines work from different frames of reference. Each is embedded in a disciplinary discourse that shapes the concerns, priorities and even the very language of its representatives – they may use the same words in different ways and different words for common concepts. These challenges were increased in the second half of the twentieth century, during the era of disciplinary separatism. The same period that saw tremendous internal advances in different fields was a period in which different fields stopped talking to one another, and did not follow one another's advances. The resulting problem is strikingly encapsulated by an aphorism of Ludwig Wittgenstein (2009: 235, II.xi.327): "Wenn ein Löwe sprechen könnte, wir könnten ihn nicht verstehen" ['If a lion could talk, we would not be able to understand it'].[1] In spite of their interrelationships and interdependence, communication presents an obstacle between disciplines insofar as their representatives – immersed in a particular academic discourse's concerns and priorities – effectively speak different languages. (Frog with Latvala 2012: 11–12.) Overcoming these thresholds and opening cross-disciplinary discussions was a primary objective of the first phase of the VAF project.

This first phase was accomplished through multidisciplinary seminars hosted by the Department of Folklore Studies, University of Helsinki, in 2011 (see further Aalto 2011). These two-day seminars were methodologically oriented to opening cross-disciplinary discussion. All speakers were invited and the seminars were made free and open to the public. In many seminars, the central question of each participant in both presenting and listening to papers is: 'How is this useful to me?' In our seminars, participants were asked to arrive with the questions: 'How is what I do useful to scholars from other disciplines? How can I help to make the data, resources and insights from my field intellectually accessible to scholars from other fields? How can I help scholars from other fields to avoid using data or resources from my field inappropriately?' In order to promote discussion and facilitate understanding, each twenty-minute presentation was followed by a forty-minute period for questions. This seminar model provided a rich venue for the lively negotiation of perspectives from diverse areas of knowledge – an essential environment for sorting through the many *fibulae* and *fabulae* among the resources of different disciplines in working toward cross-disciplinary understandings of what can and cannot be said about the *facts* relevant to the Viking Age in Finland.

Discussions and debates engaged in the seminar continued into a virtual workshop environment (on which, see further Frog with Latvala 2012). The virtual workshop was organized and maintained in 2012 and part of 2013 around the circulation of selected working papers among all participants. This was done during the processes of peer-review orchestrated by the editors and the subsequent period of revision for publication. Participants in the virtual workshop were encouraged to contact and consult one another directly as well as to cross-reference other contributions and open dialogues with other papers. (*Throughout this volume, cross-references are indicated by the author's name appearing in small capitals.*) The virtual workshop was later briefly reopened in 2014, when we received comments from the peer-reviewers of the volume as a whole organized by the editor of the Studia Fennica Historica series and during the process of finalizing the text for publication. This collection is therefore the product of more than three years of discussion among the contributors in order to negotiate a broad understanding developed from the synthesis of diverse perspectives offered by many disciplines. However, this volume is simultaneously accessible as a multidisciplinary collection with clearly distinguishable approaches and points of view that posit different scientific disciplines in relation to the topic under investigation.

Perspectives in Dialogue

Across recent decades, there have been increasing movements toward interdisciplinary cooperation, yet our experience was that images of other disciplines generally tended to be rooted in what those disciplines were when they began closing off from one another – i.e. in the state of research, research methods and methodologies current in the 1960s and 1970s. There was a lack of awareness of the tremendous internal advances that has characterized individual disciplines since that time. Consequently, interdisciplinary endeavors by outsiders to a field often engaged outdated research and methodologies. Opening discussion across disciplines was a significant step in changing those perspectives. In some cases, current views and understandings in different disciplines were considered quite striking. For example, many were surprised by the perspective from historical linguistics that most of Finland and Karelia were Sámi language areas in the Viking Age. Introducing current perspectives into an extensively multidisciplinary discussion environment situated every discipline's data in new light, generating innovative new perspectives and new understandings leading to new knowledge. These discussions opened new research questions and provided foundations for further investigations that are fully interdisciplinary in nature. Perhaps the most significant overall outcome of discussion was the general consensus that every discipline was dependent on others in order to appropriately contextualize its data, and therefore that interdisciplinary discussion and networking is essential. The chapters brought together in *Fibula, Fabula, Fact* are a concrete product of the discussions and the insights that these enabled. As a totality, they help to contextualize the results in individual disciplines within a wider picture by presenting discussions across a broad range of disciplines. These chapters are particularly oriented to carry forward the raising of awareness of the potentials and limitations of different disciplines in order to provide essential foundations for informed multidisciplinary research on the Viking Age in Finland.

The title of the Viking Age in Finland project presents two intersecting areas of discussion: the 'Viking Age' as a period of time and 'Finland' or the related historical territories as a geographical and cultural space. As was observed above, these two sides of investigation are invariably concerned with inhabitants of these territories during these periods. The chapters of this volume are organized according to these three different, yet inseparable spheres of discussion: *Time*, *Space*, and *People*. Each section offers introductions to material from different disciplines allowing the reader to consider the many facets of these broad thematic areas from multiple, complementary perspectives. The introductory chapter that opens the volume offers a synthetic overview of the current and developing perspectives on of the Viking Age in Finland. This is followed by the section on *Time*, constituted of six chapters that discuss, from the perspectives of different disciplines, how the Viking Age emerges as a period, the relevance and significance of that period as a historical era, and how that period has been presented, constructed and construed in later academic and popular discussion. This is followed by the section on *Space*, constituted of seven chapters offering diverse and complementary discussions of the geographical territories concerned, the social construction of places and their relationships, and the problems surrounding identifying places in earlier periods with particular linguistic-cultural groups when the distribution of language areas has changed radically across the intermediate centuries. The final section is *People*, constituted of six chapters concerned with the populations that inhabited these times and places, their cultures and the changes that took place within them, their identities and the riddles of meaningfulness and valuations in the social environments of earlier periods. An afterward draws the volume to a close with a look at some of the common threads that weave these many chapters together and also reveals certain lacunae in the study of the Viking Age in Finland, considering both challenges and potentials for future research. Together, these twenty-one contributions unfold a multidimensional image of the role and significance of the Viking Age in Finno-Karelian areas of habitation. Together, these diverse contributions with their many and various perspectives and approaches reveal that the Viking Age in Finland was a transitional era characterized by radical changes that comprehensively reshaped the Finno-Ugric cultural environments in this part of the globe.

Helsinki,
1st April 2014
Joonas Ahola & Frog

Notes

1 Richard Macksey employed this quotation in the same capacity nearly half a century ago, when he opened the international symposium "Les Languages Critiques et les Sciences de l'Homme" ['The Languages of Criticism and the Sciences of Man'] (Macksey 1971: 13).

References

Aalto, Sirpa. 2011. Conference Report: The Viking Age in Finland Seminars: 28th–29th April, and 11th–12th November, 2011, Helsinki, Finland. *RMN Newsletter* 3: 38–42.

Frog with Pauliina Latvala. 2012. Opening Cross-Disciplinary Dialogue: A Virtual Workshop on Methodology. In Frog & Pauliina Latvala (eds.). *Approaching Methodology*. RMN Newsletter 4 (special issue). Helsinki: Folklore Studies, University of Helsinki. Pp. 7–19.

Macksey, Richard. 1971. Lions and Squares: Opening Remarks. In Richard Maksey & Eugenio Donato (eds.). *The Structuralist Controversy: The Languages of Criticism and the Sciences of Man*. Baltimore: John Hopkins Press. Pp. 1–14.

Wittgenstein, Ludwig. 2009. *Philosophical Investigations*. Ed. P. M. S. Hacker & Joachim Schulte. 4th edn. Malden: Wiley-Blackwell.

Acknowledgements

The present volume could not have been realized without the support and participation of numerous individuals and institutions. This publication is an outcome of the Viking Age in Finland (VAF) project, which was built on the energetic and enthusiastic work and effort of the founding organizing committee members, Lassi Heininen, Sirpa Aalto and Ville Laakso, in addition to the editors of the present volume. Their contributions to discussions and debate in every venue have been very fruitful and inspiring. This group was later complemented by Teija Alenius and Anna Wessman, who have believed in this research project and been equally ready to participate in it and contribute to discussion. These individuals have played key roles in shaping the development of the project and of discussion of which *Fibula, Fabula, Fact – The Viking Age in Finland* is a key outcome. The work and support of this organizing committee has been essential in the formation of this volume.

The editors would like to express their gratitude to the Finnish Cultural Foundation, for its generous financial support for the project. This enabled the organization of three public scholarly seminar-workshops of the VAF project as well as the workshops of the organizing committee in which the project was arranged and coordinated. The present volume is developed on the basis of the first two seminar workshops, held in Helsinki: "Viikinkiaika Suomessa: Suomen viikinkiajan määrittely eri tieteenalojen lähestymistapojen valossa – The Viking Age in Finland: The Viking Age in Finland Defined in the Light of the Approaches of Different Disciplines" (28th–29th April 2011) and "Viikinkiaika Suomessa: Kulttuurienväliset yhteydet ja niiden merkitys Suomessa viikinkiajalla – The Viking Age in Finland: Cross-Cultural Contacts and Their Significance in Finland in the Viking Age" (11th–12th November 2011). We are grateful to Folklore Studies and the broader Department of Philosophy, History, Culture and Art Studies of the University of Helsinki for hosting the two seminars.

We would also like to thank the authors of the present volume, who have shown admirable open-mindedness and eagerness to participate in this endeavour. These scholars have been ready and willing to share, evaluate and discuss the results of the sometimes narrow fields of research that they represent with both representatives of other fields as well as with the general public. These authors have also participated in making this volume as concise as possible, cross-referencing their discussions with other chapters of the book as well as by providing commentaries on other discussions. This volume would not have been possible without their work, and their willingness to engage with other contributions has both enriched and helped to unify this book as a whole.

Our gratitude also goes to the many participants of the seminar workshops, through whose discussion the contributions to this volume were significantly shaped. Especially important has also been the numerous anonymous peer-reviewers, who made available their time and expertise to help ensure the scientific quality of the present volume. Their number is not small and their contributions have been crucial to strengthening the individual chapters. Finally, we would like to thank the many people who have offered their support and stimulated the work with their interest - we hope that this volume meets your high expectations.

– *The Editors*

Introduction

Joonas Ahola & Frog

Approaching the Viking Age in Finland

An Introduction

> ... *could the desire for raiding be impossible for a people who, once the Viking pirates had stopped, made all of the eastern and southern shores of the Scandinavian peninsula insecure, even burning magnificent Sigtuna – right at the heart of Sweden – to the ground.* – Julius Krohn (1883: 83).

Ideas of 'Vikings' and images associated with them dance in popular imagination, shaping understandings of what life was like in Finland before the establishment of Christianity. The degree to which the Viking Age has been embraced in popular culture contrasts with the paucity of work that has in fact been done on this period and its relevance for Finnish and Karelian history. Today, a common, instinctive lay-reaction to mentioning Finland in connection with the Viking Age is to wonder: 'Were there Vikings in Finland?' This simple question conceals the problem of how 'Vikings' are understood and what we mean by 'Finland'. It betrays the challenge of considering how this historical period and the activities associated with it may have significantly impacted and even shaped the development of many different cultures. Almost paradoxically, this question simultaneously contrasts with the central role in modern popular culture of images and information associated with Vikings and the Viking Age that are used to fill out the representations and imaginings of pre-Christian Finland in the Middle Ages.

The Viking Age is a term used to refer to a period of history in Northern Europe in the late Iron Age, often defined as roughly 800–1050 AD. It is a period characterized by the mobility and expansion of Germanic populations from Scandinavia. In spite of the several multidisciplinary volumes that have been produced on the Viking Age in the past few decades, Finland has been left outside of these discourses. Extensive research has been done on the cultural and historical significance of this period for Germanic cultures of Scandinavia and for other cultures to the west. Increasing attention has also been given to the Sámi cultures in the north and to Russia in the east. Present-day Finland is politically and culturally so much closer to other Nordic countries that it has been largely forgotten in discussions of the Viking Age. Nevertheless, medieval sagas describe adventures of heroes in Finland, a major trade route passed along the Finnish coast, and the famed trading center near Lake Ladoga – Staraya Ladoga – is in a territory of Karelia. Moreover, the Viking Age appears to have had a crucial role in shaping Finnish and Karelian cultures: it is a potentially pivotal transitional period in their history, and essential for understanding their eventual emergence into the cultures we know today. Thus, the question of the potential significance of the Viking Age in Finland remains distinct from the question of whether there were Finnish Vikings.

The present collection has been organized to meet the interest and need to open and explore the Viking Age in Finland. Research in this area has been diffuse and even neglected in many fields across the past half century. This volume draws together current views, perspectives and possibilities from a wide range of research disciplines. These multiple views have opened dialogues with one another and thereby advance toward truly interdisciplinary perspectives on the Viking Age in Finland. A significant challenge in developing this area is that the research done in each discipline is most often oriented to other specialists within that particular field. It is therefore often difficult for enthusiasts, students and specialists from other fields to access (or even to find) up-to-date information and understandings. In addition, the language barrier has left international research largely unaware of much work that has been done in Finland and Karelia. A central priority of this collection is accessibility. Contributions offer introductions to the sources, research and understandings of particular fields and thematic areas relevant to the Viking Age in Finland. These introductions are intended to be reader-friendly to non-specialists in a language that is internationally accessible. The volume is intended to raise informed awareness about the Viking Age in Finland among the interested public and also to provide foundations for conversant interdisciplinary cooperation and research in the future.

This introductory chapter sets out to offer a general overview to the topic of the Viking Age in Finland, with a look at sources, discussions, challenges and controversies connected with this dynamic area of interest. It orients a reader by offering a broad survey and synthesis of the information and multiple perspectives offered by the other contributions to this collection (cross-references will be inserted with the author's name in small capitals). It is built on the discourse that evolved through the seminars out of which this publication has developed and discussions with the many participants in those events. Ideological and political tones and intentions have affected and coloured conceptions about the Viking Age throughout history, and it is therefore necessary to open this introduction with an overview of the political history of the discourse surrounding it. This will provide an essential background when turning to different conceptions of the Viking Age and issues of sources and methodology that have developed in relation to that history. The later sections of this chapter will offer synthetic overviews of the three thematic centers of the collection – *Time*, *Space* and *People* – in relation to which the concepts entailed in the 'Viking Age' and 'Finland' will be generally assessed in terms of their relevance for this part of the world. This introduction will offer a valuable frame of reference when approaching individual contributions and their dialogues with one another, as well as having value as an introduction to the topic more generally.

The Viking Age, Romanticism and Nationalism

The term 'Viking Age' has origins in nineteenth century Sweden. Sweden lost its eastern territories (Finland) to Russia in the Finnish War (1808–1809), and in this historical environment, the glorious ancient Germanic past found relevance. The word *víking* is first recorded on rune stones, of which the earliest is probably from the ninth century, and where it was used in connection with expeditions across the seas.[1] Icelandic sources from the thirteenth century unambiguously use the expression *fara í víking* ['to go raiding'] in connection with sea-raiding, and the word for a person conducting such activities, *víkingr*, hence meant 'pirate'. The use of the term took another direction in its revival through Romanticism. In 1811, the Götiska Förbundet was founded – called in English the 'Geatish Society' or 'Gothic League' – and Erik Gustaf Geijer published a poem called "Vikingen" ['The Viking'] in the society's magazine *Iduna*. "Vikingen" celebrated the adventurous life of a sea-raider, glorifying the nineteenth century equivalent of a rock'n'roll mentality: 'live hard – die young'. Artists delighted in creating images of these Germanic warriors and Esaias Tegnér composed a romantic imitation of the medieval heroic sagas, "Frithiofs saga" (1820–1825), that rapidly found fame throughout Europe. By the end of the century, the period to which these inspiring heroes belonged was considered so important that it developed its own unique term: *vikingatiden* – 'The Viking Age'.

The notion of the Viking Age was bound up with Nordic national romanticism and also with Pan-Scandinavianism, which emphasized the common roots of Scandinavian cultures. The period has been referred to in scholarly discussion with a number of different terms. Variation in these terms reflects different political trends (Aalto), different periods of research practices (Laakso) as well as the properties of the different source materials and their suitability for temporal categorization (Ahola). The earliest historical sources offering developed depictions of Scandinavian cultures were concerned precisely with the Viking Age, its adventurous warrior-poets and the martial achievements of the first kings to build 'nations' (as seen through the eyes of Romanticism) in that part of the world. The Viking Age was politically and ideologically coloured already in the process of identifying it as a distinct and significant period in history. The term developed into a technical designation for a historical period almost by accident, as an outcome of its mounting popular and political social use. It became a period named for 'Viking' activities that was formally defined as beginning in about 800 – or concretely in 793, marked by an attack in the

British Isles as the earliest recorded so-called 'Viking raid' – and ending in about 1050 – or more concretely in 1066 with the Battle of Stamford Bridge. Oddly enough, the site of the battle considered to mark the end of the era of 'Vikings' was less than 250 kilometers away from the raided abbey at which the period officially began. In this light, it is not surprising that the predominant image of the era is characterized by violence and domination by Scandinavians. However, raiding and warfare were only a small part of this period and reflect only a perhaps exceptional part of the populations living in Northern Europe at that time.

In Finland, the Viking Age was also discussed in the spirit of Romanticism. In 1809, the Swedish Empire lost Finland to the Russian Empire. The Russian Empire made Finland an autonomous Grand Duchy and indulged its elevation of Finnish language and culture with aspirations to nationhood: this provided an efficient means to break down the long-standing ties to Sweden. This indulgence opened the possibility to discuss Finnish culture in indigenous terms. During the period of the Grand Duchy (1809–1917), the models for identity were adopted either from the west or from indigenous folk culture. Opening the construction of the identity of this new political ethnos was unbounded. Distinctions between Finnic languages and dialects had not yet been defined: at that time, the 'Finnish' language began in the capital of Helsinki, spilling outward with no clear and fixed distinction of where language and culture became 'not-Finnish'. To complicate matters, the borders of the Grand Duchy of Finland were political rather than cultural and they cut straight through the territory of Karelia. This led to nationalist dreams and aspirations of creating a 'Greater Finland' (*Suur-Suomi*), inclusive not only of Karelians, but of all groups that could be considered to share in this ethnic identity – even Estonians could be identified as 'Finns'. These ideas served as an ideological basis for the aggressive warfare by which Finland attempted to expand its territory during World War II. At the same time, the cultural heritage of all of these groups could thus be appropriated and treated as 'Finnish' because it was seen as reflecting that common heritage. Much as the archaic sagas and poetry of medieval Iceland were appropriated in the service of 'Swedish', 'Danish' and even 'Germanic' identities, folk culture especially from Karelia and Ingria were, for example, central in the development of Elias Lönnrot's national epic *Kalevala* and provided profound inspiration for the national romantic art of Akseli Gallén-Kallela and the music of Jean Sibelius. Although medieval historical sources were lacking, kalevalaic poetry was readily compared and interpreted as equivalent to the medieval eddic poems and interpreted on the same premises (Ahola). The images and motifs of this poetry were read through popular Viking Age imagery as a significant frame of reference for interpretation. This frame enabled the construction of 'Finnish' Vikings and a proud heritage and national history of bold warrior-poets independent of the Swedes and other nations (Wilson 1976: 50–58).

As the Finnish language gained a stronger position in society across the nineteenth century, a counter-movement began among the Swedish-speaking population, and the magazine *Vikingen* ['The Viking'] was founded in 1870. This magazine was intended to support the cultural identity of the Swedish-speaking population (Aalto). Swedish had been the (politically) dominant language in Finland for centuries, and change in language politics was significant. Differences in language were seen to also reflect racial differences in an era when race structured the discussion about nations.[2] The Swedish national movement in Finland claimed racial supremacy as a justification of social supremacy and the privileged position of their language (Hämäläinen 1985).

The Romantic image of the blonde Viking warrior as an ethnic ideal and icon of racial superiority was certainly not exclusive to Swedish speakers, and marks of this history of discourse continue to show up in discussions of the Viking Age in Finland. This powerful image was also bound up with the construction of images of Finnishness already in the nineteenth century, reflected, for example, the paintings of kalevalaic heroes by Akseli Gallén-Kallela and in the descriptions of these heroes by the linguist Julius Krohn (1883). And this image was, of course, taken up in the defeated Germany following World War I for the racial ideology and propaganda of the evolving national socialist movement. World War II had significant impacts on the orientation of research. The ideology of constructing and championing a unifying ethnic identity developed a new, charged association with Nazism and the appeal of drawing on Germanic models in building images of Finnishness changed. The long-standing interest in constructing connections with Germanic cultures was shaken and increasing attention was turned to Russia and the cultures there. This turn was also in accordance with the new political situation in which Finnish institutions were encouraged to help maintain the status quo with the Soviet Union. These processes did not happen overnight: in research, it took time to develop new directions and approaches; a generation had to pass for the paradigms to truly change. Sirpa Aalto suggests that it was not until the 1980s that Finnish scientific discussion surrounding the Viking Age departed from the dichotomy between genuine Finnish or Swedish culture (see also Raninen & Wessman). Even today, the voices, tensions and oppositions of this complex and emotionally charged past echo up into the present (cf. Heininen *et al.*).

The 'Viking Age' emerged as a term and concept through Romanticism and it has evolved continuously in dialogue with the uses of 'Vikings' as tools of nationalism and ethnic identities. As a consequence, a single historical period on the verge of prehistory was defined and elevated as a period that could offer images to reflect and represent ideas and ideals relevant to current needs. The choices of the images used and their interpretations reciprocally constructed how the Viking Age was viewed and understood. In Finland, the Vikings have been used as ideological tools both in order to differentiate 'Finns' from 'Scandinavians' and also to identify with them as similar, equal (Raninen & Wessman). At moments of national weakness, Vikings have provided a powerful image of strength, capability and independence that whole cultures have been able to identify with. Even though this primarily served political interests and was centered in public discussion, it also inevitably affected scientific research.

Assumptions, Presumptions and the Problems They Pose

For more than a century, the Viking Age has been upheld in circulating discourse with idealized visions and a romantic aura as the manly era of adventure, force and violence. These visions still colour conceptions. Modern popular ideas of this period are dominated by images of horned helmets and sword-wielding warriors raiding and exploring otherworldly wildernesses in square-sailed ships. In Finland, popular imaginings of local history in the Iron Age tend to fluctuate between extremes of peaceful, drumming, tree-hugging shamans and tall, blond, sword-wielding Viking warriors reliant on their courage and physical strength. The national epic *Kalevala* provides names and plots, but the visualization of their roles and environs as well as how they are interpreted all take shape by imagining them through compelling images drawn and developed, with their powerful mystique, from other cultures. The images of shamanism come primarily from Sámi culture, viewed through the lens of New Age philosophy commingled with environmentalism, while the images of Vikings are built from Germanic culture, continuously re-envisioned through fantasy genres and current images of alternative popular culture identifiable with 'wild', 'untamed' and physically powerful individuals at the peripheries of social order. These images are misleading and have very little to do with history, producing profound chimeras of modern social imagination. There is no evidence of drum-beating Finnish shamans, and in fact no evidence of horned helmets used anywhere in Northern Europe in the Viking Age.[3] Deconstructing these images of 'Vikings' and of the 'Viking Age' is more important because we are naturalized to them beginning already in childhood, and the more popular, vital and compelling the image, the more likely it can shape our ideas and interpretations unconsciously. Even those who attempt to maintain historical accuracy tend to emphasize aspects of the Viking Age which are prominent and popular (or visually attractive) at the time they are working, and this reciprocally strengthens the romantic heroic image of the era.

The development and circulation of fabricated images is not unique to popular culture. Across the decades, every academic discipline has constructed and negotiated similar images, as well as construed images of other disciplines and built up ideas about approaching the 'Viking Age' and 'Finland' within each particular field. It is essential to develop shared conceptions and images in order to have a common frame of reference for discussion. Resources and perspectives within a discipline are generally quite advanced and sophisticated today, yet every discipline's perspective is haunted by a diversity of blind spots, preconceptions and infusions of popular images. Within a discipline, conceptions and images are constantly being negotiated around the source material and themes with which it connects. At those nexuses, a discipline's conceptions and images will be very critically assessed and well-grounded. Where images and interpretations extend beyond these, moving away from the reliable centers of the particular field, they will normally rely increasingly on generalizations that may be current in the field or more closely connected to stereotypes rooted in popular images. Stereotypical conceptions are produced in both scientific and popular discourses, and these can affect the result of research and also the reception of those results.

The problem of stereotypical conceptions in the construction of images surrounding the Viking Age in Finland can be alleviated and overcome by engaging with the disciplines that deal with the relevant area. In scientific discourses, this problem is especially connected with a movement toward disciplinary separatism in the second half of the twentieth century. Disciplinary separatism was connected to changes in source-critical standards. The source materials or results from other fields had not infrequently been used with intuitive interpretations according to their value for a particular argument. This sort of interdisciplinary work was heavily criticized as of low scientific value. At the same time, there was a lack of respected methods for combining disciplines or disciplinary sources, which closed off research from questions that would require an interdisciplinary approach. Attention shifted to within the more methodologically secure disciplinary sphere – sometimes without even recognizing where interdisciplinary perspectives were needed. As a consequence of this turn, many of the views outside of a particular field's nexuses of focused negotiation are rooted in the first half of the twentieth century and, from other perspectives, these views can appear quite outdated. This includes the biases against different fields, research questions and whole types of data – biases that every discipline has built up through the long, ongoing history of discourse. Such biases are not infrequently bound up with issues surrounding ideas, methods and source materials that were current for the particular discipline half a century ago. Put another way, most of these views ultimately derive from an era when craniology was an area of study for differentiating (and defining) racial groups – a discipline built up around measuring the size and shape of people's heads and that was ideologically loaded with connotations of an ethnic hierarchy of superiority. Craniology has been abandoned (although osteology, which studies bones in a wider sense, has wide-ranging applications). Today, physiological or biological trace evidence that could be considered to reflect population movements and interactions in prehistory is associated with a field that did not even exist as such at that time: genetics. Most methods and research from that era were not surrounded by the sort of moral and ethical controversies through which craniology was devalued in the public sphere. Since more fundamental methodological problems tend not to receive media coverage, outdated approaches and scholarship are easily taken up outside of the relevant field. This does not mean that the views are necessarily 'wrong', but they tend, at the very least, to be unrefined and carry misleading connotations or interpretations. These views require reassessment in relation to disciplines and research today. It is necessary to deconstruct biases and suppositions, placing the different perspectives in dialogue with one another to develop a more dynamically unified, reliable and sustainable perspective.

A positive outcome of the period of disciplinary separatism was the tremendous internal progress and development in disciplines through which the Viking Age has traditionally been approached, such as archaeology, history, linguistics and folklore studies. These have been complemented by new disciplines enabled by technologies, such as genetics (Salmela), palaeoecology (Alenius) and palaeoclimatology (Helama). There are also other younger disciplines, such as geopolitics (Heininen *et al.*) that can be tested against the Viking Age to yield new perspectives and information. Whereas advances like carbon dating and electronic databases are linked to progress in technologies, many other advancements have been methodological, such as source-critical approaches and methods for interrelating diverse data in the field of history, or practical strategies and sensitivity in archaeological excavation. Of vital importance has been the continuous development of research infrastructures that have resulted from the extensive correlation of data and analyses in each field. For example, the negotiation of literally thousands of etymologies have produced remarkably sophisticated models for the phonetic development of different languages and their contacts against which individual cases or research questions can be considered. Similarly, 'mapping' typologies of archaeological finds through space and time has enabled the fibula on the cover of this collection to be identified as a type that developed and was produced only in territories of Finland during the Viking Age (Kivikoski 1938) and certain burial practices being particular to territories of Finland in that period (Wessman 2010). Dendrochronology has been enabled by the accumulation and correlation of evidence of annual tree growth extending back from the present to before the Viking Age, producing a timeline as a research infrastructure against which any preserved piece of wood with a sufficient series of rings can be compared, and its growth pattern can then be dated to a specific sequence of years. These advances and infrastructures are, in many respects, almost revolutionary. They demand the critical reassessment of earlier data, interpretations and even of whole research paradigms. Returning to original research material in the light of modern methods, theories and infrastructures can thus produce new information, whether this is a fresh look at archival texts or a new archaeological excavation of an earlier site. When this is combined with the breadth of new information that has been produced, the new perspectives that emerge can themselves prove revolutionary.

In many cases, great internal disciplinary advances did not produce new, better-informed understandings of the Viking Age in Finland. This was in part owing to general changes in disciplinary orientation. Historical linguistics, for example, skipped past the Viking Age to concentrate on the earliest possible Germanic contacts being identified in the Bronze Age; folklore studies constructed strong biases against all historical investigations and focused almost exclusively on synchronic contexts of data collection. Knowledge and understandings that were produced within the separatist mentality were often either limited in scope or have proven unsustainable from the perspective of other disciplines. A single field of research can only produce very limited or highly conditional knowledge solely on the basis of research material specific to that field. When the image each discipline has of others often reflects the priorities, methodologies and interests prominent before they closed off from one another – envisioning them as they were in perhaps the 1960s – this can compromise arguments and interpretations by reliance on obsolete methods and interpretations that appear outdated by half a century. Outdated conceptions and stereotypes of other disciplines may have simply been recycled for generations and they continue to pose a potential pitfall to interdisciplinary research today, a pitfall that is sometimes difficult even to effectively address. Because disciplines developed independently of one another to varying degrees, they now often have different (if overlapping) frames of reference, which presents challenges when attempting to discuss and negotiate their various perspectives. As long as disciplines are closed from one another, our understanding of history remains uneven. Cross-disciplinary dialogue is crucial.

Some patterns in the way people think about the Viking Age in Finland have a much longer history and have been so prevalent that it is challenging to step outside of them and assess them critically. In international research and popular discourse, Scandinavians and Scandinavian sources dominate discussions of the Viking Age as a historical period to such a degree that Finland and Estonia tend to be conceived in relation to the Scandinavians and Scandinavian sources: even local cultural phenomena and their developments are frequently interpreted in relation to Scandinavian influence or the lack thereof. Similarly, the language shift of West Uralic (Finno-Ugric) populations with the spread and rise to dominance of Slavic language during this period tends to be discussed separately from the formation of the early Rús' state, which is discussed in relation to a Scandinavian elite while the role of the Finnic peoples has been neglected.[4] Rather curiously, Baltic cultures have for most fields tended to remain almost entirely outside these discussions although some of them "probably had a stronger Scandinavian presence and livelier maritime contacts during the Viking Age than Finland did" (Raninen & Wessman). These tendencies are the result of a number of factors, such as the relatively few significant archaeological findings, the limited scope of much research, and the language barrier which prevents most western scholars from becoming familiar with research in Finnic, Baltic or even Slavic languages. The factors are compounded by the politicization of the Viking Age and its use as a tool in constructing national identities, as foregrounded by Sami Raninen & Anna Wessman. Another major factor is the history of discourse itself, which in a sense constructs the field of vision of scholars, what receives attention, what questions get asked, and what does not. The resulting image is thus inclined to be very simplistic, especially from the point of view of the Finnic and Baltic cultures.

Other patterns of thinking belong to much broader discourses. A catch-phrase of recent discussions has been: 'Only archaeology can offer any truly new information about the Viking Age in Finland.' This is a false statement that confuses the uncovering of raw source material with information produced through the correlation, analysis and interpretation of data. This sort of claim reflects the international trend to devalue research in the humanities and give prestige status to natural sciences (even if archaeology in fact studies human cultures). Such a claim is blind to the reality that each discipline is dependent on others in order to appropriately approach specific data and assess its relevance and relationships to socio-historical processes. It should be rephrased: 'Only archaeology is likely to offer any truly new raw source material relevant to the Viking Age in Finland.' All fields are capable of producing new information about the Viking Age through the analysis and interpretation of data. In disciplines where questions of this area of inquiry have long remained unaddressed, the production of new information is almost inevitable owing to the tremendous advances in methods, methodologies and research infrastructures in different disciplines across the last half-century. However, no one discipline can produce understandings of the Viking Age in Finland outside of dialogues with other fields. It is through precisely these dialogues that stereotypes and presumptions are broken down and sustainable knowledge and understandings are attained. It is also where cross-disciplinary dialogue is active that the most new and sustainable information and understandings are developed. The present volume is the product of stimulating precisely that sort of cross-disciplinary dialogue.

Sources for the Viking Age in Finland

Perhaps the greatest challenge to approaching the Viking Age in Finland is not only that the sources are limited but also that they are so diverse that they can be difficult to relate to one another. Moreover, every discipline is characterized by its own types of central source materials and is not equipped to deal with many others. Whereas research on the Viking Age in Scandinavia or in Russia has a longstanding history of maintaining dialogue across quite diverse data, such as written history, early examples of oral poetry and archaeological evidence, there are no written documents from Finland in the Viking Age or, unlike for Scandinavia or Russia, for many centuries thereafter. There are some foreign runic inscriptions that mention locations in Finland (SCHALIN), but these present almost no information. Some foreign medieval literature presents reports of visits to and adventures in relevant territories, but these are not objective ethnographic reports: these works are normally hundreds of years later than events they describe and their representations of Finnic and Sámi cultures are often transparent projections of Germanic ideas of social order and of 'otherness' (FROG; KOSKELA VASARU). In fact, there are almost no descriptions of Finland and Karelia during the Viking Age at all – although there were attempts to use Elias Lönnrot's *Kalevala* (1834–1835; 1849) as a source, and later to use the nineteenth and early twentieth century oral epic traditions on which *Kalevala* was based (AHOLA). This produces the problem that there is no portrayal of culture, practices and mentalities of the Viking Age in Finland that can be taken as a starting point – there is no image that we can turn around and look at from different sides, comparing it and contrasting it with other

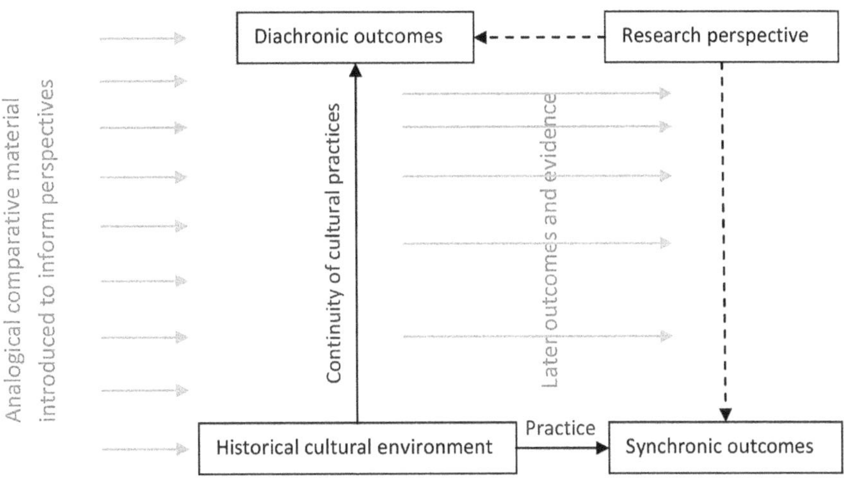

Figure 1. Illustration of tangible evidence as outcomes of synchronic processes in diachronic perspective, and intangible evidence as outcomes of diachronic processes in synchronic perspective, both of which present different aspects of a common historical cultural environment.

evidence in order to consider where it is accurate or inaccurate. However problematic the images that written sources present for studies of the Viking Age Norsemen and Viking Age Rús', they nevertheless provide a centralized frame of reference for inquiries by a full spectrum of disciplines when discussing their research. The initial images given by the written sources provided a platform for different disciplines to develop and negotiate a more dynamic understanding – which could become in many respects quite different from the initial facade offered by written texts. Without that initial frame of reference, the different disciplines are challenged to construct it from their diverse material in the very process of attempting to negotiate it for a common, critical understanding.

Source evidence for the Viking Age can be generally grouped into two classes describable as 'tangible evidence' and 'intangible evidence'. Tangible evidence is physically connected with the Viking Age in some way, such as evidence from archaeology. Intangible evidence lacks this physical connection to the Viking Age. This is evidence that has been preserved culturally through language or social practices. Although these two broad types of evidence have the potential to offer different types of access to a common cultural era, they are in most cases separated by a period of many centuries – centuries during which the culture underwent tremendous social changes and a transition to Christianity. These two classes of data are complemented by a third category of analogical material. Analogical material does not necessarily have any connection to the Viking Age or even to Finland, but can be employed as a sounding-board in order to approach evidence where sources are limited. This basic model is illustrated in Figure 1.

Tangible evidence reflects outcomes of synchronic processes and practices. In other words, something happened or was done in the Viking Age, whether natural or cultural, and the tangible evidence was produced as a consequence. These outcomes do not present the processes themselves. For example, tree rings are the outcomes of natural processes that reveal information about the climate at that time. Pollen is similarly an outcome of natural processes that reveals information about crops and flora: if we can identify *when* the pollen was produced, it informs us about plants growing at that time. This does not inform us *how* people practiced agriculture or *how* the climate affected their lives. In the same way, a burial is produced through cultural practices that take place at a certain time. An archaeological excavation can reveal the outcomes of those burial practices, but the practices themselves can only be extrapolated from what is found: the remains of a building are not the same as the earlier standing structure, nor the same as the process of building it. Outcomes of natural processes like annual tree growth occur in relation to variables in the environment with mathematical regularity. Outcomes of cultural practices are in relation to social constructions of meaning, but for the Viking Age, we lack the frames of reference in which meanings were produced. In both cases, the outcomes as evidence can be considered indicators of the processes that they reflect. The outcomes of natural processes and cultural practices intersect, for example, in the analysis of bones from a cremation burial that can reveal information about physical aspects of the cremation itself, like the temperature of the fire. Even where something can be identified as the outcome of a meaningful act, it may not be possible to determine how or why the act was significant. It is also not always clear what has been done with meaningful intent on the one hand and, on the other hand, what may be the Viking Age equivalent of a lost wallet or a discarded beer can and some cigarette butts. The problem posed by this material is that we have only a diachronic perspective on synchronically produced data, and only tiny traces survive of all of the evidence produced by these processes when they actually occurred.

Intangible evidence has been preserved culturally rather than physically – with the noteworthy exception of the genetic data of current populations. This class of evidence includes both cultural practices, or things people do, and what we will call cultural resources as a general term for popular knowledge, language, stories, symbols and so forth connected to communicating, understanding and acting. In contrast to the case-specific quality of tangible evidence, intangible evidence has circulated socially as a historical process, so any relevance of this evidence to the Viking Age must be approached outside of any specific cases. In other words, something was established in culture in the Viking Age or became established in that period and it continued to be used in some form until the present day – or whenever it was documented between the Viking Age and the present. This might be connected with something as narrow and specific as a feature in the local landscape in the case of a place name or even potentially a story about that place, or it might be something as widely circulating as the word for 'barley', the epic song of the creation of the world or techniques used when building a certain type of boat. Intangible evidence depends on a continuous history of social use, which implies a continuous history of social relevance. If cultural practices or cultural resources are not used, they are not learned by later generations and disappear. (Genetic data parallels the transmission of cultural evidence albeit with a dependence on relationships between the physicality of individuals rather than their social practices.) In order to be used, they have to have some sort of relevance to the people who use them (AHOLA). Adaptation and change is inevitable in long-term continuities of use and relevance (cf. Honko 1981: 22). This means that the evidence that can be accessed is no longer the same as it was in the Viking Age – it can only offer potential indicators of the cultural practices and cultural resources of an earlier time: the pronunciation of place-names change (SCHALIN); the semantics of words may adapt to new and different meanings (HÄKKINEN); epic, myth and rituals adapt to new ideologies and changing technologies (FROG). This also implies that the majority of cultural practices from that period and their living diversity have vanished, irrecoverably. The situation with this data is therefore the opposite of the situation with tangible data: rather than diachronic perspectives on outcomes of synchronic processes, this data offers (more or less) synchronic perspectives on the outcomes of diachronic processes. The difference is therefore not simply 'when' the data was produced, but also in the possibility to approach practices as living social phenomena.

Tangible and intangible evidence can be approached as two sides of the same coin: both connected in very different ways to social environments of cultural practices. The practical ideal of tangible and intangible data rapidly becomes complicated in realities of the evidence. Tangible evidence may have had a long history in material culture before being deposited in a Viking Age burial or an object produced in the Viking Age may have maintained a role in culture for centuries thereafter (Wessman 2010: 64, 98–101). Similarly, intangible evidence is frequently reflected in medieval, late medieval or even early modern materials that are described from foreign perspectives (cf. KOSKELA VASARU; Kirkinen 1970: 129–136), from a critical perspective of Christian authors with ideological and political agendas (cf. Anttonen 2010: 48–57), or when the evidence of cultural practices appears somehow dislocated from the earlier historical environment leaving its potential relevance to the Viking Age less certain (e.g. AHOLA; Saarikivi 2007: 212, 224–225). As a consequence, several disciplines may be relevant to considering particular data. Relating these two classes of data to one another is, however, challenging and often problematic, especially when there is a great chronological gap between them. When approaching the Viking Age in Finland, this divide is not only greater than for that for the Viking Age in Scandinavia or Russia but, much more significantly, the dialogue between them has never developed: the build-up to a critical mass of negotiating common frames of reference has never fully materialized. This obstacle is not insurmountable, and the present collection is a major step toward overcoming it.

Analogical comparative material has proven crucial to the development of frames of reference when approaching evidence of the environments and cultural practices of earlier periods. The use of analogical material has become particularly vital in archaeology and has also been essential in the development of research infrastructures in many disciplines. Analogical material is not connected to the Viking Age in Finland in any direct way. Instead, this material provides models that may present parallels and reflect patterns in historical processes and cultural practices that can be drawn on to inform perspectives where data is limited. That tree-rings can be related to climate and pollen to agricultural practice is taken for granted precisely because tree-growth and pollen production in the Viking Age can be compared analogically to these processes in more recent times. Similarly, approaches to the phonetic history of language, variation in the lexicon and connections with toponymy are approached within extensive frameworks of analogues that have been developed into general models for approaching language change. Analogical material is no less important in other areas of research when approaching conversion processes in medieval Europe or early Christian writers' descriptions of vernacular cultural practices. Such material is quite often used for methodological insights when approaching limited data. It is used when approaching persistence and change in oral poetry traditions, for anthropological and sociological frames of reference when approaching burial practices reflected in archaeological data, and so forth. Analogical data has been fundamental in the development of theoretical models for considering processes and practices as social realities.

Each field can offer different and complementary perspectives of potentially quite wide-ranging scope connecting in different ways to diverse aspects of culture and to the factors producing or resulting from socio-historical processes. Triangulating these perspectives – observing their intersections and how different phenomena appear from different sides – presents a more developed image than any one field could hope to accomplish alone. However, this cannot be done by simply lining the views of different disciplines up in a row. It is also frequently difficult to determine, among widely disparate data, what it is actually relevant to compare. The term *relevant indicator* is here used as a discipline-neutral term that provides a cross-disciplinary tool for relating such diverse data. A 'relevant indicator' is direct or indirect evidence of cultural processes, cultural practices or of human activity. A relevant indicator is always an *indicator of* and may be a relevant indicator of multiple things simultaneously. For instance, the quantity of weapons in Viking Age graves of Southwest Finland is relatively large even in Scandinavian terms. The use of these weapons in graves is simultaneously a relevant indicator of burial practices; of the value of weapons as status symbols; of cultural contacts; potentially of beliefs connected to the afterlife – and so forth. This is essentially an indexing tool for identifying intersections of data associated with cultural practices, contacts, broad areas of activity, specific meanings and so forth. In other words, this is a tool for organizing data to consider what data belongs together. This might be for comparison and contrast, such as considering weapons in these burials with other relevant indicators of weapons as status symbols, or the presence of this symbol with other relevant indicators of beliefs about the afterlife. It could also be for a grouping around a sphere of cultural activity, for example relevant indicators of other practices associated with burial, such as probable ritual lamenting as an essential part of the ritual process. The development of categories of cross-disciplinary relevance and grouping data potentially relevant for consideration together is the first step in triangulating perspectives of different disciplines.

When using 'relevant indicator' as an indexing tool, it is essential to maintain open dialogue with other perspectives across disciplines. This is particularly important regarding generalizations of scope. For example, the most emblematic markers of the Viking Age in Finland, such as the round fibulae and certain burial forms mentioned above, are distinctive relevant indicators of culture and cultural practices unique to Finland at that time. However, these markers cannot be generalized to be representative of the whole of Finland as exclusive forms, nor do they represent exclusively the Viking Age. Taken alone, any one relevant indicator is often ambiguous and potential; it is through their correlation and accumulation that individual indicators increase in probable significance in relation to their particular contexts. To take the example of weapons in the Viking Age graves mentioned above, their probabilities of being relevant indicators of cultural contacts is enabled by research infrastructures related to different weapon types that permit the identification of imports (cf. Raninen & Wessman). The identification of weapons as probable relevant indicators of status and potentially of beliefs connected to the afterlife develop especially in dialogue between the burial as a context and analogical data of the roles and significance of items appearing in burials both locally and internationally. On the other hand, intuitively inferring that the presence of weapons in the Viking Age graves is a relevant indicator of war-like raiding activities may seem 'only natural' from a modern perspective informed by popular discourse and its images of the Viking Age. However, this would be a generalization of the scope of the symbol's implications on the basis of our own constructions and biases that must be cautiously guarded against (cf. Korpela). The burial practices do not present a connection to war-like activities *per se*. The burials show that the weapons were symbolically meaningful, but not that they were meaningful *because* the weapons were actively used in raiding activities, let alone because they were used on raids by the people with whom they were buried. This remains only a possibility and requires extensive correlation with other relevant indicators of raiding in order to be critically assessed. The dating of finds and the analysis of their contexts is a process of contextualizing them as potential relevant indicators while the interpretation of the cultural relevance of individual forms of objects requires dialogue across fields.

Time

Time is an unbroken continuum. The academic periodization of history along that continuum is, perhaps inevitably, superficial. Periodization is a tool of research that is meant to help build model-like cultural contexts according to different periods of time in order to provide shared frames of reference for discussions concerning the history of different cultures. Accordingly, the periods themselves are largely constructs that reflect conformity to European historical discourse, and these shared frames of reference are centered outside of Finland. The periods therefore do not necessarily accurately reflect cultures and their historical transitions east and north of the Baltic Sea. The transitions between different periods present an additional issue when talking about one historical period as different from another. Societies and cultures seldom undergo rapid changes simultaneously on all levels, even when they experience a large-scale occupation by a foreign culture. As a rule, significant cultural changes take place across long periods of time. This is especially important to bear in mind concerning early periods in history when societies were dispersed as networks of communities with long continuities in their forms of livelihood, as in Viking Age Finland. Generalizations about a period therefore tend to highlight certain features or phenomena in culture as opposed to others, and the differences between the periods that came before and after as opposed to the continuities and fluid historical processes of change that allowed transition from one to the other. As cognitive beings, we construct categories from occasional examples and construct full images from scattered parts: the coherent understanding we construct for the Viking Age is developed precisely through the features and phenomena that get highlighted. Once established, periodizations tend to be maintained because they are normally used for categorizing new information rather than being reassessed themselves. Some of the issues of concern in this volume are precisely the appropriateness or inappropriateness of the 'Viking Age' as a period for Finland.

The use of terms from European historical discourse presents particular issues when approaching Finland, which is peripheral to (or simply outside) their basic frames of reference. Historical periods are first broadly constructed according to the inorganic materials that characterize tools and weapons in archaeological evidence: the 'Stone' Age, the 'Bronze' Age, the 'Iron' Age. Such terms are always somewhat misleading insofar as, for instance, artefacts made of stone and bronze were still in wide use long into the Iron Age. On the other hand, these periods are also used as being to some degree relative to a cultural area, hence the Iron Age began later in this part of the world than in, for example, Central Europe. It extended from approximately 500 BC to AD 1050, or for about one and a half millennia, almost coincidentally concluding the Viking Age with the Christianization of the North (cf. the legal conversion of Iceland in AD 1000) as the beginning of the so-called Middle Ages for cultures in this part of the world (see e.g. Salo 1992). Within the Iron Age, periodization is on an absolute chronology according to historical cultures that had a significant impact in Europe: the Early 'Roman' Iron Age, the 'Merovingian' or 'Vendel' Period, the 'Viking' Age. Here, for example, the Merovingian Period is commonly used with reference to the period that preceded the Viking Age in the history of Finland, yet the Merovingians ruled the Franks (from the fifth to the eighth century) and their direct influence did not extend as far as

Finland. This period is also frequently referred to as the Vendel Period, a term for the corresponding period in Swedish history. The Viking Age, as the end of the Iron Age, was followed by the so-called Crusade Period or Early Middle Ages (1050–1300), during which the Church was supposed to have become established in Southwest Finland. This, however, began well after 1050 and probably rather differently than was previously thought: politically organized religious 'crusades' to the eastern side of the Baltic Sea seem not to have begun at least for another century. The use of these terms has helped to situate cultures in Finland in relation to the rest of Europe at that time. The difficulty that they present is that many of these terms are largely arbitrary to the specific histories of cultures to the east and north of the Baltic Sea.

Applying the periodization of Western Europe as a template for the history of cultures in Finland has significant problems. First, Finland was peripheral or even beyond the periphery of the historical processes with which these periods have been developed – with the exception of the Viking Age, which belongs to a periodization specific to Northern Europe. For example, even mediated cultural and historical impacts from the Roman Empire appear to have been negligible (Raninen & Wessman). The history of cultures in Finland and Karelia were undeniably interfaced with the changing geopolitical environment of the north, but its western geographical and economic ties remained more immediate. When the Roman Empire fell in the end of the fifth century, it was in conjunction with the extensive population movements of the so-called Migration Period. The Migration Period was not simply characterized by the mobilization of populations from the steppe, but also by the significant mobilization of Germanic populations that traced their origins back to Scandinavia. This period of mobility from Scandinavia appears to correspond to a period of climatic warming trends that also affected Finland (cf. Helama). Already in the fourth century, the presumably Finnic language cultures of coastal Finland began encroaching inland, and Germanic mobility of the Migration Period probably not only produced direct interactions with Finnic groups but was also potentially a factor in the advancement of their settlements into more secure inland territories (Salo 2000: 68–69).

Following the fall of the Roman Empire, the Frankish Kingdom or Empire emerged as the center of power, comprising approximately the area of present-day France, western Germany and the Benelux countries, through which the Merovingian Period is identified. In Swedish historiography, this period is named for the parish where a prominent grave from this period was found (Vendel), identified with an indigenous center of power. However the period is designated, it is characterized for Northern Europe as the era between the mobility and expansion of the Migration Period and of the Viking Age. Insofar as these two periods are relevant to the history of cultures in Finland, the intermediate period can also be meaningfully distinguished. In Sweden, population movements and activities directed outward did not simply 'stop' at the end of the Migration Period. Contacts across the Baltic Sea appear instead to have increased. Across the end of the Migration Period and beginning of the Vendel Period, there appear to be immigrations from

Sweden to Åland on a significant (if ambiguous) scale (Callmer 1994: 18; cf. Roeck-Hansen 1991) and the trading town in Grobiņa, Latvia, was founded around AD 650 (Carlsson 1983: 38; Thunmark-Nylén 1983: 307). Marked changes in material culture associated with Germanic contacts are evident in western Finland from *c.* AD 600, or the Vendel or Merovingian Period (Lehtosalo-Hilander 1984: 289–292). Other changes in material evidence are also evident beginning from about that time (Kuusela), and, following a drop in the use of ceramics and iron production that have been considered to mark the spread of Proto-Sámi in the first millennium BC, the Sámi become manifest again in the archaeological record in the eighth century (Carpelan 2006: 81). Trade east of the Gulf of Finland had developed sufficiently by the mid-eighth century for Scandinavians to play a significant role in the founding of Staraya Ladoga (Old Norse *Aldeigjuborg* ['Fortified Town of Ladoga'][5]), the trading center south of Lake Ladoga. However, these processes were not unique to populations of Sweden: populations from Southwest Finland were also moving into this region at the end of the Vendel Period and in the Viking Age, which has equally been connected to economic factors including trade as well as population growth (Uino 1997: 141, 161, 178–179).

The Viking Age is noteworthy because, although it is named for activities in Germanic cultures, those activities were in direct and continuous interaction with populations of Finland and Karelia. In addition, the same or corresponding phenomena that stimulated the activities among Germanic peoples of this period may have also affected populations across the Baltic Sea, although these populations may not have responded to those stimulating factors in the same way. In Scandinavia, the population grew dramatically and it has been suggested that the land could not provide requirements for the traditional system of inheritance (mainly in Norway and Denmark), which pushed young men to seek wealth elsewhere (Brettell 2000: 105–110). In Finland, the period does in fact correspond with a marked variation in climate, during which Finland was warmer and drier than during preceding and later periods, although the annual weather also fluctuated remarkably, potentially making agriculture unpredictable (Helama). The data on settlements and changes in population density remains too scattered to be critically assessed (Laakso), while pollen analysis and related palaeoecological data as yet similarly only offer dispersed, localized pictures (Alenius). Nevertheless, this seems to correlate with relevant indicators of population growth in the eighth century and immigration from Southwest Finland to the vicinity of Lake Ladoga mentioned above.

In Scandinavia, the centralization of royal power increased the distance between men and their rulers on the one hand and created tensions between centralized rulers and local chieftains on the other. Although there are not indications of such centralization of authority within Finland, the process that took place in Scandinavia involved attempts to expand authority through conquests and taxation, and attempts at taxation may have reached across the Baltic Sea. It also created conditions favourable to small-group enterprises for trade or raiding oriented outside the centralized areas of authority. It was therefore not simply a period identified by cultural processes within Scandinavia, but rather as a period characterized by the interaction of cultures in Northern Europe, among which Scandinavians played a central role. This was especially enabled by sophisticated sailing technologies that Scandinavians had developed during the two previous centuries. Viking ships were lean and light with a shallow draught, enabling them to sail right onto gently sloping shores and row out again after an attack. The same ships that were suited to the open sea were equally suited to navigating even relatively narrow and shallow rivers. The period was thus not in isolation from the histories and developments in other cultures. The Viking expeditions to Europe were launched in interaction with the Europeans, as an outcome of historical processes that affected the whole of Europe. The raids did not come 'out of the blue' even if contemporary lamenting descriptions may give such impression. (See Barrett 2008.)

Raiding Scandinavians primarily made quick hit-and-run attacks on remote, minor population centres. These targets were (at least in principle) protected by strong rulers: the first Viking attacks took place when Offa ruled Mercia and when Charlemagne ruled the Frankish Empire close to its fall. The Scandinavians selected their targets presumably on the basis of the absence of a permanent military presence combined with the possibility of accomplishing the raid without allowing time to organize a defence. These strong military powers have been suggested to have reciprocally provided Scandinavians with a model for maintaining mobile armies by plunder as practice (Hernæs 1997). The collapse of the Frankish Empire in the ninth century was accompanied by a period of governmental instability from which the Holy Roman Empire arose as the new primary center of Europe. This political environment facilitated if not nurtured Scandinavian hostile activity along the coasts to the west. The activities of Viking war-bands and traders, however, seem to have been primarily oriented to immediate financial gain rather than conquest and the expansion of political authority. Even where Viking-like activities were associated with extended royal authority (such as extorting 'taxes'), that royal authority was, in essence, implemented through privateers such as a members of the king's bodyguard or even visitors from abroad rather than enacted by an established network and hierarchy of officials. This seems to be a phenomenon of the transitional period in which the extension of royal authority occurred: models for localized rule were stretched in scope while adapting foreign models, but stable ritual and bureaucratic apparatuses for executing large-scale authority had not yet become established.

As noted above, the Viking Age is customarily marked as beginning and ending in relation to events that took place on British soil: an attack on the monastery of Lindisfarne in 793 and the defeat of the king of Norway, Haraldr *harðráði*, at the Battle of Stamford Bridge in 1066. The signifiers that are chosen to identify a period easily dominate its characterization. The signifiers used to illustrate temporal differences from preceding and following eras can nevertheless easily be marginal within the scope of cultural reality or not equally prominent across a whole area. These dates identify warlike activities that may have been characteristic of Viking activities to the west but are not necessarily accurate of activities oriented to the east (Heininen *et al.*). This highlights that the process of distinguishing the Viking Age reflects perspectives. It also raises the question of whether the periodization of the Viking Age according to westward-oriented contacts – a periodization that highlights raiding – is accurate and relevant for eastward-oriented activities in which trade may have been far more significant. This consequently opens to question the relevance of this dating for eastward-oriented activities.

Although raiding took place on the coasts of the Baltic Sea, contacts in the Circum-Baltic area nevertheless exhibit a long-term continuity of positive cross-cultural relations (Heininen *et al.*). The raiding strategies undertaken from the open sea or in archipelagos were also hardly viable along the great eastern river routes. The Scandinavians began moving along these river routes already in the sixth century and were involved in establishing numerous centers for trade both before and during the Viking Age, such as Staraya Ladoga in the eighth century. Merchandise was transported along these river routes between the Baltic Sea and Byzantium on the one hand, and between the Baltic Sea and Perm or even as far as Baghdad on the other. Scandinavians seem to have traded mainly in furs and weapons, but it has been suggested that silver coming up from the Caliphate also drew large number of Scandinavians to the east (Duczko 2004: 61–64). This suggestion is supported by the evidence of a huge increase of Caliphate silver in Scandinavia during the Viking Age (see Talvio). The silver trade underscores that Finland was not merely a periphery of Western Europe but was also interfaced with the 'east' (from the perspective of Western Europe) – and indeed the territories under discussion are in fact cut through by today's customary border between Eastern and Western Europe. Independent of the fate of the Frankish state, the 'Abbisad dynasty took power (*c.* 750) and established furs as characteristic of luxury among the elite. This consequently created a rather abrupt demand for furs in the south (Kovalev 2001) and was a key factor in the opening of the silver trade. According to dendrochronology, Staraya Ladoga was founded in or before AD 753 (Kuz'min 2008), and thus it is not clear that its establishment was connected to the opening of silver trade *per se*, but the silver trade can at least be attributed with Staraya Ladoga's later significance.

The collapse of the Frankish Kingdom and the flow of silver from the south were among a constellation of factors that appear linked to the centralization of power in the expanding kingdoms of Scandinavia. Alongside these kingdoms, a corresponding centralization of power took place in Novgorod. This produced a disruption in the trade in eastern silver during the mid-tenth century – an interruption which corresponds to both the apparent break-down of the economy of Åland and the collapse of the trading center of Birka (Heininen *et al.*). The silver does not appear to have been used by the local cultures of the Finnish mainland and Karelia (Talvio): most likely silver was a commodity of 'middle men' who were oriented to trade outside of the region (Raninen & Wessman). It can nevertheless be inferred that fur trade became economically significant to the cultures of this area. Trade appears to have been generally more prominent in Scandinavian activities to the east and is well reflected in the goods from Scandinavia preserved in the archaeological record of Finland and Karelia (HEININEN *ET AL.*). From this standpoint, trade may have been a more important signifier of the Viking Age in Finland than raiding, in contrast to the perception in the British Isles.

Insofar as different disciplines concentrate on different materials, the signifiers through which the Viking Age is identified and characterized can vary, which impacts how the period is perceived in different fields. For several disciplines dealing with tangible evidence, the Viking Age is an almost arbitrary period: it is merely a particular period of time in the past, or an approximate temporal context for a given moment in which tangible evidence was produced. There may be a near-complete reliance on other disciplines for constructing the period, as for example in climatology or palaeoecology. For these and other disciplines, the Viking Age as a period from 800–1050 can appear so close to the present or such a narrow span of centuries that it is difficult to pinpoint. In linguistics, for example, the periodization of the history of Finnic languages is a relative chronology on the basis of internal development and differentiation to which other factors are secondary (KALLIO). The challenge this presents is the correlation of that relative chronology with absolute chronologies developed through disciplines such as archaeology (TOLLEY). In etymological studies of loan-words, the Viking Age cannot be differentiated within a longer historical period on the basis of phonetic and semantic features alone (HÄKKINEN), thus a narrow approach to the Viking Age is not a useful tool for periodization within the field, and corresponding challenges are faced in toponymic research (SCHALIN). Research on kalevalaic poetry has identified a number of images and motifs with the 'Viking Age', but in this material the Viking Age is both narrow and remote: the identification of material with the Viking Age is predominantly through images of the period constructed outside the field of folklore studies, and in most potential cases, it is difficult to advance beyond a probability of origin sometime in the Iron Age (AHOLA). Similar problems are faced in comparative mythology, where certain radical changes appear to have occurred in North Finnic mythologies, but these can only be approached according to a relative chronology and it is difficult to situate them more narrowly than the Iron Age (FROG). The Viking Age becomes still more difficult to pinpoint in genetic data, which considers relative chronologies of mutation on a much different scope (SALMELA). On the other hand, the conventional dating of 800–1050 as a period has also guided the absolute chronology of Finnish archaeological material to group and interpret evidence within these dates – i.e. ascribing material to an artificially imposed period rather than developing a periodization directly in dialogue with that material. As already mentioned, there are indicators of differences from earlier and later periods in this material, such as the round fibulae and distinctive burial forms (LAAKSO; cf. KUUSELA). The beginning and end of the eastern silver trade equally exhibits a rough correlation, active to varying degrees roughly from the second half of the eighth century to the end of the tenth century (Talvio),[6] about half a century off from the customary dates for the Scandinavian Viking Age as 800–1050. Another observable difference from the previous era is a shift in cultural connections predominantly to the west rather than to the east or south, and especially to connections with Scandinavia. The domination of cultural contacts with Scandinavia characterize the Viking Age in Finland, yet those contacts had nevertheless already developed centuries earlier, as observed above.

When approaching the Viking Age in Finland, identifying it with the period 800–1050 remains practical as a frame of reference shared with international research. On the other hand, this dating is more arbitrary than accurate for Finland or Finno-Karelian territories of habitation and we therefore propose it be reassessed. As stressed above, this dating is based on westward-oriented 'Viking' raiding activities, especially in the vicinity of York, with no direct connection to processes east of the Baltic. Its correlations in Finland have been produced by viewing data through the period rather than considering periods from the data. As the Viking Age transpired differently and with a different orientation east of the Baltic, it is appropriate to consider alternative dates for its periodization in Finland. Developments beginning already in the Vendel Period have been introduced above and the extensive expansion of settlements and migration, paralleling the corresponding phenomenon among the contemporary Scandinavians, appear to characterize the Viking Age in Finland, as discussed below. However, the movement especially from Western Finland to territories of Karelia around Lake Ladoga become apparent in the eighth century (Uino 1997: 174–179), the century before the Viking Age officially began in the west. Any date for the beginning of the period will be to some degree arbitrary in the continuum of cultural history. However, whereas the Viking Age in the west is marked as beginning with the first documented raid, we propose an earlier date marked by the founding of the multicultural trade center Staraya Ladoga, dated to 753 at the very latest. This situates the date relative to the territories and cultures in question, placing emphasis on the significance of trade, as well as correlating with the development of trade routes to the south and Finnic migrations from the west into the Ladoga region.

Correspondingly, the cultural processes characterizing the Viking Age in Finland did not simply stop with the dissolution of raiding activities to the west, nor does 1050 mark aggressive conversions to Christianity in Finland and Karelia that are customarily considered to define the transition from the Iron Age to the Middle Ages. However, the dating of the end of the Viking Age to 1050 leaves a gap in periodization. The subsequent era is conventionally called the Crusade Period. This term is commonly associated with the crusades in the Baltic Sea region and the crusades to Finland, which makes it anachronistic, although the name most probably originally referred to the European crusades on Jerusalem, with no clear connection to Finland. Swedish King Erik IX's initial crusade to Finland, linked to the legendary Bishop Henry, presented as the first bishop of Finland, was said to have taken place around 1150. This would antedate the Baltic or Northern Crusades east of the Baltic that began *c.* 1200. The historicity of this first crusade has been questioned (Harrison 2005: 422–423). Following the discussion of Per Olof Sjöstrand, a bishopric seems not to have yet existed in Finland when the archbishopric in Uppsala was founded in 1164. On the other hand, Swedish missionary activity among the Finns is soon indicated by a papal letter from the early 1170s and Church documents suggest that a bishopric was founded by around 1200 with its bishop under the authority of the archbishop of Uppsala. (Sjöstrand 2014.) Burial customs that are linked to Christianity in the archaeological record seem to become generally established in south-western Finland (the western cultural area in Map 4 below) across *c.* 1000–1150 (Huurre 1979: 224). The significance of these changes in practices will be returned to below, but they are in any case indicators that missionary work may have been facilitated by earlier positive contacts with Christianity. However, this process was most likely quite limited in geographical scope.

The true first crusade (i.e. a military campaign sanctioned by the Church) to Finland may have only come in 1249, following the defeat of Swedish forces at the Battle of Neva in 1240. Tension and conflict connected with religion had already been on the increase in the region, with the Northern Crusades against the heathens of Livonia (from the Gulf of Riga) in the last years of the twelfth century, Papal permission in 1229 for sites of pagan worship in Finland to be appropriated by the Church (FMU 77), and papal requests for sanctions against trade with un-Christian 'Russians' until they stopped causing trouble for the Christian Finns (FMU: 74–76). At this time, the Holy Roman Empire increasingly became a unifying center of Western Europe, entering into a complementary relationship with emerging states. Religious, political and economic aims to some degree converged or became almost interchangeable. The Battle of Neva likely resulted from an attempt to gain control of trade in the Ladoga region, a defeat that presaged Erik XI's so-called Second Swedish Crusade to 'Finland' (Tavastia, Fi. Häme) in 1249. This took (territories of) Finland under Swedish rule beneath the aegis of converting the pagan population through military force (Lind 1991). This occurred close to the end of the 'Crusade Period' (1050–1300), a term which thus generally seems more confusingly paradoxical than helpful as a tool for thinking about the history of Finland. Of course, it took the eastern and western Churches centuries to spread their authority throughout these territories, some of which were very slow to change from the cultural environments characteristic of Finnic territories through much of the Iron Age (KORPELA). The Second Crusade may appear limited in scope relative to Finland and Karelia, but it marks the division of Finland and Karelia as aligned with religiously and politically distinct spaces which culminated in the official division of the area in 1323 with the Treaty of Nöteborg. This crusade signifies the politicization of space in the spreading struggle between Sweden and Novgorod – representing eastern and western Christianity. In this sense, 1249 marks the assertion of political, economic and religious authority in the region (HEININEN *ET AL.*), and to that degree can be considered to annex Finland and Karelia into the Middle Ages.

It is impossible to avoid artificiality in dating a historical period and the validity of such a periodization is inevitably relative to different types of evidence, different regions and for different spheres of life in the past. Although the majority of contributions to this collection retain the conventional Scandinavian dates for the Viking Age (AD 800–1050), a longer periodization of the Viking Age in Finland appears both appropriate and generally more viable for multidisciplinary research negotiating the Viking Age in Finland and Finno-Karelian cultural areas. A periodization of this sort is necessary for attaining a *holistic cultural overview* for which interdisciplinary research is a tool. We therefore propose that dates for the Viking Age in Finland be assessed as from AD 750–1250. For both practical reasons of reference to the Scandinavian Viking Age and particular relevance to certain categories of data and certain territories (see e.g. Laakso) this can be distinguished as the *Early Viking Age in Finland* (750–1050) or *Viking Age Proper* (800–1050) and *Late Viking Age in Finland* (1050–1250).

Space

In international research, the territories associated with North Finnic populations in the Viking Age have usually been conceived as a periphery: it might appear on maps as a wholly uninhabited wilderness or perhaps only inhabited along a narrow stretch of the northern coastline of the Gulf of Finland, occasionally even depicted as a 'Viking' colony. This is largely a consequence of a lack of information penetrating those discussions, leaving a huge geographic expanse little more than a question mark. It is similarly common to presume that 'Finland' has always been inhabited by 'Finns' – mainly because the historical spread of language and culture has never really penetrated into popular discourse or even fully into interdisciplinary discussion. Once again, the main problem has been a lack of information and a perpetuation of views that in many cases were developed in the nineteenth century. It is therefore important to deconstruct ideas that are easily taken for granted and reframe them in a new multidisciplinary perspective. In this section, concentration will be on social, geographical and political spaces. This will include certain questions related to language distributions as well as the terms 'Finn' and 'Finn-land', whereas the discussion of cultures will be left to the following section on *People*.

Opening cross-disciplinary discussion on spaces associated with 'Finland' and other territories inhabited by North Finnic cultures meets the immediate challenge that different disciplines do not approach geographical space in precisely the same way. For climatology, defining a localized geographical area for discussion is rather like placing a picture frame over part of the fluid continuum of the atmosphere of the globe. Alternately, the study of place names is connected to the formal features of geographical spaces, while in archaeology, materials are predominantly connected to very specific locations, and not infrequently there is a tension between modern national borders and perspectives on cultural areas in earlier periods. Thus, research on the Viking Age has generally concentrated on excavations conducted in Finland and Scandinavia. On the one hand, these are also the territories where the earlier research has produced the most material, and on the other, access to perform excavations in Russia is limited. This can produce unbalanced perspectives or sometimes information simply stops at the threshold of a modern political border. These disciplines create very strong connections between 'spaces' and 'places'. Conversely, DNA, language and traditions are carried and developed socially over time, and their distribution in the present could be quite different from what it was a thousand years ago. Disciplines dealing with these types of information may face challenges of accessing research materials across national borders, but national borders may be more significant for historical process in different territories regarding the change, development or disappearance of material studied. Discussions of cultural history and genetically identified groups a millennium ago tend to be divorced from places – space becomes abstract, vague, and easily shifts into the background. In all of these cases, the disciplines that study historical cultures attempt to sketch cultural areas on the basis of evidence that is not confined by modern state borders. The use of "Finland" in the title of this volume is to be read as a provocative anachronism – an anachronism that is deconstructed in many chapters from different perspectives. It is therefore useful to begin this collection with a broad overview of the topic that can provide the reader with a frame of reference.

Every discipline can bring its own insights to discussion. Although archaeological data is often fixed to specific locations with very little information about the spaces between them, it is possible to draw conclusions that extend beyond individual excavations on the basis of different taxonomies and patterns of development (Laakso). Likewise, place names can be explored for relevant indicators of the distribution of languages, and hence the groups of peoples who used those languages (Leiviskä). These perspectives can then be placed in dialogue with evidence from linguistics, history, folklore studies and so forth in order to develop increasingly dynamic models that help to fill in the gaps in our understandings and develop an image of cultural spaces and their distributions in earlier periods.

Space simultaneously contains both the concept of a place and the concept of mobility. These two dimensions are visible in settlement patterns. Livelihoods play a central role in the social construction of spaces and their significance: how areas are identified, defined, distinguished and related to one another. The social construction of spaces is in relation to uses, usefulness and potential benefits, as well as what is familiar as opposed to unfamiliar. What is important or unimportant, valuable or useless, safe or dangerous would likely be seen very differently by groups primarily reliant on hunting and fishing as opposed to those heavily reliant on pastoral nomadism or by those invested in agricultural practices in a fixed location. In addition, the maritime environment of the southern and western coasts and archipelagos was quite different from the vast forests of the inland regions with their innumerable lakes and rivers and colder winters, and also different from the open mountainous landscape in the farthest north. These sharply different environments had implications for both the mobility and livelihoods of people inhabiting them, and therefore the people inhabiting them cannot be presumed to have been culturally uniform. The life on the coasts – and hence also the culture – undoubtedly differed from that inland, at least to some degree (see Map 1, below).

Mobility is a primary factor in the construction of space in relation to livelihoods, and there were tremendous changes in these during the Viking Age in Finland (AD 750–1250) and also in the centuries just preceding it. It is difficult to define a historical cultural area with precision. Land areas surrounded by bodies of water may appear solid on maps and it seems quite natural to conceive of these as cultural areas. This is also the case regarding Finland, which seems rather like a broad peninsula. In reality, bodies of water have been cultural contact zones throughout history, whereas forests have been entities and obstacles that separated groups from one another. Bodies of water provided an organizing framework for the development of networks of settlements in inland Finland in the Viking Age. The Gulf of Bothnia connected cultures inhabiting Sweden and Western Finland. The bodies of water provided livelihoods, such as fishing, seal hunting and bird hunting, as well as means of transportation, and they thus provided the essential conditions for trade and other kinds of contacts between people. The bodies of water also included a potentially threatening element during the Viking Age. Hill forts became common in the course of the period throughout the areas where land cultivation was practiced. They were typically constructed on hills located in the vicinity of water ways. These constructions may have functioned simultaneously as production sites for handicrafts intended for trade – secure sites for stores of marketable goods – as well as places for trading and defensive constructions in case of an attack, although their precise uses and significance remain obscure. (See Taavitsainen 1990.)

Very little is known about the potentially quite mobile communities that must have been primarily reliant on hunting and fishing and what kind of migration patterns these may have had (cf. Salo 2000). At the same time, the products from hunting seem to have been the key to trade in Finland, Karelia and in other territories around the White Sea. This would seem to suggest collective hunting activities oriented to the production of a significant surplus beyond the needs of a community. Travel over long distances may have been essential to this in order to reach, in the appropriate season, sites for trade in coastal areas along the Baltic Sea and Gulf of Finland, Lake Ladoga or the White Sea. Agriculture was playing an increased role in the Viking Age and centuries surrounding it, with different practices arriving from both east and west. The maintenance of fields in the same area affected the construction of the landscape and its importance. This created, for example, a differentiation between the domesticated landscape, delineated and developed through human labour, and the forest. It likely also significantly impacted the conceptualization of relationships with ancestors and the unseen world, for example with the concentration of the deceased kin-group in a cemetery as a permanent site in the local landscape inhabited (in some sense) by the dead (Siikala 2002: 121–138, 310). Consequently, these impacts would both construct cultures and contrasts between them.

The arrival of slash-and-burn agriculture in the east appears to have been first assimilated by Vepsian linguistic groups, and DENIS KUZMIN draws attention to a direct correlation between where Vepsian place names from the period are found and where the landscape was suited to this agricultural practice. This not only suggests a correlation of the landscape with livelihoods as cultural practice, but also between the livelihood with its technologies and a predominant language associated with those who assimilated the cultural practice. Agriculture also does not mean that settlements were unmoving. Slash-and-burn agricultural practices were founded on regularly clearing new fields and periodically changing the site even of the homestead in relation to the land being used. Where cultural life had agricultural practices as a stable center, communities were most likely still heavily dependent on a mixed economy that probably involved long periods of groups away at seasonal hunting or fishing sites and perhaps on long journeys for trade. Slash-and-burn agriculture could also be practiced as a seasonal use of landscape resources that might be at considerable distances from the homestead. The practices associated with livelihoods not only constructed space, but also place – they made locations identifiable and meaningful. Through the different types of mobility, cultural groups with the same and different livelihoods met and interacted. Populations therefore constructed these spaces and places in relation to one another, and, by implication, constructed their identities in relation to one another.

One obstacle in the development of perspectives on the Viking Age in Finland is a longstanding presumption that 'Finland' has always been inhabited by 'Finns', and if a culture was in 'Finland', then 'Finnish' must have been their language. Projecting modern understandings of 'Finns' and 'Finnishness' on the cultures of the Viking Age is as anachronistic as discussing Viking Age 'Finland' in terms of modern national borders (cf. KUUSELA). Toponymy reveals that the Sámi language was earlier spread throughout Finland, with a substrate of probable Sámi language evidence even found in Finland Proper (Salo 2000; Aikio 2007; cf. KALLIO), as well as through Karelia (KUZMIN). The Viking Age appears to have been characterized by dynamic movements among North Finnic populations including the migrations from western territories toward the Ladoga region and movements of Finnic language groups to the region of the (Northern) Dvina River basin on the White Sea, as reflected in archaeological material and toponymic evidence (Saarikivi 2006: 31–33). Janne Saarikivi observes:

> Finnic must have been spoken in the Dvina basin even in the 12th century, at the time of the appearance of the first documentary sources. It is interesting to note that at this period most of present-day Finland was still linguistically Sámi. Thus, the Finnic language area was geographically substantially different in the medieval times than at present. [...] the oldest Finnic language form in this area [the Dvina basin] was probably the closest to the southern group of Finnic languages, most notably, South Estonian. (Saarikivi 2006: 295.)

The identification of the people on the White Sea called 'Bjarmians' in Old Norse and Old English sources as speaking a Finnic language (Koskela Vasaru; cf. Frog) has supported an image of Finnic languages predominating in an unbroken continuum across all of 'Finland'. However, toponymic evidence contradicts this picture and suggests that the Bjarmians may not have been a North Finnic group at all: they may instead have been another (South Finnic or Inland Finnic) linguistic-cultural group (or several groups) participating in population movements that were stimulated in this part of the world at that time. The predominance of Finnish and Karelian across these regions in later periods is largely the outcome of processes subsequent to the Viking Age. However, the Viking Age – especially as the somewhat more flexible period of 750–1250 – seems to have been an essential phase in that process.

The social construction of territories as spaces and how these were regarded from the perspectives of different groups has an extremely long history, much of which is seen from the vantage of Germanic linguistic-cultural groups. The problematic question of whose 'land' was 'Finn-Land' presents a useful tool for framing issues of the history of cultures and their contacts in this part of the world. Evidence of 'Finns' in fact goes back roughly 2000 years. The origin of the word 'Finn' is uncertain[7] and it is not used as an ethnonym by either Finnic or Sámi speakers (Orel 2003: 103; Valtonen 2008: esp. 382). Although the terms 'Finn' and 'Finland' seem to make their first appearances through Germanic languages, Latin and Greek are the languages in which they are first documented. The Roman historian Tacitus already makes a brief reference to the *Fenni* (< Proto-Germanic sg. **finnaz*) in *Germania* 46 (late first century AD). He differentiates them from larger Germanic and Sarmatian (Indo-Iranian) linguistic-cultural groups. Tacitus describes them as the most primitive hunter-gatherers in his ethnographic survey. Half a century later, Ptolemy refers to the *Phinnoi*, and different groups of 'Finns' are distinguished in later post-Classical histories, such as the 'Skriði-Finns' and the 'Tir-Finns'. By the Viking Age, Germanic speakers employed the term *finnar* (singular *finnr*) for Sámi populations and only occasionally for North Finnic speakers, whereas North Finnic speakers were also identified by other more specific ethnonyms, such as Old Norse *Kvenir*. (See e.g. Grünthal 1997; Valtonen 2008; Aalto 2011.)[8] This has led to a common view that Tacitus's *Fenni* were in fact Sámi, mainly as the only known highly mobile linguistic-cultural group in more recent centuries. However, the term may have originally been used to refer to an unrelated linguistic group, and it should be stressed that usage of Sámi language in discussions of its distribution does *not* equate to a shared cultural or ethnic identity, and indeed such historical identities would be quite different than we tend to view them today.

Much like presumptions that 'Finland' was always inhabited by 'Finns', it is often forgotten that the Sámi were not always the 'northern neighbours' of Germanic populations. This tendency has been complemented by a general avoidance of considering the presence of any linguistic-cultural groups in the area that are not attested in more recent times, thus any groups identified and distinguished in the sources tend to be identified directly as the ancestors of present groups. However, a so-called 'Palaeo-European' linguistic-cultural group or groups are believed to have pushed into that region long before the Sámi (Carpelan 2001), and traces of this language are evident as a linguistic substrate (Saarikivi 2006: 295, 297; KUZMIN). These linguistic-cultural groups were still likely present in inland Finland and Karelia, or in any case in Northern Fennoscandia (cf. Aikio 2012) at the beginning of the Iron Age. It has been suggested that the Finnic language speakers appear to have learned the names of major rivers in, for example, Satakunta, Finland Proper and possibly deep into the Gulf of Finland from Germanic speakers by sometime around 500 BC, which would indicate that Germanic languages were established in those areas and possibly as far west as Lake Ladoga when Proto-Finnic speakers arrived (Koivulehto 1987; Helimski 2008: 75–76; Janhunen 2009: 209–210; Heikkilä 2014). Ante Aikio (2006) has shown that the Proto-Sámi language likely underwent a rapid spread, beginning in the centuries before Tacitus was writing. He considers it not unreasonable to correlate this with the spread of the Kjelmøj Ceramic Culture (*c.* 700 BC – AD 300) associated with Proto-Sámi by archaeologist Christian Carpelan (2006: 80; see discussion in Aikio 2006: 46–47; cf. however also Saarinen & Lavento 2012). The area of spread seems to have started centrally from (roughly) in the vicinity of inland territories of southern Finland and perhaps Lake Ladoga, and gradually to have progressed across Karelia and Finland and onto the Scandinavian Peninsula (and very likely also to the north and possibly to the northeast as well: cf. Saarikivi 2004; Aikio 2007: 192). It is likely that other West Uralic (Finno-Ugric) languages were among those already spoken in these territories. Toponymy reveals that many place names that the Sámi adopted were from a language or languages that were neither Indo-European nor West Uralic and that these were adopted from speakers of Palaeo-European languages (Aikio 2006; Saarikivi 2006: 257–288), as was vocabulary related to, for example, flora and fauna especially in the north (Aikio 2009). It seems most probable that the indigenous populations did not simply go extinct but rather adopted the Sámi language. As mobile cultures, a great variety of speech communities may have co-existed in interaction in these regions, potentially for millennia (Saarikivi & Lavento 2012). Thus, at the beginning of the Iron Age, Palaeo-European groups were likely the immediate northern neighbours to Germanic groups on the Scandinavian Peninsula, and there is no reason to assume that Sámi language groups were the immediate eastern neighbours of Germanic speakers in coastal Finland. Inland populations gradually seem to have shifted over to Proto-Sámi and Proto-Finnic groups began establishing an increasing presence in coastal areas. These processes were likely still ongoing at the first mention of 'Finns' by Tacitus (cf. Aikio 2006). The ethnonym 'Finn' could originally have designated these neighbours of Germanic populations that later assimilated the Sámi language. (See Maps 1 and 2.) The general topic of how groups identify and distinguish themselves and one another will be returned to in the following section. The purpose here is simply to highlight the problematics of these identifications from the perspective of research.

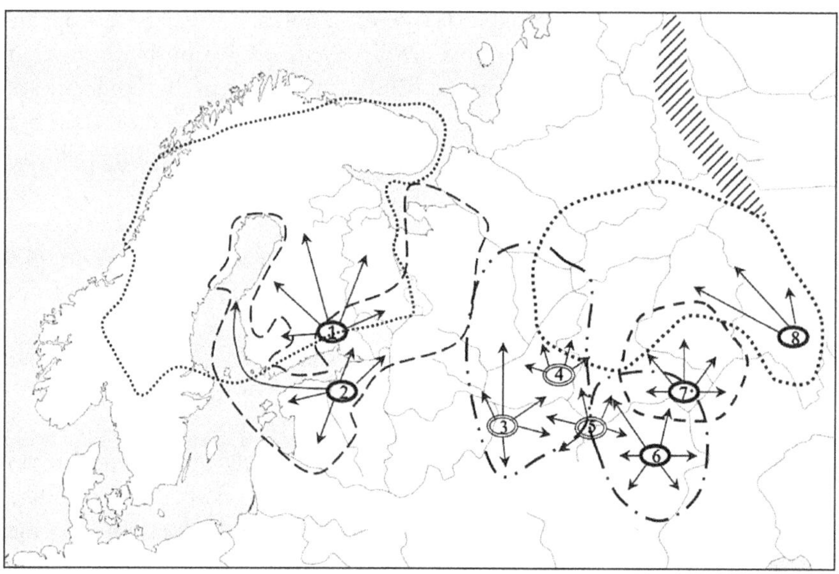

Map 1. Western Uralic linguistic homelands and their maximal spread across the Iron Age. Small circles indicate the hypothesized approximate Urheimat or 'homeland' of the language group, the area where its proto-language has supposedly been spoken. Larger enclosed areas indicate an approximate area of spread of daughter dialects or languages of these proto-languages during the Iron Age. Larger areas of spread indicate only that the language can, with a reasonable degree of probability, be considered to have been spoken within the area, without excluding the possibility of additional languages being spoken within the same area or that the language in question may also have been spoken in additional areas.

The map pictures five attested language groups and their protolanguages, Proto-Finnic, Proto-Sámi, Proto-Mordvin, Proto-Mari and Proto-Permian. All these have, with all certainty, existed, but notable problems are related to reconstruction of their speaking areas, or the early spread of their daughter languages or dialects. It also includes three hypothetical Finno-Ugrian groups, Meryan, Muroman and Meshcheran, which presently have no living daughter languages. Everything related to these languages is uncertain to the extreme.

Key: 1. Proto-Sámi, 2. Proto-Finnic, 3. Proto-Merya, 4. Proto-Muroma, 5. Proto-Meshchera, 6. Proto-Mordvin, 7. Proto-Mari, 8. Proto-Permic.
(Map and legend reproduced from Saarikivi & Frog 2014; see article for discussion.)

At the beginning of the Viking Age, speakers of North Finnic languages seem to have inhabited only or primarily southern territories of what are now Finland and Karelia. Most of the areal diversity in the Finnic language area is on the south side of the Gulf of Finland, and the centre of the language area was almost certainly there as well, the area of present-day Finland being a kind of a linguistic periphery. Sámi languages predominated in most territories and were very possibly spoken by multiple groups that might appear as different cultures in the archaeological record (see Saarikivi & Lavento 2012: 200–201). The possible presence of other undocumented languages should also not be dismissed, particularly in light of Sámi contacts with Nenets somewhere west

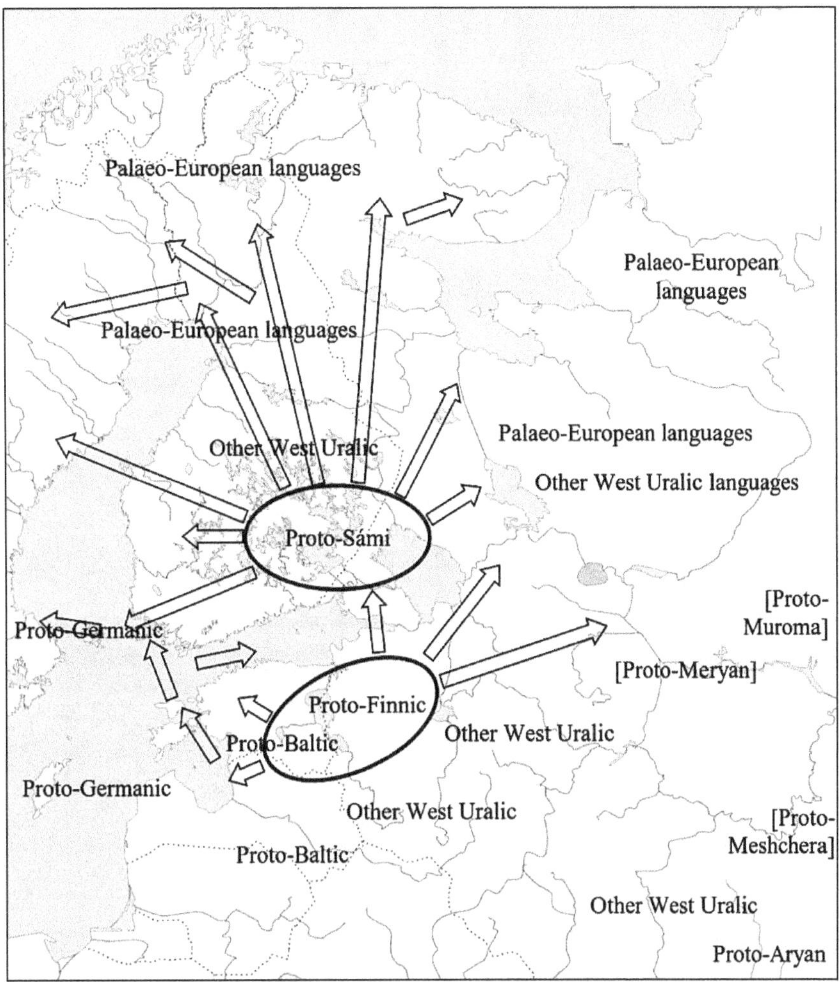

Map 2. Model of the spread of Finnic and Sámi languages from around the beginning of the present era. (Map and legend reproduced from Saarikivi & Frog 2014; see article for discussion; cf. also the view in Kallio*.)*

of the (Northern) Dvina already in the Viking Age (Hultkrantz 1985: 18–19). Christian Carpelan (2006: 81) observes that Palaeo-European languages may have still been current in areas of Fennoscandia into the Viking Age and perhaps into the Middle Ages. Language families and language isolates have survived among small populations in parts of Siberia and Northeast Asia up to the present day, and a conservative persistence of cultural practices or life ways of such a group might leave little distinctive in the archaeological record (see also Saarikivi & Lavento 2012). South Finnic or other types of Finnic languages were potentially spoken in the south-eastern area of the White Sea, and other Finno-Ugric languages and perhaps additional unknown languages as well could have been spoken in those northern territories east of Karelia. (See Map 3.)

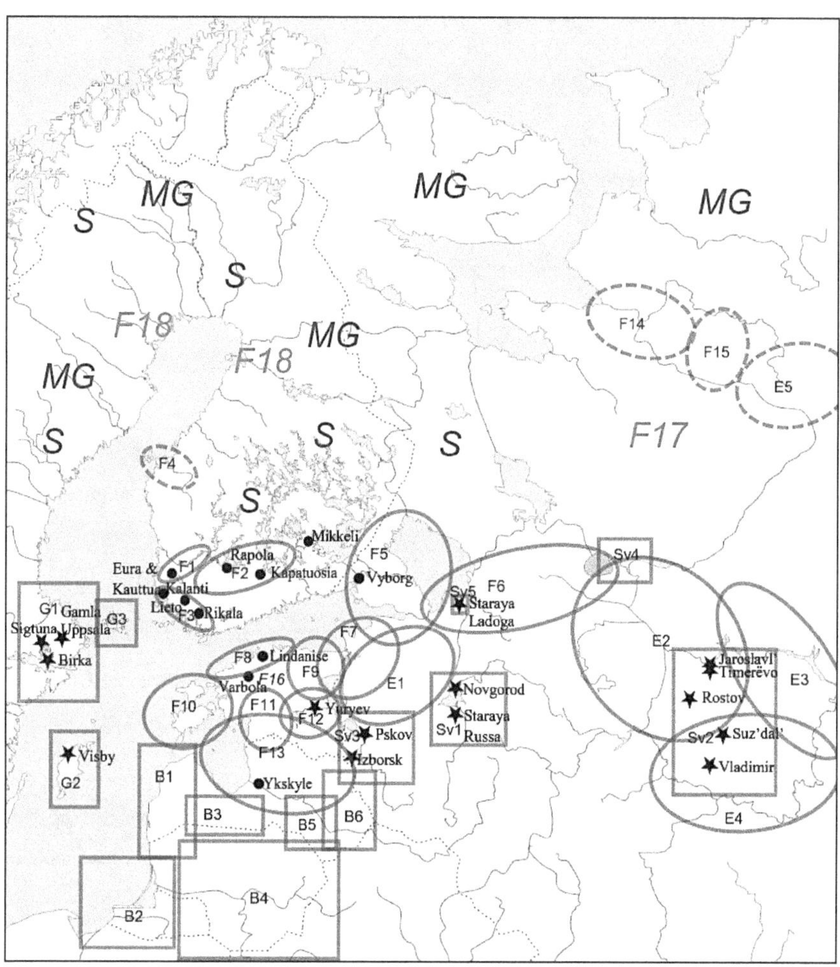

Map 3. Finno-Ugrian, Germanic, Baltic and Slavic groups in Northern Baltic Sea region around AD 1000. Stars indicate significant sites of settlement and trade that were, with certainty, established by AD 1000; dots indicate corresponding sites in the Finnic speaking regions, that were probably established by AD 1000. Circles indicate approximate areas of distinguishable tribal/ethnic entities associated with Finnic and Finno-Ugrian languages that are mentioned in the historical sources or established in the archaeological record with a reasonable degree of certainty; squares indicate similar tribal/ethnic areas associated with Indo-European languages; a dashed line indicates that the cultural area or identity under consideration is uncertain; labels without circles indicate that specifying group identities and/or their locations are problematic on the basis of historical and archaeological sources. However, they are reconstructed in their approximate areas on the basis comparative and reconstructive historical linguistic methodologies.

Key: F = **Finnic tribes** – **F1**: *Satakunta (historically attested in the twelfth century);* **F2**: *Häme (Kanta-Häme);* **F3**: *Suomi (Varsinais-Suomi or Finland Proper);* **F4**: *Kyrön kulttuuri - the area of early agricultural habitation in the Bothnia region (not necessarily Finnic):* **F5**: *Iron Age Karelia;* **F6**: *Early area of the Vepsians;* **F7**: *Early area of the Votes (on the basis of the borders of Vote Pjatina ['District']);* **F8**: *Revala maakond ['District'];* **F9**: *Virumaa maakond ['District'];* **F10**: *Saare;* **F11**: *Sakala;* **F12**: *Ugandi;* **F13**: *Livonia;* **F14**: *Bjarmia (Finnic speaking area mentioned in the Scandinavian*

sagas); **F15***: Sura poganaja (Finnic speaking area mentioned in fourteenth century Russian chronicles);* **F16***: Other Finnic (Pre-Estonian) groups (groups that subsequently appear in the Chronicle of Henry of Livonia as Harju, Alempois, Nurmekond, Mõhu, Vaiga, etc.);* **F17***: Vaga river basin (that, on the basis of historical documentation, represented people with Finnic anthroponyms in the fourteenth century and has a rich Finnic substrate nomenclature);* **F18***: Kvens (or early Bothnian Finnic settlement mentioned in the sagas; not necessarily Finnic).* **B = Balts - B1***: Curonians;* **B2***: Old Prussians;* **B3***: Semgalians;* **B4***: Lithuanians;* **B5***: Selijans;* **B6***: Latgalians.* **Sv = Slavs - Sv1***: Novgorodians;* **Sv2***: Central Russian principalities (Rostov-Suzdal, Vladimir, Jaroslavl);* **Sv3***: Principality of Pskov;* **Sv4***: Lake Beloye (Scandinavian, Slavic, West Uralic multicultural centers linked to Rostov at early stage, and later to Moscow);* **Sv5***: Staraya Ladoga (Scandinavian, Slavic, West Uralic center linked to Novgorod).* **G = Scandinavians - G1***: Svear;* **G2***: Gotlanders;* **G3***: Ålanders.* **E = Other (extinct) Finno-Ugrian groups - E1***: 'Chuds';* **E2***: Meryans;* **E3***: Muromas;* **E4***: Meshcheras;* **E5***: Toimicy poganaja.* **S = Sámi groups. MG = Mobile groups***; other hunter-gatherers (some of them probably Sámi, but many of which must have spoken other languages), some of whom also practiced limited forms of agriculture.*
(Map and legend reproduced from Saarikivi & Frog 2014; see article for discussion; cf. also Kallio; Koskela Vasaru; Raninen & Wessman.)

Language areas and the areas of the distribution of particular cultural features are not always concomitant. Language is considered today as an essential marker and emblem of ethnic identity, at least in the modern Western / European context. It is interfaced with almost every area of culture and social behaviour to varying degrees and provides an essential medium for communicating culture. However, language is also a resource and tool for communication that becomes associated with social networks, economic opportunities and potentially with prestige. This has become quite apparent in today's cultures with the roles and valuation of the English language. Ethnographic research in Lapland across the past few centuries has revealed the blurring of boundaries between languages and cultures, revealing individuals and groups that can be considered culturally to be, for example, Finnish, Sámi or Norwegian, but who would linguistically be associated with a different group. Prior to the establishment of state borders, groups and cultures developed and negotiated their own territories, local areas and the degree to which these were open or closed, as well as centers where different groups or cultures could strategically come together for trade or other cooperation.

These boundary areas and more concentrated centers can be described as *contact zones*, "or social spaces where cultures meet, clash, and grapple with each other, often in contexts of highly asymmetrical relations of power" (Pratt 1991: 34). Interpersonal contacts could also give rise to linguistic and cultural exchange. The merging of cultural features and cultural similarities is characteristic of 'border' areas and naturally results in some members of one group or culture accumulating so-called 'cultural capital' of another – i.e. cultural knowledge and skills that are valued as resources and might be marketable, such as ship-building techniques (cf. Planke 2011) or even threatening, such as ritual magic (cf. Vaitkevičienė 2008). The spaces associated with a cultural group would not be uniform: networks might be more or less dispersed, possibly among groups of other cultures, and contacts and interactions between groups and cultures would not be the same in all areas. However, certain contact zones would no doubt be established and socially recognized, like sites for trade, and within such contact zones, language itself becomes a valuable – and potentially even marketable – cultural resource. Bilingual or multilingual individuals and communities in Finland and Karelia (especially speakers of Finnic and Norse languages) probably served as valuable intermediaries for the Scandinavians approaching eastern Finno-Ugric areas (Heininen *et al.*). Although North Finnic populations do not seem to have participated extensively in eastern trade, they had the advantage of speaking a language significantly closer to the majority populations inhabiting territories to the south and especially to the north and east. These populations were still predominantly a continuum of Finno-Ugric languages and dialects at that time; they only later underwent a language shift to Slavic. To the west, Norsemen primarily interacted with speakers of Germanic languages or at least of other Indo-European languages. Finno-Ugric languages are so different from these – in an era when these languages were learned by ear and experience rather than through formal education – that the potential value of a multilingual intermediary for conducting trade or other business should not be underestimated.

When mobility is complemented by social networks with information about potential available resources, these may result in relocation and resettlement. The interests and priorities associated with livelihoods led to valuating spaces as potential resources. Such valuations combined with the more temperate climate of the Viking Age and the availability of technologies to result in migrations. The development of trade networks may have highlighted the economic opportunities for trade and drawn groups from Southwestern Finland and also Scandinavians to the east. 'Migrations' are often imagined in terms of large populations advancing across a continent in organized groups. This might be to some degree true of certain migration patterns, but migrations can also result from individuals, families and households seeking opportunities and resources where there is less competition or greater potential for gain. Recent research has highlighted that immigration takes place within networks, through existing contacts, and that these contacts are directly connected to the pull-factors of immigration – i.e. the factors that make people *want* to go precisely to a particular area (see e.g. Massey *et al.* 1993; Haug 2008: 588–590). It is very rare that immigration takes place without contact networks, prior knowledge and expectations concerning the destination. The principles of these processes are equally relevant to the Viking Age. Social networks provide essential information about where opportunities may be – they construct the relative value of inhabiting different (and sometimes unseen) spaces – while the practicalities and potentials of mobility condition where people actually go. Consequently, the movements of people were conditioned by contact networks and the practicalities of physically relocating. Bodies of water were thus potentially a central factor in directing the course of settlement patterns

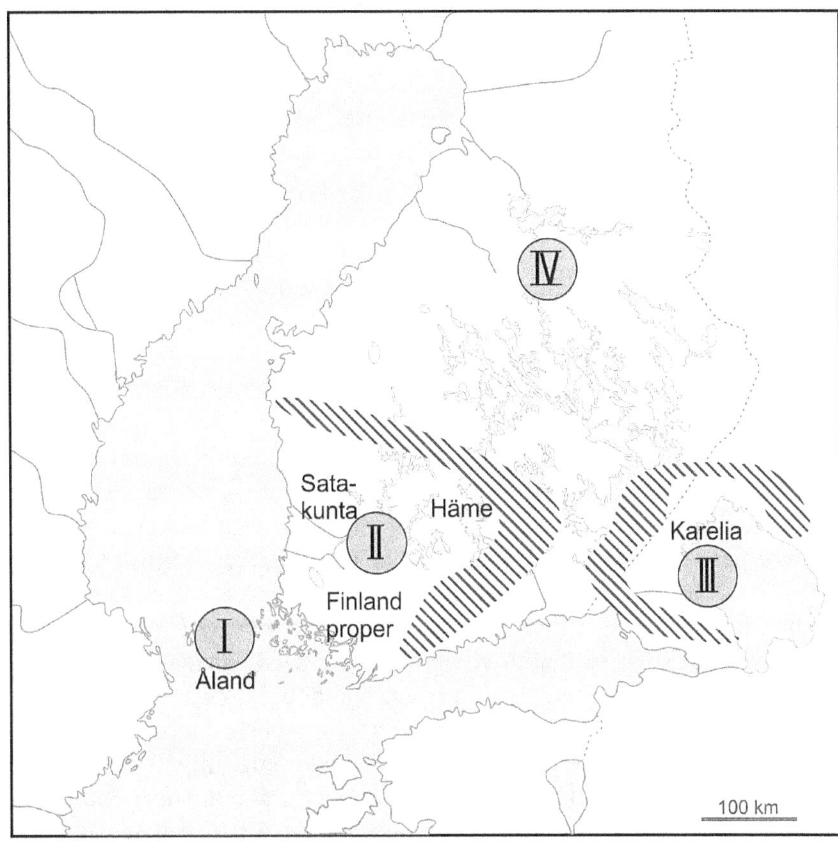

Map 4. Classic division of Iron Age 'Finland' into four cultural areas. (Adapted from Huurre 1979: 158–172.)

and determinants on the location of major settlements both in Finland and Karelia. At the same time, language and especially multilingualism must have been crucial factors in the development of networks that enabled mobility and migration across cultural areas. It therefore does not seem accidental that evidence of migrations in the Viking Age appear connected not only to waterways, but that settlement seems to precipitate in contact zones and in locations that could serve as contact zones with established inland communities (HEININEN *ET AL.*).

Research literature has traditionally differentiated four cultural areas of Iron Age Finland. These, as illustrated in Map 4, are (I) the archipelago area of the Åland Islands; (II) the western area; (III) the eastern area; and (IV) the northern area.

Beginning from the west, the archipelago area of the Åland Islands (I) appears to have been connected to the cultural sphere of the Svear of the Lake Mälaren area in the Viking Age. As noted above, there seems to have been significant immigration from Sweden to Åland during the Vendel Period and it is likely that some form of Old Norse was spoken in Åland already at that time (Ahola *et al.* 2014). They also exhibit a clearly different set of burial practices from mainland Sweden, suggestive of different beliefs about the otherworld (Raninen & Wessman). Imported artifacts, especially significant amounts of Arabic silver coins found in Åland in relation to finds elsewhere in Finland and Karelia, are relevant indicators that Åland had a more active role in the trade voyages on the Eastern Route (Talvio). This clearly distinguishes it from other territories addressed here.

In the western area of Finland (II), Scandinavian influence was especially strong in south-western Finland. The district of Satakunta [literally 'Hundred-District'] is likely a translation of the Germanic term 'hundred' to designate an administrative district in the Iron Age (see Salo 2000: 114–128). If this is the case, the name would be a relevant indicator that political structures spanned the Baltic Sea, and those structures would construct a political space with territories to the west rather than with the rest of what is today considered Finland (Heininen *et al.*). However, the place name could potentially significantly predate the Viking Age and the political structure would not itself be an indicator of the dominant language. Although western and southern coastal areas of Finland are characterized by Swedish speaking populations today, this is attributable to settlement processes that began during the Middle Ages (Meinander 1983; Tarkiainen 2008: 44–63). Place name evidence suggests that there were not Germanic language settlements in these areas in the Viking Age (Schalin), although this does not exclude the possibility of multilingualism in the area established already earlier – which would certainly be a valued competence for engaging in trade and is a likely precondition of the reception of many cultural influences. Satakunta therefore does not appear to have been a Viking Age Germanic 'colony'. Although the Scandinavian influence is quite pronounced, archeological findings such as Luistari (Lehtosalo-Hilander 2000b) indicate that an indigenous material culture developed in this area in the Viking Age.

The westernmost part of the southern coast, known as 'Finland Proper', formed an area of habitation that was separated from Satakunta by a forest zone. In this area, settlements were concentrated at the ends of long bays, and the Viking Age trading post excavated in Hiittinen (cf. Raninen & Wessman) indicates that trade was conducted at sites located at a distance from settlements. This is a potential indicator that the contacts with foreign traders predominantly concerned only a part of the society and that trade was organized in a way that kept outsiders at a distance from the rest of the community and homesteads. Archaeological evidence indicates that the inland territory of Häme also belonged to the western cultural area, principally owing to the Salpausselkä ridge system that runs roughly east to west across southern Finland. This geological feature separated Häme from the Gulf of Finland and produced basins for the remarkably extensive systems of inland lakes and rivers that characterize the area and that allowed ready access to the west. There was an eastward expansion of the population of Häme and apparently also immigration from Satakunta and Finland Proper along the Gulf of Finland to Karelia (Uino 1997; Saksa 1998). The population also expanded north along the coasts of the Gulf of Bothnia during the Viking Age (cf. Leiviskä), which is a likely location of

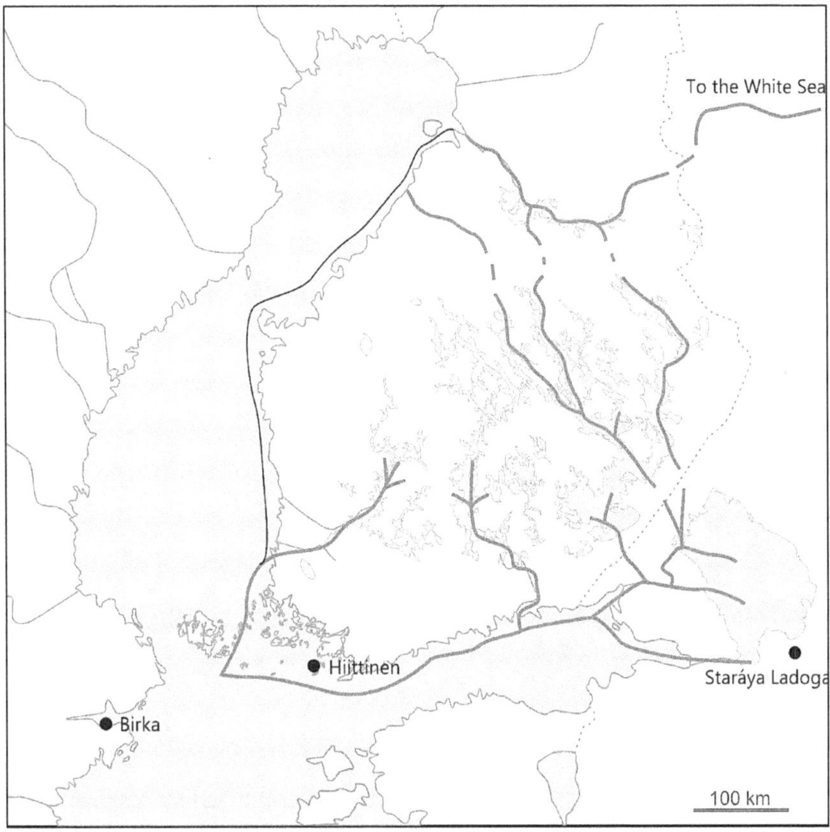

Map 5. Significant water routes of Finland (source: Julku 1967).

the 'Kvenland' mentioned in medieval Germanic sources. This migration process extended during the eleventh century, when additional inhabitants from Häme and Satakunta settled in the river valleys (Mäkivuoti 1992). Sámi settlement still prevailed in this area as well, but the earlier, predominantly Scandinavian influence in this area was superseded by the Finnic culture (Vahtola 1980; 1992).

The eastern cultural area (III) developed on the western and northern coasts of Lake Ladoga through the interaction between indigenous Finnic populations and immigrants from the western Finnish cultural area. The Ladoga region seems to have been a predominantly Finnic language area. It became one of the most important cultural contact zones of the Viking Age. Lake Ladoga was at the intersection of trade routes from the Baltic Sea to the west, from territories around the White Sea to the north, territories of Perm to the east and Byzantium to the south. The merging of especially the immigrating and indigenous Finnic groups in this environment led to the development of specifically Karelian culture during the Viking Age (Uino 1997). The relationship of the population movements and contacts in this region to the separation of North Finnic dialects into separate languages is unclear (see Kallio), but the distinctively Karelian culture

Map 6. Water routes of the Viking Age, including those associated with Scandinavian and Slavic trade routes, major routes through Finland and Karelia, and also trade routes through north-eastern Eurasia which extended these trade networks through additional cultural areas.

had fully developed by the turn of the millennium (Huurre 1979), or in the eleventh century at the latest (Uino 1997: 179, 204). Karelian settlements were centered around the mouths of water routes leading to the north along the northern and western coasts of Lake Ladoga (Julku 1967; Pöllä 1992: 437–438). The location of Karelian settlements is a relevant indicator that Karelians participated in these trade networks involved with the northern fur trade (Heininen *et al.*).

The cultures and settlements between the western and eastern territories are in many respects unclear. The area between Salpausselkä and the Gulf of Finland (where the capital Helsinki is today) has offered few signs of permanent settlement during the Viking Age. This has been presumed to reflect the restlessness and insecurity caused by the Eastern Route with potential threats of raiding, or possibly that South Finnic groups conducted satellite farming in the area across the sea (cf. Alenius), without establishing permanent settlements, as Huurre (1979: 158–159) has suggested. However, data is simply lacking. In the tenth century, the spread of western populations led to the establishment of an important settlement centre further east on the inland side of Salpausselkä in the Savo region, close to where the town Mikkeli is today. The settlers seem to have been from the western cultural area, presumably arriving via water routes passing through Häme, but the archaeological evidence reveals a gradual increase of signs of the eastern culture across the following centuries (cf. KUZMIN). Only few finds have been made on the western side of Karelian Isthmus, on the northern coast of the Gulf of Finland. It is doubtful that this lack of archaeological finds reflects that there was no one there, considering the potentially favorable living circumstances. The problem may be that the data is simply too limited and future archaeological finds could radically revise images of these areas.

The fourth, northern cultural area of Finland (IV) is both the largest and most difficult to approach. The cultures of Åland, the western areas and the eastern areas all are especially identified and approached through permanently cultivated fields and cemeteries. The indicators of culture and lifestyle that this evidence offers has been both preserved and identified precisely because of its connections to particular places. Cultural groups with more mobile ways of life left fewer indicators of their existence that were both sufficiently concentrated and historically enduring to offer an image of them in the archaeological record. This has led to the overall picture of settlements in Finland and Karelia to be biased and weighted to those groups with livelihoods of a fixed-settlement type. (LAAKSO.) The northern cultural area is also several times larger than the other cultural areas taken together, and yet offers relatively few archeological finds (cf. KUUSELA), and territories closer to the White Sea have not received as much study as those farther south. Nevertheless, it is reasonable to assume that the whole of Finland was more or less populated (cf. Carpelan 2006: 81) and that different peoples were sufficiently mobile to maintain ongoing contact for trade and exchange through extensive networks.

The mysterious northern area is characterized by several different ecological environments, including coasts on different bodies of water, inland forests and the tundra-like area of Lapland. The living conditions in the northern inland area differed radically in environment from the coasts, and very different livelihoods were likely central to these populations, with emphasis on hunting and fishing rather than on farming. It should be noted that although the domestication of reindeer as draught animals has a long history and the Sámi are often considered a reindeer-herding people today, reindeer herding seem only to have developed as a significant or common means of livelihood among Sámi across the Middle Ages – i.e. after the Viking Age – and under changing social circumstances and economic pressures (Hultkrantz 1985; cf. Aikio 2009: 206). Closer to the arctic north, in Lapland, the cold conditions and natural environment required still different kinds of livelihoods (Kankaanpää 1997). The northern cultural area of Finland cannot be assumed to be a homogenous cultural area and was more likely inhabited by multiple cultural groups. This hypothesis is supported by medieval Germanic descriptions of the Bjarmians and multiple distinct Sámi groups in the area of the White Sea (see KOSKELA VASARU). Very little is known about many of the cultures that were neighbours of the

Pre-Finnish and Pre-Karelian cultures, but reciprocal influence through these contact networks is likely (cf. Frog). Future research on these cultures and their roles in the cultural processes that were taking place in Northern Europe may lead to significant revisions of how cultures in these territories, and in Northeast Europe more generally, are understood.

The four cultural areas discussed above, into which Iron Age Finland is customarily divided in research, are developed mainly on the basis of archaeological evidence. These hardly depict the actual cultural distribution in each area concerning all cultural spheres, such as language, rituals and livelihoods. Even this sort of simple map is leaves many open questions, such as the identity of 'Kvenlanders' or their cultural influence in the North (see Kuusela). The comparison of different possible maps drawn on the basis of different sources and perspectives gives a glimpse of the complexity and fluidity of cultural phenomena that are connected to Finland as a large, concrete place.

The social construction of spaces in Finland and Karelia changed dramatically across the Viking Age. Just as mobility and population movements centrally characterized the Viking Age in the Germanic world, mobility played a central role in defining the Viking Age in Finland. Certain factors that presented essential conditions for this process were changes in climate and developing technologies within broader contact networks. The change in climate affected both the usability of spaces, for example in relation to agricultural practices, and alleviated the potential harshness of the inland climate more generally (Helama). It also increased possibilities for mobility. This is most pronounced in the opening of a sea route via the Barents Sea to the White Sea for trade. It also doubtless impacted the periods during which water routes inland were viable, and possibly the viability of overland routes as well (cf. Heininen *et al.*; Kuusela). Lassi Heininen has repeatedly stressed that mobility of the Viking Age defined Northern Europe as a unified area for the first time owing to networks of this type (see Heininen *et al.*). Mobility also seems to have redefined conceptions of spaces, how they relate to one another, and the relations of cultures inhabiting them in this period (Korpela).

A key factor that emerged in this process was Lake Ladoga as a nexus of long-distance trade routes that were rapidly opening with the changes in technology. Unlike the Norse Vikings, Finnic populations were not oriented to expansion outward via the open sea. Instead, they were oriented north and east, with particular attention to inland water routes. Interestingly, there does not appear to have been a competition in settlement of these areas with the Norse cultural expansion, although these areas clearly participated in cultural exchange and were vital to extended trade networks. Although these territories often appear peripheral from the perspective of Viking Age Germanic cultures, the pull of immigration to the Ladoga region in particular and its situation at the intersection of extended trade routes to the north, south, east and west suggest that it was a center, and not just a center for populations of Finland and Karelia, but also for Estonia and regions to the south, as well as for regions further east – a center for territories and cultures with less direct contact and connection to Germanic cultures and populations. The Viking Age in Finland can therefore be characterized through mobility and expansion that redefined cultural spaces in relation to extensive networks, much as it has been defined for Norse cultures, but with a different directional orientation and with a different center.

People

Perhaps the most subtly implicit aspect of all discussions surrounding the Viking Age is its anthropocentricity – it is always, in one way or another, connected with people. Interest and concerns invariably return to connections with what people did, their identities, beliefs, languages, relationships to one another and to other groups and cultures. People are integral to any phenomenon related to culture and cultural history. Nevertheless, an inclination to abstract and idealize different aspects of culture – as though they were somehow independent of the people who used them – has predominated across the long history of scholarship. The rising awareness of the significance of the individual and social processes has had a transformative effect on how history and cultural processes are viewed.

'People' are physically embodied social beings. It is easy to lose sight of the physicality of people in the past when the individuals themselves have become so remote from the present. It is equally easy to forget that people organize objects, spaces and practices in relation to their bodies and to the physical environment that surrounds them. Perhaps more challenging is the awareness that individual and social identities are constructed through exposure to and participation in cultural practices. People are social beings, and participate in communities. This leads individuals to develop roles *in relation to one another* as well as identities of social networks and communities *in relation to others*. This relational aspect produces perspectives on features of similarity or difference in language, dress, behaviour and other cultural practices. Such features become regarded as distinctive markers of different roles or groups; they can form constellations (e.g. language, dress and adornments) that, when they are encountered together, act as markers for different types of identities. In other words, the features become meaningful according to social discourses concerning who uses them and who does not (cf. Agha 2011). In many pre-modern cultural environments, transitions between roles and identification with different social groups could be stringently regulated and carefully managed through ritual practices (cf. van Gennep 1960). Consequently, the markers of those roles and identities would become charged as a meaningful and important distinction that would allow them to become quite pronounced. Rather than existing constantly and universally, anything that is potentially meaningful, and how it is socially perceived alone or in combination with other features, is subject to an on-going process of *enregisterment* (Agha 2007). In other words, features are in a continuous process of being identified as having meaningful associations with different roles, groups and cultural practices.

In archaeology, for example, jewellery, weapons or other artefacts included in a burial are all considered potential relevant indicators of the identity of the individual buried, as are the practices involved in the funerary rites, such scattering cremated remains or placing them in a pot; burying a body prone or curled up; orienting a grave east–west or north–south. These are all expressions of cultural practices, and therefore indicators of culture. These expressions are also connected to identities and roles within that culture, such as man and woman, warrior and queen, lord and slave. It can also be presumed on the basis of analogical evidence that language and other cultural practices were also enregistered, allowing them to function as relevant indicators of different roles and of belongingness to different social groups and networks.

The archaeological record primarily reflects one type of community in the social realities of the Viking Age – the physical and embodied community. It is therefore easy to overlook the fact that not all social beings were physically embodied according to modern understandings. One such alternative community is comprised of the dead. Burial practices both reflect and reinforce understandings of the dead and ideas about what follows death. Within the framework of pre-modern cultures of the North, funerary rituals disintegrated an individual from the living community and ensured that individual's integration into a community of the dead. Analogical evidence and probable continuities in later folklore suggest that interactions with a community of the dead did not stop with the funeral rites. Interaction was maintained through organized commemoration rituals and also through non-ritual visits, although these too might be regulated by taboos or require actions such as a food offering. This in fact continued to be the case in Russian Karelia, although the traditions waned in the nineteenth century and were greatly disrupted during the Soviet period (Konkka 1985). These activities were done with an understanding that the dead had reality as a community and the community of the dead had the potential to help or harm individuals among the living and to influence their livelihood more generally (cf. Stepanova 2011; 2012). Similarly, divine beings were recognized as having residences and even communities in remote otherworld locations. The nature of these residences and communities could vary significantly across cultural groups because they were almost certainly imagined centrally through the culture's own types of residences, social structures and livelihoods, and viewed through that lens (cf. Durkheim 1915). Thus, hunter-gathering cultures are unlikely to situate their divine beings as living on fixed farmsteads or in walled fortresses while agricultural communities living in fixed structures are unlikely to continue imagining their gods living in tents – or if they did, this would reflect the enregisterment of these alternative dwellings and ways of living. In other words, it would reflect how people regarded them in relation to their own livelihoods. Most often forgotten, however, is that the landscape itself was almost certainly regarded as inhabited or alive with mythic forces – i.e. that a lake or a forest was an entity with power to take or give – and it was a social reality that hunting, fishing, travel, tending livestock, building boats and so forth all required ongoing relationships with the unseen communities of the immediate landscape. Ritual practices as well as taboos were almost certainly aspects of maintaining relationships with unseen beings and forces both close by and far away. (Cf. Siikala 2002; Stark 2002.) When considering individual and social identities in relation to others during the Viking Age, it is necessary to remember that perceived realities of social networking extended beyond the physical into unseen social realities – into mythic worlds in the immediate landscape, and also in remote otherworld locations.

Another side of understanding people, individual identities, and the identities of social and cultural groups in the Viking Age is that all of these identities also connected with history and historical identities. A universal aspect of every predominantly oral society is the maintenance of history – stories of kin, significant ancestors and events as well as of exemplar figures associated with broader social networks – and this was certainly also the case in the Viking Age among the different cultures inhabiting Finland and Karelia. Although it is difficult to say what the particular narratives may have been, extensive fields of burial mounds in Åland physically manifested the history of kin groups in the landscape (Tomtlund 2005). In Finland, collective burial fields on level ground were similarly situated to have visual prominence (Wessman 2010). Burial grounds on islands and in copses of special trees as familiar from later traditions (Stark 2002: 147–154) would similarly play a significant role in enregistering the landscape – making it meaningful to those who inhabit it – although early burial grounds of this type, lacking structures of earth or stone, have not necessarily left directly observable traces into the present day. Most likely, the enregisterment of the landscape involved a rich process of narration, addressing everything from fishing in different lakes and who drowned in a certain river to forests known for causing people to get lost. These histories would thus not simply enregister the landscape and its relationships to communities of the living and the dead narrating and being narrated, but also its relationships to other communities of the living and of the unseen world.

Not all beings considered historical were necessarily physically embodied. The most central and prominent heroes common across a cultural group are often far more mythic than real. Such epic figures have a mythic role for a cultural group: they present exemplar representations of identities, practices and social order (cf. Honko 1998: 20–29; Foley 2004). This does not exclude the possibility that there could be a kernel of historical individuals and events in the background of them (cf. Byock 1990; Reichl 2007: 22–50). However, their status in living communities is very often connected to a vague era that precedes and leads to the establishment of a current social world order, providing mythic models that can be used to reflect on and negotiate social realities in the present, while being at least somewhat dislocated from them (Frog 2014). A significant amount of knowledge and understanding of unseen worlds and their inhabitants as well as explanations for ritual practices are communicated and negotiated through narratives about things that have 'happened' – history. These may be so-called belief legends about how the thunder-god split a certain stone or how a neighbour was attacked in his sleep by a supernatural being (cf. Jauhiainen 1998). However, the history of living communities will almost inevitably extend back to the creation of the world and the establishment of the present world order. Such accounts will nonetheless interface with what is current in the society, reflecting and affirming it, informing the significance of ritual, social practices and taboo behaviours, as well as providing resources for negotiating social roles, structures and relationships between groups (Siikala & Siikala 2005; Tarkka 2005: ch. 5; 2012). It is possible to extrapolate that such traditions of history and narration were prominent and significant in constructing history, group identities, enregistering the landscape and even constructing understandings of the world itself. However, it is very difficult to access in any concrete form what these were during a remote period (see Frog 2012b). Belief legends, epic history and even mythology itself were continuously updated and negotiated to make them current for the communities of people handling them, incorporating new or alternative concepts, images, technologies and understandings – they evolved in dialogue with culture rather than culture simply evolving around them (cf. Frog 2011b; Valk 2012). (Frog.) The diversity of complex cultural practices apparent in the archaeological record suggest a plurality of cultures inhabiting these geographical territories during the Viking Age. This highlights that traditions constructing such histories and models may have varied significantly across these diverse groups, with some shared even across languages while others may even have been consciously opposed.

Generally speaking, identification with an ethnos is linked to a constellation of features seen as conventionally belonging together. This is a social construction (Barth 1969; cf. Weber 1968: 385–398): the particular features and their constellations become enregistered as characteristic of one group as opposed to others, probably including, for example aspects of language, dress and other external presentation, social behaviours and cultural practices, and they may extend to physiological features. Ethnicity is in a sense the subjective side of the objective realities of culture (e.g. Baden 1995: 33) – i.e. the features of culture that are perceived as emblematic of bearers of that culture within the same or other groups. Geoff Emberling (1997: 296) has asserted that “Understanding ethnicity [...] is a necessary precondition to adequate understanding of the past” precisely because understanding ethnicity is a key to understanding the meaningfulness of different features of culture in communities under investigation. For the Viking Age, identification of someone with an ethnos simply means that the person will look, speak and act differently from a person of another ethnos, and this will be linked to expectations and valuations by whoever makes the identification. In a sense, the term ethnos simply denotes a category of broad scope for an extended social group, within which more specific constellations of features linked to particular roles, social activities and so forth may be seen as characteristic of one ethnos as opposed to another. This does not mean that every individual will share in all of these features, such as *necessarily* (fluently) speaking the same language; nor does it mean that the features will be exclusive, such as *not* speaking another language. The process of differentiation is a process of building categories, and it leads to the characterization of all of the groups involved. Ethnonyms in general tend to be used when referring to others rather than to one's own ethnic group, much as a person (in most language environments) is more likely to refer to himself or herself with a pronoun like 'I' or 'we' rather than saying his or her own personal name (de Castro 1998: 476). Such terms for categories of people develop intuitively around perceived constellations of features rather than being analytical and scientific.

Language is one of the most central markers of social identities but it is by no means clear to what degree Germanic or Slavic speakers distinguished between different Sámi or Finnic languages or other Uralic languages in Northwest Europe. Cultural practices or dress may have been more significant in this regard. Ethnonyms also get linked to place names, as observed in such terms as *Finnland* ['*Finn*-Land'] and *Bjarmaland* ['Land of the Bjarmians'], from which the appropriate ethnonym may either be inferred (*Finnar* ['Finns'], *Bjarmar* ['Bjarmians']) or the ethnonym may itself refer to the place (*Finnlendingar* ['Finnlander'], *Íslendingar* ['Icelander']). Especially where differences are great or contacts are remote between the group using the ethnonym and the group to which it refers, these terms can easily be transferred or simply get mixed up. Thus, as Denis Kuzmin points out, many Karelians refer to the (also Karelian) populations just to the north of them as 'Lapps', and in one local area, they refer to themselves as 'Lapps' and to their language as 'Lappish'. To return to the issue of the 'Finns' introduced above, it is uncertain when the terms Finmark (Old Norse *Finnmǫrk* ['*Finn*-Forest']) and Finland (Old Norse *Finnland* ['*Finn*-Land']) became established. By the beginning of the Viking Age (750/800), *Finnmǫrk* seems, in the west, to have clearly referred to Sámi language areas of Norway. In eastern areas, the term for Sámi seems to have been *Lappir* (['Lapp' cf. Ru. *Lop*']), in which case people in Sweden may have simply used *Finnar* for people living in *Finnland*. This complements the riddle of to whom the term *Finnar* originally referred by whether or how they were distinguished from 'Lapps'. Whereas toponymy may provide evidence of the population history of a certain area based on the language history of the place names (Leiviskä), the distribution of place names containing ethnonyms such as 'Lapp' (Salo 2000), 'Chud' (Rahkonen 2011) and 'Finn' does not resolve the identity of the culture that lived in those places that was perceived as 'other'.

Ethnographic data reveals that societies relying on hunter-gatherer livelihoods are often characterized by quite small speech communities of perhaps only a few hundred speakers, which can be considered the probable situation for many of the groups in inland and northern Finland and Karelia during the Viking Age. The size of these speech communities is a function of the size and complexity of those societies. (Saarikivi & Lavento 2012: esp. 210, 212.) The smaller the speech community, the more likely that social networks require interactions across speech communities and that exogamous marriage (i.e. taking a partner from 'outside' the family or kin) will be across communities, with especially women moving across ethnic groups (cf. Saarinen & Lavento 2012: 197). The existence of networks of smaller communities also increases the probability of familiarity or competence in the practices and traditions of other groups (or even practices common to certain networks) in a potentially dynamic multicultural arena. At the same time, the smaller networks through which language change must be negotiated and the potential for competency across languages and cultural practices connected to different groups leaves it more or less impossible to reconstruct how or even whether language and collective identity were ideologically linked in such communities (Saarinen & Lavento 2012: 212).

The spaces of Finland and Karelia were clearly inhabited by diverse linguistic groups in the Viking Age, even if their precise distribution is unclear, and the number and variety of these groups is potentially far greater than is customarily estimated. The Viking Age seems to coincide with the break-up of the North Finnic dialect continuum into distinct languages that later come to be distinguished as Finnish, Karelian, Vepsian and Ižorian, while the majority of Finland and Karelia appear to have been inhabited by speakers of Sámi languages (Aikio 2006; 2009; Kallio; Kuzmin). The degree of linguistic diversity in the far north remains unknown. The picture is complicated by population movements that appear to have been characteristic of the Viking Age in Finland (*c.* 750–1250), especially from the western cultural area east and north (Leiviskä) as well as the probable establishment of some form of Finnic language communities on the White Sea (Koskela Vasaru). Whatever incited these movements, Lake Ladoga was emerging as a vital cultural contact zone even before the eastern trade routes had fully opened (Uino 1997). Pulls for immigration no doubt also brought Germanic and Slavic settlers – at least to the area of Lake Ladoga as a vital center for economic opportunity (cf. Kuz'min 2008) – and the same pulls may have drawn settlers from other, less documented cultures as well. Linguistic evidence suggests that Christianity was carried into the Finnic cultural areas through Slavic contacts already at the beginning of the Viking Age (Häkkinen; Kallio), probably along trade routes of which Lake Ladoga was a nexus. Other potential relevant indicators of exchange can be found in the lexicon associated with these areas of culture in the term *kalma* ['grave; burial ground'] found across Finnic and Mordvin languages[9] that appears to be cognate with Old Swedish *kalm* ['burial mound; cairn'], not otherwise attested in any Germanic language (Kylstra *et al.* 1997–2012 II: 25). Although there is tremendous evidence of cultural influences entering Finnic cultures from Germanic and later Slavic models (Häkkinen), all cultural influences should not be assumed to have been unidirectional and they may have potentially been quite complex (cf. Frog 2011a).

Åland was very likely a cultural contact zone (see also Ahola *et al.* 2014). It nevertheless presents a riddle because the languages spoken there remain uncertain. There seems to have been a (probable) discontinuity in a significant proportion of Ålandic place names following the Viking Age, although there is not an indication of corresponding discontinuity in habitation – leaving a mystery (Roeck Hansen 1988). Similar questions surround the cultures near the White Sea and especially the so-called Bjarmians. Although place-name evidence suggests migrations to the area of the Northern Dvina basin by South or Inland Finnic populations in the Viking Age, the area also soon drew Slavic speakers until, in the documented era, Finnic languages have disappeared from the region (Saarikivi 2006: 295). These Finnic populations probably traded with Norsemen on the White Sea (KOSKELA VASARU) whereas northern territories of present-day Finland reveal indicators of the movement of goods – and therefore people – between the Gulf of Bothnia overland (probably) all of the way to the White Sea (KUUSELA). These, however, must have been predominantly Sámi language areas at that time, if not areas of other West Uralic language groups. These northern regions also offer indications of contacts with Permian (Kama) culture to the east that are not present in the western and eastern cultural areas of Finland or in Sweden (Huurre 1983: 421; Zachrisson 1987). This suggests that there may have been extended trade networks for which the White Sea region was more central, rather than all networks being channelled through the region of Lake Ladoga. The Viking Age appears not only to have been characterized by movements of Germanic populations, but also by movements of populations inhabiting territories of Finland, Karelia and Åland, as well as other cultures further east.

Religion and subscription to a mythology, certain beliefs or an ideology are also all potentially prominent markers of beliefs, but these are often much more difficult to identify in history. Eastern and western Christianity, Islam and Judaism were coherent religions that were carried and spread along these routes. These religions are more easily approached on the one hand because they are familiar and recognizable institutions today. On the other hand, the image that the modern religions present us with are highly stable: they are maintained by vast bureaucracies and supported by developed communication networks that enable them to conserve order and fundamentals of uniformity across thousands and thousands of globally distributed communities. In addition, the Reformation in the west and the Reforms of Patriarch Nikon in the east were responses to precisely the sorts of variation and syncretism produced by medieval conversion processes and the synthesis of Christianity into local traditions (or vice versa, depending on one's perspective). The modern image of these world religions is not accurately representative of these religions as they penetrated into the many and diverse cultures of Northeast Europe in the Iron Age. Jesus and Mary might simply complement an established mythology and be reinterpreted through it, as can be seen in kalevalaic poetry traditions of Karelia still in the nineteenth and twentieth centuries (see Siikala 2002). It should also be remembered that the bureaucratic apparatuses of organized religions were not able to supervise and assert authority over those who claimed identity as 'Christians' at the peripheries of their reach (Frog 2014). Moreover, most major conversion efforts were concentrated on establishing a unifying 'Christian' identity at a broad social level. It was a social process that involved staking out fields of social ritual practices over which religious authorities sought to assert control and influence. A not insubstantial part of this process was connecting religious identity to trade: in many places, Christians would only be allowed to trade with Christians, or with those who had received the sign of the cross as a sort of prelude to baptism. However, for those who identified themselves as 'Christians' in the Viking Age and in the Middle Ages, it is important to recognize that "their Christianity was a self-characterization" (Lotman 1990: 130) rather than necessarily corresponding to any form of Christianity that we would recognize today.

As was apparent in the discussion on the crusades above, the arrival of Christianity was uneven to say the least. Although loan words suggest that the earliest Finnic contact with Christianity seems to have been from the east, archaeological evidence suggests that significant impacts on cultural practices first got a foothold in the west (see also Korpela). Conversion processes focused especially on public, social ritual practices with less (or no) concern for personal, subjective 'faith' before the Middle Ages (cf. Sanmark 2004). Burial rites were particularly prominent in this process because these were considered emblematic of belief traditions: the dead should be buried without cremation (so that the deceased would have a body to resurrect on Judgement Day); grave goods should not be included, as these were connected to non-Christian ideas about what happens to the dead following the burial rite. It was observed above that changes in burial practices during the Viking Age in the western cultural area (Map 4), or in Finland Proper, Satakunta and Häme, can be directly associated with Christian models: burial became prominent in contrast to cremation already in *c.* 1000, and grave goods disappear from the archaeological record by *c.* 1150 (Huurre 1979: 224). These features have therefore been interpreted as evidence of Christianity being generally established in that area (cf. Tolley 2009 I: 34). However, this change in practices appears independent of activities organized by the Church (Frog 2014). It is far from clear how this should be interpreted, especially as "most symbolic action, even the basic symbols of a community's ritual life, can be very unclear to participants or interpreted by them in very dissimilar ways" (Bell 1992: 183). Although these changes are clearly of symbolic significance, they were nevertheless negotiated within communities on the peripheries of the Church's moderating bureaucratic mechanisms. For example, they could still be complemented with practices such as lamenting, which people continued to feel was not only important, but even necessary for the deceased to reach the otherworld or the living community would suffer the consequences. Ritual lament traditions remained vital in many Finnic Orthodox areas into the twentieth century, and even somewhat into the twenty-first. In the western cultural areas, it seems to have survived until the Lutheran Reformation, which was followed by strategic and aggressive measures to displace these practices that had survived in the wake of the Catholic conversion. (Stepanova 2011; 2012.) The fields over which Christianity asserted authority were also in many respects quite limited: the Christian institutions had no corresponding apparatus to replace many cultural practices that were considered essential to the livelihoods of different communities. These included practical rituals related to health and defence from forces in the unseen world, weather, hunting, agriculture and so forth. Christian prescriptions related to socially central ritual practices were also practically realized on a very limited scope and in particular details. These could therefore be integrated as complementary to existing systems of rituals (which potentially continued for several days in the case of a wedding or a funeral). In practice, *Christianity could not be completely exclusive of vernacular ritual and religious practice* because it simply did not offer equipment for dealing with the majority of activities and concerns in people's lives. In all cases, Christianity and its adaptation was local rather than a uniform, modern ideal. Consequently, the changes in burial practices observable in the western cultural area may reflect a vernacularization of Christianity rather than conversion *per se* (Frog 2014; cf. Nordberg 2012: 136–138).

The movement of cultural practices related to mythology, ritual and beliefs through networks of trade and communication was certainly not limited to major religions. This is highlighted by curious burial rituals employing a bear-paw[10] amulet made of clay that is widely found in Åland (with an example in mainland Sweden) and throughout the Jaroslavl' area (a West Uralic cultural area at that time), including at the Viking Age trade center at Timerëvo (Callmer 1994). The connection between these centers may be directly related to multilingual competence as a resource that could have potentially bolstered the role of Ålanders in trade along the Eastern Route (HEININEN ET AL.; Ahola *et al.* 2014). Once such a role was established, such competence would no doubt be encouraged, if it were economically advantageous, and maintained directly in relation to those trade networks. Changes in ritual practices suggest the assimilation and adaptation of conceptions about the dead, death, the otherworld, and potentially also about their relationship to living communities. Changes in vocabulary such as *kalma/kalm* mentioned above, are equally relevant indicators that such changes may have potentially entered East Norse cultural areas through contacts with Uralic populations. The bear-paw amulet example highlights the potential complexity of these processes: this clearly symbolic ritual practice is concentrated precisely in contact zones where Germanic and Finnic and related West Uralic populations were engaged in intensive interaction. This example not only illustrates the movement of cultural practices, but also the emergence of prominent practices precisely in environments of multicultural interaction.

An essential part of contextualizing the Viking Age is situating the radical developments associated with that period in relation to what came before and after it. The correlation of language with archaeological material has proven notoriously difficult (Saarinen & Lavento 2012). As highlighted above, the triangulation of archaeological data with toponymy and historical linguistics reveals that the linguistic map of the region was very different in the Iron Age and later Middle Ages than what we would expect today. Considering the distribution and spread of probable Finnic and Sámi language areas across the Iron Age and Middle Ages leaves open questions regarding how long and to what degree languages earlier established in these inland territories may have survived. In other words, it is uncertain whether or to what degree there may have been a rapid and extensive *language shift*. A language shift is the adoption of a new primary language for social practice by a group of language speakers (Dressler 1981). This has happened widely in the historical period, for example in the Americas, Russia, India, Australia, and is presently seen among Sámi as well as in Karelia where Russian increasingly predominates. However, the same process seems to have happened repeatedly through history. There seems to have been a language shift to Proto-Sámi across much of Fennoscandia already in the early Iron Age. This was presumably among smaller speech communities, in which not only innovations but even a complete language shift could be more easily negotiated. The Viking Age appears to have established the essential conditions for the later language shift of Sámi to Finnish and Karelian.

Modern analogues generally seem to exhibit a pattern according to which language shifts are not simply a product of cultural contacts, but a complex social process, among which social prestige and economic advantage seem particularly prominent – and interfaced with social change and changing cultural practices to a remarkable extent (e.g. Kamwangamalu 2003). In other words, a change of language seems normally to be indicative of a change in society and the way of life (although not necessarily the reverse). Thus if the spread of the Sámi language and assimilation of other languages established in Finland, Karelia and on the Scandinavian Peninsula is connected in the archaeological record with the Kjelmøj Ceramic Culture (Carpelan 2006; cf. Aikio 2006: 46–47; see also Saarinen & Lavento 2012), the ceramics with which this culture is associated should be recognized as only one technology and signifier in a potentially complex constellation. Moreover, that one signifier may have been attached to a different complex – a quite different language and ethnicity – and only later became connected with the Sámi language, while that complex would itself have to be adaptable across new ecological environments and alternative livelihoods in different parts of the north.

Sámi was subsequently superseded in the spread of North Finnic languages with the assimilation of significant populations of Sámi speakers. This spread is connected to the increased mobility along seafaring trade routes and inland waterways as discussed above. Although the specific processes remain obscure, the archaeological record of the Viking Age reveals increased agricultural practices and shifts to greater dependence on agrarian economies through influences coming from both east and west. Unto Salo has recently argued on basis of local histories that, in part of the Satakunta province, the earliest populations practicing slash-and-burn agriculture as a supplement to their livelihood were Sámi speaking, and that these were later displaced by the advancement of Finnic language groups inland with the corresponding agricultural practices (Salo 2000: 49; see also Aikio 2007: 162–163). If Salo is correct, this would highlight that a language shift is not solely dependent on any single group or community, but dependent on networks of communities in interaction in long-term historical processes. In other words, Sámi would not likely survive for many generations in only one community within a broader network and environment where a Finnic language became the *lingua franca* across communities – not unless there were other factors and networks that would support (enregister) its value and continued use (cf. Frog 2012b: 47).[11] The combination of external cultural influences combined with mobility and migration seem to have resulted in both the diversification of North Finnic dialects into different languages and also their spread northward in conjunction with cultural practices that characterized these linguistic groups. The interesting factor is that the resulting language shift was connected with a more extensive cultural shift that displaced fundamental features of earlier ways of thinking (Frog).

Only the outcomes of these processes are seen in many types of data, both in tangible evidence and in intangible culture. Among these, the genetic evidence gathered from present-day populations is exceptionally difficult to approach. Territorial differences in genetic evidence cut in an arc across Finland from Karelia to Ostrobothnia. This arc of genetic differences exhibits curious correlations with linguistic and folklore evidence – i.e. differences at the level of language and cultural practices along the same arc.[12] The complexity of these processes involving numerous factors should not be underestimated. This is especially evident observing that slash-and-burn agriculture in the east appears to have been particularly characteristic of Vepsian linguistic-cultural groups for some time, and to the degree that where it was practiced, Vepsian appears to have been spoken. Karelians assimilated these practices from Vepsians during the Viking Age (750–1250), but apparently owing to the language ideology or the potential prestige or economic advantage with which Karelian was enregistered, these speakers did not assimilate the Vepsian language. Instead, the spread of the Karelian language involved not only a language shift of Sámi speakers but also of Vepsian speakers. (Kuzmin.) It remains uncertain how precisely this should be approached with regards to the spread of North Finnic languages across these territories and how that relates to indigenous populations who may have been linguistically and culturally assimilated in that process.

Changes and continuities in cultural practices and livelihoods are reflected in the archaeological record, as are contacts between cultural groups and the 'movement' of cultural practices – even if the movement of embodied individuals in the transference of these cultural practices remains only inferred, as does its relationship to language. As emphasized above, it is necessary to recognize that cross-cultural contacts did not begin in the Viking Age. Since the Pre-Roman Iron Age, "the communities that lived in south-western Finland participated rather intensively in the trans-regional systems of ritual and material exchange in the northern Baltic Sea region" (Wickholm & Raninen 2006: 154). The reflection of these contacts and social hierarchies in early fixed-settlement communities suggest that there were communities in coastal Finland participating in so-called peer-polity interaction (on which, see Renfrew 1986). In other words, individual centralized regional communities negotiated power and authority in relation to one another though networks rather than being subordinated to a common dominant central authority such as a king (in the early Germanic context, see Storli 2000: 93–96). The correlation of archaeological and linguistic data is always problematic, but these settlements were very likely predominantly North Finnic in language and very likely multilingual environments. From the perspective of Europe as a cultural center, these communities appear peripheral, but within the network of communities engaged in interaction on the Baltic Sea, these communities may have been perceived much differently. As mentioned above, the name of the district Satakunta may derive from a Germanic term for an administrative district, and if Germanic cultures were already long established in coastal areas of Finland when Finnic groups arrived, the Finnic groups may simply have entered into already existing networks that spanned the Baltic Sea. On the eastern side, Ladoga was peripheral from the perspective of Byzantium, yet it manifested as a center among the northern trade routes with Finnic cultures in a central position mediating between east and west. Centers and peripheries are always related to perspectives (Korpela), and the same sites that may appear peripheral in broad geopolitical perspective were also likely central for trade networks of populations in inland Finland and Karelia. Livelihoods based on fixed habitation rather than mobility were likely a significant factor in Finnic populations developing stable positions in centers for these trade networks and centers for the mediation of cultural goods, practices and linguistic influences. Especially the groups that later emerge as Finns and Karelians appear to have situated themselves precisely at the heart of contact zones of Finno-Ugric and Indo-European cultures from the northern half of the Baltic Sea to Lake Ladoga. At the same time, from the perspective of inland cultures in the region, Finnic cultures and Finnic languages were situated in relation to – and potentially identified with – centers of culture, political authority and economic opportunity. If this was the case, a consequence would be the enregisterment of Finnic language and culture with potential for international mobility and personal advancement.

The important contact zones reveal juxtapositions and syntheses at the level of ritual practices, including the so-called cemeteries under level ground into which 'foreign' models were gradually assimilated (Wickholm & Raninen 2006). At the same time, continuities in these practices through the Viking Age provide valuable indicators of continuity in culture that appears to correlate with historical Finnic population movements already mentioned. These practices reflect cultural semiotics – the systems of meaningful symbols, images, motifs and representations of which language is only one part. The treatment of the embodied dead reflects the practices that both realized and communicated understandings of death, the dead, communities of the dead, relationships with them, and also how to conduct such relationships and interactions. These practices can be presumed to have been meaningful to the people who performed them and to interface with and realize aspects of belief systems current at that time. For instance, the fact that the number of weapons in Viking Age graves of Southwest Finland is relatively large even in Scandinavian terms (Lehtosalo-Hilander 1984) tells about the value of weapons as status symbols and about beliefs connected to the life after death. The relevance of these weapons to actual activities of combat and warfare in the period remain more ambiguous because *their context only offers indicators of certain areas of meaningfulness*. Rituals and beliefs themselves cannot be reconstructed, but it is possible to generalize on the basis of analogical data that these rituals had an essential role in the maintenance of relationships between the embodied living community and the unseen community of the dead. Evidence of ritual practices, mythology and its uses in the Viking Age in Finland are almost exclusively accessible through the intangible data and continuities of cultural practices. These have been historically removed from the period and in many cases disconnected from earlier spheres of cultural activity, but insights are still possible by placing the evidence in broader comparative perspective. On the other hand, there is a remarkable amount of such data available on Finno-Karelian mythology, rituals, beliefs and associated practices, and this offers a much more dynamic and multidimensional perspective than is possible with, for example, the sources for Old Norse mythology from the Middle Ages, although the difference in sources presents different methodological challenges and different limitations on what the data can, in fact, reveal about the Viking Age.

Most evidence of traditions related to mythologies survived into recent centuries for extensive documentation precisely because these mythologies were upheld by ritual specialists – some even into the present century. In other words, mythologies continued to be used and enregistered as socially significant as well as magically powerful. These specialists include healers and magical specialists as well as ritual lamenters, and each of these different specialists, like the Christian priests who sometimes lived in the same communities, had somewhat different (if overlapping) mythologies (Frog). These can also be situated in broader historical and comparative perspectives. Insofar as ritual lamenting appears to be part of the common Finnic linguistic-cultural heritage and also to have been essential to several cultures in the Circum-Baltic region, it is fairly certain that the rites in the Viking Age involved lamenters as female ritual specialists who probably ensured that the deceased individual successfully made the transition from the living community to the otherworld and became integrated into the community of the ancestors (Stepanova 2011; 2012). Other ritual specialists were also probably involved in rituals related to burial and interacting with the dead, but the later material does not enable developing coherent perspectives on these roles and their relationships to one another, let alone the full ritual process. Comparative evidence suggests that the Sámi populations of Finland and Karelia practiced a form of Northern Eurasian shamanism as part of their Uralic heritage (Frog), and this probably involved unconscious trance states and soul-journeys to remote otherworld locations paralleling practices in later documented Sámi cultures (cf. Bäckman & Hultkrantz 1978; Hoppál 2010; Rydving 2010). Stating anything more precise is problematized by the fact that the Sámi language groups of most of Finland and Karelia cannot be assumed to have historically developed practices exactly identical to Sámi cultures to the north, and their language and traditions were never documented directly. Conversely, North Finnic specialists in healing, magical practices and interaction with supernatural powers such as gods seem to be a culturally unique phenomenon with a marked discontinuity from Finno-Ugric shamanic traditions. This institution of specialist, his mythology and traditions developed particularly in relation to Germanic influences sometime during the Iron Age in the western cultural area (Siikala 2002; 2012; Frog 2012a; 2013). This specialist carried the mythology of kalevalaic poetry and a complex ideology on which his abilities and belief in the efficacy of his art was dependent. This tradition appears rooted in images and ideologies that are developed from the same complex of mythology and warfare that eventually produced the mentality associated with the Norse Vikings, a mentality that created and supported the cultural dominance of central concepts and values, such as duty and fate, which were necessary to prepare a young man to risk his life on raiding expeditions (Price 2002) and seem already to have been manipulated as a tool in the Migration Period (Gunnell 2013). The process by which this Finno-Karelian tradition spread remains unclear. However, it seems likely to have moved with the expansion of groups from the western cultural area, establishing it in Karelia, and thence spreading with the North Finnic languages (Siikala 2012). This makes the assimilation of Sámi populations in those areas particularly remarkable, because it was equally a process of conversion, resulting in a shift not only in language but also in mythology and the associated ideology (Frog 2013). This seems to have been an essential part of adopting a new social identity that was networked among individuals and across different communities in interaction.

Although Christianity is raised as an indicator of a transformative transition from the Iron Age to a new era, this followed the same sort of patterns related to cultural contacts and transitions that had been experienced by cultures again and again throughout history. In all cases, these transitions appear associated with changes in the construction of social identities and/or life ways. This is highlighted by the 'mythology shift' of the Sámi that accompanied their language shift to Finnish and Karelian, but it is equally implied for the other Uralic and Palaeo-European language groups in their corresponding shift to Sámi, although their indigenous mythologies and ritual practices remain a mystery. The most significant differences in the case of Christianity were: *a*) that this new religiously based cultural identity was rapidly advancing to a common and unifying European identity, an identity of an extreme scope that characterized the Middle Ages; and *b*) that it was attached to an extensive bureaucratic apparatus that enabled it to maintain coherence in spite of its magnitude. North Finnic magical specialists and lamenters did not reject the Christian God, Mary and Christ: they assimilated these into their own belief systems and could even view themselves as Christians. This was possible because pressures to conform their understandings of Christianity and Christian practices to those of a Church authority were too remote to exert influence in more than an extremely gradual social process (cf. Korpela). These processes highlight the degree to which languages, beliefs and cultural practices are all associated and interact in complex systems as a historical process. At the same time, this emphasizes how vital and dynamic the many and diverse cultural interactions must have been during the Viking Age.

In all of these processes, the vast and amorphous entity of a 'language', 'religion' or 'culture' is in reality comprised of the knowledge and understandings of individuals in communities – individuals who form networks and interact with one another. Within those communities, individuals develop perspectives and the world is enregistered around them. The Viking Age was characterized by numerous factors that had revolutionary impacts on the identities of people and groups, both in terms of how they saw themselves and how they saw others. Mobility, technology and climate are not by themselves enough to generate revolutions in culture; it requires people, with attitudes, ideas, goals and desires. The Viking Age brought about a transformation not only in language but also in culture and beliefs in a pivotal stage that set in motion the spread of North Finnic cultures and led to the cultures we recognize today.

Transition as a Characterizing Feature

The Viking Age emerges as a valid term and concept for approaching the history Finland and Finno-Karelian territories of habitation and appears relevant to these areas. The traditional dating for the period as AD 800–1050 is in relation to events in England connected with raiding activities. This dating is based on events that function as emblematic signifiers of the period. In addition to being geographically remote, the activities and contacts that characterized this period to the east of Scandinavia had a different orientation, especially where these extended inland along water routes. In addition, the Viking Age is conventionally viewed as the last period of the Iron Age before entry into the Middle Ages. The transition between these periods is characterized by the official conversion to Christianity which marks 'medievalization', or participation in European Christian identity with associated technologies and practices such as writing. More properly, the transition is marked by the conversion of emerging states as political entities, entities that assimilated a shared Christian identity and allegiance with the authority or power (even if not a practical means) to conform their populous to a Christian image of public social behaviour and practices. Christianity in some forms began reaching Finland during the Viking Age, but it advanced much more slowly: these territories were both remote from centers of the spreading religion and Christianity was 'new' here, whereas the Roman culture, from which Germanic Scandinavia had already been receiving influences since the beginning of the Migration Period, was Christian (Fabech 1999: 459). When this is not taken into consideration, a 'gap' is produced in the periodization between the Viking Age and the entry of Finland into the Middle Ages, which is customarily 'patched' in discussion as the 'Crusade Period', a term which is awkward because it is disjointed from crusades in the Baltic Sea region. The Viking Age in Finland has here been calibrated to accord with the more significant role of trade for the activities of 'Vikings' directed to the east, and according to events relevant to the annex of Finland and Karelia into the Middle Ages. This produces dates of approximately AD 750–1250, based on the key signifiers of the founding of Staraya Ladoga by 753, marking the opening of significant trade networks, and the so-called Second Swedish Crusade in 1249, marking the politicization of these territories for annexation by expanding Christian nation-states. Although the actual dates are no less arbitrary for dating the Viking Age than two conflicts in York are for the west, these are key dates in the history of the region and are also relevant as a period as reflected in the data under consideration.

What characterizes the Viking Age in this part of the world is mobility, the contact networks that this enabled and the migrations which followed on those networks. Mobility played a correspondingly central – if different – role in characterizing the Viking Age in Finland as it did for the Norsemen. When considering the Viking Age in this part of the world, concentration has been on broad cultural areas that are associated with territories of what are recognized as Finland and Karelia today. These territories extend into inland regions and cannot be clearly delineated by coastlines as can the majority of the Scandinavian Peninsula, Denmark, Iceland and so forth. These areas were inhabited by mobile cultures that have left only limited evidence on the archaeological record, but they were involved in these processes nonetheless. Rather than attempting to delineate spaces with strict borders, the networks of travel, trade and migrations have received emphasis here in accordance with the flexibility of the territories themselves during this period.

Above all, the Viking Age was an anthropocentric phenomenon, and from that perspective, it is a period characterized by transitions of remarkable magnitude across the north. Mobility and contacts transformed outlooks on the world and perceptions of it. A new mythology, ideology and religious institution appears to have spread with migrations and become dominant across North Finnic cultures as the linguistic-cultural groups of Finland and Karelia took on the distinctive identities that become the cultures and languages known today. In this period, the North Finnic dialect continuum broke up, so that especially Finnish and Karelia could become distinct languages and correspondingly distinct cultures in the archaeological record. Sámi cultures reappear in the archaeological record as the ancestors of the Sámi languages known today. It also appears important for linguistic-cultural groups that underwent language shifts. This is evident in the probable South Finnic population that immigrated to the (Northern) Dvina River basin, identifiable with 'Bjarmians' of medieval sources, and possibly for other small Finno-Ugric groups that may have inhabited regions in the north. More speculatively, if any additional Uralic or Palaeo-European languages survived in these regions into the beginning of the Viking Age, it is not unlikely that the changes in Sámi cultures during this period could have motivated and concluded language shifts, eclipsing them entirely. Encounters with Christianity began across this period, as this religion gradually became established on a limited basis in the southwest, and the period ended with the advancement of crusades establishing political and economic authority over the area which would soon be formally divided between Sweden and Novgorod. Most significantly, the period established foundations for Finnish and Karelian to assimilate a whole branch of the Sámi language and become dominant languages in the region, sweeping across territories from the Gulf of Finland to the White Sea.

Acknowledgement: We would like especially to thank Janne Saarikivi for his valuable comments on the question of languages, their historical distribution and spread, as well as the many other colleagues whose discussion and comments have helped strengthen this overview. Frog's contribution to this chapter was completed within the framework of the Academy of Finland Project "Oral Poetry, Mythic Knowledge and Vernacular Imagination: Interfaces of Individual Expression and Collective Traditions in Pre-Modern Northeast Europe" of Folklore Studies, University of Helsinki.

Notes

1 Inscription Sm10 memorializes *Toki víkingʀ* ['Toki the Viking']; DR161 reads *með víkingum* ['with Vikings'] and Vg61 *í víkingu* ['on a Viking raid'] both referring to journeys or adventuring to the west (cf. Heininen *et al.*); U617 memorializes a *víkinga vǫrðr* ['Viking watchman'].

2 This is exemplified in the theories of Arthur de Gobineau (1852–1855) and, in the Finnish context, for instance in the writings of August Sohlman (1855) and later, Artur Eklund (1914).

3 The former image is a relatively recent development related to the international interest in shamanism since the mid-twentieth century. The image of horned helmets became popular a century earlier: it is probably rooted in medieval monks depicting anyone they saw as evil with horns when illustrating manuscripts – manuscripts in which Vikings were described as horrible pagans who attacked and robbed helpless monks in their cloisters. Another source for the misconception could be Danish Bronze Age ritual helmets and other scattered artefacts (from the Grevensvænge hoard) which were incorrectly dated in the eighteenth century to the Iron Age, while on Viking Age artefacts that were superficially interpreted, the 'horns' actually appear to be birds turning to face one another (Gunnell 1995).

4 Debate has returned to the so-called 'Varangian problem', which directed discussion to the dispute between Normanist vs. anti-Normanist origins (see e.g. Sørensen 1968). The earlier research tended to highlight the Finnic (Finnish) impact, even on rather weak grounds (see Latvakangas 1992). The actual role of Finnic or Finno-Ugric peoples in this process still requires further assessment (cf. also Schalin).

5 The Old Norse term *Aldeigja* is considered etymologically related to 'Ladoga' with metathesis in the first syllable (*La-* > *Al-*). The etymology of this hydronym is disputed (see e.g. Janhunen 2009: 204–207) and the problems related to developing an etymology that is both reasonable and cogent could be related to origins of the place name in a language that is neither Uralic nor Indo-European.

6 The earliest hoard from the Ladoga region cannot have been deposited before 786 (Talvio), but silver had presumably already begun changing hands in the region before large quantities were deposited as hoards.

7 The proposed etymology from a Germanic term related to the verb 'to find' (e.g. Grünthal 1997) seems to have found popularity, presumably because it resonates with ideas of wandering hunter-gatherers. Etymologically, however, this cannot account for the form *fenni* used by Tacitus in the first century, at which time the proposed ethnonym would have been rendered in Latin as something more like ***fentani*.

8 The ethnonym 'Chud' found in medieval sources has often been interpreted as referring to Vepsians or otherwise to Finnic linguistic-cultural groups generally, but a strong argument has recently been put forward that there was a particular linguistic-cultural group identifiable with this ethnonym slightly further to the

south and, although probably Finno-Ugric/Uralic, this group did not speak a Finnic language (Rahkonen 2011).

9 Mordvin belongs to the Volgic branch of the Finno-Ugric language family. After Sámi, Mordvin is the closest (living) language related to Finnic, both linguistically and geographically. These languages are separated geographically today by a wide Russian language area, but in the Viking Age there was a continuum of Finno-Ugric linguistic-cultural groups between them which later underwent a language shift. Common vocabulary in Finnic and Mordvin languages is frequently a relevant indicator that the words were likely established across that entire intermediate continuum.

10 Although these amulets have been suggested to represent a beaver's paw (for discussion, see Callmer 1994), it seems most probable that, if associated with the mythic power of the animal or animal totemism, it is intended to represent the paw of a bear. In contrast to the beaver, which was significant as an economic resource (cf. Jonuks 48–49), the bear was a significant animal and symbol bound up with mythic and mythological conceptions especially prominent among Finno-Ugric cultures, while bear skins and claws were also otherwise ritually present in a number of Germanic burial practices (see further Frog 2014).

11 In his study of Sámi loanwords in North Finnic languages, Ante Aikio (2009: 212–213) proposes that the prominence of pejoratives "in part reflects the sociolinguistic conditions at the time of borrowing. During the expansion of the Finnic farmers scornful attitudes towards the foraging 'Lapps' have probably been common." (Aikio 2009: 213.)

12 For an overview, see Norio 2003: 463–465.

References

Sources

FMU – Finsk medeltidsurkunder. http://extranet.narc.fi/DF/index.htm

Sm10 Runic inscription: "Sm 10 (Sm10) – Växjö domkyrka". Runic Dictionary. Available at: http://abdn.ac.uk/skaldic/db.php?if=runic&table=mss&id=16359

DR161 Runic inscription: "DR 161 (DR161) – Hune". Runic Dictionary. Available at: http://abdn.ac.uk/skaldic/db.php?id=18986&if=runic&table=mss&val=&view=

Vg61 Runic inscription: "Vg 61 (Vg61) - Härlingstorp". Runic Dictionary. Available at: http://abdn.ac.uk/skaldic/db.php?id=16592&if=runic&table=mss&val=&view=

U617 Runic inscription: "U 617 (U617) - Bro k:a". Runic Dictionary. Available at: http://abdn.ac.uk/skaldic/db.php?id=17439&if=runic&table=mss&val=&view=

Literature

Agha, Asif. 2011. Commodity Registers. *Journal of Linguistic Anthropology* 21(1): 22–53.

Ahola, Joonas, Frog & Johan Schalin. 2014 (in press). Language(s) of Viking Age Åland: An Irresolvable Riddle? In Joonas Ahola, Frog & Jenni Lucenius (eds.). *The Viking Age in Åland: Insights into Identity and Remnants of Culture.* Annales Academiae Scientiarum Fennicae Humaniora. Helsinki: Academia Scientiarum Fennica.

Aikio, Ante. 2006. On Germanic–Saami Contacts and Saami Prehistory. *Journal de la Société Finno-Ougrienne* 91: 9–55.

Aikio, Ante. 2007. The Study of Saami Substrate Toponyms in Finland. *Onomastica Uralica* 4: 159–197.

Aikio, Ante. 2009. *The Saami Loanwords in Finnish and Karelian*. Oulu. Available at: http://cc.oulu.fi/~anaikio/slw.pdf (last accessed 12.01.2013).

Aikio, Ante. 2012. An Essay on Saami Ethnolinguistic Prehistory. In Riho Grünthal & Petri Kallio (eds.). *A Linguistic Map of Prehistoric Northern Europe*. Suomalais-Ugrilaisen Seuran Toimituksia 266. Helsinki: Société Finno-Ougrienne.

Anttonen, Veikko. 2010. *Uskontotieteen maastot ja kartat*. Tietolipas 232. Helsinki: Suomalaisen Kirjallisuuden Seura.

Bäckman, Louise, & Åke Hultkrantz. 1978. *Studies in Lapp Shamanism*. Stockholm Studies in Comparative Religion 16. Stockholm: Almqvist & Wiksell International.

Bader, Veit Michael. 1995. Ethnische Identität und ethnische Kultur: Grenzen des Konstruktivismus und Manipulation. *Forschungsjournal Neue Soziale Bewegungen* 8(1): 32–45.

Barrett, James. 2008. What Caused the Viking Age? *Antiquity* 82(3): 671–685.

Barth, Fredrik. 1998 [1969]. Ethnic Groups and Boundaries. In Fredrik Barth (ed.). *Ethnic Groups and Boundaries: The Social Organization of Cultural Difference*. Long Grove: Waveland Press. Pp. 9–38.

Bell, Catherine. 1992. *Ritual Theory, Ritual Practice*. Oxford: Oxford University Press.

Brettell, C. 2000. Theorizing Migration in Anthropology: The Social Construction of Networks, Identities, Communities and Globalscapes. In C. Brettell & J. Hollifield (eds.). *Migration Theory: Talking across Disciplines*. London: Routledge. Pp. 97–136.

Byock, Jesse L. 1990. Introduction. In *The Saga of the Volsungs: The Norse Epic of Sigurd the Dragon Slayer*. Berkeley: University of California Press. Pp. 1–29.

Callmer, Johan. 1994. The Clay Paw Burial Rite of the Åland Islands and Central Russia: A Symbol in Action. *Current Swedish Archaeology* 2: 13–46.

Carpelan, Christian. 2001. Late Palaeolithic and Mesolithic Settlement of the European North: Possible Linguistic Implications. In Christian Carpelan, Asko Parpela & Petteri Koskikallio (eds.). *Early Contacts between Uralic and Indo-European: Linguistic and Archaeological Considerations*. Helsinki: Suomalais-Ugrialainen Seura. Pp. 37–53.

Carpelan, Christian. 2006. Etnicitet, identitet, ursprung? Exemplet samerna. In Vesa-Pekka Herva (ed.). *People, Material Culture and Environment in the North: Proceedings of the 22nd Nordic Archaeological Conference, University of Oulu, 18–23 August 2004*. Oulu: Oulun Yliopisto. Pp. 75–82.

Carlsson, Anders. 1983. *Djurhuvudformiga spännen och gotländsk vikingatid*. Stockholm Studies in Archaeology 5. Stockholm: Stockholms Universitet.

de Castro, Eduardo Viveiros. 1998. Cosmological Deixis and Amerindian Perspectivism. *Journal of the Royal Anthropological Institute* 4(3): 469–488.

Duczko, Wladyslaw. 2004. *Viking Rus: Studies on the Presence of Scandinavians in Eastern Europe*. Leiden / Boston: Brills.

Dressler, Wolfgang. 1981. Language Shift and Language Death: A Protean Challenge for the Linguist. *Folia Linguistica* 15(1–2): 5–28.

Durkheim, Émile. 1915 [1912]. *The Elementary Forms of Religious Life*. Trans. J. W. Swain. London: Allan & Unwin.

Eklund, Artur. 1914. Ras, kultur, politik. In *Svenskt i Finland: Ställning och strävanden*. Helsingfors: Söderström. Pp. 1–22.

Emberling, Geoff. 1997. Ethnicity in Complex Cocieties: Archaeological Perspectives. *Journal of Archaeological Research* 5(4): 295–344.

Fabech, Charlotte. 1999. Centrality in Sites and Landscapes. In Charlotte Fabech & Jytte Ringtved (eds.). *Settlement and Landscape: Proceedings of a Conference in Århus, Denmark, May 4.7 1998*. Moesgård: Jutland Archaeological Society. Pp. 455–473.

Frog. 2011a. Circum-Baltic Mythology? – The Strange Case of the Theft of the Thunder-Instrument (ATU 1148b). *Archaeologia Baltica* 15: 78–98.

Frog. 2011b. Ethnocultural Substratum: Its Potential as a Tool for Lateral Approaches to Tradition History. *RMN Newsletter* 3: 23–37.

Frog. 2012a. Confluence, Continuity and Change in the Evolution of Mythology: The Case of the Finno-Karelian Sampo-Cycle. In Frog, Anna-Leena Siikala & Eila Stepanova (eds.). *Mythic Discourses: Studies in Uralic Traditions*. Studia Fennica Folkloristica 20. Helsinki: Finnish Literature Society. Pp. 205–254.

Frog. 2012b. The Parallax Approach: Situating Traditions in Long-Term Perspective. In Frog & Pauliina Latvala (eds.). *Approaching Methodology*. RMN Newsletter 4. Helsinki: Folklore Studies, University of Helsinki. Pp. 40–59.

Frog. 2013. Shamans, Christians, and Things in between: From Finnic–Germanic Contacts to the Conversion of Karelia. In Leszek Słupecki & Rudolf Simek (eds.). *Conversions: Looking for Ideological Change in the Early Middle Ages*. Studia Mediaevalia Septentrionalia 23. Vienna: Fassbaender. Pp. 53–98.

Frog. 2014 (in press). Mythology and Identity: Approaching Archaeological Evidence of Viking Age Åland. In Joonas Ahola, Frog & Jenni Lucenius (eds.). *The Viking Age in Åland: Insights into Identity and Remnants of Culture*. Annales Academiae Scientiarum Fennicae Humaniora. Helsinki: Academia Scientiarum Fennica.

Geijer, Erik Gustaf. 1811. Vikingen. *Iduna* 1.

van Gennep, Arnold. 1960 [1908]. *The Rites of Passage*. Chicago: University of Chicago Press.

de Gobineau, Arthur. 1853–1855. *Essai sur l'inégalité des races humaines*. Paris: Firmin Didot Fréres.

Grünthal, Riho. 1997. *Livvistä liiviin: Itämerensuomalaiset etnonyymit*. Castrenianumin toimitteita 51. Helsinki: Helsingin Yliopisto.

Gunnell, Terry. 2013. The Acceptance of Óðinn as a Preparation for the Acceptance of God? In Joonas Ahola, Frog & Jenni Lucenius (eds.). *The Viking Age in Åland: Insights into Identity and Remnants of Culture*. Studia Mediaevalia Septentrionalia 23. Vienna: Fassbaender.

Haug, Sonja. 2008. Migration Networks and Migration Decision-Making. *Journal of Ethnic and Migration Studies* 34(4). Pp. 585–605.

Hämäläinen, Pekka Kalevi. 1984. Suomenruotsalaisten rotukäsityksiä vallankumouksen ja kansalaissodan aikoina. In Aira Kemiläinen (ed.). *Mongoleja vai germaaneja? - Rotuteorioiden suomalaiset*. Historiallinen arkisto 86. Helsinki: Suomen Historiallinen Seura. Pp. 407–420.

Harrison, Dick. 2005. *Gud vill det! - Nordiska korsfarare under medeltiden*. Stockholm: Ordfront Förlag.

Helimski, Eugene. 2008. Ladoga and Perm Revisited. *Studia Etymologica Cracoviensia* 13: 75–88.

Hernæs, P. 1997. Storpolitikk og vikingtog på slutten av 700-tallet. In I. Fuglestedt & B. Myhre (eds.). *Konflikt i forhistorien*. Stavanger: Arkeologisk museum i Stavanger. Pp. 57–67.

Hultkrantz, Åke. 1985. Reindeer Nomadism and the Religion of the Saamis. In Louise Bäckman & Åke Hultkrantz (eds.). *Saami Pre-Christian Religion: Studies on the Oldest Traces of Religion among the Saamis*. Acta Universitatis Stockholmensis: Stockholm Studies in Comparative Religion 25. Stockholm: Almqvist & Wiksell International. Pp. 11–28.

Huurre, Matti. 1979. *9000 vuotta Suomen esihistoriaa*. Helsinki: Otava.

Huurre, Matti. 1983. *Pohjois-Pohjanmaan ja Lapin historia I: Pohjois-Pohjanmaan ja Lapin esihistoria*. Oulu: Pohjois-Pohjanmaan maakuntaliiton ja Lapin maakuntaliiton historiatoimikunta.

Janhunen, 2009. Some Additional Notes on the Macrohydronyms of the Ladoga Region. *Studia Etymologica Cracoviensia* 14: 203–212.

Jauhiainen, Marjatta. 1998. *The Type and Motif Index of Finnish Belief Legends and Memorates*. FF Communications 267. Helsinki: Academia Scientiarum Fennica.

Jonuks, Tõnno. 2005. Archaeology of Religion: Possibilities and Prospects. *Estonian Journal of Archaeology* 9(1): 32–59.

Julku, Kyösti. 1967. Oulujoki karjalaisten kaukoliikenteen väylänä keskiajalla. *Studia Historica: Acta Societatis Historicae Ouluensis I*. Oulu: Oulun Historiaseura. Pp. 65–98.

Kallio, Petri. 2006. On the Earliest Slavic Loanwords in Finnic. In Juhani Nuorluoto (ed.). *The Slavicization of the Russian North*. Slavica Helsingesia 27. Helsinki: Department of Slavonic and Baltic Languages and Literatures at Helsinki University. Pp. 154–166.

Kamwangamalu, Nkonko M. 2003. Social Change and Language Shift: South Africa. *Annual Review of Applied Linguistics* 23: 225–242.

Kankaanpää, Jarmo. 1997. People in Cold Environments - Ihmisiä kylmillä mailla. In Eeva-Liisa Schulz & Christian Carpelan (eds.). *Varhain pohjoisessa - Early in the North: Maa - The Land*. Helsinki Papers in Archaeology 10. Helsinki: University of Helsinki. Pp. 103–123.

Kirkinen, Heikki. 1970. *Karjala idän ja lännen välissä I: Venäjän Karjala renessanssiajalla (1478–1617)*. Helsinki: Kirjayhtymä.

Kivikoski, Ella. 1938. Likarmade spännen från vikingatiden. *Finskt museum* 45: 10–28.

Koivulehto, Jorma. 1987. Namn som kan tolkas urgermanskt. In Lars Húlden (ed.). *Klassiska problem inom finlandssvensk ortnamnsforskning*. Studier i Nordisk filologi 67. Helsingfors: Svenska Litteratursällskapet i Finland. Pp. 27–42.

Konkka, Unelma. 1985. *Ikuinen ikävä*. Helsinki: Suomalaisen Kirjallisuuden Seura.

Kovalev, R. K. 2001. The Infrastructure of the Northern Part of the 'Fur Road': Between the Middle Volga and the East during the Middle Ages. *Archivum Eurasiae Medii Aevii* 11: 25–64.

Krohn, Julius. 1883. *Suomalaisen kirjallisuuden historia I: Kalevala*. Helsinki: Suomalaisen Kirjallisuuden Seura.

Kuz'min 2008 = Кузьмин С. Л. 2008. Ладога в эпоху раннего средневековья (середина VIII — начало XII в.) In *Исследования археологических памятников эпохи средневековья*. СПб. Pp. 69–94.

Kylstra, A. D., Sirkka-Liisa Hahmo, Tette Hofstra & Osmo Nikkilä (eds.). 1991–2012. *Lexikon der älteren germanischen Lehnwörter in den ostseefinnischen Sprachen* I–III. Amsterdam: Radopi.

Latvakangas, Arto. 1992. Suomalaisteoria: Varjagiongelman historiografinen sivupolku. In Kyösti Julku (ed.). *Suomen varhaishistoria: Tornion kongressi 14.–16.6.1991*. Rovaniemi: Pohjois-Suomen historiallinen yhdistys. Pp. 249–294. (With an English summary.)

Lehtosalo-Hilander, Pirkko-Liisa. 1984. Suomen nuoremman rautakauden esineistö kansallisuusolojen heijastajana. In *Suomen väestön esihistorialliset juuret*. Bidrag till Kännedom av Finlands Natur och Folk 131. Helsinki: Societas Scientiarum Fennica. Pp. 283–301.

Lehtosalo-Hilander, Pirkko-Liisa. 2000a. *Kalastajista kauppanaisiin: Euran esihistoria*. Eura: Euran kunta.

Lehtosalo-Hilander, Pirkko-Liisa. 2000b. *Luistari IV: Luistari: A History of Weapons and Ornaments*. Suomen Muinaismuistoyhdistyksen Aikakauskirja 107. Helsinki: Suomen Muinaismuistoyhdistys.

Lind, John H. 1991. Early Russian–Swedish Rivalry: The Battle of the Neva in 1240 and Birgir Magnusson's Second Crusade to Tavastia. *Scandinavian Journal of History* 16(4): 269–295.

Lotman, Yuri M. 1990. *Universe of the Mind: A Semiotic Theory of Culture*. Trans. Ann Shukman. Bloomington: Indiana University Press.

Massey, D. S., J. Arango, G. Hugo, A. Kouaouci, A. Pellegrino & J. E. Taylor. 1993. Theories of International Migration: A Review and Appraisal. *Population and Development Review* 19(3): 431–466.

Mäkivuoti, M. 1992. Rautakauden asutus Pohjanrannalla. In Kyösti Julku (ed.). *Suomen varhaishistoria: Tornion kongressi 14.–16.6.1991*. Rovaniemi: Pohjois-Suomen historiallinen yhdistys. Pp. 343–355. (With an English summary).

Meinander, Carl Fredrik. 1983. Om svenskarnes inflyttningar till Finland. *Historisk Tidskrift för Finland* 1983(3): 229–251.

Nordberg, Andreas. 2012. Continuity, Change and Regional Variation in Old Norse Religion. In Catherina Raudvere & Jens Peter Schjødt (eds.). *More than Mythology: Narratives, Ritual Practices and Regional Distribution in Pre-Christian Scandinavian Religions*. Lund: Nordic Academic Press. Pp. 119–151.

Norio, Reijo. 2003. Finnish Disease Heritage II: Population Prehistory and Genetic Roots of Finns. *Human Genetics* 112: 457–469.

Tarkiainen, Kari. 2008. *Sveriges österland: Från forntid till Gustav Vasa*. Stockholm: Atlantis.

Orel,Vladimir. 2003. *A Handbook of German Etymology*. Leiden: Brill.

Planke, Terje. 2011. Båt og mønster. In *Fra kaupang til bygd: Festskrift for Ragnar Pedersen*. Hamar: Hedmarksmuseet og Domkirkeodden. Pp. 173–195.

Pöllä, Matti. 1992. Laatokan länsirannikon asujaimiston etnisen koostumuksen muutokset rautakaudella ja Karjalan synty. In Kyösti Julku (ed.). *Suomen varhaishistoria: Tornion kongressi 14.–16.6.1991*. Rovaniemi: Pohjois-Suomen historiallinen yhdistys.

Pratt, Mary Louise. 1991. Arts of the Contact Zone. *Profession* 1991: 33–40.

Price, Neil S. 2002. *The Viking Way: Religion and War in Late Iron Age Scandinavia*. AUN 31. Uppsala: Department of Archaeology and Ancient History.

Rahkonen, Pauli. 2011. Finno-Ugrian Hydronyms of the River Volkhov and Luga Catchment Areas. *Journal de la Société Finno-Ougrienne* 93: 205–266.

Reichl, Karl 2007. *Edige: A Karakalpak Oral Epic as Performed by Jumabay Bazarov*. FF Communications 293. Helsinki: Finnish Literature Society.

Renfrew, Colin 1986. Introduction: Peer-Polity Interaction and Socio-Political Change. In Colin Renfrew & John F. Cherry (eds.). *Peer-Polity Interaction and Socio-Political Change*. Cambridge: Press Syndicate of the University of Cambridge. Pp. 1–18.

Roeck Hansen, Birgitta. 1988. Settlement Change and Agricultural Structure in the Late Iron Age and Medieval Åland. *Geografiska Annaler* 70B(1): 87–93.

Rydving, Hakon. 2010. *Tracing Sami Traditions: In Search of the Indigenous Religion among the Western Sami during the 17th and 18th Centuries*. Oslo: Institute for Comparative Research in Human Culture.

Saarikivi, Janne. 2004. Über die saamischen Substratennamen des Nordrusslands und Finnlands. *Finnisch-Ugrische Forschungen* 58: 162–234.

Saarikivi, Janne. 2006. *Substrata Uralica: Studies on Finno-Ugric Substratein Northern Russian Dialects*. Tartu: Tartu University Press.

Saarikivi, Janne. 2007. Finnic Personal Names on Novgorod Birch Bark Documents. In Juhani Nuorluoto (ed.). *The Slavicization of the Russian North*. Slavica Helsingensia 32. Helsinki: Department of Slavonic and Baltic Languages and Literatures, Helsinki University. Pp. 196–246.

Saarikivi, Janne, & Mika Lavento. 2012. Linguistics and Archaeology: A Critical View of an Interdisciplinary Approach with Reference to the Prehistory of Northern Scandinavia. In C. Damm & J. Saarikivi (eds.). *Networks, Interaction and Emerging Identities in Fennoscandia and Beyond. Papers from the Conference Held in Tromsø, Norway, October 13–16 2009*. Helsinki: Suomalais-Ugrilainen Seura. Pp. 177–239.

Saarikivi, Janne, & Frog. 2014 (forthcoming). Reconstruction of Historical Language Distribution and Change East of the Baltic Sea (with Consideration of the Problem of Ethnic Identities). *RMN Newsletter* 9.

Saksa, Aleksandr. 1998. *Rautakautinen Karjala: Muinais-Karjalan asutuksen synty ja varhaiskehitys*. Joensuu: Joensuun yliopisto.

Salo, Unto. 1992. Raudan synty. *Sananjalka* 34: 103–122.

Salo, Unto. 2000. Suomi ja Häme, Häme ja Satakunta. In Jukka Peltovirta (ed.). *Hämeen käräjät I*. Hämeenlinna: Hämeen heimoliitto. Pp. 18–231.

Sanmark, Alexandra. 2004. *Power and Conversion: A Comparative Study of Christianization in Scandinavia*. Occasional Papers in Archaeology 34. Uppsala: Department of Archaeology and Ancient History, Uppsala University.

Siikala, Anna-Leena. 2002. *Mythic Images and Shamanism: A Perspective on Kalevala Poetry*. FF Communications 280. Helsinki: Suomalainen Tiedeakatemia.

Siikala, Anna-Leena. 2012. *Itämerensuomalaisten mythologia*. Helsinki: Suomalaisen Kirjallisuuden Seura.

Siikala, Anna-Leena, & Jukka Siikala. *Return to Culture: Oral Tradition and Society in the Southern Cook Islands*. FF Communications 287. Helsinki: Academia Scientiarum Fennica, 2005.

Sjöstrand, Per Olof. 2014 (in press). History Gone Wrong: Interpretations of the Transition from the Viking Age to the Medieval Period in Åland. In Joonas Ahola, Frog & Jenni Lucenius (eds.). *The Viking Age in Åland: Insights into Identity and Remnants of Culture*. Helsinki: Academia Scientiarum Fennica.

Sohlman, August 1855. *Det unga Finland*. Stockholm.

Sørensen, Hans Christian. 1968. The So-Called Varangian-Russian Problem. *Scando-Slavica* 14 (1): 141–148.

Stark, Laura. 2002. *Peasants, Pilgrims, and Sacred Promises: Ritual and the Supernatural in Orthodox Karelian Folk Religion*. Studia Fennica Folkloristica 11. Helsinki: Finnish Literature Society.

Stepanova, Eila. 2011. Reflections of Belief Systems in Karelian and Lithuanian Laments: Shared Systems of Traditional Referentiality? *Archaeologia Baltica* 15: 128–143.

Stepanova, Eila. 2012. Mythic Elements of Karelian Laments: The Case of *syndyzet* and *spuassuzet*. In Frog, Anna-Leena Siikala & Eila Stepanova (eds.). *Mythic Discourses: Studies in Uralic Traditions*. Studia Fennica Folkloristica 20. Helsinki: Finnish Literature Society. Pp. 257–287.

Storli, Inger. 2000. Barbarians of the North: Reflections on the Establishment of Courtyard Sites in North Norway. *Norwegian Archaeological Review* 33(2): 81–103.

Taavitsainen, Jussi-Pekka. 1990. *Ancient Hillforts of Finland*. Suomen Muinaismuistoyhdistyksen Aikakauskirja 94. Helsinki: Suomen Muinaismuistoyhdistys.

Tarkka, Lotte. 2005. *Rajarahvaan laulu: Tutkimus Vuokkiniemen kalevalamittaisesta runokulttuurista 1821–1921*. Helsinki: Suomalaisen Kirjallisuuden Seura

Tarkka, Lotte. 2012. The Sampo: Myth and Vernacular Imagination. In Frog, Anna-Leena Siikala & Eila Stepanova (eds.). *Mythic Discourses: Studies in Uralic Traditions*. Studia Fennica Folkloristica 20. Helsinki: Finnish Literature Society. Pp. 143–170.

Tegnér, Esaias. 1820–1825. *Frithiofs saga*. Available at: www.runeberg.org/frithiofs/.

Thunmark-Nylén, Lena. 1983. Gotland och Ostbaltikum. In Jansson, Ingmar (ed.). *Gutar och vikingar (Gutes and Vikings)*. Stockholm: Statens historiska museum. Pp. 306–322.

Tolley, Clive 2009. *Shamanism in Norse Myth and Magic* I–II. FF Communications 296–297. Helsinki: Academia Scientiarum Fennica.

Tomtlund, Jan-Erik. 2005. *Vikingatid på Åland*. Mariehamn: Museibyrån.

Uino, Pirjo. 1997. *Ancient Karelia: Archaeological Studies*. Suomen muinaismuistoyhdistyksen aikakauskirja 104. Helsinki: Suomen Muinaismuistoyhdistys.

Vahtola, Jouko. 1980. *Tornionjoki- ja Kemijokilaakson asutuksen synty: Nimistötieteellinen ja historiallinen tutkimus*. Rovaniemi: Pohjois-Suomen historiallinen yhdistys.

Vahtola, Jouko. 1992. Pohjois-Pohjanmaan rannikon asutuksen synty. *Suomen varhaishistoria. Tornion kongressi 14.–16.6.1991*. Studia Historica Septentrionalia 21. Jyväskylä. Pp. 613–621.

Vaitkevičienė, Daiva (ed.). 2008. *Lietuvių užkalbėjimai: Gydymo formulės – Lithuanian Verbal Healing Charms*. Vilnius: Lietuvių literatūros ir tautosakos institutas.

Valk, Ülo. 2012. Thunder and Lightning in Estonian Folklore in the Light of Vernacular Theories. In Frog, Anna-Leena Siikala & Eila Stepanova (eds.). *Mythic Discourses: Studies in Uralic Traditions*. Studia Fennica Folkloristica 20. Helsinki: Finnish Literature Society. Pp. 40–67.

Valtonen, Irmeli. 2008. *The North in the Old English Orosius: A Geographical Narrative in Context*. Mémoires de la Société Néophilologique de Helsinki 73. Helsinki: Sociétéì Néophilologique.

Weber, Max. 1968. *Economy and Society; An Outline of Interpretive Sociology*. Ed. Guenther Roth & Claus Wittich. Berkeley: University of California Press.

Wessman, Anna. 2010. *Death, Destruction and Commemoration: Tracing Ritual Activities in Finnish Late Iron Age Cemeteries (AD 550–1150)*. Iskos 18. Helsinki: Finnish Antiquarian Society.

Wickholm, Anna, & Sami Raninen. 2006. The Broken People: Deconstruction of Personhood in Iron Age Finland. *Estonian Journal of Archaeology* 10: 150–166.

Wilson, William A. 1976. *Folklore and Nationalism in Modern Finland*. Bloomington: Indiana University Press.

Zachrisson, Inger. 1987. Östliga kontakter under nordsvensk vikingatid och tidig medeltid. In Kyösti Julku (ed.). *Nordkalotten i en skiftande värld: Kulturer utan gränser och stater over gränser*. Studia Historica Septentrionalia 14(1). Rovaniemi: Pohjois-Suomen historiallinen yhdistys. Pp. 188–204.

I

Time

Introduction

VIKING AGE IN FINLAND

The Viking Age is first and foremost a historical period. One of the central concerns of this volume is the relevance and significance of this period to 'Finland' and to Finno-Karelian regions of habitation. Before turning to the problem of territories and their relevance from the perspective of different disciplines, it is first necessary to gain perspectives on the Viking Age as a period. The Viking Age and its relevance emerge quite differently in the material examined in different disciplines. This makes it more significant that the 'Viking Age' has been constructed through academic and popular discourses across the past two centuries. The definitions for when this period began and ended continue to be negotiated around historical events and activities concentrated west of the Baltic Sea region in Northern Europe. The six chapters of this section provide necessary perspectives on how this period and its relevance emerge from the perspective of different disciplines. The broad introductory discussions and frames of reference provided by these chapters will benefit a reader as the questions, problems and information presented here are engaged and explored from different perspectives in subsequent parts of this volume.

Clive Tolley opens this section with a broad introduction to the potentials, problems and limitations of approaching our topic from the perspective of linguistics. He presents an overview that will be readily accessible to non-specialists. On the one hand, Tolley highlights the difficulty in correlating the relative chronologies of linguistic etymologies with the rather short target period of 800–1050 on an absolute chronology. On the other hand, he stresses the difficulty in correlating cultures that are identified according to linguistic criteria in one period with cultures that are identified according to archaeological criteria in a period centuries earlier. Although this chapter is focused on language and linguistics, the discussion it offers is generally relevant to fields concerned with data that has been transmitted historically through and across cultures: it outlines essential problematics of attempting to approach an earlier historical period through data that results from outcomes of diachronic processes.

Ville Laakso turns attention to archaeology and the potentials, problems and limitations of approaching the Viking Age through this discipline. Although archaeological data presents outcomes of synchronic processes that can be more reasonably situated on an absolute chronology, the dates of absolute chronologies must be correlated with the diversity of cultures that existed at that time and this data must also be situated in relation to earlier and later periods. Laakso highlights the unevenness of the distribution of archaeological data and its limitations. He also considers problems of where and how this data has been used. Whereas Tolley considers the problematics of correlating linguistically defined cultures with archaeological evidence, this chapter presents the other side of the coin, considering the problematics of correlating archaeologically defined cultures with cultures identified through languages in later periods. This discussion provides a valuable background for subsequent chapters addressing archaeological materials and data produced as synchronic outcomes of cultural and natural processes that happened during the Viking Age.

The outcomes of synchronic processes not only reveal information about cultures, but also about the environment. Samuli Helama approaches the Viking Age from the perspective of climatology. He draws back the focus from small language groups and localized archaeological cultures in order to situate the Viking Age in the broader context of the history of climate variation and change. Changes and variation in climate provide an invaluable frame of reference for understanding population movements and changes in cultural networks, mobility and livelihoods in the Viking Age. Helama shows that there is a correlation between the Viking Age as a historical period and changes in climate relevant to mobility, livelihoods and cultural practices. The chapter situates these changes in relation to global patterns and shows their interconnectedness with geological events on different continents that seem otherwise remote. The scope of this chapter valuably reveals how transient the Viking Age appears in the history of this part of the world, and indeed how small 'Finland' seems when situated in a global context.

Following a discussion on the scope of global climate, Tuukka Talvio draws attention back to items small enough to hold in one's hand: he considers the Viking Age from the perspective of numismatics – the study of coins – offering a valuable overview of coins found in Finland from the Viking Age proper. Coins provide an exceptional type of material for study. These resources are especially connected with trade, ornamentation and depositions, as well as having other connections with aspects of culture. Coins are also more enduring in the archaeological record than many other cultural products and are therefore more likely to be preserved as evidence. Moreover, these socially circulating artefacts connect to a great diversity of research questions, ranging from cultural contacts and socio-economic structures to cultural valuation systems and even ritual practices. Whereas Helama related climatic patterns independent of human activity to the Viking Age as a historical period, Talvio illustrates the relevance of the Viking Age in historical periodization through evidence of changes in cultures and cultural practices that become apparent through numismatics. At the same time, this chapter observes that the conventional dates for the historical period of the Viking Age (800–1050), based on historical events far to the west, do not wholly coincide with the corresponding processes in Finland.

The problem of identifying culturally relevant dates for the Viking Age in Finland returns the reader to the issue that the 'Viking Age' as a historical period is in fact a construct negotiated in both academic and popular discourses. This aspect of discussion is taken up by Sirpa Aalto, who looks at the appearance of 'Viking Age' as a term in discussions and studies of the past two centuries. Aalto considers how this term, its use and avoidance are entangled with nationalist discourses and the negotiation of cultural identities. She gives special attention to how the term has been used surrounding the construction of Finnishness in the Finnish language on the one hand, and, on the other, the maintenance of a cultural identity of Swedish language populations of Finland during the changing social and political environments of a modernizing nation-state. This chapter emphasizes that discussions surrounding the Viking Age as a historical period can never be wholly disentwined from the contemporary discourse environment in which it is discussed.

Petri Kallio brings the section to a close by turning from questions of 'Finnish' national cultural identity to questions of Finnic languages and their distribution in the Viking Age. Whereas Tolley focused on the problematics of identifying the Viking Age in later linguistic evidence, Kallio outlines a long-term chronology of the development and break-up of Finnic languages and situates the Viking Age in relation to that chronology. Through correlations of linguistic, archaeological and toponymic data, this chapter offers the reader a perspective on the dispersal of Finnic languages, their variety and distribution into the Viking Age. The perspective it offers on the history of language development and spread reveals that Finnic languages were most likely not spoken in the majority of the territories where Finnish and Karelian are found today. The cartographic distribution of languages in the Viking Age was much different than in later periods. This work prepares the reader for the discussion of social and cultural space in the following section. The insights it offers can be placed fruitfully in dialogue with perspectives from research on archaeological cultures and on other linguistic-cultural groups.

The six chapters of this section are, on the one hand, independent treatises representing various points of view both of different disciplines and the perspectives within those disciplines. On the other hand, they together demonstrate that the Viking Age was a constituent of the past of Finland. They simultaneously reveal its relevance – both for the contemporary inhabitants of the relevant territories and as a tool and resource in discourses of later periods – simultaneously showing that it can be extremely elusive from the perspective of any one discipline. These chapters also expose how, as a period in the history of this part of the world, the Viking Age can be – and has been – interpreted in various ways according to the point of view, context of discourse, and nature of the evidence on which the interpretation is based. Individually, these chapters show a tendency to focus on questions of developments in time within the available evidence, yet they also extend in scope beyond the temporal spheres of the Viking Age in Finland to connect with many intersecting themes that are woven through the contributions, anticipating discussions in following sections and knitting them tightly into dialogue with the other chapters brought together in this volume.

Clive Tolley

Language in Viking Age Finland

An Overview

The present chapter aims to offer a broad overview of the topic of language in Viking Age Finland, and is intended mainly as an introductory contextualisation for non-linguists. It does not seek to offer any new research insights, for which the reader is directed to the more specialised contributions in the present collection, but rather to give some idea of the areas which call for investigation and the challenges inherent in doing so.

Finland has long been the meeting place not only of different languages, but of different language families – and all the indications are that this truism was reflected particularly strongly during the Viking Age. My aim here is to set out a few aspects of the framework within which any investigation of the linguistics of Viking Age Finland must take place, with reference to other chapters within the present collection, to which this essay acts as a general introduction.

Most Finns are aware of the official bilingualism of the country: both Finnish and Swedish have the status of officially recognised languages. In fact, a further official language (or rather set of closely related languages) needs to be added to this list: the Sámi language(s) of Lapland. If we move back in history a mere hundred years, Russian was also acknowledged as an official language of Finland. These four languages, all still vital players in the region, have formed the protagonists of a linguistic drama which has been acted out not just since the Viking Age, but for millennia: the Viking Age is the setting for just one scene in a play of many acts. Others too, such as the Baltic languages (now represented by Latvian and Lithuanian, but once widespread across a much greater area of Prussia, Northwest Russia and, most likely, over into Finland), have played a significant part in this drama. Perhaps the Finns learnt to build bridges from the Balts, for they took the word *silta* ['bridge'] from them; yet, although they also borrowed the word *hammas* ['tooth'], we must beware of concluding that ancient Finns had no teeth (the old word was probably *pii*, confined now to flint, and the tines of a fork). Some players in distant days, probably three millennia or more ago, may seem from our modern perspective like strange partners: yet it is clear that speakers of an ancestral dialect from which Finnish derives danced hand-in-hand on that stage with speakers of languages which gave rise to those spoken now in Iran and much of India (including the Sinhalese of far-distant Srilanka), from whom they borrowed the word for heaven/sky (*taivas*) and the *sampo*, one of the central, mysterious artefacts of Finnish folk poetry (see Ahola). These borrowings must have taken place close to the steppe, probably somewhere near where the Volga crosses it (roughly to the south of Udmurtia, Finno-Ugric-speaking to this day), for in ancient days the steppe was inhabited by Indo-Aryan speakers, and to their north in the taiga were spoken ancestral Finno-Ugric dialects.[1]

These stages in the linguistic development of Finnish and its encounters with other languages are not directly relevant to the study of the Viking Age: yet they illustrate some of the sort of issues we face. Lexical borrowings (loanwords) may indicate adoption of new technologies like bridge-building, and may tell us something about the source and time of the borrowings; but examples like *hammas* illustrate how careful we must be in drawing conclusions, and also pose us further questions – why does a language give up its normal word for 'tooth'; or, taking an example borrowed (before the Viking period) from a Germanic language, why did ancestral Finns stop calling their mothers *emä* and use the foreign word *äiti*? The ancient Indo-Aryan loans point to an external religious influence with implications for the origins and development of some central aspects of folklore and mythology recorded centuries, indeed millennia, later. These are just some of the areas of cultural history and the sorts of question that a consideration of language history may enable us to elucidate. The examples I have given are very well known; it is hoped, naturally, that we may be able to bring rather less well-known, or indeed wholly unresearched, examples to bear on the study of Viking Age Finland.

What then can be said, in general terms, of the linguistic atlas of Viking Age Finland? The map changes, of course, as our research increases, and the present essays contribute to this research base. It is likely that in the centuries preceding the Viking Age, speakers of ancestral Finnish dialects lived in limited areas close to the western and southern coasts; by the Viking Age, settlement was spreading inland and eastwards towards Karelia. Such areas of agricultural settlement may be identified archaeologically, and these are usually interpreted as Finnish-speaking regions: it should be remembered, however, that nothing in the linguistic evidence *necessitates* a precise correlation between areas of early Finnish speech and these areas of settlement (which are themselves always subject to revision in the light of new archaeological evidence). Close to the Finnish speakers, but probably somewhat further inland, away from areas of intensive settlement, dwelt Sámi speakers: varieties of Sámi were spoken in inland Finland and Karelia (as noted by Kuzmin) for centuries after the Viking Age. The Sámi language had spread some centuries earlier from a base in southern Finland and already reached Lapland, displacing earlier and probably unrelated languages, but the extent to which these other languages were still spoken in northern Fenno-Scandia in the Viking Age is an open question (with implications for what was actually meant by Old Norse *Finnr*, for example, a word taken to refer to Sámi, but possibly with wider connotations).[2] Whatever the motivation for the Sámi expansion (as yet largely unresearched), our notions of trade, warfare and other forms of contact throughout the prehistoric period will be altered by a deeper understanding of it. In the eastern part of Finno-Karelian varieties of Finnic were or had been spoken which survive only as a substrate element (discussed below) in Karelian dialects; again, the spread of this East Finnic and its contacts remain a matter of debate. Bordering on the Finnic region dwelt the Chud: it remains unclear who these people were, and what language they spoke (possibly a non-Finnic, but still closely related Finno-Ugric language: see Kallio), but they were within the ambit of the Norse Varangians, and hence may have played a significant part in cultural contacts at this time. As Kaisa Häkkinen emphasises, Finnic speakers were also in contact with Slavic speakers, beginning from the time Slavs penetrated as far north as Novgorod, i.e. approximately the Viking Age. A number of loans surviving in Finnish illustrate a focus upon trade in such contacts, and later upon Christianity (the first Finnish contacts with which appear, on linguistic evidence, to have taken place rather earlier with the Orthodox Russians than with the Catholic Swedes). Norsemen too were in direct contact with Slavs during the Viking period, as Rus (originally Swedish, later slavicised) traders passed down the main waterways of Russia towards Constantinople. It was between Finns and Swedes on the west (and later south) coast of Finland that the most persistent and deepest contacts were maintained. Such contacts went back many centuries before the Viking period, and continued after it.

* * *

Let us adumbrate a few of the challenges in attempting to flesh out this simplified picture of language in Viking Age Finland.

To begin with a definitional problem: the concept of 'Viking Age Finland' itself presents difficulties. As anyone with even a slight knowledge of the history of the country will be aware, the borders of the state of Finland have changed constantly – most recently with the loss of parts of Karelia to Soviet Russia in the aftermath of the Second World War. Some, looking back through history, may be aware of a series of treaties dividing the territory of Finland between the empires of Sweden and Russia, back to the first we have any record of, that of Nötholm (Pähkinäsaari) in 1323, which marked the conclusion to an extended period of skirmishes between the two powers, delineating the spheres of influence on a line running approximately from Vyborg (Viipuri) to Uleåborg (Oulu). Before this date, the territory of Finland had long been a borderless region subject to influences from both west and east (and indeed south), with speakers of a number of languages, including ancestral forms of Finnish and Sámi, scattered across this area of cultural interchange. The particular forms of this interchange, and the players within it, are the subject of investigation in many fields, including linguistics. One point on which all researchers agree, however, is that 'Finland' in the modern sense is not a meaningful construct for the prehistoric period: it serves as a convenient shorthand for the territory encompassed by modern Finland, but of necessity includes surrounding areas too when used in reference to the distant past.

Comparable difficulties arise with the notion of the Viking Age. This period, taken to cover AD 800 to 1000, is largely derived from Scandinavian, rather than Finnish, history, and even in its original context was not meant to imply any sudden changes at either end of the time span: this is all the more true when the term is applied to Finland. From a linguistic point of view, such a brief period would only be meaningful if we had datable written sources to trace linguistic development in fine detail: but we have no such written records in Finnish. We must therefore rely on linguistic reconstruction, which almost always works on much longer time scales than a couple of centuries, and is moreover generally relative rather than absolute: we can often determine that one linguistic change (such as in pronunciation) must have taken place before another, but without external datable testimony, it is generally impossible to assign absolute dates to these changes.

Thus, in order to discuss Viking Age Finland, a consideration of the wider geographical and chronological contexts is unavoidable, and hence the presentations offered here bring in considerations of the prehistory of Finnish and Scandinavian languages, and extend into Karelia as far as Lake Onega, and southwards into Estonia and indeed down to Novgorod. The present collection does not include consideration of Sámi languages of Lapland, but such an investigation will extend the arena further outside the bounds of modern-day Finland.

A further, rather more fundamental, challenge to anyone attempting to draw general conclusions about the linguistic situation of Viking Age Finland is the paucity of research undertaken hitherto in this area. Considerable work has been undertaken on the development of the Finnish written language, from the late Middle Ages on; within prehistoric (i.e. pre-written) linguistics most scholarly attention has been focused on the development of Finnish and related languages of a considerably older period, concluding approximately with the Roman period. This is a particularly fascinating period from a linguistic perspective: it was the one in which Finnish and related languages (Estonian, varieties of Karelian, and more distantly related Sámi) became distinguished as a group within the wider Finno-Ugric family of languages, with far-reaching changes such as loss of many sounds such as *č* or *š* (to oversimplify), and the adoption of many loanwords, borrowed from ancestral forms of the Germanic and Baltic languages. Whilst such changes cannot in themselves be dated very closely, it is generally agreed that the period in question covered at least the Bronze and Iron Ages. After the Roman period Finnish remained fairly stable, at least in phonemic terms (the sounds of the language), and probably also in lexical terms (the vocabulary). A great deal of effort has gone into pushing back the relative age of the earliest loans from Germanic and Baltic languages. Yet surprisingly little attention has been paid to the development of the Finnish language after this 'interesting' phase, and hence we know relatively little either about internal developments within the language, or about the loanwords which entered it during this period. Typical of the characteristic scholarly interest in very ancient prehistorical linguistics is Tette Hofstra's important thesis of 1985, which summarised and considered research in the previous quarter century on contacts between Germanic and Finnic, but barely mentioned the Viking period. Another quarter of a century has now passed, and we are in need of a similar fresh survey – but even if such a survey were conducted it would not add very much more in terms of the Viking Age: hence, there is a need for new research to be undertaken and presented. Hofstra's work sets a precedent for how to present such a new survey, with its consideration of the phonological backgrounds (the sound systems and structures) of the languages and their effects on the form of loanwords, and a typology of loans. An important advance has been made in the field of Germanic–Finnish linguistic contacts with the publication of the *Lexikon der älteren germanischen Lehnwörter in den ostseefinnischen Sprachen* (1991–2012).

As soon as we attempt to refine any general outline of the linguistic situation of Viking Age Finland, as was given earlier, we begin to climb what appears an exponential curve of difficulties. Let us take just one issue: Finnish–Germanic contacts. We are dealing with reconstructed forms in both languages: Finnish was wholly unwritten at this period, and Norse was only sparsely recorded in often unclear runic inscriptions. Norse had undergone rapid change from about 600 to 800, but thereafter remained relatively stable until well after the Viking period. Finnish underwent many substantial changes at an earlier period, concluding, as noted, around the early Roman time, after which it did not alter greatly in phonological terms. One problem with drawing conclusions from comparisons between reconstructed languages is that a feature which disappears from a language cannot be reconstructed: for example, many more Germanic loans could in principle have been taken into Finnish but subsequently disappeared, which would alter our perceptions of the extent and type of cultural contact; this caveat to the conclusions we draw always needs to be borne in mind. As far as dating is concerned, we should in principle be able in many cases to distinguish loans borrowed before and after *c.* 800, since loanwords in Finnish will reflect the fairly rapidly changing forms of the Norse originals up to this date, but in practice the phonological form of only a few words is such as to allow us to place them even approximately in the Viking Age.[3] Häkkinen takes one example, *auskari* ['bail'] which happens to show sufficient characteristics for us to be able to assign an approximate date: the *r* indicates a borrowing after Norse rhotacism (a regular change of *z* to *r*), but before Swedish monophthongisation of *au* to *ö*; a Viking Age setting is justified phonologically, and corresponds to a seafaring era when bailing out ships would have been a particularly frequent activity. We are given a few such examples in the present collection, yet it is evident that to date no systematic study of such loans, or even survey of existing work on them, has been made, so our knowledge remains piecemeal. It is only when the painstaking work of a more thorough investigation has been carried out that we will be in a position to draw any general inferences about the extent and type of cultural contact in the Viking Age.

It needs to be emphasised, especially for non-linguists, that any references to languages which today have standardised forms, such as Finnish or Swedish, in fact refer to a series of closely related dialects: national languages received standard forms only in very recent centuries, a process which requires strong political centralisation of a form completely absent in Viking Age Finland. We may be confident that the areas in which 'Finnish' or 'Old Norse' were spoken in fact comprised patchworks of dialects, each of which was probably spoken in a very small area (by a few hundred people or so); to be more accurate, even the notion of 'dialect' is fluid, since every individual speaks in a slightly different way, or to put it in linguistic terms, has his or her own *idiolect* – and an idiolect may be further subdivided, since an individual uses different registers depending on when and who they are talking to, and a person's language also changes over their lifetime. What exists in a language is the result of just a very minute portion of a language at an earlier stage being passed on, and never in wholly unaltered form, to succeeding generations: so any reconstruction merely glimpses a few snatches of what a language was like in former times, with whole dialects, and indeed languages, which may at the time have been prominent, having disappeared without trace. We are often confronted by apparently aberrant forms of words when, for example, considering loanwords: it may often be the case that a word has been borrowed from a dialect which has otherwise simply disappeared. Any such conclusion has to be drawn tentatively, but in principle, with enough work, it may be possible to build a picture, however indistinct, of the dialectology of prehistoric Finland and prehistoric loans, which in turn may reveal interesting information about the geography of contact.

The dialectal nature of languages in the Viking period poses further questions: how did loans actually take place? Did one Finnish-speaking coastal settlement (or initially one person within that settlement) decide to use the word the Norse sailors were using for their bail, *auskari*, and through trade or other contacts with other settlements the word was adopted more widely? Or did several settlements adopt the word independently – with some of them, perhaps, differing in their interpretation of what the Norsemen were actually saying, giving rise to the variant form *äyskäri*? We may imagine various scenarios, but the existence of a loanword implies a challenge of explanation of how it spread, often through several dialects or even languages (for example, it seems that all the words in Sámi taken from Baltic languages were borrowed twice: first of all by Finnish speakers, and then from these Finns by Sámi speakers). The distribution of a loanword is an indication of its importance and of cultural history, and much work remains to be done in this field, particularly with regard to the Viking period.

Loanwords are, of course, not the only type of linguistic investigation that calls for attention. Another is onomastics, the study of names, and in particular place names (which may, in fact, themselves be loanwords). As Johan Schalin points out, place names undergo a sort of para-linguistic development, not necessarily following the same sound-change rules at the same rate as ordinary words, for example: they therefore require specialist treatment. Place names may reveal a great deal about changing cultural trends, for they often follow patterns which change over time, and, as Schalin indicates, they may reveal changing settlement patterns between Swedish and Finnish speakers. Theophoric names are those containing a divine name, and their study may provide us with information about the spread of cult in prehistory; an example is names containing *oksi* ['bear'] which may relate to the traditional bear-wake ceremonies preserved in Finnish folk tradition. Whilst place-name studies in some countries, such as England, have been extensive and carried out over many decades, the field remains underdeveloped in Finland, so a significant potential for important conclusions to be drawn remains.

Any linguistic investigation also needs to take into account the material culture, usually established through archaeology, palaeobotany and other sciences, and the political situation: the Viking Age is characterised by mass movements of at least the warrior elite and traders, which can be established through historical sources and archaeology. Within the present collection, Häkkinen in particular emphasises the need to take account of material culture when determining what can be said of linguistic contacts: thus, although *humala* ['hop'] could, as far as its phonology goes, be borrowed from Proto-Germanic, it is known that hops came into use in beer-making only in the Viking period, so a borrowing at this period is much more likely (anything later being excluded because of sound changes in Swedish). This example illustrates the sort of facet of cultural history it is hoped may be unveiled through linguistic study.

Linguistics needs to take account of the findings of other disciplines, but any discipline should remain true to its own principles. One of the greatest temptations for historical linguists, concerned with reconstructing and analysing linguistic circumstances from past ages, is to attempt not merely to correlate their findings with those of archaeology, but to infer linguistic conclusions on the basis of archaeological evidence. This is a logically unfounded methodology, but one which has been indulged in rather frequently within Finnish linguistics. In particular, even though it is a well-understood principle within linguistics that linguistic continuity or change bears no necessary correlation with material continuity or change – in other words, there can be a change or none at all in what language people speak without this showing any signs in the archaeological record – this is precisely the fallacy that has all too often been adopted.

The overarching principles that need to be adopted in our linguistic research are, then, on the one hand to remain true to the principles of linguistic research, and on the other to adopt a nuanced approach when interfacing with other disciplines, taking account of the many strands of evidence rather than adopting any one model established on, for example, archaeological grounds without full consideration of the implications.

Fortunately, more nuanced approaches are now beginning to be adopted within linguistics; an example is Ante Aikio's critique of the assumption that Sámi must have been spoken in Lapland since the mesolithic, on the grounds that there is no observable break in material culture in the archaeological record (Aikio 2006). Aikio points out, on the basis of linguistic evidence, that Sámi up to the Roman period must have been spoken in a limited region of southern Finland, whence it spread rapidly into Lapland some centuries later. His proposal is based firmly on linguistic grounds: it is an inductively established fact that, in primitive societies, a language cannot maintain its coherence over huge geographical areas for anything but short lengths of time. All the Sámi languages are so close that they must derive from one dialect, spoken by definition in a limited area at an earlier period; that area must have been in southern Finland, since there are no grounds for placing speakers of early Finnish in any other area, and the Sámi language shows many loans taken from Finnish (which cannot have been made later, because of their particular phonological form). Hence the unavoidable conclusion that Sámi must have spread fairly rapidly from southern Finland into Lapland at a point which linguistic change and other factors determine must have been roughly in the Roman or post-Roman period.

Yet the archaeological evidence of continuity of culture in Lapland is not merely swept aside in this scenario, merely the crudeness of its interpretation as an indication that Sámi 'must' have been spoken there since the mesolithic. Aikio, by contrast, interprets the continuity as being reflected linguistically in what is termed the *substrate* element in Sámi. A substrate is a part of a language (usually vocabulary, but it can include phonetic or grammatical structures too) which is derived from another language previously spoken in an area where the new language is adopted; it is all that is left as an indigenous core when a new language is taken over from outside. The identification of substrate elements can be contentious, but is based on the principle of identifying words, sounds or structures that do not adhere to forms that could have been inherited: e.g. if a word has no cognates ('cousins', inherited from an antecedent form of the language: e.g. Finnish *piimä*, Estonian *piim*) in other related languages, or is not borrowed from any other identifiable language, and particularly if it has a sound structure aberrant from the norm of the language, it may be inherited from a lost and displaced language. Substrates are typically found when a population adopts a new language, but not a new culture (or at least preserves major elements of its existing culture), and adapts the terms, for example for specialist tools and tasks, but also for names of geographical features, from the old language into the new. Finnish shows apparently non-Finno-Ugric substrate elements at least in place names such as *Päijänne*; Sámi, apart from geographical terms, also has a large substrate element – identified as such largely on the basis of its uniqueness to Sámi (there are no related words in other Finno-Ugric languages, so the words are not inherited from that ancestral source) – concerning aspects of life typical to the far-northern Sámi culture (such as Northern Sámi *njálla* ['arctic fox'], *vieksi* ['young common seal']). The implication therefore is that people switched languages (while preserving something of their old language), not that they abandoned their cultural heritage. Why such a linguistic change should have taken place remains to be investigated; similar examples have been suggested elsewhere, such as the adoption of Indo-European languages in northern India in antiquity, which has been interpreted as being the adoption of a *lingua franca* for trade purposes with Indo-European traders from the steppe to the north: such examples may serve as paradigms for investigation of circumstances in prehistoric Finland. Whatever the particular historical explanation for the linguistic landscape of modern Lapland, it is the large substrate element in Sámi languages, representing the remnants of languages spoken before the adoption of Sámi in the far north and hence of cultural continuity, that corresponds to the archaeological record of continuity.

Substrates affect more than just Sámi, however. When the massive changes in Finnish prehistory which resulted in (approximately) the existing consonant system of modern Finnish were first identified and analysed, it was suggested that the impetus for them was provided by Germanic influence or even a Germanic substrate: speakers of Germanic dialects were unable to pronounce sounds like *š* or *č*, and so accommodated the whole sound system of Finnish to their way of speaking (ironically, Germanic languages are nowadays full of such sounds, whereas Finnish lacks them: but the converse was true some two or more millennia ago). It is also recognised that the Germanic languages almost certainly have a substantial substrate element, inherited from earlier languages spoken in northern Europe: some have – with very little grounds – sought to identify this substrate element as Finno-Ugric. The point to draw is that even though substrate studies may become fanciful, they continue to form an essential element in historical linguistic analysis, offering the potential to uncover at least hints of cultural continuity and change from long ago. The constant language shifts in border areas between Finnish and Swedish in Finland might be said to represent a patchwork of substrate elements between the two languages, as SCHALIN helps to illustrate in his study of place names.

As we proceed to investigate the linguistics of Viking Age Finland, I would like by way of summary to isolate a few matters that need to be borne in mind:

1. The reconstruction of earlier stages of a language is always a levelling process, which involves the explanation of anomalies in a current language as arising from earlier regularities. It is impossible to reconstruct anomalies which have disappeared, precisely because reconstruction is necessarily rule-based, and anomalies are those features which do not fit the rules. Thus, earlier forms of languages would have had far more anomalies than their reconstructed forms allow for. This may sound an abstruse argument, but it has significant implications. One of them is dialectal variation, which is a form of anomaly: proto-languages always look homogeneous, whereas there was certainly huge dialectal variation which has simply left no trace, or very little. Both Proto-Norse and Proto-Finnic would have occurred in more varied forms than it is possible to reconstruct. This is a point which is taken up in different ways by SCHALIN, who points out differences in phonology of borrowings between Finnish and Swedish in different areas, by KUZMIN, who notes differences in the now vanished Sámi dialects of Eastern Karelia from any existing dialects spoken in Lapland, and by KALLIO, who notes the existence of East

Finnic, also now vanished (other than as a substrate element in some eastern North Finnic languages). Thus, linguistic reconstruction tends to pull in one direction, towards an ever more homogeneous and regular linguistic landscape with fewer and fewer languages the further back we go, whereas we know the reality to have been quite the contrary, with languages as irregular as ever, broken into myriad varying dialects, and bordered by many other unrelated languages which have disappeared with almost no trace.

2. Related to the first point is the geographical spread of a language. In the last few years some researchers such as Aikio have emphasised the impossibility of some proto-language geographies, such as the notion that Proto-Uralic could have been spoken over an area extending from the Baltic to the Urals, which is in direct contradiction to what is observed in living languages of roughly comparable cultural peoples such as the Khanty, where there are vast differences from one river valley to the next. Aikio has pointed out that where linguistic homogeneity exists over a wide geographical area, this is bound to be the result of fairly recent and rapid spread of the language – or more specifically of one form (dialect) of a language (it is clear that other Sámi dialects once spoken in Finland and Karelia ceased to exist). Hence Sámi cannot have been spoken as a cohesive entity over almost the whole of Finland, Karelia and Lapland for any length of time: determining the status of the Sámi language in the Viking Age has implications for the questions of linguistic contact with Norse speakers. Aikio's observations are carefully framed in relation to the cultural, and particularly political, status of the linguistic community concerned: in more hierarchically controlled societies, there is a greater likelihood of some form of standard language being imposed over wider regions for longer periods, and such relative differences may be relevant in considerations of the different languages involved in Finland.
3. Substrates are attracting increasing attention within linguistic research. There is a need to look more systematically at substrates in Finnic, Sámi and Germanic languages, and draw out their implications. Conclusions concerning cultural continuity, and potentially the handing down of traditions, may be profound: thus, for example, much of the substrate in Sámi languages appears to relate to aspects of lifestyle characteristic of the far north, the implication being that the way of life may have continued even when the language changed. Substrate studies should inspire a more nuanced approach to questions of cultural and linguistic interaction.
4. An important field of study for enlightening our understanding of contact in the Viking Age is place-name research. In the present collection, this is Schalin's special focus in this volume. Place names such as Tafæistaland indicate continuous contact from the Viking Age onwards between Finnish and Swedish speakers, but the details of etymology in such names is often obscure, and, as the discussion of *Köyliö* and *Ahvenanmaa* illustrates, a complex series of linguistic moves to and fro between Finnic and Germanic often appears to have taken place. Schalin also draws

out the implications of historical sources, in particular a thirteenth-century list of Finnish coastal place names, which appears to confirm that there was no Swedish settlement further east than Hangö at this stage. As a general conclusion, there was clearly prolonged contact in Finland between Swedish and Finnish speakers, but we cannot form any detailed picture, either geographically or chronologically, of what was going on in prehistory without considerable amounts of work such as that undertaken by SCHALIN. Even when such work has been done, it is clear that a great deal of uncertainty will remain.

5. Theophoric names (in a wide sense) in particular may act as keys to unlock ancient cult practices. There is considerable interest now in such names, which have been investigated in Scandinavia, and to an extent in Finland. Further work in this area should prove illuminating, especially in its potential to link with research into folk tradition and belief.
6. We must be careful in assessing the implications of loanwords. It is essential to form a chronological typology of loans, to determine what areas of culture were particularly affected at different periods. Here we also need to account for the lack of Finnic loans in Norse languages, and consider the cultural implications. A typologically comparable example is the situation in England a few centuries before the Viking Age, when over several centuries Germanic speakers settled the country and turned the predominant language from Celtic to English: there are practically no loanwords apart from place names from Celtic into English, yet it has been shown that the cultural influence must have been considerable both in material and intellectual culture.
7. There is often an assumption that all Viking Age Germanic loans in Finnish must be from East Norse (Swedish), yet a more refined approach needs to be adopted. We know of at least one merchant at this period who sailed around the eastern Baltic, named Wulfhere, who was probably English, and Frisians were great traders too at this time. We must therefore be aware of the possibility of western Germanic influence upon Finnish. Also, the Viking Age saw increasing contact between some Sámi and West Norse (Norwegian) speakers. How far can we detect differences between East and West Norse influences within the Finnic/Sámi area? The *Lexikon der älteren germanischen Lehnwörter in den ostseefinnischen Sprachen* recognises many Germanic loans without any Norse reflexes, and this work needs to be analysed and built upon.
8. Warriors and traders from Sweden are known to have passed along the Gulf of Finland and on down into Russia from about the eighth or even seventh centuries. Yet further work is needed to establish how far these Norse speakers penetrated inland, and how involved the inhabitants of Finland were in this eastern travel, in order to give a background for the linguistic borrowings which may have taken place.
9. A more subtle approach is needed to some known historical phenomena. Of particular importance here is the coming of Christianity. This is often viewed as an almost overnight change which affected Sweden in the eleventh to the twelfth century and Finland a century or so later.

Yet missionary work in Sweden goes back much further than this, and familiarity with Christianity even further. At least the coastal region of Finland was similarly subject to some Christian influence long before the supposed date of the conversion. In linguistic terms, therefore, we cannot assume that all Christian terms must be late-medieval borrowings. At present, it appears on linguistic grounds as if the earliest contacts with Christianity occurred with the Russian Orthodox Church – but this picture may possibly change with a more thorough examination of the dating of Christian loanwords in general. Extending this argument, there is a need to look at how far the many supposedly late-medieval loans from Swedish may in fact be from an earlier period.

10. Much of the source material for linguists is the language itself, its vocabulary and forms of speech (including for example dialectal forms). Sometimes, however, sources may take the form for example of ancient documents or literary works. In such cases, caution needs to be exercised in interpretation: thus Schalin takes a justly sceptical view of the earliest Norse source to mention 'Finlanders' (*Finnlendingar*) and its context. In this case, it is possible to construct arguments over the identification of a place called Herdalar in skaldic (courtly) verses composed around 1008, but such arguments may be worthless if – as is more than likely, given the particular way proper names tend to be invented and used in skaldic poetry – the name is a pseudo-name, 'Army Vale', invented for poetic effect by the poet.

As things stand in the present state of research, we lack a clear perception, based on linguistic evidence, of the culture and cultural relations that existed in the Finnish area between the Roman period and the Middle Ages. It is to be hoped that some of the matters outlined here will be taken up in the course of work carried out in the context of the Viking Age in Finland project.

Notes

1 The literature on Finnish prehistory, and prehistoric language, is, of course, extensive; the generalised nature of the present chapter militates against giving long bibliographical lists of items which are mainly too specific to suit the present context, though the reader is referred to the other works in the collection, where further bibliographical references will be found. A good introduction to the topics outlined here, which focuses on prehistory in the light of linguistic evidence, is Häkkinen 1996. I hesitate to recommend something as old as Hakulinen 1941, but it still functions as a useful survey of the development and structure of Finnish which is essentially linguistically based, and is both broad in its remit and specific in the many examples cited – though much would need revising in the light of more recent research, particularly in the extent and dating of loanwords. A further useful collection of essays, of not too abstruse a nature, is Paunonen and Rintala 1984 (though further research conducted since then would again to some extent call for an update). Further essays on prehistory and proto-languages (though mainly antedating the Viking Age) are found in collections such as Carpelan, Parpola & Koskikallio 2001, and Fogelberg 1999. A collection of essays by Koivulehto,

who did much to further work on the linguistic relationships of Finnish with its neighbours, with implications for the Viking Age, is Koivulehto 1999. Surveys not focused on Finnish may also offer insights into relations with other language groups: Mallory 1991 (on Indo-European prehistory), for example, is useful.

2 'Norse' is a term used as a collective designation of the North Germanic languages (Icelandic, Faroese, Norwegian, Danish, Swedish, in modern nation-state terms) or of their common ancestor (Old Norse); the term is sometimes used just in reference to West Norse (Icelandic, Faroese, Norwegian), but in Viking times the differences between West and East Norse were, as far as our evidence allows us to see, minor, and it is most convenient to use the term Norse in reference to all North Germanic languages and their speakers.

3 The matter is made even more complex by the delayed phonemicisation, and hence potential non-reflection in loanwords, of some changes we know to have taken place, such as umlaut – an anticipatory sound change of vowels, such that a vowel is for example fronted, such as *o* to *ö*, when the next syllable has a front vowel like *i* in it: in other words, although the sound change had taken place, speakers did not immediately perceive the new sound as forming a distinct category, or phoneme, in the language; an example in English is the distinction between aspirated and non-aspirated *p* in *pit* and *spit* respectively, which native speakers would simply class together as one 'p' sound, i.e. they are *allophones* of one *phoneme*.

References

Aikio, Ante. 2006. On Germanic–Saami Contacts and Saami Prehistory. *Journal de la Société Finno-Ougrienne* 91: 9–55. (Available at: http://www.sgr.fi/susa/91/aikio.pdf)

Carpelan, Christian, Asko Parpola & Petteri Koskikallio (eds). 2001. *Early Contacts between Uralic and Indo-European: Linguistic and Archaeological Considerations.* Suomalais-Ugrilaisen Seuran toimituksia 242. Helsinki: Suomalais-Ugrilainen Seura.

Fogelberg, Paul (ed.). 1999. *Pohjan poluilla: Suomalaisten juuret nykytutkimuksen mukaan.* Bidrag till kännedom av Finlands natur och folk 153. Helsinki: Societas Scientiarum Fennica.

Häkkinen, Kaisa. 1996. *Suomalaisten esihistoria kielitieteen valossa.* Tietolipas 147. Helsinki: Suomalaisen Kirjallisuuden Seura.

Hakulinen, Lauri. 1941. *Suomen kielen rakenne ja kehitys* I–II. Helsinki: Otava.

Hofstra, Tette. 1985. *Ostseefinnisch und Germanisch: Frühe Lehnbeziehungen im nördlichen Ostseeraum im Lichte der Forschung seit 1961.* D.Litt. thesis, Rijks-universiteit te Groningen. Groningen: van Denderen.

Koivulehto, Jorma. 1999. *Verba mutuata.* Suomalais-Ugrilaisen Seuran toimituksia 237. Helsinki: Suomalais-Ugrilainen Seura.

Lexikon der älteren germanischen Lehnwörter in den ostseefinnischen Sprachen I–III. 1991–2012. Ed. A. D. Kylstra, Sirkka-Liisa Hahmo, Tette Hofstra & Osmo Nikkilä. Amsterdam / New York: Rodopi.

Mallory, James Patrick. 1991. *In Search of the Indo-Europeans: Language, Archaeology and Myth.* London: Thames and Hudson.

Paunonen, Heikki, & Päivi Rintala. 1984. *Nykysuomen rakenne ja kehitys.* Tietolipas 95. Helsinki: Suomalaisen Kirjallisuuden Seura.

Ville Laakso

The Viking Age in Finnish Archaeology

A Brief Source-Critical Overview

In Finnish archaeology, the Viking Age (Fi. *viikinkiaika*), AD 800–1050, is known as one of the six Iron Age periods – the others being the Pre-Roman Iron Age (*c.* 400–1 BC), the Roman Iron Age (AD 1–400), the Migration Period (AD 400–600), the Merovingian Period (AD 600–800) and the Crusade Period (*c.* AD 1050–1150/1300, the end of the era depending on the area of the country).[1] From an archaeological point of view, the Viking Age is a distinctive period of the Finnish Iron Age – as are the other periods, each in its own way. First and foremost, characteristic of the period is the very small amount of contemporaneous written sources on Finland – documents written inside the area of the present country do not exist at all. This obviously gives the archaeological material a very central role in research. The aim of this chapter is to present – especially for a reader from outside the discipline – a concise assessment of the state, the possibilities and the limitations of archaeological research on the Viking Age in Finland.

The Adoption of the Term

At the end of the nineteenth century, it was not possible to use a very accurate periodisation concerning the prehistory of Finland, simply because few reliable methods of exact absolute dating existed.[2] At that time, it was common to crudely divide the Iron Age into an older and a younger phase; the limit was set at *c.* AD 700 (see e.g. Aspelin 1875: 139; Hackman 1905: 1–6; Nordman 1924: 1n.2). A more detailed and accurate periodisation was soon needed, and adopted, as the number of archaeological sites and finds accumulated, and as the understanding in dating different phenomena developed.

Since the beginning of the writing of history, the 'Vikings' have been known to have been a part of ancient history in the Baltic Sea region. Already in the nineteenth century Finnish archaeologists had sporadically used the term Viking Age even when referring to the Finnish area, especially when writing about connections with Scandinavia (see e.g. Appelgren 1897; Hackman 1905: 312).

Among the first Finnish archaeologists to use the term in a systematic manner was Carl Axel Nordman (see Nordman 1921; 1924). In his classic study on the Iron Age of Karelia from 1924, he openly favours using the periodisation "common in Scandinavia" (Nordman 1924: 1n.2). Influence from Scandinavia may be explained by the facts that Nordman (1892–1972) came from a Swedish-speaking family and had worked in Denmark for several years prior to the above-mentioned publications (on his career, see Meinander 1973).

Also the archaeologist Aarne Michaël Tallgren (1885–1945) soon adopted the term in his general work on Finnish prehistory, *Suomen muinaisuus* (1931: 159), which was the first part of a larger series of books on the history of the country. Writing about the Late Iron Age, Tallgren explains: "let us call it by the term which in fact belongs to Scandinavia, but is suited in connection with all the countries around the Baltic Sea, the Viking Age."[3] From here on, the term was firmly established in use in archaeology (cf. AALTO).

From early on, the period was dated to *c.* AD 800–1050, as it is today (e.g. Tallgren 1931: 153, 191).[4] The dating, of course, was also adopted from Scandinavia, and is originally based on West European written sources. However, the limits of the period suit Finnish archaeological material reasonably well. The distinctiveness of the period is at its beginning evidenced by the appearance of round convex brooches, and at the end by their replacement by small penannular brooches, as well as changes in forms of burial.[5] On the other hand, it should be noted that very accurate dating of artefact types is not usually possible – the margin of error is typically several decades, as in this case (on chronology on the basis of archaeological material, see Sarvas 1971; 1972; TALVIO).

The name for the previous period, the Merovingian Period, was adopted in a similarly determined manner, being, however, not based on the Swedish *Vendeltid* ['Vendel Period'], but on (German) *Merowingerzeit* ['Merovingian Period'], a term used in Central Europe, Norway, and partly also in the Baltic countries (see Salmo 1938: v). The applicability of the term has raised some criticism for the fact that the Frankish Merovingians had nothing to do with Finland (e.g. Huurre 2004: 117–118).[6] It took longer – several decades – for this term to be fully established in Finnish archaeological discourse (see e.g. Sarvas 1981 and the chronology in Kivikoski 1973), but it remains the sole term used today. It is interesting to note that in fact all the names for the Finnish Iron Age periods are formed on the basis of information from foreign written sources.

Using the term Viking Age in connection with Finland could also have been criticised, since no Viking colonies existed on Finnish soil, and inhabitants of the mainland area apparently did not take part in Viking trips, or at least not on a large scale (on the possible 'Finnish Vikings' see e.g. Tallgren 1931: 190; Kivikoski 1961: 208, 225; Lehtosalo-Hilander 1991). However, adopting the term does not seem to have raised public debate in Finnish research. The water route of the Varangians (Old Norse *Væringar*,

Greek *Varangoi*, Slavic *Varjagy*) towards modern-day Russia passed close by the Finnish south coast, and as the archaeologist Matti Huurre (2004: 118) has put it, the trips towards the east greatly influenced the Finnish area, too. Thus, from an archaeological point of view, the term 'Viking Age' should still be considered a perfectly useful tool. A similar term is also used by archaeologists in Estonia and Russia.

The State of Research

Archaeological research on the Viking Age has been reasonably lively in Finland. The period has taken a notable role in studies published on various areas of the country, such as Kymenlaakso (Miettinen 1998) and Karelia (Uino 1997; 2003; Saksa 2010). Important types of sites, for example house-floors (Uino 1986) and cemeteries (Shepherd 1999; Wessman 2010), have been researched. Excavation results of substantial sites, such as Luistari in Eura (Lehtosalo-Hilander 1982a–b; 2000), Varikonniemi in Hämeenlinna (Schulz & Schulz 1993; see also Taavitsainen 1990: 166), Kyrksundet in Hitis (Edgren 1995), Orijärvi in Mikkeli (Mikkola & Talvio 2000) and Pörnullbacken in Vörå (Viklund & Gullberg 2002), have been published.

Studies of key types of artefacts concern coins (Talvio 2002), weapons (Creutz 2003; Mäntylä 2005) and different types of ornaments (e.g. Asplund 2005). A variety of social and cultural aspects have been touched upon as well (e.g. Meinander 1980; Lehtosalo-Hilander 1982c; 1993; 1997).[7]

The research on various topics and areas remains far from inclusive, however. Many basic subjects of research, such as settlement sites, are still relatively poorly understood. Many of the publications concerning artefact types are quite old, and there are also unsolved problems concerning artefact chronology. The dating of several types of antiquities – such as hill forts – needs further study. There is also no thorough up-to-date standard reference monograph on the Finnish Viking Age, or on the Iron Age in general.

At present, research topics and subjects on the period are not determined primarily by scientific needs, but instead by building activity, research grants, personal interests of individual scholars and coincidences. The number of researchers with serious interests in this period is small. Cremation cemeteries of the Viking Age exhibit fragmentary and scattered remains and have find contexts that are hard to interpret; these cemeteries seem not to be as popular as research topics as later inhumation graves with intact artefacts preserved in their original positions. It should, however, be said that there is quite a lot of primary archaeological research material from the Viking Age – especially when compared with previous periods of the Iron Age. The research potential of this material is substantial.

The Main Characteristics of the Period

The present-day archaeological view of the Viking Age in Finland is largely based on cemeteries, since far fewer sites of other types have been registered. Even large parts of the artefacts in museum collections originate from burial sites. Based on the existing material, it is known that the densest settlement existed in the areas of Finland Proper, Häme, Savo and Karelia - but only within certain limited parts of each province. This traditional assessment has remained very stable for decades (see e.g. Tallgren 1931: 159, 192, 208; Edgren 1992: 221–233; Huurre 2004: 134). In the archaeological discourse, these central areas are known as the areas *with cemeteries*.

During this period, settlement in the country was more widespread than before, and it was also expansive towards areas previously unpopulated. On the other hand, settlements seem to have disappeared from some areas where they existed during previous periods. The most important of these is South Ostrobothnia in the western part of the country.[8]

The settlements in the core areas are considered to have consisted of hamlets, and livelihood was based mainly on farming and cattle-raising (e.g. Huurre 2004: 187–189). All in all, the population remained reasonably sparse, and did not - according to estimations - exceed some tens of thousands in the whole area of the country (e.g. Huurre 2004: 259).

Forms of burial were similar more or less throughout the central area: cairns with cremations and level-ground cremation cemeteries (Fi. *polttokenttäkalmisto*).[9] Even the artefact types used in these areas were largely uniform, or "general Western-Finnish" (Fi. *yleislänsisuomalaista*, a term used by Huurre 2004: 170; see also e.g. Kivikoski 1961: 213, 257–259).

Exceptions to this rule exist in the westernmost part of the country: some areas in Satakunta, where inhumation cemeteries were already used (e.g. Edgren 1992: 222), and in the Åland Islands, where the prevailing burial form was a mound, similar to the ones in Sweden (e.g. Tallgren 1931: 167; Edgren 1992: 227–229). Artefacts used in the Satakunta area were similar to the types used in most other parts of the country, but even in this context the Åland Islands are similar to Scandinavia.[10]

In the largest parts of the core settlement areas, characteristic of the period are certain types of ornaments: penannular brooches, convex round brooches and equal-armed brooches.[11] On the Finnish mainland, most types of jewellery can be characterised as being domestic in origin (see e.g. Kivikoski 1961: 198; Huurre 2004: 181). On the other hand, weaponry largely consisted of types that were used throughout wide areas in Europe (see e.g. Kivikoski 1961: 199; Huurre 2004: 196–204). Burial forms are distinctive and differ from the ones used in most of the neighbouring areas.

In the east, the area with largely similar features in the material culture extended to Karelia on the western shore of Lake Ladoga. Level-ground cemeteries existed to some extent even in Estonia and even in Latvia (see Wessman 2010: 19), but on the eastern shores of Lake Ladoga burial traditions were already different (e.g. Kochkurkina 2004).

Settlement Archaeology

One of the definite strongpoints of archaeology is working with the developments and changes in settlement. Its dynamics are reasonably easy to comprehend in the above-mentioned core areas of Viking Age Finland. However, a major research problem is the situation in the areas outside of them, in the vast hinterlands that actually comprise most of the country. These areas are characterised by single graves or stray finds of artefacts, neither of which are customarily considered as proof of permanent settlement.[12]

Interestingly, especially palaeoecological studies have demonstrated the presence of agriculture in many parts of these in-between areas (see e.g. Taavitsainen *et al.* 1998; Alenius & Laakso 2006; Alenius 2011). Archaeologists often interpret this evidence as signs of wilderness utilisation (Fi. *eränkäynti* or *kaukonautinta*), originating from somewhere in the core areas (on this phenomenon, see e.g. Taavitsainen *et al.* 1998: 236–247). In cases where there is palaeoecological proof of slash-and-burn cultivation, it is plausible that the farmers may have resided only temporarily in these areas, but in cases with evidence of field cultivation, even permanent settlement in the in-between areas must be considered plausible. In the latter cases, the lack of archaeological sites connectable with these settlements remains a major problem, at least within the discipline.

One factor affecting the view of settlement is the dating of different cultural phenomena. In archaeology, single finds and sites can often be dated quite accurately with the help of coin finds or the radiocarbon method, for example. At the same time, the exact period of use of many important artefact types remains uncertain. For example, it is known that a certain type of ceramics was used for several centuries during the Iron Age, but it is not known exactly when it was adopted or fell out of use in different areas of Finland. When this type of ceramics is found, for instance at a settlement site, it is not possible to determine on the basis of this material alone whether the site was used in the Viking Age or several centuries earlier – or both.

Another factor is the difficulty of understanding the variety of different types of sites. For example, different livelihoods affected the choice of settlement locations, and different religious beliefs produced different types of graves. Archaeological research often looks for certain kinds of site at certain expected locations, and will not find the ones in unexpected locations – sites which in fact might be quite common in the area in question. In the future, many of the problems connected with settlement archaeology will undoubtedly be overcome with the help of new research, and the results will probably change the way we understand the Viking Age.

It is likely that the areas that were most densely populated in the prehistoric era are better represented in the known material than the areas at peripheries. It seems to be more difficult to find archaeological remains of the less dense Iron Age populations, even through determined research.[13] It is unfortunately not unusual that new finds are interpreted on the basis of old ones, instead of being used to revise old conceptions.

The deficiencies of present-day settlement archaeology are demonstrated, for example, by the fact that new sites are every now and then found in areas previously considered as uninhabited (see e.g. Jansson 2011). A recent example of this development can be found in Ruokolahti parish in south-eastern Finland. There, local metal detector hobbyists have in recent years found several new cemeteries, indicating permanent settlement in the Viking Age (see Pylkkö 2011). An area previously characterised by only stray finds has – mainly by accident – been raised in status to a central area of settlement. It is notable that, prior to the finds, professional archaeological surveys aimed at locating new sites found no cemeteries or settlement sites in the same areas.

On the other hand, the fact still remains that, in the areas where cemeteries have been found, we can also be confident that contemporary permanent settlement did exist. Thus, areas without known sites were not necessarily empty of settlement, but cemeteries are positive proof of settlement.

Environment, Livelihood and Connections

People always live in close connection with their (natural) environment, and archaeology can contribute to the study of this relationship. Most often this is done in co-operation with geologists or biologists. In the context of the Viking Age, such studies have involved especially the history of agriculture, for example the relationship of settlement and soil types (Orrman 1991) or plant remains from excavations (e.g. Aalto 1997; Lempiäinen 1999; 2011). Archaeology can provide samples for researchers of other fields – such as plant remains for palaeoecologists – from datable cultural contexts. Artefacts and archaeological remains – in the case of the Viking Age, items such as sickles, scythes, or remains of ancient fields – can sometimes tell very directly about the means of livelihood.

The existing material forms a reasonably solid base for studying trade and cultural relations. An important source of information on economy and trade relations is coins and coin finds (see Talvio). Similarities and differences between different types of artefacts from different areas are vital in this respect as well. This kind of research requires thorough knowledge of large amounts of material, including from neighbouring areas, and it is not a very popular theme of research at present. Even studies of technology are relevant here, since new technologies are often imported.

On the basis of similarities in artefacts, especially in the south-western part of Finland, the lively Baltic connections of the Merovingian Period were during the Viking Age slowly replaced by connections with Sweden in the west.[14] In the eastern part of the country Scandinavian contacts existed as well. For this area, however, it is more difficult to verify whether there were direct contacts with areas in Scandinavia, or whether they were rather directed towards the Varangian centres south of Lake Ladoga, such as Staraya Ladoga (the latter seems more probable).[15]

All in all it can be asserted that studies of environment, livelihood and contacts have great potential for research on the Finnish Viking Age.

Identity and Religion

Matters of identity can to some extent be touched upon by archaeological means and materials, but this type of study is much more complex and open to interpretation than those mentioned above. Probably for this reason the topic has not been popular among archaeologists studying the Finnish Viking Age.

From the point of view of archaeology, artefacts were used by an individual and they may tell something about the identity of the person who used them. On the other hand, burial customs tell first of all about the world view of the community that was responsible for the burial practice.[16] In the prevailing Viking Age level-ground cremation cemetery, remains of several individuals were often scattered collectively in the same area, and it is not usually possible to investigate the identity of individuals based on this material (cf. Wickholm & Raninen 2006). Towards the end of the period, adoption of the inhumation burial custom presents new opportunities for this type of research: in single inhumation graves, it is possible to discern individuals and their possessions.

It is possible to say quite a lot about questions of religious beliefs, especially on the basis of burial customs, but mainly on a rather general level (on the archaeological study of Viking Age religion in the area, see e.g. Shepherd 1999). Trying to understand people's thoughts always requires extensive interpretation, and often help from other disciplines – such as from the study of religion or folkloristics – is essential. In the case of the Viking Age, analogies from the historical period can be used, but – because of the several centuries and numerous generations in between – with great caution.

In the context of the Finnish Viking Age, a major change was the adoption of inhumation burial instead of cremation. In most areas, this took place at the end of the period. This change must be considered as one of the most important pieces of evidence for the Christianisation process in the area.

Some Christian artefacts, such as cross pendants, are used as proof of the same process, but this type of source material is more sensitive to interpretation as random phenomena and does not necessarily reflect the religious beliefs of their owners, yet alone whole societies. According to present archaeological knowledge, the Christianisation of Finland was a process that lasted for several centuries; it was merely in its early stages in this area during the Viking Age.[17]

Ethnicity and Language

Especially problematic fields of research from an archaeological point of view are matters concerning the ethnicity of ancient peoples. It is common to discern *cultures* – territorial groups formed on the basis of artefacts, structures or sites that bear similar traits, but it is often impossible to say what and how complex the processes behind these common features were. In the context of the Finnish Viking Age – and of the Iron Age in general – the term *culture* is not commonly used in this sense.

As far as the Iron Age is concerned, jewellery has often been seen as a reflection of people's identity, acting as a mark of distinction from other groups. A common ethnos may be behind the common features of an archaeological culture, but this is almost impossible to verify on the basis of archaeological material alone. This is a universal problem within the discipline, involving all prehistoric periods and places (on archaeology and ethnicity, see e.g. Jones 1997).

On the basis of the archaeological material, there is clear settlement continuity in the Finnish core settlement areas from the Merovingian Period through the Viking Age and into historical times. Based on this observation, it has been considered plausible that the cemeteries of these areas already represent the Finnic population that is well documented in the first written sources from the sixteenth century or earlier. On the other hand, the question about the ethnicity of people living outside the core areas is to some extent still unclear for archaeologists, and the question is debated (see e.g. Huurre 2004: 151–157). There is little solid evidence, such as settlement sites or cemeteries, reflecting the presence of this population during the Viking Age.[18] Because of lack of known archaeological sites, it is not possible to follow the material culture of the inhabitants of this area up to the period with historical sources that provide information on their ethnicity. It is quite possible that the lack of known sites is a problem connected with the approaches and methods of archaeology: they simply have not been found yet.

Another problematic field of study is language. It may not leave any remains in the material heritage, and the Finnish Viking Age represents an area and a period from which there are practically no preserved contemporaneous finds that would provide sources on language. An archaeological *culture* may have had a common language, but – again – it is impossible to verify this on an archaeological basis alone. One application of co-operation in this field has been the comparison of certain types of prehistoric artefacts with the linguistic terms relating to them (see e.g. Salo 1989). Another possible field of co-operation involves place names: archaeological evidence concerning settlement continuity sometimes can – and in many cases should – be used to estimate their age. In Finland, comparative studies between archaeology and linguistics have so far concentrated on periods older than the Viking Age (see, however, e.g. Salo 2007).

Concluding Remarks

All in all, most of the problems of interpretation described above are not characteristic just of the Finnish Viking Age, but involve most periods with few or no written sources. There are complex variables connected with the process of accumulation of the archaeological material, and artefacts kept in museum collections do not form a representative sample of past human life. Our present knowledge of prehistory is highly dependent on research funds and interests, intensity of land use and several other factors. Major changes are still possible to the view provided by archaeology on the Viking Age of Finland.

It is a traditional view that primary archaeological material lacks the built-in thought processes that are typical, for example, of contemporaneous written sources. However, it is equally obvious that archaeologists need to make rigorous interpretations when trying to understand the first-hand sources, which are often random fragments of past material cultures. In many cases, archaeology is highly dependent on co-operation with other disciplines.

In the end, it is still necessary to remember one of the main strengths of archaeology: it is possible to acquire plenty of new primary research material by field work – unlike, for example, in the study of medieval written documents.

Notes

1 The Iron Age periodisation is nowadays rather well settled, but the exact chronology of some of the periods often varies by a few decades. Sometimes the Iron Age is subdivided into an older, a middle and a younger phase (*c.* 500 BC – AD 400, 400–800 and 800–1150/1300 respectively). Also, the term Early Metal Period (*c.* 1500 BC – AD 400) is often used, having an effect on the chronology at the earlier parts of the Iron Age.

2 With the term *Finland*, I refer to the area of the so called historical Finland. This also includes those areas ceded to Soviet Union in the Second World War, the largest of which was the former historical Finnish Province of Karelia. On the other hand, it should be stressed that some parts of Karelia have never been part of Finland (on the different areas of Karelia, see Uino 1997: 13–16).

3 Literally, *viikinkikausi* ['the Viking period']. There was no earlier name for the same exact period, since it was first discerned at the same time.

4 In the western part of the country the end of the period is often set at *c.* AD 1025 (see Sarvas 1971; Sarvas 1972; cf. Talvio) and in the eastern part *c.* AD 1100 (see Uino 1997: 113).

5 E.g. Kivikoski 1961: 193–195, 229–242; Sarvas 1971: 59; Edgren 1992: 215, 249–253; Huurre 2004: 181–182.

6 The same can be said about The Roman Iron Age, too.

7 I have listed here only reasonably recent publications and concentrated on the ones in more widely used languages. In these publications, it is possible to find references to most important older sources, many of which are still relevant.

8 See e.g. Edgren 1992: 221–233; Huurre 2004: 131–134; on Ostrobothnia and different interpretations, see Herrgård & Holmblad 2005: 190–205; Holmblad & Herrgård 2013: 193–214; Kuusela 2013.

9 E.g. Huurre 2004: 132, 169–170; on research problems related to cemeteries of this type, see Taavitsainen 1992.

10 See e.g. Tallgren 1931: 189–190; Edgren 1992: 222, 227–229; Huurre 2004: 161, 164–166.

11 E.g. Tallgren 1931: 180–181; Kivikoski 1973: Abb. 656–1031; Huurre 2004: 181–184.
12 See e.g. Tallgren 1931: 208–223; Huurre 2004: 124, 254–156; on northern parts of the country, see also KUUSELA.
13 See e.g. Tuovinen 2002: 255–269; Alenius & Laakso 2006; Asplund 2008: 366–369; Tuovinen 2011.
14 See e.g. Kivikoski 1961: 205–209; Huurre 2004: 159–162; RANINEN & WESSMAN.
15 See e.g. Uino 1997: 179–184; on the general background for the areas southeast of Finland, see e.g. Nosov 2001; Kochkurkina 2004; Uino 2006.
16 For a case study, see Raninen 2005; see also the section on ethnicity and language below.
17 On Christianisation, see e.g. Lehtosalo-Hilander 1987; Salo 1989; Valk 1998; Hiekkanen 2002; Laakso 2014.
18 E.g. Huurre 2004: 151–154, 171–172, 264–266; cf. e.g. Taavitsainen 2003: 30–31, 37.

References

Aalto, Marjatta. 1997. Cultivated Plants of Finnish Iron Age. In *Славяне и финно-угры: Археология, история, культура: Доклады российско-финляндского симпозиума по вопросам археологии.* СПб.

Alenius, Teija, & Ville Laakso. 2006. Palaeoecology and Archaeology of the Village of Uukuniemi, Eastern Finland. *Acta Borealia* 2006(2): 145–165.

Alenius, Teija. 2011. From Forest to a Farmland: Palaeoenvironmental Reconstruction of the Colonization of Western Uusimaa. In Mika Lavento (ed.). *Maritime Landscape in Change: Archaeological, Historical, Palaeoecological and Geological Studies on Western Uusimaa.* Iskos 19. Helsinki: The Finnish Antiquarian Society. Pp. 87–116.

Appelgren, Hjalmar. 1897. Svenskarnas inflyttning i Finland. *Finskt Museum* 1897: 17–29.

Asplund, Henrik. 2005. The Bear and the Female: Bear-Tooth Pendants in Late Iron Age Finland. In Sari Mäntylä (ed.). *Rituals and Relations: Studies on the Society and Material Culture of the Baltic Finns.* Suomalaisen Tiedeakatemian Toimituksia Humaniora 336. Helsinki: Academia Scientiarum Fennica. Pp. 13–30.

Asplund, Henrik. 2008. *Kymittæ: Sites, Centrality and Long-Term Settlement Change in the Kemiönsaari Region in SW Finland.* Turun yliopiston julkaisuja B 312. Turku: University of Turku.

Creutz, Kristina. 2003. *Tension and Tradition: A Study of Late Iron Age Spearheads around the Baltic Sea.* Theses and Papers in Archaeology N.S. A 8. Stockholm: Stockholm University.

Edgren, Torsten. 1992. Den förhistoriska tiden. In Märtha Norrback (ed.). *Finlands historia* I. Esbo: Schildts. Pp. 9–270.

Edgren, Torsten. 1995. "...De Aspø usque Ørsund. vi. Inde usque Hangethe. iij...": An Archaeological Research Project Concerning One of the Harbours in Finland's South-Western Archipelago Referred to in "the Danish Itinerary". In Olaf Olsen, Jan Skamby Madsen & Flemming Rieck (eds.). *Shipshape: Essays for Ole Crumlin-Pedersen on the Occasion of his 60th Anniversary February 24th 1995.* Roskilde: The Viking Ship Museum. Pp. 203–212.

Hackman, Alfred. 1905. *Die ältere Eisenzeit in Finnland I.* Helsinki: Alfred Hackman.

Herrgård, Mikael, & Peter Holmblad. 2005. *Fornminnen I Österbotten från neandertalare till sockenbor.* Studier i Österbottens förhistoria 6. Vasa: Scriptum.

Hiekkanen, Markus. 2002. The Christianisation of Finland: A Case of Want of Power in a Peripheral Area. In Guido Helmig, Barbara Scholkmann & Matthias

Untermann (eds.). *Centre Region Periphery: Medieval Europe Basel 2002: Third International Conference of Medieval and Later Archaeology: Preprinted Papers* I. Basel: Archäologische Bodenforschung Basel-Stadt. Pp. 488–497.

Holmblad, Peter, & Mikael Herrgård. 2013. *Luolamiehistä talonpojiksi: Pohjanmaan muinaisuus sanoin ja kuvin.* Vaasa: Scriptum.

Huurre, Matti. 2004. *9000 vuotta Suomen esihistoriaa.* 8th edn. Helsinki: Otava.

Jansson, Henrik. 2011. Burials at the End of Land: Maritime Burial Cairns and the Land-Use History of South-Western Uusimaa. In Georg Haggrèn & Mika Lavento (eds.). *Maritime Landscape in Change: Archaeological, Historical, Palaeological and Geological Studies on Western Uusimaa.* Iskos 19. Helsinki: Finnish Antiquarian Society. Pp. 117–151.

Jones, Siân. 1997. *The Archaeology of Ethnicity: Constructing Identities in the Past and Present.* London: Routledge.

Kivikoski, Ella. 1961. *Suomen esihistoria.* Suomen historia I. Porvoo: WSOY.

Kivikoski, Ella. 1973. *Die Eisenzeit Finnlands: Bildwerk und Text.* Helsinki: Finnische Altertumsgesellschaft.

Kochkurkina, Svetlana. 2004. The Chronology of the Kurgans of the South-East of Lake Ladoga. In Pirjo Uino (ed.). *Fenno-Ugri et Slavi 2002: Dating and Chronology.* Museoviraston arkeologian osaston julkaisuja 10. Helsinki: National Board of Antiquities. Pp. 36–45.

Kuusela, Jari-Matti. 2013. *Political Economy of Bronze- and Iron Age Societies in the Eastern Coast of the Bothnian Bay ca. 1500 BC – AD 1300.* Oulu: Juvenes Print.

Laakso, Ville. 2014. *Papinniemi in Uukuniemi and Related Archaeological Sites of the Eastern Orthodox Cultural Area in Finland.* Archaeologia Medii Aevi Finlandiae XIX. Suomen Keskiajan Arkeologian Seura.

Lehtosalo-Hilander, Pirkko-Liisa. 1982a. *Luistari I: The Graves.* Suomen Muinaismuistoyhdistyksen Aikakauskirja 82:1. Helsinki: Suomen Muinaismuistoyhdistys.

Lehtosalo-Hilander, Pirkko-Liisa. 1982b. *Luistari II: The Artefacts.* Suomen Muinaismuistoyhdistyksen Aikakauskirja 82:2. Helsinki: Suomen Muinaismuistoyhdistys.

Lehtosalo-Hilander, Pirkko-Liisa. 1982c. *Luistari III: A Burial-Ground Reflecting the Finnish Viking Age Society.* Suomen Muinaismuistoyhdistyksen Aikakauskirja 82:3. Helsinki: Suomen Muinaismuistoyhdistys.

Lehtosalo-Hilander, Pirkko-Liisa. 1987. The Conversion of the Finns in Western Finland. In Birgit Sawyer, Peter Sawyer & Ian Wood (eds.). *The Christianization of Scandinavia: Report of a Symposium Held at Kungälv, Sweden 4–9 August 1985.* Alingsås: Viktoria Bokförlag. Pp. 31–35.

Lehtosalo-Hilander, Pirkko-Liisa. 1991. Le Viking finnois. *Finskt Museum* 1990: 55–72.

Lehtosalo-Hilander, Pirkko-Liisa. 1993. Finnland zur Wikingerzeit: Monarchie oder gleichwertige Gesellschaft. *Karhunhammas* 15: 25–43.

Lehtosalo-Hilander, Pirkko-Liisa. 1997. Luistari in Eura: From Pagan Burial-Ground to Christian Cemetery. In Michael Müller-Wille (ed.). *Rom und Byzanz im Norden. Mission und Glaubenswechsel im Ostseeraum während des 8.–14. Jahrhunderts* I. Mainz: Akademie der Wissenschaften und der Literatur. Pp. 389–403.

Lehtosalo-Hilander, Pirkko-Liisa. 2000. *Luistari: A History of Weapons and Ornaments: Luistari IV.* Suomen Muinaismuistoyhdistyksen Aikakauskirja 107. Helsinki: Suomen Muinaismuistoyhdistys.

Lempiäinen, Terttu. 1999. Prehistoric Cultivation in Finland: Macrofossil Evidence of Cultivated Cereals. In *Environmental and Cultural History of the Eastern Baltic Region.* PACT 57. Rixensart: Conseil de l'Europe. Pp. 353–355.

Lempiäinen, Terttu. 2011. Notes on the Archaeobotanical Records of Flax (*linum usitatissimun*) in Finland. In Janne Harjula, Maija Helamaa & Janne Haarala (eds.). *Times, Things & Places: 36 Essays for Jussi-Pekka Taavitsainen.* Turku: J.-P. Taavitsainen Festschrift Committee. Pp. 192–197.

Meinander, C. F. 1973. Carl Axel Nordman. *Finskt Museum* 1972: 85–88.

Meinander, C. F. 1980. The Finnish Society during the 8th–12th Centuries. In Paula Purhonen (ed.). *Fenno-Ugri et Slavi 1978: Papers Presented by the Participants in the Soviet-Finnish Symposium "The Cultural Relations between the Peoples and Countries of the Baltic Area during the Iron Age and the Early Middle Ages" in Helsinki May 20–23, 1978*. University of Helsinki Department of Archaeology Stencil 22. Helsinki: University of Helsinki. Pp. 7–13.

Miettinen, Timo. 1998. *Kymenlaakson esihistoriaa*. Kymenlaakson maakuntamuseon julkaisuja 26. Kotka: Kymenlaakson maakuntamuseo.

Mikkola, Esa, & Tuukka Talvio. 2010. A Silver Coin Hoard from Orijärvi, Kihlinpelto in Mikkeli Rural Commune, Province of Savo, Eastern Finland. *Fennoscandia Archaeologica* 17: 129–138.

Mäntylä, Sari. 2005. Broad-Bladed Battle-Axes, Their Function and Symbolic Meaning. In Sari Mäntylä (ed.). *Rituals and Relations: Studies on the Society and Material Culture of the Baltic Finns*. Suomalaisen Tiedeakatemian Toimituksia Humaniora 336. Helsinki: Academia Scientiarum Fennica. Pp. 105–130.

Nordman, C. A. 1921. *Anglo-Saxon Coins Found in Finland*. Helsingfors: The Finnish Archaeological Society.

Nordman, C. A. 1924. *Karelska järnåldersstudier*. Finska Fornminnesföreningens Tidskrift 34:3. Helsingfors: Finska Fornminnesföreningen.

Nosov, Evgenij N. 2001. Ein Herrschaftsgebiet entsteht. Die Vorgeschichte der nördlichen Rus' und Novgorods. In Michael Müller-Wille, Valentin L. Janin, Evgenij N. Nosov & Elena A. Rybina (eds.). *Novgorod: Das mittelalterliche Zentrum und sei Umland im Norden Russlands*. Studien zur Siedlungsgeschichte und Archäologia der Ostseegebiete 1. Neumünster: Wachholtz. Pp. 13–74.

Orrman, Eljas. 1991. Geographical Factors in the Spread of Permanent Settlement in Parts of Finland and Sweden from the End of the Iron Age to the Beginning of Modern Times. *Fennoscandia Archaeologica* 8: 3–21.

Pylkkö, Ilkka. 2011. Jäämejä Jääskestä idäntielle: Etelä-Karjalan nuoremman rautakauden kontakteja uusien löytöjen valossa. *Arkeologia nyt!* 2011(1): 13–17.

Raninen, Sami. 2005. Big Men on the River Banks: Some Thoughts on the Middle Merovingian Period Weapon Burials in Finland. In Sari Mäntylä (ed.). *Rituals and Relations: Studies on the Society and Material Culture of the Baltic Finns*. Suomalaisen Tiedeakatemian Toimituksia Humaniora 336. Helsinki: Academia Scientiarum Fennica. Pp. 224–245.

Saksa 2010 = Сакса, А. И. 2010. *Древняя Карелия в конце I – Начале II тысячелетия н. э. Происхождение, история и культура населения летописной Карельской земли*. Санкт-Петербург: Нестор-История.

Salmo, Helmer. 1938. *Die Waffen der Merowingerzeit in Finnland*. Suomen Muinaismuistoyhdistyksen Aikakauskirja 42:1. Helsinki: Suomen Muinaismuistoyhdistys.

Salo, Unto. 1989. The Early Stage of Finland's Conversation to Christianity. *Byzantium and the North: Acta Byzantina Fennica* 4: 95–117.

Salo, Unto. 2007. Sastamalan kalmistonimistä ja niiiden taustoista. In Aimo Hakanen & Reino Kero (eds.). *Sata sanan juurta: Satakunnan vanhaa paikannimistöä*. Satakunta kotiseututututkimuksia 25. Harjavalta: Satakunnan Historiallinen Seura. Pp. 136–179.

Sarvas, Pekka. 1971. Ristiretkiajan ajoituskysymyksiä. *Suomen Museo* 1971: 51–63.

Sarvas, Pekka. 1972. *Länsi-Suomen ruumishautojen raha-ajoitukset*. Helsingin yliopiston arkeologian laitos, moniste 6. Helsinki: Helsingin yliopiston arkeologian laitos.

Sarvas, Pekka. 1981. Finland. In Lena Thunmark-Nylén (ed.). *Vikingatidens ABC*. Stockholm: Statens Historiska Museum. Pp. 71–72.

Schulz, Eeva-Liisa, & Hans-Peter Schulz. 1993. Hämeenlinna Varikkoniemi: Eine späteisenzeitliche-frühmittelalterliche Kernsiedlung in Häme: Die Ausgrabungen 1986-1990. (Mit einem Beitrag von Georg Haggrén). *Suomen Museo* 1992: 41–85.

Shepherd, Deborah Jeanne. 1999. *Funerary Ritual and Symbolism: An Interdisciplinary Interpretation of Burial Practices in Late Iron Age Finland.* BAR International Series 808. Oxford: British Archaeological Reports.

Taavitsainen, Jussi-Pekka. 1990. *Ancient Hillforts of Finland: Problems of Analysis, Chronology and Interpretation with Special Reference to the Hillfort of Kuhmoinen.* Suomen Muinaismuistoyhdistyksen Aikakauskirja 94. Helsinki: Suomen Muinaismuistoyhdistys.

Taavitsainen, Jussi-Pekka. 1992. Cemeteries or Refuse Heaps? – Archaeological Formation Processes and the Interpretation of Sites and Antiquities. *Suomen Museo* 1991: 5–14.

Taavitsainen, Jussi-Pekka. 2003. Lapp Cairns as a Source on Metal Period Settlement in the Inland Regions of Finland. *Acta Borealia* 2003(1): 21–47.

Taavitsainen, Jussi-Pekka, Heikki Simola & Elisabeth Grönlund. 1998. Cultivation History beyond the Periphery: Early Agriculture in the North European Boreal Forest. *Journal of World Prehistory* 12(2): 199–253.

Talvio, Tuukka. 2002. *Coins and Coin Finds in Finland AD 800–1200.* Iskos 12. Helsinki: Suomen Muinaismuistoyhdistys.

Tuovinen, Tapani. 2002. *The Burial Cairns and the Landscape in the Archipelago of Åboland, SW Finland, in the Bronze Age and the Iron Age.* Acta Universitatis Ouluensis B Humaniora 46. Oulu: University of Oulu.

Tuovinen, Tapani. 2011. The Finnish Archipelago Coast from AD 500 to 1550: A Zone of Interaction. In Mika Lavento (ed.). *Maritime Landscape in Change: Archaeological, Historical, Palaeoecological and Geological Studies on Western Uusimaa.* Iskos 19. Helsinki: The Finnish Antiquarian Society. Pp. 10–60.

Uino, Pirjo. 1986. An Iron Age Community at Ketohaka in Salo and Other Remains of Metal Period Buildings in Finland. In Elvi Linturi (ed.). *Iron Age Studies in Salo* I–II. Suomen Muinaismuistoyhdistyksen Aikakauskirja 89:1. Helsinki: Suomen Muinaismuistoyhdistys. Pp. 25–201.

Uino, Pirjo. 1997. *Ancient Karelia: Archaeological Studies – Muinais-Karjala: Arkeologisia tutkimuksia.* Suomen Muinaismuistoyhdistyksen Aikakauskirja 104. Helsinki: Suomen Muinaismuistoyhdistys.

Uino, Pirjo. 2003. Viikinkiaika n. 800–1100 jKr. In Matti Saarnisto (ed.). *Karjalan synty.* Viipurin läänin historia I. Lappeenranta: Karjalan kirjapaino Oy. Pp. 313–382.

Uino, Pirjo. 2006. The Background of the Early Medieval Finnic Population in the Region of the Volkhov River: Archaeological Aspects. In Juhani Nuorluoto (ed.). *The Slavicization of the Russian North: Mechanisms and Chronology.* Slavica Helsingiensia 27. Helsinki: University of Helsinki. Pp. 355–373.

Valk, Heiki. 1998. About the Transitional Period in the Burial Customs in the Region of the Baltic Sea. In Nils Blomkvist (ed.). *Culture Clash or Compromise? – The Europeanisation of the Baltic Sea Area 1100–1400 AD.* Acta Visbyensia 11. Visby: Gotland Centre for Baltic Studies. Pp. 237–250.

Viklund, Karin, & Kurt Gullberg (eds.). 2002. *Från romartid till vikingatid: Pörnullbacken – en järnålderstida bosättning i Österbotten.* Acta Antiqua Ostrobotniensia 5. Vasa: Scriptum.

Wessman, Anna. 2010. *Death, Destruction and Commemoration: Tracing Ritual Activities in Finnish Late Iron Age Cemeteries (AD 550–1150).* Iskos 18. Helsinki: Suomen Muinaismuistoyhdistys.

Wickholm, Anna, & Sami Raninen. 2006. The Broken People: Deconstruction of Personhood in Iron Age Finland. *Estonian Journal of Archaeology* 10(2): 150–166.

Samuli Helama

The Viking Age as a Period of Contrasting Climatic Trends

Climatic variations occur on all scales, affecting life on Earth with concomitant influences on society. Improving our understanding of climate behaviour, its causes and consequences, requires an aggregation of increasingly diverse sources of information to produce the records of climate variability. While the meteorological stations are continuously monitoring the contemporaneous state of the atmosphere, they have typically been in operation for only a century or two. Much longer records of climate variability can be obtained using substitute data in the form of proxy observations (Fritts 1976; Bradley 1999). Such records are necessary to unearth the long history of climatic variations and to reveal the full spectrum of climatic changes. Proxy records and reconstructions of past climate variability based on proxy data form the basis of palaeoclimate analyses. Palaeoclimate reconstructions spanning historical episodes or prehistoric cultural phases can subsequently be used to throw light on the possible climatic influences on these occasions. In the Nordic context, an intriguing period for such comparisons may be the Viking Age, during which the Norse voyages and settlements in Greenland and America were probably safeguarded by an improved climatic phase (Lamb 1995). Yet the Nordic countries constitute a region where the success of historical agricultural food production has been tightly linked to contemporaneous climate fluctuations (Holopainen & Helama 2009; Holopainen *et al.* 2012), the palaeoclimatic approaches thus providing essential, yet largely unexplored means for historical, archaeological, human ecological and anthropological studies.

Tree-Ring Chronologies as Palaeoclimate Proxies

Proxies are climate-sensitive records of geological, biological, glaciological or palaeontological evidence or historical archives. Natural proxies commonly originate from physical, chemical or biological properties (e.g. pollen) of lake, sea or peatland sediment archives (Bradley 1999). Yet tree-rings tell of past climate. In a dendrochronological approach, tree-ring chronologies are examined to rigorously build the growth histories of old and ancient trees. Given that the growth of the studied trees is strongly correlated with temporal variations in temperature or precipitation, the tree-ring chronologies take the form of proxy data and they can be exploited for palaeoclimate analyses (Fritts 1976; Sheppard 2010).

Tree-ring cores can be extracted from old living trees and the resulting chronologies commonly extend over the past few centuries. Conventionally, tree-rings are observed under the microscope, and the data of consecutive widths are saved to form dendrochronological series. Tree-ring chronology is constructed by cross-dating the individual series in a process where the unique synchrony of the wide and narrow rings ensures the correct temporal alignment of the series according to calendar years (Douglass 1941; Stokes & Smiley 1968; Yamaguchi 1991). Non-climatic portions of growth variations are to be removed from the initial tree-ring series prior to climatic interpretations using statistical examination (Fritts 1976; Esper *et al.* 2003; Helama *et al.* 2004). Importantly, processing the tree-ring properties in many trees from a given region allows the averaging of the several series to robust estimates of growth variability. Actually, the benefit of tree-rings as palaeoclimate proxies is the dating precision and exactness of the data. Occasionally, tree-rings have been thought to measure past climate fluctuations over short times but not record the long-term trends (e.g. Broecker 2001). This issue is known to be linked to the removal of non-climatic growth variations from the series and can, at least partly, be surmounted by state-of-the-art methods (Esper *et al.* 2003; Helama *et al.* 2004).

The temporal extent of the chronologies can be lengthened using the tree-ring data measured from wood materials of historical, archaeological or palaeontological provenance. In Finland, the building of very long tree-ring chronologies has been possible using a combination of living trees and ancient remains of trunks preserved in the lake sediments as subfossils (Eronen 1979; Eronen *et al.* 1999; 2002; Helama *et al.* 2010b). These assemblages comprise tree-ring data from several hundred standing and dead pines (*Pinus sylvestris* L.) whose series have been rigorously cross-dated into mean chronologies of millennial length. In Finland, the longest chronologies are presently those originating from Lapland and south-eastern Finland, spanning the past 75 and 14 centuries, respectively (Eronen *et al.* 1999; 2002; Helama *et al.* 2005; 2008). In fact, the long tree-ring chronology of Finnish Lapland is among the longest continuous chronologies worldwide and as such a precious type of climatic calendar over much of the post-glacial period, spanning both historic and prehistoric times. In Eurasia, there are, however, several other tree-ring chronologies of similar length (Pilcher *et al.* 1984; Grudd *et al.* 2002; Hantemirov & Shiyatov 2002; Naurzbaev *et al.* 2002; Nicolussi *et al.* 2009), the longest chronology extending into glacial times (Friedrich *et al.* 2004).

Towards Palaeoclimate Reconstructions

Topically, the long chronologies of Lapland and south-eastern Finland both exhibit direct palaeoclimate significance. In northernmost Lapland, tree growth is governed by summer temperatures and the tree-ring chronologies correlate especially well with the mean temperatures in July; this has been illustrated by repeated dendroclimatic comparisons in the region (Lindholm 1996). In order to reconstruct the summer temperature variability, the tree-ring chronology was regressed against instrumental data from a local weather station (Karasjok; 69° 28′ N; 25° 31′ E) to represent temperature variations on a Celsius scale (Helama *et al.* 2010b). This dendroclimatic reconstruction accounts for more than 40 per cent of the total observed temperature variance over the calibration period (AD 1877–2004) (Fig. 1a). On longer timescales, the correspondence between the observed and reconstructed climate variability is even better (Fig. 1b). The reconstruction shows low temperatures during the cool decades at the end of the nineteenth century, and high temperatures during the warmer decades during the 1920s and 1930s, and it follows the more subtle cooling and warming over the later part of the twentieth century.

In south-eastern Finland, the dendroclimatic correlations indicate suitable circumstances for precipitation reconstruction (Helama & Lindholm 2003). The pines of the region benefit from increasing moisture during the early part of the growing season, as implied by significant tree-ring correlation with the precipitation sum of the May–June season (Helama *et al.* 2005). In order to build up the palaeoclimate reconstruction in the region, mean and variance of chronology were adjusted to the precipitation record (Helama *et al.* 2009a) over the calibration period (AD 1909–1993) (Fig. 1c). Here, the instrumental data was computed as the mean precipitation as observed at four meteorological stations (Savonlinna, 61° 48′ N, 28° 50′ E; Lappeenranta, 61° 05′ N, 28° 09′ E; Punkaharju, 61° 48′ N, 9° 20′ E; Tohmajärvi, 62° 14′ N, 30° 21′ E). The reconstruction accounts for 40% of the total precipitation variance. On longer timescales, the reconstruction reproduces well the regimes of drier and wetter phases as evidenced by the close correspondence between the two curves of moisture variability (Fig. 1d).

Applying the obtained dendroclimatic calibrations over the pre-calibration period, the tree-ring chronologies enabled yearly estimates of summer temperatures for 5500 BC through to AD 2005 (Helama *et al.* 2010b) and spring–summer precipitation sums for AD 660 to 1993 (Helama *et al.* 2009a). Relevant to the present purposes, these reconstructions make it possible to depict the Viking Age (AD 800–1050) climate particularities in Finland in the context of the past two thousand years. Both the temperature (Fig. 2a) and precipitation (Fig. 2b) reconstructions show evidence for highly variable climate conditions over the study period. Summer temperature variations are dominated by a strong year-to-year fluctuation, evident also for the precipitation variations. Moreover, longer-term variations are evident, as shown by the filtered curves of more subtle amplitude. Correlativity between the two reconstructions varies depending on timescale. On the year-to-year

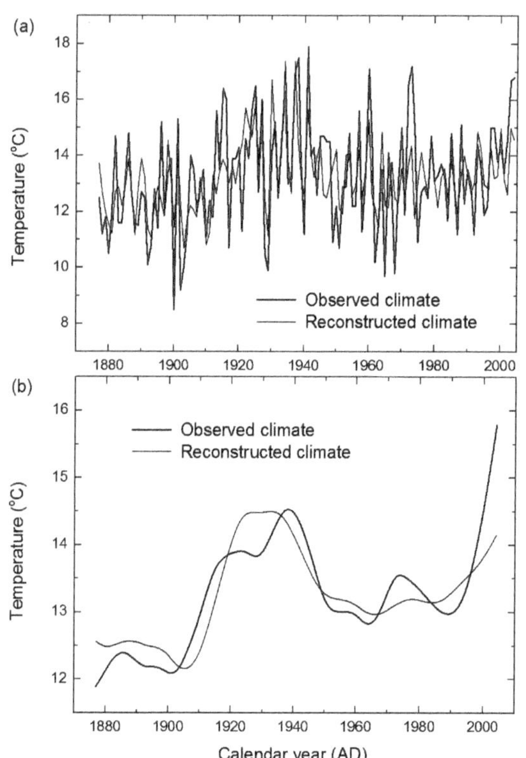

Fig. 1. Observed and reconstructed mid-summer (July) temperature (a, b) and early-summer (May-June) precipitation (c, d) variability over the corresponding calibration periods, compared as total variability (a, c) and on multi-decadal timescales (b, d).

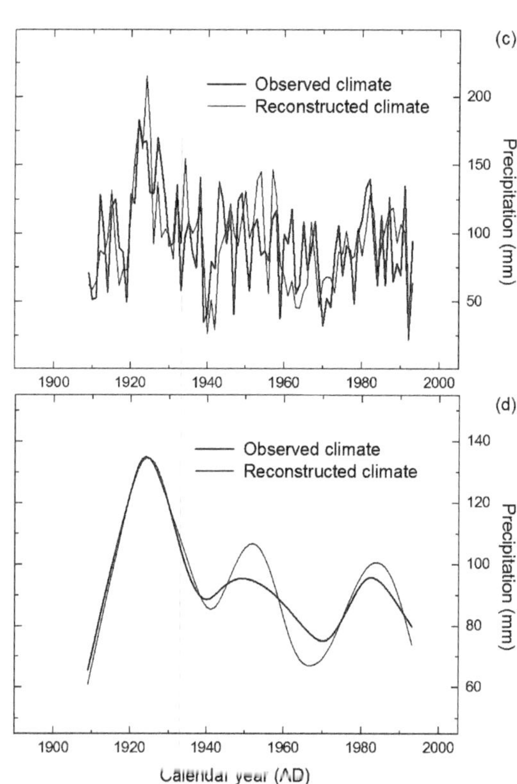

scale (thin grey lines in Fig. 2) the Pearson correlation coefficient between the reconstruction is positive (0.17) but negative for long-term (black lines in Fig. 2) fluctuations (–0.12).

Viking Age Climate Variability in Long-Term Perspective

The temperature variations of centennial and longer scales exhibit warming during the fifth to seventh centuries, tenth to twelfth centuries and over the twentieth century towards the present day; long-term cooling were experienced during the third century and seventeenth to nineteenth centuries (Fig. 2a). The long-term precipitation extremes were evident as relatively rainy intervals during the ninth, thirteenth, sixteenth and twentieth centuries, where the multi-centennial drought from the early thirteenth century, with a culmination during the eleventh to twelfth centuries and the early ninth century (Fig. 2b). With regards to the Viking Age, no precise coincidence with the above-mentioned climatic regimes could be detected. In fact, a closer look at the particular time interval shows that the Viking Age temperature and precipitation variations showed trends towards warmer climate (Fig. 3a) and, especially, dry conditions (Fig. 3b). Over these contrasting trends were superimposed the more ample variations of shorter timescales.

Calculating directly from the yearly estimates of temperatures and precipitation, it was established that the described climatic trends in fact constituted the most appreciable multi-centennial climatic changes over the past two thousand years. In detail, the most notable warming trends of similar lengths were found for the periods AD 255–504, AD 1744–1993 and, indeed, AD 788–1037, during which the slope of linear trends[1] indicated warming rates of about 0.47, 0.42 and 0.29°C per century, respectively. Thus, the rate of temperature change throughout the Viking Age (AD 788–1037) was approximately two thirds of the corresponding rate during the era of modern warming (AD 1744–1993). Naturally, both estimates are relatively rough and should not be over-interpreted. The rise of temperatures towards the end of the Viking Age is in agreement with multiple lines of evidence showing long-lasting warming in many parts of the world around AD 1000–1200. Such palaeoclimatic evidence was first presented by Lamb (1965) and recently confirmed in a proxy analysis for the northern hemisphere (Ljungqvist *et al.* 2012).

Calculation using the yearly estimates of precipitation actually quantifies the Viking Age as the period with the strongest trend towards drier conditions in the context of the full reconstruction. The slope of the regression-based trend line was found to be steepest for the period 811–1060, with a rate of precipitation reduction of about 32 mm per century. This trend could be compared only with the drying of similar character during the period 1501–1750, when the rate of precipitation reduction was approximately 20 mm per century. In other words, the hydroclimatic trend throughout the Viking Age was a uniquely anomalous feature of the reconstruction.

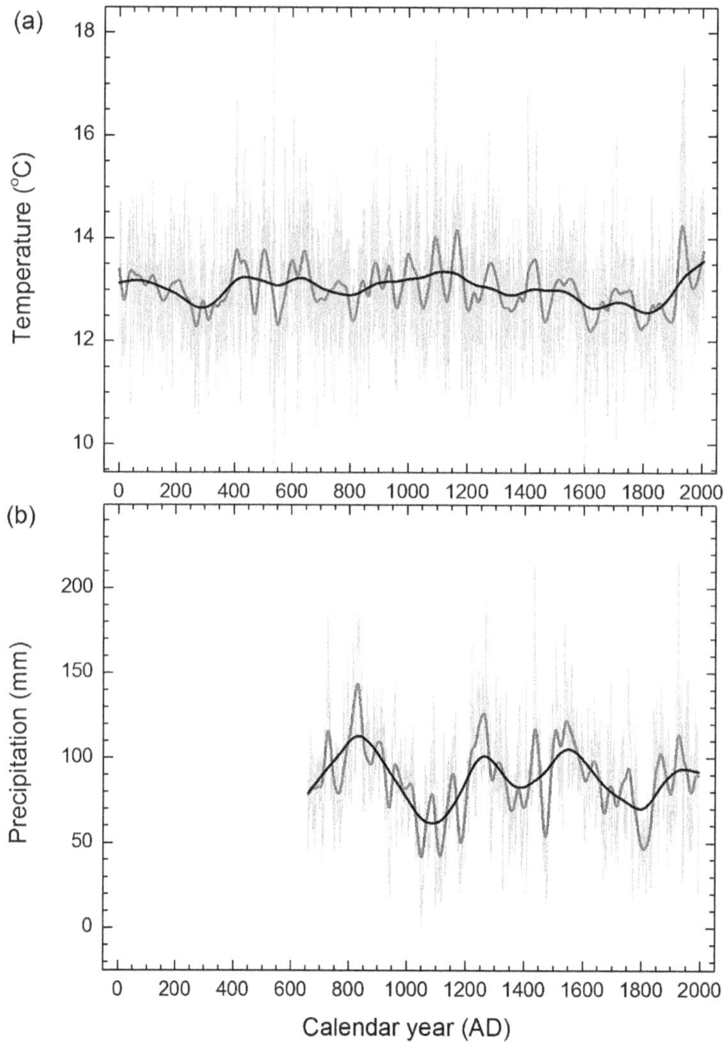

Fig. 2. Reconstructed mid-summer (July) temperature (a) and precipitation (b) variability over the past two thousand years represented as total variations (light-grey line), decadal (dark grey line) and centennial (black line) variations.

The negative trend seen in the precipitation reconstruction (Fig. 3b), and the resulting drought during the following centuries (Fig. 2b), may actually both coincide with similar hydroclimatic perturbations over various regions. This was shown in a global comparison of drought-proxies, including the reconstruction in hand, demonstrating that the summers may have been notably dry over similar times at least in England, Holland and Spain (Helama *et al.* 2009a). The origins of the climatic trends throughout the Viking Age may likewise result from climate dynamics of a considerably

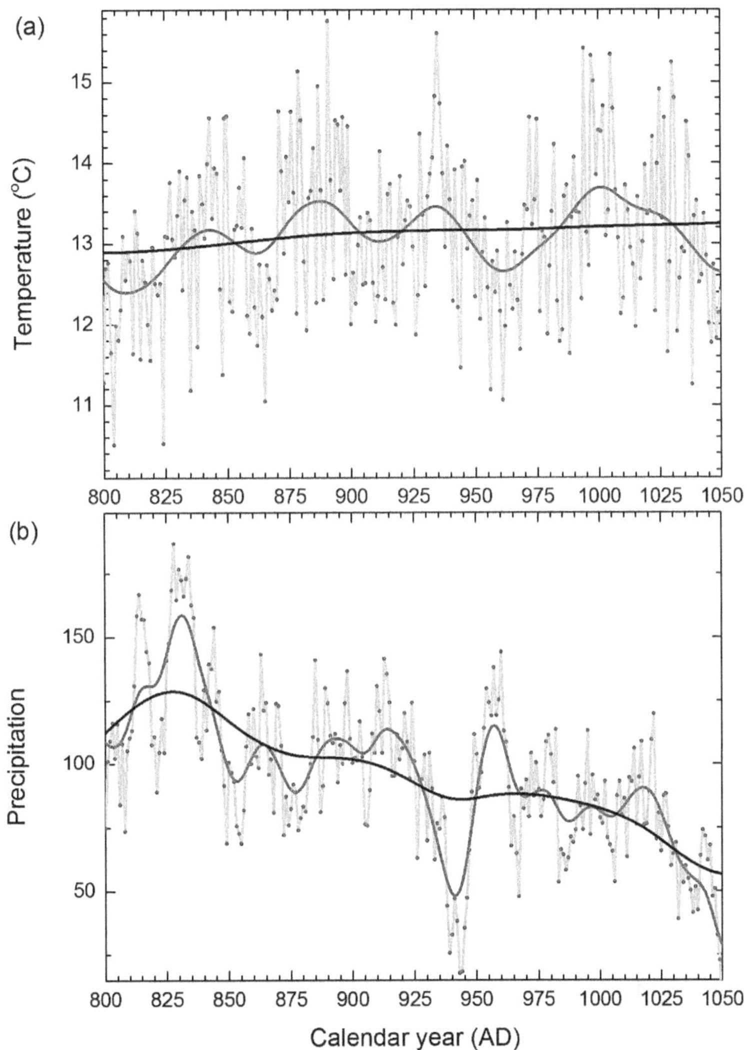

Fig. 3. Reconstructed temperature (a) and precipitation (b) variability during the Viking Age, depicted as total variations (dotted light-grey line), decadal (dark-grey line) and centennial (black line) variations.

large scale. Inferred from the proxy data in hand, the warming through the Viking Age could be seen as coincident with an intensification of the thermohaline circulation in the North Atlantic, carrying more heat from low to high latitudes (Helama *et al.* 2009b). Moreover, long-term solar activity variations may be responsible for the oceanic anomalies, whereas the involvement of ocean–atmosphere interactions is probably needed to explain the reconstructed temperature and hydroclimatic changes over the study region (Helama *et al.* 2009a; 2010b).

Viking Age Climate Variability on Decadal-to-Annual Scales

Apart from the long-term trends, the climatic reconstructions illustrate variations on shorter timescales. Concentrating on variations with periodic features, the reconstructions were exposed to spectral analyses using algorithms specifically tailored for climatic series (Ghil *et al.* 2002). Results from these analyses strongly suggest periodic temperature variability at three different periods, of about fifty-seven, four and three years (Fig. 4a). In fact, these results serve as quantifications of the visual inspection of the reconstruction variations that indeed seem to exhibit fluctuations on multi-decadal and multi-annual scales (Fig. 3a). The spectral analyses of the precipitation reconstruction revealed a strong periodicity on biennal periodicity only (Fig. 4b). On longer scales, the spectral analysis further quantified the trend of precipitation reduction over the Viking Age. A common feature found in the spectral analyses is the multi-annual variability; on these timescales, both reconstructions produce evidence of periodic features (Fig. 4). Overall, this finding implies vigorously fluctuating climate and related environmental conditions during the study period at a timescale of between two and six years.

Interestingly, the temperature variations of multi-decadal timescales (pertaining here to the approximately 57-year periodicity) particularly over the Atlantic region have previously been associated with natural instabilities of the thermohaline circulation and their climatic inferences (Knight *et al.* 2005). These findings would augment the view of strong Atlantic influence on multi-decadal climate variability through the Viking Age (Fig. 4a) as well as on the long-term climatic warming over the same period (Fig. 3a).

Moreover, the palaeoclimate data indicate notably low temperatures during the three individual years at the beginning of the study period, in AD 804, 824 and 865 (Fig. 3a). In this regard, the connection of the coolest summers and atmospheric effects of large explosive volcanic eruptions have been demonstrated to be the strongest signal of cooling during the one or two years following the eruption around the northern hemisphere (Bradley 1988; Briffa *et al.* 1998) with, interestingly, a profoundly strong cooling over the territory of Finland (Fischer *et al.* 2007). Similarly, the cooling has been detected in the high-resolution temperature-sensitive palaeoclimate records from northern Finland over the past five centuries (Helama *et al.* 2005; 2010a). Combined, these results would imply distant effects of explosive eruptions for the observed anomalously cool years at the beginning of the Viking Age. Actually, there is historical evidence of Mount Fuji, in Japan, erupting in 800–802 and 864 (Tsuya 1955; Koyama 1998a; 1998b). These findings would add to the previous evidence linking the summer cooling in AD 1709 with the Mount Fuji eruption known to have occurred in AD 1707 (Helama *et al.* 2005). The results agree with the evidence of high-level volcanic activity of Mount Fuji during the Viking Age, from the ninth to eleventh centuries, and could be further confirmed by the fact that the eruptions of 800–802, 864 and 1707 were more violent than the other eruptions during historical times (Tsuya 1955, Koyama 1998a; 1998b). The coolness of the summer 824,

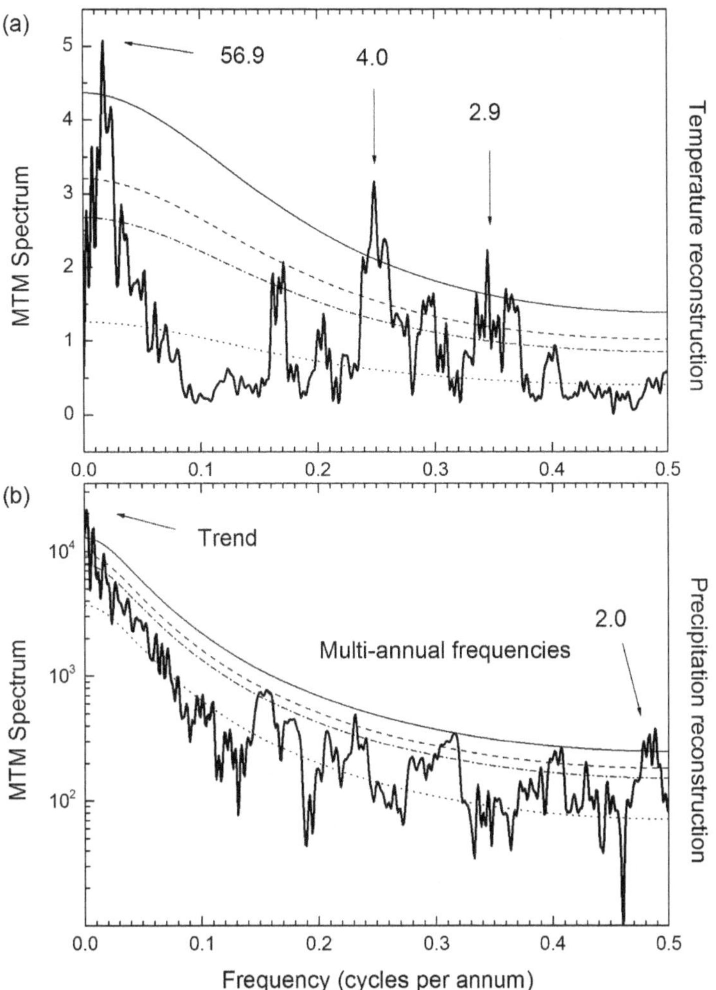

Fig. 4. Timescale-dependent characteristics of reconstructed temperature (a) and precipitation (b) variability over the Viking Age, estimated as MTM-spectrum (Ghil et al. 2002). The associated 99% (solid line), 95% (dashed line), and 90% (dash-dot line) significance levels and the red-noise background (dotted line) are shown by the four smooth curves from the lowest to the highest curve in the figure. The significant periodicities found are given as numerals.

on the other hand, could be linked with the eruption of the Popocatépetl volcano in Mexico. This eruption probably occurred during the winter of AD 822 or spring of 823 and has been estimated to have affected climate globally (Siebe *et al.* 1996). These suggestions would link with our findings of the above-mentioned cool summers in Finland. It cannot be ruled out that several other cool summers in the reconstruction also resulted from volcanic influences. Such comparisons are obscured by the lack of exactly dated information on past eruptions.

Climate Variability and the Subsistence of Inhabitants of Finland

Climatic variations in the past probably influenced contemporary human populations to a considerable extent. Long-term influences have previously been suggested with regards to the Viking Age, when the amelioration of climate may have facilitated the Norse voyages towards Arctic regions (Lamb 1995). It is of note that this amelioration was also demonstrated here as the warming indicated by the tree-ring proxy of this study. In the study region, the climatic trends and extremes could have influenced the ancient Finns by altering their crop yields (Tornberg 1989; Solantie 1997). Indeed, such suggestions are consistent with similar relationships demonstrated for other northern areas that are marginal in terms of agriculture (Parry 1975). In this regard, the studies of pollen and macrofossil remains have evidenced *Hordeum* (barley) and *Secale* (rye) cultivation in southern part of Finland during the Viking Age (Onnela *et al.* 1996; Taavitsainen *et al.* 1998; Alenius *et al.* 2008). As indicated by an analysis of macrofossils, wheat was a species of lesser importance (Onnela *et al.* 1996).

The relationships between climate variability and crop yields may in fact be rather complex, as is known from modern agricultural practices (Mukula & Rantanen 1989a; 1989b). Knowledge about modern climatic influences cannot, however, be directly applied to past agrarian environments and historic human populations. In this context, an analysis of historically documented crop yields (Holopainen & Helama 2009) suggested that the yields of both rye and barley were markedly influenced by large-scale temperature variations as indicated by the sixteenth- and seventeenth-century evidence from south-western Finland. During the eighteenth century, the variability in barley crop yield is better explained by precipitation variables, whereas the crop yield of rye remained sensitive to temperature. It was also seen that frost damage was a constant threat and earliness in ripening a benefit (Holopainen & Helama 2009). Support for these results is found from historical accounts of south-western Finland, describing poor harvests in association with cool summers and frosts and, especially in the case of barley, with droughts, during the seventeenth and eighteenth centuries (Tornberg 1989).

On the other hand, the Viking Age populations were not fully dependent on agriculture as a subsistence source (Taavitsainen *et al.* 1998). Potentially, the food availability of hunter-gatherers could have been even more dependent on warm climate conditions than subsistence by an agrarian production. This was indicated by the long-term reconstructions of population history and environmental changes in the southern part of the country, suggesting that the populations of hunter-gatherers were affected by overall environmental productivity influencing the availability of food (Tallavaara & Seppä 2012).

Conclusions

The main aim of the chapter was to provide the Viking Age with a climatic context. This was done using the available tree-ring evidence, which was transformed into estimates of past temperature and precipitation variability in Finland. Interestingly, the Viking Age (AD 800–1050) emerged as a period of contrasting climatic trends, with continuing warming and drying of the summer climate. As the short literature survey implied, the described climatic changes were not geographically limited to Finnish conditions but at least some of them represent climatic fluctuations linked to climatic evolution of the North Atlantic sector and even on a hemispheric scale. Moreover, the reconstructed climatic variations during the Viking Age could, it may be suggested, have impacted on the subsistence of the contemporary human populations, but to an unknown degree. The simplest interpretation would indicate an amelioration of the climate as the long-term warming continued throughout the Viking Age, whereas the declining trend in hydroclimate reconstruction would imply deterioration of environmental conditions, at least putatively, in the case of barley crop yields. The single years of cool summers, in association with the distant effects of explosive eruptions, in all likelihood came with deleterious effects on agriculture. Finally, this discussion does not suggest a monocausal explanation of climate variations behind all ancient population changes. Inclusion of palaeoclimate reconstructions as complementary data for topical studies in the field of history and archaeology is recommended.

Acknowledgements: This study was supported by the Academy of Finland (#251441).

Notes

1 A trend line and its slope were calculated using least squares linear regression.

References

Bradley, Raymond S. 1999. *Paleoclimatology: Reconstructing Climates of the Quaternary*. 2nd edn. San Diego: Academic Press.

Briffa, K. R., P. D. Jones, F. H. Schweingruber & T. J. Osborn. 1998. Influence of Volcanic Eruptions on Northern Hemisphere Summer Temperature over the past 600 years. *Nature* 393: 450–455.

Broecker, Wallace S. 2001. Was the Medieval Warm Period Global? *Science* 291: 1497–1499.

Douglass, A. E. 1941. Crossdating in Dendrochronology. *Journal of Forestry* 39: 825–831.

Eronen, Matti. 1979. The Retreat of Pine Forest in Finnish Lapland since the Holocene Climatic Optimum: A General Discussion with Radiocarbon Evidence from Subfossil Pines. *Fennia* 157: 93–114.

Eronen, Matti, Hannu Hyvärinen & Pentti Zetterberg. 1999. Holocene Humidity Changes in Northern Finnish Lapland Inferred from Lake Sediments and Submerged Scots Pines Dated by Tree Rings. *The Holocene* 9: 569–580.

Eronen, M., Pentti Zetterberg, Keith R. Briffa, Markus Lindholm, Jouko Meriläinen & Mauri Timonen. 2002. The Supra-Long Scots Pine Tree-Ring Record for Finnish Lapland: Part 1, Chronology Construction and Initial References. *The Holocene* 12: 673–680.

Esper, Jan, Edward R. Cook, Paul J. Krusic, Kenneth Peters & Fritz H. Schweingruber. 2003. Tests of the RCS Method for Preserving Low-Frequency Variability in Long Tree-Ring Chronologies. *Tree- Ring Research* 59: 81–98.

Grudd, Håkan, Keith R. Briffa, Wibjorn Karlén, Thomas S. Bartholin, Philip D. Jones & Bernd Kromer. 2002. A 7400-Year Tree-Ring Chronology in Northern Swedish Lapland: Natural Climatic Variability Expressed on Annual to Millennial Timescales. *The Holocene* 12: 657–665.

Fischer, E. M., J. Luterbacher, E. Zorita, S. F. B. Tett, C. Casty & H. Wanner. 2007. European Climate Response to Tropical Volcanic Eruptions over the Last Half Millennium. *Geophysical Research Letters* 34: L05707, doi:10.1029/2006GL027992.

Friedrich, Michael, Sabine Remmele, Bernd Kromer, Jutta Hofmann, Marco Spurk, Klaus Felix Kauser, Christian Orcel & Manfred Kuppers. 2004. The 12,460-Year Hohenheim Oak and Pine Tree-Ring Chronology from Central Europe: A Unique Annual Record for Radiocarbon Calibration and Paleoenvironment Reconstructions. *Radiocarbon* 46: 1111–1122.

Fritts, H. C. 1976. *Tree Rings and Climate*. London: Academic Press.

Ghil, M., M. R. Allen, M. D. Dettinger, K. Ide, D. Kondrashov, M. E. Mann, A. W. Robertson, A. Saunders, Y. Tian, F. Varadi, & P. Yiou. 2002. Advanced Spectral Methods for Climatic Time Series. *Reviews of Geophysics* 40: 1003, doi: 10.1029/2000RG000092.

Hantemirov, Rashit M., & Stepan G. Shiyatov. 2002. A Continuous Multimillennial Ring-Width Chronology in Yamal, Northwestern Siberia. *The Holocene* 12: 717–726.

Helama, Samuli & Markus Lindholm. 2003. Droughts and Rainfall in South-Eastern Finland since AD 874, Inferred from Scots Pine Ring-Widths. *Boreal Environmental Research* 8: 171–183.

Helama, Samuli, Markus Lindholm, Mauri Timonen & Matti Eronen. 2004. Detection of Climate Signal in Dendrochronological Data Analysis: A Comparison of Tree-Ring Standardisation Methods. *Theoretical and Applied Climatology* 79: 239–254.

Helama, Samuli, Markus Lindholm, Jouko Meriläinen, Mauri Timonen & Matti Eronen. 2005. Multicentennial Ring-Width Chronologies of Scots Pine along North-South Gradient across Finland. *Tree-Ring Research* 61: 21–32.

Helama, Samuli, Kari Mielikäinen, Mauri Timonen & Matti Eronen. 2008. Finnish Supra-Long Tree-Ring Chronology Extended to 5634 BC. *Norsk Geografisk Tidsskrift* 62: 271–277.

Helama, Samuli, Jouko Meriläinen & Heikki Tuomenvirta. 2009a. Multicentennial Megadrought in Northern Europe Coincided with a Global El Niño-Southern Oscillation drought Pattern during the Medieval Climate Anomaly. *Geology* 37: 175–178.

Helama, Samuli, Mauri Timonen, Jari Holopainen, Maxim G. Ogurtsov, Kari Mielikäinen, Matti Eronen, Markus Lindholm & Jouko Meriläinen. 2009b. Summer Temperature Variations in Lapland during the Medieval Warm Period and the Little Ice Age Relative to Natural Instability of Thermohaline Circulation on Multi-Decadal and Multi-Centennial Scales. *Journal of Quaternary Science* 24: 450–456.

Helama, Samuli, Alar Läänelaid, Hanna Tietäväinen, Marc Macias Fauria, Ilmo T. Kukkonen, Jari Holopainen, Jan K. Nielsen & Ilmari Valovirta. 2010a. Late Holocene Climatic Variability Reconstructed from Incremental Data from Pines and Pearl

Mussels: A Multi-Proxy Comparison of Air and Subsurface Temperatures. *Boreas* 39: 734–748.

Helama, Samuli, Marc Macias Fauria, Kari Mielikäinen, Mauri Timonen & Matti Eronen. 2010b. Sub-Milankovitch Solar Forcing of Past Climates: Mid and Late Holocene Perspectives. *Geological Society of America Bulletin* 122: 1981–1988.

Holopainen, Jari & Samuli Helama. 2009. Little Ice Age Farming in Finland: Preindustrial Agriculture on the Edge of the Grim Reaper's Scythe. *Human Ecology* 37: 213–225.

Holopainen, Jari, Ian J. Rickard & Samuli Helama. 2012. Climatic Signatures in Crops and Grain Prices in Nineteenth-Century Sweden. *The Holocene*, doi: 10.1177/0959683611434220.

Knight, Jeff R., Robert J. Allan, Chris K. Folland, Michael Vellinga & Michael E. Mann. 2005. A Signature of Persistent Natural Thermohaline Circulation Cycles in Observed Climate. *Geophysical Research Letters* 32: L20708, doi: 10.1029/2005GL024233.

Koyama, Masato. 1998a. Reevaluation of the Eruptive History of Fuji Volcano, Japan, Mainly Based on Historical Documents. *Bulletin of the Volcanological Society of Japan* 43: 323–347.

Koyama, Masato. 1998b. Reevaluation of the 800–802 A.D. Eruption of Fuji Volcano, Japan, and Its Influence on the Ancient Traffic Network around the Volcano, Based on Eruptive Deposits and Historical Records. *Bulletin of the Volcanological Society of Japan* 43: 349–371.

Lamb, H. H. 1965. The Early Medieval Warm Epoch and Its Sequel. *Palaeogeography, Palaeoclimatology, Palaeoecology* 1: 13–37.

Lamb, H. H. 1995. *Climate, History and the Modern World.* 2nd edn. London / New York: Routledge.

Lindholm, Markus. 1996. *Reconstructions of Past Climate from Ring-Width Measurements of Scots Pine (*Pinus sylvestris *L.) at the Northern Forest Limit in Fennoscandia.* Publications in Sciences 40. Joenssu: University of Joensuu.

Ljungqvist, F. C., P. J. Krusic, G. Brattström & H. S. Sundqvist. 2012. Northern Hemisphere Temperature Patterns in the Last 12 centuries. *Climate of the Past* 8: 227–249.

Mukula, J., & O. Rantanen, 1989a. Climatic Risks to the Yield and Quality of Field Crops in Finland: III. Winter Rye 1969–1986. *Annales Agriculturae Fenniae* 28: 3–11.

Mukula, J., & O. Rantanen, O. 1989b. Climatic Risks to the Yield and Quality of Field Crops in Finland: VI. Barley 1969–1986. *Annales Agriculturae Fenniae* 28: 29–36.

Naurzbaev, Mukhtar M., Eugene A. Vaganov, Olga V. Sidorova & Fritz H. Schweingruber. 2002. Summer Temperatures in Eastern Taimyr Inferred from a 2427-Year Late-Holocene Tree-Ring Chronology and Earlier Floating Series. *The Holocene* 12: 727–736.

Nicolussi, K., M. Kaufmann, Thomas M. Melvin, J. van der Plicht, P. Schießling & A. Thurner. 2009. A 9111 Year Long Conifer Tree-Ring Chronology for the European Alps: A Base for Environmental and Climatic Investigations. *The Holocene* 19: 909–920.

Parry, M. L. 1975. Secular Climatic Change and Marginal Agriculture. *Transactions of the Institute of British Geographers* 64: 1–13.

Pilcher, J. R., M. G. L. Baillie, B. Schmidt & B. Becker. 1984. A 7,272-Year Tree-Ring Chronology for Western Europe. *Nature* 312: 150–152.

Sheppard, Paul. R. 2010. Dendroclimatology: Extracting Climate from Trees. *Wiley Interdisciplinary Reviews: Climate Change* 1: 343–352.

Siebe, Claus, Michael Abrams, José Luis Macías & Johannes Obenholzner. 1996. Repeated Volcanic Disasters in Prehispanic Time at Popocatépetl, Central Mexico: Past Key to the Future? *Geology* 24:399–402.

Solantie, Reijo. 1997. Ilmaston, maankäytön ja väestön kolmiyhteys Suomessa vanhan maatalouden aikana ['The Tripartite Interdependence of Climate, Land Use and Population in Finland during the Old Agricultural Era'] (abstract in English). *Finnish Meteorological Institute. Meteorological Publications* 35: 1–73.

Stokes, Marvin A. & Terah L. Smiley. 1968. *An Introduction to Tree-Ring Dating.* Chicago: University of Chicago Press.

Tallavaara, Miikka, & Heikki Seppä. 2012. Did the Mid-Holocene Environmental Changes Cause the Boom and Bust of Hunter-Gatherer Population Size in Eastern Fennoscandia? *The Holocene* 22: 215–225.

Tornberg, Matleena. 1989. Ilmaston- ja sadonvaihtelut Lounais-Suomessa 1550-luvulta 1860-luvulle. *Turun Historiallinen Arkisto* 44: 58–87.

Tsuya, Hiromichi. 1955. Geological and Petrological Studies of Volcano, Fuji, V: 5. On the 1707 Eruption of Volcano Fuji. *Bulletin of the Earthquake Research Institute University of Tokyo* 33: 341–383.

Yamaguchi, David K. 1991. A Simple Method for Cross-Dating Increment Cores from Living Trees. *Canadian Journal of Forest Research* 21: 414–416.

Tuukka Talvio

The Viking Age in Finland

Numismatic Aspects

Hoards of coins and/or non-monetary silver are a typical feature of the Viking Age in the whole of northern Europe. Compared with neighbouring areas, the Finnish finds are relatively modest, but the regional differences in the distribution of the hoards within Finland are still problematic. The find material has not been significantly increased since the monograph *Coins and Coin Finds in Finland AD 800–1200* by the present author was published twelve years ago (Talvio 2002), although metal-detectorists have in recent years made many single finds and even found clusters of coins which probably derive from hoards dispersed by the tilling of the soil.

Before discussing the distribution of the hoards we should, however, pay attention to the chronological division between the Viking Age and the so-called Crusade Period. In Finland as elsewhere, the beginning of the Viking Age is usually dated to *c.* 800, but when did it end? In Sweden the ending of the Viking Age is generally dated to 1100 (Thunmark-Nylen 1981: 285) but in Gotland, because of the continuing coin imports, it is considered to have lasted until 1150 (Jonsson 1992: 79–81; Jansson 1983: 9). In Finland, on the other hand, the last phase of the Iron Age is divided into the Viking Age, from 800 to 1025 or 1050, and the subsequent Crusade Period, which in western Finland continued until 1150 and in Karelia until 1300.

Originally the term Crusade Period seems to have been applied in Finland mainly to the last phase of the Karelian Iron Age. A. M. Tallgren, for example, divided the Late Iron Age in his textbook on Finnish prehistory into the 'Viking Age' (AD 800–[1050–]1100]" and the 'Crusade Period' (AD 1050–[1100–]1300) but the chapters dealing with these periods are named "The Late Iron Age in West Finland (*c.* 800–1100)" and "The So-Called Age of the Crusades: The Late Iron Age in Karelia [1100–1300]" (Tallgren 1931: 16, 159, 190). Considering that the crusades to the Holy Land began in 1096 and to the Baltic area in 1147, and that the so-called First Crusade to Finland is supposed to have taken place in the 1150s, it seems odd that the beginning of a period named after the Crusades is in Finnish archaeological literature now usually dated to 1025.[1]

The date 1025 is in fact primarily based on the numismatic dating of certain graves in the Humikkala cemetery at Masku (Sarvas 1972: 19–20, 23–24), but the dating of the coins in question – imitations of Byzantine silver coins and one genuine coin of Basil II (978–1025) – is in fact much too uncertain to be used for the re-dating of a whole archaeological period (Talvio 2004: 126). A simple solution would be to rename the period 1050–1150 the 'Late Viking Age', or something similar. In Karelia, the 'Crusade Period' would still be a good name for the years 1150–1300.

Coins in the North before the Viking Age: Roman Silver and Gold

Before the Viking Age, there were two separate periods of imported coinage in the northern lands. First, Roman silver coins, *denarii*, were imported during the Roman Iron Age (Horsnæs 2010: 173–177). Nearly 8,000 denarii are known from Sweden and 4,500 from Denmark, most of them dating from the second century AD. They seem to have been brought to the north mainly through Poland (Lind 1988: 137; Bursche 1993: 297–303), but Norway, Finland and the East Baltic lands apparently did not profit much from this import. From Finland, for instance, only two denarii are known, both of them now lost, in addition to a number of copper coins, some of them possibly, and a few certainly, secondary finds (Talvio 1982).

The denarii were in the fifth and sixth centuries followed by Late Roman and Early Byzantine gold coins, known as *solidi* (sg. *solidus*). About one thousand solidi have been found in Scandinavia, most of them again from Sweden and Denmark. The finds are strongly concentrated on the islands of Öland, Gotland and Bornholm – and again there are very few coins from Finland, Norway and Estonia, and apparently none from Latvia, Lithuania or north-western Russia. The Finnish material consists of four coins (to be precise, 3½) from southern Ostrobothnia, but there is information of a few solidi having been found in the same area already in the eighteenth century (Talvio 2009).

Eastern and Western Silver

After the ending of the solidus import, hardly any coins are known from the North before the Viking Age, with the exception of the eighth-century *sceattas* (small silver coins issued in southern Britain and Frisia), which in recent decades have been found in south-western Scandinavia. The beginning of the Viking Age as a historical phenomenon is usually dated to *c.* 800, partly on the basis of the raids in Western Europe and partly because of the import of Islamic silver coins, *dirhams*, which is generally thought to have begun about the same time. As has been pointed out by T. S. Noonan, substantial imports of eastern silver would not have been possible before the ending of the long war between the Khazars and the Arabs in the late eighth century (Noonan 1980).

The earliest dirham hoard from northern Russia, found at Staraya Ladoga, has a *terminus post quem* concealment date of 786 (Kirpichnikov 1990: 65–66). The eastern imports climaxed in the early tenth century. From that time probably dated a hoard from the shore of Lake Ladoga which is reported to have weighed more than a hundred kilograms, theoretically consisting of more than 35,000 coins (Markov' 1910: 130–131). Soon after the middle of the tenth century, however, the dirham import started to decline, ceasing almost entirely in the 960s. At the end of the century, the flow of eastern silver began again, but only on a small scale, and soon after 1000 it ended completely.

In "The Impact of the Silver Crisis in Islam upon Novgorod's Trade with the Baltic" (1988), Noonan writes that there were:

> developments affecting Russian silver exports to the Baltic [...] which were quite independent of dirham imports into European Russia from the Islamic world. Long before the export of dirhams from the Islamic world began to decline, the re-export of dirhams from European Russia to Sweden and perhaps other parts of the Baltic had decreased markedly. (Noonan 1988: 430; cf. Noonan 1990: 255; 1994: 230–234.)

However, he also points out that the silver content of the dirhams declined in the second half of the tenth century (Noonan 1988: 437–438), and this may well have been the main reason why their importation to Scandinavia declined.[2]

West European coins were very rare in Scandinavia in the heyday of the eastern silver, but in the late tenth century, at the same time as the dirham imports declined, Anglo-Saxon and German pennies began to appear in finds, and in the 990s they became plentiful (Jonsson 1992: 81–82). Western European money has since then always been important for the northern lands, but the Viking Age imports of silver pennies were strongly reduced in the second half of the eleventh century, after the introduction of local monetary systems in Denmark and Norway. The situation may also have been influenced by the circumstances within Germany, which in the later eleventh century was the most important export area. According to a somewhat controversial theory, the so-called *Fernhandelsdenar*[3] was replaced in the twelfth century with a system of regional coinages (Hatz 1974: 185–186; Kilger 2000: 33–5). The decline of coin imports from England has usually been connected with the abolition of the tax known as *heregeld* in 1051 (Jonsson 1976: 27).

Table 1 should give a fairly representative picture of the Viking-Age coin finds from the Baltic area:[4]

Table 1. Survey of coins from the eighth to the twelfth centuries found in the Nordic Countries and Baltic lands, with the three major elements presented separately. Sources: Jonsson 1992, Molvõgin 1995 (for Estonia), Talvio 2002 (for Finland). The figures for Finland do not include finds from former Finnish Karelia.

	Islamic	*German*	*English*	*Total*
Denmark	5,100	24,000	14,500	57,900
Norway	400	3,300	3,300	10,700
Mainland Sweden & Öland	15,300	16,200	6,300	44,800
Gotland	49,800	62,200	25,800	145,800
Poland and Polabia	30,000	150,000	4,500	250,000
Latvia	2,200	2,100	200	5,200
Estonia	5,000	10,500	2,000	17,500
Finland	1,700	3,800	1,000	7,000
Russia	100,000	50,000	3,500	155,000
Total	209,500	322,100	61,100	693,900

As we can see, the Finnish finds account for only about one per cent of the Viking Age coins found in the countries surrounding the Baltic Sea. From a local point of view, the 7,000 coins are, however, a substantial collection, especially when compared to the very small number of Roman and Late Roman coins surviving from the earlier periods – as noted above, only four solidi are known from Finland. However, if we conjecture that the coins mentioned in the eighteenth century sources which are now lost were also four in number, the total would have been eight solidi, or one per cent of the Swedish find material. Considering how much non-monetary gold the Swedish finds contain, the difference is in fact much larger (Talvio 2009: 273). The 7,000 coins from Viking Age Finland still account for less than 4 per cent of the Swedish finds.

These 7,000 coins do not give us the right to speak of a monetary economy in Viking Age Finland. The coins were only a form of bullion which could be used both for transactions and as material for jewellery. However, minted silver probably enjoyed a higher value than its equivalent weight of ordinary bullion, for it was easy to handle and coins must have been recognised as normally being of good silver. The small folding scales that are met with in Viking Age graves were necessary utensils at a time when coins struck according to several different weight systems were in circulation together.

Regional Differences: The 'Satakunta Question'

An interesting fact concerning the province of Satakunta is that the rich inhumation cemeteries of this area contain – in addition to a considerable number of coins and coin fragments – more scales than are known from the rest of Finland put together. There is, however, only one (eleventh-century) hoard from the province, and it comes from Lempäälä near the border of Tavastia, which is a province with numerous hoards (Talvio 2002: 119–123). How are the differences in the distribution of hoards to be explained?

When in the eleventh century silver hoards became common on the mainland, they were concentrated on the south-western coast of Finland Proper and in the lake district of Tavastia. Writing on the finds in 2002, I suggested that traders operating on the coast of Finland Proper played a central role in the imports, and the hoards of that area belonged to them, while in the case of Tavastia the hoards were connected with the organisation of the fur trade. Although most of the evidence concerning the fur trade naturally postdates the Viking Age, it is interesting to note that the origins of the 'Ox Road' (*Hämeen härkätie*, connecting Finland Proper with the Vanaja Lake District in Tavastia) are now dated to the Late Iron Age (Masonen 1989).

A possible explanation for the almost total absence of Viking Age hoards in Satakunta seemed to be that the trading there was based more on barter (goods exchanged for goods) than a 'silver economy'. According to this interpretation, the silver that was available was usually converted into other goods rather than hoarded. This would mean that there were in Finland in the later Viking Age two systems of trading. Both employed money (silver), but in differing degrees. The 'wholesale dealers', who sold furs and other goods to overseas merchants, acquired considerable sums of money and used it to obtain their merchandise from inland areas. Local dealers also used money, but much of their trading was based on bartering - for silver was, after all, just another expensive import product, and its value tended to fluctuate (Talvio 2002: 122–123).

Discontinuity of Settlement in Åland?

In the case of Åland, the problem is that the dirham hoards come to an end soon after the middle of the tenth century. This must have been connected with the ending of the eastern imports, but unlike mainland Finland, they were not followed by a flow of western silver. Helmer Salmo believed that the population of Åland had decreased or even wholly disappeared in the late tenth century as a result of the unruly times (Salmo 1948: 421–424). Mårten Stenberger, too, paid attention to the apparent ceasing of archaeological finds in Åland around 1000 (Stenberger 1964: 799–802). The linguist Lars Hellberg has completed the picture by his theory that the present place names of Åland date from post-Viking times (Hellberg 1987). From a numismatic point of view, one can add that Viking Age coins are usually found not only in hoards but also as single and cumulative finds and in graves. All four find categories are well enough represented in Åland until around 960. The total lack of all kinds of coin finds from the following two centuries simply cannot be accidental, for in all the neighbouring areas - Estonia, mainland Finland and Sweden - coins from the eleventh century are more numerous in the finds than the dirhams. It would be difficult to think that the people of Åland voluntarily reverted to barter economy after the plentiful silver imports of the ninth and tenth centuries.

Coins reappeared in Åland in the twelfth century. The earliest medieval coins are Gotlandic pennies, and as the coin type in question was introduced around 1140, the finds have also usually been thought to begin in the twelfth century (e.g. Talvio 2002: 109f). According to a recent study by Nanouschka Myrberg, only four of the 116 early Gotlandic coins found in Finland can be dated earlier than 1220. Three of them are from Finström church in Åland (Myrberg 2008: 318). If there are four coins from the years 1140–1220 and 112 from the years 1220–1288 (51 of them from the churches of Åland), it seems unlikely that even the four earlier ones would date from the beginning of their minting period – they need not belong to the twelfth century at all. Considering that the earliest stone churches of Åland are now dated to the thirteenth century (Hiekkanen 2003: 54), this is hardly surprising.

The only non-Gotlandic coin found in Åland that has been dated to the twelfth century is a supposed penny of Knut Eriksson (1167–1196) from Finström church. It is, however, a small fragment, and in their publication of the coin finds from Finström church, Kenneth Jonsson and Lars O. Lagerqvist (1975: 5ff) do not consider its attribution certain. If, then, even the earliest coin from Svealand found in Åland is a small fragment that *may* date from the last quarter of the twelfth century, one can hardly speak of a monetary history of Åland during that century. In the thirteenth century, the situation was already very much different: the Geta hoard, consisting of 850 bracteates with the *terminus post quem* of 1275, is the earliest medieval coin hoard from Finland (Talvio 2007: 120).

Local Minting in Finland in the Eleventh Century

Not all coins in Viking Age Finland were imported from afar: there was also some – but apparently very little – local production. This become known when Pekka Sarvas in 1973 published a listing of the Byzantine coins found in Finland, which also included fifteen imitations of Byzantine coins that he considered to be locally made (Sarvas 1973; Talvio 1994). Ten of the imitations were based on the coins of Basil II (976–1025) and five on those of Roman III (1028–1034) and/or Constantine IX (1042–1055). Since then, the material has doubled. It is quite clear that at least a part of the imitations – especially the later ones – must have been struck somewhere in south-western Finland, but it no longer seems probable that all the Basil II imitations are of Finnish origin. On the other hand, it is clear that the 'Finnish' group also includes crude imitations of Islamic dirhams. A new type of imitation was found in the summer of 2011 (Talvio 2012), prompting a new investigation of the whole material. This work has not yet been completed.

Notes

1 The same dating is used in the archaeological exhibition of the Finnish National Museum.
2 I am grateful to Kenneth Jonsson for his comments on this question.
3 The term refers to the important role of German silver coins in the Baltic trade in the late tenth and the eleventh centuries.
4 Most of these figures are now 10–20 years old but we must also take into account that some of the largest figures (like those for Russia and Poland) are in any case only rough estimates.

References

Bursche, A. 1993. Pourquoi les *denarii* frappés apres 194 étaient-ils absents dans le Barbaricum? In Tony Hackens & Ghislaine Moucharte (eds.). *Actes du XIe Congrès International de Numismatique II*. Louvain-la-Neuve: Séminaire de Numismatique Marcel Hoc. Pp. 297–303.

Hatz, Gert. 1974. *Handel und Verkehr zwischen dem deutschen Reich und Schweden in der späten Wikingerzeit*. Stockholm: Kungl. Vitterhets-, Historie- och Antikvitetsakademien.

Hellberg, Lars. 1987. *Ortnamn och den svenska bosättningen på Åland. 2nd edn*. Helsingfors: Svenska Litteratursällskapet i Finland.

Hiekkanen, Markus. 2003. *Suomen kivikirkot keskiajalla*. Helsinki: Otava.

Horsnæs, Helle W. 2010. *Crossing Boundaries: An Analysis of Roman Coins in Danish Contexts I*. Studies in Archaeology and History 18:1. Copenhagen: The National Museum of Denmark.

Jansson, Ingmar, 1983. Gotland och omvärlden under vikingatiden: En översikt. In I. Jansson (ed.). *Gutar och vikingar*. Stockholm: Statens Historiska Museum. Pp. 207–247.

Jonsson, Kenneth. 1976. Vikingatidens myntimport. In Helge Pohjolan-Pirhonen (ed.). *Kulturhistorisk Lexikon för Nordisk medeltid från vikingatid till reformationstid* XX. Helsingfors: Akademiska Bokhandeln. Cols. 25–28.

Jonsson, Kenneth. 1992. Hoards and Single-Finds from the Middle and Northern Baltic Sea Region c. 1050–1150. In A. Loit, E. Mugurevics & A. Caune (eds.). *Kontakte zwischen Ostbaltikum und Skandinavien im frühen Mittelalter*. Studia Baltica Stockholmensia 9. Stockholm: Almqvist & Wiksell. Pp. 79–89.

Jonsson, Kenneth & Lagerqvist, Lars O. 1975. Mynten från Finströms kyrka, Åland. *Åländsk odling. Årsbok 1974*. Mariehamn: Ålands Folkminnesförbund. Pp. 5–30.

Kilger, Christoph. 2000. *Pfennigmärkte und Währungslandschaften: Monetarisierungen im sächsisch-slawischen Gränzland ca. 965–1120*. Commentationes de nummis saeculorum IX–XI in Suecia repertis. Nova series 15. Stockholm: Kungl. Vitterhets-, Historie- och Antikvitetsakademien.

Kirpichnikov, A. N. 1990. Old Ladoga Dirhems. In *Fenno-ugri et Slavi 1988*. Iskos 9. Helsinki: National Board of Antiquities. Pp. 63–7.

Lind, Lennart. 1988. *Romerska denarer funna i Sverige*. Stockholm: Rubicon.

Markov' 1910 = Марковъ, А. 1910. *Топографія кладовъ восточныхъ монет*. С.-Петербургъ: Типографія Императорской Акадміи Наукъ.

Masonen, Jaakko. 1989. *Hämeen härkätie: Synty ja varhaisvaiheet*. Tiemuseon julkaisuja 4. Helsinki: Valtion painatuskeskus.

Myrberg, Nanouschka. 2008. *Ett eget värde. Gotlands tidigaste myntning, ca 1140–1220*. Stockholm studies in archaeology 45. Stockholm: Stockholms universitet.

Noonan, Thomas S. 1980. When and How Dirhams First Reached Russia: A Numismatic Critique of the Pirenne Theory. *Cahiers du Monde russe et soviétique* 21(3–4): 401–469.

Noonan, Thomas S. 1988. *The Impact of the Silver Crisis in Islam upon Novgorod's Trade with the Baltic: Oldenburg - Wolin - Staraja Ladoga - Novgorod - Kiev*. Bericht der römisch-germanischen Kommission 69. Frankfurt am Main: Kommission des deutschen archäologischen Instituts. Pp. 411–417.

Noonan, Thomas S. 1990. Dirham Exports to the Baltic in the Viking Age. In Kenneth Jonsson & Brita Malmer (eds.). *Sigtuna Papers: Proceedings of the Sigtuna Symposium on Viking-Age Coinage 1-4 June 1989*. Commentationes de nummis saeculorum IX–XI in Suecia repertis. Nova series 15. Stockholm: Kungl. Vitterhets-, Historie- och Antikvitetsakademien. Pp. 251–257.

Noonan, Thomas S. 1994. The Vikings in the East: Coins and Commerce. In Björn Ambrosiani & Helen Clarke (eds.). *Developments around the Baltic and the North Sea in the Viking Age*. Birka Studies 3. Stockholm: Riksantikvarieämbetet. Pp. 215–236.

Salmo, Helmer, 1948. *Deutsche Münzen in vorgeschichtlichen Funden Finnlands*. Suomen Muinaismuistoyhdistyksen Aikakauskirja 47. Helsinki: Suomen Muinaismuistoyhdistys.

Sarvas, Pekka. 1972. *Länsi-Suomen ruumishautojen raha-ajoitukset*. Helsingin yliopiston arkeologian laitos, moniste 6. Helsinki: Helsingin yliopiston arkeologian laitos.

Sarvas, Pekka. 1973. Bysanttilaiset rahat sekä niiden jäljitelmät Suomen 900- ja 1000-lukujen löydöissä. In Pekka Sarvas & Ari Siiriäinen (eds.). *Honos Ella Kivikoski*. Suomen Muinaismuistoyhdistyksen Aikakauskirja 75. Helsinki: Suomen Muinaismuistoyhdistys. Pp. 176–86.

Stenberger, Mårten. 1964. *Det forntida Sverige*. Stockholm: Almqvist & Wiksell.

Talvio, Tuukka. 1982. Romerska myntfynd i Finland. *Nordisk Numismatisk Årsskrift* 1979–1980: 36–53.

Talvio, Tuukka. 1994. Imitations de la monnaie byzantine en Finlande. *Revue Numismatique* 1994: 146–154.

Talvio, Tuukka. 2002. *Coins and Coin Finds in Finland AD 800–1200*. Iskos 12. Helsinki: Suomen Muinaismuistoyhdistys.

Talvio, Tuukka. 2007. Coins and coin circulation in medieval Finland. In Stanis[3]aw Suchodolski E Mateusz Bogucki (eds.). *Money Circulation in Antiquity, the Middle Ages and Modern times. Time, Range, Intensity*. Warsaw–Crakow: Avalon. Pp 179–90.

Talvio, Tuukka. 2009. Gotlannin rahat Suomen 1200-luvun löydöissä. In Hanna-Maria Pellinen (ed.). *Maasta, kivestä ja hengestä. Markus Hiekkanen Festschrift*. Saarijärvi: Kulttuurien laitos, arkeologia, Turun yliopisto *et al.* Pp. 306–13.

Talvio, Tuukka. 2012. Nya vikingatida fynd från Finland. *Nordisk Numismatisk Unions Medlemsblad* 2012: 74–76.

Thunmark-Nylén, Lena. 1981. Vikingatiden. In L. Thunmark-Nylén *et al.* (eds.). *Vikingatidens ABC*. Stockholm: Statens Historiska Museum. Pp. 284–286.

Sirpa Aalto

Viking Age in Finland?

Naming a Period as a Historiographical Problem

In Finnish historiography the use of the term Viking Age cannot be taken for granted. In archaeology, the Iron Age is an established term for a period from *c.* 500 BC to AD 1050/1300 in Finnish history, and it follows the periodisation of Christian Jürgensen Thomsen (1788–1865), who used the terms Stone Age, Bronze Age and Iron Age in his book published in 1836 (Immonen 2008: 78; Tommila 1989: 112). The Viking Age (800–1050) and the Crusade Period (1050–1150) form together the Late Iron Age in Finnish history, but also other, more indefinite terms such as the Pagan/Heathen period (*pakanakausi*), the Pre-Christian period (*esikristillinen kausi/aika*) or the Tribal Age (*heimokausi*) have been used in the past (see Raninen & Wessman). The purpose of this chapter is to examine the Finnish academic discourse in four journals from the turn of the twentieth century up to the twenty-first century in order to determine what kind of terminology is used of the Viking Age and why. The periodisation of the past and the use of certain names for periods reflect the time and place where they were developed. It is important to be conscious of the fact that choosing a name for a period is always a comment.

Both historians and archaeologists have participated in writing about the Viking Age or more generally the Late Iron Age in Finland. Therefore, it is interesting to examine whether these two disciplines have had different approaches to the period in question. My hypothesis is that the discourse concerning the Viking Age shows differences when we compare the fields of history and archaeology, because their starting points are different. It can be claimed that archaeology uses the primary sources, i.e. the archaeological material, for the study of the Viking Age and archaeologists thus provide the first-hand information. Historians, on the other hand, rely on the archaeological record because of the lack of written sources,[1] and therefore their interest has mainly been to connect the Late Iron Age to a historical timeline and continuum. The problem of dating and naming a period is not confined to the Viking Age, but applies more generally to the transition from prehistory to history (Sarvas 1971; Julku 1979; Immonen 2012).

Usually the naming of historical and pre-historical periods in Finnish historiography follows foreign examples. On the one hand, this practice is useful for scholars because it allows comparisons to be made between different cultures but, on the other hand, it does not take into account local circumstances and developments. Therefore, a name for a period that is adopted from another cultural context may be unsuitable.

As an example of the kind of difficulties involved when a name for a period is adopted from another culture, we may take the Middle Ages. In the European context – especially when it comes to Southern and Central Europe – the Middle Ages extends from *c.* 500 AD to 1500, which means that it includes the Viking Age. In the Finnish, context the Middle Ages extends from 1150/1300 to *c.* 1500, leaving the Viking Age as part of prehistory. The Middles Ages is divided into the Early, High and Late Middle Ages, and this division was applied to Finnish history, too. This kind of division – used for example by the Finnish historian Jalmari Jaakkola (1881–1964) – was more than artificial because the terms referred to different periods in Central and Southern Europe than they did in Finland. It is generally accepted that the Middle Ages did not begin in Finland Proper (south-western Finland) before the 1150s and even later in other parts of Finland. When it comes to the northernmost part of Finland, we could ask whether there has ever been a period that could be called the Middle Ages. (Jaakkola 1938; 1944; 1950; Mäkivuoti 1992: 6–11)

Building the Myth of a Nation

The question of the term 'Viking Age' and its use in the Finnish context is intertwined with the general discourse on shaping the Finnish past. In the nineteenth century, the Finnish past was in a way invented and reworked in order to legitimise the Finnish people, culture and language. The past was also used for the legitimisation of independence. This was in accordance with the ideas of Romanticism, which called for people to become aware of themselves as a nation and of their historical task. (Tommila 1989: 65, 71; Fewster 2000b: 108; Klinge 2010: 191.)

In academic discourse of the end of the nineteenth century and the first half of the twentieth century, Finnish group identity was based on an imagined greatness in the past. The building blocks of this Finnish identity were features of culture that distinguished the Finns from their neighbours, and supposed connections with some larger Finno-Ugrian 'family'. The construction of Finnish identity and history is a classic example of how literary sources (or even lack thereof) but also fictional stories are inevitably involved with how we depict, reconstruct and create the past and what kind of terminology we use (Korhonen 2006: 18).

The periodisation of the Finnish past was not relevant until the nineteenth century, when in the wake of Romanticism, it was important for Finnish scholars to trace the history of the 'Finnish people'. Scholars had to ponder, for instance, whether the periodisation of Swedish history was suitable for

Finnish history. Different names were suggested for the period before the Middle Ages, but in general it came to be described in terms of religion. The period was called 'pre-Christian' (Gustaf Renvall), 'the heathen period' (Gabriel Rein) or more neutrally 'ancient times' (Adolf Ivar Arwidsson). (Tommila 1989: 80–81.)

Because Finland had first been part of Sweden and then part of Russia, it was important for nationalistic history-writers to find something unique in the Finnish past and in Finnish culture. One example of this uniqueness was the *Kalevala*, an epic of Homeric scope developed on the basis of traditional folk poetry by Elias Lönnrot (1802–1884), first published in 1835 and then in an extensively revised and expanded second edition in 1849. Lönnrot himself thought that he was reconstructing the past when he composed the *Kalevala* (Lönnrot 1964: iv–v). When it was published, the *Kalevala* was used almost without critique as a source for history, although some scholars, such as Julius Krohn (1835–1888), were critical about the historicity of the poems. Julius Krohn's son Kaarle Krohn (1863–1933) went further in his hypotheses and he compared the heroes of the *Kalevala* with the Vikings and saw Scandinavian influence in them. (Wilson 1976: 55, 104–105; see AHOLA.)

In the nineteenth century the uniqueness of the Finnish people was emphasised by considering it as a specific entity that had migrated during a certain period to Finland. The character of the Finns had supposedly come about as a contrast to that of neighboring peoples. This kind of thinking was typical in the age of Romanticism, when a people or nation was defined according to dialectical ideas as something opposed to its counterpart (Rantanen 1997: 220; Klinge 2010: 127).

Discourse in the Historical Journals

The data for this chapter covers the Finnish historical journals *Suomen Museo – Finskt Museum*, *Historiallinen Aikakauskirja*, *Historisk Tidskrift för Finland* and *Muinaistutkija*. These journals were issued in 1894, 1903, 1916 and 1984 respectively. Finnish archaeologists published in the first three journals before the archaeological journal *Muinaistutkija* was issued. It was not a scientific periodical in the beginning, but it will be taken into account when looking at the discourse at the end of the twentieth century and the beginning of the twenty-first century. The purpose in this case is not to concentrate on the scientific value of the texts but on Viking Age discourse as a whole.

The material covers the period between 1894 and 2011 and consists of 113 articles, notes and book reviews written either in Finnish or Swedish.[2] The data was examined qualitatively, in order to look at how the name Viking Age or equivalent terms for it were used. The scholarly field of the authors was also examined. Owing to limitations of space, the scope of this chapter does not include the discourse in the nineteenth century, which would require extending the survey of source material and discussion to the numerous general surveys of Finnish history and also popular journals.

The discourse centres on the last twenty-seven years of the period examined here because of publications in *Muinaistutkija*: 48 articles out of a total 113 came out between 1984 and 2011. The discourse was concentrated in *Suomen Museo* (57 cases) whereas there were only 15 cases in *Historiallinen Aikakauskirja* and 12 in *Historisk Tidskrift för Finland*. *Muinaistutkija* has been, naturally, a lively forum for discourse (29 cases). If we want to look at how evenly or unevenly Viking Age discourse was divided between 1894 and 2011, we must exclude *Muinaistutkija* and concentrate only on the other three journals. When *Muinaistutkija* is excluded, the data consists of 84 articles, notes and book reviews. Articles, notes and book reviews about the Viking Age came out approximately once or twice a year but not every year during the period examined. The exceptions are the years 1917 and 1918, when seven articles were published; these exceptions seem to be connected to the ongoing language dispute. I will return to this later in the chapter.

In order to examine whether there was a change during the period in question, the data was divided into two by taking the year 1945 as a watershed. This was based on the assumption that research interests were affected by the post-war political atmosphere. According to this assumption, research into the Late Iron Age decreased after the war, because the period itself was associated with the nationalistic ideology that supported Finnish expansion to the east. For example, school books that contained nationalistic ideas about Greater Finland were not approved after the war. It has been claimed that the post-war research interests in archaeology gradually shifted towards the Stone Age. (Tommila 2000: 93; Fewster 2006: 400; cf. Immonen & Taavitsainen 2011: 137–178.)

The discourse in the journals does not support the above-mentioned assumption: from 1894 to 1944, 41 articles, notes or book reviews concerning the Viking Age appeared, and from 1945 to 2011 there were 43. As the later period is fifteen years longer than the earlier period, the difference is low. Based on this result it can be asserted that the interest in the Viking Age (or the Late Iron Age in general) did not disappear after the war, but it did not flourish either. This result is consistent with that given in the article by Immonen and Taavitsainen (2011) in which Finnish archaeological publications were studied. Finnish archaeologists did not participate in constructing the right-wing ideology in Finland in the 1930s and 1940s, which tried to justify the Finnish expansion to east. Even though the nationalistic expansionist ideology made use of the results of archaeology and history, this kind of development cannot be compared with the internal development in Finnish archaeology as a science. (Fewster 2008: 107; Immonen & Taavitsainen 2011: 164.)

Although the year 1945 and the post-war years do not seem to be crucial for articles concerning the Viking Age, it would still be worth looking at the content of those articles that came out right after the war. The content and language of the articles could be compared with the pre-war situation in order to find out whether they reflect the contemporary political situation. For example, did the phrasing of research questions differ markedly, or were the conclusions somehow different?

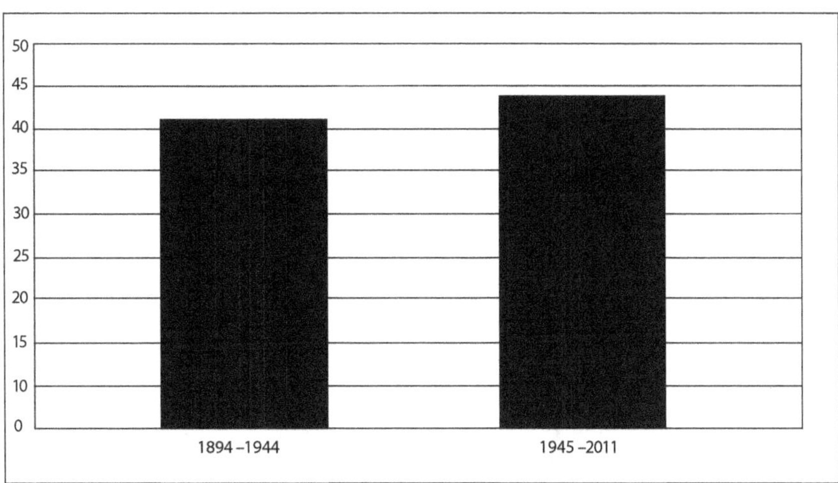

Table 1. Articles forming the data for this study published before and after 1945.

Whose Field?

Although the data in this study consisted of journals in the fields of history and archaeology, it is evident that mainly archaeologists were involved in the discourse. If scholars who were most active, writing at least two articles about the subject, are listed, the total number is nineteen (*Muinaistutkija* is again excluded from this data in order to look at the whole period 1894–2011). They wrote altogether around 72 per cent of the articles. Of these scholars, fifteen were archaeologists and four historians or philologists. When *Muinaistutkija* is included in the data, the total number of authors is sixty-seven. Of those authors who wrote about the Viking Age or whose topic was somehow related to it, only fourteen were historians,[3] which shows that the topic has been mainly dealt with in the field of archaeology.

From this data we can conclude that historians did not participate in the discourse very actively, which is understandable given the nature of the sources. Their use of the term 'Viking Age' is not consistent, which may reflect their uncertainty in naming the period.[4] However, historians could not avoid the Viking Age completely, since, together with the Crusade Period, it forms the transition from prehistory to history. Historians writing general surveys have to rely on archaeological results and use the periodisation that is conventional in the field of archaeology. They are seldom eager to propose new nomenclature for a prehistoric period even if they have not always been satisfied with the conventions used in archaeology. (Julku 1979: 223; Tommila 1989: 112; Vahtola 2003: 22.)

If we examine the articles in *Muinaistutkija*, it is obvious that the discussion concerning the Late Iron Age is lively and that archaeologists use the term 'Viking Age' with ease.[5] Maybe because it is often difficult to date artefacts exactly, archaeologists prefer to keep the timespan wide. This is evident, for instance, when two periods are combined in the discourse

('Merovingian-Viking Age' or 'Viking Age/Crusade Period'), or terms such as the Late Prehistoric or Late Iron Age are used in order to give a wider timespan.[6] Different word usages between archaeologists and historians could be explained by different traditions. Naming a period is a technical tool for an archaeologist, for example to date artefacts, but for historians it may have a different meaning. For a historian, a period reflects changes in a continuum and these changes are often more abstract in nature.

The results presented above show that the scholarly interest in the Viking Age did not decrease after the war. But somehow the political atmosphere after the war must have affected the discourse because a difference emerges in how the term 'Viking Age' is used before and after it. The data show that equivalent terms were used more often before the war than after it. Pre-war scholars such as Hjalmar Appelgren (1897a: 17–26; 1897b: 17–29; 1903: 21–23; 1907: 73–76), Johannes Aspelin (1895: 49–58; 1907: 111–113; 1915: 78), Juhani Rinne (1906: 54–72; 1909: 136) and Väinö Voionmaa (1894: 41–44; 1918; 1925) all used the term 'Heathen Period'. Their convention follows the word usage that originated in the nineteenth century, when religion was taken as the starting point when defining the name for a period. 'Heathen Period' was a convenient term, because it was not confined to specific years and because the transition from heathenism to Christianity was long. Yet at the same time other scholars – Aarne Tallgren (1909: 100–110; 1914: 30–38; 1915: 46–61; 1918: 1–10; 1936: 231–241), Helmer Salmo (1933: 22–43) and Jouko Voionmaa (1937: 47–50) – consistently used the term 'Viking Age'. All of the above-mentioned scholars were archaeologists except for Väinö Voionmaa.

For those writing Finnish history in a nationalistic spirit, it really mattered what kind of terminology was used of the past. We may take as an example the historian Jalmari Jaakkola, whose ideas about the Middle Ages but also the period preceding it have strongly affected Finnish historiography. Although Jaakkola basically agreed with Kaarle Krohn's ideas about the Scandinavian contacts in the past, the term 'Viking Age' was not an option for him. He emphasised in a nationalistic spirit that there must have been internal development of culture in Finland without any external influences. His thoughts reflected a nationalistic ideology in Finnish historiography. Jaakkola himself was willing to use a term like 'Varangian history' (*varjagihistoria*) for the last period in Finnish prehistory, which shows that he wanted to be independent in his choice of terminology. (Jaakkola 1954; Wilson 1976: 104–105). It remains to be explained why some of the pre-war scholars used the term 'Viking Age'. Aarne Tallgren, Helmer Salmo and Jouko Voionmaa were all archaeologists, and at least Tallgren was clearly oriented to the international scholarly community, which could explain his word usage. Nonetheless, further research concerning all the publications and backgrounds of the above-mentioned scholars would be needed in order to cast light on this matter.

From the academic discourse in the journals that were chosen as material for this chapter, the following conclusions can be drawn. Archaeologists have been more eager to use the term 'Viking Age' than historians, which may derive from the fact that they tend to look at connections. Historians writing in the pre-war years, on the other hand, seem to have avoided the term 'Viking Age' but also research relating to it, because the first written sources are from the Middle Ages. The general interest in the medieval period in the nineteenth century must be one of the reasons why it was depicted as a period that gave birth to the Finnish 'nation' and linked it to civilisation (meaning Christianity) (Tommila 1989: 190; Fewster 2006; Klinge 2010: 52).

The data used in this study derive from journals alone and do not allow for drawing further conclusions. Comparison between scholars who have concentrated on the study of the Viking Age would be useful in this case. It is interesting that there seems to be more variation in the word usage when it comes to scholars writing in Finnish than in Swedish, but the Viking Age discourse has a different background among Swedish-speakers in Finland. The discourse in Swedish will be dealt with in the next section.

Vikings as Symbols for the Language Dispute

In the nineteenth century and at the beginning of the twentieth century, some members of the Swedish-speaking minority in Finland still cherished the thought that they were descended from Vikings, or even from some Proto-Germanic tribe, who had settled in Finland before the Finns migrated there. The theory was not widely accepted and it was mainly promoted by some Finnish-Swedish enthusiasts, the so-called Svekomans, such as Axel Olof Freudenthal (1836–1911). He published a Swedish newspaper called *Vikingen* ['The Viking'] (on which, see Mörne 1916) and he claimed that a Viking called Thorer Helsing had once moved to the southern coast of Finland, called Uusimaa (Newland). (Kemiläinen 1993: 146–147; Huldén 2002: 15–38; Klinge 2010: 51.)

This theory must be seen in the context of the language dispute: it was of the utmost importance for the Swedish-speaking minority to prove that they were also entitled to live in Finland, when at the same time their Finnish-speaking opponents advocated the abolition of the Swedish language in Finland and argued that the Swedish speakers were not actually Finns. Moreover, the Svekomans had promoted the Vikings as their symbol. This language dispute is also reflected in the journals. As mentioned above, seven articles which dealt with the last period of prehistory, and thus also the roots of the Swedes in Finland, were published in 1917 and 1918.[7] As the usage of the term 'Viking Age' seems to have some connection with the language dispute in Finland, it is necessary to examine it further with Finnish and Swedish material such as monographs and schoolbooks from the nineteenth century and the first half of the twentieth century.

The Viking Age does not appear to have been a more popular subject in *Historisk Tidskrift för Finland* than in other journals (see the section above), although the Vikings were brought into the language dispute that had been raging in Finland since the latter half of the nineteenth century.

One reason could be that the heated debate on the supposed Viking origin of the Swedish speakers had calmed down by 1916, when *Historisk Tidskrift för Finland* was first published. In the discourse concerning the Viking Age in *Historisk Tidskrift för Finland*, archaeologists do not stand out among the authors (Hackman 1917; Meinander 1983; Taavitsainen 1994).

In Swedish texts, the term *vikingatiden* ['the Viking Period'] is generally used, but surprisingly Swedish-speaking scholars or scholars writing in Swedish in Finland use the term 'heathen period' (*hednatiden*) too.[8] On the one hand, it could be that scholars writing in Swedish were hesitant to use 'Viking Age' in a Finnish context, although the most romantic ideas about the Swedish Viking ancestors of the Swedish-speaking minority belonged to the end of the nineteenth century. On the other hand the term 'heathen period' was convenient as it defined a period in relation to Christianity or lack of it. At the same time, the heathen period bore the implication of being uncivilised and even savage. One could also interpret this as a sign that it was not unproblematic to speak of the Viking Age in the Finnish context – after all, Finland became independent in the same year as two of the articles were published.

At the turn of the twentieth century, the Finnish intelligentsia consisted mostly of speakers of Swedish; because of the language dispute, the intelligentsia was itself divided. This division affected the whole discourse on Finnish prehistory, and it had more concrete consequences for the choice of professors of history, for what kinds of associations were founded, and for who was accepted as a member of these associations (Mylly 2002: 179). The situation was a nightmare for those scholars who wanted to be impartial. For example, the historian Zacharias Topelius (1818–1898) wrote to his colleague Wilhelm Lagus in January 1886 and explained why he did not attend the founding meeting of the Swedish Literary Association in Finland. In his letter, Topelius said that he was afraid that the founders of the association were trying to build a *vikingafäste* ['Viking fortress'] and that he did not want to be involved in this kind of activity, which would divide the people (Topelius to Lagus 25.1.1886). The fact that Topelius uses the term 'Viking fortress' shows how the Vikings were associated with the Svekomans.

Although the Svekomans had a mission to prove that the Swedish-speaking population had been in Finland before the Finns, the more moderate Finnish-Swedish scholars did not participate in their efforts. These scholars represented so-called 'cultural Swedishness' (*kultursvenskhet*), and they did not see it as necessary to artificially create a Finnish-Swedish 'people'. For example, Carl Gustaf Estlander (1834–1910), who was one of these moderates, accused his Finnish colleagues of trying to create artificial lines and borders between the people in the past (Engman 2000: 43–45). The language dispute was a difficult political question in Finland in the 1920s and 1930s, but the worst excesses were curbed. It would not have benefited the Swedish-speaking minority during this period if they had been associated too strongly with Vikings or with the Germanic Battle Axe Culture, which had been done at the turn of the century. This kind of association would have labelled them as politically unreliable citizens or even as dangerous. (Fewster 2000b: 119.)

The language dispute subsided little by little among Finnish scholars during the 1940s (Ahtiainen & Tervonen 1990: 26). It was put aside after the war and replaced by the threat from the 'third direction'. Suddenly the Finnish and Swedish common past was an attractive object of research and showed more positive sides than before. The Late Iron Age was not in the focus of research for political reasons, although it did not cease or decrease markedly.[9]

Before the war, Finnish historiography concentrated on legitimising the Finns as a nation, so it would have been difficult to use terminology – in this case the 'Viking Age' – that was thought to pertain to neighbouring peoples, i.e. the Scandinavians in general (Mylly 2002: 288). As is usual in constructing a group identity, the content of the group identity is born out of a dichotomy between us and them (Jenkins 1996: 24, 80–81; Rantanen 1997: 220; Eriksen 2002:19). This explains why some pre-war scholars preferred to use other terms than the 'Viking Age'. This made-up dichotomy was most pronounced in the pre-war period, when the myth of the Finnish nation was forged. Two popular books that were published before the Winter War can be mentioned as an example: Aarno Karimo's *Kumpujen yöstä* (esp. the second part concerning the Late Iron Age) was a popular history book with some general information and lively illustration, whereas Väinö Kainuu's *Finnit tulevat* was a novel (Karimo 1930; Kainuu 1936). These works juxtaposed the 'ancient Finns' and the Vikings.

The Vikings and the Viking Age are still entwined with the past of the Swedish-speaking Finns. In the 1970s and 1980s some enthusiasts forged rune stones in Ostrobothnia and fabricated a Viking Age stone-setting burial because they wanted desperately to find their Viking past: they felt that their group identity was building on that. (See RANINEN & WESSMAN).

The 1980s as a Turning Point?

In 1980, a multidisciplinary seminar was organised in Tvärminne that changed the long-lived paradigm of Finns as late settlers in Finland. As a result, the so-called continuity theory, which emphasised the continuity in settlement in Finland since the end of the Ice Age, was widely adopted. The paradigm replaced the old migration theory, according to which the forefathers of the Finns had arrived in Finland after the birth of Christ. This change of paradigm in archaeology also affected the discourse concerning the Viking Age, because the theory of the Viking ancestors of the Swedish-speaking minority was buried once and for all in academic discourse.

After the seminar in Tvärminne the Viking Age in general raised interest and got publicity. Extensive excavations, begun already before the 1980s, were made in Luistari, south-western Finland, where rich burials from the Late Iron Age were discovered, and these excavations were also followed by the media. Later, towards the end of the 1980s, excavations in Varikkoniemi, Hämeenlinna, raised popular interest, but also critiques and discussions among scholars. In both cases the term 'Viking Age' (or 'Period') were used in articles related to these excavations (Lehtosalo-Hilander 2000; Schulz & Schulz 1990). It could be argued that enthusiasm for the Viking Age since the 1980s caused over-interpretation of some archaeological data in Finland.[10]

Although research on the Viking Age seems not have diminished after the Second World War in Finland, it did not enjoy much popularity either before the 1980s. The fact that there was a change in the political atmosphere after the collapse of the Soviet Union cannot be neglected. Globalisation and Finland's membership in the EU have affected the research indirectly: it is a trend in several fields of research to study contacts, networks and cultural impacts. The international research concerning the Viking Age over the past twenty years or so has also focused on contacts.[11]

The interest in the Late Iron Age is inevitably intertwined with the *Kalevala* in Finland, as mentioned at the beginning of this chapter. In 1985, when the *Kalevala* was celebrating its 150th anniversary, a multidisciplinary seminar was held in Helsinki and some of the papers were published in an edited volume (Linna 1987). The book did not try to offer a new synthesis of the Viking Age in Finland, but was criticized for being merely a collection of articles (Vilkuna 1989). It is, however, a sign that the Late Iron Age as a period raised general interest.

Archaeological excavations in Finland and Karelia have shown that there was a peculiar culture in these areas in the Late Iron Age, but that there were contacts with neighbouring areas, too (see Laakso). Since the 1980s, archaeological research has continuously introduced new information but understandably the results usually only relate to the excavation in question or to a particular group of artefacts (cf. Uino 1997; Saksa 1998; Lehtosalo-Hilander 2000; Talvio 2002). The old paradigm that emphasised how the Finns had developed their own culture virtually without contacts with their neighbours is rejected, but it has still not been replaced by a new paradigm.

From the Late Iron Age to the Viking Age?

In the mid-nineteenth century, Finnish historian Zacharias Topelius posed the question of whether the Finns had a history. In 1875 the historian Georg Zacharias Forsman (also known by his translated Finnish name, Yrjö Koskinen) answered this question by saying that "the Finnish people want to have their own history, and thus they have it" (Jussila 2007: 18). This manifests how history is consciously shaped and created. The last prehistoric period in Finnish history was used to shape the Finnish past. Therefore choosing a name for this period is a statement.

'Finnishness' was defined in the nineteenth and early twentieth centuries in contrast to the neighbouring peoples to the east and west. Hence it was impossible to use symbols that were associated with these neighbours. As the Swedes (and the Swedish-speaking Finns) had adopted the Vikings as their symbols, they did not fit into the concept of what was thought to be Finnish. In academic discourse, the Vikings did not play a major role, because Finnish history and the concept of the Finns as a 'nation' were based on belonging to the Finno-Ugrian 'family'. In pre-war scholarship, Finnish prehistory before the annexation to Sweden was seen as some kind of 'Age of the Finnish Tribes', which had shaped the Finnish mentality and longing for independence. This must be one of the reasons why it has been difficult to link a concept such as the 'Viking Age' to the Finnish past, because the word itself implies a connection with Scandinavia. Moreover, the question of the Viking Age in Finland was entangled with the language dispute, especially at the beginning of the twentieth century.

It could be argued that the Second World War marks some kind of watershed if we consider how Finnish historians created the Finnish past: pre-war scholars who were engaged with nationalistic history-writing often used such terms as the 'Heathen period' to describe the last prehistoric period in Finnish history. There were, however, those who consistently used the term 'Viking Age', which seems to imply that their view of the Finnish past was different. The reasons for this may be the scholarly background, contacts abroad, the time of writing and personal opinion. Based on the data in historical journals, it can be concluded that scholars used the term 'Viking Age' interchangeably with equivalent terms, especially before the Second World War, but this needs to be confirmed by further study on the nineteenth-century material, the nineteenth-century monographs in particular.

It is now accepted in the field of history that objectivity is something that a scholar aims at, but without the possibility of altogether avoiding subjectivity. The naming of a period implies a degree of subjectivity. As this chapter has shown, 'Viking Age' as a term in Finnish historiography is and will be used differently depending on time, place or forum, and political situation.

In Finnish historiography, it has been the task of archaeologists to study the Viking Age, but taking into account the transitional character of the period, much more could be gained by an interdisciplinary approach and, for example, by applying retrospective methods. New perspectives in writing history, such as 'history from below', have also revealed how limited a historian may be if he takes into account just the written documents (Burke 2001: 5). The future will show how the Viking Age is adopted in Finnish historiography, but more important is how the period will be interpreted and construed in the academic discourse of the future.

Notes

1 There are no written records from the Viking Age written by the inhabitants of Finland. However, there are some references to Finns and Finland in foreign sources. On written culture in Finland, see Heikkilä 2010.

2 There were eight articles concerning the Viking Age in other languages but they were not included because the focus was on the Finnish and Swedish discourse. Also *Fennoscandia Archaeologica* was excluded because the focus was on discourse in Finnish and Swedish.

3 Von Törne 1917: 284–294; Voionmaa T 1918: 1–35; Voionmaa V 1918: 36–45;

1925: 113–128; Forsman 1942: 91–108; Kerkkonen G 1950: 105–107; 1953: 1–27; Jaakkola 1954: 329–350; Kerkkonen M 1971: 213–230; Anthoni 1975: 233–238; Gallén 1981: 357–361; Jutikkala 1981: 312–324; Vahtola 1989: 122–126; Orrman 1990: 32–42; Sjöstrand 1998: 408–432; Jokipii 2002: 228–242. In few cases the author represented another field of humanities than history and archaeology.

4 Historians have variably used the term Viking Age (5 cases) or other, equivalent terms (8 cases).

5 Lehtosalo-Hilander 1984: 3–6; Rankama 1984: 20–22; Hirviluoto 1985: 20–23; Salo 1988: 11–13; Ikäheimo 1988: 10–12; Uino 1989: 3–6; Söyrinki-Harmo 1990: 7–11; Hirviluoto 1996: 2–7; Raninen 2003: 13–28; Kirjavainen & Riikonen 2005: 30–44; Aartolahti 2011: 26–35.

6 Pohjakallio 1995: 4–6; Vuorinen 1997: 45–48; Mikkola 1999: 39–50; Taivainen 1999: 15–21; Wickholm & Raninen 2003: 2–14; Mikkola 2004: 31–40.

7 Hackman 1917: 199–211; Karsten 1917; Lukkarinen 1917: 1–7; von Törne 1917; Tallgren 1918; Voionmaa T 1918; Voionmaa V 1918.

8 Karsten 1917: 159–198; von Törne 1917: 284–294; Hirviluoto 1970: 17–23; Meinander 1983: 229–251.

9 Tommila 2000: 93; Ahtiainen & Tervonen 1996: 124–125; Engman 1990: 58; cf. Immonen & Taavitsainen 2011.

10 Schulz & Schulz 1990; on the discussion, see Taavitsainen 2005.

11 Cf. Hansen 1996; Roslund 2001; Price 2002; Barrett 2003; Gustin 2004; Adams & Holman 2004; Brink 2008.

References

Sources

Letter from Zacharias Topelius to Wilhelm Lagus 25.1.1886. J.J.W. Lagus, Coll. 113:8 National Library, Helsinki.

Abbreviations

HAik = Historiallinen Aikakauskirja
HTF = Historisk Tidskrift för Finland
SHS = Suomen Historiallinen Seura
SKS = Suomalaisen Kirjallisuuden Seura
SLS = Svenska Litteratursällskapet i Finland
WSOY = Werner-Söderström osakeyhtio

Literature

Aartolahti, Akuliina. 2011. Rautakauden Sysmässä asutusyksiköitä metsästämässä. *Muinaistutkija* 2: 26–35.

Adams, Jonathan & Holman, Katherine (eds.). 2004. *Scandinavia and Europe, 800–1350: Contact, Conflict, and Coexistence.* Turnhout: Brepols.

Ahtiainen, Pekka & Tervonen, Jukka. 1990. Historiatiede oman aikansa tulkkina: Katsaus suomalaisen historiankirjoituksen vaiheisiin viimeisen sadan vuoden ajalta. In Pekka Ahtiainen et. al (eds.) *Historia nyt: Näkemyksiä suomalaisesta historiantutkimuksesta*. Historiallisen yhdistyksen julkaisuja 5. Juva: WSOY. Pp. 11–38.

Ahtiainen, Pekka & Tervonen, Jukka. 1996. *Menneisyyden tutkijat ja metodien vartijat: Matka suomalaiseen historiankirjoitukseen*. Helsinki: SHS.

Anthoni, Eric. 1975. Tidiga svenska förbindelser med Finland. *HTF* 4: 233–238.

Appelgren, Hjalmar. 1897a. Suomen kirveet pakanuuden aikana. *Suomen Museo* 4: 17–26.

Appelgren, Hjalmar. 1897b. Svenskarnes inflyttning i Finland. *Finskt Museum* 4: 17–29.

Appelgren, Hjalmar. 1903. Muinaislinna Räntämäellä. *Suomen Museo* 10: 21–23.

Appelgren, Hjalmar. 1907. Linnavuori Kuhmoisissa. *Suomen Museo* 14: 73–76.

Aspelin, Johannes. 1907. Mailta ristimättömiltä, paikoilta papittomilta. *HAik* 1: 111–113.

Aspelin, Johannes. 1915. Norjan ja Perman välisiä suhteita. *Suomen Museo* 22: 78.

Aspelin, Johannes. 1985. Kansan muistot ruotsalaisten ristiretkistä Suomeen. *Suomen Museo* 2: 29–58.

Barrett, James (ed.). 2003. *Contact, Continuity, and Collapse: The Norse Colonization of the North Atlantic*. Turnhout: Brepols.

von Bonsdorff, Carl.1919. Finlands förra ställning inom det svenska riket. *HTF* 4: 173–206.

Brink, Stefan (ed.). 2008. *The Viking World*. London and New York: Routledge.

Burke, Peter. 2001 [1992]. The New History: Its Past and Its Future. In Peter Burke (ed.). *New Perspectives on Historical Writing*. Pennsylvania: Pennsylvania State University Press. Pp. 1–24.

Engman, Max. 2000. Historikernas folk. In Fewster 2000a: 31–46.

Eriksen, Thomas Hylland. 2002 [1993]. *Ethnicity and Nationalism*. London / Sterling, Virginia: Pluto Press.

Fewster, Derek (ed.). 2000a. *Folket. Studier i olika vetenskapers syn på begreppet folk*. Helsingfors: SLS.

Fewster, Derek. 2000b. Fornfolket i nutiden: Arkeologins politiska budskap. In Fewster 2000a: 107–124.

Fewster, Derek. 2006. *Visions of Past Glory: Nationalism and the Construction of Early Finnish History*. Studia Fennica Historica 11. Helsinki: SKS.

Fewster, Derek. 2008. Arkeologisen tutkimuksen historia Suomessa. In Petri Halinen *et al.* (eds.). *Johdatus arkeologiaan*, Tampere: Gaudeamus. Pp. 97–108.

Forsman, Karl. 1942. Kring en "kugghamn" i östra Nyland. *HTF* 3: 91–108.

Gustin, Ingrid. 2004. *Mellan gåva och marknad: Handel, tillit och materiell kultur under vikingatid*. Lund studies in Medieval Archaeology 34. Lund: University of Lund.

Hackman, Alfred. 1917. Om Nylands kolonisation under järnålder och andra därmed sammanhängande frågor. *HTF* 3: 199–211.

Halinen, Petri *et al.* (eds.). 2008. *Johdatus arkeologiaan*. Helsinki: Gaudeamus.

Hansen, Lars Ivar. 1996. Interaction between Northern European Sub-arctic Societies during the Middle Ages: Indigenous Peoples, Peasants and State Builders. In Magnus Rindal (ed.). *Two Studies on the Middle Ages*. KULTs skriftserie 66. Oslo: Norges forskningsråd.

Heikkilä, Tuomas (ed.). 2010. *Kirjallinen kulttuuri keskiajan Suomessa*. Helsinki: SKS.

Hirviluoto, Anna-Liisa. 1985. Moottoritiekö Rapolan linnavuoren juurelle? *Muinaistutkija* 2: 20–23.

Hirviluoto, Anna-Liisa. 1996. Yläneen Anivehmaanmäen ja Varsinais-Suomen rannikkoalueen yhteydet viikinkiajalla. *Muinaistutkija* 2: 2–7.

Huldén, Lena. 2002. När kommo svenskarna till Finland? In Ann-Marie Ivars & Lena Huldén (eds.). *När kommo svenskarna till Finland?* Helsingfors: SLS 646. Pp. 15–38.

Ikäheimo, Markku. 1988. Mikä on Kuralan kylämäen kokeiluverstas? *Muinaistutkija* 3: 10–12.

Immonen Visa. 2012. The Mess before the Modern: Karen Barad's Agential Realism and Periodization in Medieval Archaeology. In T. Äikäs, S. Lipkin & A.-K. Salmi (eds.). *Archaeology of Social Relations: Ten Case studies by Finnish Archaeologists*. Oulu: University of Oulu. 12. Pp. 7–32.

Immonen, Visa, & J.-P. Taavitsainen. 2011. Oscillating Between National and International: The Case of Finnish Archaeology. In Lozny, Ludomir (ed.). *Comparative Archaeologies: A Sociological View of the Science of the Past*. New York: Springer. Pp. 137–178

Immonen, Visa. 2008. Tieteellisen arkeologian kehitys. In Petri Halinen *et al.* 2008: 78–91.

Jaakkola, Jalmari. 1938. *Suomen varhaiskeskiaika*, Porvoo: WSOY.

Jaakkola, Jalmari. 1944. *Suomen sydänkeskiaika*, Porvoo: WSOY.

Jaakkola, Jalmari. 1950. *Suomen myöhäiskeskiaika*, Porvoo: WSOY.

Jaakkola, Jalmari. 1954. Muinaisen Kukinjoen kauppapiiri. *HAik* 4: 177–187.

Jenkins, Richard. 1996. *Social Identity*. London / New York: Routledge.

Jokipii, Mauno. 2002. Ensimmäinen ristiretki Suomeen: Myyttiä vai todellisuutta. *HAik* 3: 228–242.

Julku, Kyösti. 1979. *Suomen varhaishistorian periodisointi*. Eripainossarja 59. Oulu: Oulun yliopisto, historian laitos. Pp. 220–223.

Jussila, Osmo. 2007. *Suomen historian suuret myytit*. Helsinki: WSOY.

Jutikkala, Eino. 1981. Pohjanmaa ja paiserutto. *HAik* 4: 312–324.

Kainuu, Väinö. 1936. *Finnit tulevat*. Porvoo: WSOY.

Karimo, Aarno. 1930. *Kumpujen yöstä: osa 2*. Porvoo: WSOY.

Karsten, T. E. 1917. De nordiska ortnamnen som historiska minnesmärken med särskild hänsyn till Finland. *HTF* 3: 159–198.

Kemiläinen, Aira. 1993. *Suomalaiset, outo Pohjolan kansa. Rotuteoriat ja kansallinen identiteetti*. Historiallisia tutkimuksia 177. Helsinki: SHS.

Kerkkonen, Gunvor. 1950. Tre seglande bröder. Landnam enligt sägen och hävd. *HTF* 3-4: 105–117.

Kerkkonen, Gunvor. 1953. Hiisibygderna såsom pälsvarustaplar för handeln vid Finska vikens skeppsled. *HTF* 1: 1–27.

Kerkkonen, Martti. 1971. Esihistorialliset Häme ja Suomi. *HAik* 3: 213–230.

Kirjavainen, Heini, & Jaana Riikonen. 2005. Tekstiilien valmistuksesta Turussa myöhäisrautakaudella ja keskiajalla. *Muinaistutkija* 3: 30–44.

Klinge, Matti. 2010. *Suomalainen ja eurooppalainen menneisyys: Historiankirjoitus ja historiakulttuuri keisariaikana*. Helsinki: SKS.

Korhonen, Kuisma. 2006. General Introduction: The History/Literatue Debate. In Kuisma Korhonen (ed.). *Tropes for the Past: Hayden White and the History/Literary Debate*. Amsterdam / New York: Rodopi. Pp. 9–20.

Lehtosalo-Hilander, Pirkko-Liisa. 1984. Suomen rautakauden kuva. *Muinaistutkija* 2: 3–6.

Lehtosalo-Hilander, Pirkko-Liisa. 2000. *Luistari: A History of Weapons and Ornaments*. Suomen Muinaismuistoyhdistyksen Aikakauskirja 107. Helsinki: Suomen Muinaismuistoyhdistys.

Linna, Martti (ed.). 1987. *Muinaisrunot ja todellisuus: Suomen kansan vanhojen runojen historiallinen tausta*. Historian aitta 20. Jyväskylä: Gummerus.

Lönnrot, Elias. 1849 [1964]. *Kalevala*. Helsinki: SKS.

Luoto, Jukka. 1984. Pohjanmaan autioituminen ja sen syyt. *HAik* 3: 205–208.

Luoto. Jukka. 1997. Suomen varhaiskristillisyydestä. *HAik* 2: 124–127.

Mäkivuoti, Markku. 1992. Mikä on keskiaika? *Muinaistutkija* 2: 6–11.

Meinander, Carl Fredrik. 1983. On svenskarnes inflyttningar till Finland. *HTF* 3: 229–251.

Mikkola, Esa. 1999. Halikonjokilaakson rautakautiset muinaisjäännökset eli inventoinnin ihmeellinen maailma. *Muinaistutkija* 1: 39–50.

Mikkola, Esa. 2004. Pälkäneen Pyhän Mikaelin kirkon raunioiden kaivaukset v. 2003. *Muinaistutkija* 1: 31–40.

Mörne, Arvid. 1916. *Från Saima till Vikingen*. Borgå: Holger Schildts förlag.

Mylly, Juhani. 2002. *Kansallinen projekti. Historiankirjoitus ja politiikka autonomisessa Suomessa*. Turku: Kirja-Aurora.

Pipping, Hugo. 1919. Till frågan om bosättningsförhållandena i Östra Nyland. *HTF* 1: 1–30.

Pohjakallio, Lauri. 1995. Terra Tavastorum - Hämäläisten maa: Esihistorian näyttely keskiaikaisessa Hämeen linnassa. *Muinaistutkija* 4: 4–6.

Price, Neil. 2002. *The Viking Way: Religion and War in Late Iron Age Scandinavia*. Aun 31. Uppsala: Uppsala University Press.

Raninen, Sami. 2003. Länttä, etelää, itää: Hajapohdintoja rautakaudesta. *Muinaistutkija* 4: 13–28.

Rankama, Tuija. 1984. Helsingin yliopisto RASI-projekti. *Muinaistutkija* 2: 20–22.

Rantanen, Päivi. 1997. *Suolatut säkeet. Suomen ja suomalaisten diskursiivinen muotoutuminen 1600-luvulta Topeliukseen*. Helsinki: SKS.

Rinne, Juhani. 1906. Halikonlahdenseudun muinaisesta kaupasta. *HAik* 1: 54–72.

Rinne, Juhani. 1909. Lieto: Muinaislinnoja. *Suomen Museo* 16: 136.

Roslund, Mats. 2001. *Gäster i huset. Kulturell överföring mellan slaver och skandinaver 900 till 1300*. Lund: Vetenskapssocieteten i Lund.

Saksa, Aleksandr. 1998. *Rautakautinen Karjala*. Joensuu: Joensuun yliopisto.

Salmo, Helmer. 1933. Suomesta löydetyt tanskalaiset 1100-luvun rahat. *Suomen Museo* 40: 22–43.

Salo, Unto. 1988. Katsaus Turun yliopiston arkeologiseen kenttätutkimukseen v. 1987. *Muinaistutkija* 1: 11–13.

Salo, Unto. 1995. Kristinusko ennen kristinuskoa Suomessa. *HAik* 1: 12–19.

Sarvas, Pekka. 1971. Ristiretkiajan ajoituskysymyksiä. *Suomen Museo* 78: 51–63.

Schulz, Eeva-Liisa, & Hans-Peter Schulz. 1990. Varikkoniemi in Hämeenlinna: Trading Site from the Viking Period. *Iskos* 9: 75–80.

Söyrinki-Harmo, Leena. 1990. Ihmiset kohtaavat. *Muinaistutkija* 4: 7–11.

Taavitsainen, Jussi-Pekka. 1994. Östra Tavastland son samfälld erämark. *HTF* 3: 391–412.

Taivainen, Jouni. 1999. Paluu menneisyyteen: Tyrvännön asutushistoriaa rautakaudelta keskiajalle. *Muinaistutkija* 3: 15–21.

Tallgren, Aarne M. 1909. Muinainen Bjarmaland. *HAik* 5–6: 100–110.

Tallgren, Aarne M. 1914. Rautakauden polttokalmisto Liedossa. *Suomen Museo* 21: 31–38.

Tallgren, Aarne M. 1915. Ristimäki gravfält. *Finskt Museum* 22: 46–61.

Tallgren, Aarne M. 1918. Nya järnåldersfynd från Aura ådal. *Finskt Museum* 25: 1–10.

Tallgren, Aarne M. 1936. Varhaishistoriamme: Vastinetta professori Jaakkolalle. *HAik* 3: 231–241.

Talvio, Tuukka. 2002. *Coins and Coin Finds in Finland AD 800–1200*. Helsinki: Suomen Muinaismuistoyhdistys.

Tommila, Päiviö. 1989. *Suomen historiankirjoitus: Tutkimuksen historia*, Porvoo: WSOY.

Tommila, Päiviö. 2000. Historia. In Päiviö Tommila (ed.). *Suomen Tieteen historia: Osa 2*. Porvoo / Helsinki / Juva: WSOY. Pp. 66–139.

von Törne, P. O. 1917. Några östnyländska ort- och sockennamns ålder. *HTF* 4: 284–294.

Uino, Pirjo. 1989. Karjalan kunnailta. *Muinaistutkija* 1: 3–6.

Uino, Pirjo. 1997. *Ancient Karelia*. Helsinki: Suomen Muinaismuistoyhdistys.

Vahtola, Jouko. 1989. Vanhojen runojen alkulähteillä. *HAik* 2: 122–126.

Vahtola, Jouko. 2003. *Suomen historia: Jääkaudesta Euroopan unioniin*. Helsinki: Otava.

Vilkuna, Janne. 1989. Muinaissuomalaisen yhteiskunnan loiston etsintää? *HAik* 2: 121–122.

Voionmaa, Jouko. 1937. Uusi muinaislinna Vesilahdelta. *Suomen Museo* 44: 47–50.

Voionmaa, Tapio. 1918. Gotlannin suuruudenaika ja Suomi. *HAik* 1: 1–35.

Voionmaa, Väinö. 1894. Suomen ruotsalaisen väestön alkuperästä. *Suomen Museo* 1: 41–44.

Voionmaa, Väinö. 1918. Suomen historialliset oikeudet Ahvenanmaahan. *HAik* 1: 36–45.

Voionmaa, Väinö. 1925. Oman maamme heimot ja niiden historiallinen tutkiminen. *HAik* 2: 113–128.

Vuorinen, Juha-Matti. 1997. Rakentamisesta Raision Mullissa rautakauden lopulla ja varhaiskeskiajalla. *Muinaistutkija* 4: 45–48.

Wickholm, Anna, & Sami Raninen. 2003. Rautakautinen riesa: Polttokenttäkalmistojen problematiikka. *Muinaistutkija* 2: 2–14.

Wilson, William. 1976. *Folklore and Nationalism in Modern Finland.* Bloomington / London: Indiana University Press.

Petri Kallio

The Diversification of Proto-Finnic

As languages constantly change, any language spoken in a large enough area sooner or later begins to diversify. Thus, linguistic diversification often follows language dispersal, but does not necessarily do so, because in addition to regional dialects there are also social dialects. Now, linguistic diversification occurs on all levels of language structure, such as phonology, morphology, syntax and lexicon. Yet only phonology and morphology have played a greater role in dialectology, because syntax is much harder to reconstruct, whereas lexicon is usually considered too unstable to be used as evidence of linguistic classification (cf. also Salminen 2002: 44–45). Nonetheless, even lexical evidence can fully agree with phonological evidence whenever it is used thoroughly enough (see e.g. Larsson 2012 on the case of Ume Saami).

As far as Proto-Finnic dialectology is concerned, linguistic classifications have been based primarily on phonology and secondarily on morphology (see e.g. Viitso 2003: 132–139). Very few scholars, such as Terho Itkonen (1972; 1983), have dealt with lexical evidence, but unfortunately he (like most Finnish scholars at that time) treated Estonian as a monolith without acknowledging the deep diachronic gap between North and South Estonian. It was not until Pekka Sammallahti (1977) that the suggestion first emerged that South Estonian was the earliest offshoot of Proto-Finnic, the idea of which was initially based on only one, albeit most convincing, phonological isogloss. While his approach can therefore be called qualitative in the sense that he concentrated on the best possible evidence, there is also the quantitative approach by Tiit-Rein Viitso (1985; 2000), whose evidence consisted of numerous more or less convincing phonological and morphological isoglosses. Yet Sammallahti and Viitso reached largely the same conclusions on Proto-Finnic dialectology, as I discuss below in further detail.

So what exactly can we learn from all this? In spite of the complexity of linguistic diversification in general, individual phonological isoglosses can still lead to correct linguistic classifications. Indeed, sound changes somewhat resemble genetic mutations (cf. Salmela), in that they are, by nature, random (or, more precisely, unpredictable) and irreversible (although certain sound changes producing needless formal variation can secondarily be reversed by analogy). Hence, phonological evidence is as close to scientific as comparative linguistics can get. The only problem is that some sound changes, such as losses of unstressed vowels, are so usual that they can independently occur in different times and at different places. Needless to say, such sound changes should be of lesser value when dialects are subgrouped, but they must not be ignored either, because there is also no reason to suppose that the earliest phonological isoglosses could only include unusual sound changes.

The First Dialectal Split: Coastal Finnic vs. Inland Finnic

As mentioned above, Sammallahti (1977: 133) was among the first to suggest that South Estonian (> Võro, Mulgi and Tartu in Estonia; †Leivu and †Lutsi in Latvia; Seto and †Kraasna in Russia) was the earliest offshoot of Proto-Finnic, based on the fact that although the Proto-Finnic clusters **kt* and **pt* elsewhere merged as **ht* (> Livonian *ʼd* + the lengthening of the preceding vowel), the South Estonian outcome was **tt*:

> Proto-Finnic **koktu* > Finnish *kohtu*, Karelian *kohtu*, Veps *koht*, Estonian *kõht* ~ Võro *kõtt* ['uterus, belly']

> Proto-Finnic **vakto* > Finnish *va(a)hto*, Karelian *voahti*, Veps *vaht*, Votic *vaahto*, Estonian *vaht*, Livonian *vǭʼ* ~ Võro *vatt* ['foam']

Note that a secondary South Estonian development **ht* > **tt* can be rejected, because the original Proto-Finnic cluster **ht* (< **št*) remained as such also in South Estonian:

> Proto-Finnic **lehti* > Finnish *lehti*, Karelian *lehti*, Veps *leht*, Votic *lehti*, Estonian *leht*, Livonian *lēʼḑ*, Võro *leht́* ['leaf']

While Sammallahti never named these two earliest Proto-Finnic dialects, Viitso (1978: 97–104) has called them Ugala (> South Estonian) and Marine (> other Finnic languages), which correspond to my Inland Finnic and Coastal Finnic, respectively (Kallio 2007: 243). Although Viitso has mostly preferred to rely on phonology, his most striking evidence comes from morphology, namely the Coastal Finnic present tense third person singular ending **-pi* (> **-βi* after non-stressed syllables) (Viitso 2000: 170; 2003: 143–144):

> Proto-Finnic **anta-βi* ~ **anta* > Finnish *antaa* (dial. *antavi*), Karelian *antau*, Veps *andab*, Votic *annaʙ*, Estonian *annab*, Livonian *ãndab* ~ Võro *and* ['gives']

Remarkably, Coastal Finnic **-pi* must be considered an innovation, because Inland Finnic *-Ø goes back to Proto-Uralic *-Ø (Janhunen 1982: 34–35).

Now I have also discussed some further Coastal Finnic innovations, such as *c > *s (Kallio 2007: 241–242):

> Proto-Finnic **cika* > Finnish *sika*, Karelian *sika*, Veps *siga*, Votic *sika*, Estonian *siga*, Livonian *sigā* ~ Võro *tsiga* ['pig']
>
> Proto-Finnic **kaca* > Finnish *kasa*, Karelian *kasa*, Veps *kaza*, Votic *kasa* ~ Võro *kadsa* (cf. Karelian *katša*) ['point, edge']
>
> Proto-Finnic **keüci* > Finnish *köysi*, Karelian *keysi*, Votic *tšöüsi*, Estonian *köis*, Livonian *kieuž* ~ Võro *köüdś* ['rope']
>
> Proto-Finnic **süci* > Finnish *sysi*, Karelian *sysi*, Votic *süsi*, Estonian *süsi*, Livonian *si'ž* ~ Võro *hüdsi* ['(char)coal']

Certain clusters containing **c* deserve special treatment. For instance, Proto-Finnic **kc* and **pc*, as expected, became Coastal Finnic **ks* and **ps*, but merged as Inland Finnic **cc* (cf. Proto-Finnic **kt* and **pt* > Coastal Finnic **ht* vs. Inland Finnic **tt* above; Kallio 2007: 236–237):

> Proto-Finnic **kakci* > Finnish *kaksi*, Karelian *kaksi*, Veps *kakś*, Votic *kahsi*, Estonian *kaks*, Livonian *kakš* ~ Võro *katś* ['two']
>
> Proto-Finnic **lapci* > Finnish *lapsi*, Karelian *lapsi*, Veps *lapś*, Votic *lahsi*, Estonian *laps*, Livonian *läpš* ~ Võro *latś* ['child']

An even more interesting cluster was **ck* (< **čk*) which was preserved in Inland Finnic, whereas its Coastal Finnic outcome was **tk* (cf. my simpler but chronologically more problematic formulation in Kallio 2007: 233–234):

> Proto-Finnic **kacku* > Finnish *katku*, Estonian *katk* ~ Võro *katsk* (cf. Karelian *k(o)atšku*, Veps *katšk*) ['fumes, plague']
>
> Proto-Finnic **kickë-* > Finnish *kitkeä*, Karelian *kitkie*, Veps *kitkta*, Votic *tšitkõa*, Estonian *kitkuma*, Livonian *kitkõ* ~ Võro *kitskma* ['to weed']
>
> Proto-Finnic **nocko* > Finnish *notko*, Karelian *notko*, Veps *notk*, Votic *nõtko*, Estonian *nõtk* ~ Võro *nõtsk* ['dell']
>
> Proto-Finnic **pucki* > Finnish *putki*, Karelian *putki*, Veps *butk*, Votic *putkõ*, Estonian *putk*, Livonian *puţk* ~ Võro *pütsk'* ['tube']

Remarkably, both Karelian and Veps can irregularly have an affricate (cf. Karelian *katša*, *k(o)atšku*; Veps *katšk*), which Terho Itkonen (1981: 17–19; 1983: 216–217) already plausibly derived from his postulated East Finnic substrate spoken at the bottom of the Gulf of Finland before the Late Iron Age arrival of Proto-Ladogan (a.k.a. Proto-Karelo-Veps). Strictly speaking, East Finnic should in fact be considered Para-Finnic rather than Finnic, because it has no descendants among the modern Finnic languages. In any case, as affricates are retentions from Proto-Finnic, they do not serve as evidence of a subgroup containing East Finnic and Inland Finnic. Besides, such a subgroup would have been geographically problematic, because their speech areas were most likely separated by the so-called Chuds, whose Finnicness has now been questioned on good grounds by Pauli Rahkonen (2011). In his view, Chud was a West Uralic language that was both geographically and linguistically located between Finnic and Meryan, another extinct West Uralic language. Perhaps Chud could also even be taken as another possible source of unexpected affricates in Karelian and Veps, although those in South Estonian are better explained as inherited from Proto-Finnic (Kallio 2007: 241–242).

The Second Dialectal Split: Gulf of Finland Finnic vs. Gulf of Riga Finnic

The idea that South Estonian was the earliest offshoot of Proto-Finnic was originally only one of Viitso's three alternative classifications (1978: 97–104). Livonian used to be his second choice for the earliest offshoot of Proto-Finnic (cf. also Helimski 2006: 110), although there are hardly any innovations shared by all Finnic languages other than Livonian (see e.g. Viitso 2000: 170–171; 2003: 151). Finally, Viitso's third and last alternative was that Koiva (> Livonian and South Estonian) and Neva (> other Finnic languages) were the two earliest Proto-Finnic dialects (see e.g. Viitso 2000: 169–170; 2003: 144–147). This time there is also at least one phonological innovation shared by Livonian and South Estonian, namely the development **kn* > **nn* (Kallio 2008: 313–314):

> Proto-Finnic **näk-nüt* > Estonian *näinud* ~ Livonian *nǟnd*, Võro *nännüq* (cf. analogically Finnish *nähnyt*, Karelian *nähnyt*, Veps *nähnu*, Votic *nähnü*) ['seen']

Note the exact Livonian development **näk-nüt* > **nännüt* > **nǟnud* > *nǟnd*. As we have already seen, however, many more phonological and morphological innovations suggest that Livonian belongs to Coastal Finnic, and merely one phonological innovation cannot overrule this fact, not least because **kn* > **nn* was a most natural assimilation which can very well have occurred independently in Livonian and South Estonian. As a matter of fact, there is also another well-known assimilation, **e–ä* > **ä–ä*, seemingly shared by Livonian and South Estonian:

> Proto-Finnic **kenkä* > Finnish *kenkä*, Karelian *kenkä*, Veps *keng*, Votic *tšentšä*, Estonian *king* ~ Livonian *kǟnga*, Võro *käng* ['shoe']

> Proto-Finnic **selkä* > Finnish *selkä*, Karelian *selkä*, Veps *selg*, Votic *seltšä*, Estonian *selg* ~ Livonian *sǟlga*, Võro *sälg* ['back']

This development can be considered recent even more easily, because the earliest South Estonian grammarian Johann Gutslaff (1648) still preferred the shapes *Keng* and *Selg* (cf. *Käng* and *Sälg* in the *Wastne Testament* 1686), whereas the earliest Livonian grammarian Andreas Sjögren still had *kēn̄ga* and *sēlga* side by side with *ką̄ṅga* and *są̄lga* (Wiedemann 1861: 34–35, 97–98). Hence, we are most likely dealing with an areal innovation that in no way threatens the idea that Proto-Finnic originally split up into Inland Finnic and Coastal Finnic. However, Livonian indeed seems to have been the earliest offshoot of Coastal Finnic, which we can therefore divide into Gulf of Riga Finnic (> Livonian) and Gulf of Finland Finnic (cf. Viitso's Neva above), the latter being supported by the sporadic development **ai* > **ei* in the first syllable, often accompanied by the simultaneous fronting **a* > **ä* in the second syllable:

> Proto-Finnic **haimo* > Finnish *heimo*, Karelian *heimo*, Veps *heim*, Votic *õimo*, Estonian *hõim* (→ Võro *hõim*) ~ Livonian *aim*, Leivu *aim* ['tribe']

> Proto-Finnic **haina* > Finnish *heinä*, Karelian *heinä*, Veps *hein*, Votic *einä*, Estonian *hein* ~ Livonian *āina*, Võro *hain* ['hay']

> Proto-Finnic **laipa* > Finnish *leipä*, Karelian *leipä*, Veps *leib*, Votic *leipä*, Estonian *leib* (→ Livonian *lēba*, Võro *leib*) ~ Salaca *laibe*, Leivu *laib* ['bread']

> Proto-Finnic **raika* > Finnish *reikä*, Karelian *reikä*, Veps *reig*, Estonian *reig* ~ Võro *raig* ['hole, scab']

> Proto-Finnic **raici* > Finnish *reisi*, Karelian *reisi*, Veps *reiž*, Votic *reisi*, Estonian *reis* ~ Old Võro *raiź* ['thigh']

> Proto-Finnic **saina* > Finnish *seinä*, Karelian *seinä*, Veps *sein*, Votic *seinä*, Estonian *sein* ~ Livonian *sāina*, Võro *sain* ['wall']

> Proto-Finnic **saisa-* > Finnish *seisoa*, Karelian *seisuo*, Veps *seišta*, Votic *sõisoa*, Estonian *seisma* (dial. *sõisma*) ~ Võro *saisma* ['to stand']

> Proto-Finnic **saiβas/*taiβas* > Finnish *seiväs*, Karelian *seiväs*, Veps *seibaz*, Votic *seiväz*, Estonian *teivas* ~ Livonian *tāibaz*, Võro *saivas* ['pole']

As the development **ai* > **ei* failed to occur in numerous inherited words (cf. Finnish *aivo* 'brain', *kaivaa* 'to dig', *vaimo* 'wife', etc.), Viitso (2000: 169) has even argued that there was no such sound change: in his view **ai* and **ei* have resulted from two different sound-substitution strategies. However, his opinion that Proto-Finnic **saisa-* was borrowed from Proto-Indo-European **sta-* (*sic*, *recte* **steh*$_2$*-*) ['to stand'] is far less convincing than the general opinion that Proto-Finnic **saisa-* was inherited from Proto-Uralic (Aikio 2002: 30–31). Moreover, even though Proto-Finnic **haina* and **raici* are well-known Baltic loanwords (Kalima 1936: 99–100, 152–153), they are both also early enough to have phonologically regular cognates outside Finnic (e.g. North Saami *suoidni* and *ruoida*, respectively), which makes the idea of two different sound substitution strategies inside Finnic somewhat anachronistic. Finally, both Votic and Estonian continue to decline the outcomes of Proto-Finnic **haina*, **laipa*, and **saina*, as if their initial syllable still had **ai*:

Proto-Finnic *hainoiδa > Votic *einoja*, Estonian *heinu* (part. pl.).

Proto-Finnic *laipoiδa > Votic *leipoja*, Estonian *leibu* (part. pl.).

Proto-Finnic *sainoiδa > Votic *seinoja*, Estonian *seinu* (part. pl.).

Such declension cannot possibly have been caused by different sound-substitution strategies; the sporadic development *ai > *ei is the only sensible explanation. The reason why it mostly affected loanwords is the statistical fact that the Proto-Finnic diphthong *ai happened to be much more usual in loanwords (Uotila 1986: 211–217), even though there are also numerous loanwords where *ai remained unchanged (Kalima 1936: 72–74; Hofstra 1985: 47–49). Yet in spite of its sporadicity, *ai > *ei carries much weight in establishing the Gulf of Finland Finnic subgroup, because while it may look like a natural development for a non-Fennicist, actually it was not, since it violated vowel harmony. As the examples above show, the development was *ai > *ei rather than *ai > *ëi, although there are also instances of the latter when the stem vowel remained unfronted throughout the paradigm (cf. Votic *õimo*, *sõisoa*; Estonian *hõim*, *sõisma*). Still, here we are most likely dealing with a secondary backing *ei > *ëi (cf. Mägiste 1930: 244–249).

The Third Dialectal Split: North Finnic vs. Central Finnic

No matter which one of Viitso's three alternative classifications (1978: 97–104) is followed, in all of them Gulf of Finland Finnic eventually split into a northern and southern dialect, which he labelled Taro and Maa, respectively. These two proto-dialects also correspond to Sammallahti's Pre-Tavastian and Pre-Estonian (1984: 142), whereas I call them North Finnic (cf. already Itkonen T 1972: 92–93) and Central Finnic (because South Finnic or, more precisely, Southeast Finnic and Southwest Finnic are reserved for Inland Finnic and Gulf of Riga Finnic, respectively). Now North Finnic (> the Finno-Karelo-Veps dialect continuum) is a particularly well-founded proto-dialect, although its most striking phonological innovation *ë > *e has not recently been included in this connection (see e.g. Itkonen E 1945; Viitso 1978; Holst 2001):

Proto-Finnic *mëla > Finnish *mela*, Karelian *mela*, Veps *mela* ~ Votic *mõla*, Estonian *mõla*, Võro *mõla* ['paddle']

Proto-Finnic *mërta > Finnish *merta*, Karelian *merta*, Veps *merd* ~ Votic *mõrta*, Estonian *mõrd*, Livonian *mō̃rda*, Võro *mõrd* ['fish trap']

Proto-Finnic *tërva > Finnish *terva*, Karelian *terva*, Veps *terv* ~ Votic *tõrva*, Estonian *tõrv*, Livonian *tō̃ra*, Võro *tõrv* ['tar']

Proto-Finnic *vëlka > Finnish *velka*, Karelian *velka*, Veps *velg* ~ Votic *võlka*, Estonian *võlg*, Livonian *vō̃lga*, Võro *võlg* ['debt']

Over the past few decades, the scholarly community has unanimously preferred the more Finnocentric reconstructions **mela*, **merta*, **terva*, and **velka*, presupposing the reverse development **e* > **ë* south of the Gulf of Finland where, however, the Finnic dialects were far more diverse. Although phonological innovations may of course diffuse across dialect boundaries, from a dialectological viewpoint **ë* > **e*, occurring in only one tertiary branch of Finnic, should *a priori* be considered more likely than **e* > **ë*, occurring everywhere else. Note that these words with initial-syllable **ë* hardly ever have cognates outside Finnic, and even the only apparent exception **mëla* irregularly goes back to **melä* (cf. North Saami *mealli*, Mordvin *миле*). Thus, it is easy to agree with Jaakko Häkkinen (forthcoming) that initial-syllable **ë* was introduced to Finnic through borrowings from Baltic and Germanic. True, neither Baltic nor Germanic had initial-syllable **ë*, but since their most usual stem vowel was **a*, most Baltic and Germanic words were borrowed into Finnic as *a*-stems, which originally did not coexist with initial-syllable front vowels in accordance with Uralic vowel harmony. Remarkably, initial-syllable **ë* arose about the same time as non-initial-syllable **ë* (< **ï* or, even more probably, **ə̑* in word-medial position; Kallio 2012a), which has only been preserved in Votic and South Estonian, because non-initial-syllable vocalism in North Estonian and Livonian is more reduced:

Proto-Finnic **lainëh* > Finnish *laine*, Karelian *lai(n)neh*, Veps *laineh* ~ Votic *lainõ*, Estonian *laine*, Livonian *lain*, Võro *lainõh* ['wave']

Proto-Finnic **lakëδa* > Finnish *lakea*, Karelian *lakie*, Veps *laged* ~ Votic *lakõa*, Estonian *lage*, Livonian *la'gdõ*, Võro *lakõ* ['flat, open']

North Finnic also here had the unconditioned fronting **ë* > **e* that was further accompanied by the non-initial-syllable monophthongisation **ëi* > **ei* > **i(i)* (Kallio 2012b: 32–34):

Proto-Finnic **munëiδa* > Finnish *munia*, Karelian *munia*, Veps *munid* (dial. *munīd*) ~ Votic *munõja*, Estonian *mune*, Livonian *mu'n̦d̦i*, Võro *munnõ* ['eggs' (part. pl.)]

While the phoneme **ë* was eliminated north of the Gulf of Finland, it contrarily became far more frequent south of the Gulf of Finland, especially due to the sporadic illabialisation **o* > **ë*, which, however, obviously diffused across dialect boundaries, because its frequency gradually decreased from Votic via North Estonian to South Estonian and Livonian (see e.g. Kettunen 1930: 128–129; 1962: 131–132; Posti 1942: 6–13). Meanwhile, even though initial-syllable **ö* already occurred in Proto-Finnic (Saukkonen 1975), non-initial-syllable **ö* (< **o* after an initial-syllable front vowel) did not arise until North Finnic (Itkonen T 1980: 112–113; 1983: 218):

Proto-Finnic **näko* > Finnish *näkö*, Karelian *näkö*, Veps *nägo* ~ Votic *näko*, Estonian *nägu*, Livonian *nä'g*, Võro *nägo* ['sight']

Nonetheless, while Veps later largely lost its vowel harmony due to Russian influence (see Posti 1935; Wiik 1989), non-initial-syllable **ö* secondarily spread to some dialects of Votic (Lauerma 1993: 64–106) and even Estonian (Wiik 1988: 152–154). Now the original dialect boundary was similarly blurred in the case of the most striking North Finnic morphological innovation, the subjunctive suffix **-isi-* replacing the conditional suffix **-ksi-* (Itkonen T 1983: 365–366):

> Proto-Finnic **anta-isi* ~ **anδa-ksi* > Finnish *antaisi*, Karelian *antais*, Veps *andaiži* ~ Votic *antaissi* ~ Estonian *annaks*, Livonian *āndaks*, Võro *annas(iq)* ['would give']

Although Votic *-issi-* (< **-iksi-*) is an obvious contamination of **-isi-* and **-ksi-*, there is no reason to regard Votic as mixed, because in most other respects it is the easternmost extension of the North Estonian dialect continuum. Yet the same does not apply to Kukkuzi Votic or, as it should rather be called, Kukkuzi Ingrian/Izhorian, which in all my listed isoglosses above agrees with North Finnic. On the other hand, the Kukkuzi dialect, in spite of its massive Voticisation, does not share some of the most widespread phonological innovations south of the Gulf of Finland, such as the vocalisation of **n* before **s*:

> Proto-Finnic **mansikka(s)* > Finnish *mansikka*, Karelian *mantšikka*, Veps *manzik* ~ Votic *maazikaz*, Estonian *maasikas*, Livonian *mǭškōz*, Võro *maasik* ['strawberry']

> Proto-Finnic **pënsas* > Finnish *pensas*, Karelian *pensas*, Veps *penzaz* ~ Votic *põõzaz*, Estonian *põõsas*, Livonian *pȭzõ(z)* ['bush']

The corresponding Kukkuzi words are *mantsikka* and *pēzaz*, the former of which could be regarded as inherited (cf. Ingrian *mantsikka*, on whose affricate see Toivonen 1930: 97–98), whereas the latter could be considered a Votic borrowing, because otherwise it would be the only Kukkuzi example of such a vocalisation (Kettunen 1930: 92–94). While this vocalisation was further shared by Livonian and South Estonian, the loss of **h* after resonants could truly be considered an actual Central Finnic phonological innovation:

> Proto-Finnic **tarha* > Finnish *tarha*, Karelian *tarha*, Veps *tarh* ~ Votic *tara*, Estonian *tara*, Livonian *tarā*, Võro *tahr* ['enclosure']

> Proto-Finnic **vanha* > Finnish *vanha*, Karelian *vanha*, Veps *vanh* ~ Votic *vana*, Estonian *vana* (→ Võro *vana*), Livonian *vanā*, Võro *vahn* ['old']

South Estonian had no such loss but the metathesis **Rh* > **hR*, whereas Livonian proves nothing, because its **h* has been lost everywhere. However, both the vocalisation of **n* before **s* and the loss of **h* after resonants belong to the most natural developments that can very well have diffused across dialect boundaries (Salminen 1998: 396). As a matter of fact, Terho Itkonen

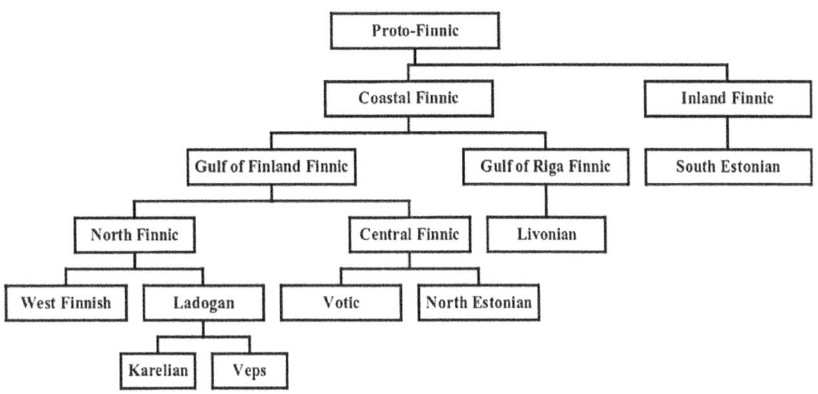

Fig. 1. The Finnic family tree.

(1983: 217–226) already acknowledged that there were very few 'South Finnic' innovations compared to many more North Finnic innovations – not least due to the fact that his postulated 'South Finnic' subgroup included not only Votic and North Estonian but also Livonian and South Estonian. Then again, there are not many actual Central Finnic innovations either, even though several innovations are shared by Votic and the eastern dialects of North Estonian (cf. **st* > **ss*, initial-syllable **o* > **ë* in polysyllabic words, etc.; Kettunen 1962: 199). All this suggests that Central Finnic was a dialect continuum rather than a uniform language.

The Finnic Family Tree at a Time and in a Space

Fig. 1 shows my proposed binary family tree from the Finnic proto-language to the seven Finnic proto-dialects in Tapani Salminen's classification (1998: 392). Admittedly, I have offered above no evidence for the Ladogan subgroup (cf. Sammallahti 1977: 125–129), which I base on the fact that the sharpest dialect boundary within North Finnic runs between West Finnish and (Karelian-based) East Finnish. Note also that my family tree omits all the directly unattested Finnic dialects, such as Terho Itkonen's postulated East Finnic substrate (1983: 209–217), which, however, may have been the source language of several Finnic place names in north-western Russia, showing the retention of both **ë* and **ai* (cf. Saarikivi 2007: 90–93).

According to Pekka Sammallahti (1977: 131–133), Proto-Finnic diversified rather slowly. In other words, he dated its initial branching into Coastal and Inland Finnic as early as the late Bronze Age (*c.* 1000–600 BC), whereas he dated its final branchings into Karelian and Veps as well as Votic and North Estonian as late as the Viking Age (*c.* AD 800–1050). Yet I am inclined to believe that Proto-Finnic diversified faster, because otherwise we would expect many more innovations in each intermediate proto-stage. Hence, I rather agree with Mikko Heikkilä (2014), who now dates the beginning of the diversification to about AD 150, based on his careful scrutiny of the most up-to-date loanword evidence. Centuries later, however, Finnic dialects were still linguistically close enough to undergo etymological nativisation, because they share Christian terminology of Slavic origin, dating to the eighth century AD at the earliest (Kallio 2006: 156–157):

> Proto-Finnic **pappi* > Finnish *pappi*, Karelian *pappi*, Veps *pap*, Votic *pappi*, Estonian *papp*, Livonian *päp*, Võro *papp'* ['priest']

> Proto-Finnic **risti* > Finnish *risti*, Karelian *risti*, Veps *rist*, Votic *rissi*, Estonian *rist*, Livonian *rišt*, Võro *rist'* ['cross']

The following important ethnonym of Norse origin is approximately of the same age (cf. Schalin):

> Proto-Finnic **roocci* > Finnish *Ruotsi*, Karelian *ruottši*, Veps *roč'*, Votic *roottsi*, Estonian *Roots*, Livonian *rūotš*, Võro *ru̯u̯tś* ['Swede(n)']

However, these seem to be among the latest Common Finnic words, after which newer borrowings no longer spread throughout the Finnic-speaking area. Thus, the diversification of the Proto-Finnic language can safely be dated to the first millennium AD, whereas the dispersal of the Proto-Finnic speakers must logically have occurred somewhat earlier. Now, according to Juha Janhunen (2005; 2009), there was a chain reaction, where the dispersal of the Slavic speakers caused the dispersal of the Finnic speakers, which in turn caused the dispersal of the Saami speakers. Yet his model must be rejected for chronological reasons. Most of all, while there might have been a minor Slavic wave to the Velikaya basin as early as the fifth century AD, the major Slavic wave to the Volkhov basin did not begin until the eighth century AD (Kallio 2006: 157). Although the Saami expansion cannot be dated with equal exactitude, the most recent studies on the topic (e.g. Aikio 2004; 2006; Häkkinen 2010; Heikkilä 2011) have more or less unanimously dated it to the first centuries AD.

Janhunen's hypothesis is not only chronologically but also geographically problematic, because in his opinion Finnic was spoken nowhere outside the Neva basin until the late first millennium AD. Yet Finnic had hundreds of Germanic loanwords dating from the Nordic Bronze Age (*c.* 1800–500 BC) onwards, although the earliest Germanic (or rather East Norse) expansion to the Neva basin did not take place until the eighth century AD (Carpelan 2006: 88–89). Finnic must therefore have been spoken further to the west, which is also confirmed by onomastic evidence. For instance, the Finnic speakers clearly knew the northern Latvian river *Gauja* at the beginning of our era, as shown by the metathetic substitution in its Finnic name *Koiva* (Koivulehto 1986: 170). Half a millennium earlier, however, they had already known the southern Finnish rivers *Eura(joki)* and *Kymi(joki)*, since their names were borrowed from the Germanic proto-language itself (Koivulehto 1987: 33–37; Schalin 2012: 392–394; Schalin). For this reason, there must have been Finnic speakers on both sides of the Gulf of Finland continually from the Pre-Roman Iron Age (*c.* 500–1 BC) onwards.

As my purpose is not to deal with Finnic glottogenesis, I do not go further back in time, but content myself with referring to Terho Itkonen's famous map of the Finnic homeland surrounding the Gulf of Finland (1983: 378). As a matter of fact, the Finnic speech area was probably even more restricted to the coastal areas than his map suggests, because it was not until the second century AD that typical *tarand*-graves spread from coastal Estonia to inland Estonia as well as northern Latvia (Lang 2007: 191–203), thus causing the separation of Inland Finnic (> South Estonian) and Gulf of Riga Finnic (> Livonian). From about AD 300 onwards, there was a similar expansion from coastal Finland to inland Finland (Salo 2004: 37–45). As all of coastal Finland, except the part protected by the Åboland archipelago, reduced its population density by the end of the Viking Age (cf. Raninen & Wessman), Gulf of Finland Finnic eventually split up into Central Finnic and North Finnic. While the former remained in northern Estonia and western Ingria, the latter expanded its area from western Finland to the Ladoga region about AD 700 (Carpelan 2006: 88–89).

The resulting Ladogan proto-language seems not to have been long-lasting either, because some of its speakers continued to expand even further to the east along the Varangian trade routes, such as that from the Neva basin through Lake Beloye as far as the Northern Dvina basin (cf. Saarikivi 2007; Koskela Vasaru). Yet all that is left now are a few scattered Veps-speaking pockets between the lakes Ladoga, Onega and Beloye. As Veps was in fact the last Finnic branch to reach its current speech area, it is no wonder that Veps dialectal differences are relatively minimal (unless we count its Karelianised variant Ludic). The remaining Karelian proto-dialect also soon began to diversify, but there is no reason to go into further details which have already been discussed elsewhere (see e.g. Salminen 1998: 401–403; Leskinen 1999: 362–364, 368–370; Kuzmin). Thus, I also leave aside the diversification of the seven Finnic proto-dialects during the second millennium AD.

References

Aikio, Ante. 2002. New and Old Samoyed Etymologies. *Finnisch-Ugrische Forschungen* 57: 9–57.

Aikio, Ante. 2004. An Essay on Substrate Studies and the Origin of Saami. In Irma Hyvärinen *et al.* (eds.). *Etymologie, Entlehnungen und Entwicklungen: Festschrift für Jorma Koivulehto zum 70. Geburtstag.* Mémoires de la Société Néophilologique de Helsinki 63. Helsinki: Société Néophilologique. Pp. 5–34.

Aikio, Ante. 2006. On Germanic-Saami Contacts and Saami Prehistory. *Journal de la Société Finno-Ougrienne* 91: 9–55.

Carpelan, Christian. 2006. On Archaeological Aspects of Uralic, Finno-Ugric and Finnic Societies before AD 800. In Juhani Nuorluoto (ed.). *The Slavicization of the Russian North: Mechanisms and Chronology.* Slavica Helsingiensia 27. Helsinki: Helsinki University Press. Pp. 78–92.

Gutslaff, Johannes. 1648. *Observationes grammaticæ circa linguam Esthonicam.* Dorpat: Johannes Vogel.

Häkkinen, Jaakko. 2010. Jatkuvuusperustelut ja saamelaisen kielen leviäminen. *Muinaistutkija* 2010(1): 19–36; 2010(2): 51–64.

Häkkinen, Jaakko. Forthcoming. *Updating the Evidence for the Proto-Finnic Illabial Back Vowels.*

Heikkilä, Mikko. 2011. Germaanisia etymologioita saamelais-suomalaisille sanoille sekä huomioita kantasaamen ajoittamisesta ja paikantamisesta. *Virittäjä* 115: 75–90.

Heikkilä, Mikko. 2014. *Bidrag till Fennoskandiens språkliga förhistoria i tid och rum.* Helsinki: Unigrafia.

Helimski, Eugene. 2006. The "Northwestern" Group of Finno-Ugric Languages and its Heritage in the Place Names and Substratum Vocabulary of the Russian North. In Juhani Nuorluoto (ed.). *The Slavicization of the Russian North: Mechanisms and Chronology.* Slavica Helsingiensia 27. Helsinki: Helsinki University Press. Pp. 109–127.

Hofstra, Tette. 1985. *Ostseefinnisch und Germanisch: Frühe Lehnbeziehungen im nördlichen Ostseeraum im Lichte der Forschung seit 1961.* Groningen: Drukkerij van Denderen.

Holst, Jan Henrik. 2001. Die Herkunft des estnischen Vokals õ. *Journal de la Société Finno-Ougrienne* 89: 57–98.

Itkonen, Erkki. 1945. Onko kantasuomessa ollut keskivokaaleja? *Virittäjä* 49: 158–182.

Itkonen, Terho. 1972. Historiantakaiset Häme ja Suomi kielentutkijan näkökulmasta. *Historiallinen Aikakauskirja* 70: 85–112.

Itkonen, Terho. 1980. Lisiä suomen rajausoppiin. *Virittäjä* 84: 101–115.

Itkonen, Terho. 1981. Zur Geschichte der *ts*-Verbindung in den westfinnischen Dialekten. In Heikki Leskinen (ed.). *Heutige Wege der finnischen Dialektologie.* Studia Fennica 24. Helsinki: Suomalaisen Kirjallisuuden Seura. Pp. 11–28.

Itkonen, Terho. 1983. Välikatsaus suomen kielen juuriin. *Virittäjä* 87: 190–229, 349–386.

Janhunen, Juha. 1982. On the Structure of Proto-Uralic. *Finnisch-Ugrische Forschungen* 44: 23–42.

Janhunen, Juha. 2005. När kom finnarna till Finland? *Sphinx* 2004–2005: 77–91.

Janhunen, Juha. 2009. Some Additional Notes on the Macrohydronyms of the Ladoga Region. *Studia Etymologica Cracoviensia* 14: 203–212.

Kalima, Jalo. 1936. *Itämerensuomalaisten kielten balttilaiset lainasanat.* Suomalaisen Kirjallisuuden Seuran Toimituksia 202. Helsinki: Suomalaisen Kirjallisuuden Seura.

Kallio, Petri. 2006. On the Earliest Slavic Loanwords in Finnic. In Juhani Nuorluoto (ed.). *The Slavicization of the Russian North: Mechanisms and Chronology.* Slavica Helsingiensia 27. Helsinki: Helsinki University Press. Pp. 154–166.

Kallio, Petri. 2007. Kantasuomen konsonanttihistoriaa. In Jussi Ylikoski & Ante Aikio (eds.). *Sámit, sánit, sátnehámit: Riepmočála Pekka Sammallahtii miessemánu 21. beaivve 2007.* Mémoires de la Société Finno-Ougrienne 253. Helsinki: Société Finno-Ougrienne. Pp. 229–249.

Kallio, Petri. 2008. The Etymology of Finnish *sauna* 'Sauna'. In Kees Dekker *et al.* (eds.). *Northern Voices: Essays on Old Germanic and Related Topics Offered to Professor Tette Hofstra.* Mediaevalia Groningana New Series 11. Leuven: Peeters. Pp. 313–319.

Kallio, Petri. 2012a. The Non-Initial-Syllable Vowel Reductions from Proto-Uralic to Proto-Finnic. In Tiina Hyytiäinen *et al.* (eds.). *Per Urales ad Orientem: Iter polyphonicum multilingue: Festskrift tillägnad Juha Janhunen på hans sextioårsdag den 12 februari 2012.* Mémoires de la Société Finno-Ougrienne 264. Helsinki: Société Finno-Ougrienne. Pp. 163–175.

Kallio, Petri. 2012b. Jälkitavujen diftongit kantasuomessa. *Fenno-Ugrica Suecana Nova Series* 14: 31–40.

Kettunen, Lauri. 1930. *Vatjan kielen äännehistoria.* Suomalaisen Kirjallisuuden Seuran Toimituksia 185. Helsinki: Suomalaisen Kirjallisuuden Seura.

Kettunen, Lauri. 1962. *Eestin kielen äännehistoria*. Suomalaisen Kirjallisuuden Seuran Toimituksia 156. Helsinki: Suomalaisen Kirjallisuuden Seura.

Koivulehto, Jorma. 1986. *Pinta* ja *rasva*. *Virittäjä* 90: 164–177.

Koivulehto, Jorma. 1987. Namn som kan tolkas urgermanskt. In *Klassiska problem inom finlandssvensk ortnamnsforskning*. Studier i nordisk filologi 67. Helsingfors: Svenska litteratursällskapet i Finland. Pp. 27–42.

Lang, Valter. 2007. *The Bronze and Early Iron Ages in Estonia*. Estonian Archaeology 3. Tartu: Tartu University Press.

Larsson, Lars-Gunnar. 2012. *Grenzen und Gruppierungen im Umesamischen*. Veröffentlichungen der Societas Uralo-Altaica 83. Wiesbaden: Harrassowitz.

Lauerma, Petri. 1993. *Vatjan vokaalisointu*. Mémoires de la Société Finno-Ougrienne 214. Helsinki: Société Finno-Ougrienne.

Leskinen, Heikki. 1999. Suomen murteiden synty. In Paul Fogelberg (ed.). *Pohjan poluilla: Suomalaisten juuret nykytutkimuksen mukaan*. Bidrag till kännedom av Finlands natur och folk 153. Helsinki: Suomen Tiedeseura. Pp. 358-371.

Mägiste, Julius. 1930. Ensi tavun vokaalivelarisaatiosta virossa. *Suomi* V.10: 244–259.

Posti, Lauri. 1935. Vepsän vokaalisoinnusta. *Virittäjä* 39: 73–89, 380–383.

Posti, Lauri. 1942. *Grundzüge der livischen Lautgeschichte*. Mémoires de la Société Finno-Ougrienne 85. Helsinki: Société Finno-Ougrienne.

Rahkonen, Pauli. 2011. Finno-Ugric Hydronyms of the River Volkhov and Luga Catchment Areas. *Journal de la Société Finno-Ougrienne* 93: 205–266.

Saarikivi, Janne. 2007. On the Uralic Substrate Toponymy of Arkhangelsk Region: Problems of Research Methodology and Ethnohistorical Interpretation. In Ritva Liisa Pitkänen & Janne Saarikivi (eds.). *Borrowing of Place Names in the Uralian Languages*. Onomastica Uralica 4. Debrecen: Vider Plusz Bt. Pp. 45–109.

Salminen, Tapani. 1998. Pohjoisten itämerensuomalaisten kielten luokittelun ongelmia. In Riho Grünthal & Johanna Laakso (eds.). *Oekeeta asijoo: Commentationes Fenno-Ugricae in honorem Seppo Suhonen sexagenarii 16.V.1998*. Mémoires de la Société Finno-Ougrienne 228. Helsinki: Société Finno-Ougrienne. Pp. 390–406.

Salminen, Tapani. 2002. Problems in the Taxonomy of the Uralic Languages in the Light of Modern Comparative Studies. *Лингвистический беспредел: сборник статей к 70-летию А. И. Кузнецовой*. Москва: Издательство Московского университета. Pp. 44–55.

Salo, Unto. 2004. Suomen ja Hämeen synty. *Suomen Museo* 2003: 5–58.

Sammallahti, Pekka. 1977. Suomalaisten esihistorian kysymyksiä. *Virittäjä* 81: 119–136.

Sammallahti, Pekka. 1984. Saamelaisten esihistoriallinen tausta kielitieteen valossa. *Suomen väestön esihistorialliset juuret*. Bidrag till kännedom av Finlands natur och folk 131. Helsinki: Suomen Tiedeseura. Pp. 137–156.

Saukkonen, Pauli. 1975. Zur Geschichte des ostseefinnischen *ö*. *Congressus Tertius Internationalis Fenno-Ugristarum I: Acta Linguistica*. Tallinn: Valgus. Pp. 357–361.

Schalin, Johan. 2012. Namnet Kymmene. In Tiina Hyytiäinen et al. (eds.). *Per Urales ad Orientem: Iter polyphonicum multilingue. Festskrift tillägnad Juha Janhunen på hans sextioårsdag den 12 februari 2012*. Mémoires de la Société Finno-Ougrienne 264. Helsinki: Société Finno-Ougrienne. Pp. 389–398.

Toivonen, Y. H. 1930. Myöhäsyntyisistä affrikaatoista itämerensuomalaisissa kielissä. *Virittäjä* 34: 91–98.

Uotila, Eeva. 1986. Baltic Impetus on the Baltic Finnic Diphthongs. *Finnisch-Ugrische Forschungen* 47: 206–222.

Viitso, Tiit-Rein. 1978. The History of Finnic *õ* in the First Syllable. *Советское финно-угроведение* 14: 86–106.

Viitso, Tiit-Rein. 1985. Kriterien zur Klassifizierung der Dialekte der ostseefinnischen Sprachen. In Wolfgang Veenker (ed.). *Dialectologia Uralica*. Veröffentlichungen

der Societas Uralo-Altaica 20. Wiesbaden: Societas Uralo-Altaica. Pp. 89–96.
Viitso, Tiit-Rein. 2000. Finnic Affinity. *Congressus Nonus Internationalis Fenno-Ugristarum I: Orationes plenariae & Orationes publicae.* Tartu: OÜ Paar. Pp. 153–178.
Viitso, Tiit-Rein. 2003. Rise and Development of the Estonian Language. In Mati Erelt (ed.). *Estonian Language.* Linguistica Uralica: Supplementary Series 1. Tallinn: Estonian Academy Publishers. Pp. 130–230.
Wiedemann, Ferdinand Johann (ed.). 1861. *Joh. Andreas Sjögren's livisch-deutsches und deutsch-livisches Wörterbuch.* St. Petersburg: Kaiserlichen Akademie der Wissenschaften.
Wiik, Kalevi. 1988. *Viron vokaalisointu.* Suomi 140. Helsinki: Suomalaisen Kirjallisuuden Seura.
Wiik, Kalevi. 1989. *Vepsän vokaalisointu.* Suomi 146. Helsinki: Suomalaisen Kirjallisuuden Seura.

II

Space

Introduction

Viking Age in Finland

The second section of this collection shifts emphasis from negotiating the Viking Age as a historical period to the geographical space under consideration. It is perhaps inevitable that individuals today think in terms of the borders of modern nation-states. These borders have been relevant to research in different ways, for example impacting archaeological investigations or the collection of folklore. However, these borders did not exist in the Viking Age. They define neither the areal distribution of archaeological cultures nor probable language areas in that period. On the other hand, when these borders are eliminated, the territories of Finland and Karelia generally blur into an indistinct wilderness. In international research, a few toponyms from Icelandic saga literature are at best vaguely situated on this part of a map – perhaps with Staraya Ladoga (Old Norse *Aldeygjuborg*) marked with a star like a settlement and a label of 'Bjarmians' somewhere on the White Sea – and viewed as a periphery or perhaps even as a staging point along the Eastern Route of Norse Viking trade. At worst, these territories are reduced to an uninhabited wilderness or only inhabited along a narrow stretch of southern coastline of Finland (occasionally depicted as a 'Viking' colony). Like the concepts 'Vikings' and 'Viking Age', these are constructs that have been circulating in academic discourses and need to be broken down and reassessed. The seven chapters constituting this section of the collection offer diverse perspectives from different disciplines on the problems of relevant and constructed space associated with Finno-Karelian areas of habitation.

Jukka Korpela opens the section by considering questions of how geographical spaces are perceived and conceptualized in different times and cultural contexts. He considers how these were constructed and construed by individuals and social groups in the Viking Age. Understandings of places and their relationships are dependent on conceptualizations of space that are socially constructed within historical contexts. Korpela highlights that these understandings of space have not always been the same and that understandings of the significance of places and their relationships are inevitably bound up with perspectives. These perspectives are in turn rooted in cultural practices, livelihoods, economic potentials and how these become valued or devalued in societies. This opening chapter presents a valuable discussion that can richly inform the background and understanding of subsequent contributions to the section.

MERVI KOSKELA VASARU builds on the opening discussion by concentrating on the Germanic construction of territories of Finland and Karelia in medieval sources with particular attention to populations encountered in trading expeditions to the White Sea. KOSKELA VASARU's contribution provides a useful illustration of the social construction of such locations in an interesting case where sea routes were opened for a few centuries owing to the climatic conditions that characterized the Viking Age and later became impassable. The chapter presents an interesting tension between the value placed on this location as an economic center for trade on the one hand, and, on the other, the remoteness from Germanic cultural centers that led it to blur with otherworldly locations. This discussion draws attention to the fact that the construction of these geographical spaces in the Viking Age was impacted by the presence of significant cultural groups that have otherwise disappeared.

JARI-MATTI KUUSELA gives further attention to these northern territories from the perspective of archaeology. This chapter offers an important overview of approaching cultural practices and changes to the face of the landscape in the archaeological record. It complements the opening discussion by engaging evidence of changing uses of space as a historical process. Whereas KOSKELA VASARU concentrates on nautical routes, KUUSELA directs attention to evidence of over-land networks that extended from the Gulf of Bothnia to the White Sea as discerned through historical changes in the distribution of stray finds in the archaeological record. The archaeological record leaves it unclear what linguistic-cultural groups may have participated in these networks, but this contribution makes it clear that the Viking Age is distinguished as a historical period by changes in the cultures and their networks in these regions as opposed to changes occurring only in territories further south.

Emphasis on trade and artefacts is then turned to settlement and agriculture by TEIJA ALENIUS, who approaches the Viking Age from the perspective of palaeoecology. Human activity impacts the physical environment of the ecology. Evidence of this impact is manifested in the synchronic outcomes of processes in nature, such as the pollen production of plants or ash resulting from slash-and-burn agriculture. ALENIUS offers a valuable introduction to the field of palaeoecology which is unfamiliar to many disciplines. Shifting focus to the southwest, this chapter considers a case on Lake Ladoga, a region considered a central area for trade and cultural contacts during the Viking Age. This case study is used to illustrate the potential, problems and limitations of the diverse data produced by research in this field.

Attention then moves from the ecology of landscapes to how these are named as MATTI LEIVISKÄ presents a practical introduction to sources and research on toponymy, or place names. Concepts, valuations and associations of place manifest in names attributed to areas and features in the landscape. Where these names become fixed and are historically maintained as a diachronic process, they can provide information about the inhabitants who produced those names. At its most basic, place names provide information about the language that people spoke, but they can also reveal information about habitation and habitation patterns, livelihoods and even population movements. LEIVISKÄ's introduction to toponymy provides an essential background for several chapters of the collection centered on this important category of information.

DENIS KUZMIN builds on LEIVISKÄ's discussion with a study of toponymy in Karelia of Sámi origin. KUZMIN's survey and discussion returns to the problem of the distribution of language groups in the Viking Age by showing that the majority of territories now associated with the Karelian language appear to have been predominantly inhabited by Sámi language speakers at that time. This chapter highlights that the Sámi language(s) spoken in these territories have subsequently disappeared and reconnects with the problem that the distribution of languages in the Viking Age was much different than in later periods. KUZMIN's discussion brings forward evidence that the Sámi language was not uniform in this region and that there were multiple distinct dialects or even multiple Sámi languages. He also includes a discussion of Vepsian culture as well as drawing attention to the fact that diverse cultures disappeared from these territories over the course of time without leaving more than trace evidence of language and verbal culture.

The section is drawn to a close by returning to the broader situation of these territories as approached from the perspective of geopolitics. LASSI HEININEN, JOONAS AHOLA and FROG emphasize the significance of the Viking Age being marked by conceptualising Northern Europe, for the first time, as a geographical space. This was accompanied by other radical changes in conceptualizations of space and the association of different spaces with economic and social power. This chapter offers a lucid and accessible introduction to current conceptions of geopolitics and how geopolitical theory can be fruitfully applied to social and cultural changes that took place in the Viking Age. It returns to the issued addressed by KORPELA with a discussion of the socio-political construction of space and relations between groups. It also anticipates the final section of this volume as emphasis shifts from the social construction of space and places to the social and cultural groups by which these were constructed and negotiated.

These seven chapters build on discussions of the preceding section, complementing, expanding and refining those perspectives with attention to the construction and conceptualization of spaces. They illustrate that a strictly delimited geographical space will not necessarily provide a relevant frame for observation and demonstrate how, within a historical period, these constructions and conceptualizations are dependent on perspectives. The contributions highlight that spaces may also be perceived very differently in research depending on the context of discussion and the point of view. It is only through the dialogues between and across these perspectives that more dynamic and wide-ranging understandings emerge. The historical circumstances of different spaces are revealed through traces of human activity. The chapters highlight, however, that it is not easy to divide space into periods of cultural or language areas on the basis of these traces alone. The dynamics between cultural centers and peripheries are shown to depend on other, temporally bounded factors such as mobility and established patterns of intercultural relations. Several chapters bring forward the additional complication that the distribution of linguistic-cultural groups in the Viking Age was not only radically different, but that approaching these groups and the dynamics of relations between them is complicated by the fact that several may have disappeared in later historical processes. Together, these chapters highlight the diversity of possibilities for defining the spatial reaches of 'Finland' in the Viking Age. They foreground that all borders drawn to depict human action and culture are artificial constructs that must be defined and critically assessed in terms of the scope of a given concern while offering allowances and flexibility for the gaps in available information. Together, the contributions of this section demonstrate that problematizing the fundamental and intuitively obvious dimension of space is fruitful and necessary when constructing an image of Viking Age Finland.

Jukka Korpela

Reach and Supra-Local Consciousness in the Medieval Nordic Periphery

The death of a human being can be defined as the cessation of his or her consciousness. To know something means to comprehend it, and this presupposes reaching it, i.e. communication between the observer and the object concerned, in other words some kind of physical and mental contact. Both human life and human history are governed by communication and its possibilities, because it is these that order how we perceive, use and comprehend our surroundings. The means of communication are not standard but have changed greatly in the course of history and depend on local physical and mental circumstances.

There are three main dimensions to consider here. Technology makes it possible to reach a target. Without a spaceship one cannot go to other planets and without a microscope it is not possible to see very small particles. Secondly, time limits the use of a certain technology. Although one could walk to the other side of the world, nobody would set out to do this. Instead, jets, cars, telephones etc. make the world smaller and easier to reach. The third dimension is truth. We are conscious of the world within the limits of a truth based on learning, experience, social norms etc., i.e. based on what society or its culture considers to be true. For medieval man, God was incontrovertibly true but black holes were not. Therefore God was an active factor in human decision-making but black holes were no more than a passive part of the natural universe.

An early-medieval army was not able to move long distances, and therefore princes could not use their armed forces as instruments for legitimising their administration and power. Armies were merely part of the commercial system deployed for collecting resources, and a permanent authority had to be established and manifested by other means, a process in which supernatural powers became important. Religion was invoked to consecrate local and supra-local power, so that resistance to such power implied rebellion against the gods.[1]

In this framework in a shamanistic culture, the shaman[2] controlled information that was vital for the community because he had a monopoly over communication with the powers of the invisible world, being the only person able to enter the worlds of the deceased and the deities. Failure to do this was a danger to the life of the society but only constant failure on his part made it possible for the people to rebel; otherwise a disloyal village inhabitant was regarded as a threat to the entire society and would soon be eliminated by other people.

According to Torsten Hägerstrand, time and space should not be separated from each other but must be studied together. Swedish scholars have stressed the concept of *räckhåll* (reachability) in their studies of the conceptualisation of our surroundings. Reachability means the area of experience that a person can reach physically and mentally, and it depends on the experiences and understanding of the person or group of people concerned. Apart from the physical possibilities for travelling to a place, it also includes social, economic, psychological and mythic dimensions.

Dick Harrison divides space into the *mikrorum* (micro-space) and *makrorum* (macro-space) and claims that the micro-space is an area of which a person has experiences, even though he may not have physically visited or seen it. The macro-space does not have much to do with physical geography, but concerns a cosmological category which encompasses the gods, the deceased and mythic phenomena.[3]

The study of communication possibilities and practices is important for an understanding of reachability. I have previously devoted a couple of articles and one monograph to the study of medieval local society on the north-eastern European periphery – how its physical and mental communication landscape was formed and later reformed during the early-modern realm-building process along with the formation of a supra-local consciousness and identity (Korpela 2006a; 2006d; 2007a; 2007b; 2008; 2011b). This development did much to alter the culture (worldview) of that society and resulted in nation formation, the definition of borders and the emergence of modern civil society.

I attempt in the present chapter to comment on the contacts that the north-eastern European peripheral societies/populations had with the emerging realms and with the reality of European Christendom and to trace the expanding understanding of the European centres with regard to the north-eastern peripheries, i.e. their incipient consciousness of more distant regions: how the 'micro-space' expanded and how the culture of the tenth to thirteenth centuries finally transformed into a European Finnish, Karelian or Russian culture. This enables us to comprehend how it was possible for a Viking Age human being in the geographical area of later Finland/Karelia to understand Vikings, their activities and identity, what they could know realistically about the so-called Vikings and how these could influence their lives in the forests, how this kind of person put himself on the map of the Viking world or Scandinavia or Europe, and how he was able to receive information about the outer world.

The time period for this chapter is not specified exactly, because in this peripheral culture the centuries or age of Vikings were relevant only after their integration into the European world. They were living with an understanding of time as cyclic and they were in fact living in the Iron Age, which is identical with the local culture of the tenth to twelfth centuries, up until the nineteenth century.

The study of this reality is not only important for gaining an understanding of medieval society, but it can also be of value for our ability to read medieval sources in the correct way. If we do not understand the cognitive limits and deviations of the authors relative to our own situation, we will not be able to use their writings. We cannot simply fall back upon our own concepts and understanding and presuppose that the chroniclers had the same consciousness as we have today.

What Is Near, and What Is Distant?

The integration of the peripheries with the centres and with the universal Christian culture of Europe was a long and heterogeneous procedure. The primitive means of communication put an absolute and understandable limit to it. It simply took a long time to reach distant places.

The Swedish nobleman Ture Bjelke complained of how difficult and troublesame the land road was from Vyborg to Oulu in 1556. Therefore people usually tried to use smaller water routes and carry boats over portages. (Handlingar till upplysning af Finlands häfder, nr. 148)

Unlike today, the medieval world was predominantly a world of water routes. It was much easier to reach another town by a river or sea than to walk a shorter distance through roadless forests. According to Adam of Bremen, a journey from Skåne to Birka took five days and from Birka to Ruzzia (River Neva?) also five days (Adam, schol. 126 (121)). Petr Sorokin has calculated that from Pskov, the travel of 65 kilometres on a land road to Novgorod took four days while from Pskov to Tartu (75 kilometres) on the lake took only one day. From the perspective of Stockholm, Vyborg and Lübeck were rather near but the inland parish of Sysmä in southern Finland was far away. (Sorokin 1997: 16, 19.)

The integration did not, however, depend only on the available means of communication and other technical matters. The degree of interest shown by groups and individuals was also important, and therefore the development could take steps both forwards and backwards.

From this perspective, Europe was a network with holes in it. One could find an abrupt periphery in the neighbourhood of a big centre, as in the case of Rome and the surrounding mountains, or Venice and the adjacent marshes. On the other hand, some very distant regions were psychologically very close to the major centres, e.g. Iceland from the eleventh to the thirteenth century. Certain central areas may also have disappeared from the map in the course of time, as happened with Iceland, Ireland and the Scottish Highlands during the late-medieval period.

In the same way, while the centres of the Viking kings in Sweden were in Götaland, this area started to decline during the reign of the *Äkta Folkungar*, whose realm was centred on Mälardalen in the east. Because of this development in the twelfth century, the Baltic Sea connection brought south-western Finland into the core area of the emerging realm, because the 'new Sweden' was a Baltic Sea realm.

There were seven parishes in the Trondenes area of northern Norway in the mid-fourteenth century and fourteen by the end of the Middle Ages, but these were all on islands and along the coast, since Norway as such did not exist in medieval times, when the area was merely 'the way to the north' (*norrvegr*). The influence of the settlements petered out inland within a couple of kilometres, after which the territory was inhabited by nomadic Sámi. The first church in this area, at Karesuando in Enontekiö, was built only in 1661.

The fact that the site of that church is still known even today as Markkina (market) testifies to the limits of information distribution and integration in that area, and also to the limits of the supra-local consciousness. The first contacts between the populations were through the ritual exchange of gifts, which did not mean a physical or psychological encounter. Later the collection of taxes was the reason for the encounter, but this was so superficial that there was still little cultural exchange. It was only proper trade that created a need to communicate and be aware of the existence of an alien world.

In the same way, we may ask about the impact of the Viking *austrvegr* on the local populations along the Gulf of Finland, beside Lake Ladoga and the River Daugava, in Narva, Velikaya and Volkhov and on the Upper Volga and Dnepr. The realm of Rus' was formed as a network of trading stations and castles in this region between the ninth and twelfth centuries, just as that of Norway was formed along the Atlantic coast of Scandinavia, and archaeological finds and other sources in the southern areas and around these centres suggest that the impact was considerable. The culture of Staraya Ladoga and Novgorod was close to that of contemporary Western European centres, and in some respects also to that of Constantinople. The inhabitants of Korela were aware of this, but I do not think that this level was reached in eastern Finland inland, e.g. in Tohmajärvi, which was connected to Lake Ladoga by a water route.

We may say that Rome was a true part of 'our world' in high-medieval Paris, Trondenes, Turku, Hauho, Staraya Ladoga and Korela, as also in Cairo, Bukhara, Herat and Samarkand, because it is mentioned in the Koran, too, but I am not at all sure whether it was familiar to the fishermen of the northern part of Lake Saimaa in the Middle Ages. Since Rome was so well known and was revered as the city of God, its influence even increased from the twelfth century onwards. Realms and parishes were tied together physically by canon law and subordinated to Rome, so that this city was much more clearly present in the everyday lives of the people of Hauho in inland western Finland than was Sigtuna or Stockholm.

The 'centre' is indeed very much a question of perspective. From the Christian point of view, the centre was Rome (or Jerusalem) and the notion of periphery meant only a mental or physical distance from that point. Although Moslems knew about Rome, the tenth-century Persian geography book *Hudud-al-alam* called Baghdad the centre of the world, and for Temür Lenk (d. 1405) it was Samarkand.

Finally, the perspectives of our own world may also obscure our understanding of the structures of the past. Of course, Vasco da Gama (d. 1524) is a well-known explorer of the water route to India, as every school girl and boy of today knows. The reasons lie in the expansion of European dominance after the sixteenth century and, in the case of Finland, our identity as Western Europeans and EU members. A Portuguese sailor forms part of our own European common past, even though the place where he lived is some 6,000 kilometres away from Helsinki. By contrast, the merchant Afanasii Nikitin, whose home town of Tver is less than 900 kilometres from Helsinki, visited India and Ethiopia in the 1470s. Russian merchants were common in Finnish towns in the fifteenth and sixteenth centuries although Portuguese traders had scarcely ever been heard of. Hence when the townspeople of Vyborg in the early sixteenth century knew something about India, the information came via Russia and not from Portugal.

Whose Truth, and Which World?

The western world of the 1950s was a uniform and therefore easily comprehensible one. There were uniform ways of living and celebrating. Today we are obliged to speak about variations within the world and a universe of overlapping worlds. The subcultures do not share each other's values, and there may be several cultures in the same urban area which have nothing to do with each other but which are well linked in real time with other similar cultures in cities on the opposite side of the world. A business man can reach another continent by jet within a few hours, but his neighbour may never have travelled abroad and an alcoholic in a suburban pub may be totally unaware of the www realities of modern civil society.

The medieval world was a world of small centres and separate cultures. Peripheries and rural areas were isolated units, and a small town could be composed of subcultures of people who had their own languages, laws, religions and so forth. but were living physically in the same place with few mutual contacts. On the other hand, they may have formed dense networks with corresponding groups in other towns, as was the case with the Jews, Armenians, North German merchants and others. The Christian subcultures had, moreover, a common supra-local basic Christian culture, which to a certain extent created a common identity all over the Christian world.

Christianity is a doctrine concerned with a universal world order, and this created a togetherness among those who were in contact with each other at the ruling level and were obliged to travel a lot. A distinguished churchman or a king would have travelled, but ordinary people did not. Thus the worldview of an ordinary man was very local, so that he would receive information on the outside world through intermediaries such as priests and tradesmen. (Korpela forthcoming b.)

The Old Russian word *mir'* means 'world', 'peace' and 'village community', and the Arab *umma* also refers to both the world and the local community in a village (the area served by one mosque). In kalevalaic poetry, the world was an island, so that home formed the world for a local community, in the sense of being its 'micro-space', and the relation of this community to the outside world was a complicated one. (Tarkka 2005: 258–266, 275–282, 286–292.)

The first route from a village to the outside world was not always the road to the next market place, and this was especially true in the northern Eurasian peripheries, where trade was not essential. The first way out went upwards, or downwards: it was the shaman's journey to the heavens or the underworld. The most important division was that between the visible world (Finn. *tämänilmainen* [literally 'this air space']) and the invisible world (*tuonilmainen* [literally 'that air space']). The idea of a world beyond the visible one did not mean something supernatural, however, but first and foremost a space beyond the immediate society. (Tarkka 1990: 238–259.)

Anna-Leena Siikala connects the understanding of the mythical Pohjola area of the Finnic epics with the understanding of time. The mythic concept of history does not make a clear and unambiguous distinction between this world and the world of the deceased. By comparison with our way of conceptualising the world, the indigenous cultures composed their mental map of symbolic meanings in a way that resulted in a quite different appreciation of physical geography, including the micro-space. The concept of space consisted of many levels rather than of long distances. (Siikala 2002: 287, 300–302, 313–323, 328–329.)

Besides hunting, the first physical contacts with the outside world were connected with the exchange of goods, which in the Merovingian Period expanded strongly in the northern European and Baltic areas, as elsewhere. The isolated island of kalevalaic poetry was connected with other worlds, which created an identity that distinguished its inhabitants from outsiders. The 'others' were tradesmen, agricultural peasants and servants of rulers. (Korpela 2008: *passim*; Hansen & Olsen 2004: 31–42.)

This view shaped the definitions of the route, the border and the truth. The invisible was present in the home village, but the road to the visible world outside became broader. This increased the flow of information and people's consciousness of the 'other' and started to marginalise the 'old'. To go out of the village was to cross a border. (Tarkka 2005: 258–266, 275–282, 286–292; Litzén 1977: 324–335.)

The traditional landscape was divided into spaces: everyday, holy, female and male spaces and so forth, and there were invisible borders that separated the home from the forest and defined certain areas as forbidden – e.g. holy hills, peninsulas, islands and lakes, which were frequently referred to in Finnish by the word *hiisi*. These belonged to the world of the deities and the deceased, which was open only to the shaman. (Anttonen 1996: 116–123.)

Even today, we can find traces of the old divisions of spaces in traditional place names. Finnish toponyms beginning with *nais-* sometimes marked places which were separated off for women. The local folklore tells that *Naislahti* ['Women's Bay'] was the place where the women used to disembark from boats on the way to Sortavala, while the men continued on Lake Ladoga around *Hiidenniemi* ['Peninsula of Hiisi']. (Koski 1967: 176–179.)

In the centre of the town of Mikkeli there is a hill called *Linnanmäki* ['Castle Hill'], and facing it one called *Naisvuori* ['Women's Hill']. The town is an early-medieval foundation and market centre, which, of course, had its own hill fort (actually several of them), but the occurrence of a possibly separate area for women is interesting in this connection. (Korpela 2008: 164–170.)

Christianisation was therefore important, because it implemented a supra-local, universal doctrine and changed the indigenous worldview of areas such as the understanding of time. According to the early Church Fathers, the Christians formed a 'universal nation' and Christianity was a historical ideology which disseminated the truths and worldview of the Middle East and the Mediterranean throughout the world. While shamanistic learning was local, and the local reality was sufficient for it, Christianity secretly instilled in all Christians a consciousness of distant people, foreign languages and other cultures. When a medieval Finnic hunter-fisher heard about wine, mustard, thorns, olives, palm trees, emperors, Pharisees and exotic animals such as lions or hyenas all mentioned in the Christian Gospels, this must have been very odd and incomprehensible to him.

The truth of the shaman was a matter of tradition, but the king's Christian truth was a matter of the future: do we own the land or do we just use it according to a moral code, do we have to pay taxes or not, and are the decisions of royal servants, Christian priests or shamans and family elders the supreme law? (Korpela 2011a: 124–136; 2011c: 331–344; 2012e: 222–240.)

The encounter of cultures also resulted in practical collisions. The forest dwellers were not visible in the eyes of the king's authorities, and these authorities did not acknowledge the rights of these people. King Albrecht of Mecklenburg gave the area of Sääminginsalo in the central Saimaa region as a fief to the noblemen Nils and Bengt Thuresson in the 1360s as if it were an uninhabited area, but there are a number of records pointing to an earlier human presence there. The inhabitants had their own system for defining the rights to use and own natural resources and to resolve everyday issues, but these things were not real from the perspective of European rulers.[4]

King Albrecht of Mecklenburg decided in February 1365 that one Matisse of Orewall had founded a farm according to the law in the wilderness of Valkeala, but the local inhabitants had expelled him from the region. The king ordered the men to return the lands to Mattisse. A folk tale also attests this Matisse, but it considers him a criminal. Following the royal declaration, Matisse had most probably taken possession of lands which belonged to somebody else according to the indigenous norms. He represented the new European order that did not acknowledge the traditional rights of use beyond the king's jurisdiction.[5]

In 1564 Judge Jesper Sigfridsson decided in Tavisalmi that the peasant Per Ollikainen could keep a field that the 'fisher peasants' had cleared. Who were these fisher peasants (*fiiskare bonder*) and why did Per Ollikainen receive their fields? According to the 'law' of slash-and-burn culture, the field belonged to the person who had cleared it, and now the king's judge was making a distinct exception in this respect. Is it possible that they were hunter-fishers who did not pay taxes and were therefore judged to be living outside the realm and beyond the king's protection? (Domböcker för Savolax 1559 och 1561–1565, p. 177.)

The Christianisation of the entire area of Finland and Karelia took a very long time, however, and, except in a few parish centres on the Baltic Sea coast (south and southwest Finland and the shores of Lake Ladoga), had not been achieved by the end of the Middle Ages. Pagan place names continued to exist and the very few Christian ones date only from the sixteenth century or later. No crosses have been added to cult stones surviving from pagan times, so that the famous rock drawing at Besov Nos on the eastern shore of Lake Onega is unique in the region in this respect.[6] This indicates superficial contacts, a lack of outside influences and therefore also a poor consciousness of Christianity and its culture and so a gap between this world and the supra-local universal Europe known by the Vikings proper.

Scholarly literature customarily divides the world into peripheries, semi-peripheries and central areas. This works well in the Central European context, but one must realise, however, that the most 'central' region of Finland, the south-western part of the country around Turku, was a European periphery in the Middle Ages. There was only one bishopric in the whole of Finland, while Calabria in southern Italy had twenty-two bishoprics at that time and even Iceland had two. The rest of Finland belonged to an outer space in the European context. But as related above, the centre is a question of perspective. From a shaman's point of view, his village was the centre of the world. According to Åke Hultkrantz, one characteristic feature of circumpolar religions is the 'world pillar', as manifested in the cult of stones and trees (Hultkrantz 1996: 31). A cup-marked-stone or other stone formation or holy tree was the local totem, forming a connection with the other world and thus serving as the centre of the community's world. A local observer would always look at the situation from his own perspective and describe it within its visible limits. Thus the results would vary and no common consciousness of the truth and the world could establish itself. This must be remembered when we read medieval texts or try to analyse the attitudes of a king or a village peasant to a concrete event that took place somewhere. While it was vital for one person, it may not even have existed for another.

The Knowledge of Rulers and Subjects

A prince would try to collect information on the affairs of his realm and send messages out in order to impose his authority. This took place through a personal network of loyal servants and allies. The information was limited, however, on account of problems of reachability, and mostly applied to the neighbourhood of local centres, i.e. parishes, castles and markets. These served as knowledge centres in their own time, and it was there that supra-local consciousness was formed and transmitted in two directions.

The centres were situated at the intersections of communication routes, e.g. confluences between two water systems, or points of contact between overland routes and waterways. These were already dwelling places in the Stone Age. (Korpela 2008: 30; Makarov 1997: 48–50.)

The people of the centres were subjects of the ruler and members of the realm, and they received information from the ruler and the Church. The consciousness of the prince was somewhat limited on this level, however, for he could control the reality of the situation, exercise his authority and collect information only in the knowledge centres. His world and the power he enjoyed in it did not reach the distant dwelling places of the hunter-fishers.

The need for new information was not the reason for forest dwellers to visit these places, however. The exchange of goods, although a frightening procedure and therefore ritualised, was almost obligatory for the forest dwellers in order to acquire certain items such as salt, iron tools and luxury goods. (Gustin 2004: 219–221; Hodges 1982: 53–57.) Similarly, this was the only way for traders to obtain furs and other forest items.

Looked at from this perspective, the Swedish–Russian peace treaty and border of 1323 never existed. The king had one perspective on it from Stockholm, and was concerned about the interests of German traders and business around the Neva, which was also in the interests of the Novgorodian lords. The division of the land areas may have interested the castellans of Vyborg and Korela, but only in the southernmost part and on a general level. The hunter-fishers of the inland area did not know anything about such a peace and did not understand the idea of dividing the land. None of the participants would have comprehended the notion of a border in the form of a line crossing the landscape, and a 'peace' meant for them not a treaty concluded after a war but above all an agreement to secure trade. (Korpela 2002: 384–397; 2006c: 454–469; Katajala 2012: 23–48.)

The prince could only increase his power and expand his world by forming new centres, i.e. by extending the parish network and building royal mansions. Tax collection was in the interests of the Church and the king, and both tried to bind more people under the control of the centre. They invited forest dwellers to till the land in the vicinity and enjoy their protection, and the forest dwellers were glad of the contact with a centre on account of their need for products. At the same time, of course, they became contaminated by its information system, their consciousness of the supra-local world expanded and they communicated this information to the outlying villages. It was the encounter between these two worlds that created a consciousness of identity and togetherness, and also of the existence of common enemies. (Korpela 2011: 331–344.)

The most important process taking place from the fourteenth to the seventeenth centuries was the territorialisation of royal power, which started with the formation of a ruling network and grew as the network became denser. The ruler gained supremacy when his network was so dense and permanent that he was able to destroy other sources of power within a certain geographical area, for then he could declare his own laws and truths that were binding on everyone. This territorialisation was important because it fixed the exact borders of absolute royal power and at the same time eliminated the influence of any similar power centre on the other side of the border. (Korpela 2012b: 168–199.)

Knowledge is power, and therefore an absolute ruler had to remain in control of information and its distribution, and simultaneously had to ensure that knowledge of other cultures was marginalised to the extent of being 'non-knowledge'. It was this latter practice that finally resulted in persecution of the shamans and other representatives of the old culture and the exercising of control over the doctrines and scholarly writings of the Church. It also led in time to the pre-modern custom of witch-hunting, control over the universities and the censorship of publications. (Korpela 2008: 289–293.)

In the Persian-Turkish world, this development of power formation and formation of supra-local consciousness took another direction than in the European Christian world. Realms were formed around local societies (the *umma*), the people of which were called the 'protected ones' (*ra'āyā/reāyā*), because the local lord took care of their well-being. There were no laws or ruler's decisions, but the lord used his absolute power to act as a shepherd of his flock according to a moral code, *şerīt*. In fact, the *umma* formed a micro-world outside of which "there existed nothing which could belong to us" (Denny 1997: 1210). (Franger 1986: 492–493.)

When absolute power was in the hands of a local lord without any legal limits, the whole of society was formed around loose coalitions of chieftains, families and clans. The supreme ruler was supported by regional warlords and was unable to involve himself in local affairs. He could remain in power only as long as he had authority over sufficient numbers of local lords. (Mukminova 1985: 17.)

These two patterns both influenced the formation of a society in the Russian area, which in turn had an impact on developments in Karelia. The basic unit of Muscovite, and later Russian, society was the village society called a *mir'* ['peace, world(!)']. This was controlled by a local lord and from the perspective of its members it meant a 'micro-world'. The village society was integrated through a very strong sense of social control, togetherness, termed in Russian *sobornost'*, which overruled laws and stressed unanimity among the people as the supreme value, so that society was placed under the authority of its leading personages. (Eklof 1981: 209–210; Budovnits & Bromlei 1986: 48–49.)

This system resulted in a controlled, limited consciousness of the distant world and underlined the role of the local village society, making the world beyond a dangerous topic and something which was of no concern to ordinary people. The concept of a border, *granitsa*, is still a frightening one in the Russian language and culture, a line which separates us from aliens. Thus, from this perspective, information and consciousness are limited to the information which the local leader allows to circulate, e.g. a strict religious adherence to the law, but nothing new. In the other direction, it limits the possibilities for the supreme ruler to establish his own authority and distribute his information at the local level, which means that such a society is even today a network of 'politicians' who distribute information to the people only to the extent that they think useful and exploit the local people as resources of their own. The consequence is that quite democratic elections tend to deliver unanimous results at the local level.

Concrete Contacts between the North-Eastern Periphery and the European Centres

The written sources point to some connections with the European north-eastern periphery from the Viking Age onwards, but only very superficial ones. These reflect a reorientation of the eastern European fur-trade routes from the region of the Upper Volga to that west of Lake Onega. The sources alone do not tell us anything, but if we combine them with the increasing number of imported artefacts from the same period to be found over the entire area, they confirm the smooth inauguration and early penetration of new cultural influences such as Christianity among the local populations. (Korpela 2008: 77–83.)

The Viking Age innovations in terms of transportation techniques reflect the same development in the area. Boats of the Mekrijärvi type and the like were introduced on the lakes and rivers of Finland, northern Scandinavia and northern Russia at this time, as they had a far better transport capacity than the old dugout canoes. According to Janne Vilkuna, the Mekrijärvi boat was the first type to be equipped with oars, as the earlier types were propelled only with paddles. One interesting fact that may connect this with the increasing Viking trade is that the Finnish word for an oar, *airo*, is a Scandinavian loan-word (cf. *åra*).[7]

On the other hand, if we look at the number of references and finds, we must admit how few there are. Byzantine artefacts are limited to only a couple, whereas this material is rather common in Scandinavia and in the Russian and Baltic areas. Christian objects are generally rare over the whole area east of Lake Päijänne and north of the Salpausselkä Ridge. (Korpela 2012a.)

South-western and western Finland were integrated into the culture of Sweden by the end of the thirteenth century, while eastern Finland, Karelia and the Dvina region were peripheral areas engaged in the fur trade and connected with the Viking trading network through waterways, mainly via Lakes Ladoga and Onega. The traditional notion of an east–west dichotomy within the area of modern Finland is a misinterpretation. A decline in artefacts dating from after the early fourteenth century reflects a re-peripherisation of the area from the perspective of European trade, which remained for next two centuries. Simultaneously, cultural contacts must have declined and only Novgorodian raids for the capture of prisoners seem to have continued. (Korpela 2008: 217–225; 2006b: 373–384; 2012c; 2012f: 275–291.)

Written culture was the prerogative of the Church, and finally, from fourteenth century onwards, of the new administration, which signified a great step towards the formation of a pan-European culture and supra-local consciousness. Western Finland was influenced by this culture in late-medieval times, and the other parts of the country were integrated into it smoothly in the course of the sixteenth and seventeenth centuries in connection with the strong pre-modern tendency for realm formation and the territorialisation of power. This in turn opened up the local cultures towards a more supra-local culture and meant an expansion of consciousness about distant areas and people. The final formation of a supra-local identity dates back only to the nineteenth century, however. (Korpela 2006: 278–286.)

From the perspective of biological contacts, the area studied here was a tightly closed one. Population growth took place from the inside without any appreciable inputs from the outside. (Korpela 2012b; forthcoming b.) This limited the distribution of new knowledge of distant regions and the consciousness of supra-locality, because practically no new people arrived in the local society with distinct information of their own.

Various innovations reached even the most remote corners of the area, of course, the first things which were introduced into the local culture normally being ones that were obviously useful. Pottery, on the other hand, remained highly conservative, and large-scale field cultivation was introduced late. Loan words related to the innovations are to be found in the various languages, but in both cases the process seems to have been very slow. (Korpela 2008: 105–111, 128–135.)

The most famous case is the Christian vocabulary. The first contacts with Christians date back to the Viking Age, and the first loan words from the east are from this period. This does not reflect any successful missionary work, but only contacts and the awareness of a novelty. A new type of shaman must be referred to in a new way, as a priest (*pappi* < *pop'*), because he was not actually a shaman. A new type of amulet must also have a name, and it was therefore called a cross (*risti* < *krest'*). (Cf. Häkkinen; Kallio.) The main Christian vocabulary as such is early modern, and the final introduction of Christianity dates to the eighteenth and nineteenth centuries, when church cemeteries were also adopted on a large scale. (Korpela 2005: 56–57; 2012a.)

However, in the interpretation of sources concerning concrete contacts one must be most careful. Artefacts and technical innovations were distributed to peripheral areas perhaps very slowly, if we think of this as an everyday procedure. For example, an object produced in Novgorod may have arrived in northern Finland through a chain of intermediators and therefore taken many years. An innovation which has been adopted in an area 'simultaneously' from the perspective of a modern observer may have been introduced into the area in question over several generations. Although scholars sometimes say on the basis of written sources that medieval Novgorodians and Karelians used to go to fish and to hunt on the Gulf of Bothnia, and also to collect taxes there (Kirkinen 1963: 141), we must think what it really meant in practice to go to fish over five hundred kilometres through pathless terrain and to transport a lot of fish home. We must also think why they would do this, as plenty of fish are available in the home lakes and rivers. Perhaps the source text had some other political context and nobody did in fact go to fish and to hunt in this way.

Geographical representations of the northeast may be expected to indicate the knowledge and consciousness that existed in the centres regarding the periphery. Medieval cartography was more of a literary genre, however, and it is only pre-modern cartography that tried to map the real world according to its physical landscape. (Lindgren 1991: 1021–1024.) Both can nevertheless be of considerable value to the scholar.

Except the twelfth-century Arabic geography of Idrisi, which is, however, in this respect problematic (Tuulio [Tallgren] 1936: map 1 and *passim*), eastern Fennoscandia did not exist on medieval maps, and the rare geographical descriptions spoke of mystic figures, as was generally the case with distant, alien regions. The Novgorodian chronicles contain several references to an area named Zavolots'e. This was a strange, remote place of long summer days and long winter nights that was inhabited by pagan prophets and fur traders. (Makarov 1997: 48–50.) This concept did not change during the Middle Ages, whereas the image of the Baltic area altered radically after the thirteenth century as it transformed from 'other' to 'ours'. (Tamm 2009: 11–35.)

The early-modern maps include Finland, which is already mentioned as a part of Scandinavia in a version of Ptolemy's map made in Ulm in 1482, although Jacob Ziegler's map of 1532 was the first to depict Finland as a peninsula. (*Vanhoja Suomen karttoja* 1967: 16–19.)

Gradually the geographical descriptions started to describe the area consistently as a part of the Christian world, but its northern and eastern margins still formed a land of witches and shamans for the sixteenth-century authors (Korpela 2008: 54). This increase in factual information coincided with the penetration of administrative functions into the periphery and the territorialisation of royal power.

Trade Ends the 'Viking Age' in Peripheries

Early trade had little to do with international commerce in the modern sense. It was an exchange of goods, sometimes a matter of robbery and frequently an encounter ritual. The main aspect was the acquisition of goods, not their sale as it is today, and therefore the early armies were not administrative instruments but commercial ones. (Gustin 2004: 11–14, 154–180, 201–203, 240–242; Hodges 1982: 53.)

The idea of gathering wealth by conducting proper business presupposes an understanding of the value added to commodities in the exchange chain. This system requires that the trader should see how much cheaper a product is in one place than in another and how much it would cost to transport the product. All primitive trade is based on the idea that the cultural value and meaning of one and the same object will change during a transition process. This differential value makes such an exchange a 'win-win situation'.

However, a straightforward exchange will not take account of a third party somewhere else who may value the commodity even more highly, and therefore the procedure must be regarded as 'primitive' rather than 'proper' trade. (Appadurai 1988: 26–29; Casanelli 1988: 236–257.)

The high-medieval Italian commercial guides already defined price levels for various products in distant markets and organised financing systems with this in mind (Francesco Balducci Pegolotti). Thus the Hanseatic League traders also transferred products between distant markets and earned additional money in this way. This was not a familiar undertaking for the forest dwellers, however, because it called for supra-local information on markets and prices. The monetary economy and money-lending reached the forests only in the pre-modern period, with the penetration of administrative functions and the parish network. It was the parish priests who were the first moneylenders in the peripheral areas.

The growth of long-distance trade also altered people's understanding of time. While the annual cycle was a reality in the forests, business planning and production needed a conceptualisation of the future. The traders had to know when the products would be ready and could be delivered to the customers and when payment would be made. Christianity supported this development, because it was a religion of linear time: the basic line governing world events proceeded from the Garden of Eden to the new Paradise and the second coming of Jesus Christ.

This changed people's understanding of distances and geography and created a concrete consciousness of 'otherness', because the needs of others formed the foundation of the new concept of trade, in which the seller rather than the customer was the active participant. This presupposed further improvements in information and communications, and the world moved from rumours and mystic beliefs to empirical facts and from prophecies to planning. The result was an expansion in consciousness of the world and the emergence of uniform linguistic concepts, as it was essential for people separated by long distances to understand each other. This created in turn many pidgin languages, such as the 'Inglis' of the North Sea coast, the Greek-Arabic-Italian mixtures of the Mediterranean and Hansa German, and it undoubtedly influenced the development of the Finno-Ugrian language of the north-eastern forest regions. Thus distant peripheries started to be connected to trade routes in a concrete fashion and to develop a supra-local consciousness that changed their worlds.

This realistic conceptualisation of the world and its resources also constituted an instrument and possibility for the formation of royal power. This was the basic reason for the king building his castle of Nyslott in the Lake Saimaa periphery in the 1470s. The local resources offered a realistic opportunity for him, he perceived them as useful and he decided to establish territorial control over them. (Korpela 2012d: 86–91.)

After this and similar actions of the fifteenth century, the Swedish and Novgorodian/Muscovite sides made a concrete and obligatory division of territories and their resources. This means that a territorial border became visible in the local culture, too, and that locals started to identify themselves more regionally and as subjects of the prince.

King Gustavus Vasa continued the policy of the building of royal mansions (*Konungx gårdh*), and he was already convinced in 1555 that the local peasants were defending *theris egenn gräntz* ['their own border'] in the area of Nyslott bailiwick against Muscovy (Konung Gustaf des förstes, no. 25, p. 509). The measures that he took and his whole way of thinking were quite typical of activities in border regions throughout Europe in his time. (Ellis 2006: 29–37.)

The development still needed time and the king's opinion was not shared by all locals. Thus, on 28 February 1559, the court of Sääminki sentenced Koszma Ukkonen to be hanged because he had been in Russia (*Ryssze landt*) and had stolen a cow and a sheep from there and "so broken the peace between the two kings". (Savon tuomiokirjat 10, 195, 219; Lappalainen 1970: 436–437.) No supra-local information about the border and his position as a subject of the king had yet reached Koszma, although his name indicates that he had been baptised. Among the locals, such court judgement cemented, for time being, the opinion of the king.

Summary

Truth and information are always a part of culture and its information system. Peripheral forest cultures of north-eastern Europe consisted of small separated co-resident groups of people. Theses populations used local resources and contacts with the outer world were mostly limited. These isolated people lacked real information about distant regions. Therefore, the Viking Age hardly existed in Finland and Karelia except in regions on the Baltic Sea shore and in the south.

The reason was not only that the locals were not interested in the European Viking world but the Vikings and Scandinavian kings and Novgorodian lords had no real interest in these distant regions either. The few contacts increased a little with Viking trade, which reached these populations through exchange of goods. With these contacts cultural influences also reached distant places and changed the local understanding of world.

The formation of Christian kingdoms (state formation) after the twelfth century also meant the approach of administration to the Finnish and Karelian regions and the founding of the first parishes. This brought European Christian influences more regularly into the core regions and caused their easy dissemination among the more distant populations.

The formation of local centres and intensification of trade are the basic reasons for the reform of indigenous people's consciousness of their surroundings. The shamanistic reality that moved between three levels of the world but at the same time within invisible borders that existed in the immediate neighbourhood, such as those between home and forest, or those marking forbidden areas, such as holy hills, peninsulas and islands, was transformed into a supra-local Christian landscape. This process was completed only in the twentieth century, but its commencement in the late Viking Age already meant an increased consciousness of distant areas and the existence of foreigners.

The understanding of this diversity and the change in information about it is necessary for the understanding of history and historical processes in the area. It enables us to understand how local populations may have received information concerning the peace treaty of 1323 and understood it as a part of their own world. Similarly this opens up a way of speaking about 'Vikings' in Finland, and of considering whether there actually were any and what the locals could know about such a phenomenon, and finally, how this understanding changed from the tenth to the eighteenth century.

Notes

1 Mann 1986: 9–10, 17–18 , 20–24 , 27–30 , 376–390, 416–446; Korpela 2008: 14–15.
2 I do not involve myself in the discussion about shamanism and shamans. I use the words here only as unspecified names for heterogeneous local traditional and non-Christian ways of living and understanding the world. On this topic in a Finnish context, cf. Frog and see also the work of Anna-Leena Siikala (esp. 1992; 2002).
3 Hägerstrand 1991: 53–54, 187–188; Harrison 1998: 50–56; Stenqvist Millde 2000: 65–66, 73–74; 2007: 113–119.
4 REA: 187; Vilkuna 1971: 225–228; Parviainen 1976: 42; cf. Lehtosalo-Hilander 1988: 150–151; Räisänen 2003: 130–131; Korpela forthcoming a.
5 FMU VIII: 6585; Mulk 1996: 69–74; Rosén 1936: 95–111; Kepsu 1990: 110–111, 139; cf. also Nahkiaisoja 2003: 168–169.
6 Villads Jensen 2009: 145–147; Selch Jensen 2009: 156–159; Savvateev 1990: 16–25.
7 Taavitsainen 1999: 310–313; Taavitsainen *et al.* 2007: 49–87; Vilkuna 1998: 256–267.

References

Sources

Adam von Bremen. *Hamburgische Kirchengeschichte: magistri Adami Bremensis gesta Hammaburgensis ecclesiae pontificum.* edition tertia. Scriptores rerum Germanicarum in usum scholarum ex Monimentis Germaniae historicis separatim editi 63. Hannoverae / Lipsiae, 1917.

Domböcker för Savolax 1559 och 1561–1565 utgivna av riksarkivet redigerade av Kauko Pirinen, Finlands äldsta domböcker I, Helsingfors, 1954.

FMU = Finlands medeltidsurkunder samlade och i tryck utgifna af Finlands statsarkiv genom Reinh. Hausen, I–VIII, Kejserliga senatens/ Statsrådets tryckeri: Helsingfors 1910–1935.

Francesco Balducci Pegolotti, *La pratica della mercatura.* Ed. Allan Evans. The Mediaeval Academy of America Publications 24. Cambridge (Mass.), 1936.

Handlingar till upplysning af Finlands häfder utgifne af A. I. Arwidsson. Norstedt & Söner: Stockholm, I–IX, 1846–1857.

Konung Gustaf des förstes registratur med understöd af statsmedel i tryck utgifvet af kongl. Riks-Archivet genom Victor Granlund, 1-29. Handligar rörande Sveriges historia, första serie. Norstedt & Söner: Stockholm, 1861-1916.

REA = Registrum ecclesiae Aboensis eller Åbo domskyrkas svartbok med tillägg ur Skoklosters codex Aboensis. I tryck utgifven Finlands statsarkiv genom Reinh. Hausen. Helsingfors 1890.

Savon tuomiokirjat 1559 ja 1561–1565. Domböcker för Savolax 1559 och 1561–1565 utgivna av riksarkivet redigerade av Kauko Pirinen, Finlands äldsta domböcker I, Helsingfors, 1954.

Savvateev, Jurij Aleksandrovič, Kamennaja letopis' Karelij. Petroglifi Onežskogo ozera i Belogo Morja, Petrozavodsk, 1990.

Vanhoja Suomen karttoja - Old Maps of Finland, Helsinki, 1967.

Literature

Anttonen, Veikko. 1996. *Ihmisen ja maan rajat: "Pyhä" kulttuurisena kategoriana*. SKS toimituksia 646. Helsinki: Suomalaisen kirjallisuuden seura.

Appadurai, Arjun. 1988. Introduction: Commodities and the Politics of Value. In Arjun Appadurai (ed.). *The Social Life of Things: Commodities in Cultural Perspective*. Cambridge / New York: Cambridge University Press. Pp. 3–63.

Budovnits, I. U., & Yu. V. Bromlei. 1986. Verv'. In *The Modern Encyclopedia of Russian and Soviet History* (1976–2011). Gulf Breeze: Academic International Press. Vol. 42, pp. 48–50.

Casanelli, Lee. 1988. Qat: Changes in the Production and Consumption of Quasilegal Commodity in Northeast Africa. In Arjun Appadurai (ed.). *The Social Life of Things: Commodities in Cultural Perspective*. Cambridge / New York: Cambridge University Press: 236–257.

Denny, F. M. 2000. Umma. In *The Encyclopaedia of Islam: New Edition, Volume X: T–U*. Leiden: Brill. Pp. 859–863.

Eklof, Ben. 1981. Mir. *The Modern Encyclopedia of Russian and Soviet History* 22: 208–223.

Ellis, Steven G. 2006. Integration, Identities and Frontiers in the British Isles: A European Perspective. In Harald Gustafsson & Hanne Sanders (eds.). *Vid Gränsen. Integration och identiteter i det förnationella Norden*. Centrum för Danmarksstudier 10. Lund: MAKADAM. Pp. 19–45.

Franger, Bert. 1986. Social and Internal Economic Affairs. In Peter Jackson & Laurence Lockhart (eds.). *The Cambridge History of Iran in Seven Volumes, Volume 6: The Timurid and Safavid Periods*. Cambridge: Cambridge University Press. Pp. 506–507.

Gustin, Ingrid. 2004. *Mellan gåva och marknad: Handel, tillit och materiell kultur under vikingatid*. Lund Studies in Medieval Archaeology 34. Stockholm: Almqvist & Wiksell International.

Hägerstrand, Torsten. 1991. Landskapet. Framtiden. In Gösta Carlestam & Barbro Sollbe (eds.). *Om tidens vidd och tingens ordning: Texter av Torsten Hägerstrand*. Byggforskningsrådet 1991:21. Stockholm: Statens råd för byggnadsforskning.

Hansen, Lars Ivar & Bjørnar Olsen. 2004. *Samenes historie fram til 1750*. Oslo: Cappelen Akademisk Forlag.

Harrison, Dick. 1998. *Skapelsens geografi: Föreställningar om rymd och rum i medeltidens Europa*. Svenska Humanistiska Förbundet 110. Stockholm: Ordfront.

Hodges, Richard. 1982. *Dark Age Economics: The Origins of Towns and Trade A.D. 600–1000*. New Approaches in Archaeology. Bristol: Duckworth.

Hultkrantz, Åke. 1996. A New Look at the World Pillar in Arctic and Sub-Arctic Religions. In Juha Pentikäinen (ed.). *Shamanism and Northern Ecology*. Religion and Society 36. Berlin / New York: de Gruyter. Pp. 31–50.

Katajala, Kimmo. 2012. Drawing Borders or Dividing Lands? – The Peace Treaty of 1323 between Sweden and Novgorod in a European Context. *Scandinavian Journal of History* 37(1): 23–48.

Kepsu, Saulo. 1990. Valkealan asuttaminen. In Risto Hamari, Timo Miettinen, Saulo Kepsu (eds.). *Valkealan historia I*. Lahti: Valkealan kunta, kulttuuri- ja kotiseutulautakunta.

Kirkinen, Heikki. 1963. *Karjala idän kulttuuripiirissä*. Historiallisia tutkimuksia 67. Helsinki: Suomen Historiallinen Seura.

Korpela, Jukka. 2002. The Eastern Border of Finland after Noteborg: An Ecclesiastical, Political or Cultural Border? *Journal of Baltic Studies* 33(4): 384–397.

Korpela, Jukka. 2005. Kristillisyys Karjalassa ja Itä-Suomessa keskiajalla. *Suomen kirkkohistoriallisen seuran vuosikirja* 2005: 54–71.

Korpela, Jukka. 2006. Die schwedische Ostgrenze von Nöteborg bis Kardis: Eine Kirchengrenze, politische Grenze oder Kulturgrenze 1323–1660? – Eine Region des Ost-West-Gegensatzes? In Jörg Hackmann & Robert Schweitzer (eds.). *Nordeuropa als Geschichtsregion*. Veröffentlichungen der Aue-Stiftung 17. Lübeck: Schmidt- Römhild. Pp. 267–286.

Korpela, Jukka. 2006a. Aspects Concerning Communication and Contact Landscape of Medieval North Eastern European Subarctic Forest Zone. In I.I. Kuropteva (ed.). *Vostočnaja Finljandija i Rossijskaja Karelija: tradicija i zakon v žizni karel*. Petrozavodsk: Izdatel'stvo PetrGU. Pp. 23–42.

Korpela, Jukka. 2006b. Beyond the Borders in the European North East. In Outi Merisalo (ed.). *Frontiers in the Middle Ages: Frontières – Frontiers: Textes et études du moyen âge*. Turnhout: Brepols. Pp. 373–384.

Korpela, Jukka. 2006c. Keskiaikainen itäraja läpi itäisen Fennoskandian metsävyöhykkeen – mikä se on! *Historiallinen Aikakauskirja* 2006(4): 454–469.

Korpela, Jukka. 2006d. Kohtaamisia keskiaikaisen Itä-Fennoskandian metsissä. In Kari Alenius, Seija Jalagin, Markku Mäkivuoti, Sinikka Wunsch (eds.). *Mielikuvien Maanosat: Olavi K. Fältin juhlakirja*. Oulu: Redactores. Pp. 166–174.

Korpela, Jukka. 2007a. Jem' i Ladoga. Slavjane i finno-ugry. In A. N. Kirpičnikov (ed.). *Kontaktnye zony i vzaimodejstvie kul'tur*. Sankt-Peterburg.

Korpela, Jukka. 2007b. Time and Space in Karelian Backwoods. In A. M. Paškov, S. G. Verigin, T. Ju. Berdjaeva (eds.). *Istorija i kul'turnoe nasledie Severnogo Priladož'ja: vzgljad iz Rossii i Finljandii*, Petrozavodsk: PetrGU: 30–37.

Korpela, Jukka. 2008. *The World of Ladoga: Society, Trade, Transformation and State Building in the Eastern Fennoscandian Boreal Forest Zone ca. 1000–1555*. Nordische Geschichte 7. Berlin: Dr. Hopf.

Korpela, Jukka. 2011. 'To the Aggrandizement of the Realm of Sweden and Christianity': Taxes and Europeanization. In Steinar Imsen (ed.). *Taxes, Tributes and Tributary Lands in the Making of the Scandinavian Kingdoms in the Middle Ages*. Trondheim Studies in History. Trondheim: Tapir Academic Press: 331–344.

Korpela, Jukka. 2011a. Aspekter till östfinska familjen under medeltiden: Indicier till ett annorlunda system. Lars Ivar Hansen, Richard Holt & Steinar Imsen (eds.). *Nordens plass i middelalderens nye Europa: Samfunnsomdanning, sentralmakt og periferier*. Speculum Boreale 16. Tromsø: Orkana Akademisk. Pp. 124–136.

Korpela, Jukka. 2011b. In Deep, Distant Forests. In Marko Lamberg, Marko Hakanen & Janne Haikari (eds.). *Physical and Cultural Space in Pre-Industrial Europe: Methodological Approaches to Spatiality*. Lund: Nordic Academic Press. Pp. 95–123.

Korpela, Jukka. 2012a. Die Christianisierung der fenno-ugrischen Peripherie Europas: Zwei Theorien und peinliche Tatsachen. In M. Salamon, M. Hardt, M. P. Kruk, A. E. Musin, P. Špehar, A. Sulikowska-Gąska & M. Wołoszyn (eds.). *Rome, Constantinople and Newly-Converted Europe: Archaeological and Historical Evidence*. U źródeł Europy Środkowo-wschodniej/Frühzeit Ostmitteleuropas 1. Kraków / Leipzig / Rzeszów. Pp. 275–285.

Korpela, Jukka. 2012b. Keskiajan yhteiskunta. In Heikkilä, Tuomas (ed.). *Euroopan keskiajan historia*. Helsinki: WSOY. Pp. 168–199.

Korpela, Jukka. 2012c. Migratory Lapps and the Population Explosion of Eastern Finns: The Early Modern Colonization of Eastern Finland Reconsidered. In Charlotte Damm & Janne Saarikivi (eds.). *Networks, Interaction, Emerging Identities in Fennoscandia and beyond*. Mémoires de la Société Finno-Ougrienne 262. Helsinki: Société Finno-Ougrienne. Pp. 241–261.

Korpela, Jukka. 2012d. Nordöstliche Fennoskandien im späteren 15. Jahrhundert. *Castella Maris Baltici* 10: 85–92.

Korpela, Jukka. 2012e. Och starec Sergej köpte land och vattenområden och skogar och fiskeplatser: Jordegendom, skenköp och det europeiska väldet i östra Fennoskandien under senmedeltiden. In Sverre Bagge (ed.). *Statsutvikling i de nordiske rikene*. Bergen: Dreyer. Pp. 222–240.

Korpela, Jukka. 2012f. Sisä-Suomen asuttaminen ja väestön kasvu myöhäiskeskiajalla ja uuden ajan alussa. *Historiallinen Aikakauskirja* 2012/3.

Korpela, Jukka. Forthcoming a. "…and they took countless captives along": Finnic Captives and East European Slave Trade during the Middle Ages. In Christoph Wizenrath (ed.). *European Slavery, Ransom and Abolition in World History, 1500–1860*. Ashgate.

Korpela, Jukka. Forthcoming b. Warum besuchte Bruno Kiew in 1008? - Praktische und ideologische Aspekte seiner Reise nach Osten. In Christian Lübke & Mathias Hardt (eds.). *Der Heilige Brun von Querfurt*. Leipzig.

Koski, Mauno. 1967. *Itämerensuomalaisten kielten hiisi-sanue: Semanttinen tutkimus I*. Turun yliopiston julkaisuja - Annales Universitatis Turkuensis, Sarja C:5. Turku.

Lappalainen, Pekka. 1970. *Säämingin historia* I:1, Pieksämäki: Säämingin kunta.

Lehtosalo-Hilander, Pirkko-Liisa. 1988. *Esihistorian vuosituhannet Savon alueella: Savon historia I*. Toinen kokonaan uudistettu laitos. Kuopio: Kustannuskiila Oy.

Lindgren, U. 1991. Karte, Kartographie. *Lexikon des Mittelalters*. Vol. 5, pp. 1021–1024.

Litzén, Veikko. 1977. Om socknen. *Historisk Tidskrift för Finland* 62: 324–335.

Makarov, Nikolaj A. 1997. *Kolonizacija severnyh okrain Drevnej Rusi v XI - XIII vekah*, Moskva: Skriptorij.

Makarov, Nikolaj A. 1997. *Kolonizacija severnyh okrain Drevnej Rusi v XI - XIII vekah: Po materialam arheologičeskij pamjatnikov na volokah Belozer'ja i Poonež'ja*. Skriptorij: Moskva.

Mann, Michael. 1986. *The Sources of Social Power. Volume I: A History of Power from the Beginning to A.D. 1760*, Cambridge: Cambridge University Press.

Mukminova, R. G. 1985. *Social'naja differenciacija naselenija gorodov Uzbekistana v XV-XVI vv.* Izd. FAN uzbekskoj SSR: Taškent.

Mulk, Inga Maria 1996: The Role of the Sámi in Fur Trading during the Late Iron Age and Nordic Medieval Period in the Light of the Sámi Sacrificial Sites in Lapland, Northern Sweden. *Acta Borealia* 13: 47–80

Nahkiaisoja, Tarja. 2003. Uudisasuttajien aika (1750–1876). In Veli-Pekka Lehtola (ed.). *Inari–Aanaar–Inarin historia jääkaudesta nykypäivään*. Oulu: Inarin kunta, 2003: 165–215.

Parviainen, Leena. 1976. Suomen vuodenaikanimet. Unpublished MA thesis, University of Helsinki, Finnish Language. Library of the Archive of Names of Research Institute for the Languages of Finland, Helsinki.

Räisänen, Alpo. 2003. *Nimet mieltä kiehtovat: Etymologista nimistötutkimusta*. SKS toimituksia 936. Helsinki

Rosén, Ragnar. 1936. *Vehkalahden pitäjän historia I: Suur-Vehkalahden asutus- ja aluehistoria n. vuoteen 1610*. Vehkalahti: Vehkalahden kunta.

Selch Jensen, Carsten. 2009. How to Convert a Landscape: Henry of Livonia and the Chronicon Livoniae. In Alan V. Murray (ed.). *The Clash of Cultures on the Medieval Baltic Frontier*. Farnham: Ashgate. Pp. 151–168.

Siikala, Anna-Leena. 1992. *Suomalainen šamanismi: Mielikuvien historiaa*. Helsinki: Suomalaisen kirjallisuuden seura.

Siikala, Anna-Leena. 2002. *Mythic Images and Shamanism. A Perspective on Kalevala Poetry*. FF Communications No. 280. Helsinki: Suomalainen Tiedeakatemia.

Singer, H.-R. 1997. Umma. In *Lexikon des Mittelalters*. Vol. 8, p. 1210.

Sorokin, Petr. 1997. *Vodnye puti i sudostroenie na severo-zapade Rusi v srednevekov'e*. Sankt-Peterburg: Gosudarstvennyj universitet.

Stenqvist Millde, Ylva. 2000. Vägar inom räckhåll: Olika nivåer av kommunikation med exempel från Dalarna och Hälsningland. *Bebyggelsehistorisk tidskrift* 39: 65–82.

Stenqvist Millde, Ylva. 2007. *Vägar inom räckhåll: Spåren efter resande i det förindustriella bondesamhället*. Skrifter från forskningsprojektet Flexibilitet som tradition, Ängersjöprojektet 12. Stockholm Studies in Archaeology 39. Stockholm: Stockholms universitet.

Taavitsainen, Jussi-Pekka, Janne Vilkuna & Henry Forssell. 2007. *Suojoki at Keuruu: A Mid-Fourteenth Century Site of the Wilderness Culture in the Light of Settlement Historical Processes in Central Finland*. Annales Academiae Scientiarum Fennicae, humaniora 346. Helsinki: Suomalainen tiedeakatemia.

Taavitsainen, Jussi-Pekka. 1999. Wilderness Commerce and the Development of Boat Types: The Remains of the Hartola Boat. In Matti Huurre (ed.). *Dig It All. Papers Dedicated to Ari Siiriäinen*. Helsinki: The Finnish Antiquarian Society. The Archaeological Society of Finland. Pp. 307–313.

Tamm, Marek. 2009. A New World into Old Words: The Eastern Baltic Region and the Cultural Geography of Medieval Europe. In Alan V. Murray (ed.). *The Clash of Cultures on the Medieval Baltic Frontier*. Farnham: Ashgate. Pp. 11–35.

Tarkka, Lotte. 1990. Tuonpuoleiset, tämänilmaiset ja sukupuoli: Raja vienankarjalaisessa kansanrunoudessa. In Aili Nenola & Senni Timonen (eds.). *Louhen sanat: Kirjoituksia kansanperinteen naisista*. Suomalaisen Kirjallisuuden Seuran Toimituksia 520. Helsinki: Suomalaisen Kirjallisuuden Seura.

Tarkka, Lotte. 2005. *Rajarahvaan laulu: Tutkimus Vuokkiniemen kalavalamittaisesta runokulttuurista 1821–1921*. SKS toimituksia 1033. Helsinki: Suomalaisen Kirjallisuuden Seura.

Tuulio [Tallgren], O. J. 1936. *Du nouveau sur Idrīsī: Édition critique, traduction, études*. Studia Orientalia VI:3. Helsinki: Edidit societas orientalis Fennica.

Vilkuna, Janne. 1998. Suomen esihistoriallisen ajan veneet – Finska båtar från förhistorisk tid. In *Människor och båtar i Norden*. Sjöhistorisk årsbok 1998–1999. Stockholm: Föreningen Sveriges sjöfartsmuseum i Stockholm. Pp. 256–267.

Vilkuna, Kustaa. 1971. Mikä oli lapinkylä ja sen funktio. *Kalevalaseuran vuosikirja*, 51: 201–238

Villads Jensen, Kurt. 2009. Sacralisation of the Landscape: Converting Trees and Measuring Land in the Danish Crusade against Wends. In Alan V. Murray (ed.). *The Clash of Cultures on the Medieval Baltic Frontier*. Farnham; Ashgate. Pp. 141–150.

Mervi Koskela Vasaru

Bjarmaland and Contacts in the Late-Prehistoric and Early-Medieval North

A short introduction will be given here to those pieces of information that the medieval written sources reveal about Bjarmaland. The main focus of the chapter is on the contacts in the very north of Europe in the late-prehistoric and early-medieval era, as seen through those sources that mention Bjarmaland. Archaeological material is introduced as a means to further expand the otherwise cursory knowledge. This material is not plentiful, but contributes nevertheless to the overall picture.

Within Norwegian and Russian research, the medieval period commences after the conclusion of Viking Age (800–1050) whereas in Finland the periodisation commonly includes the Crusade Period (1050–1150/1300) before medieval times. One can also argue that there never existed a proper medieval period in northern Finland. However, the north of Europe does not exist in a vacuum and in order to link the northernmost areas with the rest of Europe it is important to associate the area with an internationally intelligible context, and this is most easily achieved if the general periodisation is followed. Dating archaeological material precisely is difficult, especially the Late Iron Age material (and weapons in particular) in northern Fennoscandia. Both the lack of written sources and difficulties of exact dating of artefacts make it convenient to use the terms the 'late-prehistoric period' and the 'early-medieval period', with a division at the end of the Viking Age around 1050, even if dating at times is very imprecise and timeframes may stretch over the division. This division is particularly convenient from an international point of view. However, regarding the lack of written sources and the problems of precise dating of archaeological material, for all practical purposes it is possible to say that the Viking Age in the north extended until around 1250, as suggested in the introduction. There is in my opinion only one consideration that advises against this, namely that the neighbouring countries have another practise, with the medieval period commencing after 1050. Keeping a similar division of chronological periods makes it easier to communicate research internationally. (For further discussion of periodisation in the context of Finnish research, see Ahola & Frog and Aalto.)

Bjarmaland ['land of the Bjarmar'] (in Latin texts *Biarmia, Byarmia*) is a northerly area whose inhabitants are known as *Bjarmar* (in Old Norse; appearing *Biarmar* in Latin texts) or *Beormas* (in Old English) (see Jansson 1936: 39–40; Ross 1940; Haavio 1965: 47). Our knowledge of Bjarmaland is based on medieval written sources, but no area or group of people are known by these names today and this has given Bjarmaland a certain mystical aura and opened up various interpretations of the rather scant sources.

The roots of modern research go back to the sixteenth century. To begin with Bjarmaland was placed on the Kola Peninsula, whereas during the seventeenth century the location of Bjarmaland was repeatedly identified as Lapland. Another theory with roots in the research of the seventeenth century connected the Perm' area of Russia with Bjarmaland. The association of Bjarmaland with the Northern Dvina River goes back to the sixteenth century; this link started gaining popularity during the eighteenth century and remains a popular interpretation within modern research. Most scholars suggest that Bjarmaland was divided in two (*Biarmia ulterior* and *Biarmia citerior*) with one part located by the Northern Dvina River and the other on the Kola Peninsula (as indicated in Ohthere's account). (Ross 1940: 6–7; Jackson 2002: 167–170, 172; Koskela Vasaru 2008: 55–58) The idea of division is based on the interpretation of the Magnus brothers, who in 1554 and 1555 in separate works[1] interpreted the line "in ulteriorem Byarmiam navigant" in Saxo's *Gesta Danorum* (Olrik & Ræder 1931: 228) as a reference to a division of Bjarmaland. However, *Biarmia ulterior* and *Biarmia citerior* were never mentioned as such in the sources and the more correct translation of "in ulteriorem Byarmiam navigant" simply reads 'sailed on to the further coast of Bjarmaland' (Fisher 1979: 251) (or more literally translated 'sailed further into Bjarmaland').

Bjarmians have been ethnically identified with many groups of people including Karelians, Vepsians, Votes, Permians, Finns and Chuds. A number of twentieth-century researchers have suggested that 'Bjarmian' was not an ethnic name but rather a professional one and the Bjarmians were wandering traders and members of a trade organisation of mixed ethnic origin (Komi-Zyrian, Karelian, Vepsian, Sámi, Russian) (Ross 1940: 49-59; Vilkuna 1980: 647–651; Carpelan 1993: 231–233; Hansen 1996: 45–46, 51–52). The Scandinavian sources only mention contacts between Norwegians and the Bjarmians of the coastal area of the White Sea. There are no references to contacts in the more easterly area (Perm') or inland areas of the Russian north. *Historia Norvegiae* refers to *utrique Biarmones* ['two kinds of Bjarmians'] (see Ekrem & Mortensen & Fisher 2006: 54–55) but this has been regularly interpreted as a geographical division (cf. *Biarmia ulterior* and *Biarmia citerior* north and south of the Kantalahti Bay of the White Sea) rather than an ethnic one (Jackson 2002: 165–166, 170–171). The written sources contain nothing that would directly support the idea that Bjarmians were multi-ethnic wandering traders. The general setting in the sagas that mention the habitat of the Bjarmians describes permanently settled people with houses and burial grounds.[2] The descriptions of geography set Bjarmaland on the map in a way similar to how for instance

Denmark, Gotland or England are described in the same passages (see Rafn 1852: 405; Einarsson 1985: 79). There may have been inhabitants of many ethnic origins in late-prehistoric and medieval times in many of the areas that are mentioned alongside Bjarmaland, but this has not given rise to theories that people living in the area should be regarded as wandering traders. One may wonder if this assumption is attached to Bjarmaland because the area and people are not known today as opposed to the other areas that are mentioned.

In order to create an image of historical Bjarmaland, it is essential to approach the subject through the written sources. There are around thirty medieval texts[3] that mention Bjarmaland or Bjarmians. Most often Bjarmaland appears in kings' sagas (*konunga sögur*) or in mytho-heroic or legendary sagas (*fornaldar sögur*). It also appears in few Icelandic family sagas (*Íslendinga sögur*) as well as in some texts of a more geographical nature, one Anglo-Saxon text and a number of annals. The earliest source dates to the late ninth century. The majority of the texts were written during the thirteenth century (even though some of the sources have been dated to the late twelfth century and most of the mytho-heroic sagas are later than the thirteenth century), but the events they relate may nevertheless be of earlier date, and especially the kings' sagas refer to Viking Age events and the tenth century in particular in regard to Bjarmaland. One of the annals that mentions Bjarmaland is dated as late as the sixteenth century. Thus both the temporal and stylistic range of the written sources is wide and not all sources can be regarded as equally trustworthy. It is particularly important not to rely on mytho-heroic sagas alone.[4] In view of the length of the chapter it is not possible to introduce more than a selection of sources in detail, and there is space for only the most cursory discussion. For a more detailed discussion, I refer the reader to my dissertation on Bjarmaland (Koskela Vasaru 2008).

The Historicity of Bjarmaland

If medieval Scandinavian sources were the only literary proof of Bjarmaland, it might be justified to question the historical existence of the area because the sagas are in many ways far from historically reliable. Since we do not know any area as Bjarmaland today, it might be tempting to reject its historicity altogether, especially since many references to Bjarmaland in the medieval Scandinavian sources are to be found in the notoriously fantasy-filled and adventurous mytho-heroic sagas. Following the principles of source criticism, if the demands for contemporaneity (the source being written around the time of the event) and independence (several different sources of information rather than one and the same) are met, the credibility of the sources increases. In judging the historicity of Bjarmaland, these aspects are present, making a case for a historical Bjarmaland.

The oldest source available is Ohthere's account (as it is called), a late-ninth-century Anglo-Saxon textual addition to King Alfred's translation of the works of Orosius. It is significant for the historicity of Bjarmaland that this oldest extant source mentions the Bjarmians quite independently of the later Scandinavian sources. Ohthere's account is also considered as a contemporary source (Bately 2007a: 18, 27; Storli 2007: 76), which adds to its credibility.

Bjarmaland appears in the more historically oriented kings' sagas (especially in texts that refer to Eiríkr *blóðøx*[5]) as a natural part of the northern milieu in which the Scandinavians undertook so-called 'Viking' expeditions. Since the British Isles, the wide Baltic area and Bjarmaland all appear in the same context as targets of so-called 'Viking' expeditions, it appears unnecessary to question the natural assumption that Bjarmaland indeed was a part of an erstwhile geographical milieu on equal terms with the still recognisable and locatable England and the Baltic area, seen from a Scandinavian (and especially Norwegian) perspective. It is notable that all the other areas that are mentioned in this context are still identifiable today. Also, one of the motivations for writing the kings' sagas was to recount the biography of a number of kings (Knirk 1993: 362–363) and this kind of historical objective in a way anchors the general setting of this kind of saga in an actual historical environment (albeit most often reconstructed up to several hundred years after the events).

Hákonar saga Hákonarsonar, which relates the events of the thirteenth century, is one of the youngest sources available excepting the mytho-heroic sagas. It is also in principle one of the historically more reliable sagas in virtue of having been written only a few decades after the events it describes. (Schach 1993: 259–260.) In other words, the events in *Hákonar saga Hákonarsonar* are effectively placed in the actual historical environment at the time of the writing. In this text Bjarmaland is part of this current world, not part of some mythical fantasy world as in many of the mytho-heroic sagas. Both the earliest source about Bjarmaland (Ohthere's account) from the late ninth century and *Hákonar saga Hákonarsonar* from the latter part of the thirteenth century are contemporaneous to the events that they describe and Ohthere's account is also independent of the saga literature. That Bjarmaland was included in both of these texts written independently with approximately four centuries in between adds to the image that Bjarmaland had a somewhat stable position within the Scandinavian scope of the world.

Historia Norvegiae, a historical and geographical description of Norway written in Latin with *terminus a quo* in 1211, is somewhat older than the preserved sagas and partially based on sources that are independent of the sources used within the saga writing tradition (Santini 1993: 284–285). That Bjarmaland appears in this text further adds credibility for Bjarmaland as an actual historical area since being included in *Historia Norvegiae* shows that the information about Bjarmaland was not limited to one tradition of writing only.

Given the difficulties and uncertainties in identifying Bjarmaland and the Bjarmians, it is almost regrettable that Bjarmaland appears in so many mytho-heroic sagas since the fantasy elements of these sagas lessen the image of Bjarmaland as a historical area and may give rise to the notion that

Bjarmaland was imaginary rather than real. However, looking at the sources as a whole in light of their interdependence and other matters regarding their provenance, there are clear grounds to conclude that Bjarmaland and the Bjarmians did exist during the Viking Age and early-medieval times even if we cannot identify any area or group of people today with these names.

Information about the Bjarmians in the Sources

Written sources indicate the location of Bjarmaland in relation to Norway. Ohthere's account gives a sailing log with general directions and number of days used, that is, 15 days of sailing in total, starting from Hálogaland and sailing along the coast, with land on the right (starboard) and open sea on the left (port), first six days towards the north, then four days towards the east and finally five days towards the south and then up a big river (Bately 2007b: 44–45, 47). Other texts (*Historia Norvegiae*, *Haralds saga gráfeldar*, *Magnús saga berfœtts*, AM 736 I, 4°, AM 764, 4°) also indicate that Bjarmaland was located north and/or east of Norway (see Rafn 1852: 116, 404–405; Aðalbjarnarson 1941: 217; 1951: 212). Also place names like Finnmark, Kvenland, Russia and even Suzdal' (as *Suðrdalaríki* of the sources is interpreted) that appear together with Bjarmaland indicate the general location of Bjarmaland.

Three geographical names, *Gandvík*, *Terfinna land* and *Vína*, that appear in the written sources give further indications about the approximate location of Bjarmaland. *Gandvík* is mentioned for the first time in association with Bjarmaland in *Óláfs saga helga*[6] and appears also in *Hálfdanar saga Eysteinssonar* and *Þáttr Hauks hábrókar* (see Rafn 1830: 552–558; 1852: 122; Aðalbjarnarson 1945: 227–232). *Gandvík* also appears in a couple of skaldic poems, in Snorri's *Edda*, *Landafræði*, *Fagrskinna*, Flateyjarbók, *Orkneyinga saga* and *Gesta Danorum*[7] independently of Bjarmaland (see e.g. Haavio 1965: 17–18; Koskela Vasaru 2008: 384). *Landafræði* (AM 194, 8°),[8] *Fagrskinna*[9] and Flateyjarbók[10] place the northern border of Norway to *Gandvík* and based on these texts it appears clear that *Gandvík* should be looked for in the north and consequently it is most often identified as the White Sea[11] (see e.g. Ross 1951: 430; Haavio 1965: 17; Heide 2006: 25–26).

Terfinna land that is mentioned in Ohthere's account (Bately 2007b: 45) as the neighbouring area to Bjarmaland has been connected with the southern coast of the Kola Peninsula. The southern coast of the Kola Peninsula is still today called Tersky (*Terskij raion* i.e. Tersky District) and the *Terfinnas* have been identified with the Ter or Kola Sámi (Ross 1940: 6–7, 25–28). The 'Ter' names have a record of continuous use from thirteenth-century Russian (*Tre*, *Terskii bereg*) and early-fourteenth-century and sixteenth-century Scandinavian (*Trianæma*, *Trenes*) sources (Keyser & Munch 1849: 152–153; Bergsland 1982: 123; Hansen 2003: 18) up to today and have always been solely attached to the coast of the Kola Peninsula. In medieval Scandinavian written sources, the name only appears in *Ǫrvar-Odds saga* as *tyrfi/tyfni/tyfvi Finnar* (Boer 1888: 199; see also Ross 1940: 27–28).

On the basis of Ohthere's account we know that the fifteen-day sail from northern Norway to Bjarmaland followed the coast throughout the entire journey and this piece of information combined with the proximity of *Terfinna land* places the *Beormas* of Ohthere on the southern coast of the Kola Peninsula. The Varzuga River, located at the border of the Ter coast, is the most popular suggestion as Ohthere's destination (Johnsen 1923: 9; Ross 1940: 6–7; Vilkuna 1980: 647; Jackson 2002: 171; Englert 2007: 127–128). However, other rivers on the Kola Peninsula including Umba and Strelna are also mentioned, in addition to rivers in other areas like Vyg in Viena Karelia and the Northern Dvina River on the southern shore of the White Sea as the most common suggestions (Haavio 1965: 16; Carpelan 1993: 231–233; Jackson 2002: 170). Two twelfth- to thirteenth-century burials in Kuzomen' near the Varzuga River (Ovsyannikov 1984: 98–105; Jasinski & Ovsyannikov 1998: 25, 28, 30, 32, 34; see below for further details) indicate that the area was indeed inhabited. The medieval burials cannot enlighten the conditions of the Viking Age, but considering how few and far between archaeological finds are in the area, it is interesting that major medieval settlement can be established in the Varzuga River region.

The location of Bjarmaland is inexorably connected with the White Sea and a connection with the Kola Peninsula is firmly demonstrated. The third toponym, *Vína*, is not quite as straightforward. It is mentioned for the first time in connection with Bjarmaland in skaldic verses (from *c.* 970), preserved in *Haralds saga gráfeldar* in *Heimskringla* (*á Vínu borði* and *við Bjarma á Vinubakka*) (Aðalbjarnarson 1941: 217). *Vína* makes its second appearance in *Heimskringla* in *Óláfs saga helga* (*ánni Vinu*) (Aðalbjarnarson 1945: 227–232). It is also mentioned in *Egils saga Skalla-Grímssonar* (*á Bjarmalandi við Vínu*) (Nordal 1988: 93–94). Several of the later sagas including *Ǫrvar-Odds saga* (e.g. *á þá er Vína heitir; áinni Vínu*), *Hálfs saga ok Hálfsrekka* (*Vínumynni*), *Sturlaugs saga starfsama* (*ánni Vínu*) and *Bósa saga* (*Vínuskógr*) mention *Vína* as well (Rafn 1830: 626; Rafn 1850: 86; Boer 1888: 22, 24, 26, 28, 30, 32, 34; Jiriczek 1893: 21–25).

Óláfs saga helga states that *Vína* is a river. Ohthere's account also refers to a river as a final destination in Bjarmaland. Based on this, researchers most often connect *Vína* with the Russian Northern Dvina River (Finnish *Vienajoki*). However, most researchers also agree that the Northern Dvina could not have been Ohthere's destination and this would seem to imply that there were at least two rivers that were connected with Bjarmaland if the Northern Dvina was a destination of later expeditions. The main argument for connecting *Vína* and Dvina is the likeness of the names (Jackson 2002: 172). The name *Vína* corresponds directly to the name Viena whereas the relationship of *Vína* and Dvina is not so simple (Mikko Heikkilä, p.c.). It would also be advisable to consider the two other Viena names in the White Sea area as possible sources of the Scandinavian *Vína*, although neither of these is a river. The White Sea is called *Vienanmeri* in Finnish and the northernmost part of Karelia by the Kantalahti Bay is called Viena. The quotation of verses in *Haralds saga gráfeldar* demonstrates that verses were among the sources that were used to compose the saga descriptions of

Bjarmaland and this again implies that the way the author (in this case Snorri Sturluson) interpreted the verses influenced the presentation of *Vína*. The author may have had additional information that guided the interpretation, but if the verses were the only or the main source, whichever way the author interpreted the lines must have had a decisive effect.

Disregarding mytho-heroic sagas, Snorri is our main source regarding the presentation of *Vína* in Bjarmaland. *Ǫrvar-Odds saga*, *Hálfs saga ok Hálfsrekka* and *Sturlaugs saga starfsama* are probably all of them indebted to the description of Bjarmaland in *Óláfs saga helga* and in the case of *Ǫrvar-Odds saga* almost verbatim quotations leave no doubt that there is a connection between the two (Häme 1987: 187–189; Koskela Vasaru 2008: 292). In *Bósa saga Vína* is no longer a river but a forest.

Gandvík of the Scandinavian sources is generally connected with the White Sea and interestingly the westernmost bay is called Kantalahti. There is an ongoing debate whether Kantalahti or *Gandvík* is the original form, and the question is left open with standpoints that may favour either possibility (Heide 2006: 118–120; cf. Tolley 2009 I: 250). However, considering that the pre-Russian population in the area was Finno-Ugrian, it does seem reasonable to assume that a Finno-Ugrian name preceded the name *Gandvík* (Ross 1951: 429–430). In the light of this observation, it is worth considering that the existence of the name *Gandvík* refers to Scandinavian contacts with the Kantalahti Bay area (Koskela Vasaru 2011: 177–183). The southern coast of Kantalahti is known as Viena and the White Sea of which the Kantalahti is a part of is called Vienanmeri. In my opinion, it is worth considering the possibility that if *Vína* is to be connected with Viena names, a similar argument that is used to connect *Vína* with the Northern Dvina River, that is to say, likeness of the names, applies to the two other Viena names. The Kantalahti/*Gandvík* connection refers to Scandinavian contacts in the area that has two Viena names. If the Scandinavians travelling to this area were familiar with the local name Kantalahti, they may have also become familiar with other local names, including those containing the element *Viena*. The knowledge of these names may have given rise to the name *Vína* in the sagas, regardless of the name of the river(s) to which the Scandinavians travelled. Yet the possibility remains that *Vína* does refer to the Northern Dvina (Fin. and Kar. *Vienajoki* [lit. 'Viena-river']), but as long as we lack more evidence in the form for instance of archaeological finds in the Northern Dvina area, this assumption cannot be taken as a certainty.

The sources give us rather haphazard information about Bjarmaland. The Bjarmians seem to have spoken a Finnic language, quite similar to current Finnish and Karelian, as indicated by two pieces of information. Firstly, Ohthere mentions that the Sámi and the Bjarmian languages resembled each other: "Þa Finnas, him þuhte, ⁊ þa Beormas spræcon neah an geþeode" ['The *Finnas* and the *Beormas*, it seemed to him, spoke practically one and the same language'] (Bately 2007b: 45). This makes the Bjarmian language a Finno-Ugrian one. This wide definition of a language group does not exclude for instance Volga-Finnic languages or one of the Sámi languages. However, additional information in the sources would seem to point towards a Finnic language. *Óláfs saga helga* in *Heimskringla*[12] mentions the indigenous word *Jómali* as the name of a statue of a Bjarmian god ("En í garðinum stendr goð Bjarma, er heitir Jómali"[13] ['But in the yard stands a god of the Bjarmians, which is called *Jómali*']) (Aðalbjarnarson 1945: 230). This word is very close to the words for god in Finnic languages and closest of all is the Finnish and Karelian word, *jumala* (Ross 1940: 49–50). Considering that *Jómali* corresponds to *jumala* very closely and that *Jómali* is a name of a deity and that *jumala* means god (for more detailed discussion of the words see Frog), it appears highly unlikely that the correspondence is a coincidence. The body of evidence is not plentiful, but there is no other option than to try to make deductions based on the few words that we are given in the written sources. Both of the clues point towards identification within the same language group and this should add some plausibility to the conclusion that the language of the Bjarmians was a Finno-Ugrian one. *Jómali* as a name of a statue of a god is so close to the word for god in most Finnic languages that one can narrow the scope to the Finnic group. In fact, languages belonging to other language groups have never been suggested within serious research. The geographical location of the Bjarmians can be placed in approximate terms within an area that is today in north-western Russia. This area was inhabited (as far as we currently know and especially regarding pre-medieval times) by speakers of different groups of Finno-Ugrian languages (see Saarikivi 2009: 109, 113–114, 117–118), which further enhances the plausibility of the conclusion that the language of the Bjarmians was of Finno-Ugrian/Finnic origin. It is worth noting that the differences between Finnish, Karelian and Vepsian, i.e. the North Finnic languages, were not as great during the Viking Age as they are today, a whole millennium later (see Kallio) and because of their likeness, it is pointless to make any closer deductions based on one word only.

Bjarmians cannot be connected with any existing group of people and it is likely that they were a separate group of Finnic speakers in the White Sea area. Toponyms and loan words in local dialects in northern Russia indicate that Finno-Ugrian (especially Finnic) speaking populations lived in the area, which is currently completely Russian. The existence of such groups is further attested by medieval Russian chronicles that mention groups of people associated with Finno-Ugrian languages. Some of these can be identified with currently existing groups; others cannot, which implies that some groups have totally assimilated with the Russians. (Glazyrina 2000: 517–518, 521; Saarikivi 2009: 113–114, 118.) Small groups that are not mentioned in medieval Russian written sources remain anonymous to us and the Bjarmians would fit into this category.

According to Ohthere, the Bjarmians cultivated land. The wording of the source "Þa Beormas hæfdon swiþe wel gebud hira land" ['The *Beormas* had settled their land very well'] (Ohthere's Voyages 2007: 45) does not refer to agriculture directly, but the researchers have always found the implicit meaning to be that the Bjarmians "very greatly cultivated their land" (Crossley-Holland 1984: 64; see also Ross 1940: 44–45; Odner 1983: 81). Ohthere makes a clear distinction between the "well settled" land of the *Beormas* and the "wasteland" of the itinerant *Finnas* and *Terfinnas*[14] and right after mentioning that the *Beormas* had settled their land very well, he points out that the land of the *Terfinnas* was all waste. This clearly points to a difference in way of life between the *Beormas* and their Sámi neighbours, meaning that the livelihood of the *Beormas* must have included other things than hunting, fishing and fowling, making an assumption of agriculture a likely option.

A fleeting reference to dwellings in the verses in *Haralds saga gráfeldar* in *Heimskringla*[15] as well as references to burial mounds in *Óláfs saga helga* in *Heimskrigla* (see Aðalbjarnarson 1945: 227–232; a few other rather stereotypical and fantasy filled references to mounds are found in some of the mytho-heroic sagas) give further indications that the Bjarmians were permanently settled. Even if the reference to dwellings appears in a poetic context and the mound motif is generic, there is an underlying implicit level that reflects the mindset of the author. In this case the reflected image shows the Bjarmians as people who had their homeplace (indicated by dwellings and burials) in the area where the Norwegians met them.

One of the geographical accounts (AM 736 I, 4°) mentions that the Bjarmians paid taxes[16] to Russia,[17] probably by the end of the twelfth century. Also Russian medieval sources seem to suggest that the Kola Peninsula was to some extent attached to Russia and it was particularly the Karelians who extended their interest to the Kola Peninsula. A Novgorodian chronicle from the year 1216 seems to refer to Novgorodian tax-collecting on the Ter coast and there are references to summer expeditions to the southern coast of the Kola Peninsula by the mid-twelfth century by Russian settlers of the Onega and Dvina basins. "Arzuga" is mentioned as a Karelian *pogost* by 1419. (Hansen 1996: 55–57; Hansen & Olsen 2004:155–157, 160–161.)

The plural form of the words *bjarmskar kindir* ['Bjarmian kin, Bjarmian peoples' (pl.)] (verses in *Haralds saga gráfeldar* in *Heimskringla*, see above) and the reference to two kinds of Bjarmians, *utrique Biarmones*, in *Historia Norvegiae* (Ekrem, Mortensen & Fisher 2006: 54–55) would seem to imply some sort of division of the Bjarmians. However, the short references are not very clear (the semantic significance of word-choice in verses may be subordinated to stylistic or metrical requirements, making literal interpretation potentially problematic) and it is impossible to judge with any certainty whether the alluded difference had something to do with ethnicity, area or some other factor. Reference to a king of Bjarmaland (*Bjarmakonungr*) (Vigfusson 1964: 87) in *Hákonar saga Hákonarsonar* (a few other fantasy-filled references are found in some of the mytho-heroic sagas) would seem to imply that Bjarmian society was to some extent hierarchic in the eyes of a Norwegian observer. It is worth noting that in Norway the local kings were leaders of their community rather than kings in the feudal meaning of the word, and the word chieftain is perhaps a more appropriate term (see e.g. Krag 2000: 28, 49–50, 54, 67–72, 103–104). This sense of the word 'king' is perhaps more appropriate for the Bjarmian society as described as well. In any case, we should be extremely cautious in how we interpret this sort of references because the Norwegians had a tendency to ascribe kings to the foreign peoples they had contact with, and thus we also find Norwegian references to Sámi kings.

After the thirteenth century, the written sources only mention Karelians in the area that was previously connected with the Bjarmians. It is, however, impossible to connect the Bjarmians of the ninth century with Karelians since Karelian identity and culture were only beginning to develop at this time and as far as we know Karelians did not live so far north as the assumed Bjarmian area as early as the Viking Age (Saksa 1998: 15, 157, 197–198). We can speculate on the reasons as to why the written sources only mention the Karelians after a certain point in time. In addition to speaking related languages, Bjarmians and Karelians were both allies of Novgorod and involved in the fur trade (mentioned in connection with Bjarmaland in *Óláfs saga helga* and *Hákonar saga Hákonarsonar*, see Aðalbjarnarson 1945: 229; Vigfusson 1964: 70–71). These factors may have had something to do with the Bjarmians disappearing from the written sources. In other words, a certain similarity between the Bjarmians and the Karelians may have caused the presumably smaller group to assimilate with the larger after these two groups had more frequent contacts as a result of the Karelian settlement expanding gradually northwards. (Koskela Vasaru 2008: 403–408.) Something of a parallel situation is perhaps behind the assimilation process of the Karelians by Sámi on the Kola Peninsula: a Scandinavian document from 1330 states that the inhabitants of the area east of the Veleaga River (Fin. Välijoki, by the River Umba) were half Karelians and half Sámi (Hansen 2003: 17–19).

Bjarmaland and Contacts from the Viking Age until the Thirteenth Century

This section is based on a summary of the information given in the written sources that is presented in more detailed form in my dissertation (Koskela Vasaru 2008: 359–375).

Written sources refer directly only to contacts between the Bjarmians and the Norwegians.[18] These contacts were of an economic nature, both peaceful and belligerent, and continued over several centuries. The contacts are mentioned for the first time at the end of the ninth century in Ohthere's account. The last time contacts between the Norwegians and the Bjarmians appear in writing is just before the middle of the thirteenth century (discounting the more fictitious mytho-heroic sagas). The more historically oriented kings' sagas were not produced after the thirteenth century (Knirk 1993: 365) and the disappearance of Bjarmians from the written sources has partially to do with this change in the nature of the source material. Judging from the fact that no group was known as Bjarmians after medieval times the Bjarmians ceased to exist as an ethnic group. The combined effects of changing geopolitical conditions during the thirteenth century (see below) contributed to the disappearance of the ethnonym.

Norwegians had economic motives to travel to Bjarmaland. The earliest source mentions walrus ivory as an incentive,[19] whereas later sources refer to furs as the main trade article.[20] Peaceful trading was a part of the interaction but, alongside this, much more violent interaction took place in the form of looting and warfare. Some of the sagas (*Haralds saga hárfagra*, *Haralds saga gráfeldar* and *Magnús saga berfœtts* in *Heimskringla* as well as *Egils saga Skalla-Grímssonar*) mention battles, which indicates that contacts of a less peaceful nature occurred, especially during the Viking Age. According to the sources, the Norwegians as a rule instigated the aggression but there are also instances where the Bjarmians were the ones to do so, as a story in *Hákonar saga Hákonarsonar* illustrates: a group of Norwegians stayed over winter in Bjarmaland and the Norwegians were all killed after a fallout ("En um vetrinn fara Bjarmar at þeim ok drápu alla skips-hǫfnina") (Vigfusson 1964: 70). The Norwegians staying over winter in Bjarmaland would seem to indicate that the contacts between the two were not merely sporadic. A much less credible account in *Ǫrvar-Odd's saga*,[21] which is one of the mytho-heroic sagas, gives a hint of the possibility that at times Norwegians could even settle in Bjarmaland and learn the language and customs of the local populations. Naturally one cannot regard the passage as recounting an actual event. Rather, its inclusion serves to demonstrate a mindset where it was not unthinkable to place a Norwegian character in Bjarmaland over a longer period of time.

The sources only refer to Norwegian expeditions to Bjarmaland, with the exception of an account in *Hákonar saga Hákonarsonar* (Vigfusson 1964: 358) that relates that around the middle of the thirteenth century a group of Bjarmians settled in Malangen in Norway after they had been forced to leave their home. This incident hints that the relations were not necessarily always aggressive and it appears quite possible that the aggressive image of the Norwegian–Bjarmian contacts is due in part to the nature of the sources, reflecting the norms of saga themes. There was seemingly a tradition of recounting mainly (although not exclusively) kings' looting expeditions. The sources mention looting much more often than trade, but the relations may in reality have been a good deal more peaceful than many of the sources indicate. An account in *Óláfs saga helga* in *Heimskringla* (Aðalbjarnarson 1945: 227–232) indicates that it was possible to trade peacefully, but after the agreed truce the Norwegians turned to looting. This dual image of trade alongside more violent behaviour is probably largely in accordance with reality, but we should not overestimate the aggression just because it is mentioned more often in the sources that we have available.

The oldest known Norwegian expedition to Bjarmaland is dated to *c.* 875, while the next took place during the Viking Age, most probably in the early 930s, and the sources also refer to a few other expeditions during the tenth century, in 1026, at the very end of the eleventh century and finally in 1222. The sources mostly mention Viking Age expeditions made by kings that largely involved looting, although trade is mentioned as well.

Hálogaland is mentioned most often as a starting point of a Norwegian Bjarmaland expedition. Additionally, Trøndelag, Namdalen in Nord-Trøndelag and Trondheim in Sør-Trøndelag (*Óláfs saga helga*) are named. Also the more southerly part of Norway is represented in the sources

(Hordaland, Fjordane and Rogaland), although not all the sources that mention these are deemed very reliable. However, the more southerly locations appear so often that one has to suspect reasons for their inclusion. Presumably, though, the northern direction might naturally have been more tempting for people who lived in the northern parts of the country. Those who lived in the more southerly parts of Norway had other potential targets relatively nearby in a southerly direction and choosing the northerly direction would have required a special incentive.

In the written sources the kings of Norway are closely connected with Bjarmaland expeditions. Either the king himself travelled to Bjarmaland or he sent his representative or otherwise financed the expedition. In addition to kings, other wealthy persons travelled to Bjarmaland. The number of ships seems mostly to have varied between one and two, but could rise to four. The number of crew per ship can be estimated at around twenty-five on average, but could be higher depending on the size and type of the ship. In estimating the number of crew, it should be remembered that the goal of the expedition was economic profit and consequently the crew could not rise to very large numbers. On the other hand, the crew had to be large enough to be able to carry out looting effectively, for looting seems to have formed an integral part of the expeditions (cf. the truce needed in order to trade and the looting commenced as opportunity arose, as related in *Óláfs saga helga*).

The sources hint that the Norwegian Bjarmaland expeditions were profitable for one to four ships and twenty-five to a hundred crew, and it is unlikely that the expeditions would have continued over several centuries if they had not been profitable. The Norwegian Bjarmaland expeditions are described in the sources in the same manner as other so-called 'Viking' expeditions that were carried on in both western and eastern part of Europe (esp. the Baltic Sea area and the British Isles). In all probability we can consider the descriptions of Bjarmaland expeditions that are found in the sources as being as reliable as descriptions of other 'Viking' expeditions. The fact that Bjarmaland is not known as the name of an area today does not make its existence in the past less reliable than the existence of those areas that are mentioned in the same context (in this case 'Viking' expeditions) as Bjarmaland and whose locations still are recognisable today (e.g. Denmark and Scotland). Despite their current status areas that are mentioned in the same passage should be given the same credibility for as long as the source itself is oriented to reality (cf. kings' sagas and mytho-heroic sagas).

Intermarriages between the Norwegians and the Bjarmians are mentioned in the sources (*Bósa saga ok Herrauðs*, *Hálfdanar saga Eysteinssonar*, *Gesta Danorum*, *Landnámabók*), but marriage is a common literary motif, often used especially in the less historically oriented mytho-heroic sagas (Mitchell 1993: 206) and one cannot draw many conclusions based on these references. The passages with the marriage motif in *Gesta Danorum* and *Landnámabók* have a quality that resembles the descriptions in mytho-heroic sagas and consequently it is difficult to decide if the descriptions reflect reality or simply repeat formulaic motifs.

In regard to why the Norwegian expeditions to Bjarmaland apparently ceased during the Middle Ages, one may consider the many political and economic changes that first appeared during the twelfth century and continued in the thirteenth. In the Nordic countries the formation of states gathered pace during the thirteenth century and the central government tightened its control over the economy. Novgorod (and Karelians) kept expanding northwards, which provoked increased hostility with Norway, and the Mongols raided large areas in Russia. The changes in trade routes largely as a result of this in addition to the introduction of new trade articles (in particular dried fish) and possibly also an increased hostility between Norway and Bjarmaland that was in allegiance with Novgorod may all have influenced the situation. One cannot discount the possibility that deteriorating climatic conditions may also have contributed to this process (the Viking Age had been particularly favourable climate wise, on which see HELAMA). (See e.g. Johnsen 1923: 16; Hofstra & Samplonius 1995: 244; Saksa 1998: 204–205; Hansen 2003: 9; Hansen & Olsen 2001: 61, 138–9, 152–154, 165–166, 219.)

An Archaeological Perspective on Bjarmaland and Contacts in the North

Written sources do not give any clear indications of other contacts than those between the Norwegians and the Bjarmians. Archaeological material is in principle the only means of getting more information about contacts, but it is currently scarce. We do not know any Viking Age material that could confirm settlement in the assumed Bjarmian area but there are early-medieval finds that indicate settlement on the left bank of the Varzuga River near the village of Kuzomen'. The finds include ornaments mainly of the twelfth century from a destroyed cemetery, Kuzomen' I. Nearby, close to the confluence of the Kitsa and Varzuga Rivers, three other graves (Kuzomen' II) have been discovered. All the burials are dated to the twelfth to thirteenth centuries. The artefacts represent types that are typical to (western) Finno-Ugrian tribes during the medieval period.

The finds in Kuzomen' I include a West European silver coin (a denarius of Count Albert II, 1018–1064), a key-shaped amulet and an umbo-shaped plate as well as two belt buckles, two penannular brooches, three horse-shaped pendants, two bird-shaped pendants, a spearhead and a number of other metal artefacts (some of which are so corroded that it is difficult to define them more closely). A number of human bones attest to an inhumation burial ground. The key-shaped amulets are typical of the grave mounds (*kurgan*) of the south-eastern Lake Ladoga area and are quite rare outside this area. Also the two metal staves of bronze have counterparts in the south-eastern Lake Ladoga area and by Cheptsa as well as in kurgans of the Volga Kostroma area. The umbo-shaped plate (a conical pendant with spiral decoration that was originally used as boot decoration) has counterparts in an area inhabited by Finno-Ugrian tribes stretching from the Kama to the south-eastern Lake Ladoga area. Both the penannular brooches and the belt buckles have a wide distribution in the northern area (Chud'ian and Russian population) in the tenth to thirteenth centuries. Horse-shaped pendants have a wide distribution in the north-eastern Finno-Ugrian area (from Finland to the basin of the Northern Dvina River) and the type found in Kuzomen' I is most numerous in the Lake Ladoga area, the Lake Beloye area and the Vaga basin (each with three finds, e.g. Aksenovskaya and Korbala). One of the bird-shaped pendants is of a type frequently present in Russian finds (in a Finno-Ugrian context, e.g. Aksenovskaya) with main concentrations in the south-eastern Lake Ladoga area and the Lake Beloye area. Its origin is connected with the south-eastern Lake Ladoga area with the earliest finds there from the second half of the tenth/early eleventh century. The artefacts of Kuzomen' I are a mix of Finnic, Finno-Volgic and Permian forms and the artefacts are typical of two large Chud'ian areas, the Ladoga-Beloye(-Kama) area and the Volga area.

The finds in Kuzomen' II (three graves from the twelfth to thirteenth centuries) include coin-shaped pendants, a triangular pendant of bronze wire, remains of a necklace made of eight round pendants and glass beads, a penannular brooch with spiral ends (twelfth to thirteenth centuries), an iron belt ring, a small iron knife, a bronze spiral belonging to a woman's dress (with geometrical ornamentation attached to fabric on the lower part of the dress) and some fabric remains (e.g. parts of a belt); a necklace made of glass beads, two large round pendants, four round coin-shaped pendants and a round slit pendant (all of these in a very bad state of preservation), a bronze pendant shaped like a duck's foot and a bronze belt ring; a bronze belt buckle with remains of a leather belt, a round bronze belt ring, two bronze belt ring plates with three links (strap distributors) and an axe. In one of the burials, the corpse had been swaddled in bast and cloth and placed in a wooden coffin, probably of log-frame type (with a construction over the grave), while another one was made in a wooden cist and the third grave contained a body wrapped in bast. (Ovsyannikov 1984: 98–105; Jasinski & Ovsyannikov 1998: 25, 28, 30, 32, 34.)

Twelfth- to thirteenth-century burials in Kuzomen' I and II close to the Varzuga River seem to point particularly towards contacts with the (Vepsian) south-eastern Lake Ladoga area (Gurina 1984: 16). The material also shows some affinity to material in the Vaga and Beloye areas and it might be justified to say that the finds in Kuzomen' are generally connected with the Finno-Ugrian settlement[22] in northern Russia. (Gurina 1984: 16; Ovsyannikov 1984: 98–105; Jasinski & Ovsyannikov 1998: 25, 28, 30, 32, 34.) The descriptions in the sagas are too vague to make any comparisons with actual archaeological finds but on the other hand there is nothing in the saga descriptions or in the archaeological material that would be mutually exclusive. The material from Kuzomen' has been connected with a Sámi population based on both the physical features of the deceased and the general location, which is connected with Sámi settlement (Ovsyannikov 1984: 98–105), but certain features in the finds in my opinion make this suggestion unlikely. Firstly, I find it doubtful that physical features could be a reliable parameter. Secondly, the finds contain bronze spirals that were mostly used as an ornament on the hem or the apron of the female dress. They have been found in Western Finland and Karelia and they were used by Baltic tribes. Bronze spirals belong to the end of the Viking Age and the Crusade Period/early-medieval times. (Alsvik 1973: 77; see also Lehtosalo-Hilander 1980: 243–245, 256–257.)

A few finds in the Kargopol area, in the Lake Onega (Ääninen) area and in northern Karelia indicate that people lived in these regions. The finds are, however, scarce and can tell us nothing certain about the Late Iron Age and early-medieval settlement in these areas in regard to livelihood or ethnicity, but it is generally accepted among Russian historians and archaeologists that there were Sámi living on the Kola Peninsula ever since the Stone Age. (Gurina 1987: 35, 37, 41, 43, 45, 48; Carpelan 1993: 232–233; Makarov 2007: 143.) Studies of linguistics, however, seem to suggest that Proto-Sámi emerged in an area stretching from southern Finland in the west to Lakes Ladoga and Onega in the east and that Proto-Sámi had dialectally disintegrated and spread over most of the present Sámi area by approximately AD 500, causing a language shift amongst the earlier non-Sámi speaking inhabitants (Aikio 2006: 39–47). Hence the Sámi presence on the Kola cannot be pushed beyond the Iron Age whereas the medieval written sources (of both Scandinavian and Russian origin) attest that the Sámi inhabited areas in the north by the Late Iron Age.

The few northern Russian hoards found in Kem', Varzuga and Archangel (currently the only archaeological evidence from this area) connect the White Sea with the larger northern Fennoscandian cultural area that has hoards of similar character (Spangen 2005: 77–78). Northern hoards have been connected with border and transition zones where the Sámi and other ethnic groups met. In northern Norway, the other ethnic group was the Germanic population but in regard to northern Finland and the White Sea area we can only speculate who the other group(s) might have been.

In any case, silver artefacts that have been found in the hoards imply that the White Sea area had a certain economic potential. It is also possible that some of the hoards can be connected with trade, as the scales found in northern Finland would seem to suggest. In addition, Russian scholars link the northern Russian hoards with trade (Nosov *et al.* 1992: 12–14).

The hoards from the vicinity of the Varzuga and Kem' Rivers contain a collection of artefacts similar to the northern Finnish hoards and a few artefact types that have been found in the White Sea area have counterparts in the so-called stray finds in northern Finland, that is to say neckrings from Oulujoki, Koveronkoski and Vaala. The similarity would seem to refer to some sort of cultural connections between northern Finland and the coastal area of the White Sea. A single find from Uhtua and a hoard from Kem' create a hazy connection between the Varzuga and the northern Finnish Kainuu area. (Jasinski & Ovsyannikov 1998: 62; Hansen & Olsen 2004: 83–86; Koskela Vasaru 2008: 145–152.) The finds in northern Finland in general are relatively few. An analysis shows that northern Finland experienced a change of activity zone from the coastal to the inland area during AD 600–800. The activity increased as the Late Iron Age progressed and included violence and trade, as attested by finds of weapons and silver. (See KUUSELA.)

There are artefacts from the Kainuu area in Finland that have been dated between the Late Merovingian Period (550/600–800) and the Viking Age that have sometimes been interpreted as typically Norwegian. Based on this identification, it has been suggested that, before the introduction of a sea route in the ninth century, the Norwegians used a route that traversed Kainuu on the way to Bjarmaland (Tallgren 1930: 80–81; Huurre 1983: 335–337, 339, 343, 356–357, 378, 384, 391, 421). However, there are so few artefacts that can be specifically connected with Norway that this theory must remain as speculation, and in my opinion the current finds are not sufficient to support the suggestion.

The nature of archaeological material easily causes speculation. If we assume that Bjarmaland was located by the White Sea and at least partially on the Kola Peninsula as suggested by Ohthere's account, then one may wonder about a possible connection between the Varzuga River and Bjarmaland. The Varzuga River has been connected with Ohthere's destination river by many scholars (see e.g. Johnsen 1923: 9; Ross 1940: 58; Vilkuna 1980: 647; Englert 2007: 127–128) because it is a large river in an area that is indicated in Ohthere's account both in regard to vicinity of *Terfinnas* and travelling time. The medieval burials that have been found in the area of the Varzuga River constitute another feature that highlights it as an area of interest.

Archaeological material from the Kola Peninsula and Viena Karelia is scarce but current finds indicate connections between the Kola Peninsula and the south-eastern Lake Ladoga area. Looking at the provenance of the archaeological material it seems reasonable to assume that contacts existed between the Bjarmians and the Vepsians of the south-eastern Lake Ladoga region at least around the twelfth to thirteenth centuries, since archaeological material from this time with affinity to the Vepsian area has been found on the Kola Peninsula, that is connected with Bjarmaland in the written sources. Both the Karelian and the Vepsian culture formed in the early Middle Ages. The Vepsians (*Ves'* in medieval Russian sources, first mentioned in conjunction with events dated to 859 and 862) were agriculturalists and the earliest kurgans appeared from the 860s onwards. According to current knowledge there were ancient Vepsians in the southern part of Onega Karelia by the end of the Viking Age and the Vepsian area reached the northern coast of Lake Onega (Ääninen) during late-medieval times (See KUZMIN). There is no firm knowledge of this, but one may wonder if the Vepsian activity at least sporadically reached as far north as the Kola Peninsula. The burials in Kuzomen' contain a number of artefacts that show affinity with the core area of Vepsian settlement by Lake Ladoga, and this would seem to suggest at least some sort of contact, direct or otherwise.

If we consider the neighbouring areas of Bjarmaland and take into account that the Bjarmians were involved in the fur trade as stated in the written sources, we can assume that they had some sort of contacts with Novgorod, which exercised a dominant role in the fur trade in the area of northern Russia (Hansen 2003: 12, 14; Hansen & Olsen 2004: 138). Sources tell us that the Bjarmians sold furs to the Norwegians (Aðalbjarnarson 1945: 229; Vigfusson 1964: 70–71), but it would appear likely that they had other contacts, too. Considering Novgorod's central role, it is more than plausible that one of the markets for Bjarmian furs was Novgorod, either directly or through intermediaries. The fur trade was important too for the Karelians, who were associated with Novgorod, and it is likely that the Karelians came into contact with the Bjarmians because of their mutual involvement in trade. (On the peripheral fur trade in which the Karelians were engaged, see KORPELA.)

Some Thoughts and Conclusions

Our image of Bjarmaland is based on the medieval Scandinavian written sources and thus our view of this area is primarily (with the notable exception of the late-ninth-century account based on the interview with Ohthere) an interpretation put together by thirteenth-century Scandinavian authors (the later mytho-heroic sagas seem to base large parts of their image in many ways on the more factually oriented sagas). Bjarmaland is firmly placed within the geographical area of northern Europe (albeit on the fringes of it) that the Norwegians were intimately familiar with through their travels.

The importance of the international fur trade from the Viking Age onwards is often emphasised in regard to the whole of northern Fennoscandia and northern Russia (Hansen & Olsen 2004: 138). The sources indicate that the fur trade was essential for the economy of Bjarmaland as well.

The earliest sources we have available date from the Viking Age, and given the lack of anything earlier it is difficult to say anything about the potential existence of Bjarmians before this time. Archaeology offers the only chance of expanding this knowledge, but the material we have available is scarce and does not offer much that is tangible. A theory has been put forward of Norwegian expeditions to Bjarmaland through the Kainuu area in northern Finland prior to the time span covered by the written sources. In this scenario the expeditions would be pushed as far back as the late Merovingian Period (eighth century), but in effect the archaeological material to support this assumption is so slight that the theory remains speculation only. However, looking at the appearance of Bjarmian identity, the beginning of the Viking Age and the expansion of the fur trade may have provided economic incentives to settle in the White Sea area. Living further to the north would have given the inhabitants better access to hunting grounds and perhaps to furs of animals with an easterly distribution, either through their own hunting expeditions or through trade with groups of people living in the more easterly areas. As far as we know, the Bjarmian ethnic identity had its beginnings before the late ninth century, but need not be substantially older than that. Perhaps this ethnic identity as observed by Norwegians was born around this time out of the fur-trade-related interaction between the Norwegians and a certain group of people living by the White Sea.

For the Norwegians, the Bjarmians still existed around the middle of the thirteenth century. However, after this point the sources of the same quality as before were no longer produced in Scandinavia and consequently there are no written sources to document any further existence of the Bjarmians. In addition, the geopolitical situation[23] in the whole of northern Europe was changing in the thirteenth century and this may have brought about changes in the actual political situation in the Bjarmian area, perhaps resulting in the Bjarmians assimilating with the Karelian population, which was expanding its area of settlement in the north.

Economic interaction in the northern areas of Europe was also undergoing changes during the thirteenth century, and if we connect the rise of Bjarmian ethnic identity with interaction through trade, the disappearance may well, at least partially, be connected with changes within the established pattern of trade.

Notes

1 Johannes Magnus wrote in *Gothorum Sveonumque historia* (1554) "Biarmiam suppolarem regionem: quæ in Vlteriorem & Citeriorem dividitur" (Magno 1617: 10, 91, 192). Olaus Magnus wrote in *Historia de gentibus septentrionalibus* (1555) that "Biarmia duplex. Diuiditur aute*m* Biarmia, secundu*m* Saxone*m* Sialandicu*m*, in ulteriorem & citeriorem" (Magnus 1972: 9–10).

2 See *Haralds saga gráfeldar* (Aðalbjarnarson 1945: 227–232) and *Óláfs saga helga* in *Heimskringla* (Aðalbjarnarson 1941: 217).

3 For a complete list, see Ross 1940: 29–42; for approximate dating of a selection of the sources, see Jansson 1936.

4 For more information on the medieval Scandinavian sources, see e.g. Clover & Lindow 1985.

5 Ch. 32: "Þá er Eiríkr var tólf vetra gamall, gaf Haraldr konungr honum fimm langskip, ok fór hann í hernað, fyrst í Austrveg ok þá suðr um Danmǫrk ok um Frísland ok Saxland, ok dvalðisk í þeiri ferð fjóra vetr. Eptir þat fór hann vestr um haf ok herjaði um Skotland ok Bretland, Írland ok Valland ok dvalðisk þar aðra fjóra vetr. Eptir þat fór hann norðr á Finnmǫrk ok allt til Bjarmaland, ok átti hann þar orrostu mikla ok hafði sigr." (Aðalbjarnarson 1941: 134–135.) ['When Eirík was twelve years old, King Harald gave him five warships, and he went raiding, first on the Baltic, then south around Denmark and about Frísland and Saxland, and he was four years on this expedition. After that he sailed west across the sea, harrying in Scotland, Bretland [Wales], Ireland, and Valland [France], and passed four more years there. Then he sailed north to Finnmark and all the way to Bjarmaland, where he fought a great battle and was victorious.' (Hollander 1999: 86.)]
Ch. 28: "Svá segir ok Glúmr Geirason í sínu kvæði, at Eiríkr herjaði áðr en Haraldr konungr andaðisk suðr um Halland ok Skáni ok viða um Danmǫrk, ok allt fór hann um Kúrland ok Eistland, ok mǫrg ǫnnur lǫnd herjaði hann í Austrvegum. Hann herjaði ok víða um Svíþjóð ok Gautland. Hann fór norðr á Finnmǫrk ok allt til Bjarmalands með hernaði. [. . .] Ok síðan Eiríkr kom til Englands herjaði hann um ǫll Vestrlǫnd." (Einarsson 1985: 79.) ['Glúmr Geirason also says in his poem that before King Haraldr died Eiríkr plundered south around Halland and Skáney and extensively around Denmark, and he went all the way around Kúrland and Eistland, and plundered in many other countries around the Baltic. He also raided extensively round Sweden and Gautland. He went raiding north in Finnmǫrk and

all the way to Bjarmaland. [...] And after Eiríkr went to England he raided all over the British Isles.' (Finlay 2004: 59–60.)]

6 "Sigldu þá hvárirtveggju yfir Gandvík" (Aðalbjarnarson 1945: 231) ['Then both sailed across the White Sea' (Hollander 1999: 406)].

7 The preface to *Gesta Danorum* contains a geographical description that places *Gandvík* north of Norway. "Ceterum Oceani superior flexus Daniam intersecando praetermeans australem Gothiae plagam sinu laxiore contingit; inferior vero meatus eius Norvagiaeque latus septentrionale praeteriens ad ortum versus magno cum latitudinis incremento solido limitatur anfractu. Quem maris terminum gentis nostrae veteres Gandwicum dixere. Igitur inter Gandwicum et meridianum pelagus breve continentis spatium patet, maria utrimquesecus allapsa prospectans; quod nisi rerum natura limitis loco congressis paene fluctibus obiecisset, Suetiam Norvagiamque conflui fretorum aestus in insulam redegissent." (Olrik & Ræder 1931: 9.) ['The inner bend of the Ocean pierces Denmark and passes on to border the southern quarter of Götaland in a broad curve; the outer sweep increases in breadth as it streams eastwards along the coastline of northern Norway till it is walled by an unbroken arc of land and terminates in a sea which our ancestors called Gandvik. Between Gandvik and the waters to the south there is a thin strip of mainland situated between the lapping seas; if this natural barrier had not been created against the almost meeting waves, the tides, washing together in a channel, would have made an island of Sweden and Norway.' (Fisher 1980: 8–9.)]

8 *Landafræði*: "Noregr er kalladr nordan fra Vègistaf, þar er Finnmork, þat er hia Gandvik, ok sudr til Gaut-elfar. Þesa rikis ero endimork: Gandvik fyrir nordan, en Gaut-elfr fyrir sunnan, Eida-skogr fyrir austan, en Aunguls-eyiar-sund fyrir vestan" (Rafn 1852: 404–405).

9 *Fagrskinn*: "Óláfr konungr enn digri lagði þá undir sik allan Nóreg austan frá Elfi ok norðr til Gandvíkr" (Jackson & Podossinov 1997: 291).

10 Flateyjarbók (*Separate Saga of St. Olaf*): "Hann [Óláfr Haraldsson] var einvaldskonúngr yfir Noregi, svâ vítt sem Haraldr hinn hárfagri átt, frændi hans, rèd fyrir norðan Gandvík, en fyrir sunnan Gautelfr, en Eiðaskógr fyrir austan, Aungulseyjasund fyrir vestan, þessu ríki stýrdi engi einn milli Haralds hárfagra ok Ólafs ens Helga." (Rafn 1852: 496.)

11 The Arctic Ocean has been mentioned as an alternative (Jackson 2002: 171).

12 Also one of the mytho-heroic sagas, *Bósa saga*, mentions *Jómali* (Jiriczek 1893: 25) and considering the general details and themes of the text one may suspect the influence of *Óláfs saga helga*.

13 "Jómáli" and "Jómale" are manuscript variants of this name.

14 "He sæde þeah þæt [þæt] land sie swiþe lang norþ þonan; ac hit is eal weste, buton on feawum stowum styccemælum wiciað Finnas, on huntoðe on wintra ⁊ on sumera on fiscaþe be þære sæ. Ne mette he ær nan gebun land siþþan he from his agnum ham for, ac him wæs ealne weg weste land on þæt steorbord, butan fiscerum ⁊ fugelerum ⁊ huntum, ⁊ þæt wæron eall Finnas. ac þara Terfinna land wæs eal weste, buton ðær huntan gewicodon, oþþe fisceras, oþþe fugeleras." ['He said however that the land extends a very long way north from there, but it is all waste, except that in a few places here and there Finnas camp, engaged in hunting in winter and in summer in fishing by the sea. He had not previously encountered any settled land since he travelled from his own home, but there was wasteland all the way on his starboard side, except for fishermen and [wild]fowlers and hunters, and they were all Finnas, and open sea was always on his port side. But the land of the Terfinnas was all waste, except where hunters camped, or fishermen, or fowlers.'] (Bately 2007b: 44–45.)

15 "Austr rauð jǫfra þrýstir/orðrakkr fyr bý norðan/brand, þars bjarmskar kindir/brennanda, sák renna" (Aðalbjarnarson 1941: 217) ['Where [Bjarmian] folk, frightened, fled their burning dwellings' (Hollander 1999: 140)].

16 "Fyrir norðan Noreg er Finnmörk, þaðan víkr landi til lannorþrs ok svâ til austrs, áðr komi til Bjarmalands; þat er skattgilt undir Garða konúng" (Rafn 1852: 404) ['Finmark is north of Norway. Thence the land trends northeast and then again east before one reaches Bjarmaland which is tributary to the King of Russia' (Ross 1940: 39)].

17 *Hólmgarðr* (Novgorod) appears (somewhat stereotypically) in the Old Norse sources as the capital of *Garðaríki* (i.e. Russia/Rus') with the main seat of the king of *Garðar* situated in the town (see Jackson 2003: 42–43, 45). For instance, *Hákonar saga* talks about an ambassador of the king of Novgorod (*Hólmgarðr*) who came from *Garðaríki* (Vigfusson 1964: 266).

18 A few rather fictive sagas (*Gesta Danorum*, *Þattr Hauks hábrókar*, *Bósa saga ok Herrauðs*, *Hálfdanar saga Eysteinssonar*, *Sturlaugs saga starfsama*) refer to Swedish activity in Bjarmaland and in principle this could be sound information but we cannot really say anything about this on the basis of the meagre written sources (see Koskela Vasaru 2008: 419).

19 "Swiþost hē for ðider, toeacan þæs landes sceawunge, for þæm horshwælum" ['He chiefly went there, in addition to surveying the land, for the walruses]. (Bately 2007b: 45).

20 "En er þeir kómu til Bjarmalands, þá lǫgðu þeir til kaupstaðar. Tóksk þar kaupstefna. Fengu þeir menn allir fullræði fjár, er fé hǫfðu til at verja. Þórir fekk óf grávǫru ok bjór ok safala. Karli hafði ok allmikit fé, þat er hann keypti skinnavǫru marga." (Aðalbjarnarson 1945: 229.) ['When they arrived in Bjarmaland they put into a market town, and dealings [with natives] began. All those who had merchandise along sold it at full value. Thórir acquired an abundance of grey furs as well as beaver and sable pelts. Karli also had a very great amount of wares along, with which he bought many furs.' (Hollander 1999: 404.)] "ok görðu þar it mesta hervirki í manndrápum ok ránum, ok fengu stór-fè í grávöru ok brenndu silfri" (Vigfusson 1964: 71) ['and made there the greatest warfare in manslayings and plundering, and got much goods in greyskins and burnt silver' (Dasent 1964: 73–74)].

21 "Þá tekr Oddr til orða ok spyrr byrlarann tíðinda, en hann þagði við. 'Eigi þarftu at þegja, þvíat ek veit, at þú kant at mæla á norrœna tungu'. Þá segir byrlarinn: 'hvers viltu spyrja mik?' Oddr segir: 'hversu lengi hefir þú ér verit?' 'Verit hefi ek hér vetr nǫkkura.'" (Boer 1888: 26, 28, 30, 32.) ['Odd settled the man on the seat beside him and started questioning him, but he didn't say a word. "There's no point in keeping your mouth shut," said Odd, "I know you can speak Norse." "What do you want to know?" asked the man. Odd said, "How long have you been here?" "Some years," he said.' (Pálsson & Edwards 1985: 35–36)].

22 Russian archaeologists use the term Finno-Ugrian of all settlements that are deemed to be left behind by groups of people who spoke a Finno-Ugrian language. Relatively few remains of Finno-Ugrian origin have been excavated in the Russian north and they are not generally ethnically more closely identified but simply lumped together under the collective name Finno-Ugrian, which may include groups of e.g. Finnic, Finno-Volgaic or Sámi origin. The general consensus seems to be that before the spread of Russian/Slavic population the north of Russia was inhabited by groups of Finno-Ugrian peoples.

23 A global warming trend was evident around AD 1000–1200 and the Viking Age climate in the north shows a general trend towards warmer temperatures (see Helama). This in all likelihood has no direct bearing on the Bjarmians, but it is interesting to observe that the end of the warming trend is reached around 1200, an era of general changes in the north of Europe.

References

Sources

Aðalbjarnarson, Bjarni (ed.). 1941 [1962]. [Snorri Sturluson]. *Heimskringla I.* Íslenzk Fornrit 26. Reykjavík: Hið Íslendzka fornritafélag.

Aðalbjarnarson, Bjarni (ed.). 1945. [Snorri Sturluson]. *Heimskringla II.* Íslenzk Fornrit 27. Reykjavik: Hið Íslenzka Fornritafélag.

Aðalbjarnarson, Bjarni (ed.). 1951. [Snorri Sturluson]. *Heimskringla III.* Íslenzk Fornrit 28. Reykjavik: Hið Íslenzka Fornritafélag

Bately, Janet (ed.). 2007b. Text and Translation: The Three Parts of the Known World and the Geography of Europe North of the Danube According to Orosius' *Historiae* and Its Old English Version. In Janet Bately & Anton Englert (eds.). *Ohthere's Voyages: A Late Ninth-Century Account of Voyages along the Coasts of Norway and Denmark and Its Cultural Context.* Maritime Culture of the North 1. Roskilde: The Viking Ship Museum in Roskilde. Pp. 40–50.

Boer, R. C. (ed.). *Ǫrvar-Odds saga.* 1888. Leiden: E.J. Brill.

Dasent, G. W. (trans.). 1894 [1964]. *The Saga of Hacon and a Fragment of The Saga of Magnus, with Appendices.* Rerum Britannicarum medii ævi scriptores, or Chronicles and Memorials of Great Britain and Ireland during the Middle Ages 88; Icelandic Sagas and other Historical Documents Relating to the Settlements and Descents of the Northmen on the British Isles 4. Wiesbaden: Kraus Reprint Ltd.

Einarsson, Bjarni (ed.). 1985. *Fagrskinna - Nóregs konunga tal.* Íslenzk Fornrit 29. Reykjavík: Hið Íslenzka Fornritafélag.

Ekrem, Inger & Lars Boje Mortensen (eds.) & Peter Fisher (trans.). 2006. *Historia Norwegie.* University of Copenhagen. Museum Tusculanum Press. E-book.

Finlay, Alison (ed.). 2004. *Fagrskinna: A Catalogue of the Kings of Norway.* The Northern World: North Europe and the Baltic c. 400–1700 AD: Peoples, Economies and Cultures 7. Leiden: Brill.

Fisher, Peter (trans.). 1979. *The History of the Danes I: English Text.* Hilda Ellis Davidson (ed.). Haverhill: D.S. Brewer.

Jiriczek, Otto Luitpold (ed.). 1893. *Die Bósa-Saga in zwei Fassungen.* Strassburg: Verlag von Karl J. Trübner.

Keyser, R., & P. A. Munch (eds.). 1849. *Norges Gamle Love indtil 1387: Tredie Bind.* Christiania: Chr. Gröndahl.

Nordal, Sigurður (ed.). 1988. *Egils saga Skalla-Grímssonar.* Íslenzk Fornrit 2. Reykjavík: Hið íslenzka fornritafélag.

Olrik, J., & H. Ræder (eds.). 1931. *Saxonis Gesta Danorum: Tomus I: Textum continens.* Hauniæ: Levin & Munksgaard.

Pálsson, Hermann & Paul Edwards (eds.). 1985. *Seven Viking Romances.* Penguin Classics. Bury St Edmunds: Penguin Books.

Rafn, C. C. (ed.). 1830. *Fornaldar sögur Nordrlanda* I–III. Kaupmannahöfn: Hardvig Fridrek Popp.

Rafn, C. C. (ed.). 1850. *Antiquités Russes: D'après les monuments historiques des islandais et des anciens scandinaves* I. Copenhague: Frères Berling.

Rafn, C. C. (ed.). 1852. *Antiquités Russes: D'après les monuments historiques des islandais et des anciens scandinaves* II. Copenhague: Frères Berling.

Vigfusson, Gudbrand (ed.). 1887 [1964]. *Hakonar saga and a Fragment of Magnus Saga with Appendices.* Rerum Britannicarum medii ævi scriptores - Chronicles and Memorials of Great Britain and Ireland during the Middle Ages 88; Icelandic Sagas and Other Historical Documents Relating to the Settlements and Descents of the Northmen on the British Isles 2. Wiesbaden: Kraus Reprint Ltd.

Literature

Aikio, Ante. 2006. On Germanic-Saami Contacts and Saami Prehistory. *Journal de la Société Finno-Ougrienne* 91: 9–55.

Alsvik, Anne Stalsberg. 1973. *Dei skandinaviske vikingtidsfunna i Rus'-riket*. MA thesis: Universitetet i Trondheim.

Bately, Janet. 2007a. Ohthere and Wulfstan in the Old English *Orosius*. In Janet Bately & Anton Englert (eds.). *Ohthere's Voyages: A Late Ninth-Century Account of Voyages along the Coasts of Norway and Denmark and Its Cultural Context*. Maritime Culture of the North 1. Roskilde: The Viking Ship Museum in Roskilde. Pp. 18–39.

Bergsland, Knut. 1982. Tyrvi-finner. In *Kulturhistorisk leksikon for Nordisk middelalder fra vikingetid til reformationstid*. Viborg: Rosenkilde og Bagger. Vol 19, p. 123.

Carpelan, Christian. 1993. Bjarmerna. In Märtha Norrback (ed.). *Finlands historia 1*. 3rd edn. Ekenäs: Schildts. Pp. 231–233.

Clover, Carol J., & John Lindow (eds.). 1985. *Old Norse-Icelandic Literature: A Critical Guide*. Ithaca: Cornell University Press.

Englert, Anton. 2007. Ohthere's Voyages Seen from a Nautical Angle. In Janet Bately & Anton Englert (eds.). *Ohthere's Voyages: A Late Ninth-Century Account of Voyages along the Coasts of Norway and Denmark and Its Cultural Context*. Maritime Culture of the North 1. Roskilde: The Viking Ship Museum in Roskilde. Pp. 117–129.

Glazyrina, Galina. 2000. The Russian North in the Middle Ages: Some Historical Facts and Their Reflection in Old Norse Written Sources. In Ingi Sigurðsson & Jón Skaptason (eds.). *Aspects of Arctic and Sub-Arctic History: Proceedings of the International Congress on the History of the Arctic and Sub-Arctic Region, Reykjavík, 18–21 June 1998*. Reykjavík: University of Iceland Press. Pp. 517–529.

Gurina, N. N. 1984 = Н.Н. Гурина, Памятники эпохи раннего металла и раннего средневековья на кольском полуострове. In Б. А. Рыбакова (ed.). *Новое в археологии СССР и финляндии*. Доклады Третьего советско-финляндского симпозиума по вопросам археологии 11–15 мая 1981 г. Ленинград: "Наука" Ленинградское отделение. Pp. 7–16.

Gurina, N. N. 1987. Main Stages in the Cultural Development of the Ancient Population of the Kola Peninsula. *Fennoscandia Archaeologica* 4: 35–48.

Haavio, Martti. 1965. *Bjarmien vallan kukoistus ja tuho: Historiaa ja runoutta*, Helsinki: WSOY.

Hansen, Lars Ivar. 1996. Interaction between Northern European Sub-Arctic Societies during the Middle Ages: Indigenous Peoples, Peasants and State Builders. In Magnus Rindal (ed.). *Two Studies on the Middle Ages*. KULTs skriftserie 66. Oslo: The Research Council of Norway. Pp. 31–95.

Hansen, Lars Ivar. 2003. Fredstraktaten mellom Norge og Novgorod av 1326. *Middelalderforum* 2003(1–2): 6–28.

Hansen, Lars Ivar, & Bjørnar Olsen. 2004. *Samenes historie fram til 1750*. Oslo: Cappelen Akademisk Forlag.

Heide, Eldar. 2006. *Gand, seid og åndevind*. PhD dissertation. Bergen: Universitetet i Bergen.

Hofstra, Tette, & Kees Samplonius. 1995. Viking Expansion Northwards: Mediaeval Sources. *Arctic* 48(3): 235–247.

Hollander, Lee M. (ed.). 1999 [1964]. *Snorri Sturluson, Heimskringla. History of the Kings of Norway*. 3rd paperback printing. Austin: University of Texas Press.

Huurre, Matti. 1983. *Pohjois-Pohjanmaan ja Lapin esihistoria: Pohjois-Pohjanmaan ja Lapin historia I*. Kuusamo: Pohjois-Pohjanmaan maakuntaliiton ja Lapin maakuntaliiton yhteinen historiatoimikunta.

Häme, Matti. 1987. *Islantilaisten saagojen tiedot suomensukuisista kansoista ja niiden asuinpaikoista*. Lic. thesis, University of Oulu.

Jackson, Tatjana N. 2002. Bjarmaland Revisited. *Acta Borealia* 2002(2): 165–179.

Jackson, Tatjana N. 2003. The Image of Old Rus in Old Norse Literature (A Place-Name Study). *Middelalderforum* 2003(1–2): 29–56.

Jackson, Tatjana N., & Alexander V. Podossinov. 1997. Norway in Old Norse Literature: Some Considerations of the Specific Character of Scandinavian Spatial Orientation. In *"Sagas and the Norwegian Experience": Preprints: Tenth International Saga Conference: Trondheim, 3.–9. August 1997*. Trondheim: NTNU / Senter for Middelalderstudier. Pp. 281–291.

Jansson, Valter. 1936. Bjarmaland. *Ortnamns-sällskapets i Uppsala årsskrift* 1: 33–50.

Jasinski & Ovsyannikov 1998 = Ясински, М. Э., & Овсянников, О. В. 1998. *Взгляд на Европейскую Арктику Архангельский Север: Проблеиы и источники*. Vol. I. Санкт-Петербург: Российская Академия Наук.

Johnsen, O. A. 1923. *Finmarkens politiske historie*. Kristiania: Jacob Dybwad.

Knirk, James. E. 1993. Konungasögur. In Phillip Pulsiano (ed.). *Medieval Scandinavia: An Encyclopedia*. Garland Encyclopedias of the Middle Ages 1. Garland Reference Library of the Humanities 934. New York: Garland Publishing. Pp. 362–366.

Koskela Vasaru, Mervi. 2008. Bjarmaland. PhD dissertation, University of Oulu.

Koskela Vasaru, Mervi. 2011. On Bjarmaland, Vína, Viena, and Dvina. In Natalja Yu. Gvozdetskaja, Irina G. Konovalova, Elena A. Melnikova & Alexanrd V. Podossinov (eds.). *Stanzas of Friendship: Studies in Honour of Tatjana N. Jackson*. Moscow: Dmitriy Pozharskiy University. Pp. 176–183.

Krag, Claus. 2000. *Norges historie fram til 1319*. Oslo: Universitetsforlaget.

Lehtosalo-Hilander, Pirkko-Liisa. 1980. Common Characteristic Features of Dress: Expressions of Kinship or Cultural Contacts. *Fenno-ugri et slavi 1978: Papers Presented by the Participants in the Soviet–Finnish Symposium "The Cultural Relations between the Peoples and Countries of the Baltic Area during the Iron Age and the Early Middle Ages" in Helsinki May 20-23, 1978*. Helsinki: University of Helsinki. Pp. 243–260.

Makarov, Nikolaj A. 2007. The Land of the *Beormas*. In Janet Bately & Anton (eds.). *Ohthere's Voyages: A Late Ninth-Century Account of Voyages along the Coasts of Norway and Denmark and Its Cultural Context*. Maritime Culture of the North 1. Roskilde: The Viking Ship Museum in Roskilde. Pp. 140–149.

Magno, Jo. 1617 [1554]. *Gothorum Sveonumque historia*. Ex probatis antiquorem monumentis collecta & in 24 libros redacta. Secunda vice edita.. Upsalæ: Zachariæ Schureri.

Magnus, Olaus. 1972 [1555]. *Historia de gentibus septentrionalibus*. Copenhagen: Rosenkilde and Bagger.

Mitchell, Stephen A. 1993. Fornaldarsögur. In Phillip Pulsiano (ed.). *Medieval Scandinavia: An Encyclopedia*. Garland Encyclopedias of the Middle Ages 1. Garland Reference Library of the Humanities 934. New York: Garland Publishing. Pp. 206–208.

Nosov, E. N., O. V. Ovsyannikov & V. M. Potin. 1992. The Arkhangelsk Hoard. *Fennoscandia Archaeologica* 9: 3–21.

Ovsyannikov, O. V. 1984. On Trade Routes to Zavolochye in the Eleventh–Fourteenth Centuries. In Torsten Edgren (ed.). *Fenno-Ugri et Slavi 1983*. Iskos 4. Helsinki: Suomen muinaismuistoyhdistys. Pp. 98–106.

Ross, Alan S. C. 1940. *The* Terfinnas *and* Beormas *of Ohthere*. Texts and Monographs 7. Leeds: Titus Wilson of Kendal.

Ross, Alan S. C. 1951, The Place-Name Kandalaksha. In H. Draye & O. Jodogne (eds.). In *Third International Congress of Toponymy and Anthroponymy, Brussels, July 15th – July 19th 1949 II: Proceedings and Transactions*. Louvain: International Centre of Onomastics. Pp. 429–432.

Saarikivi, Janne. 2009. Itämerensuomalais-slaavilaisten kontaktien tutkimuksen nykytilasta. *Suomalais-Ugrilaisen Seuran Toimituksia* 258: 109–160.

Saksa, Aleksandr. 1998. *Rautakautinen karjala: Muinais-Karjalan asutuksen synty ja varhaiskehitys.* Studia Carelica Humanistica 11. Joensuu: Joensuun yliopiston humanistinen tiedekunta.

Santini, Carlo. 1993. Historia Norwegiae. In Phillip Pulsiano (ed.). *Medieval Scandinavia.* An Encyclopedia. Garland Encyclopedias of the Middle Ages (Vol. 1). Garland Reference Library of the Humanities (Vol. 934). New York: Garland Publishing, Inc. Pp. 284–285.

Schach, Paul. 1993. Hákonar saga gamla Hákonarsonar. In Phillip Pulsiano (ed.) *Medieval Scandinavia: An Encyclopedia.* Garland Encyclopedias of the Middle Ages 1. Garland Reference Library of the Humanities 934. New York: Garland Publishing. Pp. 259–260.

Spangen, Marte. 2005. Edelmetalldepotene i Nord-Norge: Komplekse identiteter i vikingtid og tidlig middelalder. MA thesis, University of Tromsø.

Storli, Inger. 2007. Ohthere and His World: A Contemporary Perspective. In Janet Bately & Anton Englert (eds.). *Ohthere's Voyages: A Late Ninth-Century Account of Voyages along the Coasts of Norway and Denmark and Its Cultural Context.* Maritime Culture of the North 1. Roskilde: The Viking Ship Museum in Roskilde. Pp. 76–99.

Tallgren, A. M. 1930. Bjarmienmaa. *Kalevalaseuran vuosikirja* 10: 58–83.

Tolley, Clive. 2009. *Shamanism in Norse Myth and Magic* I–II. FF Communications 296–297. Helsinki: Academia Scientiarum Fennica.

Vilkuna, Kustaa. 1980. Bjarmer och Bjarmaland. In *Kulturhistorisk leksikon for Nordisk middelalder fra vikingetid til reformationstid.* Viborg: Rosenkilde og Bagger. Vol. 1, pp. 647–651.

Jari-Matti Kuusela

From Coast to Inland

Activity Zones in North Finland during the Iron Age

This study examines the Iron Age of North Finland and focuses thematically on the economic weight of the coast during the Early and Middle Iron Age (500 BC–AD 600) and the shift of this weight to the inland zone during the Late Iron Age (after AD 600). Geographically the centre of attention is, as far as the coastal area is concerned, between the current towns of Raahe and Tornio while the inland zone contains the current provinces of North Ostrobothnia (inland areas), Kainuu and Lapland (Fig.1). In the case of North Finland, there is little use in distinguishing the Viking Age as a single period of study as this arbitrarily defined time period between 800 and 1050 AD is inextricably tied to periods both preceding and following (see Ahola & Frog). Therefore in this study this time period is merely included in what is referred to as the Late Iron Age – i.e. in this context a time period after AD 800.

Problems of Research into the Iron Age in North Finland

The Iron Age of North Finland is not a widely studied period, which is why it is still more often than not omitted from studies concerning the Iron Age of what is today Finland. Archaeologists of the University of Oulu have had a long-standing interest in this phase of prehistory. This research reached its zenith during the 1980s and 1990s, when significant archaeological excavations were carried out on several Iron Age sites, such as the Rakanmäki cemetery and the activity site in Tornio, the Välikangas cemetery in Oulu, the Tervakangas cemetery in Raahe and the Länkimaa cemetery in Kemi.[1] After this, however, the interest has somewhat waned up until recent years and, as a result, the Iron Age is still largely an unknown period in North Finland.

The problems of the Iron Age in what is today North Finland are to a large degree problems of research tradition. On the one hand, archaeologists' lack of interest in the Iron Age of North Finland over the last two decades or so and disregard of the fact that the Iron Age cultural milieu in North Finland

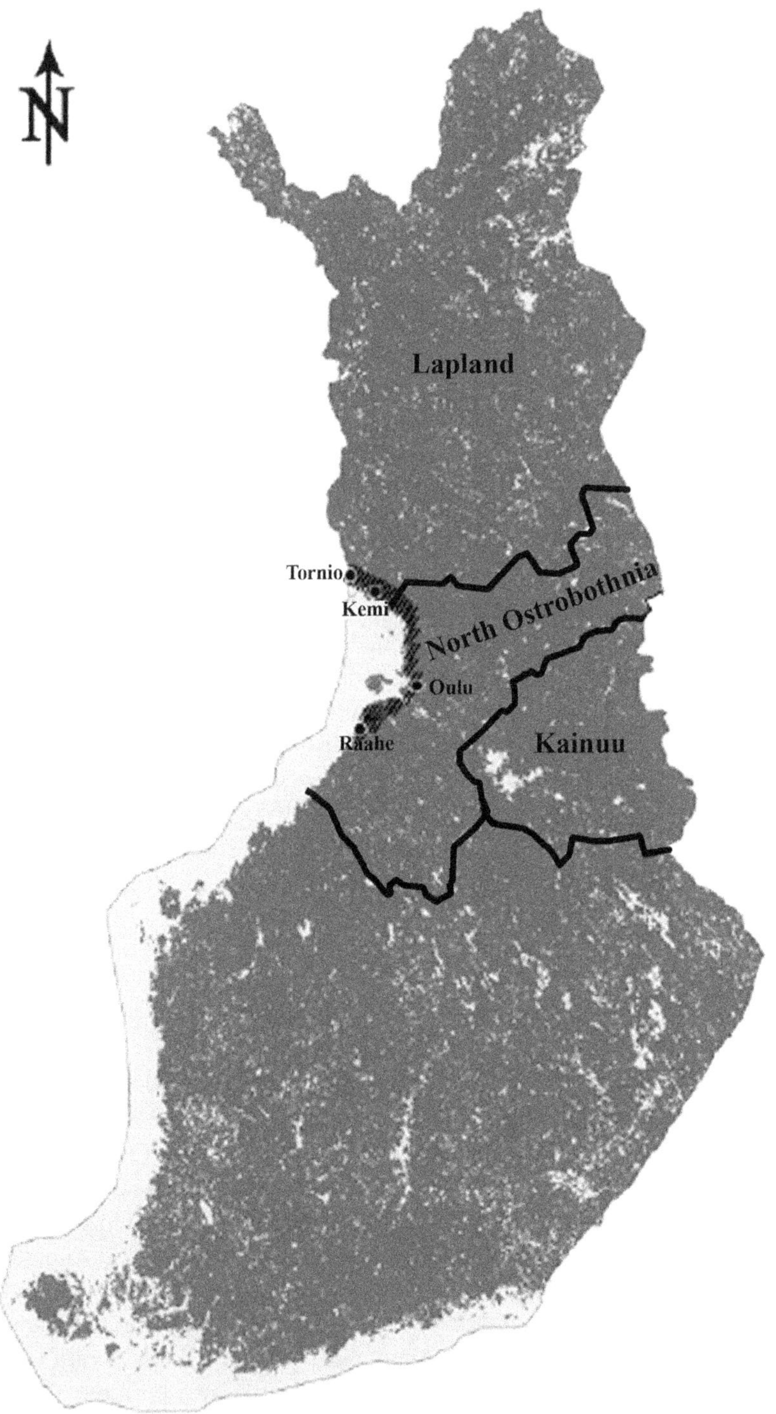

Fig. 1. Research area (North Ostrobothnia, Kainuu and Lapland) with major coastal towns marked. The thatch indicates the area referred to as coastal in the text.

significantly differs from that of the Iron Age core areas of South Finland (such as Tavastia and Finland Proper) on the other (see LAAKSO), have both contributed to the fact that, even though great strides were made during the late 1980s and early 1990s, we still know very little about the Iron Age in the area now under scrutiny. I argue that the archaeological research conducted in the 1980s and 1990s has been hampered by misunderstandings and a false premise concerning the period, resulting in a situation where North Finland is still implicitly and explicitly considered to have been more or less 'wilderness' during the Iron Age, with little or no human impact.

The false premise that has misguided Iron Age research in the north is crystallised in a dualistic approach dealing with ethnicities regarding 'Finns' (e.g. Huurre 1986: 149) and the Sámi. This results in a patterned research where archaeological material is divided between the 'Finns' and the 'Sámi' and then interpreted on the basis of this dualism.[2] This has limited the grounds on which interpretations have been made – if the archaeological material has been deemed 'Finnish' the equivalents have been sought from the core areas of Southern Finland and when they have been interpreted as 'Sámi', eyes have been turned to the historically known and somewhat ambiguous 'Lapps'. As the archaeological record in the north does not conform to either analogy, the period has remained largely unknown. Therefore often vague and ambiguous ethnicities should be abandoned in archaeological research and archaeology should not label data with ethnic terms. Instead archaeological material should be interpreted on its own merits and analogies for interpretation should be sought from general social theories utilised in other social sciences like anthropology and sociology as these have been formed in the process of studying human societies. This approach will enable an understanding of the processes behind human action, of which archaeological remains are a direct result.

The basis for the theoretical framework I use is tied closely to the social theory of Pierre Bourdieu, whose thoughts I see as having direct significance for archaeological research. It is important to ground archaeological research in a theoretical framework which has a strong link with reality – i.e. studies concerning real societies – because this prevents 'ivory-tower empiricism' where seemingly logical interpretations based on observed data are disconnected from reality because they are based on false assumptions stemming from ignorance of how the processes under study truly work (see Elias 1983; Bourdieu 1990a: 14–15; O'Brien 2007: 56–57, 66). Therefore, before turning to the archaeological data relevant for this study, I must digress and make clear the theoretical premises I operate with.

Theoretical Background: Material Culture Reflects Society's Social Space

Material culture, i.e. the material remains that form archaeological data, is the direct result of human action. Human action on the other hand can be viewed from many angles but I operate on the principle that it is a form of communication with which past societies have signalled aspects of their social world (Kuusela 2009; 2011; 2012a; Kuusela *et al.* 2010). By utilising material culture it is possible to signal aspects and properties of individuals, groups, places etc. without the need for verbal exchange, providing that the material 'code' is understandable to those observing it. To take a very simple example – a barrow built at a specific location may signal, for example, the following aspects pertaining to the location: *a*) this is a burial site; *b*) this is a sacred site; *c*) spirits live on this site, etc. Furthermore this communication may be taken to the level of individuals; for example, the size, shape or location of the barrow may further signal aspects about the individual buried within (see Kuusela *et al.* 2010; Kuusela 2011).

This should not be taken to mean that every aspect of material culture has been geared functionally towards this communication but rather that material culture, and more importantly how material culture has been used, always signals aspects of its users and therefore can be labelled communication. This is so because material culture is an excellent way to convey messages pertaining to the roles and qualities of individuals without the need for verbal verification of one's status or role in one's society with each acquaintance, and the more complex the society becomes and the more roles there appear in the social network of that society, the more need there is for such instant communication (Morris 1995: 431; Neitzel 1995: 396), or, as the proverb says: *a picture says more than a thousand words.* This is a plausible position to take as it fits well in a theoretical framework corresponding with observed human behaviour. The concept of fields, familiar from the sociological writings of Pierre Bourdieu, becomes especially useful in this context.

According to Bourdieu (Bourdieu 1985: 69–70; 1989: 16) the social space of a society is composed of social differentiation and is populated by fields encompassing specific areas of action. The position of agents in these fields is commensurate with their field-specific capital, i.e. how successful they are in the action represented by the field (Bourdieu 1985: 69–70; 1984). Fields exist relationally in the social space, forming what I call a society-specific field configuration, which means that in each society the fields of action have a different meaning and different position in the social space, i.e. different societies value different forms of action in differing ways (Kuusela & Saunavaara 2011: 207–208). As the capitals of all fields form the symbolic capital of the society (Bourdieu 1977: 183; 1989: 17; 1990b: 118–119; 1998: 48, 102), this means that the composition of symbolic capital, and therefore by definition the field configuration, varies between individual societies. Nevertheless close proximity and continuous contact make it possible for the field configurations and symbolic capital of neighbouring societies to begin to resemble each other, though they never become identical.

All this ties directly into archaeology for the reason that as archaeological material is a direct result of human action it is also a direct result of agents acting in the fields, from which follows the argument that archaeological data are, in fact, what remain of past societies' fields and field configuration and the social space that produced it. As it is possible that close contact between societies will cause their respective field configurations to resemble each other, it can be deduced that regularities observed in archaeological data become important and can plausibly be assumed to pertain to the social communication of the societies of whose actions the archaeological record is an outcome.

Before the Late Iron Age: Coasts

It would be difficult for an archaeologist to discuss a single prehistoric time period without reference to periods either preceding or following the one under scrutiny and it would be exceedingly difficult to do so with the archaeological material that forms the data used in this chapter. I must therefore ask the reader to bear in mind the fact that, in order to say something about the Viking Age, a significant portion of this chapter will be devoted to examining periods that precede the Viking Age, as only taking this long perspective will reveal and contextualise the processes that were in effect during the Late Iron Age.

Already during the Stone Age, the archaeological record in North Finland indicates that human activity was concentrated on the coasts and especially river mouths that experienced relative stability in relation to the shoreline, as the coastlines of North Finland were, and still are, subject to post-glacial land uplift, resulting in a receding shoreline (Vaneeckhout 2009). Horizontal coastline stability results in an area where the topography is steep, meaning that despite the sea level lowering vertically, the horizontal displacement of the coast is minimal. A good example of a stable milieu is the Stone Age village of Kierikki in Yli-Ii, some 50 km north of Oulu, where the coastline was stable for a very long time during the Stone Age, resulting in a long period of occupation (Vaneeckhout 2009; Costopoulos *et al.* 2012). This results in a general pattern of the archaeological record where older sites are located on higher elevations above sea level (henceforward a.s.l.) than younger sites, for example in the Oulu region the earliest Iron Age coastlines (around 500 BC) are located roughly 21–21.5 metres a.s.l. whereas the youngest known Iron Age cemetery of Välikangas, dating to the Late Roman Iron Age and Migration Period (AD 200–600), is located at an elevation of 15 metres a.s.l., corresponding with the contemporary coastline.

This pattern is naturally not without exceptions. Although it is certain that Stone Age sites cannot be located on Iron Age elevations, Iron Age sites may still be located on what would have been a Stone Age coastline. The trend of shore-boundedness is evident in the north during the periods from the Bronze Age to the Early Iron Age (Okkonen 2001; Ikäheimo 2005: 772–775; Kuusela *et al.* 2011: 182–188) but this does not mean that only the coasts were used, as the interior also has continuous signs of human activity during these periods (see Kuusela *et al.* 2011: 193–195 with citations). However, it is evident that the majority of sites known from the Bronze and Early to Middle Iron Ages are clustered on the corresponding coastlines.

In North Ostrobothnia, the sites from the Bronze and Iron Ages fall roughly into two distinctive categories – cooking pits and barrows or stone settings. A cooking pit is a type of archaeological site that mostly dates to the

Late Bronze and Early Iron Ages, roughly between 800 and 1 BC (Ikäheimo 2005: 118; Okkonen & Äikäs 2006: 21). From the area of the Oulujoki river estuary alone, between three and four hundred individual cooking pits are currently known, often clustered together (Okkonen & Äikäs 2006: 21). As to the function of the pits, there is no straightforward answer but the prevailing interpretation is that they are linked to the manufacture of seal train oil (Ylimaunu 1999; Ylimaunu *et al.* 1999: 148–153; Ikäheimo 2005: 781; Okkonen & Äikäs 2006). For the current discussion, the function of cooking pits is secondary, so suffice it to say that they signify intense human activity related to shorelines during the Bronze and Early Iron Ages.

It appears that cooking pits are in areas that have experienced relative stability in relation to horizontal shoreline displacement, i.e. how quickly the shoreline recedes. In flat and featureless areas the land uplift of, say, one metre in the vertical scale may cause the recession of the shoreline to considerable distances while steep inclines create the effect that while the land rises, the shoreline itself remains relatively stable. I examined the stability of cooking-pit sites in relation to horizontal shoreline displacement with GIS (Geographic Information Systems) by creating a 200 metre buffer around each site and then reconstructing the shoreline at one-century intervals with the aid of the shoreline displacement chronology of North Ostrobothnia (Okkonen 2003) and a 25 metre digital elevation model of the National Land Survey of Finland. With each site, I assumed that, as it is unlikely that cooking pits were constructed immediately at the edge of the water (Sandén 1995: 178; Okkonen 2003: 108–109; see also Ylimaunu 1999: 130), the actual shoreline would be at least two metres lower than the elevation of the site. With each site, I observed how long the shoreline remained within the buffer. This method is crude for several reasons – first of all, the buffer is generated around a single point and not the whole site, and secondly shoreline reconstructions are subject to uncertainties owing to local variances in land uplift (Okkonen 2003: 85–88 with citations). Also the radius of the buffer, 200 metres, is arbitrary. However, as the goal of this experiment was simply to compare sites with each other in relation to their potential shoreline stability and thus gain comparable indicative results, the apparent crudity of the method is not a key issue here. Altogether 79 cooking-pit sites from elevations corresponding with Bronze or Early Iron Age shorelines were included in the analysis. Figs. 2–3 demonstrate that the sites have a tendency to be located in areas that have remained close to the shoreline for several centuries. Altogether six sites were in unstable areas, meaning that they were within 200 metres of the shoreline for less than a century, and three were within 200 metres of the shoreline for one century or less. For the sake of clarity, these have been excluded from Fig. 2.[3] Furthermore, four sites (Hangaskangas, Kiimamaa, Korkiamaa 3 and Metsokangas) have radiocarbon dates available. Whereas the radiocarbon date of three sites correspond with the shore phase, one, Korkiamaa 3, does not. This means that the latter was not located close to the shore at the time of its use, making it an exceptional case. Excluding Korkiamaa 3, as it was not shore-bound, the median stability of the 79 sites is five centuries,

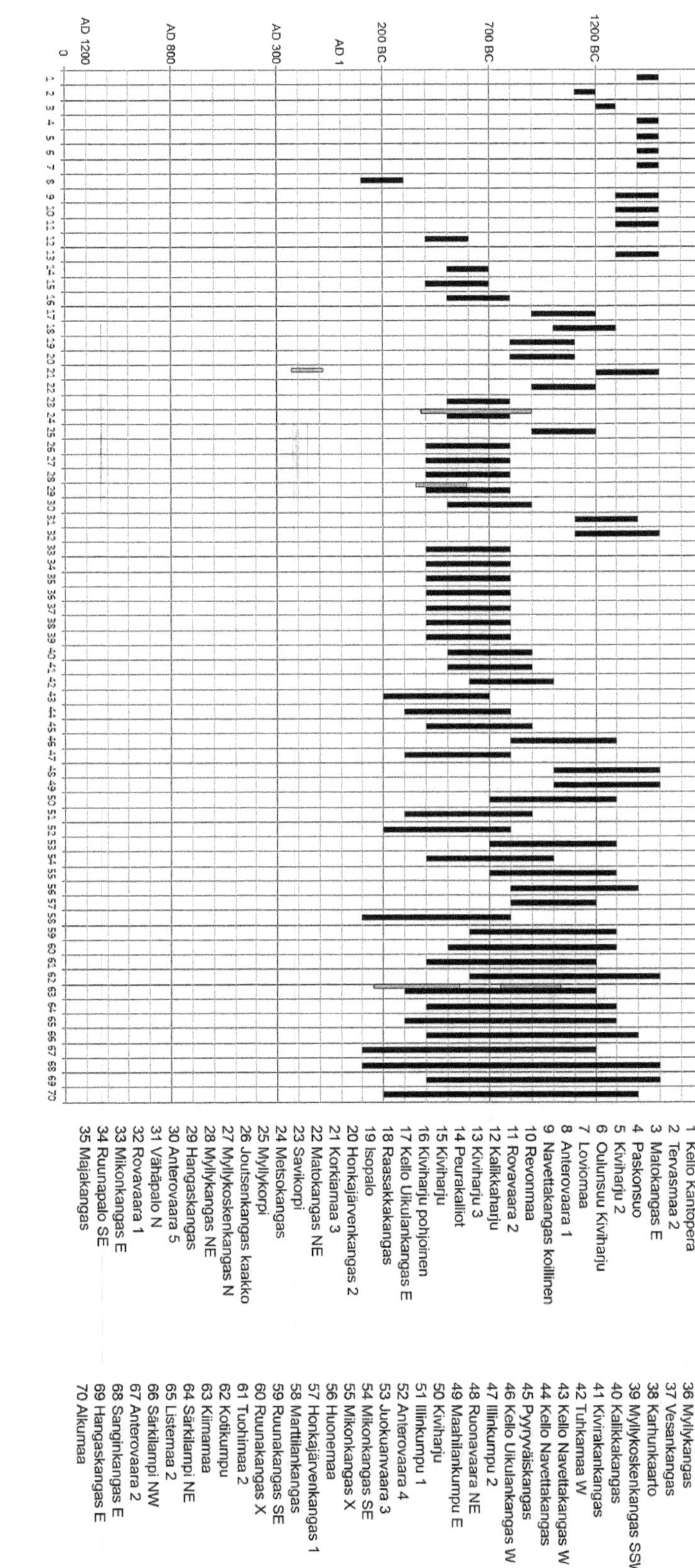

Fig. 2. Stability of cooking pit sites in relation to horizontal shoreline displacement. Grey lines indicate ^{14}C-dating.

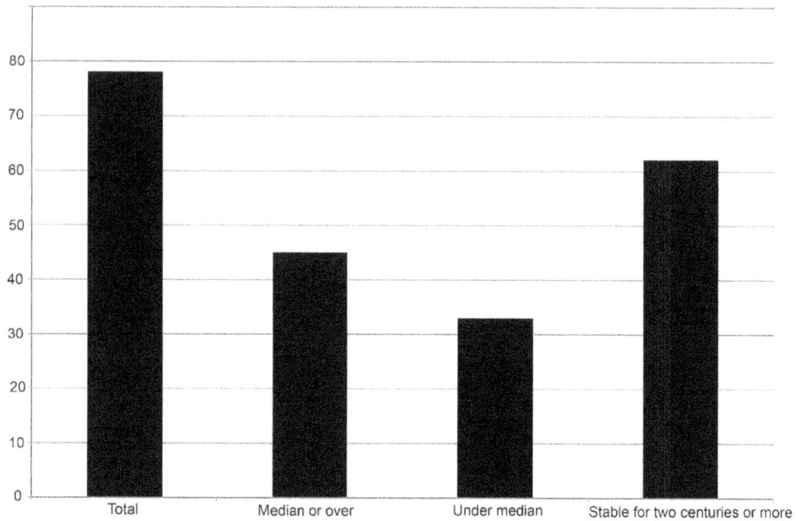

Fig. 3. Distribution of cooking pit sites in relation to their median stability (five centuries). The amount of sites that have remained stable for over two centuries is also presented.

and this is either met or exceeded by 45 sites. 62 sites remained stable, i.e. within 200 metres from the shoreline, over two centuries (Fig. 3). Therefore cooking pits seem to follow the same trend as the sites of earlier periods (see Vaneeckhout 2009) in relation to shoreline stability.

Most of the cooking-pit sites are at elevations that correspond with the Late Bronze and Early Iron Age shorelines, after which they sharply decrease in number, as can be observed in Fig. 4 (also Okkonen 2003: 169, Fig. 78). To be exact, 25 metres a.s.l., the threshold for the decline in the number of sites, is not the elevation of an Early Iron Age shoreline, but as already mentioned it is unlikely cooking pits were constructed immediately on the edge of the water (Sandén 1995: 178; Okkonen 2003: 108–109; see also Ylimaunu 1999: 130). 25 metres a.s.l. can be regarded as an appropriate threshold for Early Iron Age activities as the Early Iron Age shorelines range between 21.5 to 22.5 metres a.s.l. in the area under study.[4]

Barrows show a feature corresponding with the cooking-pit sites in that they were also constructed in relatively stable areas in relation to horizontal shoreline displacement. Figs 5–6 demonstrate this.[5] I analysed altogether 47 sites at elevations equal to or lower than 36 metres a.s.l. using the same GIS method as for the cooking-pit sites. These 47 sites include most of the known sites on the elevations equal to 36 metres a.s.l. or lower from the area under study. The earliest Bronze Age shorelines, i.e. shorelines of *c.* 1500 BC, in the study area are located roughly between 34 and 32 metres a.s.l., so assuming once more that barrows were not constructed immediately on the edge of the water, an elevation of 36 metres a.s.l. is a plausible Bronze Age activity threshold. As not all of the sites have been excavated, it is likely that not all the sites presented in Figs 5–6 are prehistoric, as it is usually very

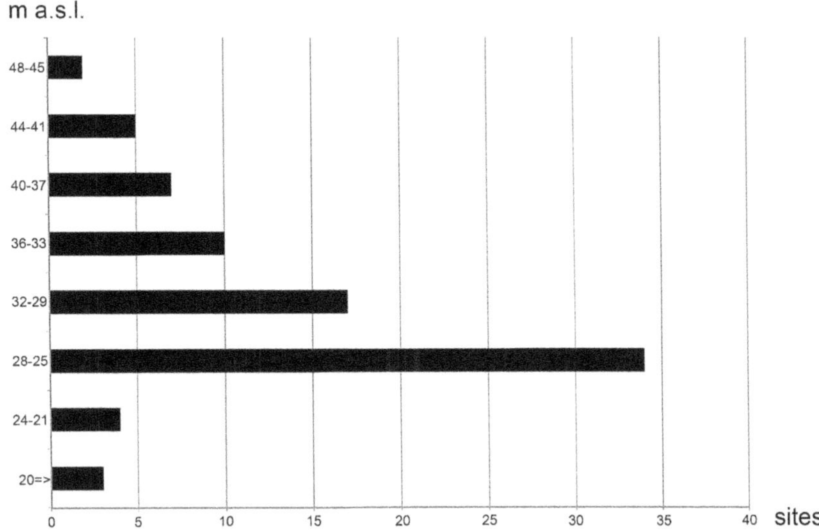

Fig. 4. Distribution of cooking pit sites in relation to elevation in meters above sea level.

difficult to ascertain with certainty the character of a stone structure with surveillance methods only (Okkonen 2003: 82–83). Even excavated barrows with typologically datable finds are problematic as it is possible that burials include finds from periods earlier than the grave itself (see e.g. Wessman 2009; 2010: 82, 96–97). Therefore, Figs 5–6 contain a margin of error that must be acknowledged. Four of the analysed sites were located within 200 metres of the shoreline for less than a century and one of them a century or less. For the sake of visual clarity these have been excluded from Fig. 5 but not from the statistics presented in Fig. 6. Among the sites, Länkimaa 1 is an exceptional case – the typological dating based on a brooch from the graves indicates that at least this burial dates from the Migration Period (AD 400–600). However, a radiocarbon sample taken from a hearth found in an activity area adjacent to the burials indicates a Merovingian Period or Viking Age date, which suggests that the burials and the adjacent activity area might not be contemporary with each other (Eskola & Ylimaunu 1993).

The analysed sites have a median stability of five centuries which is met or exceeded by 27 sites. Altogether 37 remained stable, i.e. within 200 metres of the shoreline, over two centuries. Therefore, despite the problematic case of Länkimaa 1, it appears that a plausible conclusion of the results is that proximity to the shoreline was of importance during the Bronze Age and Early to Middle Iron Age in North Finland. I will return to the interpretation of this phenomenon at the conclusion of this chapter after examining the changes that occurred during the Late Iron Age.

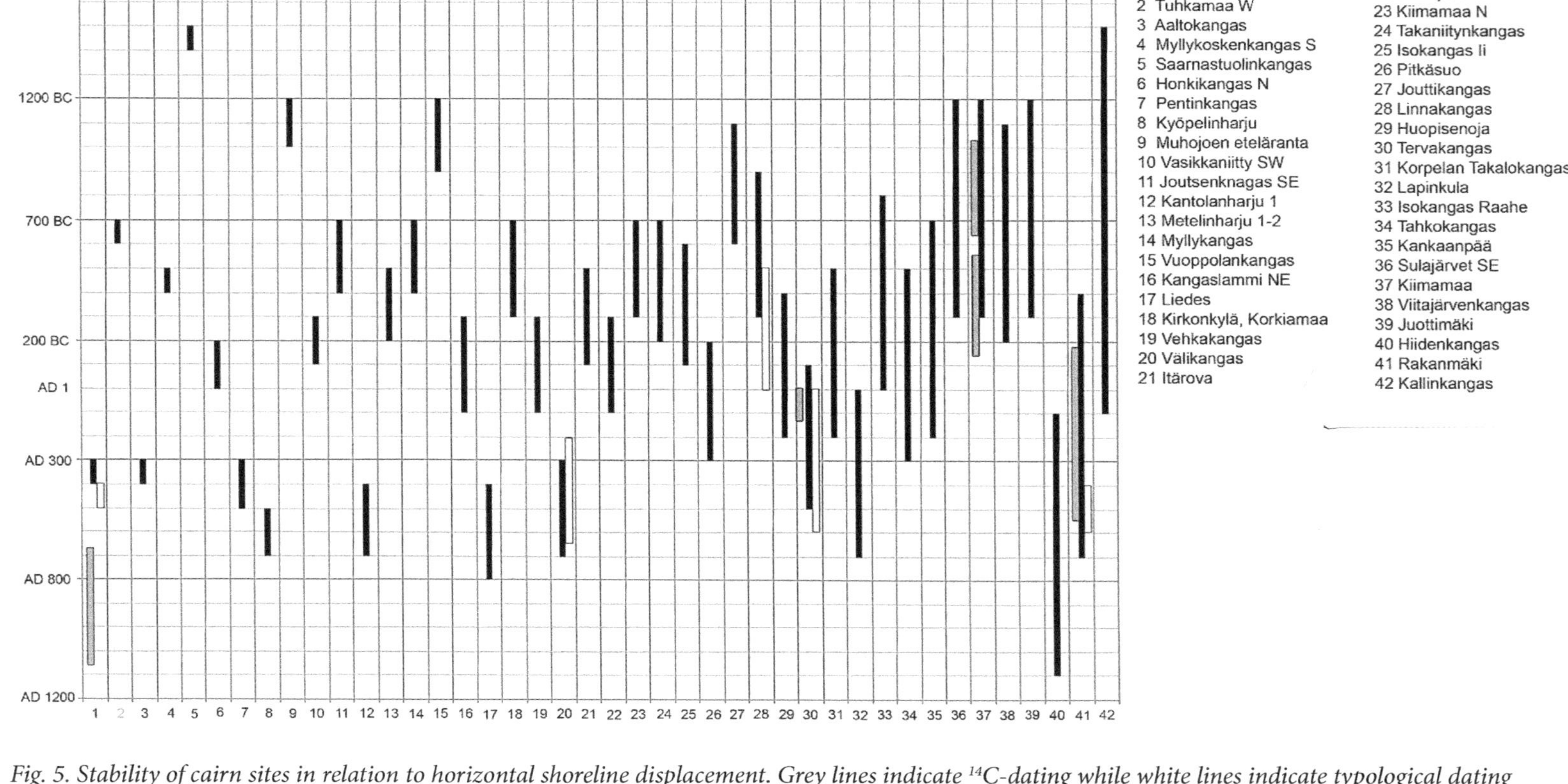

Fig. 5. Stability of cairn sites in relation to horizontal shoreline displacement. Grey lines indicate ^{14}C-dating while white lines indicate typological dating

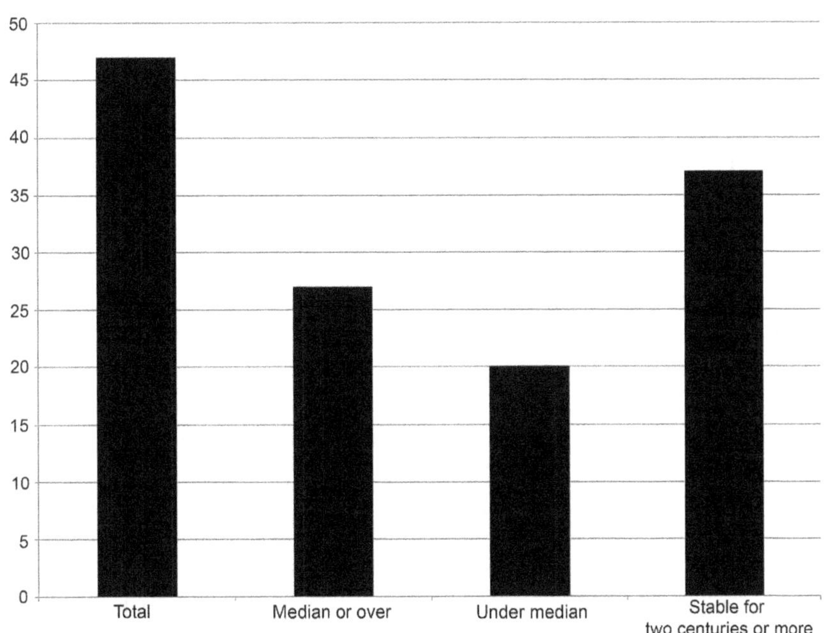

Fig. 6. Distribution of cairn sites in relation to their median stability (five centuries). The amount of sites that have remained stable for over two centuries is also presented.

The Late Iron Age: The Interior

The youngest known Iron Age barrow cemeteries in the coast of North Finland are the Late Roman Iron Age and Migration Period cemetery of Välikangas in Oulu (Mäkivuoti 1996; 2009) and the Migration Period Rakanmäki cemetery in Tornio (Mäkivuoti 1988; Kuusela 2013: appendix 1, 15). The hearth adjacent to the Länkimaa 1 burials also indicates Merovingian Period and/or Viking Age activity but the burials themselves are likely to be older. As a conclusion, from the Merovingian Period onwards, i.e. after AD 600, barrows are no longer built on the coast, breaking a tradition dating as far back as the Neolithic (Okkonen 2003). The archaeological record of the Late Iron Age consists mainly of what in archaeological terminology are called stray finds – recovered artefacts not associated with a known site. In some cases, archaeological field research has established a context for recovered artefacts, i.e. a site has later been uncovered where the artefact or artefacts were found, and technically such a find can no longer be called a stray find. Nevertheless, for the sake of clarity, I will maintain a systematic terminology and refer to all Late Iron Age artefact finds as stray finds.

As a result of stray finds not being associated with any site, they have been somewhat under-studied in archaeology with the exception of typological analyses, and have more often than not been labelled as "memoirs of travellers or immigrants from outside" (e.g. Koivunen 1975: 17–22; Huurre 1983: 342–348; Taskinen 1998: 157). I will bypass them as artefacts and ignore their typological properties. Instead, I observe them as signs of human activity, which they undoubtedly are. I will also question their labelling as signs of 'foreigners' as unconvincing.

Stray finds provide a not unproblematic set of data – or, to be more specific, the difficulties in using them as material for research are fourfold. Firstly, their number is not very significant – only around 250 artefacts dating to the Iron Age have been recovered from North Finland. As these fall into all the periods of the Iron Age, their number per period is small (see Fig. 7a–g). On the other hand, one could argue that this is a problem pertaining to archaeological material in general, so in this regard stray finds do not significantly differ from other sets of data. A more serious problem is that of context: only in a few cases has a stray-find site been studied, but when this has taken place, it has been observed that they are either directly linked to an archaeological site or to an obvious cultural milieu that should be taken into account.[6] The third problem pertains to dating. Most finds have been dated on the basis of typology, but we must remember that a typological age does not signify the age of deposition, i.e. the time that the artefact was left behind or became buried in the ground. In addition, some artefacts may have been used for a long time before deposition. Therefore typological dating can only give an approximation of the age of an artefact and can merely set an assumed *terminus post quem* dating. The fourth problem is the accuracy of the finds' spatial data. Often stray finds have been removed to an archaeological collection after a considerable time had passed since the discovery of the object. The finder, for example a local peasant, may have passed away or may not remember where the find originally came from. On only a few occasions has an archaeologist been able to study the exact find location. Recently several Iron Age finds have been obtained from North Finland as a result of the rising interest in metal detectorism as a hobby (see e.g. Kuusela & Tolonen 2011; Kuusela *et al.* 2013; Hakamäki *et al.* 2013) and in these cases the find places have often been located with relative accuracy with a GPS unit. Despite these problems, the distribution of stray finds can give important information regarding activity areas, especially during the Late Iron Age, from which period known sites are few in the current study area. When using stray-find data, the key is to examine large areas, whereby the problem of uncertain spatial data is, to a degree, mitigated.

Eliminating a False Premise

Before moving on to the interpretation, I must digress and eliminate what I consider a false premise of research regarding the Iron Age, and especially the Late Iron Age, in North Finland. I shall not view stray finds as sigs of 'foreigners' or 'immigrants' for a very simple reason: I see such an interpretation as unconvincing. First of all, there is enough evidence to argue that the deposition of these so-called stray finds is not accidental, i.e. they are not to any significant degree items that have been 'lost' (see Hakamäki & Kuusela 2013). On the contrary, in several cases the opposite is clearly

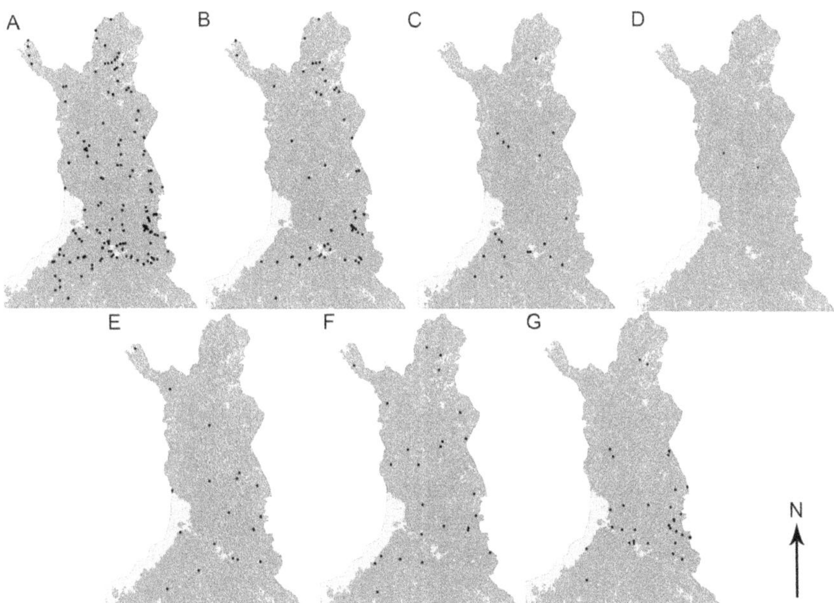

Fig. 7. Stray find distribution maps. A: Distribution of all stray finds with spatial data accurate enough to be presented in a distribution map. B: Undated finds. C: Merovingian Period or older finds. D: Merovingian Period or Viking Age finds. E: Viking Age finds. F: Viking Age or Crusade Period finds. G: Crusade Period finds. Datings are based on artefact typology.

the case and it has been confirmed that the artefacts were deposited on purpose.[7] In my view, the artefacts themselves are of secondary importance – their context matters. When stray finds have been deemed as being brought to the North by 'outsiders', the basis for this argument has been the typological link of the artefact or artefacts in question to distant areas but not the context of the find. The archaeological record of the Late Iron Age of North Finland differs significantly from that of the Iron Age core areas of, for example, Southern Finland. If stray finds are not 'lost' items but were left purposefully at a certain place, one basically has to make a choice between two interpretations. The artefacts have either been hidden by these assumed 'foreign visitors' or they are the product of the actions of members of local communities; or, in the case of burials, they are burials of outsiders who have fallen on their journey or they are the burials of members of local communities. If we choose to go with the outsiders we would have to answer the question: why? – why would an outsider hide the artefacts in such a manner or why were their remains not taken home but given a burial significantly differing from the burial practices of their home regions (see Taavitsainen 2003)? Occam's razor compels me to acknowledge the fact that the answer which makes fewer assumptions is that stray finds are the product of the actions of local communities and not of immigrants or foreign visitors. This is in accordance with the theoretical framework presented above in this chapter – different societies value fields of action in different manners thus resulting in different patterns of action. This means that the archaeological record of societies inhabiting different regions should differ from each other when compared. Therefore instead of trying to come up with complex explanations justifying the labelling of Iron Age material in the north as the product of immigrants, the evident differences should be acknowledged as simply being the result of the actions of different local societies. This explanation not only fits well with the social theory used in this chapter but it is directly corroborated by archaeological evidence, as can be deduced from the two examples below.

That a typological link does not mean a concrete link between two places is demonstrated in the case of a single find from Suomussalmi – a crucible for bronze jewellery typologically dated to AD 400–800 and linked to the Volga region (Huurre 1983: 332). Is this a sign of a bronzesmith who came from the faraway Volga to what is today Suomussalmi to manufacture bronze jewellery, or a product of a local community that has received the idea for this particular type of jewellery via interaction between neighbouring societies, who in turn may have received its jewellery or ideas for jewellery through interactions with their neighbouring societies etc.? I see local production and ideas received through, for example, trade relations once more as a more likely scenario because this eliminates the complex explanation required for the 'Volgan' bronzesmith arriving in the distant north for some reason. Another warning against too rigid a use of artefacts as evidence of direct cross-cultural links is provided by Kristina Creutz's (2003) study of the Late Iron Age spearheads of the Petersen type M. These typologically similar spearheads were formerly thought to have been imported all over the Baltic Sea area from Gotland but Creutz has convincingly demonstrated that this is not the case – they are found all over the Baltic because they were made all over the Baltic (Creutz 2003). Therefore artefacts may have a completely different place of origin than their typology might suggest.

What this naturally means is that artefacts are very poor proof of immigration or ethnicities and therefore they should not be used to track, or date, for example, linguistic changes or 'waves of immigration'.

Of the 253 finds used in this study, 160 have spatial data accurate enough (within 1 km of accuracy) to be used in distribution maps. These are presented in Fig. 7a–g, where the finds are classified in the following categories: *a*) all finds, *b*) undated, *c*) Merovingian Period or older, *d*) Merovingian Period or Viking Age, *e*) Viking Age, *f*) Viking Age or Crusade Period and *g*) Crusade Period. Referring to the above-mentioned problems pertaining to dating, presenting the finds in categories by period is misleading but justified to demonstrate that the number of stray finds seems to increase during the Late Iron Age. The change in the number of finds is further demonstrated in Fig. 8. The finds from the Merovingian Period or earlier are significantly more numerous than those of the Merovingian–Viking Age period largely because the majority of finds of the former category are oval fire-striking stones that are dated from the Early to Middle Iron Ages (Huurre 1983: 332–333) and thus cannot be given a more accurate dating estimate than before the Merovingian Period or Merovingian Period. Owing to their rather

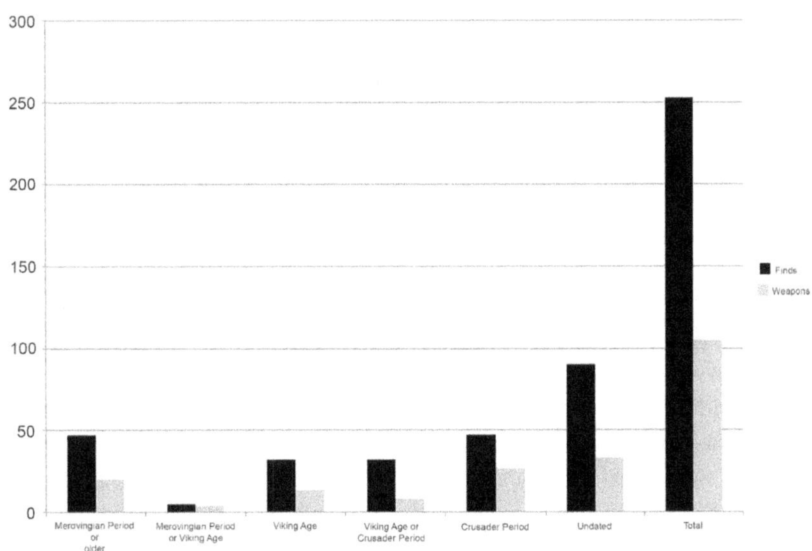

Fig. 8. Stray finds distributed in chronological classes. The black bar represents all finds and the grey bar weapon finds.

wide dating, some of the oval fire-striking stones could well belong to the Merovingian–Viking Age period and thus diminish the seeming difference between these two phases of the Iron Age.

Interpretation: Social Change in the Iron Age of North Finland

Archaeological material is clustered on sites and areas that have been, in one way or another, important for the community of whose actions the archaeological record is a result. As material culture is a form of social communication, areas and sites with archaeological material are places of importance pertaining to social communication (Kuusela *et al.* 2010; Kuusela 2011).

From the Early to Middle Iron Age, a general trend is evident: the coasts dominate the archaeological record. Most of the barrows are built in coastal areas whereas the interior is represented with a more incomplete picture where stray finds seem to be the main indicator of Iron Age activity. This might tempt an archaeologist to draw a line on the map where the coasts are dominated by the 'barrow culture' and the interior by the 'stray-find culture' but this picture is not clear-cut as inland barrows do exist (Okkonen 2003: 42–43; Taavitsainen 2003) and stray finds have been recovered from the coastal areas, although the clear majority of them are from inland. Nevertheless two zones of somewhat differing ways of producing material culture seem to be evident during the Early and Middle Iron Ages, which would suggest that the coastal and inland societies had different respective field configurations, meaning that the composition of their symbolic capital was different, at least with regard to how it was manifested in material culture. The reason for this, as I suggest, might be tied to the environment and economy.

The shoreline stability as a common feature of the Bronze to Middle Iron Age sites is an interesting one. Returning now to the cooking pits and their function: their exact function is not self-evident but the general field with which they are associated may perhaps be deduced. If they are connected with the manufacture of seal train oil or the processing of other maritime goods such as salmon (see Okkonen & Äikäs 2006: 30–31), they are economic in function. On the other hand, if they are, as their designation suggests, used in the preparation of food (Hvarfner 1963; Gustafson *et al.* 2005) they are also economic in function and, taking into account that the archaeological record in the coast clusters along the coast, the prepared food would very likely be mostly marine in nature (see Kuusela 2013: 89–95). This would explain their close relatedness to the sea – if they were used for the production/consumption of maritime goods, then it is only reasonable that they would be located on optimal sites for such activity. Also the sheer number of cooking pits in the north has been seen as an indication that the production/consumption, or whatever the pits were used for, reached levels that, perhaps a bit tongue-in-cheek, have been termed "almost industrial" (Ikäheimo 2005: 781; Okkonen & Äikäs 2006: 29). This would indicate the social significance of the action that the cooking pits are related to and thereby also signify the importance of the sea. This is supported by the fact that the contemporary burials, barrows and stone settings are also located in correspondingly stable areas along the contemporary coast. As burials are places of ritual and of significance to the community that built them, this should be seen as a link between economic and religious importance (on this, see Kuusela *et al.* 2010). This would suggest that in the field configuration of the coastal communities, the economic factors related to the sea held an important place and therefore archaeological material was naturally clustered on sites corresponding with this ideology, i.e. sites strongly associated with the sea.

It is noteworthy that the age of cooking pits and barrows, signifying an era of intense activity, corresponds with contemporary developments elsewhere in Europe – the Bronze Age was a time of extensive social networks that connected the regions of Europe with each other (Kristiansen 1998). Sometime around 500 BC, the beginning of the Iron Age according to the Finnish chronology, this social network came under duress and at least partially broke down (Kristiansen 1998: 247, 290–291; Cunliffe 2008: 317–321, 348–351). This dating of the possible collapse is interesting because it seems to correspond with the North Ostrobothnian coastal phase, after which the number of both barrows and cooking pits radically decreases. Therefore it seems likely that the north was closely connected with other areas of Europe already during the Bronze Age as the collapse of the Late Bronze and Early Iron Age social network probably extended in its effects to the coasts of what is today North Ostrobothnia (Kuusela *et al.* 2011: 193). Without a doubt a social change occurred at the beginning of the Iron Age but this change would not alter the underlying theme – the coasts remained important as cemeteries were still erected in stable coastal zones, which means that the field configuration of coastal communities still resembled that of earlier times. Furthermore, the evident change during the Early Iron Age did not change the relationship between the coastal and inland zones – the coastal areas retained their distinctive position when compared to the inland zone, implying that the importance of the coast as a zone of activity continued. A more drastic change occurred some time after AD 600.

After AD 600 the coasts are empty of the barrow cemeteries which were common in earlier times, and the Iron Age record goes relatively silent until the beginning of the Viking Age in the ninth century. However, as already mentioned, many of the stray finds from the Early to Middle Iron Age are oval fire-striking stones, whose dating cannot be established more accurately than being either Merovingian Period or older. Therefore how 'empty' the Iron Age record truly is after AD 600 is difficult to ascertain. It has recently been suggested that, in the interior, the Middle Iron Age, i.e. the time between AD 300 and 600, may have been a time of depopulation (Lavento 2011: 60–61) but the archaeological record at least in North Finland indicates that if there ever was an empty period, it occurred in the Merovingian Period, i.e. somewhere between seventh and ninth centuries AD. A recent article focusing on radiocarbon dates with an attempt to reconstruct the population development in what is today Finland sees no evident decline during the Middle Iron Age in the area now under study (Tallavaara *et al.* 2010). I myself would be cautious in considering depopulation as the reason for the change evident in the archaeological record between AD 600 and 800 and would rather see this as a period of social change pertaining to the field configuration of the coastal communities, during which the archaeological record forms into a configuration dominated by stray finds. It is worth emphasising that stray finds are not only a phenomenon of the Late Iron Age as they are represented in the inland zones throughout the Iron Age, as Figs 7c–g and 8 demonstrate, but that after AD 600 they become almost the only feature in archaeological material both in the coastal and inland zones. This suggests a change in the field configuration of coastal societies, where material culture was now used in a way akin to inland zones, but it appears that some differences remained.

One has to be careful when operating on a detailed level with a small dataset such as Iron Age stray finds, which is why I am cautious in drawing too advanced an inference on the basis of the distribution of artefact types. But one feature does warrant closer scrutiny. When observing the distribution of stray finds, one is drawn to the fact that weapons – that is axes, scramaseaxes, spearheads and swords – have, with one exception (see Hakamäki *et al.* 2013b), only been recovered from the interior, as can be observed from Fig. 9. Iron Age weapons have been recovered as burial finds from the coasts but they are not common, only two cemeteries having yielded weapon finds – Välikangas in Oulu and Tervakangas in Raahe. The former is notable for the fact that it contained a significant number of weapons – seven of the twelve burials in total contained weapons (Mäkivuoti 1996: 100–104) – whereas of the eight excavated burials of the Tervakangas cemetery weapons were found in only one grave (Leppiaho 2005: 23–24).

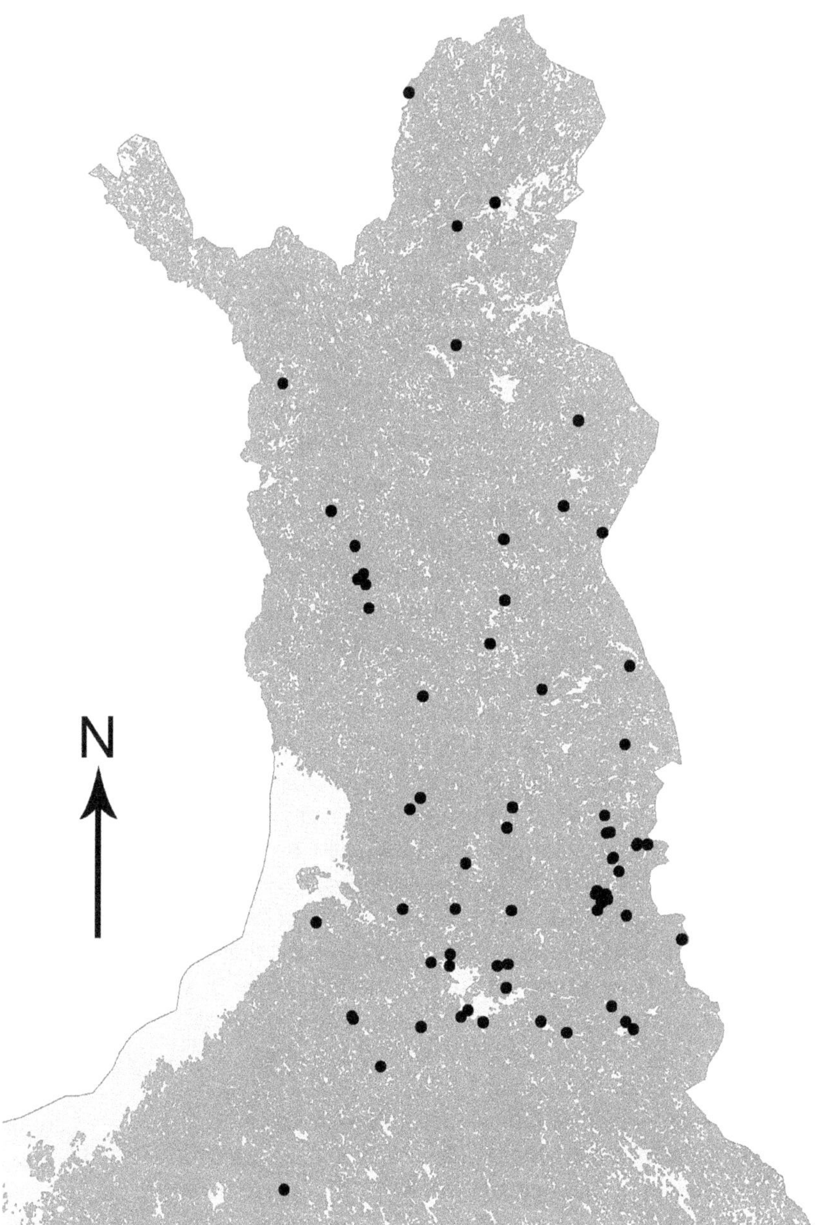

Fig. 9. Distribution map of weapon finds.

As a find type, weapons are interesting owing to the connotation they carry – they are tools of violence. Granted, axes are also regular tools and it can be argued that spears may also be used in hunting but these other functions do not exclude their purpose as fighting weapons. Also, as the find material includes artefacts whose function as weapons of war cannot plausibly be argued against – two swords, a few battle-axes and scramaseaxes – one has to seriously consider the possibility that weapon finds have, at least partially, a symbolic meaning pertaining to violence. The basis for this reasoning is once more the premise that material culture is social communication. If artefacts that can be associated with violence are a recurring feature in the material culture, a conclusion can be drawn that the concept of violence was part of the social structures of the society (see Raninen 2006: 8–9; Kuusela 2012b). This is interesting taking into account the fact that weapon finds seem to some extent to increase during the Late Iron Age, as Fig. 9 demonstrates, while at the same time a specific stray-find type – silver deposits – appears in the archaeological record of North Finland. Human activity has been interpreted as increasing in North Finland, and in Finland more generally, during the Late Iron Age (Huurre 1992: 86–87; see also KOSKELA VASARU; RANINEN & WESSMAN), and the increasing number of stray finds agrees with this interpretation. In this light, the silver deposits may indicate that this activity has partly been economic, as the silver was brought from elsewhere to be traded in the north. As weapon finds also seem to increase during this period, one is tempted to suggest that this increased activity may not have been completely peaceful and violence may therefore have been emphasised in the ideology of local communities. If this is the case, the absence of silver and weapon finds, and indeed the relatively scarce number of Iron Age finds in general, from the coastal area would suggest that, whereas the zone of activity resulting in relatively plentiful archaeological record of the Early and Middle Iron Ages was in the coastal area, at the beginning of the Viking Age at the latest this had moved into the interior (Kuusela 2013: 147–154; Kuusela 2014).

Conclusions

What the Iron Age archaeological record in the area under study seems to indicate is a change in the zones of activity resulting in a plentiful archaeological record in what is today North Finland. The emphasis of this activity shifted from the coast to the interior zone approximately between AD 600 and 800, and this activity probably increased as the Late Iron Age progressed. Considering that stray finds include silver hoards and a significant number of weapons, it seems plausible to suggest that this activity was associated with things that included, but were not limited to, such spheres of action as violence and trade.

NOTES

1 E.g. Mäkivuoti 1984; 1988; 1996; Forss & Jarva 1992; Eskola & Ylimaunu 1993.

2 See e.g. Koivunen 1975: 17–22; Huurre 1983; 1992; Carpelan 1992; Forss & Jarva 1992: 70–71; Mäkivuoti 1996: 119; Taskinen 1998: 152–155; Ylimaunu 1998; Jarva *et al.* 2001: 44–47; Oksala 2009.

3 Fig. 2 includes two sets of data when available. The first (black line) shows the time the site has remained within 200 metres of the shoreline whereas the grey lines (when present) indicate radiocarbon dates if available. It should be remembered that a radiocarbon dating only indicates the time margins within which the feature

is dated. Therefore the grey line does not signify the total period of use but the period within which a specific single event may be positioned temporally. Sample IDs for the radiocarbon analyses are Hel-3833 for Hangaskangas, Hel-3236, Hel-3682 and Hela-50 for Kiimamaa, Hel-3824 for Korkiamaa 3 and Beta-183716 and Beta-184632 for Metsokangas.

4 Fig. 4 is inaccurate in the sense that it deals with the site's elevation above sea level with a single value whereas most sites have several cooking pits situated on slightly differing heights. Therefore a more exact way to represent the data would be to use the elevation of individual pits but as such data was not at my disposal during the time I made my analyses, Fig. 4 will have to suffice as it still probably demonstrates a true phenomenon where the construction of cooking pits seems to sharply decline at the beginning of the Iron Age (also Okkonen 2003: 169, Fig. 78). It is noteworthy that the barrows and stone settings, that is burial sites, of the Bronze and Iron Ages follow a similar pattern - 25 metres a.s.l. seems to be a climax in the number of individual barrows after which there seems to be a relatively sharp decline in their number (Okkonen 2003: 140, Fig. 49).

5 Fig. 5 includes three sets of data when available. The first (black line) shows the time the site has remained within 200 metres of the shoreline. The grey lines (when present) indicate radiocarbon dates if available (see note 1 concerning the interpretation of radiocarbon dates) and the white lines (when present) indicates the typological dating. Typological datings can be very wide as some artefact types have remained in use for long periods of time. Radiocarbon samples from Kiimamaa and Rakanmäki have not been taken from the excavated burials but from an activity area adjacent to the burials. Of the Rakanmäki series of dates, sample Hel-2431 indicates a deviation from the rest, whereas all the other samples gave dates from the Early to Middle Iron Ages, sample Hel-3421 indicates a medieval age (fourteenth to fifteenth century). This could indicate activity on the site during medieval times but considering that it is the only exception in an otherwise uniform series of datings, contamination of the sample could also be a possibility. Sample IDs for the radiocarbon analyses are Hel-3235 for Länkimaa 1, Hela-88–89 for Tervakangas and Hel-2223–2228 and Hel-2427–2432 for Rakanmäki. For Kiimamaa see n. 1.

6 E.g. Huurre 1983: 389–390; Taskinen 1997; Okkonen 2013; Kuusela & Tolonen 2011; Kuusela *et al.* 2011: 196–198; Kuusela *et al.* 2013; Hakamäki *et al.* 2013; Hakamäki & Kuusela 2013.

7 Huurre 1983: 389–390; Taskinen 1998; Ojanlatva 2003; Kuusela & Tolonen 2011: Kuusela *et al.* 2013; Hakamäki *et al.* 2013.

References

Bourdieu, Pierre. 1977. *Outline of a Theory of Practice*. Cambridge: Cambridge University Press.

Bourdieu, Pierre. 1984. *Distinction: A Social Critique of the Judgement of Taste*. London: Routledge & Kegan Paul.

Bourdieu, Pierre. 1985. *Sosiologian kysymyksiä*. Tampere: Osuuskunta Vastapaino.

Bourdieu, Pierre. 1989. Social Space and Symbolic Power. *Sociological Theory* 7(1): 14–25.

Bourdieu, Pierre. 1990a. The Cult of Unity and Cultivated Differences. In P. Bourdieu, L. Boltanski, R. Castel, J. Chamboredon & D. Schnapper (eds.). *Photography: A Middle-Brow Art*. Stanford: Stanford University Press. Pp. 13–72.

Bourdieu, Pierre. 1990b. *The Logic of Practice*. Cambridge: Polity.

Bourdieu, Pierre. 1998. *Practical Reason: On the Theory of Action*. Cambridge: Polity.

Carpelan, Christian. 1992. Juikenttä: Näkokulma saamelaiseen yhteiskuntaan. In Kyösti Julku (ed.). *Suomen Varhaishistoria. Tornion kongressi 14.–16.6.1991*. Rovaniemi: Pohjois-Suomen Historiallinen Yhdistys. Pp. 34–44.

Costopoulos, André, Samuel Vaneeckhout, Jari Okkonen, Eva Hulse, Ieva Paberzyte & Colin D. Wren. 2012. Social Complexity in the Mid-Holocene Northeastern Bothnian Gulf. *European Journal of Archaeology* 15(1): 41–60.

Creutz, Kristina. 2003. *Tension and Tradition: A Study of Late Iron Age Spearheads around the Baltic Sea*. Theses and Papers in Archaeology N.S.A. 8. Stockholm: Stockholm University.

Cunliffe, Barry. 2008. *Europe between the Oceans: 9000 BC – AD 1000*. New Haven / London: Yale University Press.

Elias, Norbert. 1983. *The Court Society*. New York: Pantheon Books.

Eskola, Sanna & Timo Ylimaunu. 1993. *Kemin Länkimaan rautakautisen kalmiston ja asuinpaikan tutkimus 1992*. Arkeologian tutkimusraportti 5. Oulu: Arkeologia, Historian laitos, Oulun yliopisto.

Forss, Aulis & Eero Jarva. 1992. Raahen seudun varhaishistoria Saloisten Tervakankaan löytöjen valossa. In Kyösti Julku (ed.). *Suomen varhaishistoria: Tornion kongressi 14.-16.6.1991*. Rovaniemi: Pohjois-Suomen Historiallinen Yhdistys. Pp. 57–75.

Gustafson, Lil, Tom Heibreen & Jes Martens (eds.). 2005. *De gåtefulle kokegroper*. Oslo: Kulturhistorisk museum, Fornminneseksjonen & Universitet i Oslo.

Hakamäki, Ville & Jari-Matti Kuusela. 2013. Examining the Topography and Social Context of Metal Age Artefact Finds in Northern Finland. *Fennoscandia Archaeologica* 30: 95–106.

Hakamäki, Ville, Jari-Matti Kuusela, Mika Sarkkinen & Rosa Vilkama 2013a. Utajärven Viinivaaran itäpään rautakautisen löytöpaikan kaivaus ja kartoitus kesäkuussa 2013. *Muinaistutkija* 2013(4): 2–11.

Hakamäki, Ville, Aki Hakonen, Mikko Moilanen & Jari-Matti Kuusela. 2013b. Pohjoissuomalainen miekkalöytö viiden vuosikymmenen takaa. *Artefactum* 2. http://www.artefacta.fi/tutkimus/artefactum/2 (accessed. 23.5.2014).

Huurre, Matti. 1983. *Pohjois-Pohjanmaan ja Lapin esihistoria*. Kuusamo: Pohjois-Pohjanmaan maakuntaliiton ja Lapin maakuntaliiton yhteinen historiatoimikunta.

Huurre, Matti. 1986. Esihistoria. In Matti Huurre & Jouko Keränen (eds.). *Kainuun historia 1*. Kajaani: Kainuun Maakuntaliitto. Pp. 5–200.

Huurre, Matti. 1992. Kainuun hämärä kausi: Aika ennen savolaista uudisasutusta. In Kyösti Julku (ed.). *Suomen varhaishistoria: Tornion kongressi 14.–16.6.1991*. Rovaniemi: Pohjois-Suomen Historiallinen Yhdistys. Pp. 85–94.

Hvarfner, Harald. 1963. Storkok vid Holmajärvi. *Norrbotten, Norrbottens läns hembygdförenings årbok* 1963: 215–222.

Ikäheimo, Janne. 2005. Re-Assessing the Bronze Age of Coastal North Ostrobothnia: The Lower Oulujoki River Valley. In Joakim Goldhahn (ed.). *Mellan sten och järn: Rapport från det 9:e nordiska bronsålderssymposiet, Göteborg 2003-10-09/12*. Gotarc Serie C. Arkeologiska Skrifter 59. Göteborg: Göteborgs universitet, Institutionen för arkeologi. Pp. 772–784.

Jarva, Eero, Markku Niskanen & Kirsti Paavola. 2001. Anatomy of a Late Iron Age Inhumation Burial of Hiukka at Nivankylä (Rovaniemi, Finnish Lapland). *Fennoscandia Archaeologica* 18: 27–49.

Koivunen, Pentti. 1975. *A Gilded Relied Brooch of the Migration Period from Finnish Lapland*. Acta Universitatis Ouluensis. Series B, Humaniora 4. Oulu: University of Oulu.

Kristiansen, Kristian. 1998. *Europe before History*. Cambridge: Cambridge University Press.

Kuusela, Jari-Matti. 2009. Masters of the Burial Grounds: Elites, Power and Ritual during the Middle Iron Age in Vähäkyrö. *Fennoscandia Archaeologica* 26: 39–52.

Kuusela, Jari-Matti. 2011. Itsensä elävänä hautaavat ruumiit: Vainajat hautapaikkansa suunnittelijoina rautakaudella. In Janne Ikäheimo, Risto Nurmi & Reija Satokangas (eds.). *Harmaata näkyvissä: Kirsti Paavolan juhlakirja*. Oulu: Kirsti Paavolan juhlakirjatoimikunta: Pp. 107–115.

Kuusela, Jari-Matti. 2012a. Style as Distinction: Burials Reflecting Distinction and the Development of Social Stratification of the Iron Age Elites of Southern Ostrobothnia, Finland. In Tiina Äikäs, Sanna Lipkin & Anna-Kaisa Salmi (eds.). *Archaeology of Social Relations: Ten Case Studies by Finnish Archaeologists*. Studia Humaniora Ouluensia 12. Oulu: University of Oulu. Pp. 155–180.

Kuusela, Jari-Matti. 2012b. Tools of lethal play. Weapon burials reflecting power structures and group cohesion during the Iron Age in Ostrobothnia, Finland. In Ragnhild Berge, Marek E. Jasinski & Kalle Sognnes (eds.) *N-TAG Ten. The Proceedings of the 10th Nordic TAG Conference at Stiklestad, Norway 2009*. BAR S2399. Oxford: Archaeo Press. Pp. 275–289.

Kuusela, Jari-Matti. 2013. *Political Economy of Bronze- and Iron Age Societies in the Eastern Coast of the Bothnian Bay ca. 1500 BC–AD 1300*. Oulu: University of Oulu.

Kuusela, Jari-Matti. 2014. Pohjois-Suomen rautakauden kuvasta. *Muinaistutkija* 2014(2): 27–43.

Kuusela, Jari-Matti, Janne Ikäheimo, Ville Hakamäki, Rosa Vilkama & Anna-Kaisa Salmi. 2013. Suutarinniemi: The Late Iron Age/Early Medieval Cemetery in Ii (Northern Ostrobothnia, Finland). *Fennoscandia Archaeologica* 30: 126–132.

Kuusela, Jari-Matti, & Juha Saunavaara. 2011. Ajatuksia päätöksenteosta arkeologian ja historian tutkimuskohteena. *Faravid* 35: 205–220.

Kuusela, Jari-Matti, Jasse Tiilikkala, Riku-Ville Vaske & Jari Okkonen. 2011. Keskus-periferiamalli Pohjois-Suomen rautakauden asutusdynamiikan tarkastelun apuna. *Faravid* 35: 177–204.

Kuusela, Jari-Matti, & Siiri Tolonen. 2011. A Late Iron Age Site from Siikajoki, North Ostrobothnia, Finland. *Fennoscandia Archaeologica* 28: 79–84.

Kuusela, Jari-Matti, Samuel Vaneeckhout & Jari Okkonen. 2010. Places of Importance and Social Communication: Studying the Pre-Roman Cairn Field of Viirikallio in Laihia, Finland. *Estonian Journal of Archaeology* 14(1): 22–39.

Lavento, Mika. 2011. The Migration Period in the Finnish Inland: Cultural Relations between the Populations When Pottery Making Came to an End? In Janne Harjula, Maija Helamaa & Janne Haarala (eds.). *Times, Things & Places: 36 Essays for Jussi-Pekka Taavitsainen*. Turku: J.-P. Taavitsainen Festschrift Committee. Pp. 50–63.

Leppiaho, Annika. 2005. "Kivikehiä pirunpellossa": Raahen Saloisten Tervakankaan rautakautinen kalmisto. MA thesis, University of Oulu.

Mäkivuoti, Markku. 1984. Kempeleen Linnakankaan lapinrauniotutkimus kesällä 1983. *Faravid* 7: 29–37.

Mäkivuoti, Markku. 1988. An Iron-Age Dwelling Site and Burial Mounds at Rakanmäki, Near Tornio. *Fennoscandia Archaeologica* 5: 35–45.

Mäkivuoti, Markku. 1996. Oulun Kaakkurin Välikankaan rautakautinen kalmisto. Lic. phil. dissertation, University of Oulu.

Mäkivuoti, Markku. 2009. Huomioita eräiden Kaakkurin kalmiston esineiden ajoituksesta ja alkuperästä. In Janne Ikäheimo & Sanna Lipponen (eds.). *Ei kiveäkään kääntämättä: Juhlakirja Pentti Koivuselle*. Oulu: Pentti Koivusen juhlakirjatoimikunta. Pp. 183–194.

Morris, Craig. 1995. Symbols to Power: Styles and Media in the Inka State. In Christopher Carr & Jill Neitzel (eds.). *Style, Society, and Person*. New York & London: Plenum Press. Pp. 419–433.

Neitzel, Jill. 1995. Elite Styles in Hierarchically Organised Societies: The Chacoan Regional System. In Christopher Carr & Jill Neitzel (eds.). *Style, Society, and Person*. New York & London: Plenum Press. Pp. 393–417.

O'Brien, Denis Patrick. 2007. *History of Economic Thought as an Intellectual Discipline.* Cheltenham / Northampton: Edward Elgar Publishing.

Ojanlatva, Eija. 2003. A Late Iron Age Silver Deposit Found at Nangunniemi, Inari, Finland. *Fennoscandia Archaeologica* 20: 115–119.

Okkonen, Jari. 2001. Cairns and Cultural Landscape: An Attempt to Define Stone Age and Bronze Age Land Use and Territoriality in Ostrobothnia, Finland. *Faravid* 25: 23–35.

Okkonen, Jari. 2003. *Jättiläisen hautoja ja hirveitä kiviröykkiöitä: Pohjanmaan muinaisten kivirakennelmien arkeologiaa.* Acta Universitatis Ouluensis. Humaniora B52. Oulu: Oulun yliopisto.

Okkonen, Jari. 2013. Kuusamon Pyhälahden myöhäisrautakautisen raha-aarteen konteksti ja muinaisjäännösmaisema. *Faravid* 37: 7–18.

Okkonen, Jari & Äikäs, Tiina. 2006. Oulun seudun varhaismetallikautiset keittokuopat: Käyttötarkoitus ja konteksti. *Faravid* 30: 17–32.

Oksala, Hilkka. 2009. Sámi Past in the NW Forest Lapland in Finland: Tradition and Change from the Stone Age up to Historical Times. In Petri Halinen, Mika Lavento & Mervi Suhonen (eds.). *Recent Perspectives on Sámi Archaeology in Fennoscandia and North-West Russia: Proceedings of the First International Conference on Sámi Archaeology, Rovaniemi, 19–22 October 2006.* Iskos 17. Helsinki: The Finnish Antiquarian Society. Pp. 144–161.

Raninen, Sami. 2006. Tuskan teatteri Turun Kärsämäessä II: Väkivalta varhaisrautakauden kontekstissa. *Muinaistutkija* 2006(3): 2–22.

Sandén, Erik. 1995. An Early Bronze Age Site on the Coast of Västerbotten, Sweden, with Hair-Tempered Pottery. *Fennoscandia Archaeologica* 12: 173–180.

Taavitsainen, Jussi-Pekka. 2003. Lapp Cairns as a Source of Metal Period Settlement in the Inland Regions of Finland. *Acta Borealia* 20(1): 21–47.

Tallavaara, Miika, Petro Pesonen & Markku Oinonen. 2010. Prehistoric Population History in Eastern Fennoscandia. *Journal of Archaeological Science* 37: 251–260.

Taskinen, H. 1998. Suomussalmen Tyynelänrannan hautalöytö. In K. Julku (ed.). *Rajamailla IV 1997.* Rovaniemi: Pohjois-Suomen historiallinen yhdistys. Pp. 147–158.

Vaneeckhout, Samuel. 2009. Aggregration and Polarization in Northwest Coastal Finland. Socio-Ecological Evolution between 6500 and 4000 cal BP. PhD dissertation, University of Oulu.

Wessman, Anna. 2009. Levänluhta: A Place of Punishment, Sacrifice or Just a Common Cemetery? *Fennoscandia Archaeologica* 26: 81–105.

Wessman, Anna. 2010. *Death, Destruction and Commemoration: Tracing Ritual Activities in Finnish Late Iron Age Cemeteries (AD 550–1150).* Iskos 18. Helsinki: The Finnish Antiquarian Society.

Ylimaunu, Juha, Ylimaunu, Timo & Okkonen, Jari. 1999. Hylkeenpyynnin kehityksestä ja merkityksestä Itämerellä esihistoriallisella ajalla. *Faravid* 22–23: 131–158.

Ylimaunu, Timo. 1999. Iin Hangaskankaan keittokuopan rasva-analyysi, *Faravid* 22–23: 125–130.

Ylimaunu, Timo. 1998. Interpreting Sites: A Preliminary View of the Iron Age Sites at the Northern Bothnian Gulf. In Kjersti Dahl, Mia Krogh & Ingrid Sommerseth (eds.). *Jeger - Samlere.* Kontaktstencil 40. Trømsø: Fellenordisk råd för arkeologistudenter. Pp. 27–42.

Teija Alenius

Pollen Analysis as a Tool for Reconstructing Viking Age Landscapes

The long and continuous sediment cores from lake sediments are desirable archives for palaeo-environmental reconstructions. The sediment cores preserve records of past environmental changes, and provide information about the development and change of anthropogenic activity through time.

In optimal conditions, lake sediments and peat layers preserve long and undisturbed archives of fossil pollen records. The value of accumulated sequences of pollen in lake sediments and peat deposits lies above all in its possibility of characterizing vegetation over a long period of time. While archaeological material is fragmentary and provides a horizontal timeframe, pollen analysis provides a continuum over time. Nowadays, pollen analysis can be considered as one of the fundamental tools in understanding the palaeoecological changes related to vegetation, and development and change of human activities through time.

The results are usually presented as pollen percentages, pollen concentrations (grains cm−3) and pollen accumulation values (grains cm−2 yr−1). The advantage of accumulation values over percentages is that they allow one to estimate the presence of individual species independently for each species, while pollen percentages depend on the presence of all the other taxa in the pollen sum (Hicks 1997). The critical question is how to derive the actual quantitative measures of vegetation covers from pollen percentages, concentrations and accumulation values. Thanks to research work done during the past twenty years, we now have a much better understanding of the link between the pollen spectrum and both the vegetation and the spatial scale of vegetation that can be inferred from pollen records. In this paper, some recent advances in the field of palynology are presented that are important when interpreting the stratigraphic pollen diagrams, namely pollen production (PPE) and pollen source area (RSAP). In addition, an example of a standard pollen percentage diagram is presented from Lake Kirjavalampi, which is in the northern archipelago of Lake Ladoga. In this diagram, Viking Age land use is clearly reflected in a 10 centimetre interval of a sediment sample that is altogether 170 centimetres long.

Pollen is best preserved in anaerobic conditions, such as lake sediments and peat bogs. Small lakes, deep for their area with no major through flows, usually record continuous sedimentation and are best suited for reconstructing past terrestrial environments (Bennett & Willis 2001). Varved sediments that are preserved in meromictic and dimictic lakes with a permanent or seasonal oxygen deficit in the bottom water layers are desirable archives in pollen stratigraphical studies. They reflect the annual cycle of sedimentation because there is little post-depositional disturbance (e.g. Saarnisto 1986). Before its final burial, pollen may be affected by various sedimentary processes internal to a lake. The degree of resuspension from the shallower areas of the lake basin, redeposition, focusing and biological mixing in the sediment all depend on the morphometry of a lake basin (e.g. Birks & Birks 1980). In general, very shallow lakes, those less than 2 metres in depth, are more open to sediment re-suspension and mixing (Evans 1994).

In addition to pollen, pollen slides may contain a wide range of other microfossils. Among the microfossils are fungal and algal spores, seeds, tissue fragments and charcoal particles. Charcoal particles provide evidence of natural and human-induced fires in the palaeoenvironment. According to Pitkänen *et al.* (2001) the average fire interval in eastern Finland for dry sites was with a range of 130–180 before any major human influence and, in the period of active land use, the mean fire interval was reduced to *c.* 40 years.

Pollen Production

Production of spores and pollen varies for different species. In general, anemophilous (wind pollinated) species produce substantial amounts of pollen, because they depend on wind to disperse pollen and produce a large number of grains (e.g. Vuorela 1973). In contrast, entomophilous (insect pollinated) plants may produce only a few hundred thousand pollen. As a result, pollen rain composition comprises different proportions of taxa that originate from species that produce small amounts of locally dispersed pollen and pollen from wind pollinated species are produced in large quantitates and spread over large areas. This is also the case with pollen of the species that is the most important indicator of cultivation: *Cerealia* pollen. In relation to wind pollinated *Secale* (rye), pollen of autogamous *Hordeum* (barley) and *Triticum* (wheat) releases very little pollen into the air (Vuorela 1973). Therefore *Secale* pollen is overrepresented in the pollen analytical results in relation to poorly produced and dispersed *Hordeum*. It has been demonstrated that the pollen of *Hordeum* is poorly represented even in the immediate vicinity of the fields (Vuorela 1973; Bakels 2000).

Today, pollen productivity estimates are available in nine study areas of Europe for 15 tree and 18 herb taxa (Broström *et al.* 2008; Poska *et al.* 2011; Abraham & Kozáková 2012; Twiddle et al. 2012; Bunting et al. 2013). Collection of pollen productivity estimates from different geographic areas is necessary because the pollen productivity of a plant species can vary greatly between vegetation regions. (Abraham & Kozáková 2012; Twiddle et al. 2012; Bunting et al. 2013.)

For the studies, modern pollen and vegetation data has to be collected. Modern pollen samples are obtained either from moss polsters or from lake sediments. The vegetation surveys are designed to obtain distance weighted plant abundance around pollen sample. Once the modern pollen and vegetation data are available pollen productivity estimates are obtained using extended R-value (ERV) models (Parsons & Prentice 1981; Prentice & Parsons 1983; Sugita 1994). In the model, so called 'distance-weighted plant abundance' corrects the biases caused by the size and type of sedimentary basin of pollen, species-specific pollen dispersal, and spatial distribution of the plant species surrounding the sedimentary basin. Usually pollen productivity estimates are expressed relative to one of the taxa, usually *Poaceae* (the meadow grasses), involved in the calculation.

Pollen productivity estimates in open and semi-open cultural landscapes of southern Sweden revealed that most of the common tree taxa in the region produce 6–8 times more pollen per unit area as *Poaceae*. In Finnish Lapland, the pollen productivity estimate was for *Pinus* (pine) 8.4, *Betula* (birch) 4.6 in Finnish Lapland (Räsänen *et al.* 2007). That leads to dominance of high pollen producers and long distance dispersal pollen taxa such as *Betula*, *Pinus*, *Alnus* (alder) and *Quercus* (oak) in the pollen diagrams.

Among the herbs and shrubs, *Juniperus communis* (juniper), *Calluna vulgaris* (heather), *Filipendula* (meadowsweet), *Plantago lanceolata* (ribwort plantain), *Potentilla* type (cinquefoil), *Ranunculus acris* type (meadow buttercup), *Galim* type (bedstraw) and *Rumex acetosa* type (sorrel) are the highest pollen producers (Hjelle 1998; Broström *et al.* 2004). Among the tree taxa, the low pollen producers are *Fraxinus* (ash), *Salix* (willow), *Tilia* (lime) and *Ulmus* (elm).

The Source Area of Pollen

In general, the relationship between basin size and pollen source area has been well known for a long time; larger sedimentary basins collect pollen from larger areas than smaller basins (Jacobson & Bradshaw 1981). Thanks to the achievements of the research projects during the last 20 years, the understanding of the source area of pollen in the sediment of a peat sample has greatly improved.

The pollen source area has been defined in various ways. In 1994, Sugita launched the concept of "Relative Source Area of Pollen" (RSAP). This is defined as the area beyond which the correlation between pollen deposited at the site and the surrounding vegetation does not change. Background pollen coming from beyond the relevant source area of pollen becomes nearly constant between sites, and thus the relevant source area of pollen is the spatial scale appropriate for detecting variations in local vegetation from pollen records. It has been demonstrated that in very large lakes, small vegetation patches cannot be recorded in the pollen data because substantially large amounts of pollen come from source assemblages further away (Sugita 1994). According to computer simulations, the Relevant Source

Area in a fully forested environment from the lake edge is 50–100 metres for forest hollows, 300–400 metres for small lakes with a radius of 50 metres and 600–800 metres for medium size lakes with a radius of 250 metres (Sugita 1994). In a recent study from northern Michigan (Sugita *et al.* 2010) the RSAP was estimated as the area in a 126-metre radius from forest hollows. In the cultural landscape of Denmark, pollen spectra from medium sized lakes with radius of *c.* 100–500 metres gave the estimate of *c.* 1700 metres for the relevant source area of pollen. This estimate is in close agreement with the results obtained from the cultural landscape of the hemi-boreal forest zone in Estonia, where the RSAP for 40 lakes with an average radius of approximately 100 metres (22–274 m) led to estimates of the Relative Source Area of Pollen varying between 1500–2000 metres (Poska *et al.* 2011). In the simulations it is generally expected, that all pollen is transported to the place of deposition from air. However, in the lakes, where there are inflowing streams, the proportion transported from the catchment may be substantial (Peck 1973; Bonny 1978).

Simulation-based calculations have demonstrated the relevant source area of pollen is primarily an expression of the patterning of the vegetation e.g. size of the vegetation patches within the landscape (Nielsen & Sugita 2005). The change in the Relative Source Area of Pollen estimates for the same sized basins is especially profound when the mean patch size of land-cover changes considerably. In Skåne, Southern Sweden, for example, the Relative Source Area of Pollen was found to vary between 600–1200 metres between the Early Neolithic, Late Bronze Age, Viking Age and Middle Ages, whatever the size of the basin (lake or bog, 25–250 metre radius) (Hellman *et al.* 2009). The explanation for the differences in the Relative Source Area of Pollen was variable patch size and spatial distribution of the patch sizes in the landscape through time. In the small basins with a radius of 25–70 metres, the Relative Source Area varied between *c.* 1200–2300 metres, and for larger basins with a radius of 250 metres the Relative Source Area of Pollen varied between 2000–3000 metres.

Land-Use History on Riekkalansaari Island in the Northern Archipelago of Lake Ladoga

The western and northern shores of Lake Ladoga are renowned for their rich archaeological finds from the Late Iron Age and Crusade Period, representing an indigenous Karelian culture (Uino 1997). Archaeological data indicate that the original cultural development in the western Ladoga region started in the Merovingian Period (AD 600–800), but this, in its early stages, was masked by traded artefacts that show predominantly external influences. In the archaeological material, the establishment of agriculture as the principal subsistence source and the consequent population growth can be seen from the 11th and 12th centuries. In order to provide an insight into the early stages of settlement history on Riekkalansaari Island in the northern archipelago of Lake Ladoga, pollen analysis was constructed from Lake Kirjavalampi

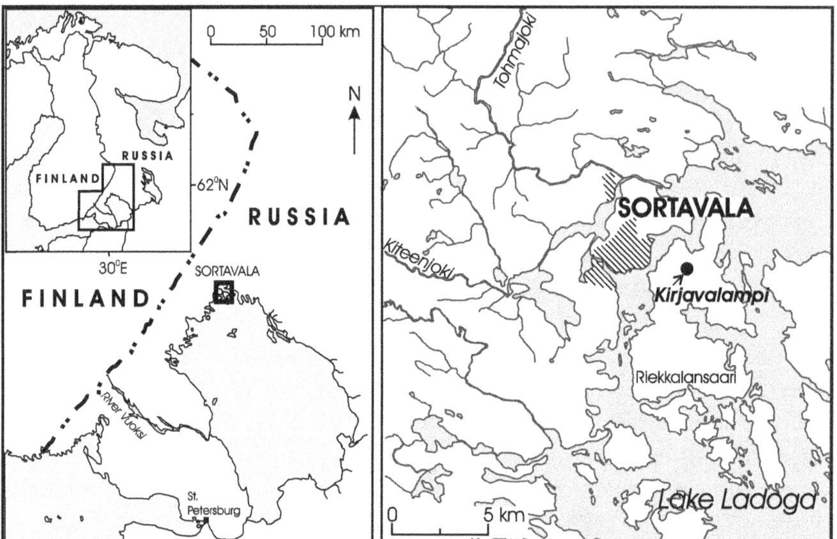

Fig. 1. Location of Lake Kirjavalampi, in the northern archipelago of Lake Ladoga (Alenius et al. 2004).

a small lake, *c.* 2.4 hectares and the maximum depth of 4 metres situated on the Riekkalansaari Island (Alenius *et al.* 2004) (Fig 1.). The studied lake is situated close to the dwelling site of Nukuttalahti, which probably represents the scanty traces of the indigenous Metal Period culture.

Lake Kirjavalampi became isolated from Lake Ladoga when the River Neva was formed as a new outlet for Lake Ladoga *c.* 1300 BC. As a consequence, the level of Lake Ladoga rapidly dropped and extensive lowland areas were exposed. Only one small brook enters Lake Kirjavalampi and the lake also has only one outlet (to Lake Ladoga). Because there are no major streams entering into the lake that could carry a substantial amount of pollen, it can be argued that the pollen content in the sediment mainly represents the airborne pollen from the pollen source area and also from the drainage area, which around Lake Kirjavalampi is *c.* 94 hectares. Based on the simulations discussed above, it can be hypothesized that the relevant source area of airborne pollen in this lake is in a range of 600–1700 metres. However, during Lake Kirjavalampi's history, the Relative Source Area of Pollen has likely varied because the patch size and spatial distribution of patches had varied.

In the Fig. 2 pollen percentages for the main arboreal pollen are presented together with some important herb pollen types that give an overview of the land use around the lake. In addition to pollen percentages, the charcoal particle concentration (charcoal particles per cm^3), species richness and sediment loss-on-ignition (LOI) are presented. Species richness is estimated by rarefaction analysis where all the pollen counts are standardized to a fixed number of grains (Birks & Line 1992). Generally speaking, species richness remains low in a fully forested environment whereas the highest values in species richness are yielded by diverse practices in land use involving a variety of methods, such as slash-and-burn cultivation, cultivation in permanent fields and grazing. 'Loss-on-ignition' refers to the relative amount of organic matter in the sediment (Bengtsson & Enell 1986). This factor can be used, for example, to detect increased erosion within the lake catchment resulting from lake isolation, changes in water level and – above all – human activities in the catchment.

A pollen diagram covering thousands of years is generally rather complicated and in order to work with the diagram, it is usually divided into local pollen assemblage zones that are relatively uniform periods in the sediment with the regard to pollen content. Zonation can be done visually or with computer programs, such as stratigraphically-constrained cluster analysis (CONISS) (Grimm 1987). The Lake Kirjavalampi pollen diagram has been divided into six local Pollen Assemblage Zones (PAZ Kir 3, 4a, 4b, 4c, 5, 6). The horizontal lines extending over the diagrams mark the zone limits. The dating in the Lake Kirjavalampi pollen diagram is based on the tree radiocarbon dates from the sediment and consequent age-depth model. The median probabilities of the calibrated radiocarbon dates are presented on the right-hand side of the diagram.

In the Lake Kirjavalampi pollen diagram, no indications of human activity were found in zone Kir 3, between 172–114 cm of the sediment sample and covering the time period of *c.* 1300 BC – AD 70. Pollen diversity remains low and the pollen data mainly indicate arboreal data. The first indications of apparent human land-use activities date to AD 70 (in Kir 4a). Small-scale land clearance is implied by the clear decrease in spruce pollen frequencies. At the same level, the mineral content of the sediment starts to increase, visible in loss-on-ignition values, indicating increased soil erosion in the vicinity.

Rye cultivation is recorded from the beginning of the subzone 4B from 97 cm upwards, placing the onset of cultivation to *c.* AD 600 (i.e. to the beginning of the Merovingian Period). This result correlates with archaeological evidence from Riekkalansaari, where the oldest archaeological find is a cairn-type grave dated to *c.* AD 500. Further finds on Riekkalansaari Island include a hoard and a Late Iron Age cremation cemetery with finds dated to AD 950–1100, and jewellery dated to AD 1150–1250. An increase in the charcoal particle concentration coincides with the beginning of rye cultivation and is therefore likely to be connected to slash-and-burn cultivation. At this stage, forest clearance appears to have been fairly limited: the proportion of the boreal trees/herbs indicate that the landscape was still forested. However, the sudden increase in the number of pollen types from AD 600 onwards indicates that human disturbance has increased the structural diversity in the landscape.

According to the pollen data, land use also continued at the same low intensity through the Viking Age. In the pollen diagram, this time period is registered as an interval that is only 10 cm total, between *c.* 83–93 cm in the sediment sample. During the Viking Age, the landscape still remained relatively closed as boreal trees still constitute 90% of the total pollen. The high concentration of charcoal particles and decrease in spruce and rye

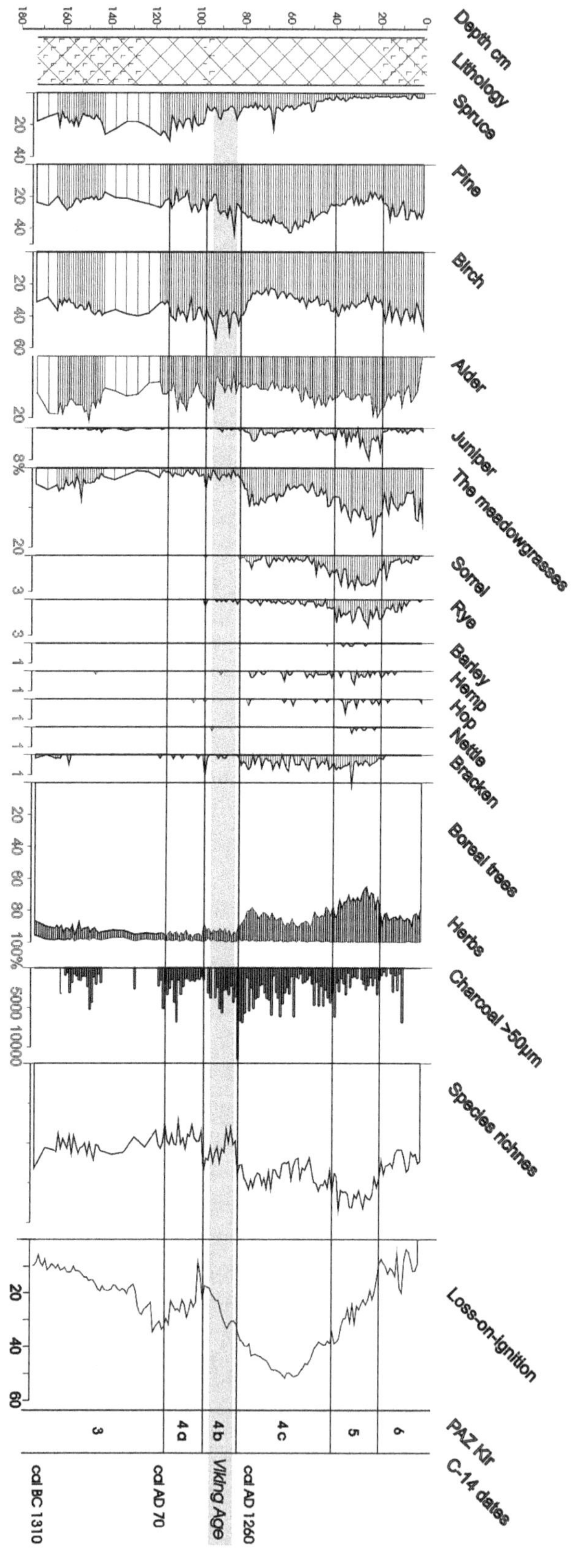

Fig. 2. Pollen percentage diagram from Lake Kirjavalampi. The shaded bar extending across the diagram indicates the Viking Age (modified from Alenius et al. 2004).

pollen suggests that cultivation was of the slash-and-burn type. It is possible that, during the Viking Age, the island was at least somewhat remote and used mainly for its resources while the actual settlements were situated further away. Land use has obviously caused changes in the sediment type. The loss-on-ignition curve, for example, shows that the organic content in the sediment starts to increase together with pollen of water lily, indicating slight eutrophication of the lake. It is interesting that both *Humulus* (hop) and *Cannabis* (hemp) types of pollen increase in the pollen diagram from around the Viking Age. Kaisa Häkkinen discusses hops from a linguistic perspective: according to her, hops became important as an ingredient for beer at the beginning of the Viking Age. Unfortunately there is always the risk of misidentification, because morphological differences between the pollen of hops and hemp are very small.

Intensification of the land-use activities with an open cultural landscape of fields and grazing areas is recorded 82 cm onwards, from the beginning of subzone 4C, *c.* AD 1200 onwards. In the pollen data, development of the landscape is reflected by increasing frequencies of herb and shrub pollen, and in decreasing frequencies of arboreal pollen. These results correspond well with the archaeological material, where the establishment of agriculture as the principal subsistence source and consequent population growth can be seen during the 11th and 12th centuries. Saksa (1998) relates this to an economy based on cereal crop cultivation, animal husbandry and the fur trade.

It is worth noting that pollen percentages do not give reliable estimates of the degree of openness of the landscape. Recently developed Landscape Reconstruction Algorithm (LRA) based vegetation reconstruction (Sugita 2007a–b) overcomes this fundamental problem in pollen analysis for quantitative reconstruction of vegetation. It has proven to be a significantly more accurate than pollen percentages alone (Sugita *et al.* 2010). In Denmark, the application of LRA demonstrated that the degree of openness of the landscape during the last 3000 years was much higher than it appears from uncorrected percentage pollen diagrams (Nielsen & Odgaard 2010).

In Kir 5, at 40–19 cm and from the eighteenth to the twentieth century, pollen data shows the strongest presence of apophyte and anthropochore pollen in the entire sequence studied. The total proportion of grasses reaches its maximum at 35% of the total pollen sum. The highest abundances of rye, sorrel, juniper and meadow grasses are also recorded. According to Heikinheimo (1915), the area of slash-and-burn cultivation amounted to over 75% of the land in the northern and north-western areas of Lake Ladoga during the period AD 1700–1850, and the landscape of eastern Finland was generally open and largely devoid of mature coniferous forests. The charcoal data, however, shows the decline in fires during this period. It is historically known that crop cultivation in Sortavala parish was already predominantly based on permanent fields by the year 1637 (Saloheimo 1977). This is probably due to the extent of the fine-grained water-deposited soils that are well suited for field cultivation on the shore of this lake. This plausibly explains the low values of charcoal particles at

Kir 5. The concomitant increase of minerogenic matter in the sediment can be interpreted as indicating increased soil erosion due to modernisation in field agriculture. Furthermore, increasing weed pollen, such as that from *Brassicaceae* (brassica) *Centaurea* (knapweed) and *Urtica* (nettle) can be associated with permanent field cultivation and settlements. Diverse land-use practices yielded the highest values in species richness, a phenomenon that is clearly seen in the pollen data in Kir 5. In the uppermost zone, representing the twentieth century, it is possible to see a clear decline in species richness, as well as in pollen types indicative of intensive land use.

Concluding Remarks

Pollen analytical studies provide information about past vegetation and above all about changes in vegetation, such as the transition from undisturbed landscapes to cultural landscapes. The picture, however, is distorted by the limitations of pollen analysis itself, related to differences in pollen production and dispersal and also to various factors in the sedimentation processes. Nevertheless, pollen analysis remains the most important method for the reconstruction of the history of vegetation and of past environments of different periods, such as the Viking Age. Pollen analysis can tell how people in the Viking Age modified the vegetation around them and it can provide data on a wide range of human activities, such as contemporary land-use techniques like slash-and-burn cultivation, field cultivation, grazing, animal husbandry, use of fire and the species of plants that were cultivated. Recent developments in pollen modeling and landscape reconstruction allows the visualization of past landscape changes related to human activity on a more quantitative basis. Nevertheless, cooperation with different disciplines such as archaeology, history, folklore, macrofossil studies and osteology remains necessary to elucidate the data from pollen analysis in order to provide a broader picture of that cultural environment.

References

Abraham, V., & R. Kozáková. 2012. Relative Pollen Productivity Estimates in the Modern Agricultural Landscape of Central Bohemia (Czech Republic). *Review of Palaeobotany and Palynology* 179: 1–12.

Alenius, T., E. Grönlund, H. Simola & A. Saksa. 2004. Land-Use History of Riekkalansaari Island in the Northern Archipelago of Lake Ladoga, Karelian Republic, Russia. *Vegetation History and Archaeobotany* 13: 23–31.

Bakels, C. C. 2000. Pollen Diagrams and Prehistoric Fields: The Case of Bronze Age Haarlem, the Netherlands. *Review of Palaeobotany & Palynology* 109: 205–218.

Bengtsson, L., & M. Enell. 1986. Chemical Analysis. In Berglund, B. E. (ed.). *Handbook of Holocene Palaeoecology and Palaeohydrology*. Chichester: Wiley. Pp. 423–451.

Bennett, K. D., & K. J. Willis. 2001. Pollen. In J. P. Smol, H. J. B. Birks & W. M. Last (eds.). *Tracking Environmental Change Using Lake Sediments*. Dordrecht: Kluwer Academic Publishers. Vol. 3, pp. 5–32.

Birks, H. J. B., & J. M. Line. 1992. The Use of Rarefaction Analysis for Estimating Palynological Richness from Quaternary Pollen-Analytical Data. *The Holocene* 2(1): 1–10.

Bonny, A. P. 1978. Recruitment of Pollen to the Seston and Sediment of Some Lake District Lakes. *Journal of Ecology* 64: 859–887.

Broström, A., S. Sugita & M.-J. Gaillard. 2004. Pollen Productivity Estimates for the Reconstruction of Past Vegetation Cover in the Cultural Landscape of Southern Sweden. *The Holocene* 14(3): 368–381.

Broström, A., A. B. Nielsen, M.-J. Gaillard, K. Hjelle, F. Mazier, H. Binne, J. Bunting, R. Fyfe, V. Meltsov, A. Poska, S. Räsänen, W. Soepboer, H. Steding, H. Suutari & S. Sugita. 2008. Pollen Productivity Estimates of Key European Plant Taxa for Quantitative Reconstruction of Past Vegetation: A Review. *Vegetation History and Archaeobotany* 17: 461–478.

Bunting, M. J., J. E. Schofield & K. J. 2013. Estimates of Relative Pollen Productivity (RPP) for Selected Taxa from Southern Greenland: A Pragmatic Solution. *Review of Palaeobotany and Palynology* 190: 66–74.

Evans, R. D. 1994. Empirical Evidence of the Importance of Sediment Resuspension in Lakes. *Hydrobiologia* 284: 5–12.

Grimm, E. 1987. CONISS: A Fortran 77 Program for Stratigraphically Constrained Cluster Analysis by the Method of Incremental Sum of Squares. *Computers Geosciences* 13: 13–35.

Heikinheimo O. 1915. Kaskiviljelyksen vaikutus Suomen metsiin. *Acta Forestalia Fennica* 4: 1–264, 1–149.

Hellman, S., M. J. Gaillard, J. M. Bunting & F. Mazier. 2009. Estimating the Relevant Source Area of Pollen in the Past Cultural Landscapes of Southern Sweden: A Forward Modelling Approach. *Review of Palaeobotany and Palynology* 153: 259–271.

Hicks, S. 1997. Pollen Analogues and Pollen Influx Values as Tools for Interpreting the History of a Settlement Centre and Its Hinterland. In U. Miller & H. Clarke (eds.). *Environment and Vikings: Scientific Methods and Techniques.* Birka Studies 4.II.3: Stockholm / Rixensart, 137–150.

Hjelle, K. L. 1998. Herb Pollen Representation in Surface Moss Samples from Mown Meadows and Pastures in Western Norway. *Vegetation History and Archaeobotany* 7: 79–96.

Jacobson, G. L. Jr., & R. H. W. Bradshaw. 1981. The Selection of Sites for Paleovegetational Studies. *Quaternary Research* 16: 80–96.

Nielsen, A. B., & B. V. Odgaard. 2010. Quantitative Landscape Dynamics in Denmark through the Last Three Millennia Based on the Landscape Reconstruction Algorithm Approach. *Vegetation History and Archaeobotany* 19: 375–387.

Nielsen, A. B., & S. Sugita. 2005. Estimating Relevant Source Area of Pollen for Small Danish Lakes around AD 1800. *The Holocene* 15(7): 1006–1020.

Parsons, R. W., & I. C. Prentice. 1981. Statistical Approaches to R-Values and Pollen-Vegetation Relationship. *Rev Palaeobot Palynol* 32: 127–152.

Prentice, I. C. 1985. Pollen Representation, Source Area, and Basin Size: Toward a Unified Theory of Pollen Analysis. *Quaternary Research* 23: 76–86.

Prentice, I. C., & R. W. Parsons. 1983. Maximun Likelihood Linear Calibration of Pollen Spectra in Terms of Forest Composition. *Biometrics* 39: 1051–1057.

Poska, A., V. Meltsov, S. Sugita & J. Vassiljev. 2011. Relative Pollen Productivity Estimates of Major Anemophilous Taxa and Relevant Source Area of Pollen in a Cultural Landscape of the Hemi-Borela Forest Zone (Estonia). *Review of Palaeobotany and Palynology* 167: 30–39.

Peck, R. M. 1973. Pollen Pudget Studies in a Small Yorkshire Catchment. In H. J. B. Birks & R. G. West (eds.). *Quaternary Plant Ecology*. Oxford: Blackwell. Pp. 43–60.

Pitkänen, A., K. Tolonen & H. Jungner. 2001. A Basin-Based Approach to the Long-Term History of Forest Fires as Determined from Peat Strata. *The Holocene* 11(5): 599–605.

Räsänen, S. 2001. Tracing and Interpreting Fine-Scale Human Impact in Northern Fennoscandia with the Aid of Modern Pollen Analogues. *Vegetation History and Archaeobotany* 10: 211–218.

Saarnisto, M. 1986. Annually Laminated Lake Sediments. In B. E. Berglund (ed.). *Handbook of Holocene Palaeoecology and Palaeohydrology*. Chichester: John Wiley. Pp. 343–370.

Saksa, A. 1998. Iron Age in Karelia: The Emergence and Early Development of Ancient Karelia. *Studia Carelica Humanistica* 11: 1–258.

Saloheimo, V. 1977. Asutuksen kasvun rajat: Taloluvun kehitys ja sen tekijöitä Laatokan-Karjalassa1500–1764. Publications of the Karelian Institute 27. Joensuu: University of Joensuu.

Sugita, S. 1994. Pollen Representation of Vegetation in Quaternary Sediments: Theory and Method in Patchy Vegetation. *J Ecol* 82: 881–897.

Sugita, S., M. J. Gaillard & A. Broström. 1999. Landscape Openness and Pollen Records: A Simulation Approach. *Holocene* 9: 409–421.

Sugita, S., T. Parshall, R. Calcote & K. Walker. 2010. Testing the Landscape Reconstruction Algorithm for Spatially Explicit Reconstruction of Vegetation in Northern Michigan and Wisconsin. *Quaternary Research* 74: 289–300.

Twiddle, C. L., R. T. Jones, C. J. Caseldine & S. Sugita. 2012. Pollen Productivity Estimates for a Pine Woodland in Eastern Scotland: The Influence of Sampling Design and Vegetation Patterning. *Review of Palaeobotany and Palynology* 174: 67–78.

Uino, Pirjo. 1997. *Ancient Karelia: Archaeological Studies - Muinais-Karjala: Arkeologisia tutkimuksia.* Suomen Muinaismuistoyhdistyksen Aikakauskirja 104. Helsinki: Suomen Muinaismuistoyhdistys.

Vuorela, I. 1973. Relative Pollen Rain around Cultivated Fields. *Acta Bot Fennica* 102: 1–27.

Matti Leiviskä

Toponymy as a Source for the Early History of Finland

The main goal of this chapter is to introduce the onomastic method and what it has to offer for the study of early history in Finland. The basis of this chapter lies in my licentiate thesis, where I have studied the early settlement history of the Siikajoki river valley in Northern Ostrobothia (Leiviskä 2011). The main questions in my study were: *a*) where and when did the first settlers come to the region; *b*) who used the area before the permanent settlement; and *c*) how did the settlement history vary in different parts of the area. One source material in this study was the oldest settlement names, including personal names, household names and village names. Another source was names of natural features such as rivers and lakes. Even though the study focuses on settlements, it was necessary to include names of natural features because the names of the places which were used for hunting or as a route or waterway can provide much information about the early history of the area. (Ainiala 2008: 123.) Also, many village and household names are based on names of natural features and hence too strict a limitation would be problematic.

The geographical delimitation of my study was the Siikajoki river valley, which includes the main bed of the River Siikajoki and all the minor streams flowing into it. In the sixteenth and seventeenth centuries, this area constituted one large parish, which was called Siikajoki. Today, the research area is divided into three municipalities: Siikajoki, Siikalatva and Pyhäntä. Chronologically, the thesis focused on the time from the Viking Age or Middle Ages (the periodisation is extremely indeterminate in Northern Finland) to the seventeenth century, because over that time period the settlement attainted the main lines of its later shape, as can still be seen today. However, some important place names appear only in younger source material, so the chronological limits could not be too strict.

In previous studies, the settlement history of the Siikajoki river valley was considered clear, and a rather young phenomenon, apart from on the coast of the Gulf of Bothnia. Therefore, some of my main questions were: *Was the settlement history of Siikajoki river valley really so simple as studies have hitherto assumed? Were the first settlers on the coast, on the mouth of the river*

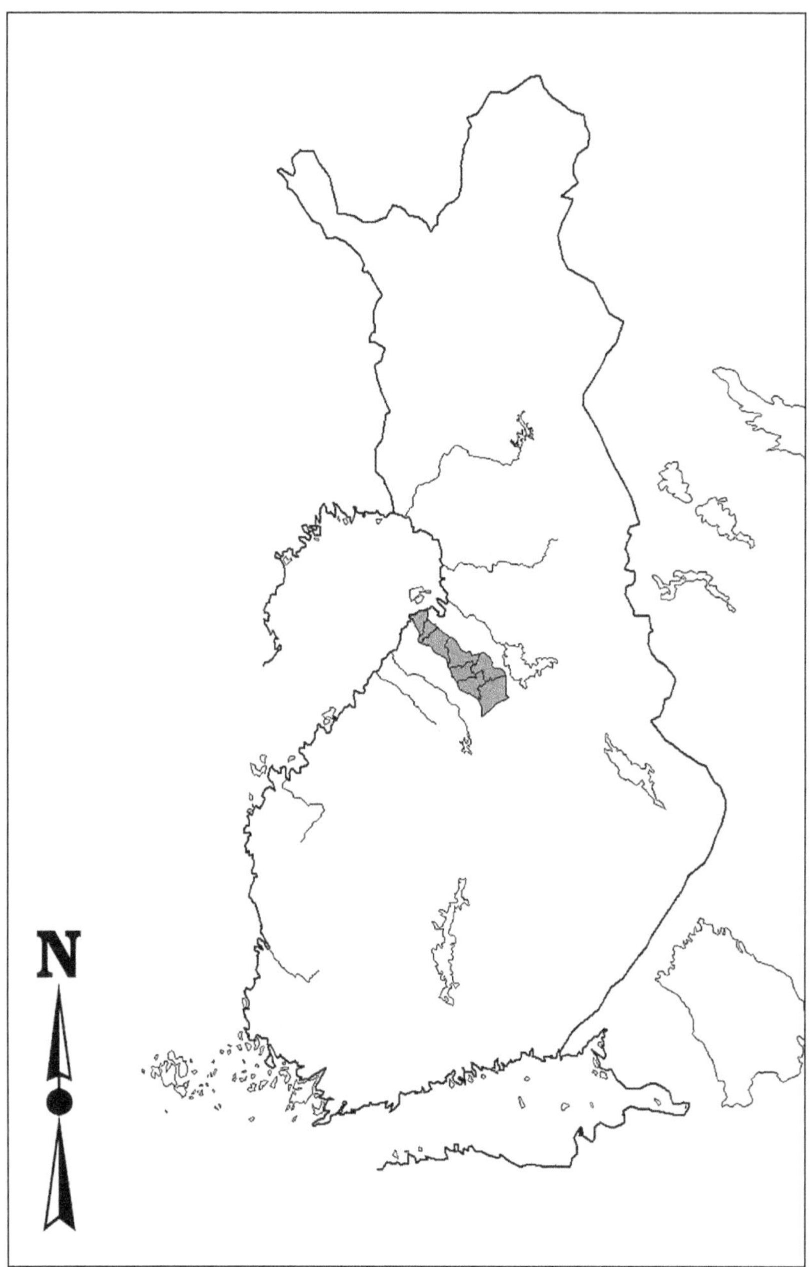

Fig. 1. Location of the old Siikajoki parish and river valley. Map drawn by Matti Leiviskä.

Siikajoki, mainly from western Finland, and did the Savo people settle first in the uninhabited uplands of the river valley during the sixteenth century, as it is commonly claimed? Or did the process start much earlier and was it more complicated than commonly supposed? In order to answer these questions, it was necessary to study the settlement history of the region as a whole and use all of the potential source material.

The results of the study were encouraging. Briefly, the thesis provided much new information about the chronology and origin of the settlement in the Siikajoki river valley, with some indicators even relating to Viking Age settlements. It also provided a new view of the settlement dynamics in one region in Northern Finland. In later sections, I present some examples of the research results, but first it is necessary to introduce the main sources and the methods which were used in the study.

Source Material

In investigating the history of settlement in the Siikajoki river valley, I used two main sources: firstly, the old tax registers, and secondly, toponyms (place names). In the case of place names, the best sources can be found in the Names Archive of the Research Institute for the Languages of Finland. This archive contains over 2.6 million place name entries, mainly from Finland but also from nearby areas. Furthermore there is large collection of personal names and place names gathered from old documents. The main collection of place names was gathered by interviewing local people village by village. The first collecting programme of Finnish toponyms was begun in 1878 by the Finnish Antiquarian Society, the predecessor of the Finnish National Board of Antiquities. The quality of these early collections is, alas, quite variable and mainly poor for systematic research because material was not gathered from every part of the country. Systematic collection of place names was begun in 1915 by many different organisations. Since then, collectors have mainly been trained linguists and students. In the 1990s, it was estimated that the Names Archive already contained 95 per cent of the place names in Finland. Later, these estimates have been questioned because new studies indicate that toponyms form a dynamic, living and constantly changing system. Nonetheless, we can say that the Names Archives collections provide sufficient materials to study the settlement history of Finland.[1]

Although the Names Archive's collections are unique and offer invaluable source material for research, there are many problems which must be taken into consideration when evaluating the information they provide. Firstly, the material is not homogeneous; the quality depends on the region, the collector and the time when the information was gathered (Virrankoski 1978: 14). Generally, the older collections are better than the younger ones and more information is gained from the countryside than from dense population centres. From the perspective of settlement history, the most fertile collections were gathered from country villages during the 1960s and 1970s. Before the 1960s, there were no adequate and comprehensive instructions for the collectors and hence background information on the names remained scarce. (Närhi 1978: 57–58; Ainiala 2001: 8.) After the 1970s, the main problem was the depopulation and structural change of the countryside and the reduction in numbers of older informants. For this reason, many minor names, for example field names, have been lost. (Kiviniemi 1990: 32–33.) In some places, the problem is also the incoherence

Tavastkenkä

tavaskeŋkä : tavaskeŋŋällä

Pyhäntä

Suurin Pyhännän kylä. Yhteen aikaan
Tavastkengällä on asunut yli puo-
let koko Pyhännän väestöstä.
Kylän nimi on joidenkin kertojien
mukaan saanut alkunsa Tavastkengän-
järvellä sattuneesta tapahtumasta,
ks. Tavastkengänjärvi.
Kerrotaan myös, että alue olisi ollut hämäläisten vanhaa metsästys-
maastoa.
Kerrotaan, että Tavastkengän ensimmäinen asukas on ollut Koljosessa
(ks. Koljonen), jolloin Kestilän

Pyhäntä
Sirkka-Liisa Savinen
1972

Jatkuu

Fig. 2. A typical name note from the Names Archive of the Research Institute for the Languages of Finland. Tavastkenkä is one of the old villages in the Siikajoki river valley.

of the collection, when there have been many different collectors over several decades. The best possible situation is when one competent collector has gathered all the information from the same area.

As was mentioned above, the Names Archive contains 2.6 million place name entries from Finland and nearby areas. The average name density in Finland is about 6–7 names per square kilometre, but this varies greatly depending on the place (Kiviniemi 1990: 35). From the whole Siikajoki river valley, for example, there are about 28,000 name notes, which were all thoroughly scrutinised for the thesis. The number of notes is approximately the same as the actual number of independent names in the area. Every note contains a headword, consisting of the place name in its standard language form. Under that is the same name as pronounced in the local dialect, then different forms of the name, the location of the place referred to and brief clarification about the type of place (a house, hill, river etc.). More details about the name and the place may follow below this basic information, e.g. a folk tale or a local etymology. (Närhi 1978: 56–57.)

Most of the toponyms in the Siikajoki river valley, as also in the rest of Finland, are commonly used names of little interest from the perspective of settlement history. These names, e.g. *Kivimäki* ['stone hill'] or *Riihipelto* ['a field near a drying barn'], can be found in almost every corner of the country. Once such names are discarded, the remaining names usually have some rare constituent parts or appellatives. In the Siikajoki river valley, discarding commonplace names reduced the count from 28,000 to about 1,100 names. Finally, about 150 name series were left, which all contained one or several place names. For example *Jylhänkangas*, *-koski*, *-niska* and *-ranta* in Pulkkila village form one name series, which is studied together with all other *Jylhä*-names from the research area.

Toponyms are of essential importance when studying the history of periods which lack continuous or sufficient written sources. In Finland, this means particularly the Late Iron Age or the Middle Ages. From the beginning of the 1540s, the number of written sources increases remarkably and, in addition to place names, settlement history can be studied in light of personal names and other information appearing in tax registers. These documents list the people who paid taxes in the region. Information is divided according to parishes, regions and villages, mainly in geographical order. In the sixteenth century, the tax register contained mainly just the village names and personal names, commonly just the name of the owner of the farm. Household names rarely appear until the middle of seventeenth century, but many of them had been used for much longer.

Old taxation documents are excellent sources for research into old settlement names, especially village names, personal names and household names. As material for comparison, all the name material gathered from other documents from the same period can be used. It is important to take into account that many sixteenth-century personal names had moved from their original position already by the seventeenth century because of the intense migration during the previous century. Therefore, the comparative material has to be approximately from the same century, and preferably from the same decade, if possible. There is also a large collection of names gathered from old documents in the Names Archive, but there are certain matters to consider when using these collections. Firstly, there is a high probability of error when using these handwritten notes, because the writer could have read the name wrong from the original document. Especially when there is only one single name occurrence in the archive, it must be used with great caution. Usually it is better to check every name from the original document before using it in research. For this purpose, there are reference markings in every note. In addition to the tax registers, many old names can be found in younger documents, for example from district court records from the beginning of seventeenth century or from maps, map descriptions and other documents made for the general parcelling out of land during the late eighteenth century.

Methods

Toponyms have been used as a source in many local history and settlement history studies since the late nineteenth century. Great names such as Väinö Voionmaa, Jalmari Jaakkola and Armas Luukko used place names in their argumentation concerning the settlement history of Finland. The main problem of these early-twentieth-century studies was the scarcity of the source material and the researchers' pointed search for evidence to back up their own arguments. Some later historians, such as Pentti Virrankoski, have used toponyms in much better and more objective ways. The main developers of the modern onomastic method in Finland are Viljo Nissilä and Eero Kiviniemi, both professors of the Finnish language. Their methods have been used and developed by many later scholars since the 1960s and 1970s. In Northern Finland, the most important onomastic research so far has been the doctoral thesis of historian Jouko Vahtola, in which he studied the origin of the settlement of the Tornionjoki and Kemijoki river valleys. This study changed the traditional picture of the early history of Northern Finland in many ways.

The methods used in my thesis were onomastic and historical. It is said that the name of a place is also the memory of a place. Names can conserve information of events over centuries, even millennia, and because of this capacity, they are one of the rare sources we have from the time before written sources in Finland. Place names have been passed from generation to generation as lore or, in some cases, in written documents. They are very stable relics, unless total depopulation happens. Yet not even place names can tell about the past if the lore is completely broken. Preservation does not, however, require a permanent population, but instead permanent human influence on the region, for example in the form of regular hunting or fishing trips.[2]

Toponyms can be preserved, perhaps with some phonetic changes, even if a large new ethnic group comes to a region. A place name's capacity to remain unchanged is commensurate with the size and stability of the named object. The name of a large lake or a river is better preserved than for example that of a small field, because larger objects also have a larger user group. It is also significant where the place is located, because near a dense population centre various new names that indicate ownership (*Väinönpelto* ['Väinö's field']) or land use (*Myllymäki* ['Mill Hill']) can easily overwhelm an antecedent name stratum. In outlying districts, however, it is possible to find a very old name stratum, even of names of small places, because the pressure to change names has not been so substantial.[3] In the case of very old names, there is a possibility that, in spite of their stability, their pronunciation could have changed over the centuries. Some of the regular changes are caused by alteration of the local dialect, but some changes are irregular and case-specific. One of the most common reasons for changes to place names is ellipsis (shortening). For example *Perioja* can become *Peroja* and *Syväjärvi* can change to *Syväri*. In these cases, the original can often be found on old maps or documents or by comparing it with similar cases elsewhere. (Virrankoski 1978: 14–17; Vahtola 1984a: 83, 89–90.)

Toponyms can provide information about the past livelihoods in the region, for example about farming and hunting, but they have much more significance when research is carried out on whence or when the first inhabitants arrived. The main idea of researching settlement history through place names is that when new settlers arrive in a region, they also bring new kinds of names along with them. If similar names can be found in two different areas, it is possible that they had some connection in the past. Conclusions cannot be drawn from just one or two names; several common names or name types are needed. (Nissilä 1968: 54–55; Vahtola 1984a: 84.) When there are enough names, they can be studied on the basis of three factors: *a*) the original language of the names; *b*) the contents of the name; and *c*) the geographical distribution of names, name types and appellatives used in them. (Kiviniemi 1978b: 22; Vahtola 1984a: 85.)

A name can be of significance from the perspective of the history of the settlement even if it is based on a different language from that of the modern population of the region, such as Sámi or Swedish. In the upland of the Siikajoki river valley, there are names such as *Mella-*, *Rova-* and *Vuohto-*, which all have Sámi counterparts. In these cases, originally foreign names need to be distinguished from those that have only a foreign element, because many loanwords are also used in place names. Drawing a line between these two options is not always easy, but it is necessary because they suggest different histories. If an entire toponym can be shown to be a loan, it usually means that there were two different human populations with different languages that were at least in contact, or maybe even integrated with each other. On the other hand, a foreign appellative in a word does not mean that a foreign group of people lived in the region, because these kinds of loanwords could have been adopted in other areas and spread thereafter. In addition to names of clearly foreign origin, there may be place names that contain some dialectal words, used only in certain regions of the country.[4]

Alongside the linguistic background, it is also important to research the meaning and factual content of the names, because people did not give names to a place without reason. In the present day, that original meaning may be more or less unclear or even impossible to recognise, but it was often some distinguishing characteristic that marked out the place from others nearby. The ways to do this have varied depending on the time, culture, source of livelihood and many other factors. Common aspects of contemporary culture and land use are rarely found alone in names because of their non-specificity. If there are lots of birch forests in a village, almost no names containing the word *koivu* ['birch'] would be found in that village. But if the village is mainly covered with conifer forests, every place with birches may be named according to this one characteristic. Correctly decoded, the factual content of a name can assist in solving its origin and even its date. If a name is believed to have a foreign origin, the meaning of the place name should suit the place. Some characteristics that the place now lacks could have been present at some point in history. Especially these kinds of altering characteristics can be useful in dating the naming process. On the coast of the Gulf of Bothnia, for example, there are many names like *saari-* ['island'] that are associated with the sea but are many kilometres away from the modern coast. These names can be dated with the help of the post-glacial rebound, which causes the rise of the land and fall of the sea level. When the exact location and elevation of a named place is known, it can easily be calculated when it was under water or rose above sea level.[5]

Many toponyms hold a meaning that refers to sources of livelihood, beliefs or cultural features, which can be connected to some specific group of people or to a certain time period. Place names that contain a name for a tribe or cultural group such as *Hämeen-* ['of Tavastia'] or *Karjalan-* ['of Karelia'] are important for the study of settlement history because they indicate that some particular ethnic group has used the region or even lived there. These kinds of name also presuppose another ethnic group living or using the same region because names that refer to one tribe or cultural group are given by another group. Many personal names can also be connected with certain populations (e.g. Swedish or Karelian personal names), but it is often hard to say whether they are the result of direct or indirect contacts. (Vahtola 1984a: 104–112.)

The toponyms of a region did not develop all at the same time, but instead there are many strata of place names with different origins and different ages. By comparing the geographical distribution of the names, we can investigate the proportion of names of a given age between different settlement layers, and possibly establish the date of the settlement. This method also works on a wider scale. Modern onomastic studies of historical settlement are focused not so much on individual names as on the geographical distribution of the names on a regional and national scale. Names could have spread by being transplanted with migration from an original settlement, when the same names have been given to similar places even when the meaning was already unknown. On the other hand, it seems that most place names are based on established naming models and traditional nomenclature patterns. Many of these models were used over the whole Finnish language area and so conclusions about historical settlement cannot be inferred from them. For many other models, however, it is peculiar that they have been used only by certain groups of people or that they have been active only for a specific period of history. This means that if the geographical distribution of place names and name types in Finland is investigated and similarities are found between two places, a settlement and/or migration link between these areas may be surmised. It is crucial that assumptions should not be made on the basis of just one or two names. In the best cases, the distribution of names can provide useful information even when the background of the name is not so striking.[6]

The Toponymy of the Siikajoki River Valley

In the Siikajoki river valley there are at least six strata of names of different origin. I introduce the most significant of them here. In the upper parts of the river valley, the oldest name stratum seems to be of Sámi origin. Many names of smaller lakes and other waterways are based on Sámi words, for example the lake *Vuohtojärvi* in the village of Piippola and *Mellassalmi* in the parish of Pyhäntä (*vuohčču* and *miel'li* in North Sámi). Map 3 shows the geographical distribution of the names which begin with the word *mella*. (Itkonen T. I. 1920: 9; SPnk: s.v. 'Vuohtajärvi', 'Vuohtomäki', 'Vuotso'; Aikio 2009: 263, 289) The northern distribution of these names also supports the supposed Sámi origin. Because there are no traces of Sámi people in the oldest written sources from this region, we have to assume that they had already disappeared by the middle of the sixteenth century. Therefore the Sámi place names have to be much older, at least from the Middle Ages or even from the Viking Age.

The oldest or the second-oldest name layer in the Siikajoki river valley seems to be Tavastian because most of the names of larger waterways and other important terrain names have counterparts in Tavastia and upper Satakunta. Names of western Finnish origin occur even in the upper parts of the river valley, which was inhabited by Karelian and Savo people from the middle of the sixteenth century. Therefore these western names have to be older, maybe even from the Viking Age. For example the name of the lake *Iso Lamujärvi*, the largest lake of the valley and one of the source lakes of the River Siikajoki, contains the word *lamu* ['flat, wide']. This word appears in place names in many parts of Finland, but originally it was used mainly in upper Satakunta, as we can see in Map 4.

Names of eastern Finnish origin occur in all parts of the Siikajoki river valley, even on the very coast of the Gulf of Bothnia. The population of the coastal villages has traditionally been considered as of western origin, but eastern personal names can also be found in the oldest tax registers. The eastern population was of Karelian origin and had moved to the coast of the Gulf of Bothnia during the Middle Ages. Karelian words occur only in smaller place names, which indicates that this name stratum is younger than the Sámi or the western Finnish layer. In Map 5 are all the names including the word *rivi*, which is known from the Karelian Isthmus in the sense 'underwater rocks or sandbank' (SKES: s.v. 'rivi'). In the Siikajoki river valley, it appears in the name of the torrent *Rivinkoski* in the parish of Kestilä.

In the Siikajoki river valley there are only a few place names which have counterparts in the south-western parts of Finland, in Finland Proper and in lower Satakunta. Therefore we can assume that there was little migration from these regions to the shores of the Siikajoki. One of the few names with counterparts in Finland Proper is *Ruonaoja*, a small ditch in the village of Siikajoki. The word *ruona* ['accretion, muddy bay'] is widely known in place names on the western coast of Finland. (Pitkänen 1985: 222–225, 229; Mikkonen & Paikkala 2000: s.v. 'Ruonala'.)

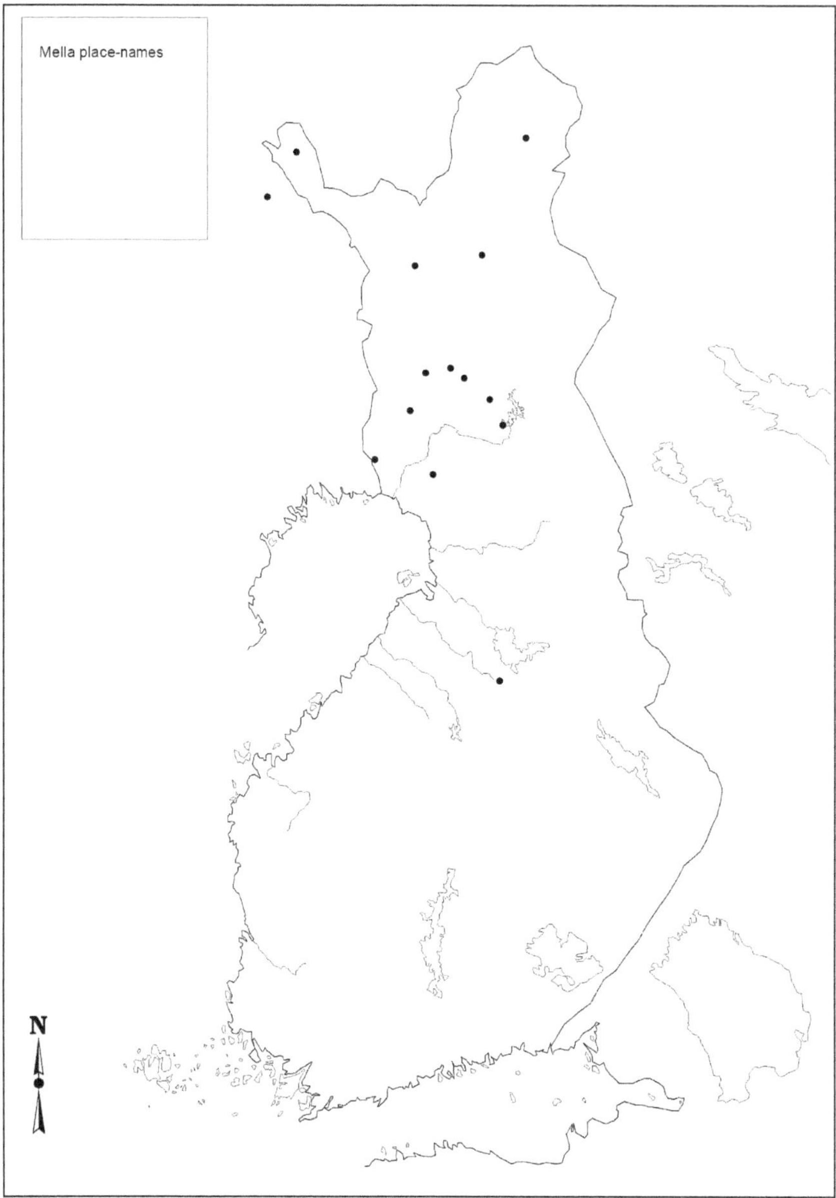

Fig. 3. Geographical distribution of the place names including the word mella-. Map drawn by Matti Leiviskä.

Names of Scandinavian origin are very rare in the Siikajoki river valley. Some names can be found on the coast of the Gulf of Bothnia, near the Siikajoki estuary, but it is usually hard to say whether the name was originally Swedish or just based on a Swedish loanword. For example the name of the lake *Vartinjärvi* in the village of Siikajoki is probably based on the Swedish word *svart* ['black, dark'].

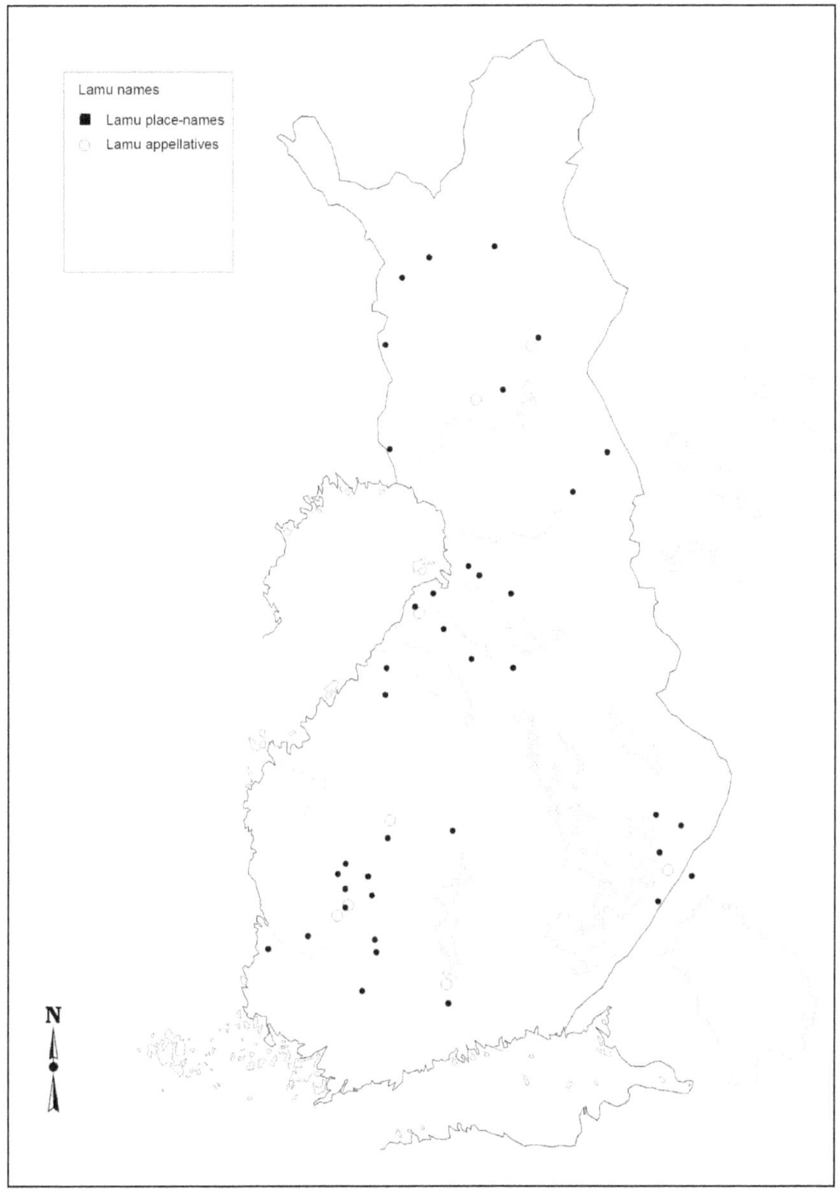

Fig. 4. Geographical distribution of the place names including the word lamu. Map drawn by Matti Leiviskä.

The name stratum in the Siikajoki river valley seems to be very similar to that found by Jouko Vahtola in the Kemijoki river valley. The layer of Sámi place names could be the oldest but it has been preserved only in outlying districts. Most of the great waterways and terrain names have western Finnish, especially Tavastian, origins. Some of these names may date back to the Viking Age. The eastern Finnish name layer can be considered to be the youngest, but in the coastal village of Siikajoki it may nonetheless have medieval roots.

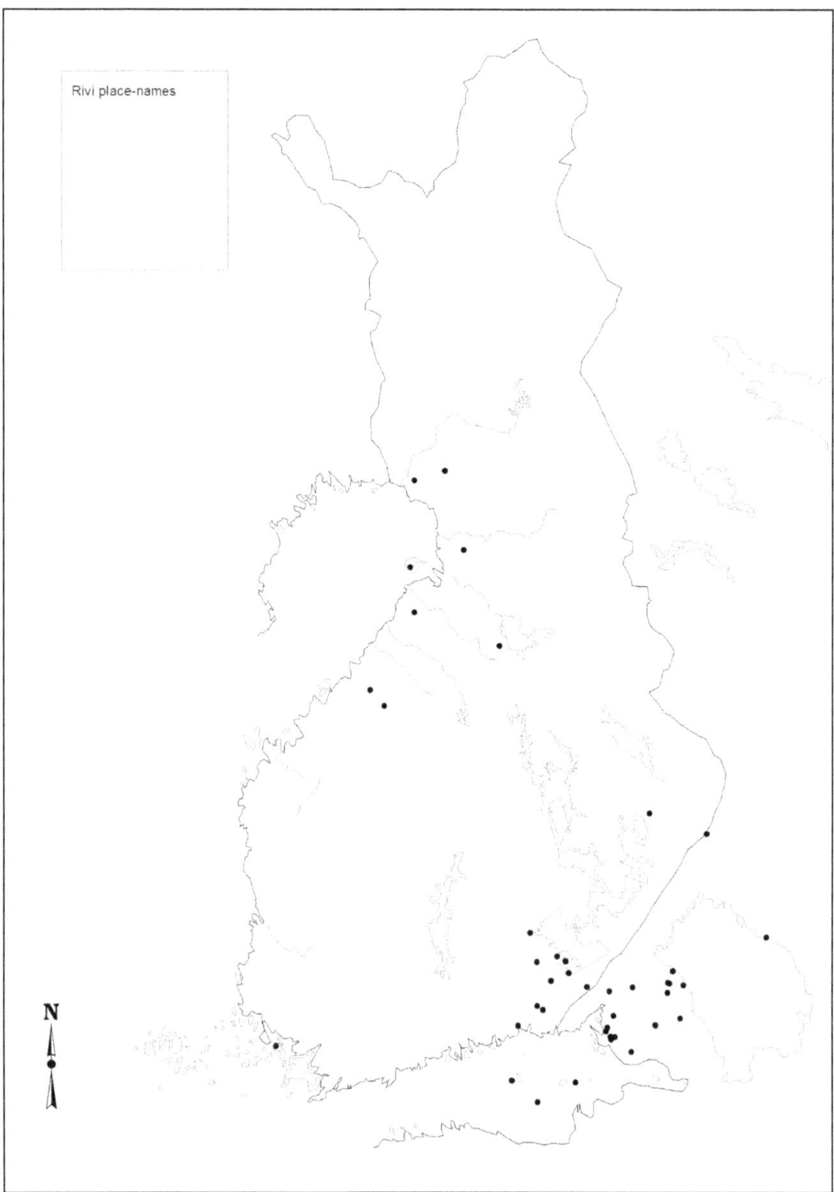

Fig. 5. Geographical distribution of place names including the word rivi. Map drawn by Matti Leiviskä.

Summary

In conclusion it can be said that toponyms are the only plentiful, easily available and regionally unbiased source material from the early history of Finland. The same thing cannot be said of the traditional sources for historical study or of archaeology, because in both cases the source materials are rare and geographically clustered. A viable study of place names requires the handling of huge numbers of names, because one name may be misleading

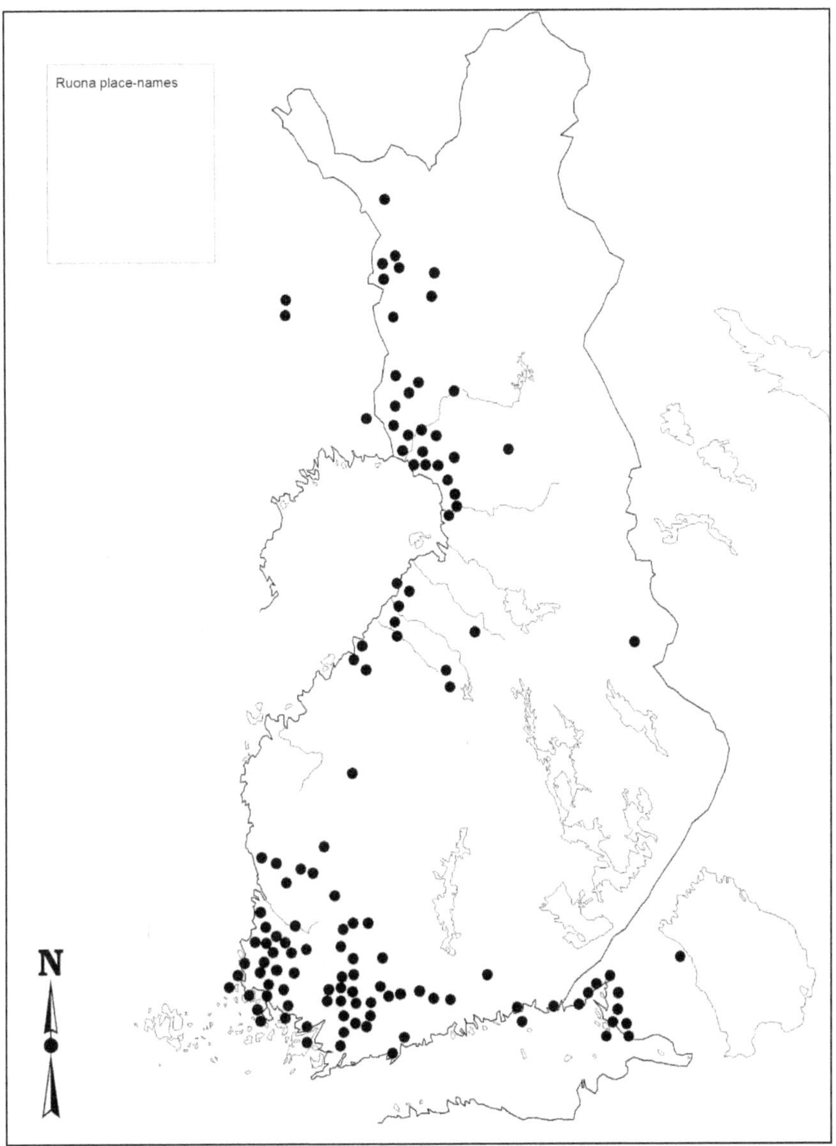

Fig. 6. Geographical distribution of the name Ruona. Map drawn by Matti Leiviskä; the original map drawn by Saulo Kepsu (2003) is preserved in the map collections of the Names Archive.

but large numbers can reveal the truth. The best possible results can be achieved with the assistance of other branches of science, such as history, archaeology, geography, linguistics and genetics.

Although the sources of onomastics have been available for decades, they have regrettably been but seldom used. There is still much to research and to discover and many questions concerning Finland's early settlement history need closer study. In many places the most 'modern' studies are very old, even from the beginning of the twentieth century. Even though onomastics has demonstrated that it is of great value when studying the early history of Finland, the origin of many focal Finnish population centres is still covered with thick mist. From the perspective of Northern Finland, the most important research subject would be the settlement history of the Kyröjoki river valley in Southern Ostrobothnia. The mystery of the Sámi settlement in inland Finland has not been solved, and much remains to be clarified in the settlement history of Savo before the sixteenth century. Further areas to research can be found from the old heartlands of Häme, Karelia, Satakunta and Finland Proper. Onomastic research on these heartland areas could enlighten the origins of settlement history in the whole of Finland, bud sadly in these cases research has not proceeded so far during the last few decades. The work would be immense, but with modern computers and other technical solutions, it is much easier to work with large collections of names than before. Perhaps the time has finally come to take up the challenge and really begin to study the history of the place names of Finland.

Notes

1 Kiviniemi 1978b: 21; 1990: 33; Närhi 1978: 52–53, 61–62; Vahtola 1980: 84–85; Ainiala 2001: 9; homepage of the Research Institute for the Languages of Finland (http://www.kotus.fi/?l=en).
2 Nissilä 1968: 56; Kiviniemi 1978b: 21–22; 1978a: 73–77; Vahtola 1980: 13–14; 1984a: 82–83; 1990: 1.
3 Nissilä 1968: 56; Kiviniemi 1978a: 73–77; Virrankoski 1978: 12–13; Vahtola 1980: 13; Kiviniemi 1990: 36–43; Ainiala 1997: 238.
4 Kiviniemi 1978b: 22–23; 1984: 329–332; Vahtola 1984a: 85–89; 1990: 5.
5 Kiviniemi 1978a: 80–82; Kiviniemi 1978b: 24–25; Kiviniemi 1984: 327, 331–332, 335–337; Vahtola 1984a: 104.
6 Kiviniemi 1975: 12–13, 50–53; 1977: 4–9, 207–208; 1978a: 84–88; 1984: 337–338; Vahtola 1984a: 91–93; 1990: 3; Ainiala 2008: 118.

References

Sources

Collections of the Names Archive of the Research Institute for the Languages of Finland.

Literature

Aikio, Ante. 2009. *The Saami Loanwords in Finnish and Karelian.* Oulu: Oulun yliopisto, Giellagas-instituutti.

Ainiala, Terhi. 1997. *Muuttuva paikannimistö.* Suomalaisen Kirjallisuuden Seuran Toimituksia 667. Helsinki: Suomalaisen Kirjallisuuden Seura.

Ainiala Terhi. 2001. Paikannimistön keruun tavoitteet ja tulokset. In Kaija Mallat, Terhi Ainiala & Eero Kiviniemi (eds.). *Nimien maailmasta.* Kieli 14. Helsinki: Helsingin yliopiston suomen kielen laitos.

Ainiala, Terhi, Minna Saarelma & Paula Sjöblom. 2008. *Nimistöntutkimuksen perusteet*. Tietolipas 221. Helsinki: Suomalaisen Kirjallisuuden Seura.

Alanen, Timo. 2004. *Someron ja Tammelan vanhin asutusnimistö: Nimistön vakiintumisen aika*. Oulu: Oulun yliopiston, suomen ja saamen kielen ja logopedian laitos, suomen kieli.

Collinder, Björn. 1964. *Ordbok till Sveriges lapska ortnamn*. Uppsala: Kungl. ortnamnskommissionen.

Húlden, Lars. 2001. *Finnlandsvenska bebyggelsenamn: Namn på landskap, kommuner, byar i Finland av svenskt ursprung eller med särsklild svenskt form*. Helsingfors: Svenska litteratursällskapet i Finland.

Häkkinen, Kaisa. 1997. *Mistä sanat tulevat: Suomalaista etymologiaa*. 2nd edn. Tietolipas 117. Helsinki: Suomalaisen Kirjallisuuden Seura.

Häkkinen, Kaisa. 2005. *Nykysuomen etymologinen sanakirja*. 3rd edn. Helsinki, WSOY.

Itkonen, T. I. 1920. Lappalaisperäisiä paikannimiä suomenkielen alueella. *Virittäjä* 24: 1–11.

Itkonen, T. I. 1948. *Suomen lappalaiset vuoteen 1945*. Helsinki: WSOY.

Kepsu, Saulo. 1981. *Pohjois-Kymenlaakson kylännimet – Village Place Names in Northern Kymenlaakso*. Suomalaisen kirjallisuuden seuran toimituksia 367. Helsinki: Suomalaisen Kirjallisuuden Seura.

Kepsu, Saulo. 2005. *Uuteen maahan: Helsingin ja Vantaan vanha asutus ja nimistö*. Helsinki: Suomalaisen Kirjallisuuden Seura.

Kiviniemi, Eero. 1971. *Suomen partisiippinimistöä: Ensimmäisen partisiipin sisältävät henkilön- ja paikannimet*. Suomalaisen Kirjallisuuden Seuran Toimituksia 295. Helsinki: Suomalaisen Kirjallisuuden Seura.

Kiviniemi, Eero. 1975. *Paikannimien rakennetyypeistä*. Suomi 118:2. Helsinki, Suomalaisen Kirjallisuuden Seura.

Kiviniemi, Eero. 1977. *Väärät vedet*. Suomalaisen Kirjallisuuden Seuran Toimituksia 337. Helsinki, Suomalaisen Kirjallisuuden Seura.

Kiviniemi, Eero. 1978. Paikannimistö systeeminä. In Kiviniemi, Eero (ed.). *Nimistöntutkimus ja paikallishistoria*. Paikallishistoriallisen Toimiston Julkaisuja 2. Helsinki: Paikallishistoriallinen Toimisto. Pp. 73–89.

Kiviniemi, Eero. 1978. Paikannimistö asutushistoriallisen tutkimuksen lähdeaineistona. *Faravid: Pohjois-Suomen Historiallisen Yhdistyksen vuosikirja* 2: 21–28.

Kiviniemi, Eero. 1984. Nimistö Suomen esihistorian tutkimuksen aineistona. In *Suomen väestön esihistorialliset juuret*. Helsinki: Societas Scientiarum Fennica. Pp. 327–346.

Kiviniemi, Eero. 1990. *Perustietoa paikannimistä*. Suomalaisen Kirjallisuuden Seuran Toimituksia 516. Helsinki: Suomalaisen Kirjallisuuden Seura.

Leiviskä, Matti. 2007. Vanhan Salon pitäjän kylännimistö. *Faravid: Pohjois-Suomen historiallisen yhdistyksen vuosikirja* 31.

Leiviskä, Matti. 2011. Siikajokilaakson asutuksen synty: Nimistöhistoriallinen tutkimus Siikajokilaakson asutuksesta keskiajalta 1600-luvun puoliväliin. Licentiate thesis. Oulu: University of Oulu.

Luukko, Armas. 1954. *Pohjois-Pohjanmaan ja Lapin historia II*. Oulu: Pohjois-Pohjanmaan ja Lapin Maakuntaliittojen Historiatoimikunta.

Mallat, Kaija. 2007. Naiset rajalla: Kyöpeli, Nainen, Naara(s), Neitsyt, Morsian, Akka ja Ämmä Suomen paikannimissä. Helsinki: Suomalaisen Kirjallisuuden Seura.

Mikkonen, Pirjo, & Sirkka Paikkala. 2000. *Sukunimet*. Keuruu, Otava.

Nissilä, Viljo. 1939. *Vuoksen paikannimistö I*. Suomalaisen Kirjallisuuden Seuran Toimituksia 214. Helsinki: Suomalaisen Kirjallisuuden Seura.

Nissilä, Viljo. 1948. Pohjois-Pohjanmaan karjalaista nimistöä. *Virittäjä* 1948: 215–243.

Nissilä, Viljo. 1957. Slaavilaisia aineksia nimistössämme. *Virittäjä* 1957: 49–70.

Nissilä, Viljo. 1968. Asutushistoriallinen nimistötutkimus. In Antero Penttilä (ed.). *Paikallishistoria tänään*. Helsinki: Paikallishistoriallinen Toimisto. Pp. 54–74.

Nissilä, Viljo. 1975. *Suomen Karjalan nimistö*. Joensuu: Karjalaisen kulttuurin edistämissäätiö.

Nissilä, Viljo. 1976. *Suomen Karjalan ortodoksinen nimistö*. Lappeenranta: Viipurin Suomalainen Kirjallisuusseura.

Närhi, Eeva Maria. 1978. Suomen Nimitoimiston kokoelmat tutkimuksen lähdeaineistona. In Eero Kiviniemi (ed.). *Nimistöntutkimus ja paikallishistoria*. Paikallishistoriallisen Toimiston julkaisuja n:o 2. Helsinki: Paikallishistoriallinen Toimisto. Pp. 52–72.

Pitkänen, Ritva Liisa. 1985. *Turunmaan saariston suomalainen lainanimistö*. Suomalaisen Kirjallisuuden Seuran Toimituksia 418. Helsinki, Suomalaisen Kirjallisuuden Seura.

Räisänen, Alpo. 2003. *Nimet mieltä kiehtovat: Etymologista nimistöntutkimusta*. Suomalaisen Kirjallisuuden Seuran Toimituksia 936. Helsinki: Suomalaisen Kirjallisuuden Seura.

Räisänen, Alpo. 2006. *Kainuun kieltä ja paikannimiä*. Studia Carelica Humanistica 21. Joensuu: Joensuun yliopiston humanistinen tiedekunta.

Saarikivi, Janne. 2006. *Substrata Uralica: Studies on Finno-Ugrian Substrate in Northern Russian dialects*. Tartu: Tartu University Press.

Saloheimo, Veijo. 2006. *Viipurinkarjalaiset kotona ja maailmalla 1541–1620: Viipurinkarjalaisten sukunimien esiintyminen muualla Suomessa ja lähialueilla liikkuvuuden mittarina*. Suomen Sukututkimusseuran Julkaisuja 57. Helsinki: Suomen Sukututkimusseura Ry.

SKES = *Suomen kielen etymologinen sanakirja* I–VI. 1955–1978. Helsinki: Suomalais-Ugrilainen Seura.

SMS = *Suomen murteiden sanakirja* I–VIII. 1986–2009. Kotimaisten Kielten Tutkimuskeskuksen julkaisuja 36. Helsinki.

SSA = *Suomen sanojen alkuperä. Etymologinen sanakirja*. 1992–2000. Suomalaisen Kirjallisuuden Seuran Toimituksia 556. Kotimaisten Kielten Tutkimuskeskuksen Julkaisuja 62. Helsinki.

Vahtola, Jouko. 1980. *Tornionjoki- ja Kemijokilaakson asutuksen synty: Nimistötieteellinen ja historiallinen tutkimus*. Studia Historica Septentrionalia 3. Rovaniemi: Pohjois-Suomen Historiallinen Yhdistys.

Vahtola, Jouko. 1984. Onomastinen metodi Suomen varhaishistorian tutkimuksessa. In Eero Kuparinen (ed.). *VIII Suomalais-Neuvostoliittolainen yhteiskuntahistorian symposiumi Turussa 2.–6.9.1984*. Turun Historiallinen arkisto 41. Turku: Turun Historiallinen Yhdistys.

Vahtola, Jouko. 1990. *Nimistöntutkimus ja Pohjois-Suomen varhaishistoria*. Eripainossarja 241. Oulu: Oulun Yliopiston Historian Laitos.

Vahtola, Jouko. 1992. Pohjois-Pohjanmaan rannikon asutuksen synty. In Kyösti Julku (ed.). *Suomen varhaishistoria, Tornion kongressi 15.–16.6.1991: Esitelmät referaatit*. Studia Historica Septentrionalia 21. Rovaniemi, Pohjois-Suomen Historiallinen yhdistys. Pp. 613–621.

Vahtola, Jouko. 1999. Saamelaisten esiintyminen Suomessa varhaishistoriallisten lähteiden ja paikannimien valossa. Paul Fogelberg (ed.). *Pohjan poluilla: Suomalaisten juuret nykytutkimuksen mukaan*. Helsinki: Suomen Tiedeseura. Pp. 109–116.

Virrankoski, Pentti. 1978. Mitä historiantutkija odottaa nimistöntutkimukselta? In Eero Kiviniemi (ed.). *Nimistöntutkimus ja paikallishistoria*. Paikallishistoriallisen Toimiston Julkaisuja 2. Helsinki: Paikallishistoriallinen Toimisto. Pp. 9–23.

Denis Kuzmin

The Inhabitation of Karelia in the First Millennium AD in the Light of Linguistics

In Russia, the term 'Viking Age' is rarely used in the study of linguistics and cultural history. The corresponding period is instead referred to as the early Middle Ages. This period was important from the perspective of Karelian and Vepsian culture and language because these ethnic groups formed during this time, although this occurred largely outside the borders of today's Republic of Karelia. In the late Viking Age, Finnic groups (ancient Vepsians and Karelians) moved from the region of their origins to begin settling in the southern part of what is now the Republic of Karelia and in Eastern and Southeast Finland (cf. Kallio). These territories are associated by their cultural history, although they are separated by the Finland–Russia border today, and they are central within the ethnogenesis of Finnic peoples. The archaic cultures of these territories share a significant number of common features that developed in relation to cultural contacts, and for this reason, the study of the Viking Age in Finland also requires the study of the ethnohistorical processes that took place in adjacent regions. The aim of this chapter is to provide a general overview of the population of the Republic of Karelia in the Iron Age.

Karelia until AD 1050 in the Light of Archaeological Evidence

Geographically, definitions of 'Karelia' refer to broad concepts that are not all consistent. Karelia is a territory in Russia and partly in Finland. Finnish Karelia is considered to consist of the Karelian Isthmus, Ladoga Karelia and the regions commonly called North and South Karelia. Today, Russian Karelia is politically defined through the Republic of Karelia, consisting of Viena Karelia and Aunus Karelia. Another Karelia in Russia is the so-called 'Daughter Karelia' (*tytär-Karjala*) which consists of Novgorod Karelia and Tver Karelia. Dialects of Finnish Karelian were spoken in Finnish Karelia. In Russian Karelia are spoken Karelian, Livvi (*livvi*, not to be confused with *liivi*, Livonian) and Ludic (Map 1). The Karelian language has been spoken on the Finnish side of the border in the northernmost parishes of North

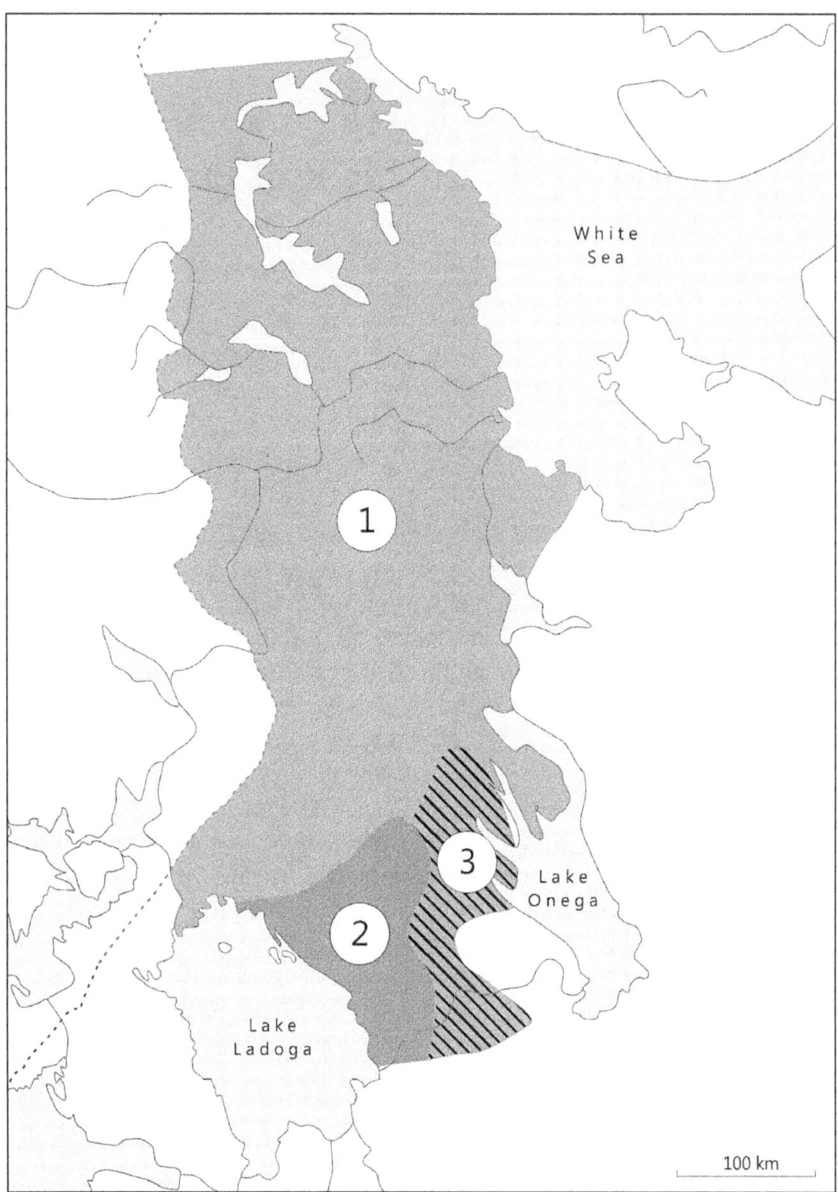

Map 1. Dialect areas of Karelian. Key: 1. Karelian proper dialects; 2. Livv dialects; 3. Ludic dialects.

Karelia, in eastern Kainuu, as well as in the territory formerly called Border Karelia and also known as Ladoga Karelia (Torikka 2004). The present chapter addresses Karelia as inclusive of the present-day Republic of Karelia, areas of the former Ladoga Karelia still within the Finnish border and the easternmost part of the parish of Ilomantsi. Russian Karelia has been an area of numerous ethnic and linguistic contacts over the course of history. According to Russian archaeologists, it is possible to distinguish a chronology of at least nine successive cultural layers that indicate continuous habitation from the Palaeolithic era up through the present, and spanning a period of nine thousand years (Kosmenko 1996a: 18).

The pioneers of the Mesolithic era were fishers and hunters whose primary game consisted of deer and elk. The bones of these and other game are found in large quantities at settlements located by lake shores. There are at least two separate groups of archaeological findings from this era which represent different cultures: one around Lake Onega and the other from the northern and south-western parts of Russian Karelia.

Archaeologists cannot answer the questions of precisely who the representatives of these prehistoric cultures were or what languages they spoke. Nevertheless, the Bronze Age culture characterized by textile ceramics – the so-called Textile Ceramic or Netted Ware Culture (*c.* 1900–500 BC; see Map 2) – has been considered to be connected to the spread of Finno-Ugric languages into Karelia and Finland. (Kosmenko 2008: 23.)

The culture of the Forest Sámi developed in Karelia in the second half of the Iron Age and in the early Middle Ages (Kosmenko & Kotshkurkina 1996: 379). In the western and northern parts of Karelia and in eastern and central Finland, for example, the so-called Luukonsaari Culture prevailed from the first millennium BC up to about AD 500. This culture apparently was connected to the predecessors of the Sámi people (Kosmenko 2008: 23). Settlements that belonged to this culture have been found for instance in the southern part of Aunus Karelia (e.g. in Säämäjärvi).

The early medieval evidence is divided by archaeologists into two separate culture groups. One is characterized by robust handmade ceramics with a distribution area that covers the southern part of the Lake Onega drainage basin (including the mouth of Uikujoki River and Lake Säämäjärvi). The other is characterized by settlements without traces of ceramics in western and northern parts of Karelia (Kosmenko 1996b: 272). Archaeological remains without ceramics are common throughout eastern Fennoscandia, and this phenomenon is commonly connected to the ancient Sámi (Kosmenko & Kotshkurkina 1996: 379). For instance, settlements without traces of ceramics in Säämäjärvi have been dated from the tenth to the twelfth centuries even though individual finds date even as late as the fourteenth century (Kosmenko 2008: 23). The same period of the Mid and Late Iron Age (approximately AD 350–1050) in Finland's interior and northern regions is occasionally labelled the 'Sámi Iron Age', also characterized by a scarcity of archaeological finds.

According to archaeological studies, the settlement in Aunus Karelia and on the northern shore of Lake Onega in the Late Iron Age can be identified with the early Vepsians. It is characterized by robust handmade ceramics (in Russian *grubaja lepnaja keramika*). This type of ceramics is close to the ceramics of the contemporary Kurgan Culture of the south-eastern shore of Lake Ladoga (Kosmenko 1996a: 21; 2008: 24).

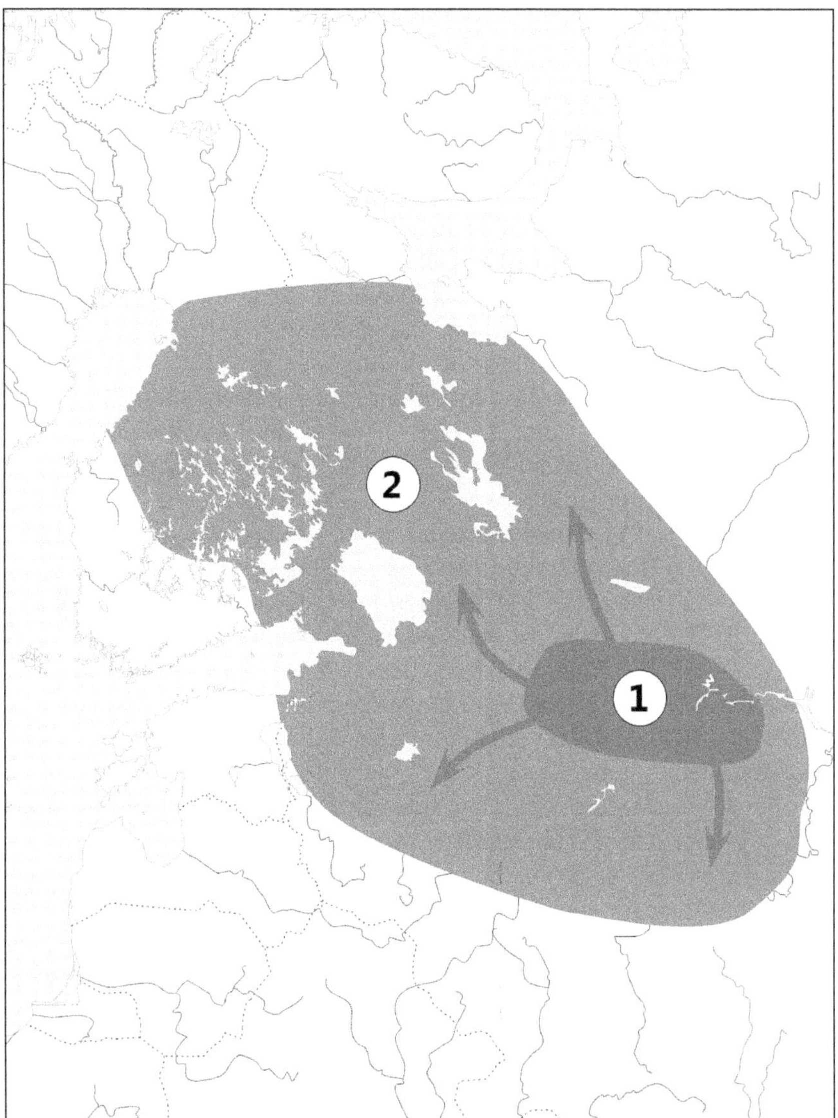

Map 2. The spread of textile ceramic into Karelia and Finland. Key: 1. area of origin; 2. extent of spread. (Source: Carpelan & Parpola 2001: 89).

The Sámi

The earliest layer or substrate of place names that can be reliably dated in the area of Karelia is linguistically Sámi in origin. The Sámi have lived in Karelia for centuries. This is also visible in the vocabulary of the Karelian language, in features of Karelian culture and in place names in Karelia with origins in Sámi. An area spanning across Lake Ladoga, Lake Onega and Lake Beloye (Fi. Valkeajärvi, Ru. Beloe ozero) has been considered the core area of Proto-Sámi. The Sámi proto-language has been believed to be spoken around the time of the birth of Christ and possibly in the first centuries thereafter (Saarikivi 2011: 113). Proto-Sámi is divided into two dialects, the northern dialect and the southern dialect. The southern dialect was spoken in the area of present-day Karelia and Finland (Korhonen 1981: 49-50). The spread of the Sámi languages appears to have been rather rapid and to have reached central Scandinavia by the ninth to the eleventh centuries. This presumption is necessary in the light of the phonological shape of place names borrowed from Scandinavian languages into Sámi (Bergsland 1995).

The earliest documents concerning the area of present-day Karelia are from the late Middle Ages. These do not mention Sámi on the Aunus Isthmus or in southern areas of what is now Russian Karelia. The same sources reveal, however, that potentially Sámi people inhabited the eastern shore of Lake Onega. This is suggested, for example, in the biography of the monk Lazar Muromsky. In this text, Lazar complains that he is harassed by the local population called *lop'* (Russian: лопь > Lappish) and *čud'* (Russian: чудь > Chud – ? today Vepsians). The hagiography tells that the chief of the 'Lapps' lived at the shore of *Rondo ozero* ['Lake Rondo'] (? today Lake Randozero) (Pashkov 2003: 10). According to this saint's biography, the monk Lazar founded the Muromsky monastery or the Svyat-Uspensky monastery on the cape of Murom on the eastern shore of Lake Onega in the middle of the fourteenth century (Pashkov 2003: 7).

In the beginning of the seventeenth century, 'reliable local lore' (= testimony given by oath) was recorded from an inhabitant of the village of Porajärvi in Selgi Pogost according to which Lappish people still lived in the area in the middle of the fifteenth century (*Istorija Karelii*: 90). Preserved documents indicate a Sámi minority at the end of the sixteenth century, but only in the northern parts of the former Aunus Governorate and in the area of Viena Karelia.

Karelian settlement advanced from the south across the interior of present-day Karelia – Sámi lands – from the thirteenth century onwards. The former Sámi areas became a part of the 'Korela land' (in Russian *Korelskaja zemlja*) of the Votic Fifth[1]. Simultaneously, the area extending from north of Lake Säämäjärvi to Lake Pääjärvi was called the Lapp pogosts or Forest Lapland (Karelian: *Lappela*, RussK: *Lešaja Lop'*). This seems to testify to the fact that precisely the Sámi were the preceding inhabitants of that area. Forest Lapland served as fishing and hunting grounds for Karelians and, in the course of time, permanent Karelian settlements also appeared there.

The Lapp pogosts were created as administrative units during the rule of Ivan III at the end of the fifteenth century. The area in question began as a narrow wedge from the north of Lake Säämäjärvi in Aunus Karelia and reached to the White Sea in the north and the present-day border of Finland. The area is also called Novgorod Lapland. It consisted of seven pogosts: Lintujärvi, Semšijärvi, Selgi, Paatene,[2] Rukajärvi, Suikujärvi and Paanajärvi (*Istorija Karelii*: 312).

Vocabulary Derived from Sámi[3]

It is possible to conclude that the Sámi used to populate the entire area of present-day Karelia. The forms of Sámi language spoken in Karelia have not been preserved. They disappeared when the language border between the Finnic and Sámi languages moved north, from the thirteenth century onwards (Korhonen 1981: 49–50).

It is very probable that part of the Sámi were assimilated into the Finnic populations (for instance Karelians and Vepsians) and possibly also into Russian populations. This is indicated by loanwords in dialects of Karelian, Vepsian and Russian languages which derive from Sámi. A number of these reflect terminology for terrain and fauna:

Example Set 1: Terms Related to Terrain

RussK *арешник* (arešnik) ['bare rock'] < **ārē* ['boulder area'] (> SámK *ā'rešm*)

Karelian *čiekerö, kiekerö,* RussK *кегора, тегора* (kegora, tegora) ['snow field damped as the pasture of reindeer'], < **čiekęr* ['winter pasture of reindeer'] (> SámN *čiegar*)

Karelian *čokka* ['hill'] < **ćokkę* ['peak of a hill, hillock'] (> SámN *čokka*)

RussK *чолма* (čolma) ['sound'] < **čoalmē* ['sound'] (> SámN *čoalbme*)

Karelian *eno* ['deep spot, a channel (in a river, stream); the center of a river where the current is strongest; an unfrozen calm river'] < **eanō* ['great river'] (> SámN *eatnu*)

Karelian *guba*[4], *kupa,* RussK *губа* (guba) ['bay'] < SámN *gohppi* ['round bay'] (Janne Saarikivi, p.c.)

Karelian *jok(k)oh, jokkohut* ['track of reindeer (deer, elk pack, rabbit) in snow or earth; road, path; trap path']; *jokoš* ['footprint of a deer'] < SámK *čuokkac, čuə*^{g}*kas* ['winter road']

Karelian *jänkä* ['great bog'], RussK *янга, янговина* (janga, jangovina) ['soggy spot in a bog, boghole, depression, wet spot'] < **jeaŋkē* ['bog'] (> SámN *jeaggi*)

Karelian *kenti, kentti, kenttä* ['open, even, dry grass or sandland, a field'], Vepsian *kend, kendäk* ['shore of a body of water; edge of bog'], RussK *кент* (kent) ['small forest'], *кенда* (kenda) ['rather high sandy lake shore; high spot on a bog which grows hay; rather high heath with sandy ground'] < **kientē* ['natural meadow'] (> SámN *gieddi,* I *kieddi*)

Karelian *korgo,* RussK *корга* (korga) ['rocky shallow, underwater rock'] < **kuorkō(j)* ['shoal, islet, ledge'] (> SámN *guorgu*)

RussK *кошка* (koška) ['shallows'] < **koškē* (> SámN *guoika,* SámK *kǭšḱ*^{E} ['shallow'], *kǫšḱ*^{E} ['dry'])

Karelian *kotkova, kuotkuo, kuotkut, kuotkuva,* RussK *коткуй* (kotkui) ['(narrow) neck of land'] < **kuotkō(j)* ['isthmus'] (> SámN *guotku*)

Karelian *kuršo, kuržu* ['wet, thicketed depression; thicket'] < **korsę* ['ravine, depression'] (> SámK *guršu,* SámK *kurhce)*

Karelian *könkäs, köynäs* ['waterfall'] < **keavŋēs* ['waterfall'] (> SámI *kievŋis)*

Karelian *n'uoru,* RussK *нюра* (n'ura) ['underwater shallows in a body of water'] < **ńuorę* ['shallows'] (> SámN *njuorra,* SámK *n'uǫrr*ᵃ, *ñurr)*

Karelian *näčäkk/ä, -ö* ['(of ground) moist, wet'], RussK *няша, няча* (n'aša, n'ača) ['muddy shore or bottom of a body of water'] < SámK *ń'eş̌şe* ['mud; trash']

Karelian *oaje, uaje* ['quagmire, boghole, soft spot in a bog, closed up spring'] < **ājęk* ['spring'] (> SámN *ája: ádjaga)*

Karelian *pahta, puahto,* RussK *naxma* (pahta) ['steep rock face, precipice, rock, rocky hill'] < **pāktē* ['rock'] (> SámN *bákti,* SámK *pą̇x̄t*ᴱ)

Karelian *poža, poša* ['bay'] < **poaššō* ['back of a hut or back corner'] > ['bay'] (> SámN *boaššu,* this has been considered a Finnic loan, compare SSA II: 383)

Karelian *ruopas,* RussK *ропака, ропаки* (ropaka, ropaki) ['heap of stones or ice'] < **roapē* ['heap of stones, rocky hillock']

Karelian *tunturi, tundurvuara,* RussK *тундра* (tundra) ['treeless mountain; peak of a tree-covered hill'] < **tōntęr* ['uplands'] (> SámN *duottar,* SámK tūndar)

Karelian *vuara, vuaru,* RussK *варака* (varaka) ['forest growing hillock, hill'] < **vārē* ['tree-covered hill'] (> SámN *várri)*

Example Set 2: Terms for Fauna

Karelian *alli, al'l'eikka* RussK *аллейка* (alleika) ['long-tailed duck'] < SámK *allo`ɔ̄k*ᵃ̊ ['long-tailed duck']

RussK *чабар(а), чабра, чебар* (čabar(a), čabra, čebar) ['young gull, gull fledling'] < SámK *čėȧbar* ['great black-backed gull']

Karelian *čiekšo, sieksu, kiekki* ['osprey'] < **čiekčę* ['osprey'] (> SámN *čiekčá)*

RussK *чухарь* (čuhar') ['wood grouse'] < **ćukčē* ['wood grouse'] (> SámN *čukcá,* SámK *čuxč)*

Karelian ? *kapšakka* ['isopod'], RussK *капшак, капшачок* (kapšak, kapšačok) ['isopod'], RussA *капчак* (kapčak) ['parasitic sea worm'] < SámK *kāptsa* ['sea worm']

Karelian *koittassu, kosotus* ['four-year-old male raindeer'] < **koasVttēs* (> SámN *goaistas,* SámK *koisttas* ['five-year-old reindeer'])

Karelian *kojama* ['male salmon, large salmon'] < SámI *koáijim,* SámI *kǫ̌ą̆ijä`m* ['large male salmon']

Karelian *kondie, kon'd'ii,* Vepsian *kon'd'i* ['bear']< **kuomčę* ['bear'] (> SámN *guovža,* SámI *kuobžâ)*

Karelian *kumpši, kumša*, RussK *кумжа* (kumža) ['lake trout, small trout'] < **kuvčā/ē* ['trout'] (> SámN *guvžá*)

Karelian *kuntous, kuntassu, kuntushärkä* ['three-year-old male reindeer'], RussK *кундус* (kundus) ['three-year-old male reindeer'] < SámN *gottodas, goddâs* ['four-year-old male reindeer']

Karelian *kuuja* ['lake trout'] < **kuvčā/ē* ['trout']

Karelian *kuukšo(i), kuukša*, RussK *кукша* ['Siberian jay'] < ** kuoksẹŋkẹ* ['Siberian jay'] (> SámK *kūzvŋ̄*^{g}*k̦*)

Karelian *kärččä*, RussK *керча, керца, кирчак* (kerča, kerca, kirčak) ['stone loach'] < SámK *k'ertts*^{s}*, kerts* ['stone loach']

Karelian *muržu*, RussK *морж* (morzh) ['walrus'] < **moršẹ* ['walrus'] (> SámN *morša*, SámK *mor̄š*^{A})

Karelian *n'abuaga, n'avuaka*, RussK *навага* (navaga) ['navaga, a small species of fish in the cod family Gadidae'] < SámK *nāva*^{g} ['navaga']

Karelian *n'orppa*, RussK *нерпа* (nerpa) ['ringed seal'] < **noarvē* ['seal'] (> SámN *noarvi*, SámK nụər̄j^{e})

Karelian *paltassu*, RussK *палтас, палтус* (paltas, paltus) ['halibut'] < **pāltēs* ['pallas'] (>SámN *bálddis*, SámK. *pāl̄dẹṣ)*

RussK *пертуй* (pertui) ['small White Sea cod'] < SámK *per*^{d}*-tai̯* ['cod']

RussK *пинагар, пинагорь* (pinagar, pinagor') ['lumpsucker'] < SámK *pinn*^{a}*garr*$^{(a)}$ ['lumpsucker']

RussK *сайда* (saida) ['pollack'] < **sājδē* ['pollack'] (> SámN *sáidi*, SámK *sạ̄i̯Ḏ*^{E}*)*

Karelian *t'iiksei, t'iikšei*, RussK *тикшуй*, pik*šui* (tikšui, pikšui) ['haddock'] < SámK *tịk̄sa* ['haddock']

Karelian *tinta, tiinda*, RussK *тинда* (tinda) ['small salmon, salmon fry']; *tintti* ['perch fry'] < SámK *tịn̄*^{d}*t*$^{(A)}$ ['small salmon']

Karelian *urakka*, RussK *урак* (urak) ['one year old male reindeer'] < SámS *årēk, varēk* SámN *varit* ['male']

RussK *вальчак, вольчаг* (val'čak, vol'čag) ['salmon; female salmon'] < SámK *vạ̄ld'žē*^{g} ['fresh water salmon']

Karelian *vuajin* (gen. *vuatimen*), *важенка* (važenka) ['female deer, female reindeer'] < **vāçẹm* ['female reindeer'] (> SámN *váža*, SámK *vài̯j*$^{(a)}$*, vā*$^{d'}$*ž)*

Karelian *vuonnelo, vuonnilo*, RussK *вонделица* (vondelica) ['one year old female reindeer'] < SámK *vuońal* ['one year old female reindeer']

Karelian *vuoveršo, vuorsa, vuorso* ['two year old reindeer, primarily female'] < SámN *vuovers*, SámI *vyevers* ['two year old reindeer, primarily male']

Example Set 3: Other Loanwords

Karelian *čole* ['fish entrails, intestines or guts'] < **čoalē* ['intestine'] (> SámN *čoalli*)

Karelian *čumu* ['heaped measure, of heaped measure'] < **čomę̑* ['heap'] (> SámN *čopma*)

Karelian *čuna*, RussK *тюни, чунки* (t'uni, čunki) ['reindeer sledge; sledge'] < **ćoanē* ['sledge'] (> SámK *čuəņņ^e*, SámN *čoanohus*)

Karelian *čura* ['side, edge; direction'] < **čorō* ['side, brim, edge'] (> SámN *čorrut* ['on one's side']

Karelian *čurmuine* ['a small amount of something, quantum'] < **čormę̑* ['fistful'] (> SámN *čorbma* ['fist'])

Karelian *juovuo* ['to follow, especially of reindeer'], *juovottua* ['to lead'] < SámN *čuovvut* ['to follow']

Karelian *keikkalo*, *kilkalo*, *keikaro*, RussK *кейкала, кейкало* ['piece of wood on the neck of a reindeer with the owner's name written on it'] < SámN *gilkor*, SámK *ḱe`lgȧ`l, ḱ'eṷ̄ᵍk̄al* ['piece of wood with the owner's mark on it, for instance on the neck of a reindeer']

Karelian *kerosa* ['a raindeer sledge without the stern plank'], RussK *керёжа, керес* (ker'oža, keres) ['a Sámi sledge'] < SámK *ḱeŗŗeș*, SámN *gieres* ['a reindeer sledge']

Karelian *kollo(h), kolloš* ['a line of reindeer tied to one another'] < SámN *goallus* ['a line of reindeer without burdens tied to one another']

Karelian *kualua*, *kualada* ['wade'] < **kālē-* ['wade'] (> SámN *gállit*)

Karelian *käšäš, käšäyš* ['a reindeer's collar made of leather'] < SámK *keässas* ['a reindeer's collar made of a hide or of leather strap']

Karelian *n'ulkata* ['(of a reindeer) to run evenly'] < SámN *njolggástit* ['to jog']

Karelian *nuoska*, *nuoskie* ['moist, wet'] < **ńuockę̑* ['moist, wet'] (> SámN *njuoska*)

Karelian *ola*, *olas* ['a groove on a ski bottom'] < **oalē-s* ['a groove on a ski bottom'] (> SámN *oalis: oallá*)

Karelian *palis*, *palin*, *palkini* ['reindeers' area of movement, reindeers' pastures; a reindeer herding company of a village consortium'] < SámN *bálges*, SámI *paalgas* ['a regular summer habitat of reindeer or sheep']

Karelian *panka* ['a bell holder of a reindeer; a reindeer's headstall'] < **pāŋkē* (> SámN *bággi* ['a reindeer's headstall']

Karelian *piiksi* ['a bird's breastbone or its ridge'] < **piksę̑* ['a bird's breastbone'] *(> SámN *biksa*; SámK *pik̄s^(A)*)

Karelian *počko, počkous, počkuus* ['a reindeer's pulling lead'] < SámK *pọ̄askas, pu̯aᵗskas* ['a sledge's pulling lead']

Karelian *puoska, puosku* ['(derogatory) of a child: brat'] < **puockę̮* ['brat']

Karelian *raitijoija* ['to herd reindeer'] < SámN *ráidi* ['a hired reindeer herder']

Karelian *raito, kelkkaraito, pororaito,* RussK *paйда* (raida) ['a line of teams of reindeer'] < **rājtō* ['a line of reindeer pulling sledges or carrying loads'] (> SámN *ráidu)*

RussK *сигостега, чивастега, чигостега* (sigostega, čivastega, čigostega) ['a reindeer herder's lasso'] < SámK *čā̂·vostąk, čovstək* ['a reindeer herder's lasso']

Karelian *suopunki* ['a lasso made for catching reindeer'] < **suoppe̮nje̮* (>SámN *suohpan,* SámI *suoppânj* ['a lasso made for catching reindeer']

Karelian *tokka* ['a reindeer herd'] < **toakkē* ['a lot, a herd'] (> SámN *doahkki,* SámI *toakki,* SámK *tọ̄ą̆ʾķ'ķᴱ*)

Karelian *tolva* ['(a reindeer's) trot'], *tolvata* ['to trot'], *tolvual'l'a* ['(of a reindeer or a cow) to run loose'] < **toalvē* (> SámI *tuálvi,* SámN *doalvi* ['(a reindeer's) trot']

Karelian *toraš* ['icicle'], RussK *mopoc* (toros) ['pack ice'] < SámK *tōras* ['a block of ice, a bank of ice on a sea shore']

Karelian *tunka* ['a dish made of a reindeer's rectum and fat, and of grits'] < **toŋkē* (> SámI *togge,* SámN *doggi* ['a reindeer's maw (abomasum)']

Karelian *vuotto-, vuotturaippa* ['a reindeer's pulling lead'] < SámN ? *vuottaráipi* ['a reindeer's pulling lead']

The majority of the vocabulary that is of Sámi origin consists of terms that were once connected to livelihoods new to the settlers (e.g. related to hunting sea animals or to reindeer herding) and to the new types of familiar livelihoods (e.g. sea fishing, deer hunting in a new environment, etc.). Obviously, new words were not invented on the basis of indigenous vocabulary: they were loans from the original population of the area. It is notable that many of the designations for the fish in the White Sea have direct parallels in the Sámi dialects of the Kola Peninsula. It has already been mentioned above that part of the Sámi population in Karelia most likely changed language through a phase of bilingualism. This would have offered great potential for preserving Sámi vocabulary that belonged to everyday life. Furthermore, new vocabulary was undoubtedly also adopted through intercultural marriages and through trade connections.

It should be mentioned that a considerable portion of the words mentioned above are known both in the Karelian dialects of Viena Karelia and in the Russian dialects of the west coast of the White Sea. In other words, the vocabulary is shared across historically unrelated languages in the area that is connected to the statements about the Sámi in early documents. On the other hand, about half of the lexical matter of Sámi origin mentioned above is also encountered in southern dialects of Karelian and Vepsian, as well as in the Northwest dialects of Russian that are all spoken far away from the areas in which the modern Sámi languages are spoken.

These include, for instance, the following loanwords (for the etymologies of these terms, see Example Sets 1–3 above):

RussK *arešnik*, RussK *čolma*, Karelian *guba*, RussK *guba*, Karelian *jok(k)oh, jokkohut*, RussK *janga*, Karelian *kenti, kenttä*, Vepsian *kend(äk)*, Karelian *korgo*, RussK *korga*, Karelian *kotkova*, Karelian *kuržu*, Karelian *n'uoru*, RussK *n'ura*, Karelian *näčäkk/ä, -ö*, Karelian *uaje*, Karelian *poža*, Karelian *ruopas*, RussK *ropaka*, Karelian *tundurvuara*, Karelian *vuara, vuaru*, RussK *varaka*, Karelian *alli, al'l'eikka*, RussK *alleika*, Karelian *čiekšo*, RussK *čuhar'*, Karelian *kon'd'ii*, Vepsian *kon'd'i*, Karelian *kuukšo(i)*, RussK *kukša*, Karelian *čole*, Karelian *čumu*, RussK *čunki*, Karelian *čura*, Karelian *čurmuine*, Karelian *kualua*, Karelian *nuoska*, Karelian *ola(s)*, Karelian *puoska, puosku*.

Sámi Place Names and Earlier Substrates

Place names have an important role in investigations of language history and prehistory. This is for two main reasons. First, place names have been preserved from periods for which written sources are lacking. Second, place names are established in the area in which they are being used. Many significant and economically important formations of nature were given names already at an early stage. Most often, place names have also been preserved well if there has been a continuity of settlement in the area.

Compared to other sources for the study of prehistory, place names are extremely numerous. If the same name types appear in different contexts, their connections to ancient forms of language can be verified. Hence, place names comprise a versatile historical source material that reflects the settlement and culture of each region, nature and features characteristic to its scenery, and also the livelihoods and the usage of the area. In addition, place names that are connected to religion and beliefs comprise a specific group.

The place names of Karelia may provide information about ancient Sámi settlements. The old form of community among the Sámi was *siida* (SámN) < **sijtę* ['(winter) village']. It was formed by a group of families that had common areas of settlement and usage. Each family roamed across its own area for nine months of the year and for the three winter months, it stayed in the *siida* (Vilkuna 1971). It is likely that the following place names in the Republic of Karelia reflect this form of community: *Siidniemi*[5] (a village, the volost of Pyhäjärvi) and *Siidarvi* (Lake Jängärvi, the volost of Porajärvi). Place names beginning with *Ši(i)d-* have also been found in the Vepsian nomenclature, where they seem to be connected to a group of place names: *Šid'järv* (Russ. *Sidozero*) (the river area of Kapša, Leningrad Oblast), *Šid'järv* (Russ. *Šidozero*) (The river area of Lid, Leningrad Oblast). According to historians, the social organization based on *siida*, or a winter village, which was later connected to reindeer herding, may have evolved in the Late Iron Age (Halinen 2011: 158, Carpelan 2003: 70–71).

Other place names of Sámi origin also reveal information about the historical period in Karelia that is characterized by the Sámi. Nevertheless, it must be noted that a considerable share of the names of the largest bodies of water remain obscure even on the basis of the Sámi language. This indicates that before the Sámi, there lived people in Karelia that spoke languages that are not known. Marks of these peoples have remained in archaeological evidence and in the nomenclature. For example, a considerable number of words in modern Sámi languages do not have parallels in other Finno-Ugric languages. For example, geaðgi ['stone'], *njárga* ['cape'], *ája* ['spring'], *bákti* ['rock'], *roavvi* ['an area ravaged by forest fire'], *vuotna* ['fiord'], *gáisa* ['a snow peaked mountain'], *lismi* ['the end of a rapid'], *leakšá* ['a forested valley'], *lu'smm* ['head of a river'], *suotnju* ['a big swamp'], *njálla* ['an arctic fox'], *morša* ['a walrus'] are such words (Saarikivi 2011: 104–105). These words can be substrate borrowings that have once been borrowed by the Sámi from the indigenous population. In other words, the forefathers of the Proto-Sámi assimilated the preceding Palaeo-European population that had earlier lived in the northern Fennoscandia, although the origins of this population are not clear. There are, however, also signs of this population in archaeological remains.

The marks of this unknown language (or languages) are observable in the nomenclature. A considerable number of common nouns depicting the terrain among the substrate words listed above appear widely within the nomenclature of the Sámi territory. They also appear in the place nomenclature of Karelia and adjunct areas which had earlier been Karelian but have become Russian, especially in the central and northern parts of the Republic of Karelia. In these cases, it is reasonable to believe that these exceptional terms were adapted from Sámi into these other languages – that they were mediated through Sámi, whatever the language of the origin of the particular terms. The distribution of the place names comprised of these terms may correspond with the settlement area of this ancient Sámi population which, for some reason, did not extend to the east and to the southeast, or to the area of present-day Archangel and Vologda.

There are also many other examples in Karelia of place names that have not been attributed a convincing Sámi or Finnic etymology. The names of the lakes *Päijärvi* (Finn. *Pääjärvi*, Sam. *Bejauri*), *Tuoppajärvi*, *Kuittijärvi* and *N'uokkajärvi* are examples of such place names. In fact, among the names of the thirty largest lakes in the Republic of Karelia, only two are of Finnic origin: *Himol'anjärvi* (Porajärvi) and *Roukkulanjärvi* (Repola). The etymology of the names of many other lakes likewise remains obscure, and this is also true concerning the names of rivers.

On the other hand, some of the largest lakes have names that can be explained on the basis of either Sámi languages or Proto-Sámi. For example, it is possible to trace the name of the second-largest lake in Europe, *Ääninen* ['Onega'], to Sámi: (Vepsian *Änine*, Karel. *Iänizjärvi*): < **ēnē* ['much, large'] (Mullonen 2002: 281). This is equally possible with the name of Lake *Uikujärvi* (variant. *Vuikkajärvi*) < **Vuikakoski* < **vēkę̑* ['power; powerful, strong'] or **vę̑kę̑* ['fast-flowing'] (Mullonen 2007: 202). A similar case is Lake

Säämäjärvi (Karelian *Siämäjärvi*) < Proto-Sámi **sāmē-* < Pre-Sámi **šämä* ['Sámi'] (> Finnish *häme-*) (Mullonen & Mamontova 2008: 26).

More nomenclature of Sámi origin is met in the central and northern parts of modern day Karelia where Sámi are known to have still lived from the sixteenth to the nineteenth centuries. On the other hand, there are rather many place names in southern Karelia that reflect a Sámi heritage. For example, many of the names of the parishes in southern Karelia are from the Pre-Finnic period: *Videle*, *Vieljärvi* (< **vitel-*, origin unknown) *Kotkadjärvi* (Proto-Sámi **kuotkō(j)* ['isthmus'], *Kuujärvi* (Proto-Sámi *kukkē* ['long']), *Vuohtajärvi* (**uktị̯* ['passage, route']), *Munjärvi*, *Kontupohja* ? (Proto-Sámi **kontē* ['wild deer']), *Suoju*, *Siämäjärvi* (Proto-Sámi **sāmē* ['Sámi']).

The parish names in Finnish Ladoga Karelia seem to be Finnic, at least by their linguistic form, except *Ilomantsi* (Karelian *Il'manči*), which is without doubt Sámi in origin (see below): *Salmi*, *Imbilahti* (Finnish *Impilahti*), *Suistamo*, *Korbiselgä* (Finnish *Korpiselkä*), Suojärvi, *Sovanlahti* (Finnish *Soanlahti*). In my opinion, this shows that the Finnic (Karelian) population has a relatively long history in this area. Nevertheless, there are also place names in this territory that have origins in the Sámi period.

Place names that originate from the Sámi settlement[6] of the southern parts of the Republic of Karelia are presented in Example Set 4. These are found both as names of topographic formations and as names of bodies of water. Part of the names are micro-toponyms.[7]

Example Set 4: Place Names in Southern Parts of the Republic of Karelia

Čolmazenlambi (var. Džolmazen-) (Vegarus, Suojärvi), ? *Čolmala* (a farm) (Melaselkä, Ilomantsi), *Čolmankoski* (Sagila, Leningrad Oblast), *Čolmanjogi* (Koskenala, Leningrad Oblast), *Čolmužguba* (a bay) (Garnitsi, Äänisniemi), *Čolmuži* (a village) (Äänisniemi), < **čoalmē* ['strait, channel']

Čieksanoja (Työmpäinen, Salmi), *Čieksanniemi* (Vuottoniemi, Ilomantsi), *Čieksunsalmi* (Finnish Sieksunsalmi) (Tolvajärvi, Korpiselkä), *Sieksniemi* (Nuamoilu, Suoju), *Sieksenjogi* (Sieksi, Riipuskala) < **čiekčẹ* ['osprey']

Čilmitjärvi, -suo, -jogi (Pečynselgä, Nekkula) < **ćẹlmē* ['eye']; > (cf. RussK *чильма* (čil'ma) ['boghole; moss; peatland'] – this word is not met in modern Sámi languages but the phonological shape of the word indicates Sámi origin (see Saarikivi 2006: 46)

Čuksoilambi (Ussuna, Munjärvi) < **ćukčē* ['wood grouse']

Ellingilambi (Vaaksaus, Suojärvi), *Elli* (an island) (Sumeria, Impilahti), *Elinlambi* (Tolvajärvi, Korpiselkä), *Elinlammit*, *Elisenpuro* (Maukkula, Ilomantsi), *El'midd'ärvi*, *El'mičoja* (Elmitjärvi, Vuohtjärvi), *Elmyzjärvi* (Juustjärvi, Porajärvi), Elmyzjärvi (Suarenpiä, Repola), *Elmizjärvi* (Pääkönniemi, Jyskyjärvi), *Elmanka* (a river) (Šaidoma, Kontupohja), ? *Ielimäzenoja* (Ahi, Tulemajärvi), ? *Eloisuo* (Koivahanselgy, Tulemajärvi), < **elē* ['upper'], **ẹlēmus* ['uppermost']

Ilmahansuo (Sammatus, Nekkula), *Ilmasuo* (Lumatjärvi, Kotkatjärvi), *Ilmeänluodo* (Rajakondu, Videle), *Ilmananselgy* (Iudankylä, Vieljärvi), *Ilomančinjärvi* (Ilomantsi), *Ilmolampi* (Ilomantsi), *Ilmačinvuara* (Jängäjärvi, Porajärvi), *Ilmetjoki* (Ilmee, Hiitola), *Ilöntjärvi* (Sarka, Suistamo), *Ilemguba, Ilemozero* (Čebolakša, Kontupohja), *Ilemenza* (puro) (Pulozero, Petrovskij Jam) < **e̯lēmus* ['uppermost'], **e̯lmē* ['sky' > *'upper']

Ienimäjogi, -järvi (= Ienine) (Mägriä, Nekkula), ? *Inämvongu* (a river bend) (Suonu, Tulemajärvi) ? < **ε̄ne̯m* ['land']

Jaurunselgä (Jalovaara, Suistamo), *Jaurumalambi, Jaurunvuara* (Pölkkylä, Paadane) < **jāvrē* ['lake']

Jänkäsuari (Ilomantsi), *Jängihuuhtu* (Vieljärvi), *Jängärenjärvi, Jängärvi* (Stekki, Vieljärvi), *Jängähänjogi* (Lintujärvi), *Jangozero* (järvi) (Jangozero, Puutoinen) < **jeaŋkē* ['a mire']

? *Kaina(i)zjärvi, -vuaru* (Liävyniemi, Vieljärvi), *Кайнос* (an island) (Äänisessa, Äänisenniemi), *Каин-наволок* (a cape) (Tolvuja, Ääniesniemi), *Кайнеостров* (Sennaja Guba, Äänisniemi < **kε̄jnō* ['route']

? *Karadsalmi* (Karatsalmi, Suojärvi), *Karasozero* (Karasozero, Äänisniemi; Puutoinen) < **kāres* ['narrow']

Kend'd'ärvi (Kend'd'ärvi, Munjärvi), *Кендийгуба* (*Kendijguba*) (a bay) (Kutkostrov, Kontupohja) < **kientē* ['field, lawn']

Korsumäki (Hunttila, Impilahti), *Korzu* (a village) (Säämäjärvi) < **korse̯* ['ravine, depression']

Kuačkulakši (Lahtenkylä, Siämäjärvi), *Kočkovnavolok* (a cape) (Šala, Puutoinen), *Kotkazlambi* (Tiudia, Kontupohja), *Kotkassuo* (Nimijärvi, Munjärvi), *Kotkudoja*[8] (Kortašši, Munjärvi), *Kotkadniemi* (Kaničanselgä, Munjärvi), *Kotkatniemi* (Salmi), *Kotkanaho* (Leppäsyrjä, Suistamo), *Kuotkunselgy* (Ignoila, Suojärvi), *Kotkadmäget* (Priäzy, Pyhäjärvi), *Kotkano* (an island) (Njuhča, Vienanmeri), *Kutkuniemi* (Kompakka, Rukajärvi), *Kutkuvuara* (Soimavuara, Porajärvi), *Kuutkupohja* (a bay) (Lubasalmi, Porajärvi), *Kutkostrov* (an island) (Kutkostrov, Kontupohja) < **kuotkō(j)* ['isthmus']

? *Koude(niemi)* (Martniemi, Munjärvi) < SámI *kuovda-* ['centre']

? **K(u)avasuari* (Russian *на Кавы-острову (1610)*, Karelian *Eloisuari)* < **kāve* ['a bend']

Kuolizjärvi, Kuolizma (Kuolismaa, Ilomantsi), *Kulišmajogi* (Pyörittäjä, Suistamo), *Kuoluužoja* (Jängärvi, Porajärvi), *Koležmareka* (joki), *Kolemžozeri* (a lake) (Koležma, Vienanmeri), *Kolonža* (a brook) (Kalakanda, Puutoinen) < **kōlē* ['fish']

Kuukkausjärvi (Vaaksaus, Suojärvi), *Kuukkauksensuo* (Sellinkylä, Paadene), ? *Kukkaniemi* (Impilahti), *Kukkajärvi* (Kukkajärvi, Vieljärvi), *Kuukonjogi* (Suona, Tulemejärvi), *Kuukasdärve* (Konnunkylä), *Kukkahanoja, Ku(u)kas* (a meadow) (Mägriä, Nekkula), *? Kukkojogi* (Veskelys, Säämäjärvi), *Kuujärvi* (RussK record

Kukozero) (Kuujärvi), *Kukolovo* (a long lake) (Virma, Vienanmeri), *Kukkozero* (a lake) (Ščepina Gora, Petrovskij Jam) < **kukkē* ['long']

Kuudamlambi (Ol'koilu, Vuohtjärvi), *Ku(u)damjärvi, -jogi* (Elmitjärvi, Säämäjärvi), *Kuudamaizenjärvet* (Pälväjärvi, Porajärvi), *Ku(u)damolakši* (Kuudamolakši, Porajärvi), *Кудомгуба* (Kudomguba) (Votlajärvi, Puutoinen) < **koδę* ['to spawn']

Kälgälambi (Vuontele, Suojärvi), *Kälgäjärvi* (Vegarus, Suojärvi), *Kälkäjärvi* (Mutalahti, Ilomantsi), *Kälgäjärvi* (Prokkola, Puadene) < SámK. *kialg* ['forest soil growing lichen']

Kätkäjärvi (Ilomantsi), *Ket'kozeo* (Vorenža, Petrovskij Jam; Šuikujoki, Vienanmeri; Virma, Vienanmeri) < **kēδkē* ['rock'] or **kētkē* ['wolverine']

? *Leibärenoja* (Heččula, Vieljärvi) < SámI *lejbi* ['alder']

Lidžmanlahti (Vegarus, Suojärvi), *Lid'zmanrand* (Novikuo, Kuujärvi), *Lizmoi* (a ditch) (Viidana, Suoju), *Ližmejärvi* (Lizmajärvi, Kontupohja), *Lidžmindärvi* (Lidžmi, Pyhäjärvi), *Ližmnavolok* (Vatnavolok, Kontupohja) < SámS *lisme* ['mud, dirt'], SámN *lisma* ['water moss']

Luzmanlahti (Suojärvi), *Luzmand'ogi* (Nimijärvi, Munjärvi), *Luzmanoja* (Peldoine, Pyhäjärvi) < SámK *lu̇šm̄ᵉ* ['head of a river']

Nivanjärvi (Sarka, Suistamo), *Nivad'ogi* (Jyrkänmägi, Munjärvi; Kortašši, Munjärvi), ? *Lapinniva* (quiet waters) (Korpiselkä) < **ńęvē* ['a place with a current, small rapids']

N'uhčaozero (Kiži, Äänisniemi), ? *N'učkina reka, N'učkin kangas* (Solomanni, Suoju) < **ńukcę* ['swan']

N'uoru (an isthmus) (Suojärvi), *N'uoru* (a meadow) (Hyrsylä, Suojärvi), *N'uoru*[9] (an island) (Nuamoila, Suoju), *N'uorunniemi* (Kolatselgy, Tuulemajärvi) < **ńuorę* ['shoal']

Nälmääjogi (Hukkala, Suojärvi), *Nälmänniemi* (Nälmyniemi, Vieljärvi), *Nälmyjärvi* (Liävyniemi, Vieljärvi; Inžuniemi, Siämäjärvi) < **ńālmē* ['mouth; mouth of a river']

Oibozero (Kažma, Äänisniemi) < **ōjvē* ['the rounded peak of a mountain']

Olonec (a river) (Aunus) < **ōlō+nčē* ['floodwater']

Oskajärvet (Saarivaara, Korpiselkä), *Oskarvi* (Čuiniemi, Siämärvi), *Oškutjärvi* (Nuamoila, Suoju) < **vōsk-* ['perch']

? *Päččikoski* (Suonu, Tulemajärvi), *Pečjeboloto* (Šaidoma, Kontupohja), ? *Pečeha* (a grassfield) (Kutkostrov, Kontupohja) < **pēcē* ['pine']

Petuzd'ärvi (Inžuniemi, Siämäjärvi), ? *Petäranta* (Kuolismaa, Ilomantsi), ? *Petreka* (a river) (Kiži, Äänisniemi) < **pętę* ['back part'; modifier 'back']

Podzanguba (a bay) (Pyhäjärvi), *Počeverje* (a field) < **Pod'žavieri* (Kuzaranda, Äänisniemi) < **poaššō* ['back part or back corner of a Sámi hut'] > 'bay'

Polga (niemi), *Polgešlamba* (Koikinitsi, Uikujärvi) < **pālk* ['path; deer path']

Pälärvi, Päländ'ogi (Päläjärvi, Munjärvi), *Pälizjärvi* (Lintujärvi), *Päljärvi* (Pölkkylä, Paadene), *Pälärvi* (Vitsataipale) *Pälozero* (a lake) (Lapina) < **pε̄ljē* ['an ear'] > ['edge, side']

Ruoksunnurmet (Viidana, Suoju), *Ruoksonrandu* (Paušoila, Säämäjärvi), ? *Ruoksuo* (Tavoimägi, Kontupohja) < SámK *ruokse* ['moss']

Šodd'ärvi < **Šondärvi* (RussK *Шондозеро = Шомозеро*) < **šōnte-* ['to cleave, to divide']

Suolužmägi (Suoluzmägi, Suoju), ? *Suolanpalte* (a slope) (Kuikkaniemi, Suojärvi), ? *Suolumua* (a field) (Lunkula, Salmi), < **sōlōj* ['island']

Torazjärvet (Kaitajärvi, Suojärvi), *Torazjärvi* (Vennyr, Vuohtjärvi; Torasjärvi, Kotkatjärvi), *Tora(s)suari* (Ruvankylä, Siämärvi) < **toarēs* ['crosswise'], see also SámK *tōr(r)os* ['block of ice, bank of ice on a sea shore']

Vablok (saari) (Äänisniemi) < Proto-Sámi **vāvlē* ['passage']

Viiksinjoki, -lampi (Korpiselkä), *Viiksinselkä* (Ilomantsi), *Viiksijärvi* (Viiksijärvi, Munjärvi; Lizmajärvi, Kontupohja), *Viiksinjogi* (Tiudia, Kontupohja) < **vēksi* ['a river between bodies of water; (geo.) sound']

Vilmärvi, Vilmienoja (Luazari, Puadene), *Vil'mozörko* (a lake) (Mihejeva Sel'ga, Kontupohja) < Proto-Sámi **vēlmē* ['quiet waters in a river (a long stretch of quiet waters in a river; a deep, calm river between two lakes)']

Volozero (a lake) (Äänisniemi; Povenets), ? *Vuolussuo* (Kindahankylä, Siämärvi), ? *Vuolahsellinkoski* (Torazjärvi, Kotkatjärvi), < SámK *vu̯əl̦l̦ᵉ* ['lower']

Vuoččijoki (Lehmivuara, Korpiselkä), *Vuožarvi* (Vuohtjärvi), *Vožosel'ga* (a hill) (Luza, Puutoinen) < SámN *vuohčču* ['a long, narrow swamp']

Änine (=Iänizjärvi) (Ääninen ['Onega']), *Jänisjärvi, Janatjogi* (= *Jananus-, Jänis-*) (Suistamo), *Väneguba* (a bay), *Jäniostrov* (an island) (Tikonitsi, Petrovskij Jam), *Vänäreka* (a river) (Vožmogora, Petrovskij Jam), *Jäneozero, -moh* (a lake, a swamp) (Luza, Puutoinen), *Eningilambi* (Sellinkylä, Puadene) < Proto-Sámi **ε̄nē* ['much'] > 'great'

Many of the name stems above appear in a rather wide area from the Kola Peninsula to at least Lake Beloye in the south and to the (Northern) Dvina River in the East (e.g. *čolm-, el-, jang-, jaur-, kuk-/kukas-*). It must be observed that the mentioned name stems are derived from the early Proto-Finnic vocabulary that is common to both the Finnic and Sámi languages. Therefore, the wide distribution of the name stems in Northwest Russia would indicate the area inhabited by a population that spoke this ancient parent language.[10] Then again, it is apparent that the Sámi language that used to be spoken in Karelia was not similar to the Sámi languages of today: it differed from these in many features. On the basis of the recorded nomenclature, it is possible to conclude that the 'Sámi' language that was spoken in Karelia was not a consistent language form. It is possible to find parallels to the nomenclature and vocabulary in different dialects of the Sámi languages. In connection with this, it is good to bear in mind that part of the lexical matter that appears widely in the Sámi nomenclature has been recorded only in the northern and central parts of Karelia. In other areas, the nomenclature bears traces of Sámi substrate languages that may have deviated from the present-day Sámi languages to a considerable degree.

An illustrative example of this kind is the case of the Proto-Sámi diminutive affix **-ńće-*. Two genetically close affix variants of this have been recorded in Karelia: *-nčV (*-ńče)* and *-нжа/-нза (*-ńdźe)*, of which one appears in both Karelian and Russian nomenclature and the other only in Russian hydronyms in the southern part of the Lake Onega region and in south-eastern Karelia (including the eastern parts of the Archangel Oblast at the border of present-day Karelia).

Example Set 5: Place Names with the Two Variants of the Proto-Sámi diminutive affix **-ńće-*

-nčV: *Ilmančisuari* (Jänkäjärvi, Porajärvi), *Korkančivuara* (Kostovaara, Oulanka), *Livončinoja* (Nuozjärvi, Vieljärvi), *Lotenčansuari* (Viččataipale), **Ōlōnčē* (RussK *Olonec*) (a river, Aunus), *Pelončozero* (RussK *Пелончозеро*) (a lake, Kočkamozero, Vuigajärvi), *Pizančajärvi* (RussK *Пизанец*) (Puadene), *Povenča* (RussK *Повенец*) (a settlement, Povenec), *Rievenči* (a bay, Lohilahti, Kiestinki), *Uomančijärvi* (Rukajärvi)

-nžV: *Verenža* (RussK *Веренжа*) (an island, Vodlajärvi), *Vorenža* (*Воренжа*) (a part of a river, Vorenža, Sumozero), *Ilemenza* (*Илеменза*) (a river, Pulozero, Sumozero), *Kolonžozero* (*Колонжозеро*) (a lake, Kalakunda, Puutoinen), *Naglinža* (*Наглинжа*) (a rapid, Vodlajärvi), *Parmanža* (*Парманжа*) (a river, Njuhčozero Archangel Oblast), *Romen'ža* (*Роменьжа*) (a river, Vorenža), *Uhtinža* (*Ухтинжа*) (a brook, a bay, Vodlajärvi), *Šigerenža* (*Шигеренжа*) (a brook, Vožmogora, Vuigajärvi)

It may be assumed that the areal *-nčV/-nžV* has a dialectal background which is interpretable on an ethno-linguistic basis. In this case, on basis of the distribution of the affix evidence, the form of the substrate language that was used in the eastern and southeastern parts of the Lake Onega region differs from the substrate dialect that was spoken in the western part of Karelia. The border between the two dialects was potentially located along a line connecting the Aunus Isthmus – Lake Onega – Lake Uikujärvi – River Uikujoki – the White Sea (Map 3). North and west from this line, the *-nčV* affix was used in hydronyms, whereas east and southeast from this line the *-nžV* affix was used. For example, names for the lake *Pelončozero* (*Пелончозеро*) (Kočkamozero, Vuigajärvi), for part of a river *Vorenža* (*Воренжа*) (Vorenža, Sumajärvi), and also hydronyms with the same stem, *Ilmančisuari* (Jänkäjärvi, Porajärvi) and *Ilemenza* (a river, Pulozero, Sumajärvi) are in neighboring areas. The same suffix type is also attested in the Finnish nomenclature that originates in Sámi: *Il'mančinjärvi* (Ilomantsi),

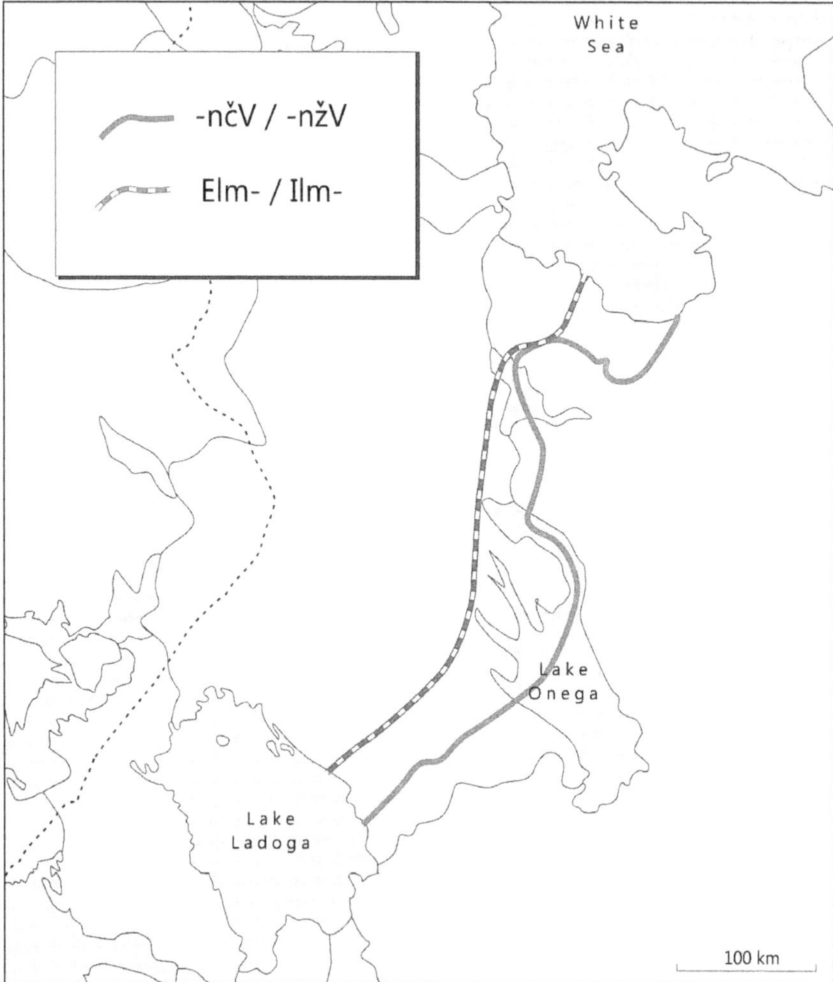

Map 3. Borders of ilm-/elm- and -nčV/-nžV toponym areas.

Kuvansi(njoki), *Kuvansinkoski* (Joroinen), *Kuvansi* (a lake, Suonenjoki/Leppävirta), *Syvänsi* (a lake, Joroinen/Jäppilä) (NA), which may indicate that a consistent Sámi language (or closely related dialects of this language) was once spoken in both the western parts of Karelia and in eastern Finland.

In addition to the *-nčV/-nžV* affix, the nomenclature in Karelia reveals two place name clusters that are interesting from the point of view of the language history of Sámi: *Ilm-* and *Elm-*. This is a case of two phonetic variants of the same place name type deriving from the Proto-Sámi word **elmē-* ['upper'] (Finnish *ylä-mä*) (< **ülä*). The linguistic form of the name stems provides an opportunity to analyze their distribution in the light of the different phases of the development of the Sámi language. The border between these types in the territory of Karelia is along the line connecting Rajakontu – Tulemajärvi – Vieljärvi – Säämäjärvi – the northwest part of Lake Onega – the eastern side of Lake Uikujärvi (Map 3). Place names formed from the name stem *Elm-* appear on the north side of this line while place names formed from the name stem *Ilm-* occur south of it. Place names that belong to the *Ilm-* type have also been recorded in the present-day Leningrad Oblast and in eastern parts of the Archangel Oblast, outside of the Republic of Karelia, and there is one appearance in Karelia north of this line, in Jänkäjärvi (Porajärvi).

Example Set 6: Place Names with the Two Variants of Proto-Sámi **elmē-* ['upper']

Elm-: *El'midd'ärvi, El'mičoja* (Elmitjärvi, Vuohtjärvi), *Elmyzjärvi* (Juustjärvi, Porajärvi), Elmyzjärvi (Suarenpiä, Repola), *Elmizjärvi* (Pääkönniemi, Jyskyjärvi), *Elmanka* (a river) (Šaidoma, Kontupohja), *Ielimäzenoja* (Ahi, Tulemajärvi) etc.

Ilm-: *Ilmahansuo* (Sammatus, Nekkula), *Ilmasuo* (Lumatjärvi, Kotkatjärvi), *Ilmeänluodo* (Rajakondu, Videle), *Ilmananselgy* (Iudankylä, Vieljärvi), *Ilomančinjärvi, Ilmolampi* (Ilomantsi), *Ilmačinvuara* (Jängäjärvi, Porajärvi), *Ilmetjoki* (Ilmee, Hiitola), *Ilöntjärvi* (Sarka, Suistamo), *Ilemozero* (Čebolakša, Kontupohja), *Ilemenza* (puro) (Pulozero, Petrovskij Jam) etc.

It is therefore possible to talk about two Sámi dialects on the basis of the form of the first vowel of the type. One, realizing *Elm-*, was close to the late Proto-Sámi and the other, realizing *Ilm-*, was close to early Proto-Sámi (Mullonen 2002: 241). However, this issue requires further assessment, because place names with the prefix *El-* have been recorded rather distant from Karelia, in the areas of Archangel and Vologda (Saarikivi 2006: 196–197).

Vepsians and Karelians[11]

An 'Old Vepsian' settlement seems to have been established in the southern parts of Aunus Karelia as early as in the Viking Age. This is indicated by the burial mound culture that prevailed between the tenth and thirteenth centuries in the southern Olonets Karelian area along the Vitelenjoki River (RussK Vidlica), the Tuuloksenjoki River (RussK Tuloksa) and the Aunuksenjoki[12] River (RussK Olonka). The burial mound cemeteries of this area have clear connections to the burial mound culture found along the southeast coast of Lake Ladoga, which may indicate that the population moved from the south to the north.[13] The cultural formation of the Old Vepsians took place in the vicinity of the southern coast of Lake Ladoga (Sedov 1997; Itkonen 1983) and the oldest kurgans appeared on the southeast coast of Lake Ladoga in the 860s (Map 4). Soon after this, they spread to the lower parts of the Paksujoki River and the Ojattijoki River. Evidence of Old Vepsian settlement and of the impact of their culture has also come to light in excavations of the kurgans on the Onega Peninsula on the northern coast of Lake Onega. The connections between these and the burial mound culture on the southeast side of Lake Ladoga indicates that the population moved from the south to the north (Saksa 1998: 120, 124). It should be noted that this population is from a later period than the population in Aunus Karelia. It has been concluded on the basis of archaeological studies that the 'Old Vepsians' inhabited three primary areas: the valley of River Šeksnajoki south of Lake Beloye, the valley of the Suda River southwest of Lake Beloye, including the valleys of rivers that flow into Lake Ladoga from the southeast – Ojatti (RussK Ojat'), and also Säässynjoki (RussK Sjas') and Paksujoki (RussK Paša) (Kochkurkina 2006: 182–186). The Old Vepsians are mentioned with the ethnonym *ves'* in Russian chronicles that recount events between the years 859 and 862, when a group of tribes invited the Varangians (i.e. Vikings) to rule them. The Old Vepsians mentioned in the Primary Chronicle are presumed to have lived in the Lake Beloye region already during the 860s (Letopisi: 160).

There is also linguistic evidence of an Old Vepsian population in Aunus Karelia. Old Vepsians apparently supplied the basis for the population of the entire Aunus Isthmus, and their language was the foundation of both Livvi and Ludic (cf. Map 1). This is demonstrated by, among other things, Aunus Karelians, Luds as well as both the northern and western Vepsians using the same ethnonym of themselves, namely *lyydi* (< Russian *ljudi* ['people']). Livvi was also spoken in Finnish Ladoga Karelia, for example in Salmi, Impilahti, southern Suistamo and eastern Suojärvi. The lexical basis of the dialect of Karelian in Suojärvi is obviously Livvi and so close to the dialects in Aunus that the communication between Karelians who lived in Suojärvi and the proper Aunus Karelians does not cause problems. This can be interpreted as an indication that the Livvian population in Suojärvi became linguistically Karelian in the seventeenth century, following the Treaty of Stolbovo. During that time, speakers of Karelian proper immigrated to the area from the western parishes of the Käkisalmi Province that had been conquered by the Swedes (Laasonen 2005: 111).

The spread of Livvi in the area of Ladoga Karelia may indicate that the Old Vepsian population once inhabited an area that extended to Harlu in the west. This kind of an areal distribution could potentially be explained by particular ecological and geographical circumstances. The Old Vepsians apparently used land that was suitable for slash-and-burn cultivation. The soil type characteristic of the southeast shore of Lake Ladoga extends precisely to the area of Impilahti (O. Jarovoi, p.c.). This correlation implies that the technique and form of the slash-and-burn cultivation was a determinant on the extent of the area occupied by the Old Vepsian population. Perhaps this is why the present-day Vepsian areas on Lake Onega were settled by the Vepsians much later than Aunus Karelia. The rocky coast of Lake Onega, the marshes in the water division area and the unfertile soil are poorly suited to farming. V. V. Pimenov (1965), among others, argues that the Vepsian population on the southwest coast of Lake Onega originates in the fourteenth century at earliest.

The northern limit of the Old Vepsian ethnic territory also corresponds to the zonal border of the central taiga forests. It can therefore be concluded that the range of the Vepsian population in the north depended on climatic and geographical factors, which then again indicates that the old Vepsians

Map 4. The spread of Viking Age kurgans around Lake Ladoga.

conducted agriculture. This conclusion is further strengthened by, for example, the distribution of place names with the prefixes *Niini-* ['linden-'] and *Lin-* (RussK *липа* ['linden']) in Kareli – e.g. *Niiniseľgy* (*Нисельга*), *Lipovaja seľga* (*Липовая сельга*), *Lipovyj bor* (*Липовый бор*), etc. The distribution of the name stem corresponds with the real range of linden trees in Karelia. Linden grows in fertile soil and agriculture is often connected to its range. The range of linden in Karelia lies on the south side of the line between Värtsilä – Säämäjärvi – Sunku. In the eastern parts of Karelia it is met only to some extent around the rivers Vodlajoki and Kolodajoki in the Puudos area (Puutoinen). The distribution of many place name types with Vepsian origins has a corresponding northern border. This indicates that the agricultural practices of the Old Vepsians had a significant role in the settlement of the Aunus Isthmus area and the eastern region of Lake Onega (Karelian place name atlas, manuscript).

Place names that are formed from ethnonyms also refer to the Old Vepsians. These appear predominantly in the southern parts of Republic of Karelia;[14] for instance, *Vepsniem'* (Kontupohja), *Vepsänmua, -polvi* (Tiitanniemi Vuohtjärvi), *Vepsänvuara, -lambi* (Kumsjärvi, Mändyselgä), *Vepsälambi* (Sellinkylä, Paadene), *Vepsino* (Virma, White Sea), *Венсозеро, Веснаволок, Венсгуба* (Kontupohja). The Karelian population in the Paatene Volost and the Porajärvi Volost in central Karelia refer to the Luds, who live to the south of them, as 'Veps' or 'Vepsians'. This can be considered without a doubt as evidence of an earlier Vepsian population in the area. Place names beginning with *Vepsä-*, *Vepso-* or *Vepsu-*[15] have also been recorded in Finland today, especially in its eastern parts (Valonen 1980: 72). They are found in the Karelian nomenclature of Ladoga Karelia as well, such as, *Vepsäjärvi* (Salmi) (mentioned in a source from 1621) and *Vepsonselgy* (Orusjärvi, Salmi). Vepsä(läinen) ['Veps(ian)'] is also a Finnish surname, the distribution of which is predominantly in eastern Finland (SSN 1988: 847). These uses of the ethnonym can be considered evidence of Vepsian immigration (Valonen 1980: 74).

The Vepsian substrate in the southern dialects of Karelian offers incontestable evidence of the presence of Old Vepsians in southern parts of Russian Karelia. Nevertheless, there are relatively few place names that are convincingly of Vepsian origin. A problem is that in charting the distributions of closely related peoples, the criteria for ethnic place names are often unreliable. The vocabulary that is used in Aunus Karelian and Vepsian place names is predominantly derived from a vocabulary that is common to both Vepsian and Karelian, and it cannot be used for the identification of origins in either of the two closely related languages. A researcher's task is therefore to seek identification criteria or place name models that would enable the differentiation between place names of these two ethnic groups (on relevant methodology, see also Leiviskä). A primary factor for differentiation may be the vocabulary used in the nomenclature, which may belong, for example, to only one of the Finnic language groups and lack equivalents in the other language group, or which may only have a very limited use in one of the two language groups. On these bases, certain word stems seem indeed to be of Vepsian origin: *Čuhuk-* ['hill, hillock'], *Kuara-* ['bay'], *Palte-* ['slope'], *Pauni-* ['a small grassland in a forest'], *Pehk-* ['decayed'], *Purde-* ['a spring'], *Sara-* ['a (small) tributary'], *Vadai-* ['a swamp that grows stunted wood'] and *Vuaž* ['a wide swamp (area)']. These word stems have a fairly limited distribution in the nomenclature of present-day Aunus Karelia (Karelian place name atlas, manuscript). For the time being, it is difficult to say anything concerning when the place names listed above originated. It is very probable that they originate as early as the period immediately following the Viking Age.

The present state of research leaves it almost impossible to identify Old Karelian elements in the nomenclature that would have origins in the Viking Age. Old Karelians are believed to have begun settling the area of the present-day Republic of Karelia during the thirteenth century (Bubrih 1947: 37).[16] Then again, it is not reasonable to exclude the possibility that the early hunting expeditions of the Karelians were directed to the territories of present-day Karelia already in the Viking Age, even if there is no direct evidence of this.

Conclusions

It is possible to follow the history of Karelia continuously back in time for 8000–9000 years through archaeological evidence. At the same time, it remains almost impossible to say which groups of people are represented by the earlier archaeological cultures (that existed before the first millennia BC) or what languages they spoke. Substrate loans from the unknown Palaeo-European languages, representative the oldest identifiable linguistic substrate are found in Sámi languages of today as well as in place names in Karelia: it has frequently proven impossible to provide a convincing Finnic or Sámi etymology for many hydronyms in particular. It can therefore be assumed that the speakers of unknown ancient languages in the early archaeological cultures were assimilated by the forefathers of the Sámi, most likely during the first millennium AD.

During the Iron Age and in the early Middle Ages, the culture of the forest Sámi evolved in Karelia. In the light of linguistic evidence, the Sámi seem, in the Viking Age, to have still inhabited the majority of the present-day Republic of Karelia and apparently also of the neighboring areas. Traces of the Sámi period of Karelia have best been preserved in borrowings into Karelian, Vepsian and Russian dialects and especially in place names. There are many place names of Sámi origin in all parts of Karelia. A major part of these are names for rather large bodies of water and geographical features. On the basis of the place names, it is also possible to conclude that Sámi language forms were spoken in Karelia that differed from present-day Sámi languages. This is testified by linguistic elements in the vocabulary and nomenclature that have lexical equivalents in both different dialects of present-day Sámi languages and also beyond the borders of Karelia (e.g. in the Archangel, Vologda and Leningrad Oblasts). The existence of Sámi borrowings and numerous place names of Sámi origin make it possible to suppose that a remarkable portion of this Sámi population was assimilated into the Finnic settler populations of Karelia.

The Finnic population on the coasts of Lake Ladoga in the area of Aunus Karelia is rather old. It was based on the Old Vepsians, whose gradual movement to the North began in the tenth century AD. Karelians from the northwest side of Lake Ladoga began populating Karelia during the thirteenth century. Over time, both the Sámi and the majority of Vepsians were assimilated to the Karelian language. Finally, it should be observed that the Old Vepsians can be considered to have been a farming culture in the Viking Age to a greater extent than the Old Karelians, whose economy was based predominantly on fishing, hunting and trade that was based on products acquired through these means. However, agriculture seems to have had some significance also among the Old Karelians since the Viking Age (Simola 2003: 110).

Linguistic Abbreviations

SámI – Inari Sámi language
SámK – Sámi vernaculars of the Kola Peninsula (Kildin and Ter Sámi)
SámN – Northern Sámi language
SámS – Sámi vernaculars in Sweden
RussK – Russian dialects in Karelia
RussA – Russian dialect in Archangel District

NOTES

1 The Votic Fifth (Russian *Vodskaja pjatina*) was one of the basic administrative units within the principality of Novgorod.
2 In Karelian, the designation *lappi* or *lappalainen* ['Lapp'] usually refers to the population living north from the speaker, be it Sámi or Karelians (Bubrih 1947: 39–40). It is a peculiar fact that the Karelians in Mäntyselkä and Paatene used the designation *lappalainen* of themselves and called the Karelian language that they spoke *lappi*.
3 The following literature concerning Sámi language has been used in developing this section: Aikio 2009; Fasmer 1986; Itkonen 1958; Itkonen 1986; Kert 2002; Kortesalmi 1996; Lehtiranta 1989; Nielsen 1979.
4 The Karel. *kuba* ~ *guba* and Rus. *guba* ['bay'] do not show an exact phonological correspondence to the Sámi word *gohppi* (< *kuppē). On the other hand, only limited research has been conducted regarding the phonological relationships of elements of Sámi origin in the Northern Russian dialects. For this reason, there is rather little information on the types of adaptation models and rules that have been employed when adopting words of foreign origin into the Slavic language system. It must be noted, however, that both the Sámi *gohppi* and Russian *guba* refer to the same concept. In addition, Russian *guba* occurs mainly only in the Russian dialects spoken in Northwestern Russia, particularly in Karelia and neighbouring areas. The same apparently applies to the Karelian word *näčäkkä* ['moist, wet (e.g. of land)'] and Rus. *näčä*. It is worth mentioning here that the phoneme *č* appears secondarily in several Karelian words, i.e. there are many words where this *č* phoneme occurs in the place of an original *s*: Karel. *čičiliusko* ~ Fin. *sisilisko* ['viviparous lizard'], Karel. *nyčä* ~ Fin. *nysä* ['stub'], Karel. *tylčetä* ~ Fin. *tylsyä* ['to dull'], Karel. *čurčettua* ~ Karel. *sursettua* ['to burble']. It seems that at some point, *č* ~ *s* variation has been a favourable phenomenon in Karelian.
5 It is possible that also *Siidoikoski* < **Siidakoski* (Kuittinen, Nekkula), *Сидосуо* < **Siidasuo* (Luzma, Repolan volosti), *Ситозеро* < **Siidajärvi* (Vozmogora, Uikujärvi) and *Ситьручей* < **Siidaoja* (Puutoinen) belong to this group. However, the latter two could be based on the Karelian word *sitta* ['shit, filth, muck'].
6 This material has been prepared using the etymologies of place names of Sámi origin presented by I. Mullonen (2002: 228–306; 2008: 160–169), among others.
7 Place name material collected in Karelia served as the basis for this study. This material has been archived in the name archives (KNA) of the Institute of Language, Literature and History of the Karelian Science Centre of the Russian Academy of Sciences (ИЯЛИ КарНЦ РАН) as well as in the place name archives in the Institute for the Languages in Finland (NA).
8 Place names beginning with *Kuotk-*, *Kotk-* can also be of Finnic origin (cf. Karelian *kuotkut*, *kotkova* ['isthmus']), but the appellatives is undoubtedly borrowed into the Karelian language from Sami.

9 Karelian has the appellativ *n'uoru* 'an underground shoal', which is a borrowing from Sámi (see. *K(u)otk-)*.
10 Sámi and Finnish started to separate around the shift from the Bronze Age to the Iron Age, i.e. approximately 500–600 BC (or possibly somewhat later).
11 On early Finnic settlements, see further KALLIO.
12 Karelian, *Anuksenjogi*; Finnish also *Alavoisenjoki*. It should be mentioned that one group of scholars considers a passage in the book *De origine actibusque Getarum* ['The Origin and Feats of the Goths'] by the Gothic historian Jordanes (ca. 551 AD) to present the first mention of the Vepsians. The passage reads: "thiudos: Inaunxis Vasinabroncas Merens Mordens Imniscaris [...]" ['peoples: in Aunus vas [ves' = Vepsians], in ? Abronkas Meryas, Mordvins in Meštšora ...'] (Napolskih 2006: 100).
13 The River Vaasenijoki (Karelian *Vuažn'and'ogi*, Russian *Važinka*) had great significance in the spread of Old Veps settlement to the north from the River Svir. Irma Mullonen considers the name of the river to derived from an originally Vepsian (now lost) topographical term *vad'ž* (< **vatsV*) ['a wide marsh; a great marshland']. The diphtong in the first syllable is explainable by the use of the name in the Karelian place names system (Mullonen 2002: 289).
14 Place names beginning with *Vepsä-* have also been found in the southern and northeastern parts of Viena Karelia: e.g. *Vepsävuara* (Hiisijärvi in Jyskyjärvi) and *Vepsäjärvi* (Kälkäjärvi in Vitsataipale). Both are relatively far from the area of the main distribution of this name type. In this case, the question of possible common roots of the nomenclature of this type remains open and requires further inquiry. The stem of the place names may be a person's name without indications of ethnicity.
15 According to Riho Grünthal, the form ending in '-u' may indicate that the *Vepsu-* nomenclature has Aunus Karelian origins (Grünthal 1997: 101). On the other hand, it is conspicuous that most of these names have been met in western Finland.
16 Bubrih refers to the national borders of 1939.

References

Sources

Itkonen, E. 1986. *Inarilappisches Wörterbuch* I–III. LSFU 20. Suomalais-ugrilainen seura. Yliopistopaino. Helsinki.

Itkonen, T. I. 1958. *Kuotan- ja Kuolanlapin sanakirja* I–II. LSFU 15. Suomalais-ugrilainen seura. Suomalaisen Kirjallisuuden Kirjapaino Oy. Helsinki.

KKS = *Karjalan kielen sanakirja 1–6*. Lexica Societatis Fenno-Ugricae XVI. Kotimaisten kielten tutkimuskeskuksen julkaisuja 25. Helsinki: Suomalais-Ugrilainen Seura – Kotimaisten kielten tutkimuskeskus 1968–2005. Helsinki.

Karjalan paikannimikartasto = Кузьмин Д.В., Муллонен И.И. Топонимический атлас Карелии (рукопись (käsikirjoitus)).

Lehtiranta, J. 1989: *Yhteissaamelainen sanasto*. SUST 200. Suomalais-ugrilainen seura. Yliopistokirjapaino: Helsinki.

Letopisi = Полное собрание русских летописей. СПб., 1859. Т. VIII. С. 160.

Nielsen, K. 1979. *Lapp Dictionary. Vol. 1–5*. 2. opplag. Instituttet for sammenlignende kulturforskning. Oslo.

KNA = Научный топонимический архив ИЯЛИ КарНЦ РАН.

NA = Nimistöarkisto. Kotimaisten kielten tutkimuskeskus.

SSA = *Suomen sanojen alkuperä*. Suomalaisen Kirjallisuuden Seura: Kotimaisten kielten tutkimuskeskus, 1995 (2. painos). Helsinki, 2001.

SSN = *Suuri suomalainen nimikirja*. Otava. Helsinki. 1988.

SRGK = *Словарь русских говоров Карелии и сопредельных областей 1–6*. Издательство С.-Петербургского университета. 1994–2005.

Literature

Aikio, Ante. 2009. *The Saami Loanwords in Finnish and Karelian*. Oulu. Avaliable at: http://cc.oulu.fi/~anaikio/slw.pdf (last accessed 17.01.2012).

Bergsland, K. 1995. *Bidragtil sydsamenes historie: Skriftserie*. Senter for Sámiske studier 1. Tromsö: Senter for Sámiske studier.

Bubrih 1947 = Бубрих, Д. В. 1947. *Происхождение карельского народа*. Петрозаводск.

Carpelan, Christian. 2003. Inarilaisten arkeologiset vaiheet. In *Inari – Aanaar: Inarin historia jääkaudesta nykypäivään*. Oulu: Inarin Kunta. Pp. 28–95.

Fasmer 1986 = Фасмер, М. 1986. *Этимологический словарь русского языка*. Прогресс.

Grünthal, Riho. 1997. *Livvistä liiviin: Itämerensuomalaiset etnonyymit*. Castrenianumin Toimitteita 51. Helsinki: Suomalais-Ugrilainen Seura.

Halinen, Petri. 2011. Arkeologia ja saamentutkimus. In Irja Seurujärvi-Kari, Petri Halinen & Risto Pulkkinen (eds.). *Saamentutkimus tänään*. Tietolipas 234. Helsinki: Suomalaisen Kirjallisuuden Seura. Pp. 130–176.

Istorija Karelii = *История Карелии с древнейших времен до наших дней*. Петрозаводск: Периодика, 2001.

Kert 2002 = Керт, Г. М. 2002. *Применение компьютерных технологий в исследовании топонимии*. Петрозаводск.

Itkonen, E. 1986- *Inarilappisches Wörterbuch* I–III (1986–89). Lexica Societatis Fenno-Ugricae 20. Helsinki: Suomalais-Ugrilainen Seura.

Itkonen, T. I. 1958. *Kuotan- ja Kuolanlapin sanakirja* I–II. Lexica Societatis Fenno-Ugricae 15. Helsinki: Suomalais-Ugrilainen Seura.

Itkonen, T. I. 1983. Välikatsaus suomen kielen juuriin. *Virittäjä* 2: 190–229.

Kochkurkina 2006 = Кочкуркина, С. И. 2006. Весь. In *Современная наука о вепсах: Достижения и перспективы (памяти Н.И. Богданова)*. Петрозаводск: КарНЦ РАН. Pp. 178–211.

Korhonen, Mikko. 1981. *Johdatus lapin kielen historiaan*. Suomalaisen Kirjallisuuden Seuran Toimituksia 370. Helsinki: Suomalais-Ugrilainen Seura.

Kortesalmi, J. Juhani. 1996. *Pohjois-Vienan poronhoito*. Kansantieteellinen Arkisto 41. Helsinki: Suomen Muinaismuistoyhdistys.

Kosmenko 1996a = Косменко, М. Г. 1996. Основные проблемы и задачи теории и методики изучения древностей Карелии. In *Археология Карелии*. Петрозаводск: Карельский научный центр РАН. Pp. 8–35.

Kosmenko 1996b = Косменко, М. Г. 1996 Поселения охотничье-рыболовецких культур. In *Археология Карелии*. Петрозаводск: Карельский научный центр РАН. Pp. 272–285.

Kosmenko 2008 = Косменко, М. Г. 2008. Археологические данные и этнокультурные процессы в Сямозерье. In *История и культура Сямозерья. Издательство Петрозаводского университета*. Петрозаводск. Pp. 13–24.

Kosmenko & Kochkurkina 1996 = Косменко, М. Г., & Кочкуркина, С. И. 1996. Вопросы истории населения древней Карелии. In *Археология Карелии*. Петрозаводск: Карельский научный центр РАН. Pp. 362–387.

Laasonen, Pentti. 2005. *Novgorodin imu: Miksi ortodoksit muuttivat Käkisalmen läänistä Venäjälle 1600-luvulla*. Helsinki: Suomalaisen Kirjallisuuden Seura.

Lehtiranta, J. 1989. *Yhteissaamelainen sanasto*. Suomalais-Ugrilaisen Seuran Toimituksia 200. Helsinki: Suomalais-Ugrilainen Seura.

Mullonen 2002 = Муллонен, И. И. 2002. *Топонимия Присвирья. Проблемы этноязыкового контактирования.* Петрозаводск: Петрозаводский государственный университет.

Mullonen 2007 = Муллонен, И. И. 2007. Загадка Выга. In *Комплексные гуманитарные исследования в бассейне Белого моря.* Петрозаводск: Издательство «Острова». Pp. 200–203.

Mullonen 2008 = Муллонен, И. И. 2008. *Топонимия Заонежья: словарь с историко-культурными комментариями.* Петрозаводск.

Mullonen & Mamontova 2008 = Муллонен, И. И., & Мамонтова, Н. Н. 2008. Топонимия как отражение этнического прошлого Сямозерья. In *История и культура Сямозерья.* Петрозаводск: Издательство Петрозаводского университета. Pp. 25–38.

Napolskih 2006 = Напольских, В. В. 2006. Булгарская эпоха в истории финно-угорских народов Поволжья и Предуралья. In *История татар с древнейших времён в семи томах II: Волжская Булгария и Великая Степь.* Казань. Pp. 100–115.

Nielsen, K. 1979. *Lapp Dictionary.* Vol. I–V. Oslo: Instituttet for Sammenlignende Kulturforskning.

Pashkov 2003 = Пашков, А. М. 2003. "Житие Лазаря Муромского" в истории культуры Карелии XVIII-XX вв. *Кижский вестник (сборник статей)* 8: 3–13.

Pimenov 1965 = Пименов, В.В. 1965. *Вепсы: Очерк этнической истории и генезиса куль туры.* М. / Л.: Наука.

Saarikivi, J. 2006: *Substrata Uralica: Studies on Finno-Ugrian Substrate in Northern Russian Dialects.* Tartu: Tartu University Press.

Saarikivi, Janne. 2011. Saamelaiskielet: Nykypäivää ja historiaa. In Irja Seurujärvi-Kari, Petri Halinen & Risto Pulkkinen (eds.). *Saamentutkimus tänään.* Tietolipas 234. Helsinki: Suomalaisen Kirjallisuuden Seura. Pp. 77–119.

Saksa, Aleksandr. 1998. Vepsäläiset: Pohjolan muinainen kansa. In Mikko Savolainen (ed.). *Vepsä: Vepsänmaa.* Oulu: Atena. Pp. 120–125.

Sedov 1997 = Седов, В. 1997. Прибалтийско-финская языковая общность и ее дифференциация. *Финно-угроведение* 2: 3–15.

Simola, Heikki. 2003. *Karjalan luonto ja ihminen.* In Matti Saarnisto (ed.). *Karjalan synty. Viipurin läänin historia I.* Lappeenranta: Karjalaisen Kulttuurin Edistämissäätiö. Pp. 81–115.

Torikka, Marja. 2004. *Karjala: Kieli, murre ja paikka.* Kotimaisten kielten tutkimuskeskuksen julkaisuja 129. Helsinki: Kotimaisten kielten tutkimuskeskus. Available at: http://scripta.kotus.fi/www/verkkojulkaisut/julk129/karjala_sisalto.shtml (last accessed 03.05.2012).

Valonen, Niilo. 1980. Varhaisia lappalais-suomalaisia kosketuksia. *Ethnologia Fennica* 10: 21–98.

Vilkuna, Kustaa. 1971. *Mikä oli lapinkylä ja sen funktio.* Kalevalaseuran Vuosikirja 51. Helsinki: WSOY.

Lassi Heininen, Joonas Ahola & Frog

'Geopolitics' of the Viking Age?

Actors, Factors and Space

'Geopolitics' is commonly understood to focus on physical space, natural resources and (state) power. In addition to this classical geopolitics, however, there are other schools of thought with a broader approach that takes into consideration a wider range of factors. Among these factors are 'new' actors, identity(-ies), knowledge(s), interrelations between power and knowledge, and the 'politicization' of physical space. These critical approaches to geopolitics are rather new. It is possible to apply them to historical periods like the Viking Age, as is done here. Doing so has great potential for producing new information, to reveal new ideas and new interpretations. The discussion set out in the following pages puts forward an interpretation that the Viking Age was characterized by newly defining Northern Europe – i.e. that Northern Europe became a recognized frame within which regionalism and relations between polities and cultural groups were contextualized. Geopolitics has the tools and approaches to address precisely these aspects of the period and their interrelations with the potential to develop new understandings and interpretations of the Viking Age.

The Viking Age presented a new context that reframed relationships of time, place and the actors that used, produced and developed new kinds of factors, such as technology and knowledge, mobility, networks, identities and adaptation. This process of reframing also affected perceptions of these different factors, their associations with different groups or social and political positioning, as well as their interpretations and potential valorization. Finland is seldom mentioned in discussions of the Viking Age as a context, the processes associated with it, or when 'Vikings' are discussed more generally. However, the Finnic cultures east of the Baltic Sea comprised cultural groups that were adjacent to the Scandinavians and, despite differences in language and culture, in many ways closely interlinked with them. It is obvious that the Finnic cultures of the Viking Age cannot be described in the same terms as the Scandinavians. However, the aim of this chapter is to discuss possibilities that the main discourses (or schools of thought) of geopolitics together with their conceptual machinery may contribute to the definition of Finland in the Viking Age, particularly as related to Fennoscandia.

Every discipline is equipped to provide different sorts of information about historical periods and each is better equipped to offer information in some domains than others. The present chapter approaches the Viking Age and its relevance for populations and polities in and around what are Finland and Karelia today through the fields of international relations and geopolitics. When approaching the Viking Age in Finland, all of these disciplines – archaeology, anthropology, folkloristics, genetics, history, linguistics, philology and so forth – are concerned with outcomes from that period; none of them may access it directly. The outcomes may be synchronic, as in archaeological data, offering evidence of human activities and changes in the environment through their outcomes at that time, or they may be outcomes of a *longue durée* in human practices, such as the continued use of certain words or the telling of the same stories observed in the nineteenth or even in the twentieth century (AHOLA & FROG). The models which these different disciplines produce are always theoretical reconstructions and conceptions that are necessarily to some degree speculative, and they are realized through the imagination of the researchers. The present discussion is such an exercise from the perspective of geopolitics.

Applying Geopolitics to the Viking Age

Geopolitics deals with both geography and politics with an emphasis on the interrelationship between them. It is traditionally interpreted as focusing on physical 'space' and 'power', meaning physical space and natural resources connected with the power of a state. This is an image of *classical geopolitics* – the oldest, and if you wish, the original, school of thought on geopolitics. Classical geopolitics and its sub-theories focus on the strategic value and control of a physical space, and on the power and hegemony of a state, much of which handles so-called *Realpolitik* (Killinen 1958: 15). Here *state* refers to the institution of a nation, or a unified state as a political and administrative system, and the unified state system as the international context. This is the variety of state in which we still live, even if there are indicators of a transition into other kinds of more globalized systems, such as economic integration, 'geoeconomics', and regional or city states, as well as the social and economic systems and entities developing with the internet. *Power* means both 'might' of, and brute force by, a state, which is, if needed, "unilateral, national(istic), competitive, military power" (Newcombe 1984). Implementations of this old school of geopolitics are for example, the *resource models* (of geopolitics), emphasizing the strategic importance of natural resources and potential conflicts related to their utilization (e.g. Dalby 2002), and the *technology models*, emphasizing the strategic importance of technologies. According to this approach, geopolitical factors consist of a short list of physical space, natural resources, and power or force, particularly that of a state.

Classical geopolitics was challenged in the early 1990s by new and critical approaches that re-conceptualized the traditional definitions and interpretations. These new approaches made geopolitics a discursive practice by which to represent international politics as a 'world' characterized by particular types of places, peoples and dramas (Ó Tuathail & Agnew 1992). They occupied more room with new discourses, and new schools of thought of geopolitics were established – 'New Geopolitics' and 'Critical Geopolitics' (e.g. Moisio 2001). The new discourses and schools have a general understanding that there are other factors in addition to physical space and state power and they recognize that these additional factors are also relevant to geopolitics and should be taken into consideration. Among them is an *actor* – the fact that there are also other actors than a nation-state, particularly, people(s), such as indigenous peoples without their own state (e.g. Abele & Rodon 2007), and civil societies. There is also *identity(-ies)*, which comes together with people(s), 'social space' and economics (Jukarainen 1999). 'Geo-economics' in particular, introduced by new geopolitics, is often mentioned as the most important factor of a polity and the entire power system, and its high importance is greatly (and perhaps overly) emphasized in the globalized world of the early twenty-first century.

Correspondingly, another new school of thought, *critical geopolitics* strongly criticizes the passive or ossified interpretation of 'space' as referring exclusively to physical space. Critical geopolitics has shifted consideration to the politicizing of physical space and it has worked to bring new and additional factors into academic discussion in addition to those of classical geopolitics: (other) actors, identity(-ies), knowledge *per se* and the interrelations between power and knowledge (e.g. Jukarainen 1999; Heininen 2005), as well as the 'politicization' of physical space (Heininen 2010) as geopolitical factors. As mentioned above, geopolitics with its critical approaches is a rather new discourse. It is, however, possible to apply many factors of this critical approach to the Viking Age, especially when viewed as an era and period of economic, technical, cultural and political exchange and interrelations between peoples, settlements, polities and powers in Northern Europe and the North Atlantic. In the following pages, this chapter will first outline some initial contextualizing information and then introduce and explore a variety of geopolitical factors and their applications to the Viking Age in Finland.

Historical Context

Geopolitical perspectives foreground the interconnectedness of human history and interrelations between the past and the present and between the present and the future. This is especially true for Europe, which is geographically small, and where nations with their societies, cultures, languages, identities, and innovations have been mixed and interrelated for centuries. For example, the current university system – which has been a globally successful innovation and even a product for export – was started about a thousand years ago, at the end of the Viking Age, by the early universities in Paris and Bologna (Kolbe 2012). Once established, such systems and institutions can have a *longue durée* that can be easily overlooked and taken for granted as a 'natural' part of culture and history (cf. Barthes

1972). History also reveals degrees of continuity in the tradition of common activities and functions in the 'East–West' – or 'North meets North' – relations between the peoples, communities and regions of Northern Europe, including the North Atlantic, Fennoscandia, the White Sea area and the Urals. The conditions and consequences of the Viking Age for populations in what is now Finland and Karelia belong to the interconnectedness of the history of Europe and of Northern Europe in particular.

Links between southwest Finland and the Scandinavian Peninsula across the Baltic Sea have been ongoing and gradually increasing since the Bronze Age, as observable in the archaeological record (Huurre 1979: 107–109). It is not possible to say anything definitive about the political situations of this early period. Nevertheless, it is possible to infer that both the populations of these settlements, where limited forms of animal husbandry were practiced, and also the highly mobile hunter-gatherer communities, which have left far less evidence in the archaeological record, formed organized groups with social hierarchies and conventions of conduct that differentiated each of them from other organized groups. However simple or complex those organizations were, such groups can be broadly described as forming polities, whether associated with fixed settlements or highly mobile. Etymological evidence suggests that Germanic languages were current east of the Baltic and that their networks extended farther east to presumably into the vicinity of Lake Ladoga and presumably farther south for language contact to reach the hypothetical Proto-Finnic *Urheimat*. Proto-Germanic etymologies have been proposed for names of large rivers in western Finland (Satakunta and Finland Proper, on which see Koivulehto 1987; Janhunen 2009: 209–210; Kallio) and even for the River Neva, connecting Lake Ladoga to the Gulf of Finland (Helimski 2008: 1–2). More securely, there is evidence of loan-words in Finnic languages antedating their dispersal and separation (see e.g. Kylstra *et al.* 1991–2012). Following the discussion of Petri Kallio, the primary separation of Finnic languages seems to have been between what he refers to as Inland Finnic and Coastal Finnic, the latter referring to language use that advanced to the Baltic coast around the Gulf of Riga. Finnic language use spread as far north as the coast of Finland by *c.* the beginning of the present era.

However the spread of Finnic languages took place, it can be inferred to have involved changes in mobility and relevant technologies. The lexicon for travel by ship has been clearly influenced by Germanic loans (Hofstra 1985: 315–318), suggesting corresponding models for these technologies. The Germanic vocabulary related to fixed settlement housing construction and associated buildings can also be noted (Hofstra 1985: 318–321), especially the term e.g. Finnish *kartano* from Proto-Germanic, which designated a property or farmstead (Kylstra *et al.* 1991–2012 II: 53–54). This term is linked to conceptualizations of settled spaces, as may also be words related to agriculture, such as e.g. Finnish *pelto* ['field'] (Hofstra 1985: 309–312). A significant number of terms are also relevant to social life and social order, such as e.g. Finnish *kuningas* ['chieftain, leader', later 'king'] (Hofstra 1985: 327–330). Many of these words may likely go back to the common

Proto-Finnic language, although some of the loans from this period could be adapted across dialects after the language spread (Kallio; cf. Häkkinen). These linguistic loans suggest changes in settlement and livelihood, which in turn would involve corresponding changes in social and political structures. In addition to these early loans, the stratification of Germanic loans through the history of the Finnic languages (cf. Schalin) are indicative of more or less continuous cultural interactions since that time, from which trade may be inferred.

Correlating evidence of an archaeological culture or community with a particular language group is highly problematic (Saarikivi & Lavento 2012; Laakso). Nevertheless, symbolically significant artefacts such as swords and practices associated with burial were being adapted in coastal communities of Finland from across the Baltic Sea in the centuries surrounding the turn to the present era (e.g. Wickholm & Raninen 2006: 154–155). Whether or not these adaptations of symbols and practices were linked to changes in 'beliefs', they suggest that the construction of social identities and hierarchies forming these polities was developing in relation to other polities across the Baltic as models in a manner suggestive of peer-polity interaction. *Peer-polity interaction* describes the negotiation of power and authority between centralized regional communities through networks rather than being subordinated to a common dominant central authority (see further Renfrew 1986). This model of interaction has been argued to have been active in Germanic Scandinavia during the Migration Period and before – i.e. that there were networks of local social and political authorities that negotiated power (Storli 2000).

In Scandinavia, power was presumably negotiated through public law at some form of local and perhaps regional community assemblies. This form of the distribution of social power may have paralleled the legal structure of Iceland or Gotland as systems of loosely organized chieftains or chieftain-priests subscribing to a common law. Local authority may also have been more centralized, as in Sweden, where the king appears to have been required to tour through his realm, perhaps in a form of itinerant kingship (cf. Sundqvist 2002). It seems probable that relative authority waxed and waned among these groups and networks through history, until the Viking Age when the networks of local polities were increasingly subordinated to the centralized authority of a king. In Finland, the term Satakunta appears to be a compound of *sata* ['hundred'] and *kunta* ['district'], which could be a translation-loan of the Germanic legal administrative district called a 'hundred' (Salo 2000: 114–128; for a contesting view, see Nuutinen 1989). This would suggest that communities of coastal Finland did not simply participate in peer-polity interaction across the Baltic Sea, but that they also developed their polities on the same structural model. It also presents the possibility that polities in Finland belonged to and were somehow integrated with the same cooperative (and sometimes subjugated?) networks as those across the Baltic Sea (cf. Klinge 1983). This would be consistent with Germanic populations being established in these territories prior to the arrival of Finnic languages. Toponymic evidence suggests that new

Germanic place names were no longer becoming established by the Viking Age (SCHALIN), by which time the local North Finnic language had become dominant – although this does not preclude the ongoing use of the relevant Germanic language in the region. If this description is correct, it presents the possibility that the Finnic populations assimilated into models of social order and political structure in these regions as part of the process of adapting their livelihoods to the new environment of the existing population. In such a case, it would imply long-term continuity of political networks, and possibly sea powers (however limited in scope and magnitude), across the Baltic Sea.[1] The contact networks to the east and south are more difficult to assess, although it appears that river routes from the Baltic Sea to the Mediterranean were already being explored during the Migration Period (Naploskikh 2006).

The political structures of Finnic, Sámi and other indigenous populations remain uncertain. The loan-word *kuningas* suggests at least familiarity with social hierarchy and authority. It has been suggested that aristocratic organization and implementation of taxation was established in Estonia already at the end of the Bronze Age (Tvauri 2012: 315–317), and Valter Lang (2006) has proposed that a form of itinerant local rulers who personally circled through lands under their control was established in Estonia by the end of the Viking Age or the centuries just following it (cf. Siig 2012). Mention of 'kings' of Finnic groups in Old Icelandic sources are problematic because they may simply be a projection of familiar social structures on unfamiliar cultures, yet these mentions and for instance marks of defence being organized on a district level (hill forts) nevertheless warrant giving thought to the possibility that some polities in Finland may have been organized around some type of *kuningas* as a local political authority.

Models for centralized power and its centralization were becoming available in the Finns' vicinity especially during the Viking Age. The collapse of the Frankish Empire and the rise of the Holy Roman Empire in the ninth century coincided with the beginning of the centralization of power in Scandinavia. King Haraldr *blátǫnn* ['Blue-Tooth'] united the Danes in the middle of the tenth century, and Norway was united by King Haraldr *hárfagri* ['Fine-Hair'] by the beginning of the tenth century. There were three especially significant political areas in Sweden: the area of the Geats in southern Sweden, the area of the Svear in central Sweden around the area of Lake Mälaren where Helgö was an important centre of trade, and the island of Gotland. The two first-mentioned were united around the year 1000 by King Óláfr *skǫtkonungr* ['Treasure-King'] and were ruled as one entity. However, it was Gotland that prospered economically during the eleventh century. The Slavic settlement expanded from Kiev towards the North during the course of the Iron Age, and the first contacts between the Slavs and Finnic groups took place somewhere southwest of the Gulf of Finland around AD 400 (Kallio 2006: 157). The founding of Staraya Ladoga can be considered the establishment of Slavic influence in the Lake Ladoga area. The Russian Primary Chronicle suggests that the need for centralized power was realized in this evolving multicultural region in the latter part of the ninth century and that disagreeing groups invited rulers for themselves, which established the Scandinavian Rurikids as the rulers of the emerging Slavic state to the south (Cross & Sherbowitz-Wetzor 1953: 59–60). This could of course be a euphemistic rendering of aggressive and controversial conflicts as viewed by those who aligned themselves with the established state, affirming its validity in retrospect or perhaps whitewashing the state's establishment by foreign conquest. Whatever the case, the establishment of this polity which gradually developed into a powerful state of that era was and long remained unambiguously linked to the power structures and processes of state formation in Scandinavia. By the Viking Age, models for such power structures were prominent in the two most important directions of contact with the rest of Europe, and Finnic cultures were situated along a major route between them.

Connections between Finland and the East Baltic as well as Estonia were overshadowed by the Scandinavian connections during the Viking Age. Estonian coastal settlements were mostly gathered around fortifications (Tvauri 2012: 56–59), perhaps due to the insecurity caused by passing ships and fleets travelling on the Eastern Route. The opposite Finnish coast seems to have been largely uninhabited at this time. However, Estonian maritime culture also developed towards that of Scandinavians. Especially Saaremaa seems to have been a place where ship-borne trade and plundering grew to significant measures (Mägi 2004; 2007). The ships from Estonia presumably reached Finland as well. Generally, it may be possible to conclude that there were political organizations of different types and with different powers in the Baltic Sea region. At the beginning of the Viking Age, insular cultures seem to have played a significant role in trade and to have formed distinct polities or networks of polities, as in the cases of Gotland and Saaremaa. In parallel with this, the centralization of power seems to have been a trend in mainland areas that developed and became established especially over the course of the Viking Age.

Vikings West and Vikings East

The term 'Viking' has become a modern stereotype with an almost archetypal status, an idealized image of a 'primitive' European that has been built up out of a long history of discourse, ranging from Romantic Nationalism and Nazi images of a master race to modern open-air museums and black metal music. This image of the 'Viking' is the opposite of social order, norms of polite behaviour, the distributed responsibility of bureaucracy and the veiling of emotions and intentions beneath the composure of propriety and deceptive, two-faced manipulations of others. This image of the 'Viking' is also a symbol with which we reflect on ourselves and on our society: it is a tool for imagining what and who is 'other', manifesting fantasies of other ways that the world and people in it could be in order to consider how things are different now, for both better and worse (cf. Csapo 2004). The traditional dating of the end of the Viking Age is the Battle of Stamford Bridge in 1066, which was considered the last 'Viking raid' on 'Europe', from the perspective of especially English, French and German historians. This was not, however, a band of Viking warriors on a smash-and-grab raid; this was a large-scale invasion organized under the leadership of King Haraldr *harðráði*, ruler of unified Norway (as viewed at that time) – it was a battle resulting from one kingdom in Northern Europe attempting to take possession of the territory of another through force of arms. In order to frame the Viking Age in geopolitical perspective, it is necessary first to work past the modern stereotype of a 'Viking'.

Historically, the Viking Age is centrally characterized by Nordic raiders – 'Vikings' – who mainly roamed in Northern and Western Europe. They sailed from Scandinavia towards the West in order to explore and settle the islands of the North Atlantic. So-called Varangians (or Varjagians) were Scandinavians who sailed to the east in order to trade with the Finnic-speaking and other Uralic peoples and the Slavs, and also perhaps others who participated in the trade networks extending as far south as the Middle East. It should not be assumed that such adventurers and entrepreneurs were exclusively ethnic Norsemen. Early sources on these raiding activities are from either the perspective of the cultures being attacked by foreign 'others' who came and went like 'Vikings', or from the perspective of Icelanders and Germanic Scandinavians, who emphasized connections to their own identity in histories about their ancestors and kings. Communication is fundamental to interpersonal interaction, but partnerships and alliances were also matters of practicality and convenience. The historicity of the thirteenth century Icelandic *Egils saga* is highly problematic, but its description of a King Faravið of Kvenland nevertheless presents certain relevant information. Kvenland probably lay somewhere around the eastern and northern coasts of the Gulf of Bothnia and west of today's Kainuu region (Tolley 2009 I: 41–43; cf. KUUSELA). King Faravið formed an alliance with a force of Norsemen (Einarsson 2003: 17–18), which illustrates that such alliances were conceived as possible. Indeed, such alliances were realized with Finnic groups later in the conflicts that led up to the Treaty of Nöteborg between Sweden and Novgorod in 1323. The most famous Viking warrior-band remembered today – the Jómsvíkingar – were based in the territory of the Wends, a Slavic cultural area on the southern coast of the Baltic Sea. As Janne Saarikivi and Mika Lavento (2012: 207) have recently reminded us, the ninth and tenth century raids elsewhere in Europe led by Turkic language speakers resulted in the spread a Finno-Ugric language (Hungarian), the thirteenth century raids led by Mongolian speakers spread Turkic languages, and the spread of Slavic languages linked to the Rus' was led by speakers of East Norse. A simple correlation of language, ethnicity and mobilization in these activities cannot be assumed: groups organized for raiding and trade may also have included Finnic, Baltic or Slavic members, and separate bands from these different cultural groups may also have been performing the same activities.

Perhaps the most central aspect of the Viking Age was mobility. In spite of their violent reputation, Norsemen of this era were farmers and traders, shipbuilders and navigators, and also settlers, as is discussed from different perspectives throughout this volume. These Northerners were capable and skilful enough to build bigger boats – ships – that were light and durable, enabling them to both sail the open seas and to navigate inland river routes in the same vessels (Näsman 1991). This enabled them to advance their shoreline-based navigation techniques to travel the open seas. They were very mobile and travelled all over Europe and the North Atlantic in almost all possible directions, exploring every corner, from the White Sea to the Mediterranean, from inland regions of what is Russia today all of the way to the coasts of North America.

A great part of western travel was exploration in order to have more space for living and farming, establishing colonies in the Faroe Islands and Iceland, and on other islands in the North Atlantic, as well as establishing themselves in Yorkshire and for a time even in Dublin. They explored still further to the west, establishing colonies in Greenland and travelling to Newfoundland, establishing the first routes for travel and trade between Europe and North America. They also travelled along the European coasts, establishing colonies in Brittany of modern-day France and they circumnavigated the Iberian Peninsula. Although encounters with 'Vikings' in the British Isles and along the coasts of mainland Europe have provided Scandinavians with a notorious reputation as raiders, it is necessary to bear in mind that they also were active as merchants, conquerors and rulers. To the north, Norsemen circumnavigated the coasts of Norway and the Kola Peninsula, sailing the Barents Sea to Svalbard and the White Sea. These journeys were not for settlement, but for exploration and trade with the natives of present-day Northwest Russia, where they encountered the Bjarmians (see KOSKELA VASARU) and the various populations referred to as different types of *Finnar* who were probably speakers of Sámi languages (see e.g. Grünthal 1997; Valtonen 2008; Aalto 2011). To the east, mobility was quite different: although the Baltic Sea was sufficiently open for the swift arrival and disappearance in so-called 'Viking raids', travel farther east was along inland river routes, which structured mobility and limited the viability of such raiding. These routes passed from the Gulf of Finland to Lake Ladoga, linking Scandinavia to the emerging center of trade and interactions at Lake Ladoga, which resulted in founding more or less permanent settlements such as Staraya Ladoga already in the middle of the eighth century (Kuz'min 2008), and a bit later Novgorod, followed by additional trading centers farther east (Duczko 2004). Both these routes and those from the Gulf of Riga via the Western Dvina River also opened access to the south around this same time as a burgeoning silver trade opened from the Mediterranean along these channels (cf. TALVIO).

Finno-Ugric languages predominated in these northern and eastern territories, presenting a communication barrier that, for Norsemen, required special language skills for even simple trade. Individuals fluent in sufficiently similar languages would have been an invaluable asset in such interactions. JOONAS AHOLA & FROG have suggested that such language skills may have been a factor in the role of Ålanders in trade during this period: as a culture in a major Finnic–Germanic contact zone, Ålanders were likely competent in both Old Norse and North Finnic. Consequently, they not only played a role in the silver trade to a degree that that other territories of Finland did not (TALVIO; cf. RANINEN & WESSMAN) but also in more distant Scandinavian trading centers of Merya territories to the east, where a West Uralic language similar (if still different) to the Finnic languages was spoken.

With the exception of the insular culture(s) of the Åland Islands, the role of Finland and Karelia in the silver trade as such of this era appears minimal (TALVIO). This most probably reflects the fact that silver was not valorized in commodification for these populations. In other words, the people with the furs did not barter in silver, because coins had not developed a general position in their economies as integers of wealth. The usage of coins in Finland as mere raw material for a smith or as decorations in jewelry can be compared to the initial adaptation of coinage in Germanic Scandinavia during the Migration Period, producing the so-called bracteates - symbolic, ornamental, magical and/or ritual objects rather than economic integers as 'money' (Hauck *et al.* 1985–1989). It can nevertheless be inferred that fur trade became economically significant to the cultures of this area - otherwise Staraya Ladoga would never have been established and Norsemen would likely not have been trading on the White Sea. The emergence of the Slavic state in the south was connected with the potentially strategic control of water routes central to the silver trade in the middle of the tenth century, which interrupted the flow of silver to the north (Kovalev 2011: 13–21). Scandinavia seems to have reoriented trade to the west in the wake of the breakdown of the eastern silver trade, whereas the economy of Åland may have collapsed (TALVIO). It is not clear that the economic networks in Finland were in a position to recover or recover quickly from these economic changes or what consequences this may have had for them.

Scandinavians were mobile when exploring and trading, and they created trade networks and communications channels during this period, but they were not the only linguistic-cultural groups involved in this process. Finnic populations also mobilized in their own expansion during this period, although its extensiveness must be considered modest as related to that of the Scandinavians. These groups spread along coastal areas as well as inland in both Finland and Karelia while other Finnic populations from perhaps farther south established colonies as far north as the White Sea in the Northern Dvina river basin. At the same time, Slavic language areas spread dramatically to the east and carried their influences to the north along the river routes to influence Finnic cultures for the first time - and it was the Slavic rather than Germanic language contacts that provided Finnic speakers with their basic vocabulary related to Christianity (Kallio 2006; HÄKKINEN). None of these processes happened in isolation, as is emphasized by the early Scandinavian leadership among the Slavic Rus'. The networks of politics and trade established in this period were maintained for hundreds of years, some of which already had a potentially long history. This maintenance was dependent on communication between different trading posts, settlements and emerging political entities. The populations involved in these movements were flexible enough to apply their knowledge and adapt to the existing climate and environment of new settlements, and to the habits, culture, and administrative structures of existing settlements or centers. All of these different areas and cultures exhibit corresponding processes and interconnections with one another. However, the Viking Age manifested in different ways and with different emphases in different regions. Thus, the same technologies that enabled the raiding activities for which Vikings are best known also enabled the colonization of islands across the North Atlantic as well as trading expeditions along river routes to the east, where the Germanic activities associated with the Viking Age were quite different and were more consistent with the activities of Finnic and Slavic populations in those regions.

Space and Place

In the Viking Age, the original geographical space – Scandinavia – was extended through increased mobility to become a larger space, an international space for more extended undertakings. New connections and lines of communication were created in every cardinal direction. The exchange of culture and material goods had, of course, been ongoing for centuries. However, the extent of communication expanded tremendously during the Viking Age and, quite significantly, it expanded in scope: connectivity was reconceptualised to look beyond adjacent local and regional polities to view all of these within a frame extending from Greenland (or at least Iceland) to Novgorod, and from Bjarmaland on the White Sea to Constantinople and Jerusalem (cf. Korpela). The connotations of the term 'Viking Age' remain today almost like a warning label on a historical period, suggestive of violence and lawlessness in popular imagination. However, this was a period of economic, technical, cultural and political exchange and interrelations between peoples, settlements and powers – a period that redefined a 'new' Northern Europe and North Atlantic (Heininen 2005; Ahola 2006).

The Vikings become 'great communicators' as well as the *first* communicators across Northern Europe and the North Atlantic. In this role, Scandinavians held center stage, although the linguistic-cultural groups central in the communication and connectivity of this era had quite different dynamics east of the Baltic Sea. Nevertheless, the Vikings in a way reconceptualized Northern Europe and the North Atlantic as a 'cooperative region'. (Heininen 1998.) Before the Viking Age, communication lines had never been as direct between Scandinavia and locations as remote as Baghdad or Byzantium. This era also brought the Scandinavians into the consciousness of the Europeans. This process simultaneously involved opening Scandinavia to the rest of Europe, not least through the adoption of Christianity at the level of political polities and other structures which would, for the next millennium, provide a unifying basis of a shared European identity (cf. Frog). It is indeed perhaps not an overstatement to say that Scandinavians entered Europe before European powers, particularly the Christian Church, entered Scandinavia and elsewhere in the North. Furthermore, by travelling widely around Europe, for example, maintaining routes from the north to the Mediterranean both through the east and around the coasts to the west, the Scandinavians in a way 'drew up' the borders of Europe as they are understood in the twenty-first century (Käkönen 1998). Thus, the Vikings did nothing more nor less than redefine Europe, or define Europe as we understand it today.

Finland and Karelia appear at the periphery of Scandinavian activities. Connections of Finnic cultures in Finland to Scandinavians seems to have been quite close, as testified by artefacts that bear marks of their influence or are of Scandinavian origin (see LAAKSO). However, there are no signs of Scandinavian colonies in Finland, and only rather little evidence of the presence of Finns in Scandinavia; their activities appear predominantly attested as oriented to the north and east (see KUUSELA; KOSKELA VASARU; KUZMIN). However, these places seem to have formed significant contact zones for multiple cultures in interaction. The expansion of the Finnish settlements to the north on the Baltic Sea, on northern coast of Lake Ladoga, as well as in the river basin on the White Sea situated these communities in a position to mediate and potentially also to some degree control mobility and trade with inland communities (see AHOLA & FROG). Whereas in coastal Finland, contacts may have been predominantly with seafaring Germanic groups and inland Sámi groups as well as other (potential) indigenous populations, the Ladoga region was a center of contact between regional Finnic populations, Germanic cultures from the east, Slavic (and perhaps Baltic) cultures from the south, as well as the Uralic cultures to the north and east. In this respect, it formed a vital multicultural center, where it should not be assumed that Germanic languages played a dominant role. Lake Ladoga was situated outside of Germanic language areas and this space was peripheral to Scandinavia, to the reach of Christian polities, and in a sense also to the newly defined Europe. At the same time, precisely this peripheral positioning allowed the site of Lake Ladoga to become central as a contact zone for cultures to the west and south but also to the pagan inland forests of the north and to the east, rich in furs.

Actor(s)

Defining an 'actor' as a new factor of geopolitics allows several actors to be identified on this stage of Northern Europe. The Viking Age is characterized precisely by the introduction of new actors – the mobilized and mobilizing actors that are commonly referred to under the blanket term 'Vikings'. These actors with their societies and through their activities had geopolitical impacts. The maritime mobility and raiding activities of these actors redefined the potentialities of coastal areas and to some degree also rivers with the threat of sudden raids or the more or less spontaneous appearance of a new, hostile polity within an already politically defined space (e.g. setting up a base).

Individual actors could also play significant roles. For example, the histories of Norway attribute Haraldr *hárfagri* as a motivated actor who was first to accomplish the centralization of political power and, in a sense, with the formation of Norway as a state. Similarly, the missionary kings Óláfr Tryggvasonr and Óláfr the Saint were agents largely responsible for the Christianization of Norway and the legal Christianization of Iceland. Another major actor was the Church, which provided both resources for social control and a bureaucratic apparatus that helped enable the durability of consolidated political power under a single king (Sanmark 2004). The emerging kingdoms of Scandinavia formed larger polities than one individual could practically oversee, even with the help of a personal guard and other henchmen (on which, see Kaplan 2011: 69–75). The established hierarchical structures of a feudal system were lacking and rich or politically powerful individuals could choose their allegiance insofar as they were not under threat. The Church provided a unifying apparatus that authorized the central political authority while the king reciprocally enabled the Church to penetrate into the organization of people's daily lives at every level of society.

Redefining Northern Europe through connectivity also affected the actors on that shared stage. The formation of consolidated Scandinavian kingdoms produced those kingdoms as agents. Connecting those kingdoms to the Church was in part politically motivated owing to the critical attitude of major polities of Europe toward interactions with non-Christians, whether politically or in trade, which also held potential for serious conflicts. Defining these kingdoms as Christian united them with the common identity of Europe and situated their kingdoms in relation to other kingdoms as actors on that political stage. This process led to the valorization of continental court practices in Scandinavian kingdoms and the import of culture and cultural products (cf. Agha 2009). Corresponding processes may have occurred in Finland and Karelia. This sort of phenomenon was already observed above in the adoption of swords and Scandinavian artefacts by populations in Finland as (unavoidably) symbolic objects in ritual practices, a phenomenon which can be observed through the Iron Age.[2] Its equivalent could potentially have also occurred in interactions between Finnic groups and inland hunter-gatherer polities. The establishment of these Finnic linguistic groups at places of access to inland regions appears to have established them as small-scale polities with the language and resources for successful mediation with other foreign cultures interested in trade. If this is correct, it makes it probable that the language and culture were valorized from the perspective of the inland cultures, which presents a potential factor in the subsequent language shift of these populations in the spread of Finnish and Karelian (Ahola & Frog). These three examples – Scandinavian courts in relation to European courts, North Finnic polities in relation to Scandinavian polities across the Baltic Sea, and Finnic coastal (or equivalent) polities in relation to inland groups – potentially present parallel processes of the valorization of culture, cultural knowledge and cultural symbols in relation to perceptions of power and access to authority, while they differ in that they involve polities on very different scales.

It appears that the Viking Age resulted in fundamental changes that reoriented and restructured peer-polity interactions in the north. On the one hand, the formation of kingdoms was built on the subordination of more localized polities to a centralized authority. On the other hand, the formation of these kingdoms – and especially Christian kingdoms – redefined the agents that constituted peers as well as relationships to other polities as agents. At the same time, the Viking Age appears fundamental to the later spread of Finnish and Karelian languages across a huge geographical area, a process which may in part have begun with their positioning as polities capable of international relations. Polities of Åland and coastal Finland seem to have constituted agents that earlier engaged in peer-polity interaction with corresponding agents in Sweden and elsewhere. However, the centralization of authority across the Viking Age seems to have resulted in their subordination. This can be particularly linked to the extension of Church bureaucracy which linked them to Europe via Sweden. The precise processes remain obscure (and are still more obscure for Karelia), but it remains clear that the centralization of power in early state formations resulted in a breakdown of earlier peer-polity interaction because the actors of Finland and Karelia could not maintain themselves as peers in the interaction. Although some form of peer-polity interaction may have persisted between Finnic polities and mobile hunter-gatherer communities, their positions were eventually subordinated and redefined as parts of the larger state formations of Sweden and Novgorod, which became formalized in the division of these regions with the Treaty of Nöteborg in 1323.

Identity(-ies)

'Identity' comes with being an actor, but it is a factor *per se* from the viewpoint of critical geopolitics. At the beginning of the Viking Age, the world was without real borders and 'territoriality', as we currently understand it; it was observed from a perspective that was more limited to the immediate surroundings (Korpela). The identities of different groups could only develop in interaction with other groups, and the number of those other groups was limited by mobility. Identities are socially constructed and developed as concepts that are situated in relation to alternatives, and also in relation to the constructed perceptions of how alternative identities are situated in relation to one another. This phenomenon is particularly apparent in the construction of 'others', such as competitors, rivals and enemies and more abstract 'enemy-pictures' (e.g. Harle 1991). It also occurs in the construction of shared identities such as 'Christians', relationships of a liegeman or poet to a king or patron, as well as in the development of alignments as in the peer-polity interactions noted above, where emblems of the 'other' may be assimilated as part of identity construction (courtly entertainments, the sword as an emblem of power, language as a medium for economic success).

Models for identities changed during the course of the Viking Age. Early textual evidence reflecting Germanic ideologies makes Scandinavian identity models more possible to reconstruct. The Scandinavian expansion seems to have developed on vernacular models of the hero, with qualities of courage, endurance, ability and honour (cf. AHOLA). It may also be observed that Old Norse language (as well as Old English) seems to have resisted assimilating words from Celtic or Finno-Ugric languages. This is suggestive of an ideology of superiority and exclusion reflected at the level of the lexicon. The inherited model of identity was combined with a technological capacity for mobility which enabled exploration – an activity that suggests curiosity or adventurousness was also built into these identity models. The technology to sail on open waters had only recently been achieved in Scandinavia, and it consequently provided the potential to be more mobile than other European peoples of that time. It may be argued that 'mobility' became an important part of Scandinavian identity – or at least of what we would today identify as a 'Viking'. Raiding, conflict and conquest also became linked to this identity, but the process of redefining Northern Europe led this emerging identity to be redefined in relation to those of other agents on that stage – and thus it changed. It became Christian and adopted the characteristics of identities of continental Europe that became esteemed.

Finnic identities remain more obscure, although they exhibit a long and intimate dialogue with Germanic identities. The loan-word vocabulary suggests that they also had a corresponding interaction with the arriving Slavic culture. In contrast, there seems to have been a resistance to lexical borrowings from Sámi languages, and the words that are borrowed suggest an ideological stance devaluating those languages (Aikio 2009: 212–213), and thus presumably also the speakers of whom those languages were emblematic. This attitude is paralleled in the transformation of ritual practices and mythology that seems to have emerged under Germanic influences and in a contrastive relationship to 'shamanism', whether a vernacular Finnic tradition or in Sámi religion (FROG). There also seems to have been an early linking of these Finnic religious identities with Christianity (Frog 2013). A noteworthy factor is that the identities of Finnish and Karelian groups seem to have been valorized in some way from the perspective of inland cultural groups during the course of the Viking Age: these languages became more desirable or practical to speak on a wider basis, and the gradual spread of these groups involved a language shift of indigenous populations (cf. KUZMIN).

Perhaps among the most significant impacts of the Viking Age for identities was that their diversity was diminished through their unification. The independent status of local identities was dissolved and subordinated in relation to the development of larger, shared identities, a process in some cases directly linked to changes in peer-polity relations.

Knowledge(s)

For their time, people(s) and societies of the Viking Age seem in many respects to have been oriented toward progress and produced several new innovations. Scandinavians displayed great advances in different fields of technology – they were 'high tech' for the Middle Ages – developing, for example, superior boats or ships for the open seas. This required a higher level of knowledge and experience that not only indicates knowledge *per se*, but also the understanding of the strategic importance of knowledge – i.e. that knowledge, meaning different knowledges and different kinds of knowledge, was interpreted to mean power, as well as influence. This provides a frame in which to consider the flow of technological innovations from Germanic to Finnic cultures across the Iron Age, observing especially that Finnic cultures of the time appear to have viewed knowledge as power in a literal sense of having mythic quality (Frog 2013: esp. 62).[3]

The knowledge that manifested itself in innovations did not appear out of nowhere; it was a result of a process. The unique design of the Viking ships, for example, developed from earlier types of boats over the course of centuries. Other innovations connected to seafaring evolved in the same process as needed (Crumlin-Pedersen 1991). The technologies enabled new capabilities, and the activities and deeds accomplished through these new capabilities led to redefining objects, environmental features and phenomena according to what people were able to do, to do with them, or to do to them. In this sense, the Viking raids can equally be considered as an outcome of a process enabled by indigenous cultural heritage: the circumstances in coastal Europe enabled trade to turn into hostile offenses for rapid gain (cf. AHOLA & FROG). This technology translated into a type of *sea power*, a concept proposed by Alfred Mahan (e.g. 1918) and which became an influential sub-theory of classical geopolitics relevant to achieving and the struggle for world hegemony. This knowledge was fundamental to conquering more space through settlement, which was complemented by the maintenance of lines of communication and also lines of material resources. It also led to discoveries that were in many cases initially accidental – such as getting lost at sea and discovering Greenland, but surviving the odyssey to tell others about it, thanks to the developed maritime technology.[4] This mobility was an essential precondition of the connectivity that reconstructed Northern Europe as a unified space.

The advances in maritime technology that enabled Scandinavians to cross the North Atlantic do not seem to have been assimilated by populations in Finland, or at least not to have led to similar consequences. Masted sailing ships have an integrated position in kalevalaic epic traditions that appear to be rooted in the Iron Age (see AHOLA), suggesting that this technology was viewed as integrated into vernacular cultural practices rather than being exclusively associated with cultural 'others' (cf. FROG; AHOLA *ET AL.*). However, evidence of Finnic mobility seems to have been led to the expansion of settlement on a more localized basis with orientations along coasts and inland to the north and east. A factor may have been that these groups were in the north-eastern part of the Baltic Sea, which in practical terms made shores to the north comparatively close while coastal areas to the south already had a stronger presence of existing settlements while reaching the North Atlantic required a lengthy journey. On the other hand, activities of raiding and slaving expeditions – 'Vikings' as agents on the Baltic Sea – may have also inclined these Finnic groups to limit their activities on the sea across the course of the Viking Age: the settlements on the southern coast of Finland seem to have been abandoned for a long stretch (Salo 2000: 91–93) and the people prepared themselves better for offenses from the sea. For example, hill forts were taken into use before the Viking Age but their number seems to have increased in the course that era (Taavitsainen 1990). It is possible that this process led mobility to become associated with the identity of 'others', at least by the majority of the scattered settlements of the rural population. Then again, the contacts with strangers became more regular in the Viking Age and encouraged mobility to a greater extent than earlier: these contacts could potentially have affected the Finns' identity with regards to mobility as well. For example, the thirteenth century small ship made of planks that was found in Lapuri represents a local Finnish adaptation of Scandinavian maritime technology that may have been introduced already in the Viking Age (Alopaeus 1995), and there are strong indications that a kalevalaic epic cycle recounting maritime adventures gained popularity during the Viking Age (Ahola). Åland maintained insular communities and appears in numerous respects to have remained culturally distinct. Ålanders seem to have been oriented toward external trade, and maritime technologies were no doubt fundamental to those interests, while their robust ties to the east may be directly linked to capitalizing on knowledge of languages that could enable them to conduct business with both Germanic groups and those with languages close to Finnic (for discussion, see Ahola *et al.* 2014). Karelian identities may also have been strongly constructed on the basis of linguistic ability, which becomes a form of commodifiable knowledge with potential for both empowerment and as an economic resource: they situated their settlements especially on the northern and eastern shores of Lake Ladoga and potentially capitalized on the ability to negotiate with language groups for whom Germanic and Slavic languages might be inaccessible.

The 'Politicization' of Physical Space

All of the factors outlined above made it possible for different groups to take and conquer more physical space, land, water and natural resources. More importantly, it also enabled cultural influence on new spaces. Consequently, it became possible to transfer that growing influence into political power. This did not, however, mean an establishment of a state or of state power – at least not yet. Instead, what initially seems to have developed was power used to create and maintain political or administrative units or entities for economic, technical and cultural exchange.

The political power of Finns did not really expand to a degree in any way comparable to that of the Scandinavians. The territory of these groups expanded during the Viking Age but this should not be imagined as forming a unified political area. It most likely functioned through loose networks of quite localized polities. The immigration from south-western Finland to the northern coast of Lake Ladoga did not lead to a 'colony' but to an integration of cultures, which suggests that organizing new polities around ethnic identities was not a priority. Similarly, Staraya Ladoga quickly became an amalgamate culture representing Slavic and Finno-Ugric elements even though Scandinavians had a central role in its founding. Whether it was done strategically or simply a common cultural pattern, the settlements of Finnic groups around access points to inland river routes quite possibly involved a politicization of these spaces. Such settlements constituted the formation of a polity sufficiently strong and organized to be capable of defending those spaces, and thereby also capable of exerting regulatory control over them with potentially significant implications for trade, much as the growing polity of the Slavs exerted over routes of the silver trade.

The establishment of a new kind of cooperative region in Northern Europe was one by-product of this process. The actualization of such a region also politicized it. The areas of present-day Finland and Karelia were linked to this networked area, at the periphery of the Germanic arena. However, Finnic populations in these spaces may have found themselves in the potentially empowering position of mediating cultures at the heart of various cultural contact zones. Along the coasts of the Baltic Sea, Finnic groups presented fixed settlement sites at access points to inland regions, situating them to mediate between especially sea-faring Germanic groups and inland populations such as the Sámi. In Karelia, Finnic groups were situated at the nexus of trade routes to the north, south, east and west. These trade routes had developed from those of earlier eras, but they became especially vital during the Viking Age, when they may have held a special or exceptional status at thresholds to the political arenas of the Northern Christian world. These territories took on new significance precisely through the construction of Northern Europe as a geopolitical space – a significance which changed again with the repoliticization of these spaces when they were later divided between Sweden and Novgorod.

The features addressed here and interpreted as geopolitical factors made it possible for the populations and polities of the Viking Age to have and maintain connections between different destinations, new settlements and mainland communities. Correspondingly, connectivity made it possible to create networks for communication and trade and to maintain these, as also happened between mainland Europe and the islands of North Atlantic, as well as to create and maintain new kinds of administration and governance. This mobility and connectivity as phenomena over Northern Europe and the North Atlantic can be interpreted as indicating and implementing the politicization of physical space.

Time

All of these factors and their outcomes were cumulative: they produced a new kind of period or era. In this respect, time itself also became a new factor through which the new kind of geopolitical context began to make sense. Indeed, there was a new kind of relationship between time, place and (active) actor (with an identity). This relationship functioned as a context to produce and further develop new kinds of factors, such as technology, knowledge, mobility, networks and adaptation, and the new context provided new kinds of meanings for all of these. Cultures of Finland and Karelia seem not to have been active in outward mobility and technological innovation in a manner corresponding to that of Scandinavians, but changes in these factors and especially their outcomes appear to have had significantly impacted these populations and established the conditions which later enabled the spread of Finno-Karelian languages: the Viking Age was nonetheless a period of transition for these and other linguistic-cultural groups in the region. The population dynamics within the area of Finland and Karelia changed during this period as the population that inhabited southern parts of Finland expanded towards the east and the north and those in Karelia expanded to the north and west. Among the diverse populations in contact, Finnic groups seem centrally to have been opened to new influences through interactions with Scandinavian and Slavic peoples, which at the same time enabled the development of indigenous cultures and their consequent identities.

Perspectives

The Viking Age was a period in which changes and innovations in technology enabled forms and ranges of mobility that produced a new level of connectivity in the larger Northern European region. These developments had transformative consequences for trade connections and for social, cultural and political structures and their relations. Earlier networks for communication and trade were linked and expanded in this process as the new level of mobility enabled the maintenance of networks of trade and communication across greater distances than had previously been possible. The Norsemen were active and influential actors in the geographical space that they made available to themselves, and mobility, knowledge and internationalization (based on mobility and knowledge) became significant factors through which many Norse identities became defined. For Finns, internationalization was narrower in scope: it does not appear to have extended significantly to the south and instead seems to have been oriented north and inland. From the perspective of Scandinavians and Slavic groups, North Finnic cultures were at the periphery of the space defined by their major activities. At the same time, these Finnic cultures were at the center of the contact networks that linked the Indo-European cultures to the inland regions of Finland and Karelia as well as to the trade networks to the east: they were, in a sense, at the thresholds where actors in quite different geopolitical spaces would meet. Approaching these phenomena through geopolitical factors, including not only technology and mobility but also actors, identities and space, offer new perspectives and insights into the Viking Age with consequences for how Finland is perceived on that stage.

In the North Atlantic, new settlements of diaspora, such as in Iceland, Greenland and the Orkneys, distinguished themselves from the 'mainland' of Scandinavia to evolve as political and cultural entities in their own right. At the same time, the Norse expansion established these as a distinctive Norse peer-polity network that included the Scandinavian mainland, extending from the Baltic Sea to Greenland. On the Baltic Sea, this connectivity was equally realized: insular cultures in particular appear to have held central positions in trade while peer-polity interaction extended to the east and south, including especially Finnic and Slavic groups, of which the latter were linked by the Rurikid dynasty to Scandinavia. The main body of written sources for this period are from Iceland or western Scandinavia more generally and thus centrally reflect the network in the North Atlantic (in which Icelanders primarily participated). The networks of the Baltic Sea region and farther to the east are much less well represented.[5] Nevertheless, the Norse perspective in the medieval sources unambiguously regards this whole extended network as forming a coherent area of numerous polities in interaction. These sources emphasize especially the network of Norse polities (extending to that of the Rurikids), but also acknowledge the polities of other cultural groups as integrated in the connectivity, whether in the British Isles or the Bjarmians on the White Sea. Northern Europe was thus in a sense defined as a coherent geopolitical space for the first time, and the indicators of defining Northern Europe in this way are correspondingly indicators of the politicization of that space.

The same technologies that enabled the connectivity across Northern Europe were also significant in entering Northern Europe into the consciousness of Western Europe, and into the consciousness of the Church, even if this attention was gained through hostile 'Viking' activities. Corresponding – if more opaque – processes also occurred in the east, especially along the trade routes that carried furs from the north and silver from the south. Connectivity along these routes can be assumed to be a key factor in the introduction of Christianity to Finnic language groups through Slavic language contacts and the eastern Church. The routes of mobility both east and west in a way described Europe as a space that remains quite similar to perceptions of 'Europe' today. The dynamics of peer-polity interaction within the extended network of Northern Europe developed in tandem with the centralization of power in Norway, Denmark, Sweden and Novgorod. This process involved linking these polities to Christianity as a new (European) identity in their advancement toward state formation. A characterizing feature of the conclusion of the Viking Age is that Christianity becomes reciprocally established on the basis of the force of 'statehood-based' or 'national' authority – i.e. 'national' in the sense of a state as a or the center and its power over its territories (including peripheries) and citizens, and which emphasizes the importance of (state) sovereignty as the ultimate aim of a state as an entity. As a consequence of this, the positions and orientation of these polities developed across the Viking Age so that by the end of that era in Scandinavia (*c.* 1050) the essential conditions had been established for these polities on the one hand to orient themselves on the European stage of states and nations, and on the other to extend their power through the subjugation of the smaller polities of Northern Europe that had earlier been engaged as peers. The Viking Age thus established the conditions necessary to integrate the north into the space of Europe. It can be interpreted as a transition period of economic, technical, cultural and political exchange relevant to the interrelations between peoples, settlements, local polities and kingdoms, as well as other powers such as the Church.

Finno-Karelian polities do not exhibit indicators of the centralization of power as seen in Scandinavia or around Novgorod. The reasons for this remain unclear, although it may at least in part be related to the remoteness of these territories to the historical processes in Western Europe from which Germanic groups in Scandinavia had been assimilating models already for about a millennium; the Germanic and Slavic models for the centralization of power of the Viking Age (or perhaps a preceding period) were relatively new by comparison. Although contacts with Christianity came to these areas during the Viking Age, there is also no evidence of major polities asserting a Christian identity on the populous. Instead, the societies in these territories were eventually subordinated to larger emerging states, as those states redefined these spaces in terms of potentially acquirable assets of economic resources and/or tools in the geography of power. The processes which occurred in Scandinavia and united them with a European identity extended much more slowly to the eastern side of the Baltic Sea. In a sense, these 'pagan' regions were annexed by Europe through the Northern Crusades, in which marshal state power was used to expand territories of authority (ostensibly) in order to convert threatening 'other' identities to a European Christian identity. This process seems to have reached Finland only in the so-called Second Swedish Crusade of 1249 (Ahola & Frog). Within an interpretation of the Viking Age as a period of transition, that period appears to have advanced in stages across different polities and networks of polities rather than uniformly concluding at a single point in time (e.g. 1050). On the one hand, this means that the transition from the period characterized as the Viking Age took longer to reach some polities, such as those east of the Baltic Sea. On the other hand, it suggests that 'time' as a geopolitical factor includes not only the concept of the Viking Age as a period, but also that, for example, the 'Later Viking Age' in Finland (1050–1250: see Ahola & Frog) was situated in relation to a Scandinavia that had already entered the Middle Ages.

The Viking Age was clearly a period of the 'regional' and 'regionalism' in Northern Europe and the North Atlantic area as opposed to the 'national'. This regionalism is owing to the significant influence of the Viking societies being based on local polities and networks of such polities rather than states as national entities. Since the end of the Viking Age, the 'national' and 'statehood' have for the most part predominated, although there has been a boom of new 'regional' and 'regionalism' in (Northern) Europe since the 1980s. The Viking Age is interesting with regard to this development because it shows that the 'regional' was first in Northern Europe, and that regional cooperation itself shaped the environment, extended the populated area and developed into a political structure.

Notes

1 Considering the name of the district Satakunta as a translation loan does not resolve the period when this term became established. Owing to a probable background of the Germanic term in marshal organization, Unto Salo (2000) has considered the term to be related to Indo-European contacts and especially to influences on Germanic cultures assimilated through contacts with the Roman Empire. Inger Storli (2000) presents establishments of centralized polities in Norway of a relevant type from especially the first centuries of the present era.

2 Swords continued to be used as symbolic of power in magical practices in Karelia into the nineteenth and twentieth centuries.

3 The correlation of knowledge with power is semantically transparent in the term for the vernacular ritual specialist called a *tietäjä* ['knower, one who knows'].

4 Accounts of such events are found, for example, in the Old Icelandic works *Landnámabók* ['The Book of Settlements'], *Grænlendinga saga* ['The Saga of the Greenlanders'] and *Eiríks saga rauða* ['The Saga of Eric the Red'].

5 For example, the archaeological record attests to the significance of Åland in these networks especially with regard to trade, in addition to the islands being situated in a key position along sailing routes, yet Åland as such is not mentioned anywhere in Old Norse literature.

References

Aalto, Sirpa. 2011. *Categorizing Otherness in the Kings' Sagas.* Dissertations in Social Sciences and Business Studies 10. University of Eastern Finland: Joensuu.

Abele, Frances, & Thierry Rodon. 2007. Inuit Diplomacy in the Global ERA: The Strengths of Multilateral Internationalism. *Canadian Foreign Policy Journal* 13(3): 45–63.

Ackrén, Maria. Forthcoming. Greenlandic Paradiplomatic Relations. In Lassi Heininen (ed.). *Security and Sovereignty in the North Atlantic: Small States, Middle Powers and their Maritime Interests.* Palgrave Pivot.

Agha, Asif. 2011. Commodity Registers. *Journal of Linguistic Anthropology* 21(1): 22–53.

Ahola, Joonas. 2006. Workshop Report: Vikings in the East in Veliky Novgorod, Russia in May 10–13, 2006. In Jón Haukur Ingimundarson, Embla Eir Oddsdóttir & Gudrún Rósa Thorsteinsdóttir (eds.). *The Borderless North: Proceedings of the Fourth NRF Open Meeting.* Akureyri: The Northern Research Forum Secretariat. Pp. 68–72.

Aikio, Ante. 2009. *The Saami Loanwords in Finnish and Karelian.* Oulu. Avaliable at: http://cc.oulu.fi/~anaikio/slw.pdf (last accessed 12.01.2013).

Alopaeus, Harri. 1995. Aspects of the Lapuri Find. In O. Olsen, J. Skamby Madsen & F. Rieck, (eds.). *Shipshape: Essays for Ole Crumlin-Pedersen on the Occasion of His 60th Anniversary February 24th 1995.* Roskilde: Viking Ship Museum. Pp. 127–134.

Barthes, Roland. 1972. Myth Today. In Roland Barthes. *Mythologies.* New York: Hill & Wang. Pp. 109–159.

Bertelsen, Rasmus Gjedssø. Forthcoming. Managing Devolution and Withdrawal: Denmark and the North Atlantic 1800–2100. In Lassi Heininen (ed.). *Security and Sovereignty in the North Atlantic: Small States, Middle Powers and their Maritime Interests*. Palgrave Pivot.

Cross, Samuel Hazzard & Olgerd Shebowitz-Wetzor (eds.) 1953. *The Russian Primary Chronicle: Laurentian Text*. Cambridge MA: The Medieval Academy of America.

Crumlin-Pedersen, Ole. 1991. Ship Types and Sizes AD 800–1400. In Ole Crumlin-Pedersen (ed.). *Aspects of Maritime Scandinavia AD 200–1200: Proceedings of the Nordic Seminar on Maritime Aspects of Archaeology, Roskilde, 13th–15th March, 1989*. Roskilde: The Viking Ship Museum. Pp. 69–82.

Csapo, Eric. 2004. *Theories of Mythology*. London: Blackwell.

Dalby, S. 2002. Security and Ecology in the Age of Globalization. *Environmental Change and Security Project Report* 2002(8): 95–108.

Duczko, Wladyslaw. 2004. *Viking Rus: Studies on the Presence of Scandinavians in Eastern Europe*. Leiden / Boston: Brill.

Einarsson, Bjarni (ed.). 2003. *Egils saga*. London: Viking Society for Northern Research.

Frog. 2013. Shamans, Christians, and Things in between: From Finnic–Germanic Contacts to the Conversion of Karelia. In Leszek Słupecki & Rudolf Simek (eds.). *Conversions: Looking for Ideological Change in the Early Middle Ages*. Studia Mediaevalia Septentrionalia 23. Vienna: Fassbaender. Pp. 53–98.

Grünthal, Riho. 1997. *Livvistä liiviin: Itämerensuomalaiset etnonyymit*. Castrenianumin toimitteita 51. Helsinki: Helsingin Yliopisto.

Harle, Vilho. 1991. *Hyvä, Paha, Ystävä, Vihollinen*. Jyväskylä: Rauhankirjallisuuden edistämisseura ry., Rauhan- ja konfliktintutkimuslaitos.

Hauck, Karl, *et al.* (eds.). 1985–1989. *Die Goldbrakteaten der Völkerwanderungszeit*. I–III. Münstersche Mittelalter-Schriften 24. München: Fink.

Heininen, Lassi. 1998. *Viikingit Pohjolaa laajentamassa: Erään historiallisen aikakauden hahmottelua*. Rovaniemi: Arktinen Keskus, Lapin Yliopisto.

Heininen, Lassi. 2005. Northern European Geopolitics: Northern Dimension and 'Northernness': An Essay. In Lassi Heininen, Kari Strand & Kari Taulavuori (eds.). *Northern Dimensions and Environments*. Northern Sciences Review 2005. Oulu: Oulu University Press. Pp. 13–50.

Heininen, Lassi. 2010. Pohjoiset alueet muutoksessa: Geopoliittinen näkökulma. *Politiikka* 2010(1): 5–19.

Helimski, Eugene. 2008. Ladoga and Perm Revisited. *Studia Etymologica Cracoviensia* 13: 75–88.

Hettne, B. 1994. The New Regionalism: Implications for Development and Peace. In Björn Hettne & Andr'as Inotai (eds.). *The New Regionalism*. Research for Action. Forssa: The United Nations University, WIDER. Pp. 1–49.

Hietala, Marjatta. 2012. Historiantutkimuksen uudet haasteet. *Tieteessä tapahtuu* 2012(5): 9–14.

Hofstra, Tette. 1985. *Ostseefinnisch und Germanisch: Frühe Lehnbeziehungen im nördlichen Ostseeraum im Lichte der Forschung seit 1961*. Groningen: Hofstra.

Huurre, Matti. 1979. *9000 vuotta Suomen esihistoriaa*. Helsinki: Otava.

Janhunen, 2009. Some Additional Notes on the Macrohydronyms of the Ladoga Region. *Studia Etymologica Cracoviensia* 14. Pp. 203–212.

Jukarainen, Pirjo. 1999. Norden is Dead – Long Live the Eastwards Faced Euro-North: Geopolitical Re-Making of Norden in a Nordic Journal. *Cooperation and Conflict* 34(4): 355–382.

Käkönen, Jyrki. 1998. Näkökulmia pohjoiseen. *Ulkopolitiikka* 35(2): 83–86.

Kallio, Petri. 2006. On the Earliest Slavic Loanwords in Finnic. In Juhani Nuorluoto (ed.): *The Slavicization of the Russian North*. Slavica Helsingesia 27. Helsinki:

Department of Slavonic and Baltic Languages and Literatures at Helsinki University. Pp. 154–166.

Kaplan, Merrill. 2011. *Thou Fearful Guest: Addressing the Past in Four Tales in Flateyjarbók*. FF Communications 301. Helsinki: Academia Scientiarum Fennica.

Killinen, Kalervo. 1958. *Kansainvälinen politiikka 1: Politiikan ja strategian maantieteelliset perusteet*. Porvoo: WSOY.

Klinge, Matti. 1983. *Muinaisuutemme merivallat: Kuvitettu historiallinen luonnos*. Helsinki: Otava.

Koivulehto, Jorma. 1987. Namn som kan tolkas urgermanskt. In Lars Huldén (ed.). *Klassiska problem inom finlandssvensk ortnamnsforskning*. Studier i Nordisk filologi 67. Helsingfors: Svenska Litteratursällskapet i Finland. Pp. 27–42.

Kolbe Laura, 2012. 'Huipulle ja yhteiskuntaan': Oma kulttuuriperintö yliopistojen kilpailuvaltiksi. *Tieteessä tapahtuu* 2012(4): 27–34.

Kovalev, Roman. 2011. Circulation of Sāmānid Dirhams in Viking-Age Northern and Eastern Europe (Based on the Mints of Samarqand and al-Shāsh). Working paper presented at the Oriental Numismatics Workshop: Monetary Circulation in 10th-century Northern Europe held at Oxford University, 1st–2nd August 2011. Available at: https://www.academia.edu/1032808/Circulation_of_Samanid_Dirhams_In_Viking-Age_Northern_and_Eastern_Europe_Based_on_the_Mints_of_Samarqand_and_al-Shash.

Kuz'min 2008 = Кузьмин С. Л. 2008. Ладога в эпоху раннего средневековья (середина VIII — начало XII в.) In *Исследования археологических памятников эпохи средневековья*. СПб. Pp. 69–94.

Kylstra, A. D., Sirkka-Liisa Hahmo, Tette Hofstra & Osmo Nikkilä (eds.). 1991-2012. *Lexikon der älteren germanischen Lehnwörter in den ostseefinnischen Sprachen* I–III. Amsterdam: Radopi.

Lang, Valter. 2006. Die Wacke im vorzeitlichen und mittelalterlichen Estland: Ein Beitrag zur Erforschung der vorzeitlichen Bodennutzung und des Steuersystems. *Forschungen zur Baltischen Geschichte* [1]: 7–28.

Mägi, Marika. 2004. '...Ships Are Their Main Strength': Harbour Sites, Arable Lands and Chieftains on Saaremaa. *Estonian Journal of Archaeology* 8(2): 128–162.

Mägi, Marika. 2007. Collectivity versus Individuality: The Warrior Ideology of Iron Age Burial Rites on Saaremaa. *Archaeologia Baltica* 8: 263–272.

Mahan, Alfred. 1918. *Lessons of the War with Spain and Other Articles*. Boston.

Moisio, Sami. 1998. *Kriittinen geopolitiikka ja alueelliset uskomusjärjestelmät: Uhkakuvatutkimuksen teoriaa empiirisin menetelmin*. Turun yliopiston maantieteen laitoksen julkaisuja 158. Turku: Turun yliopisto.

Napolskih 2006 = Напольских, В. В. 2006. Булгарская эпоха в истории финно-угорских народов Поволжья и Предуралья. In *История татар с древнейших времён в семи томах II: Волжская Булгария и Великая Степь*. Казань. Pp. 100–115.

Näsman, Ulf. 1991. Sea Trade during the Scandinavian Iron Age: Its Character, Commodities, and Routes. In Ole Crumlin-Pedersen (ed.). *Aspects of Maritime Scandinavia AD 200–1200: Proceedings of the Nordic Seminar on Maritime Aspects of Archaeology, Roskilde, 13th–15th March, 1989*. Roskilde: The Viking Ship Museum. Pp. 23–40.

Newcombe, Hanna. 1986. Collective Security: Common Security and Alternative Security: A Conceptual Comparison. *Peace Research Reviews* 10(3): 1–8, 95–99.

Nuutinen, Olavi (Olli). 1989. Satakunnan synty ja Kainuun kato. *Virittäjä* 93(1): 11–49.

Ó Tuathail, Gearóid, & John Agnew. 1992. Geopolitics and Discourse: Practical Geopolitical Reasoning in American Foreign Policy. *Political Geography* 11(2): 190–204.

Renfrew, Colin 1986. Introduction: Peer-Polity Interaction and Socio-Political Change. In Colin Renfrew & John F. Cherry (eds.). *Peer-Polity Interaction and Socio-Political Change*. Cambridge: Press Syndicate of the University of Cambridge. Pp. 1–18.

Saarikivi, Janne, & Mika Lavento. 2012. Linguistics and Archaeology: A Critical View of an Interdisciplinary Approach with Reference to the Prehistory of Northern Scandinavia. In C. Damm & J. Saarikivi (eds.). *Networks, Interaction and Emerging Identities in Fennoscandia and Beyond: Papers from the Conference Held in Tromsø, Norway, October 13–16 2009*. Helsinki: Suomalais-Ugrilainen Seura. Pp. 177–239.

Salo, Unto. 2000. Suomi ja Häme, Häme ja Satakunta. In Jukka Peltovirta (ed.). *Hämeen käräjät I*. Hämeenlinna: Hämeen heimoliitto. Pp. 18–231.

Sanmark, Alexandra 2004. *Power and Conversion: A Comparative Study of Christianization in Scandinavia*. Occasional Papers in Archaeology 34. Uppsala: Department of Archaeology and Ancient History, Uppsala University.

Siig, Kristo. 2012. *Kuningamäng* ['King Game']: An Echo of a Prehistoric Ritual of Power in Estonia. *RMN Newsletter* 5: 15–22.

Storli, Inger. 2000. 'Barbarians' of the North: Reflections on the Establishment of Courtyard Sites in North Norway. *Norwegian Archaeological Review* 33(2): 81–103.

Sundqvist, Olof 2002. *Freyr's Offspring: Rulers and Religion in Ancient Svea Society*. 2nd edn. Acta Universitatis Upsaliensis: Historia Religionum 21. Uppsala: University of Uppsala.

Taavitsainen Jussi-Pekka. 1990. *Ancient Hillforts of Finland*. Suomen muinaismuistoyhdistyksen aikakauskirja 94. Helsinki: Suomen Muinaismuistoyhdistys.

Tolley, Clive 2009. *Shamanism in Norse Myth and Magic* I–II. FF Communications 296–297. Helsinki: Academia Scientiarum Fennica.

Tolvanen, Matias. 2012. Tietoa ympäristökeskustelun pohjaksi. *Tieteessä tapahtuu* 2012(3): 57–58.

Tvauri, Andres. 2012. *The Migration Period, Pre-Viking Age, and the Viking Age in Estonia*. Estonian Archaeology 4. Tartu: Tartu University Press.

Valtonen, Irmeli. 2008. *The North in the Old English Orosius: A Geographical Narrative in Context*. Mémoires de la Société Néophilologique de Helsinki 73. Helsinki: Socieìteì Neìophilologique.

Wickholm, Anna, & Sami Raninen. 2006. The Broken People: Deconstruction of Personhood in Iron Age Finland. *Estonian Journal of Archaeology* 10: 150–166.

Winterhalter, Boris. 2012. Ilmastokyynisyys vaiko ilmastoprgamaattisuus?. *Tieteessä tapahtuu* 2012(3): 49–51.

People III

Introduction

Every discussion of the Viking Age is implicitly anthropocentric: as a historical period, the Viking Age is relevant and defined in terms of people who inhabited it. Where something is not directly or indirectly relevant to people living in that period, there is no relevance for addressing it in terms of the Viking Age. However broad or narrow the discussions and studies in this volume, interest and concern inevitably return to what people did, their identities, beliefs, language, relationships to one another and to other groups and cultures with which they may have had contact. *People* has therefore been reserved for the closing section of this collection, in which the condensation of earlier discussions takes shape with increasing clarity surrounding this most subtly central aspect of the Viking Age in Finland.

Sami Raninen and Anna Wessman open this section by drawing many of the preceding themes together from the perspective of archaeology and linking them to discourses surrounding identities. Their overview of the problematics in constructing images of the past on the basis of limited evidence is placed in dialogue with the ideas and issues of the present. They highlight that it is precisely through the dialogue of the present reflecting on and bringing forward the past that images of identities both past and present are constructed. Åland provides an excellent example for the illustration of problems and limitations of sources by looking at the degree to which scholarship and popular discourses have shaped and constructed ideas about Åland across the past two centuries. Åland was a center for contacts between Germanic and Finnic populations and Åland also has a long and complex history of relationships in later discourses owing to its situation between Finland and Sweden. Raninen and Wessman offer an insightful approach to these dynamic and lively discourses, and they consider the potential for new insights and understandings enabled by triangulating diverse perspectives.

Elina Salmela carries discussion forward by addressing the topic from the perspective of genetics. This discipline focuses on people as embodied individuals in physical interaction, engaging in reproduction as a historical process. Genetic data of populations today is unusual in that, like the tangible outcomes of synchronic processes investigated through archaeology, DNA is physically realized evidence, yet like evidence of intangible heritage, this physically realized evidence only reaches us at outcomes of diachronic processes. Genetic evidence presents the difficulty that it can be transferred through movements of populations and, as became apparent in the preceding section, genetic populations can be assimilated to different dominant languages and cultural practices as a historical process. SALMELA offers an important and accessible introduction to this often intimidating field. She stresses the problematics of attempting to identify and correlate particular specific features in the outcomes of genetic processes alone, especially with a period as narrowly defined as the Viking Age Proper.

Challenges similar to those faced in approaching genetic data are also encountered in the research of traditions maintained through cultural practices. JOONAS AHOLA turns attention to Kalevala-meter epic traditions which have preserved images, motifs and narrative traditions of heroes that were current already in the Viking Age or which may even have become established in the epic singing tradition during that period. Epic and kalevalaic poetry more generally have been prominent in discussions of the Viking Age and particularly weighted owing to their powerful imagery and potential as tools in nationalist discourses. AHOLA offers a fluent overview of the central epics associated with the Viking Age and the history of arguments and discussion attempting to connect them with it. This chapter offers a lucid introduction to the problematics of using these epic poems as sources for the Viking Age as a historical period. Discussion is then extended to observe general patterns of parallels in narrative and heroic identities encountered across kalevalaic, Old Norse and North Russian heroic epics. AHOLA considers whether these could all be outcomes of cultural encounters in the changing social environments of the Viking Age that found culture-specific realizations in the forms of 'epic' of each group.

KAISA HÄKKINEN returns to the question of language in the Viking Age, focusing particularly on changes in the lexicon situated in relation to social and cultural processes. HÄKKINEN introduces the study of etymology, or the history of individual words and their meanings, in a way that will be easily accessible to non-linguists. This chapter returns to problems opened in the first section of the volume regarding the correlation of chronologies in language history with an absolute chronology. The contribution considers how evidence from linguistics can be complemented and triangulated with a diversity of data in order to produce perspectives on cultural contacts and changes that took place in a culture at earlier periods. HÄKKINEN's treatment highlights that the Finnic language-groups, however distinct in Northern Europe, has never lived in isolation. The vocabulary of the Finnic languages reveals intercultural contacts that took place in history and that have left indelible marks on this cognitive tool-set. This chapter looks at how the historical periods in which contacts took place can be distinguished and identified, and offers insights into how historical linguistics can contribute to the study of the Viking Age in Finland.

Continuing with the theme of linguistic data, JOHAN SCHALIN returns to the subject of toponymy introduced in the preceding section. SCHALIN reviews in greater detail the historical intersections of phonetic changes in languages when considering the periods of possible language contact. This provides a background for approaching place names in medieval Germanic sources that are associated with Finland. This chapter discusses the origins of numerous central place names that belong to the heart of what we consider Finland already established in the Viking Age. These place names extend from recognized contact zones of Scandinavians and Finns to Åland, and to the area of Tavastia in inland Finland, far from routes of the Scandinavian Vikings. Discussion extends even to place names that appear distinctively Finnish, such as those of *Harjavalta* or *Köyliö*. SCHALIN offers valuable insights into questions and problems of contacts between Germanic and Finnic languages and cultures in the Viking Age. Reinforcing the discussion of HÄKKINEN, this chapter shows how loan words in toponymy strongly indicate that the Finnic-speaking populations of the Viking Age maintained close contacts with the Scandinavians throughout the later Iron Age.

Drawing the section to a close, FROG takes up the theme of mythology in the Viking Age as it is reflected and refracted through diverse data produced by different disciplines. Approached from the broad perspective of mythological thinking, mythology underpins the meaningfulness of diverse symbolic strategies in culture and is relevant not only to stories about gods, but also to ritual practices, understandings of the seen and unseen worlds as well as to the strategies for interacting with them. It is also relevant to the meaningfulness of images and phenomena in both the symbolics of representation and in nature itself. Mythology has had a particularly vital position in the construction of national identities since the era of Romanticism and has continued to stimulate popular imagination. On the one hand, the vitality of material and its interpretation presents challenges to unravelling selective modern constructs from cultural heritage. On the other hand, it presents challenges to untangling the appropriate assessment and handling of source materials from poorly founded transpositions, juxtapositions and comparisons that have become commonplaces through the history of discussion. This closing chapter engages the earlier themes and discussions of the collection and places them in dialogue around a thematic nexus of mythology, centering on the social construction and negotiation of meaningfulness in the diverse and multifaceted cultures that inhabited the territories under discussion.

The Viking Age was a period of transition, and perhaps quite pronouncedly so. The transitions that took place in that period had a transformative affect on the populations that lived during that time. The distribution of linguistic-cultural groups was radically altered in combination with remarkable changes in conceptual models of the world, mythologies and social practices, not least among which was the early arrival of Christianity. The Viking Age marked the beginning of developments that would eventually lead to the distribution of languages and cultures that have become recognizable to us today. Chapters of the opening section of this collection focus on the problems of defining the Viking Age as a temporal period for this part of the world while chapters of the second section advance the problematics – if not the impossibility – of drawing cultural and political territories of that period precisely on a map according to any single factor. The chapters of this third part of the collection now illustrate how linguistic, poetic and material expression bear traces of lively intercultural contacts and exchange. Despite the relative homogeneity and distinctiveness of individual cultures that have been addressed through these many complementary studies, the cultural heterogeneity of the area under discussion becomes obvious. It is certain that there were people during the loose period of history called the 'Viking Age' in this vaguely definable area called here 'Finland', with concentration on Finno-Karelian areas of habitation, but who exactly those people were and how precisely they relate to the cultures and populations we recognize in our modern-day surroundings, is another, more intriguing question.

Sami Raninen & Anna Wessman

Finland as a Part of the 'Viking World'

Archaeology is a social science just as are history and other studies of culture. The Viking Age in particular has drawn not only archaeologists but also people from other sciences to study different phenomena. The Viking Age is media-sexy – it gets attention and has a widespread popular appeal. This means that archaeologists have to take a responsibility by commenting when the debate goes off track. Rather than present a descriptive overview of the historical and archaeological evidence for the Viking Age in Finland (see Edgren 2008; Laakso), this chapter is instead focused upon certain key issues, some of which have been sometimes misunderstood in popular debate.

What Was the Viking Age?

The Finnish Iron Age (500 BC – AD 1200/1300) is subdivided into periods with names that might be perplexing to the non-specialist since they are terms adopted from Scandinavian and continental scholarship in the early twentieth century for purely chronological and comparative purposes. For example, the early and middle portion of the Iron Age are known as the Pre-Roman Iron Age (500–1 BC), the Roman Iron Age (AD 1–400), the Migration Period (AD 400–550) and the Merovingian Period (AD 550–800). It is obvious that names like these do not meaningfully describe events or cultural processes current in the territory of present-day Finland during the first millennium AD. Similarly, the Viking Age (AD 800–1050) should be understood as a technical, rather than descriptive term of historical relevance to Finnish archaeology.

However, it is commonly considered that the concept of Vikings is not quite as misplaced for Finland as the Romans or Merovingians are. The definition of 'Viking' is problematic if the term used to define an entire people. In its narrow sense, the term Viking refers to navigators of Scandinavian origin during the ninth, tenth and eleventh centuries AD. These navigators did originate in countries neighbouring Finland, and they certainly had a much stronger impact in Finland than did, for example, the Romans, whose observable influence in Finland is limited to a small number of exotic imports. However, it is undeniable that modern day identity politics have supported and intensified the need to associate Finland with the Scandinavian

Viking Age. Thus, the perceived affinity with, and historical recognition of, the Vikings, has far more to do with twentieth- and twenty-first-century socio-politics than anything to do with the late first millennium AD.

At least since the 1930s, Finns have markedly identified themselves as a Nordic nation. It is therefore quite logical that they appropriated the most potent and widely recognized Nordic imagery – Viking symbolism – for various emblemic uses, if sometimes in a carnevalistic and parodic way, as seen in the furry horned 'helmets' worn by ice-hockey fans. Yet there is deeper significance than the peaceful competition and allegiance of sporting events.

The Finnish identity as a Nordic nation has been constructed under contradictory pushes and pulls. The Finns are separated from the majority of the Nordic peoples by a linguistic divide, as the Finnish language belongs to a language family completely different and unrelated to the Scandinavian languages (see Tolley). Because of their language, the Finns have sometimes been portrayed in more xenophobic Scandinavian discourses as a culturally and even racially alien, eastern, intrusive element in Northern Europe. On the other hand, Finnish nationalism has usually stressed that the cultural, historical and existential affiliations of the Finns are essentially western, despite some exotic oddities in the cultural heritage and mentality. This thinking was earlier based on the need to distinguish the Finns from Russians or even from Asians, with whom the Finns were sometimes associated in racialist discourses. In the present day, this has become more an issue of brand – the Finns wish to be associated with images of Nordic wealth and human development, as opposed to the alternative field of associations which is to be perceived as one of the struggling post-Communist nations, with which Finland gets easily confused.[1] On a different level, the Viking imagery is used in the negotiation of a distinct cultural and historical identity of the Swedish-speaking minority in Finland. The distinct *finlandssvensk* identity was first constructed during the late nineteenth and early twentieth centuries, when Viking romanticism had its heyday (see also Aalto). Thus Viking imagery has been used to both associate the Finns with the speakers of Scandinavian languages and to dissociate the language groups in Finland from each other.

The question nevertheless remains whether it possible to speak of Finland as an authentic 'Viking' country in a meaningful way. The answer to this obviously depends on the definition of the Viking Age. If the concept of Viking is defined as a something related exclusively to the speakers of Old Scandinavian languages, then the only region in Finland with a supportable claim to any Viking past would be the Åland Islands. The material culture of these isles had a largely Scandinavian character during the ninth and tenth centuries AD – even if it was not quite as dominant as had often been suggested (see below). There are also reasons to believe that the islanders were at least sporadically involved with the Scandinavian trade routes along the East European rivers (Callmer 1994; Talvio 2002; Duczko 2004). Otherwise, there seems to be neither archaeological nor – perhaps more tellingly – credible toponymic evidence of any Scandinavian settlement during the Viking Age in the present-day territory of Finland (see Schalin). The Finnish mainland was inhabited by early Finnish-speaking or Sámi-speaking groups, and the Swedish colonization of coastal areas cannot be proven to predate the twelfth and thirteenth centuries (Ivars & Huldén 2002).

Another, and certainly more sensible way to address the question is to forget all notions of true, ethnic 'Vikingness', and instead to outline the inter-regional developments and their influence on various societies of the period. The space will not allow us to compare Finland and Scandinavia in all possible cultural, social, economic, religious, political and other respects which would be of interest here. Instead, this discussion will be restricted to a close look at the Åland Islands, followed by a more general discussion of the most popular Viking themes – long-distance contacts, trade and warfare – in the mainland territory of the present-day Finland.

The Viking Age and the Åland Isles

According to the most recent large surveys, there are over 400 mound cemeteries and 175 building foundations dating to AD 500–1300 in the Åland Islands (Karlsson 1987: 5). The Late Iron Age settlement on the isles is characterized by sometimes quite large mound cemeteries which are situated in an agrarian landscape, close to the contemporary settlement sites. Most of the archaeologically examined cemeteries derive from AD 550 onwards, which means that not much is known of the earlier burial types. The majority of the mound cemeteries are located in the parishes of Finström, Jomala, Saltvik and Sund (Wickholm 2000a).

The material culture implies that the contacts to both east and west were frequent and vibrant, especially during the Viking Age (AD 800–1050). Approx. 1,300 Islamic coins have been found, in both hoards and burials, on the main island. Intriguingly, there is only one West European coin dated to the first half of the eighth century, found from a settlement site in Saltvik (Tomtlund 2005). These Islamic coins alone have sometimes attracted daring and potentially exaggerated archaeological interpretations of a glorious Viking Age past for Åland, in which the population would not only have taken part in Viking raids, but also played an important role in organizing them (Kivikoski 1949: 67). There is even a theory – though never accepted by other researchers – that the Viking Age town Birka, mentioned in contemporary Continental texts, was in fact situated in Åland rather than in Central Sweden (Dreijer 1969; 1974).[2]

During the end of the tenth century, the recognizable burials disappear very quickly from Åland. This is often seen as evidence of nearly complete depopulation (e.g. Hiekkanen 2010). However, some researchers have also explained this by an early Christianization, others by a re-organization of the settlements due to an economic collapse.[3] In any case, the total lack of any datable artefacts from the eleventh and early twelfth centuries is astonishing and very hard to explain. There is no clear evidence of a population wipe-out, but on the other hand, there is not enough research done in the area in order to take a stand on either part.

As was stated above, the Åland Islands are the only Finnish region with a supportable claim to a true Viking past. The material culture had a strong Scandinavian character during the ninth and tenth centuries AD, which means that both the burial customs and many of the grave goods derive from Scandinavia. Still, when it comes to the grave goods, a striking phenomenon is also the strong connection to the Finnish mainland and the Baltic areas. Archaeologists have seldom brought attention to this.

The previous archaeological research has typically concentrated on the Scandinavian identity of the population on Åland, tending to exclude elements of eastern influences in their studies. This can partly be explained by neglect or by the fact that the archaeologists working with the material have no knowledge or interest in the archaeology of the Finnish mainland. However, there might also be unconscious nationalistic goals in the background as well. Nevertheless, many Swedish archaeologists have given attention to the material from Åland. From a Swedish perspective, the islands become more interesting during the Vendel (Merovingian) Period and the Viking Age due to the fact that the population there seems to go through some kind of 'Scandinavization', which is manifested in new burial customs, such as burial mounds. This is also seen in the introduction of brooch types, such as oval and trefoil brooches, which were important parts of the female dress. However, there are clear non-Scandinavian dress details from these burial mounds, such as distinct copper alloy spirals, which are characteristic applications in Late Iron Age female dress on the Finnish mainland. These spirals imply that the ethnic or cultural identity of the Viking Age inhabitants of the islands was not as purely Scandinavian as previous research has suggested (e.g. Kivikoski 1964).

Critique can also be focused on the Finnish researchers who have taken no interest, or only very limited interest in the material from Åland. The isles are often excluded completely or given only very limited space in popular or scientific books. More attention is given to the territory lost to Russia during World War II than to the Åland Islands. This bias is related to the present-day conceptualization of ethnic spaces: because of the conspicuous Swedish-speaking identity of the Åland Islands today, many Finns tend to exclude them from the national Finnish past.

The Viking Age and the Swedish-Speaking Minority on the Finnish Mainland

It is clear that the Vikings have played an important role for the Swedish-speaking minority in Finland, especially during the end of the nineteenth century and the beginning of the twentieth century, when the Swedish-speaking identity was problematized by the dominant Finnish nationalism. This can be seen in art, literature and in history writing (e.g. Fewster 2000; 2006; Vainio 2001). However, the discussion of the 'roots' of the Swedish speaking minorities has also been vivid later, as will be shown here below.

There are many examples from different areas in Finland where the Viking Age inheritance has become an important part of the heritage debate

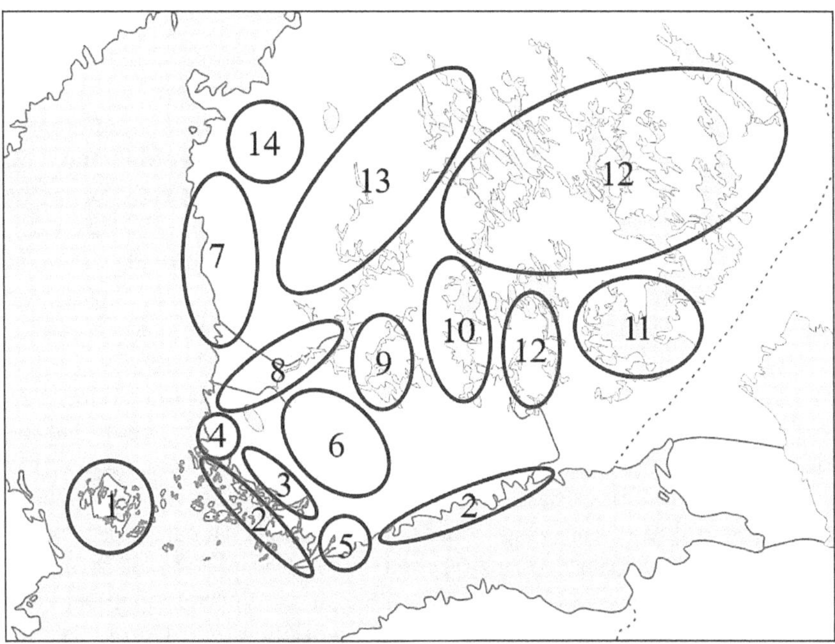

Map 1. An Interpretative Map of South and Central Finland in the Viking Age.

Key: 1. The Åland Islands: *Dense agricultural settlement, furnished cemeteries. Prominent Scandinavian cultural elements. Relative abundance of ninth and tenth century Islamic silver. Few Late Viking Age finds.* 2. Southern seaboard: *Poorly known, relatively few finds. Recent pollen evidence suggests permanent Viking Age settlements at least in some locations. Seasonal presence of fishers and traders from the South Finland interior?* 3. South-western coast (Finland Proper), eleventh century silver hoarding zone: *Relatively dense agricultural settlement, furnished cemeteries.* 4. South-western coast (Finland Proper), eleventh century silver non-hoarding zone: *Relatively dense agricultural settlement, furnished cemeteries. Few Late Viking Age finds.* 5. Western Uusimaa: *Relatively dense agricultural settlement, furnished cemeteries. Few Late Viking Age finds.* 6. South-western interior *Poorly known, relatively few finds. Some Viking Age human presence. Economic outland? Roads connecting the southwest coast to the Lakeland?* 7. Western seaboard: *Poorly known, relatively few finds. Some Viking Age human presence.* 8. River- and Lakeland of Satakunta and Pirkanmaa regions, eleventh century silver non-hoarding zone: *Relatively dense agricultural settlement, furnished cemeteries.* 9. Lakeland of Tavastia Proper, eleventh century silver hoarding zone *Relatively dense agricultural settlement, furnished cemeteries.* 10. Lakeland of Eastern Tavastia: *Some agricultural settlement. Clusters of furnished cemeteries with relatively wide distances between them. Archaeologically elusive hunter-fisher groups in some locations?* 11. Lakeland of Southern Savo and Southern Karelia: *Some agricultural settlement, but apparently less frequent than in Tavastia. Clusters of furnished cemeteries or find-sites with wide distances between them. Archaeologically elusive hunter-fisher groups in many locations.* 12. Peripheral lake districts in Eastern Finland: *Poorly known, mostly single finds. Archaeologically elusive hunter-fisher groups, but also indications of mobile or sedentary farmers at least in some locations.* 13. Watershed zone of Suomenselkä: *Poorly known, but relatively frequent single finds. Mostly if not exclusively hunter-fisher groups. Seasonal presence of South Finnish hunters and traders? A contact zone between the north-western seaboard and the interior?* 14. Southern Ostrobothnia: *Relative abundance of Pre-Viking Age finds (agricultural settlement). Viking Age poorly known, but strong evidence of continuing human presence.*

(e.g. Wickhom 2000a; 2000b; Viklund 2002; Wilson 2007; Wickholm 2008). These are mainly in the coastal areas where the Swedish-speaking minority is settled today. The Viking Age is of great importance to this minority group as it offers an evocative historical link to Sweden. However, the traditionally Swedish-speaking areas in the southern and western coasts of Finland have all been interpreted as depopulated by the Finnish archaeologists during the Viking Age.

In the 1980s, a fierce debate began between the Nationals Board of Antiquity and a group of local amateur archaeologists and enthusiasts in the Swedish-speaking areas of Ostrobothnia (Fi. Pohjanmaa) in north-western Finland. The debate originates in the almost complete lack of finds, cemeteries and settlement sites in these areas that date to the Viking Age. The local people would not accept the prevailing scholarly opinion that the Swedish minority derived from historically documented times and preferred to seek a more glorious past connected to the Vikings. When appropriate cemeteries and rune stones that could demonstrate such a past were lacking, the heritage was fabricated. This resulted in, for example, the 'discovery' of several fake runic inscriptions, which were never accepted as genuine by the Finnish Cultural Heritage administration (Taavitsainen 1980; Donner 1986).[4] The forgeries were probably made owing to a strong Swedish nationalistic affinity: the local people wanted to identify themselves with the Viking Age and they had a strong belief in an all-Swedish prehistory. These inscriptions were, and still are today, seen as authentic by some local enthusiasts (e.g. Norrman 1983). The schism between the National Board of Antiquities and the local enthusiasts went so far that a Viking Age stone-setting burial was fabricated. The artefacts, excavated by a professional archaeologist, were in fact authentic, but they had been planted in the site by unknown people only some months before the field-work (Miettinen 1984). The debate was fierce even in the Swedish-speaking newspapers (Wickholm 2000b).

This controversy resulted in a linguistic and geographical polarization between Southern Finland, with its mostly Finnish-speaking capital Helsinki, and the more rural Swedish-speaking Ostrobothnia. The local people felt that the important gentlemen in Helsinki had no real interest in peripheral archaeology and that they had been unfairly treated by the archaeologists in Helsinki (Wickholm 2000a). In 1986 the local enthusiasts in Ostrobothnia turned to Sweden and asked the archaeologists from the University of Umeå to start a research project with the aim to find the missing Viking Age in the area. This resulted in large-scale archaeological surveys and several archaeological excavations. Today, the Swedish interpretation is that the area was not deserted during the Viking Age. Instead, some Merovingian Period sites have been suggested by Swedish archaeologists to have protracted occupation into the Viking Age (Viklund 2002). In the site of Pörnullbacken in Vörå (Fi. *Vöyri*), this interpretation is strongly supported by C14 dates and artefact finds. However, there is no clear evidence of settlement sites or cemeteries being in use any longer in the area during the Late Viking Age. Also lacking are excavated and dated sites indicative of permanent settlement during the subsequent Crusade Period (AD 1050–1200). The theory of settlement continuity is mostly based on pollen analyses (Wickholm 2004). Pollen analyses indicate cultivation throughout the Viking Age. However, the Finnish researchers do not generally accept this as evidence of permanent settlement, observing that slash-and-burn agriculture was a part of a traditional long-distance resource utilization complex (Fi. *eränkäynti*) in Finland (Taavitsainen 1988). The cultivation evidence and sporadic artefact finds are explained as traces of the seasonal presence of people from South Finnish inland areas (e.g. Orrman 1991; 1993).[5]

A similar debate occurred in the Swedish speaking archipelago of Southwest Finland in 2007, when a local entrepreneur in the tourist industry published a book on Swedish place names in Finland (Wilson 2007). According to the author – who is a self-proclaimed linguist – the dominant hypothesis that the Swedish-speaking minority originated in the twelfth or thirteenth century is unsatisfying. Instead, the author wanted to prove that the Swedish-speaking minority in Finland not only dated back to the Viking Age, but to show that it could be dated even further back in the prehistory. The book can be understood as a *facsimile* from a Freudenthalian past.[6] Both the text and the pictures in that book reflect strong Viking symbolism. The debate inspired by the book was harsh, and those scholars who criticized the author were dismissed by her followers as part of the establishment or as being traditionalists (Wickholm 2008: 62).

The Finnish Mainland during the Viking Age

During the Viking Age, the Finnish mainland is roughly divided into two distinct zones. The narrow areas with furnished cemeteries were the zones inhabited by sedentary farmer communities, who also maintained hunting and fishing as subsidiary subsistence practices. As far as can be said from linguistic history and toponymic evidence, these groups were largely Finnish-speaking. They were divided into local autonomous groups (polities) with loose leadership and decision-making institutions (Asplund 2008). There is no convincing evidence of established regional leaders or institutions that could be seen to represent an early stage of an indigenous state-formation process. Weapons interred in male-gendered graves suggest that these early Finns (or Sámi) – who presumably had absolutely no idea of being Finns (or Sámi) in the present-day sense – were martial and prone to local feuding, although not necessarily into large-scale warfare (Raninen 2010).

The rest of Finland is often referred to as the "wilderness" (e.g. Taavitsainen 1990). It was inhabited by groups who are archaeologically rather elusive and are usually defined as hunter-fishers (Taavitsainen 1990; Taavitsainen *et al.* 2007). According to toponymic evidence, these must have been largely Sámi-speaking (Aikio 2006). Their lives seem to have been often mobile – for example, in Northern Lapland archaeologists have suggested that residence systems consisted of common winter settlements of local groups and dispersed summer settlements of smaller family groups (Carpelan 2003: 68, 69; Halinen 2005). However, it is difficult to tell the difference between the seasonally used settlement sites of the local hunter-fishers and the seasonally used hunting and fishing camps of predominantly agricultural groups (cf. Kumpulainen 2005). Some parts of the 'wilderness' seem, in fact, to have had fully sedentary farmer settlements (Alenius 2007), and there is evidence of at least sporadic agriculture even in North Finland. The hunter-fishers presumably had the potential to adopt small-scale slash-and-burn farming and sheep/goat rearing, even if their residence patterns were mobile.

Trade and Long-Distance Contacts

Farmer communities in Southern Finland were clearly integrated in the long-distance contact networks of the Viking Age. Many kinds of imported goods were brought into Finland through trade and also through gift-exchange related to the formation and maintenance of political alliances or social relations, and possibly through occasional raiding as well. Examples include numerous high-quality weapons, Scandinavian copper alloy ornaments, and at least occasional pieces of foreign cloth. Copper alloys must have been very important imports – not only in the form of ready-made ornaments, but also as raw material, because increasing amounts of this material was needed for the local manufacture of brooches and other ornaments and dress utensils. Copper alloy raw materials used in Northern Europe were presumably of Central European origin. Copper alloy ornaments, ingots and scrap metal were valuable enough to sometimes be hoarded and apparently also even plundered from graves (e.g. Poutiainen & Siljander 2009).

Exports must have been mostly high-value products, such as furs, and probably also slaves. The long-distance export of low-value bulk commodities like dried fish, if it existed at all, must have had a much more modest economic importance than during the fourteenth or fifteenth centuries.[7]

Although many communities in Finland had participated in long-distance exchanges long before the Viking Age, it is likely that the volume of exchanged goods now increased and the institutions of exchange were transformed and developed. The Viking Age market-place found in the isle of Hitis (Fin. *Hiittinen*) in the south-western archipelago was a completely new kind of a phenomenon (Edgren 1995). It has been suggested that it was a seasonally-used site with no permanent population (Asplund 2008: 129–133 and works there cited). Similar seasonally-used maritime market-places are known in other places around the Baltic Sea as well (e.g. Callmer 2007), and there may be other comparable sites still to be found in the coastal regions of Finland. Thus the territory of Finland certainly seems to have participated in the general development of long-distance trade and other exchange during the Viking Age. This impression is also supported by indicators of the rapid spread of external cultural influences into Finland. For example, Viking Age male dress used in Finland became in many respects similar to that on the other shores of the Baltic Sea. This evidence reflects the contacts of Finns engaging in long-distance media for expressing masculine identity rather than colonisation.

Viking Age trade of the late ninth and early- to mid-tenth centuries around the Baltic Sea was famously dominated by the eastern 'silver route' along the East European rivers (i.e. rivers in modern Russia, Belarus and Ukraine). These river-routes connected the Baltic Sea with the wealthy Moslem world. Conclusive evidence of the volume and significance of this trade is offered by nearly 400,000 Islamic silver dirhams known from hundreds of hoards found in Northern, East Central and Eastern Europe. Most of these coins were minted during the tenth century in the Samanid emirate in Central Asia. The reasons for this massive hoarding are not fully known, but most researchers now believe that these were of social or economic character (e.g. Talvio 2002; Sindbaek 2011). Religious beliefs may also have influenced the hoarding (e.g. Price 2008). The old idea that hoarding was mostly caused by warlike activities is not widely supported today, even if it should not be entirely dismissed (see below).

Seven dirham hoards of various sizes are known from the Åland Islands, while hoards from the Finnish mainland are few and mostly small. Only around 250 complete or fragmented[8] dirhams have been found in the latter, including those found in burials (Talvio 2002). This is a miniscule amount compared to the roughly 1,300 dirhams reported in the Åland Islands, 8,700 in Southeastern Baltic, 80,000 in Sweden, 37,000 in Poland, 7,500 in Denmark, 200,000 in Russia, Belarus and Ukraine, and so on (Kovalev & Kaelin 2007). It seems that many of the Finnish dirham finds were imported in a very late phase of the Islamic 'silver trade', after the year 950 – probably from Estonia (Talvio 2002: 102–104).[9] (See TALVIO.)

The lack of hoards could potentially be explained away, but we prefer the simple explanation: the Finnish mainland was really somewhat detached from the 'silver trade' and consequently had little silver during the ninth and tenth centuries. The local groups were able to obtain other kinds of prestigious or valuable imports, such as expensive Viking swords – that are actually quite numerous in Finland (Lehtosalo-Hilander 1985) – copper alloy, and so on. Nonetheless, as impressive as some of these imports are, they cannot hide the almost embarrassing rarity of dirham finds. It seems that a major form of portable wealth – silver – largely evaded ninth and tenth century Finns or Sámi. This conclusion is supported by the fact that silver ornaments are also quite rare finds. The relative lack of silver could be explained either by a surprising disinclination to obtain silver in large quantities and/or by limited economic opportunities or abilities to purchase it. The first alternative would suggest some kind of mental isolation or cultural rejection of the Viking Age 'silver fever'.[10] The latter explanation would imply that ninth- and tenth-century Finland (with the exception of the Åland Islands) was an economically peripheral part of the Viking world.

The explanation of this situation may be a geographical one: furs and slaves intended for the wealth-generating Moslem markets could be obtained in Russia. There was no obvious reason to purchase them in a remote corner like Finland, whose trade was perhaps sustained rather by the southern and western markets, which did not have much silver to offer until the late tenth or early eleventh century.[11] On the other hand, transportation costs caused by additional distance would not have been devastating when we are discussing light, high-value goods. So, perhaps some Finnish furs (and Finns or Sámi) were also, after all, sold 'down the river' in the east – but the trade was organized so that Islamic silver did not enter onto the Finnish mainland in significant quantities. This seems plausible considering the network-like character of Viking Age long-distance trade (Sindbaek 2007; 2010; 2011). In the nodal points of trade routes, great proto-urban sites were situated, and the products of the peripheries were channelled through them. The silver was probably concentrated in the hands of those who played the *intermediary role* and actively organized the transportation of goods into nodal points and between them. Those who actually trapped the furs (or slaves) and then traded them to intermediaries were not the ones to reap the largest profits.

Hypothetically, we could suggest the following pattern: *a*) fur trappers and small-scale traders (perhaps also occasional slave-dealers) from Southwest Finland (and from the north-western coast of Lake Ladoga) collected furs and other goods, some trapped by themselves and some obtained from the inhabitants of Northern, Central and Eastern Finland; and *b*) these trade-goods were then exchanged at coastal and archipelagian sites like Hitis to foreign seafaring merchants at seasonal markets.[12] These intermediary merchants may have been based at Birka, Gotland, on the Åland Islands, in coastal Estonia, etc. On a smallish and remote market-place like Hitis, there were fewer potential purchasers, and thus less demand and smaller prices to be had than in larger centres like Birka, where the intermediaries made their profits. What was perhaps lacking on the Finnish mainland were middlemen operating on a large scale, individuals and groups who would have collected truly large volumes of local merchandise and transported them directly to nodal market-centres. This pattern might explain the lack of silver from the Finnish mainland although trade still flowed in and out of the region.

Thus the Finnish mainland may have been peripheral, but it was certainly not isolated. After all, Finland shared much of its portable material culture with more central regions like Central Sweden, Gotland and the Latvian coast, although many regionally distinctive features existed as well. Furthermore, even if the hypothesis presented above is accepted, it is not necessary to assume that trade and navigation were completely in the hands of foreigners. The types of ornaments and dress utensils which were produced mostly in Southern Finland can be mentioned as evidence pointing in the opposite direction. Their distribution outside of Finland reflects contacts and possibly even movements of people with Finnish (or Sámi) origin in the wider world. Viking Age artefacts of probable Finnish origin (or Finnish inspiration) have been found in various places around the Baltic Sea, on the Scandinavian Peninsula and in Northwest Russia, as well as in few cases even further away.[13] It is interesting to note that mobility was not restricted to men: finds such as brooches and ceramic wares suggest that women from Southwest Finland may have visited and also lived on the Åland Islands and in Central Sweden, including in such places as the famous proto-urban site of Birka (e.g. Edgren 2008: 477).

Of course, Finnish finds around the Baltic Sea or in Eastern Europe are very rare compared to Scandinavian finds. It is nonetheless still probable that individuals or groups of Finnish or Sámi origin had visited places over the sea or beyond Lake Ladoga, and possibly also stayed there for long periods, even permanently. (Groups of Finnish and Sámi origin are difficult and problematic to distinguish on the basis of archaeological finds in foreign contexts because both used very similar metal ornaments during the Viking Age.) Reasons for this mobility may have included trade, diplomatic exchanges, marriages, raiding and conceivably also military service in the retinues of foreign lords – not to mention unfortunate involuntary reasons (e.g. slavery). Of course, some of the Finnish/Sámi goods found in faraway places most certainly passed through several hands instead of being carried by long-distance voyagers from Finland. However, there is no compelling reason to assume that this is the only explanation. The existence of Finnish (including Karelians) 'east-farers' during the Viking Age has been argued for by some recent researchers such as Lehtosalo-Hilander (1984; 1991) and Uino (2003: 354, 355).[14]

During the Late Viking Age (early and middle eleventh century), larger and more numerous silver hoards finally appear on the South Finnish mainland. More than 4,000 coins in 15 hoards overshadow the very limited silver import of the two previous centuries. Now the hoards contain mostly German and Anglo-Saxon coins, whose import was started around AD 1000 or slightly earlier. Some of the coins were fragmented as 'hack silver' (fragmented coins and ornaments valued by weight), and also whole or fragmented silver ornaments are present in some hoards (Hårdh 1996: 120–122; Talvio 2002). The increasing availability of silver can be seen also in the more common use of silver ornaments. This growth of portable wealth was probably a result of the fact that the major markets for northern furs were now in the west (Spiridonov 1992; Korpela 2004: 41 and works there cited). Thus, the most important fur-hunting areas were also relocated to the west, towards the Baltic Sea. This may have resulted in the formation of a new group of relatively wealthy, silver-hoarding fur-traders in some parts of Finland (Talvio 2002).[15] On the other hand, it is very likely that the possession of silver had much less significance than control of land, cattle, agricultural labour and other subsistence resources, which certainly were the most important form of wealth in these largely self-sufficient, agrarian communities.[16] It must also be noted that even the eleventh-century coin import to Finland seems rather modest compared to the contemporary affluence of western silver in some parts of Scandinavia, Slavic areas of North-Central Europe and Northwest Russia (e.g. Korpela 2004: 39).

Settlement Expansion and Colonization

During the Viking Age, furnished cemeteries became more common in the South Finnish inland, in the southern parts of the so-called Lake District. In the present-day region of Päijät-Häme (Eastern Tavastia), this growth is visible already around AD 800. In the more eastern regions of Southern Savo and South Karelia, it is clearer during the Late Viking Age (Taavitsainen 1988; 1990: 63, 71, 72). Beyond the modern Russian border, on the western coast of Ladoga, similar developments were taking place from the ninth century onwards (Uino 1997; 2003). All of this indicates a significant social and demographic transition in this large area. It was probably connected with western (presumably Finnish-speaking) colonization to at least some degree, although the earlier inland population (probably Sámi-speakers) must also have participated in this expansion as well. It is possible that the colonization and expansion were partially triggered a by growing demand for furs, which were hunted inland.

The location of larger, wealthier or more long-lasting farmer settlements deep inland – the ones with furnished cemeteries – was largely decided by agro-geological factors, such as the presence of reasonably fertile soil types that could be tilled with very primitive ploughs (Orrman 1991). At the same time, these settlements were situated along the vast Finnish lake systems, which offered excellent access to more distant hunting and fishing areas within the interior. Indeed, seasonal utilization of various long-distance resources remained an essential part of the farmer economy in this area until the late sixteenth century. The inland settlers could either hunt by themselves or obtain products from the earlier (presumably Sámi-speaking) hunter-fishers groups living around the lake-basins (Taavitsainen 1994a). Traditionally, Finnish researchers have thought that the attitude of the inland farmers towards the Sámi was highly exploitative and aggressive (e.g. Jaakkola 1935). More recently, doubts have been raised whether raiding or tribute-exaction were the best possible means to obtain anything from a dispersed and mobile population of experienced big-game hunters and archers. Considering the sheer practical difficulties of such pursuits, it seems likely that the relationship between the two groups was often peaceful, mutually beneficial and characterized by trade or gift-exchanges – at least as long as they did not enter into rivalry for the same subsistence resources.[17]

One of the most interesting facts concerning the Viking Age in Finland is that the number of various finds in 'wilderness' regions – i.e. the regions with no or very few furnished cemeteries – rises dramatically in this period (see also Kuusela).[18] This can be seen as a sign of increasing contacts between the inland farmers and hunter-fishers, and also of the proper start of market-oriented fur-hunting, whose products were largely intended for export. The control and defence of the most valuable fur-procurement areas may have become a crucial issue for maintaining wealth, power and trading contacts (Taavitsainen 1994b). When furnished cemeteries appeared in the interior, they were situated along water-routes, often at their termini or starting points (Taavitsainen 1990: 65).

Moreover, a new type of boat seems to have been introduced on Finnish lakes during the Viking Age. The so-called *Mekrijärvi* type of keel timber boat (Fi. *haapio*) was a light vessel that could be transported from one water-system to another by portages. In addition, the *ahkio*, a boat-like sledge made with a clinker technique, may be a Viking Age innovation (Taavitsainen 1999). Technological developments like these were presumably inspired by the increasing mobility of people and goods. To put it briefly, the expansionism and long-distance mobility generally associated with the Viking Age seem to manifest themselves even in the deep Finnish and Sámi peripheries – even if they were there related to movements of local groups, and only indirectly connected to the proper, Scandinavian 'Vikings'.

Violent Contacts

The Viking Age is usually stereotyped as one of endemic warfare. Yet there is not much to say about Viking Age warfare in Finland.[19] Runic inscriptions and the Old Norse literature contain some references to Scandinavian raids targeting regions usually identified as Southern Finland during the early eleventh century (Larsson 1990: 119, 120; Schalin 2008). These include at least one defeat of seaborne raiders by the local population and a couple of Norse casualties during other incidents as well. No archaeological finds can be conclusively associated with Viking Age raids. However, Salo (2000) has argued for the traditional interpretation according to which the eleventh century silver-hoards were hidden during military threats. This view has been criticized by Taavitsainen (1990: 156–158) and Talvio (2002: 117–120), who correctly stress that there may have been various social and economic reasons for depositing silver in the ground.

It has been often suggested that the Viking threat prevented the permanent inhabitation on the South Finnish coast bordering on the Gulf of Finland and even depopulated the existing settlement in Western Uusimaa in the present-day district of Raasepori (Sw. Raseborg). There is no direct evidence of this, and it is questionable if the coast was really devoid of permanent settlement given that new pollen evidence and occasional finds seem to rather suggest the existence of permanent populations in some locations (Leskinen & Pesonen 2009; Alenius 2011). Of course, *some* risks must have been involved in residence in places which were easily accessible from the sea and not too far from regularly sailed routes, as even materially poor settlements could be targeted by slave-raiders. However, the sea provided livelihood by both marine exploitation and trade, making the risk of raiding a threat faced by all people living in maritime environments in the Baltic region at this time.

There is no written information of possible Finnish raids made around the Baltic Sea or Lake Ladoga. Only in the late twelfth and early thirteenth century do we have Russian chronicles mentioning incidents whose perpetrators might have come from Southern Finland. The limited amount of the silver-finds in the region may suggest that raids were not made very often – or very successfully – during the ninth or tenth centuries. Later, some of the eleventh-century silver and other wealth found in Finland was possibly obtained by plundering.[20]

The possibility of some Finnish or Sámi men serving in foreign military retinues or in mercenary bands was briefly mentioned above. Professional warriors of the era often went into the service of foreign lords, so the idea is not necessarily far-fetched. A martial society like Viking Age Finland could presumably produce adventurers or misfits inclined to live by the sword (or axe) (cf. Ahola).[21] On the other hand, there is absolutely nothing to suggest that there would have been any major movement of warriors from Finland into foreign service, and the curious cases of special individuals are always hard to confirm archaeologically. There are nevertheless some intriguing finds that might – just might, and no more – be associated with such warriors who returned home and were buried in Finland. Space does not allow us to discuss them here, and such an interpretation of the evidence cannot advance beyond speculation (see however Edberg 1999; Hedenstierna-Jonson 2006). In any case, many such males would have died in foreign lands, where they may be archaeologically unidentifiable, as they were not necessarily buried according to the rites of their native culture.

Conclusion

Although imported prestigious materials such as silver, copper alloys, or glass-beads were not basic necessities (cf. Sindbaek 2011), it is clear that the people living in Finland went to great effort to obtain them. They somehow made the long-distance contacts as a meaningful – even essential – component of their life-worlds and social realities. Negotiations of social status and gender involved imported materials and artefacts, and it is conceivable that participation in long-distance voyages and knowledge of far-away places were important sources of individual authority and power as such. In this sense, it is clear that Finland was a part of the Viking world. However, it is very unlikely that many people in the present-day territories of Finland would have regarded themselves as a 'Viking' let alone 'Norse' in the late first millennium AD. In addition, it must be fairly acknowledged that Finland, despite its Nordic credentials, has no superior claim to Viking heritage compared to other non-Scandinavian countries around the Baltic Sea: for example, a country like Latvia probably had a stronger Scandinavian presence and livelier maritime contacts during the Viking Age than Finland did. However, Latvia is not usually included among the Nordic nations, for reasons entirely dependent on modern political history (cf. Heininen *et al.*). The Viking images that still go on rampages in our wishes, fantasies and pop culture clichés have more to do with nineteenth- and twentieth-century ideologies than the actual happenings during the late first millennium AD. This chapter is both a symptom of and – we hope – a dose of antidote to the modern-day Viking obsession.

Notes

1 It is interesting to consider comparison of Finland with Estonia, its neighbour to the south, where the ideology of 'Nordic with a twist' has recently been adopted to emancipate the country from East European and post-Soviet labels. It is not surprising that present-day Estonian archaeology gives much attention to the western and Scandinavian contacts (e.g. Kriiska & Tvauri 2008).

2 See Nuñez 1993 and 1995 for overviews of the settlement development and cultural ecology of the Åland Islands during the first millennium AD.

3 See e.g. Kivikoski 1964; Dreijer 1974; Hellberg 1980; Ringbom 1994; Roeck Hansen 1994.

4 Only one fragment from a Viking Age rune stone has been found in Finland. This piece was found in 0.5 meters deep water in Hitis in south-western Finland in 1997. It probably derives from the ballast of a ship and is hence from a secondary context (Åhlén *et al.* 1998).

5 Recently, Holmblad (in Herrgård & Holmblad 2005) and Kuusela *et al.* (2011) have presented balanced intermediate views on this issue, suggesting settlement continuity but also a social collapse or at least a thorough structural transformation in Viking Age Ostrobothnia. Regarding the linguistic ancestry of the present-day Swedish-speakers of the region, it must be noted that even undisputed settlement continuity would prove nothing of prehistoric languages spoken there, as language shifts are not rare and past languages cannot be determined from non-textual archaeological finds. The question of Iron Age languages spoken in Ostrobothnia must be left for linguists (see Ivars & Huldén 2002; Häkkinen 2010).

6 Axel Olof Freudenthal (1836–1911) was a Swedish-speaking philologist and a politician. He was one of the leading ideologists for the nationalist movement of Finland's Swedish-speaking minority in the nineteenth century. Due to certain racial views that he held, he is a somewhat controversial figure in present-day Finland.

7 See Masonen (1989), who, however, downplays the possibility of slave-trade; cf. Barrett *et al.* (2009) regarding the Viking Age fish trade.

8 The dirhems were sometimes fragmented as their value in Northern and Eastern Europe was usually measured according to their weight; a fragment of a coin could be used as a relatively low-value means of payment. Silver ornaments or their fragments could also be used as means of payment, having equal value as coins weighing the same. Fragmented coins and ornaments are generally known as 'hack silver'.

9 In addition to the dirhams, there were some other eastern imports as well: for example, the rare silken dress found in a tenth century male burial in Luistari, Eura (Lehtosalo-Hilander 1982: 171); the Islamic or Mediterranean glass beads and West Asian carnelian beads worn by females in necklaces (Lehtosalo-Hilander 1982: 130–142); the rare cowrie shells from the Indian Ocean, used in necklaces and found in three sites in Finland (Poutiainen & Siljander 2009: 87); and the metal-mounted belts of East European origin or inspiration (Lehtosalo-Hilander 1982: 152–154).

10 According to Bogucki (2007), silver was almost completely rejected in tenth-century Prussia, despite the fact that the region took active part in inter-regional trade.

11 However, Finland seems to have been in a peripheral position even in the western trade. Many categories of exclusive continental imports of the ninth and tenth centuries, such as fine ceramics or glass vessels, are almost completely lacking in the Finnish record.

12 Inhabitants of Eastern Finland presumably maintained their trade contacts around Lake Ladoga as well, where the proto-urban nodal point of Staraya Ladoga on the River Volkhov was accessible by ships (e.g. Uino 2003: 355; Korpela 2004: 46, 47).

13 Lehtosalo-Hilander 1991, 1993: 36–37; Lehtosalo-Hilander & Wahlstedt 2001; Nosov & Khvoschinskaya 2006; Spirgis 2006.

14 Already long before the Viking Age, artefacts from Central and Eastern Russia were sporadically distributed in Finland, obviously as a result of contacts between various Finno-Ugrian groups. These contacts seem to become more intense during the Merovingian Period (AD 550–800), possibly involving long-distance voyaging and direct contacts between widely separated areas (e.g. Meinander 1950: 119–123; Uino 2003: 306, 307). It is intriguing to ponder how these native contact networks may have influenced the development of Viking Age trade systems (Carpelan

2006). In addition, during the Viking Age, the possibility of internal long-distance contacts among the Finno-Ugrians should be considered. For example, the distribution of a type of firesteels seems to plausibly indicate Viking Age contacts between Finland and Eastern Russia (Lehtosalo-Hilander 1991). Indications of contacts between Eastern Finland and the Finnic (Vepsian) area on the south-eastern side of Ladoga exist as well (Taavitsainen 1990: 112, 113).

15 Interestingly, the north-western zone of South Finnish settlements (regions of northern Finland Proper, Satakunta and Pirkanmaa) completely lacks even the eleventh-century silver hoards, despite the relative wealth and presence of silver in furnished burials. This has been explained either by peaceful conditions (e.g. Salo 2000) or by some sort of social and economic difference between the silver-hoarding and non-hoarding regions (e.g. Talvio 2002 and Talvio).

16 Not much is known of the actual use of silver coins in eleventh-century Finland. With one exception (a hoard from Hattula, Tavastia Proper), the percentage of hack silver in Finnish hoards is relatively low, suggesting that silver was not commonly used as a means of payment in every-day transactions of low-value goods (Hårdh 1996: 123, 124). Probably, the use of silver was largely confined to rare, high-value purchases, and to non-market spheres of exchange: conceivably the silver could be used as political gifts, religious sacrifices or as highly specialized means of payment used to pay bridal prices, compensations, ransoms, etc. There is even a hypothesis that a major cause for the Viking raiding in general could be the attributed to a need for unmarried, young males to obtain silver for a bride-price (Barrett 2008).

17 Carpelan 1984; Taavitsainen *et al.* 2007; for a similar transformation in views concerning the relationship between the Viking Age Sámi and the Scandinavians, see Olsen 2003.

18 Regarding Central and Eastern Finland, see Taavitsainen 1990; 1994a; 1994b; 1999; Taavitsainen *et al.* 2007; regarding less-researched Northern Finland, see Huurre 1983; Kuusela *et al.* 2011; Kuusela.

19 For summaries covering most aspects in more detail than is possible here, see Taavitsainen 1990; Raninen 2010; Moilanen 2010.

20 On the meagre written evidence regarding the inland raids made by 'Kvens' (possibly a Finnic group) in Northern Fennoscandia during the Viking Age and later, see Valtonen 2008; regarding the archaeology of the 'Kvens', see Wallerström 1995.

21 A possible Scandinavian cultural/religious influence related to martial lifeways of the Viking Age is the practice of depositing (sacrificing?) weapons in water or in the ground outside of burial contexts. This phenomenon has been often overlooked in Finland, but it has been recently discussed by Luoto (2009).

References

Åhlén, Marit, Tuovinen, Tapani & Myhrman, Hans. 1998. Ett runstensfragment från Hitis. *Muinaistutkija* 1998 (1). Pp. 18–20.

Aikio, Ante. 2006. The Study of Saami Substrate Toponyms in Finland. In Ritva-Liisa Pitkänen & Janne Saarikivi (eds.). *The Borrowing of Place-names in the Uralic Languages.* Onomastica Uralica 4. Debrecen: 159–197.

Alenius, Teija. 2007. *Environmental Change and Anthropogenic Impact on Lake Sediments during the Holocene in the Finnish–Karelian Inland Area.* Publications of the Department of Geology D11. Helsinki: University of Helsinki.

Alenius, Teija. 2011. From Forest to a Farmland: Palaeoenvironmental Reconstruction of the Colonization of Western Uusimaa. In Georg Haggrén & Mika Lavento (eds.): *Maritime Landscape in Change: Archaeological, Historical, Palaeoecological and Geological Studies on Western Uusimaa.* Iskos 19. Pp. 87–116.

Barrett, James H. 2008. What Caused the Viking Age? *Antiquity* 82(317): 671–685.

Barrett, James H., Alison M. Locker & Callum M. Roberts. 2009. 'Dark Age Economics' Revisited: The English Fish-Bone Evidence. In Louis Sicking & Darlene Abreu-Ferrera (eds.). *Beyond the Catch: Fisheries of the North Atlantic, the North Sea and the Baltic, 900–1850.* The Northern World 41. Leiden / Boston: Brill. Pp. 31–59.

Bogucki, Mateusz. 2007. Coin Finds in the Viking-Age Emporium of Janów Pomorski (*Truso*) and the 'Prussian Phenomenon'. In Stanis³aw Suchodolski (ed.). *The Middle Ages and Modern Times: Time, Range, Intensity.* Institute of Archaeology and Ethnology. Warsaw / Cracow: Polish Academy of Sciences. Pp. 65–78.

Callmer, Johan. 1994. The Clay Paw Burial Rite of the Åland Islands and Central Russia: A Symbol in Action. *Current Swedish Archaeology* 2: 13–46.

Callmer, Johan. 2007. Urbanisation in Northern and Eastern Europe, ca. AD 700–1100. In Joachim Hennig (ed.). *Post-Roman Towns, Trade and Settlement in Europe and Byzantium I: The Heirs of the Roman West.* Berlin / New York: Walter de Gruyter. Pp. 233–270.

Carpelan, Christian. 1984. Katsaus saamelaisten esihistoriaan. In *Suomen väestön esihistorialliset juuret.* Bidrag till kännedom av Finlands natur och folk 131. Helsinki: Suomen Tiedeseura. Pp. 97–109.

Carpelan, Christian. 2003. Inarilaisten arkeologiset vaiheet. In Veli-Pekka Lehtola (ed.). *Inari - Aaanar: Inarin historia jääkaudesta nykypään.* Oulu: Inarin kunta.

Carpelan, Christian. 2006. On Archaeological Aspects of Uralic, Finno-Ugric and Finnic Societies before AD 800. In Juhani Nuorluoto (ed.). *The Slavicization of the Russian North: Mechanisms and Chronology.* Slavica Helsingiensia 27. Helsinki: Department of Slavonic and Baltic Languages and Literatures, Helsinki University. Pp. 78–92.

Donner, Joakim. 1986. Bidrag till kännedom om Vörårunornas ålder: Exempel på ristningsteknik använd I runskrifter och hällristningar. *Fennoscandia archaeologica* 3: 73–80.

Dreijer, Matts. 1969. Det återfunna Birka. *Åländsk Odling* 30: 3–35.

Dreijer, Matts. 1974. Åland och Bircaproblemet. *Åländsk Odling* 35: 31–47.

Duczko, Wladyslaw. 2004. *Viking Rus: Studies on the Presence of Scandinavians in Eastern Europe.* The Northern World 12. Brill: Leiden / Boston.

Edberg, Rune. 1999. Krigaramuletter från Rus' i Sigtunas svarta jord. *Fornvännen* 94: 245–253.

Edgren, Torsten. 1995. Kyrksundet i Hitis: Ett arkeologiskt forskningsprojekt kring en av "det danska itinerariets" hamnar i det sydvästra Finlands skärgård. *Budkavlen* 1995: 48–66.

Edgren, Torsten. 2008. The Viking Age in Finland. In Stefan Brink (ed.). *The Viking World.* London / New York: Routledge. Pp. 470–484.

Fewster, Derek (ed.) 2000. *Folket. Studier i olika vetenskapers syn på begreppen folk.* Skrifter utgivna av Svenska litteratursällskapet i Finland. Helsingfors: Svenska litteratursällskapet i Finland.

Fewster, Derek. 2006. *Visions of past Glory: Nationalism and the Construction of Early Finnish History.* Studia Fennica, Historica 11. Helsinki: SKS Finnish Literature Society.

Halinen, Petri. 2005. *The Prehistoric Hunters of Northernmost Lapland.* Iskos 14. Helsinki: Suomen Muinaismuistoyhdistys.

Hedenstierna-Jonson, Charlotte. 2006. *The Birka Warrior: The Material Culture of a Martial Society.* Stockholm: Stockholm University.

Hellberg, Lars. 1980. Ortnamnen och den svenska bosättningen på Åland. In *Ortnamn och samhälle* 2. Uppsala: Uppsala Universitet.

Herrgård, Mikael, & Peter Holmblad. 2005. *Fornminnen i Österbotten: Från neandertalare till sockenbor.* Acta Antiqua Ostrobotniensia, Studier i Österbottens förhistoria 6. Vasa: Scriptum.

Hiekkanen, Markus. 2010. Burial Practices in Finland From Bronze Age to the Early Middle Ages. In Bertil Nilsson (ed.). *Från hedniskt till kristet: Förändringar i begravningsbruk och gravskick i Skandinavien, c:a 800–1200*. Stockholm: Sällskapet Runica et Mediævalia. Pp. 270–380.

Huurre, Matti. 1983. *Esihistoria: Pohjois-Pohjanmaan ja Lapin historia 1*. Oulu.

Hårdh, Birgitta. 1996. *Silver in the Viking Age: A Regional-Economic Study*. Acta Archaeologica Lundensia 8:25. Stockholm: Almqvist & Wiksell.

Häkkinen, Jaakko. 2010. Jatkuvuusperustelut ja saamelaisen kielen leviäminen: Osa 2. *Muinaistutkija* 2010(2): 51–64.

Ivars, Ann-Marie, & Lena Huldén (ed.). 2002. *När kom svenskarna till Finland?* Studier utg. av Svenska Litteratursällskapet i Finland 646. Helsingfors: Svenska Litteratursällskapet i Finland.

Jaakkola, Jalmari. 1935. *Suomen varhaishistoria*. Suomen historia II. Helsinki: WSOY.

Karlsson, Marita. 1987. *Åländska husgrunder från yngre järnålder – tidig medeltid*. Mariehamn: Ålands Museum.

Kivikoski, Ella. 1949. Birka ja Suomi. *Kalevalaseuran vuosikirja* 29: 56–70.

Kivikoski, Ella. 1964. *Finlands förhistoria*. Helsingfors: Schildt.

Korpela, Jukka. 2004. *Viipurin linnaläänin synty*. Viipurin läänin historia II. Jyväskylä: Gummerus.

Kovalev, Roman & Kaelin, Alexis C. 2007. Circulation of Arab Silver in Medieval Afro-Eurasia: Preliminary Observations. *History Compass* 5 / 2. Pp. 560–580.

Kriiska, Aivar, & Anders Tvauri. 2007. *Viron esihistoria*. Suomalaisen Kirjallisuuden Seuran Toimituksia 1105. Helsinki: Suomalaisen Kirjallisuuden Seura.

Kumpulainen, Miikka. 2005. Eräsija ja eränkäynti: Sisämaan rautakauden ja keskiajan asuinpaikat. Petro Pesonen & Teemu Mökkönen (eds.). *Arkeologipäivät 2004*. Hamina: Suomen Arkeologinen Seura. Pp. 60–73.

Kuusela, Jari-Matti, Jasse Tiilikkala, Riku-Ville Vaske & Jari Okkonen. 2011. Keskus-periferia-malli Pohjois-Suomen rautakauden tarkastelun apuna. *Faravid* 35: 177–204.

Larsson, Mats G. 1990. *Runstenar och utlandsfärder*. Acta Archaeologica Lundensia 8:18. Stockholm.

Lehtosalo-Hilander, Pirkko-Liisa. 1982. *Luistari II: The Artifacts*. Suomen Muinaismuistoyhdistyksen Aikakauskirja 82:2. Helsinki: Suomen Muinaismuistoyhdistys.

Lehtosalo-Hilander, Pirkko-Liisa. 1984. Keski- ja myöhäisrautakausi. *Suomen historia* 1. Espoo: Weilin / Göös. Pp. 250–405.

Lehtosalo-Hilander, Pirkko-Liisa. 1985. Viikinkiajan aseista: Leikkejä luvuilla ja lohikäärmeillä. *Suomen Museo* 92: 5–36.

Lehtosalo-Hilander, Pirkko-Liisa. 1991. Le Viking finnois. *Finskt Museum* 1990: 55–72.

Lehtosalo-Hilander, Pirkko-Liisa. 1993. Finnland zur Wikingerzeit: Monarchie oder gleichwertige Gesellschaft. *Karhunhammas* 15: 25–43.

Lehtosalo-Hilander, Pirkko-Liisa. 2000. *Luistari IV: A History of Weapons and Ornaments*. Suomen Muinaismuistoyhdistyksen Aikakauskirja 107. Helsinki: Suomen Muinaismuistoyhdistys.

Lehtosalo-Hilander, Pirkko-Liisa (ed.). 2001. *Viikinkejä Eurassa? Pohjoismaisia näkökulmia Suomen esihistoriaan*. Eura: Euran muinaispukutoimikunta.

Leskinen, Sirpa, & Petro Pesonen. 2009. *Vantaan esihistoria*. Vantaa: Vantaan kaupunki.

Luoto, Jukka. 2009. Suomen esihistoriallisista uhrilöydöistä. In Hannu Poutiainen (ed.). *Hirviveneestä hullukaaliin: Muinaisuskomukset arkeologisen aineiston tulkinnassa*. Päijät-Hämeen Tutkimusseuran Vuosikirja 2008–2009. Lahti: Päijät-Hämeen Tutkimusseura. Pp. 12–33.

Masonen, Jaakko. 1989. *Hämeen Härkätie: Synty ja varhaisvaiheet*. Tiemuseon Julkaisuja 4. Helsinki: Multikustannus.

Meinander, C. F. 1950. *Etelä-Pohjanmaan historia I: Esihistoria*. Etelä-Pohjanmaan historia I–II. Helsinki: Etelä-Pohjanmaan historiatoimikunta. Pp. 7–236.

Miettinen, Mirja. 1984. Vörå Rejpelt Båtholmen. Unpublished excavation report. National Board of Antiquities, Helsinki, Finland.

Moilanen, Mikko. 2010. Katsaus korjausten ja käytön jälkiin Suomen rautakauden miekkalöydöissä. *Muinaistutkija* 2010(4): 2–13.

Nordman, C. A. 1944. Svenskarna i Finlands järnålder. *Nordisk Tidskrift för Vetenskap, Konst och Industri* 1944: 313–330.

Norrman, Ralf. 1983. *Vörårunorna I: En bok om runskrifterna i Höjsal och Härtull.* Jakobstad: Jakobstads Tryckeri.

Nosov, Evgeny N., & Natalia V. Khvoschinskaya. 2006. Links of the Population of Western Finland and Estonia with the Central Ilmen Region in the Context of International Trade in the Baltic Area Region in the 9th–10th Century. In H. Valk (ed.). *Etnos ja kultuur: Uurimusi Silvia Laulu auks.* Muinaisaja teadus 18. Tartu / Tallinn: Tartu Ülikooli Arheoloogia Õppetool. Pp. 147–156.

Nuñez, Milton. 1993. Searching for a Structure in the Late Iron Age Settlement of the Åland Islands, Finland. *Karhunhammas* 15: 61–75.

Nuñez, Milton. 1995. Agrarian Colonization and Settlement of the Åland Islands in the First Millennium AD. *Fennoscandia Archaeologica* 12: 113–122.

Olsen, Bjørnar. 2003. Belligerent Chieftains and Oppressed Hunters? - Changing Conceptions of Interethnic Relationships in Northern Norway during the Iron Age and Early Medieval Period. In James H. Barrett (ed.). *Contact, Continuity, and Collapse: The Norse Colonization of the North Atlantic.* Studies in the Early Middle Ages 5. Turnhout: Brepols. Pp. 9–32.

Orrman, Eljas. 1991. Geographical Factors in the Spread of Permanent Settlement in Parts of Finland and Sweden from the End of the Iron Age to the Beginning of the Modern Times. *Fennoscandia Archaeologica* 8: 3–21.

Orrman, Eljas. 1993. Where Source Criticism Fails. *Fennoscandia Archaeologica* 10: 77–82.

Poutiainen, Hannu, & Eero Siljander. 2009. Päijät-Hämeen rautakautiset aarre- ja korukätkölöydöt. In Hannu Poutiainen (ed.). *Hirviveneestä hullukaaliin: Muinaisuskomukset arkeologisen aineiston tulkinnassa.* Päijät-Hämeen Tutkimusseuran Vuosikirja 2008–2009. Lahti: Päijät-Hämeen Tutkimusseura. Pp. 82–101.

Price, Neil. 2008. Dying and the Dead: Viking Age Mortuary Behaviour. In Stefan Brink (ed.). *The Viking World.* London / New York: Routledge. Pp. 257–273.

Raninen, Sami. 2010. Sodankäynti ja soturit rautakaudella. In Hannele Klemettilä (ed.). *Suomalainen sotilas 3: Muinaisurhosta nihtiin.* Hämeenlinna: Weilin & Göös. Pp. 46–79.

Ringbom, Åsa. 1994. Dateringen av Ålands kyrkor. *Historisk tidskrift för Finland* 1994(3): 459–493.

Roeck Hansen, Birgitta. 1995. Change and Continuity: Land-Use in Åland from the Late Iron Age to the 18th Century. In A. Nissinaho (ed.). *Cultural Ecology: One Theory?* Turku: University of Turku.

Salo, Unto. 2000. Suomi ja Häme, Häme ja Satakunta. In Jukka Peltovirta (ed.). *Hämeen käräjät I.* Hämeenlinna: Hämeen heimoliitto. Pp. 18–230.

Schalin, Johan. 2008. Hårdalar, namnet Karis och den första nedtecknade händelsen i Finlands historia. *Finsk tidskrift: Kultur - ekonomi - politik* 2008(8): 414–428.

Sindbæk, Søren M. 2007. Networks and Nodal Points: The Emergence of Towns in Early Viking Age Scandinavia. *Antiquity* 81: 119–132.

Sindbæk, Søren M. 2009. Open Access, Nodal Points, and Central Places: Maritime Communication and Locational Principles for Coastal Sites in South Scandinavia, c. AD 400–1200. *Estonian Journal of Archaeology* 13(2): 96–109.

Sindbæk, Søren M. 2011. Silver Economies and Social Ties: Long-Distance Interaction, Long-Term Investments - and Why the Viking Age Happened. In Graham Campbell, Søren M. Sindbæk & Gareth Williams (eds.). *Silver Economies, Monetisation and Society in Scandinavia, AD 800–1100.* Aarhus: Aarhus University Press. Pp. 41–65.

Spirgis, Roberts. 2006. Chain Ornaments with Tortoise Brooches as a Source for Interpreting the Origin of the Daugava Livs in the 10th–13th century. In H. Valk (ed.). *Etnos ja kultuur: Uurimusi Silvia Laulu auks.* Muinaisaja teadus 18. Tartu / Tallinn: Tartu Ülikooli Arheoloogia Õppetool. Pp. 227–248.

Spiridonov, A. M. 1992. Karelians in the North of Fennoscandia in the 11–13th Centuries: A View from the East. In Kyösti Julku (ed.). *Suomen varhaishistoria: Tornion kongressi 14.–16.6.1991.* Studia Historica Septentrionalia 21. Rovaniemi: Pohjois-Suomen historiallinen yhdistys. Pp. 559–567.

Taavitsainen, Jussi-Pekka. 1980. Runskriften vid Höjsal träsk i Vörå. *Horisont* 3/1980.

Taavisainen, J.-P. 1988. Wide-Range Hunting and Swidden Cultivation as Prerequisites of Iron Age Colonization in Finland. *Suomen Antropologi* 1987(4): 213–233.

Taavitsainen, J.-P. 1990. *Ancient Hillforts of Finland: Problems of Analysis, Chronology and Interpretation with Special Reference to the Hillfort of Kuhmoinen.* Suomen Muinaismuistoyhdistyksen Aikakauskirja 94. Helsinki: Suomen Muinaismuisto-yhdistys.

Taavitsainen, J.-P. 1994a. Kaskeaminen ja metsästys erämailla. In Pekka Laaksonen & Sirkka-Liisa Mettomäki (eds.). *Metsä ja metsänviljaa.* Kalevalaseuran vuosikirja 73. Helsinki: Suomaliasen Kirjallisuuden Seura. Pp. 187–207.

Taavitsainen, J.-P. 1994b. Östra Tavastland som samfälld erämark. *Historisk Tidskrift för Finland* 1994(3): 391–412.

Taavitsainen, J.-P. 1999. Wilderness Commerce and the Development of Boat Types: The Remains of the Hartola Boat. In Matti Huurre (ed.). *Dig It All: Papers Presented to Ari Siiriäinen.* Helsinki: The Finnish Antiquarian Society / The Archaeological Society of Finland. Pp. 307–316.

Taavitsainen, J.-P., Janne Vilkuna & Henry Forssell. 2007. *Suojoki at Keuruu: A Mid 14th -Century Site of the Wilderness Culture in the Light of Settlement Historical Processes in Central Finland.* Helsinki: The Finnish Academy of Sciences.

Talvio, Tuukka. 2002. *Coins and Coin Finds in Finland AD 800–1200.* Iskos 12. Helsinki: Suomen Muinaismuistoyhdistys.

Tomtlund, Jan-Erik. 2005. *Vikingatid på Åland.* Mariehamn: Ålands Landskapsregering, Museibyrån.

Uino, Pirjo. 1997. *Ancient Karelia: Archaeological Studies.* Suomen Muinaismuisto-yhdistyksen Aikakauskirja 104. Helsinki: Suomen Muinaismuistoyhdistys.

Uino, Pirjo. 2003. Viikinkiaika. In Matti Saarnisto (ed.). *Karjalan synty.* Viipurin läänin historia I. Lappeenranta: Karjalaisen Kulttuurin Edistämissäätiö. Pp. 313–382.

Vainio, Maria (ed.) 2001. *Nylands nationshus 1901-2001.* Samling utgivna av Nylands Nation XII. Helsingfors: Nylands nation.

Valtonen, Irmeli. 2008. *The North in Old English Orosius: A Geographical Narrative in Context.* Helsinki: Socieìteì Neìophilologique.

Viklund, Karin. 2002. *Från romartid till vikingatid: Pörnullbacken - en järnåldertida bosättning i Österbotten.* Vasa: Scriptum.

Wallerström, Thomas. 1995. *Norrbotten, Sverige och medeltiden: Problem kring makt och bosättning i en europeisk periferi.* Lund Studies in Medieval Archaelogy 15:1. Stockholm.

Wickholm, Anna. 2000a. Kontinuitet - Nationalitet - Identitet: Fyndotmheten i teorins ljus i det vikingatida västra Nyland, Österbotten och Åland. Unpublished Master's thesis, University of Helsinki.

Wickholm, Anna. 2000b. Järnåldersbosättningen i Österbotten samt fyndtomheten i ljuset av runstensdebatten: Arkeologi som ett försök att legitimera sin identitet. In Marika Lindström, Laura Mattsson & Antti Pokela (eds.). *Extremt Österbotten.* Historicus Skriftserie 14. Vantaa: Historicus. Pp. 105–124.

Wickholm, Anna. 2004. Pörnullbacken: Ett brandgravfält eller brandgropsgravar? *Muinaistutkija* 2003(4): 47–51.

Wickholm, Anna. 2008. En tankeväckande men förbryllande bok om finlandssvenska ortnamn och arkeologi. *Muinaistutkija* 2008(1): 60–67.

Wilson, Paula. 2007. *Röster från forntiden: Gamla ortnamn berättar.* Keuruu: Schildts.

Elina Salmela

The (Im)Possibilities of Genetics for Studies of Population History

The genetic structure of populations – groups of interbreeding individuals – is dependent on demographic factors such as population size, movements and contacts. Conversely, the genetic composition of a population, including the genetic diversity within a population and the genetic similarities between populations, can be used to infer events of population history.[1] In principle, genetics can provide a rich and independent source of population-history information; in practice, however, its conclusions are often limited by data availability as well as by theoretical constraints.

This chapter will first describe the basic mechanisms of inheritance from parents to offspring and their interplay with other factors in producing the genetic structure of populations. It will then describe some basic principles of genetic population-history inference, followed by a discussion of the main limitations of its potential. Because the latter appear serious in the specific question of the Viking Age in Finland, actual genetic evidence related to Vikings will be touched on only very briefly, whereas further attention will be devoted to the overall genetic structure of the Finnish population, including indications of its contacts with Sweden.

The Structure of the Human Genome and Some Basic Concepts

Hereditary information is encoded by deoxyribonucleic acid (DNA), specifically in the sequence of its four constituent bases (which are typically denoted A, T, C and G). In humans, the hereditary information – the human genome – contains 3.2 billion basepairs (bp) of DNA. It consists of 23 chromosome pairs located in the cell nucleus: one pair of sex chromosomes (XY in males and XX in females) and 22 pairs of non-sex chromosomes called autosomes. Additionally, the mitochondrion, which is the energy-producing organelle of the cells, has a small (c. 17,000 bp) circular DNA of its own. Notably, less than 2 per cent of the human genome codes for proteins, and while some of the non-coding DNA has a regulatory role, the majority of the genome has no known function. (See e.g. Strachan & Read 2011.)

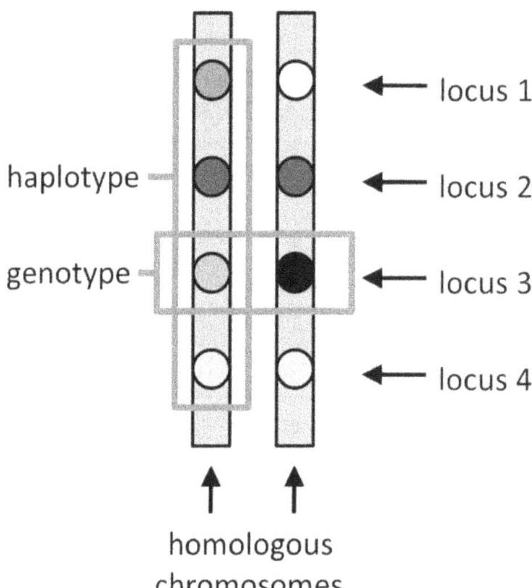

Fig. 1. A schematic representation of two homologous chromosomes (i.e. a chromosome pair). The small circles denote alleles in four loci along the chromosomes. The individual is homozygous for loci 2 and 4, and heterozygous for loci 1 and 3.

A given location in the DNA is called a locus (plural loci), and the different forms of DNA present at a locus are alleles. Loci or alleles are often loosely referred to as genes, as in the term 'gene pool', which stands for the set of all alleles of a population, although not all loci are protein-coding as a strict definition of gene would require. Humans are diploid, which means that they have two copies of each chromosome – the chromosome pair, called homologous chromosomes – and thus two copies of each locus and two alleles at each locus (Fig. 1). Within an individual, these two alleles can be identical to each other, in which case the individual is called homozygous (or a homozygote), or different, in which case the individual is called heterozygous (or a heterozygote) for the locus in question. The combination of the two alleles at a given locus in a given individual is called the individual's genotype, whereas the combination of alleles across loci on the same chromosome is called a haplotype. (NB: the term genotype can also mean the combination of an individual's alleles across multiple or all loci, often as opposed to the individual's physical appearance, its phenotype.)

Inheritance from Parents to Offspring

Of the two homologous chromosomes, an individual has inherited one chromosome from the mother and the other from the father. The same applies to the two alleles at a locus. Correspondingly, a parent transmits only one of its two alleles to an offspring; which of the two alleles this is, is

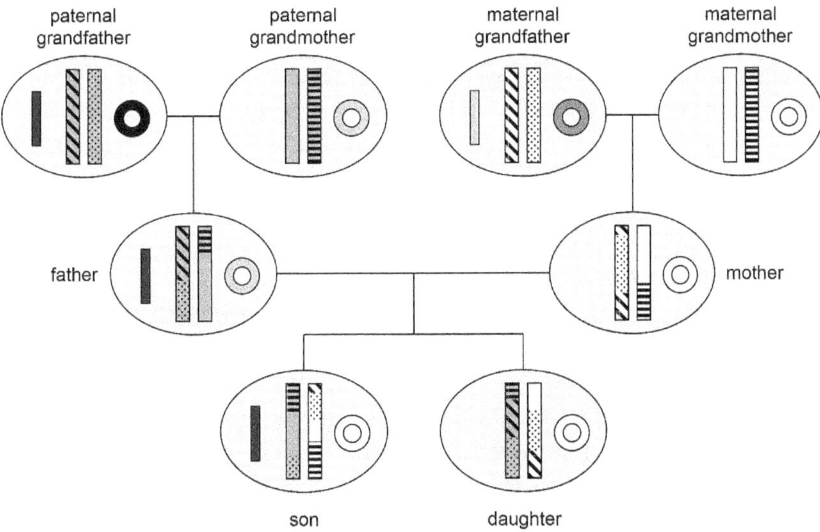

Fig. 2. The inheritance patterns of various parts of the genome through three generations. The mitochondrial DNA (circles) is inherited along a maternal and the Y chromosome (short bars) along a paternal lineage, whereas the autosomal chromosomes (pairs of long bars) recombine in each generation. (Reproduced from Salmela 2012 with permission.)

determined randomly and independently for each offspring. Exceptions to this principle include the mitochondrial DNA (mtDNA), which is passed on to the offspring solely from the mother (Fig. 2), and the sex chromosomes, where males always transmit an X chromosome to their daughters and a Y chromosome to their sons, while all offspring receive an X chromosome from their mother.

In loci that are located on different chromosomes, the principle described above applies to each locus independently, whereas in loci that are located on the same chromosome, the alleles that reside on the same chromosome (haplotype) tend to be inherited together. However, the homologous chromosomes of an individual can occasionally recombine: they change parts so that the haplotype that the offspring inherits becomes a combination of the parent's two haplotypes. The locations of recombinations along the chromosome are random, but the further apart two loci are on a chromosome, the more likely they are to recombine. On the average, there is roughly one recombination per 100 million basepairs of DNA per generation. Notably, recombinations are absent from the mtDNA, and – apart from a small pseudo-autosomal region – the X chromosome recombines only in females, while the Y chromosome does not recombine.

Processes that Govern the Genetic Structure of Populations

The same processes that transmit alleles from parents to offspring of course take place in the flow of alleles between generations in a population, but a population's genetic composition is also shaped by other phenomena. There are four factors that can change a population's allele frequencies: mutation, selection, migration and genetic drift. These factors will be detailed in the next paragraphs. Together with the inheritance mechanisms, these factors also affect the genotypes and haplotypes of the population; this interplay is described further below.

A mutation is a change in the DNA sequence – an error in the transmission of hereditary information from parents to offspring. Because a large part of the DNA is non-coding, a mutation may have no effect on an individual's phenotype (appearance). On the other hand, mutations are random changes, and on coding DNA their effect is seldom beneficial and often deleterious. Because the molecular machinery for DNA copying and error correction is extremely accurate, mutations are generally very rare: for instance the rate of single-base mutations is in the order of one per 100 million basepairs per generation (1000 Genomes Project Consortium 2010). Still, mutations are the original source of all genetic variation in populations.

Selection is a process in which the individuals with an advantageous phenotype leave more descendants than other individuals. This leads to the enrichment of their alleles in the population. It will also increase the frequency of the phenotype in question if that is genetically determined. Thus, selection produces adaptation to the environment and removes harmful mutations from the population. Selection can also affect alleles at nearby loci that are themselves not directly under selection, because their alleles tend to be inherited on the same haplotype; the phenomenon is often called genetic hitch-hiking.

In migration, individuals move from one population to another, and if they reproduce in the other population, their alleles become incorporated into it. (To be exact, the latter event should be called gene flow, but the two concepts are often used synonymously.) Migration can increase the genetic variation of the population by introducing new alleles. Meanwhile, the genetic differences between the populations sending and receiving the migrants will decrease. In this respect, even fairly small numbers of migrants can have a relatively large allele frequency-harmonising effect.

Genetic drift manifests in random fluctuations of the proportions in which the alleles of a population are transmitted to the next generation. It is essentially caused by sampling errors: for instance, while the two alleles of a genotype have an equal probability of being transmitted, one can end up overrepresented among offspring merely by chance. For example, if an individual has four descendants, there is a 12.5% chance that they will all inherit the same allele. Obviously, such fluctuations can even out on the population level when there are many reproducing individuals with the same genotype; therefore, the effects of drift are strongest in small populations. They are also cumulative across generations, and will eventually lead to the

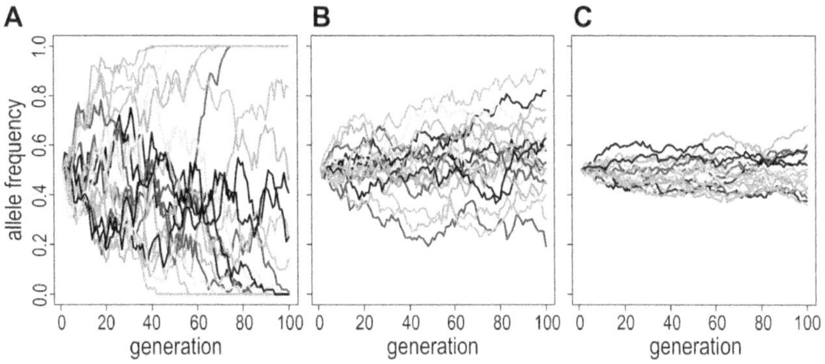

Fig. 3. The effect of genetic drift in populations with 50 (A), 300 (B) and 1500 (C) reproducing individuals. Each line depicts the frequency fluctuations of one allele through 100 generations; all panels contain 20 alleles with an initial frequency of 50 per cent. For example, in the small population (A), alleles in 14 of the initial 20 loci become fixed over the 100 generations. Note that the reported population sizes refer to the number of breeding individuals; the total census size of the corresponding population would be larger. Therefore, genetic drift can have substantial effects on the allele frequencies for example in small rural populations. (Reproduced from Salmela 2012 with permission.)

fixation of one allele per locus in the population and the loss of all other alleles. Thus, genetic drift reduces the genetic variation within a population while increasing the genetic differences between populations. These effects can be quite strong (Fig. 3); indeed, in relatively small populations, genetic drift can often override the effects of selection.

The effects of genetic drift are irreversible in the sense that once an allele becomes fixed, the genetic variation in that locus can only be restored by introduction of new alleles into the population by migrants or through mutations. Therefore, even transient reductions of population size can result in substantial loss of genetic diversity. Examples of such events include population bottlenecks, in which the population size temporarily decreases (for example because of an epidemic or a famine), and founder effects, in which a small group of individuals emigrates from a population to form a new population elsewhere. Even if such populations soon reach a size where the effects of drift are negligible, their allele frequencies can radically differ from those of the initial population.

The frequencies of genotypes in a population are determined by a simple rule – at least when a number of assumptions hold. If none of the allele frequency-changing factors listed above are in effect, the allele frequencies of the next generation will be equal to those in the parental generation, because (as stated in the previous section) the alleles to be transmitted to the next generation will be determined randomly and independently. Moreover, if the population is randomly mating, the alleles will unite at random to form the genotypes of the new generation, and the genotype frequencies will reflect the probability of the corresponding combinations. For example, the frequency of a given homozygous genotype will be the square of the frequency of the allele in question. A population whose genotype frequencies correspond to these expected frequencies is said to be in Hardy-Weinberg equilibrium (HWE); naturally, a population may not be in HWE if some of the above assumptions are not met.

In the context of population haplotype frequencies, the tendency of alleles on the same chromosome to be inherited together more often than not comes into play. Originally, when a mutation happens, it takes place on a particular chromosome and forms a new haplotype. This haplotype will then be inherited intact unless broken by a recombination event. On the population level, this results in a phenomenon called linkage disequilibrium (LD): some alleles occur together on a haplotype more often than their frequencies in the population would suggest. In addition to the rates of mutation and recombination, the level of LD in a population can depend on other factors: LD is stronger in small populations, decays faster in expanding populations, and will increase if new haplotypes are introduced to the population by migration.

Basic Principles of Genetic Inference of Population History

The processes described above affect the patterns of genetic variation within and between populations. Therefore, such patterns can be used to draw inferences on the population history events that have produced them. Of the four factors that can change allele frequencies, mutations can often be ignored in population history inference because they are generally rare and will thus have relatively little effect on the genetic composition of a population, especially in slowly mutating loci and on short timescales. The effects of selection, in turn, can be minimised – if they are not of immediate interest – by studying non-coding or neutral loci; however, as noted above, even these can be affected by selection to some degree through hitch-hiking effects. In some cases, the effects of selection can also be directly tested for. Of the remaining two factors, migration is obviously the more interesting in terms of population history events, but also genetic drift can yield information about population sizes, while the accumulation of drift-induced divergence between populations may signal a scarcity of contacts.

Like allele frequencies, the genotypic composition of a population can provide information on population history. Genotype frequencies can be compared to those expected under HWE, and differences attributed to departures from the HWE assumptions. Specifically, population substructure (the existence of subpopulations in which individuals are more likely to mate with each other than with individuals from the other subpopulations and which (can) have differing allele frequencies) will lead to a deficiency of heterozygotes in the total population compared to the HWE expectation based on overall allele frequency (Fig. 4). Such deficiencies are quantified by the F statistics (F_{ST} etc.) which measure population structure (Holsinger & Weir 2009). However, because the genotypes form anew in each generation,

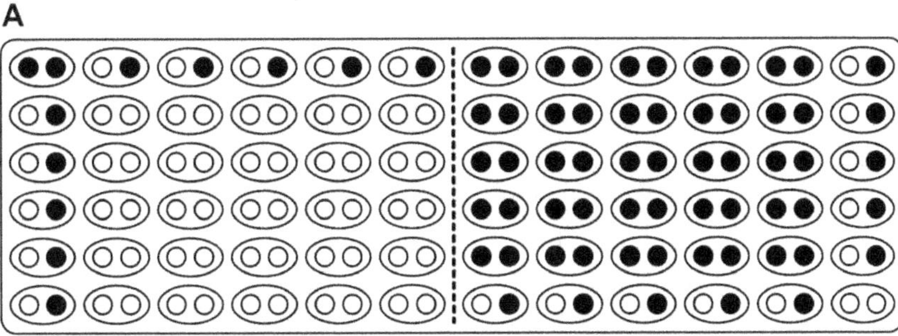

Allele frequency in total population: 1/2

Subpopulation allele frequency: 1/6 Subpopulation allele frequency: 5/6

Heterozygote frequency: 20/72 = 28%

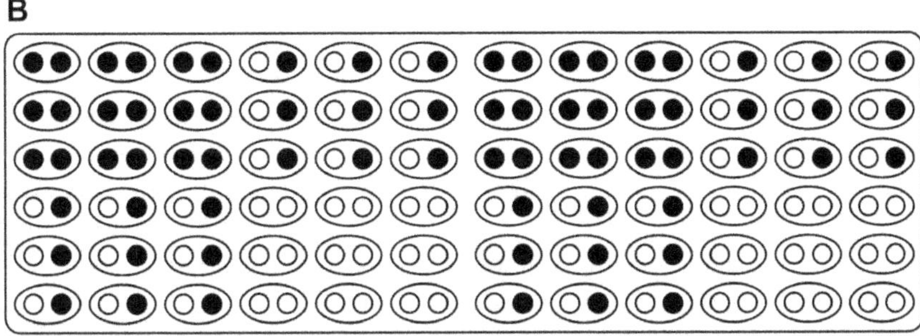

Allele frequency in total population: 1/2

Subpopulation allele frequency: 1/2 Subpopulation allele frequency: 1/2

Heterozygote frequency: 36/72 = 50%

Fig. 4. The effects of population substructure on the frequency of heterozygous genotypes. Black and white circles represent two types of alleles, and the ellipses demarcate the genotype of an individual. In (A), the population consists of two randomly mating subpopulations with differing allele frequency, while in (B), the whole population is randomly mating. Although the overall allele frequency in (A) and (B) is the same, and the subpopulations in (A) are in Hardy-Weinberg equilibrium, the subdivided population (A) harbours fewer heterozygotes than the randomly mating population (B). (Reproduced from Salmela 2012 with permission.)

their frequencies will mainly reflect the current rather than historical mating patterns.

In contrast, the effects of population history on LD are less transient, because it takes numerous generations for LD to be gradually broken down by recombinations. Therefore, the increased LD produced for example by migration or population admixture will remain detectable for a relatively long period after the actual event. Furthermore, because small and constant-size populations harbour more LD, patterns of LD can also be used to determine whether a population has recently expanded. They can also serve in the timing of genetic events (see below).

Obviously, many of the processes that produce the genetic patterns of a population are random (or probabilistic) by nature. Consequently, they may affect some loci disproportionately strongly and others hardly at all.

It is therefore advisable to base population history conclusions on data from several loci. For example genetic drift can produce patterns that by chance – i.e. in a few loci – will resemble the effects of migration, whereas actual migration will have a more consistent effect across loci, and therefore multilocus data can serve to better differentiate between the two.

In addition to observing the genetic patterns of real populations, population history inference can be complemented by the use of population simulations. These are computer models which mimic the effects that the population genetic and inheritance processes will have on the genetic composition of a virtual population which is subjected to various demographic scenarios determined by the researcher. However, it should be noted that a fit of the observed genetic patterns to those produced by a particular population simulation does not prove that the simulated scenario is the one that actually took place in the real population: many other, untested scenarios could produce an equal or better fit to the observed data. Furthermore, the simulated population scenarios are often highly simplified, not least owing to computational limitations. Thus, the value of simulations resides mostly in excluding unlikely scenarios and testing how different population history factors will affect the resulting genetic patterns. (For further discussion on population simulations in general and in the context of Finnish population history, see Sundell et al. 2010.)

Genetic data can also be utilised to estimate the timing of population events, using various approaches. Firstly, the time since a population split can be assessed from the accumulation of genetic differences between the populations through genetic drift. However, this requires the absence of subsequent migration between the populations and constant (or at least known) population sizes – neither of which are realistic assumptions in much of human population history. Secondly, the breakdown of LD can be used to infer the time of the introduction of a haplotype into a population: through generations, recombinations will have broken the initial haplotype down, and the more generations have passed, the shorter will be the stretches of the initial haplotype that are shared between individuals. This approach is often used to estimate the age of disease mutations. Similarly, timings can be based on the accumulation of mutations on the descendant copies of a DNA stretch – the more variation there is, the more time will have lapsed since the common ancestor. Although mutations are rare, on short timescales the inference can be based on fast-mutating loci. This approach, unlike the one based on LD, is applicable also to non-recombining genome regions, and is therefore typically used for the mtDNA and Y chromosome.

Limitations of Genetic Data in Interpreting Population History

In theory, the most straightforward way of unravelling the genetic structure of past populations would be to study them directly, as ancient DNA (aDNA) can be extracted from organic materials like bone and teeth. In practice, aDNA studies are seriously complicated by DNA breakdown in the source material and contaminations caused by contemporary DNA during excavation, storage and laboratory analyses (e.g. Hofreiter et al. 2001; Willerslev & Cooper 2005). Furthermore, suitable materials are not always available: for example in Finland, the acidic soil preserves organic materials poorly. Even at best, the number of available samples is usually small and may not allow a proper characterisation of the genetic variation in the past populations. Of course, even single aDNA samples can be used to address binary questions about genetic continuity between ancient and contemporary populations or to make predictions about the individual's phenotype for characteristics that have a strong genetic background for which the main contributing loci are known, such as eye color or lactose tolerance.

However, often the only possibility of studying the genetics of past populations is to base inferences on the structure of contemporary populations (as described in the previous section), but this is not necessarily unproblematic either. Firstly, different population history events can create similar genetic patterns, while the historical interpretations of the events could differ radically. For example, a given locus can harbour low genetic variation in a population as a consequence of low migration, substantial selection, significant genetic drift (which in turn can result from several scenarios of low population size), or various combinations of these factors. Secondly, the present genetic structure of a population reflects a combination of all the factors the population has been subject to throughout its history, and the signals of newer events may have covered some of the older ones; indeed, the genetic composition of a population has been likened to a palimpsest (Jobling et al. 2004), a manuscript which has been overwritten but in which some of the older text may be deciphered, with great effort, from underneath the newer writing.

Even when a past event is genetically detectable, it cannot be automatically attributed to a particular time period. Timing methods, in turn, have their limitations. Some of them are based on assumptions that may not hold for the population in question but that are often untestable. Since the methods are generally based on chance events (genetic drift, mutations, recombinations) and their accumulation, their use is limited to time intervals that are sufficiently long for a reasonable number of such events to have taken place. Even then, the confidence intervals of the resulting time estimates tend to remain wide. Furthermore, the methods as such will only provide relative time estimates; the transformation of the estimates into years or generations requires the use of mutation or recombination rates, uncertainties in which will widen the confidence intervals further. Additionally, the timings thus obtained may not directly correspond to tangible population events: if several non-identical copies of a haplotype enter a population through migration or survive a bottleneck, the resulting timing will reflect the common ancestor of these copies, which obviously can markedly predate the migration or the bottleneck. Conversely, a dramatic population bottleneck will reset the timing even for haplotypes that may already have resided in a population for millennia – therefore, genetic timings should not be directly equated with population age or migration waves.

In addition to the above constraints, the genetic inference of population history may be limited by data availability. Some decades ago, population genetic studies could only be based on blood groups and a few other proteins. After the advent of DNA analysis techniques, a lot of interest was directed to studies of mtDNA and the Y chromosome. Admittedly, their non-recombining nature allows elegant analyses, and the maternal (mitochondrial) and paternal (Y-chromosomal) inheritance pattern enable the comparison of male- and female-specific population phenomena. Nevertheless, mtDNA and the Y chromosome are only two loci, and may thus not be representative of the full history of a population (see previous section). This shortcoming has been circumvented over the last few years since it has become feasible to analyse tens or hundreds of thousands of loci (called SNPs) across the whole genome. Furthermore, the recent methodological advances in DNA sequencing, which currently make it feasible to study whole genomes of individuals at a reasonable effort, open unprecedented prospects for population genetic and population historical analyses in the near future, especially as the decreasing analysis prices will allow the sequencing of increasing numbers of individuals.

While technical advances have alleviated the problem of locus availability, the availability of individuals for study can still remain a limiting factor. In addition to the population of interest, samples or data are needed from reference populations in order to infer contacts between populations. However, the relevant reference populations are not necessarily available or known, and in the case of historical inference may not exist any more. (NB: even when reference populations are available and signs of contacts are detected, it may not be possible to infer their precise strength, because different analysis methods can produce radically differing results; see for example Fig. 1 in Alexander et al. 2009.) Moreover, it is important that the sample sizes per population are sufficiently large, because small sample sizes may underestimate the genetic variation within a population and cause bias in comparison to larger samples. Another important factor in the conclusions is the geographic scale of sampling: in the presence of fine-scale population structure, samples from a small geographic area can appear genetically more divergent from other populations than a wider sample from the same area would.

Of Vikings in Particular and Finnish Population Structure in General

In the light of the above treatment, the questions of the Viking Age in Finland are not easy to tackle genetically (at least not based on contemporary genetic data). Firstly, they involve populations that are presumably closely related to start with; it would naturally be easier to detect subsequent contacts between clearly divergent populations, for example on an intercontinental scale. Secondly, the relevant time interval is short – in fact very short relative to the usual precision of genetic timings. On the other hand, reliable timings would be needed to distinguish Viking Age genetic signals from those caused by previous or subsequent contacts, both of which are more than likely in the area in question; in this respect, genetic analyses of the Viking history of Iceland (e.g. Helgason et al. 2000; 2001) have been much more straightforward, because earlier influences can be excluded. Obviously, the limitations set by timing methods also affect the population history aspects that do not involve contacts between populations, for example the existence of local population bottlenecks.

However, an interesting case example of a possible genetic Viking influence in Finland can be found. The Viking activities in Europe have been connected to the frequency patterns of some diseases and alleles, including hereditary haemochromatosis (Milman & Pedersen 2003), multiple sclerosis (MS) (Poser 1995) and a deletion in a gene called CCR5 (Lucotte 2001; 2002; Lucotte & Dieterlen 2003). (The latter two may even be connected: Pulkkinen et al. 2004.) Interestingly, in Finland MS is enriched in three areas: in two river valleys in the province of Satakunta in south-western Finland, in the upper parts of Porvoonjoki river in eastern south Finland and in Southern Ostrobothnia. While the high MS risk in Southern Ostrobothnia probably has more to do with the role of south-western Finns in the settlement history of the area, the enrichment in Satakunta has been suggested as resulting from a Viking influence. (Tienari et al. 2004.) Obviously, this evidence remains tentative and will hardly allow any estimation of the strength of the related influence, as it is based on a highly limited number of loci (cf. above).

Other genetic influences of the Vikings on the Finnish population are definitely possible. The Finnish gene pool is mostly European, but it contains some eastern elements and shows signs of genetic drift (compatible with the historically low population size) (Guglielmino et al. 1990; Lappalainen et al. 2006; Salmela et al. 2008). There is a marked genetic difference between the south-western vs. northern and eastern parts of the country. While this east–west difference is clearly related to the extreme demographic events during the introduction of agriculture to eastern Finland, it may also partly stem from differing proportions of immigration from the eastern vs. western directions into these regions. Because the east–west difference is visible in autosomal (Salmela et al. 2008) and Y-chromosomal loci (Kittles et al. 1998; Hedman et al. 2004; Lappalainen et al. 2006) but not in mtDNA (Hedman et al. 2007), it has been suggested that it could partly reflect male-dominated migrations from Scandinavia to the western but not the eastern region (Palo et al. 2009); however, the tendency of mtDNA to display more subtle patterning than Y chromosome is close to universal. Overall, western Finns show genetic affinity to Swedes, which is pronounced not only in the Swedish-speaking areas but also in south-western Finland; interestingly, the Swedish counties that are genetically closest to western Finland are Uppsala and Västmanland (Salmela et al. 2011). Obviously, however, this affinity does not require Viking Age influence, as possible alternative times for contacts abound both before and after the Viking Age.

In addition to such overall possibilities of contact, the absence of genetic evidence (when data exists) could perhaps be utilised in some specific questions: for example a very low genetic affinity to eastern central Sweden in a given Finnish region could speak against Viking (and any other Swedish) contacts. However, many such questions would likely be too specific for a population geneticist to be aware of, and would therefore call for interdisciplinary collaboration.

Conclusions

Although a population's genetic structure is a potent source of population history information, genetics is generally most suited to tackling questions that involve relatively long time intervals and/or markedly divergent populations. While genetics has provided invaluable insights for example into the post-glacial settlement of Europe, it has not been equally pivotal in studies of several more recent events – owing on the one hand to the inherent limitations of its inference capabilities, on the other hand to the larger number of other disciplines that can provide information on these timescales. Even there, however, genetics can serve as an additional, largely independent source of information to yield evidence for or against specific hypotheses of other disciplines, which obviously could prompt interdisciplinary collaborations.

Further Reading

The basics of population genetics are covered in many textbooks; Hamilton (2009) is one of the easiest to approach. The use of population genetics in human population history inference is thoroughly dealt with by Jobling *et al.* (2004). An overview of the population structure in Finland and the Baltic Sea region in a north European context is provided by Lappalainen (2009); a more recent review which is focused mostly on Finland and Sweden can be found in Salmela (2012).

Notes

1 This chapter uses the word 'history' to refer to the past in general, regardless of the existence of written sources, i.e., to both history and prehistory.

References

1000 Genomes Project Consortium. 2010. A Map of Human Genome Variation from Population-Scale Sequencing. *Nature* 467: 1061–1073.

Alexander, David H., John Novembre & Kenneth Lange. 2009. Fast Model-Based Estimation of Ancestry in Unrelated Individuals. *Genome Research* 19: 1655–1664.

Guglielmino, C. R., A. Piazza, P. Menozzi & L. L. Cavalli-Sforza. 1990. Uralic Genes in Europe. *American Journal of Physical Anthropology* 83: 57–68.

Hamilton, Matthew B. 2009. *Population Genetics*. Chichester: Wiley-Blackwell.

Hedman, Minttu, Ville Pimenoff, Matti Lukka, Pertti Sistonen & Antti Sajantila. 2004. Analysis of 16 Y STR Loci in the Finnish Population Reveals a Local Reduction in the Diversity of Male Lineages. *Forensic Science International* 142: 37–43.

Hedman, M., A. Brandstätter, V. Pimenoff, P. Sistonen, J. U. Palo, W. Parson & A. Sajantila. 2007. Finnish Mitochondrial DNA HVS-I and HVS-II Population Data. *Forensic Science International* 172: 171–178.

Helgason, Agnar, Sigrún Sigurðardóttir, Jayne Nicholson, Bryan Sykes, Emmeline W. Hill, Daniel G. Bradley, Vidar Bosnes, Jeffery R. Gulcher, Ryk Ward R & Kári Stefánsson. 2000. Estimating Scandinavian and Gaelic Ancestry in the Male Settlers of Iceland. *American Journal of Human Genetics* 67: 697–717.

Helgason, Agnar, Eileen Hickey, Sara Goodacre, Vidar Bosnes, Kári Stefánsson, Ryk Ward & Bryan Sykes. 2001. mtDNA and the Islands of the North Atlantic: Estimating the Proportions of Norse and Gaelic Ancestry. *American Journal of Human Genetics* 68: 723–737.

Hofreiter, Michael, David Serre, Hendrik N. Poinar, Melanie Kuch & Svante Pääbo. 2001. Ancient DNA. *Nature Reviews Genetics* 2: 353–359.

Holsinger, Kent E. & Bruce S. Weir. 2009. Genetics in Geographically Structured Populations: Defining, Estimating and Interpreting F_{ST}. *Nature Reviews Genetics* 10: 639–650.

Jobling, Mark A., Matthew Hurles & Chris Tyler-Smith. 2004. *Human Evolutionary Genetics: Origins, Peoples & Disease*. Abingdon: Garland Publishing.

Kittles, Rick A., Markus Perola, Leena Peltonen, Andrew W. Bergen, Richard A. Aragon, Matti Virkkunen, Markku Linnoila, David Goldman & Jeffrey C. Long. 1998. Dual Origins of Finns Revealed by Y Chromosome Haplotype Variation. *American Journal of Human Genetics* 62: 1171–1179.

Lappalainen, Tuuli, Satu Koivumäki, Elina Salmela, Kirsi Huoponen, Pertti Sistonen, Marja-Liisa Savontaus & Päivi Lahermo. 2006. Regional Differences among the Finns: A Y-Chromosomal Perspective. *Gene* 376: 207–215.

Lappalainen, Tuuli. 2009. *Human Genetic Variation in the Baltic Sea Region: Features of Population History and Natural Selection*. PhD dissertation: University of Helsinki.

Lucotte, Gérard. 2001. Distribution of the CCR5 Gene 32-Basepair Deletion in West Europe: A Hypothesis about the Possible Dispersion of the Mutation by the Vikings in Historical Times. *Human Immunology* 62: 933–936.

Lucotte, Gérard. 2002. Frequencies of 32 Base Pair Deletion of the (Delta 32) Allele of the CCR5 HIV-1 Co-Receptor Gene in Caucasians: A Comparative Analysis. *Infection, Genetics and Evolution* 1: 201–205.

Lucotte, Gérard & Florent Dieterlen. 2003. More about the Viking Hypothesis of Origin of the Delta32 Mutation in the CCR5 Gene Conferring Resistance to HIV-1 Infection. *Infection, Genetics and Evolution* 3: 293–295.

Milman, N. & P. Pedersen. 2003. Evidence that the Cys282Tyr Mutation of the HFE Gene Originated from a Population in Southern Scandinavia and Spread with the Vikings. *Clinical Genetics* 64: 36–47.

Palo, Jukka U., Ismo Ulmanen, Matti Lukka, Pekka Ellonen & Antti Sajantila. 2009. Genetic Markers and Population History: Finland Revisited. *European Journal of Human Genetics* 17: 1336–1346.

Poser, C. M. 1995. Viking Voyages: The Origin of Multiple Sclerosis? An Essay in Medical History. *Acta Neurologica Scandinavica Suppl* 161: 11–22.

Pulkkinen, K., M. Luomala, H. Kuusisto, T. Lehtimäki, M. Saarela, T. O. Jalonen & I. Elovaara. 2004. Increase in CCR5 Delta32/Delta32 Genotype in Multiple Sclerosis. *Acta Neurologica Scandinavica* 109: 342–347.

Salmela, Elina, Tuuli Lappalainen, Ingegerd Fransson, Peter M. Andersen, Karin Dahlman-Wright, Andreas Fiebig, Pertti Sistonen, Marja-Liisa Savontaus, Stefan

Schreiber, Juha Kere & Päivi Lahermo. 2008. Genome-Wide Analysis of Single Nucleotide Polymorphisms Uncovers Population Structure in Northern Europe. *PLoS One* 3: e3519.

Salmela, Elina, Tuuli Lappalainen, Jianjun Liu, Pertti Sistonen, Peter M. Andersen, Stefan Schreiber, Marja-Liisa Savontaus, Kamila Czene, Päivi Lahermo, Per Hall & Juha Kere. 2011. Swedish Population Substructure Revealed by Genome-Wide Single Nucleotide Polymorphism Data. *PLoS One* 6: e16747.

Salmela, Elina. 2012. *Genetic Structure in Finland and Sweden: Aspects of Population History and Gene Mapping.* PhD dissertation: University of Helsinki.

Strachan, Tom, & Andrew Read. 2011. *Human Molecular Genetics.* New York: Garland Science, Taylor & Francis Group.

Sundell, Tarja, Martin Heger, Juhana Kammonen & Päivi Onkamo. 2010. Modelling a Neolithic Population Bottleneck in Finland: A Genetic Simulation. *Fennoscandia Archaeologica* 27: 3–19.

Tienari, Pentti J., Marja-Liisa Sumelahti, Terhi Rantamäki & Juhani Wikström. 2004. Multiple Sclerosis in Western Finland: Evidence for a Founder Effect. *Clinical Neurology and Neurosurgery* 106: 175–179.

Willerslev, Eske & Alan Cooper. 2005. Ancient DNA. *Proceedings of the Royal Society B: Biological Sciences* 272: 3–16.

Joonas Ahola

Kalevalaic Heroic Epic and the Viking Age in Finland

When sketching a holistic picture of the Viking Age in Finland, epic cannot be ignored. However, the conclusions drawn on the basis of this material are limited. Finno-Karelian kalevalaic poetry comprises a large bulk of poetry which was collected mainly in the nineteenth and early twentieth century and recorded mostly in writing. This collection, which represents diverse poetic genres, is united by the alliterative four-footed trochaic metrical form. Kalevalaic poetry represents topics and themes not only relevant in the contexts of its performance but also topics and themes that derive from different eras in the past. Heroic epics belong to the group of poetry within this corpus that stem from the distant past. Several generations of researchers have dated a certain share of these epic poems to the Viking Age.

The hypotheses that oral poetry from the nineteenth century can illuminate a period centuries earlier requires that this poetry, or aspects of this poetry, are conceived as survivals from the earlier period. In other words, these cultural phenomena would have to be preserved within communities with some form of ongoing use in spite of changes in the cultural context across centuries; they would reflect a cultural continuum extending all of the way from the Viking Age to the time when the poems were recorded. However, no cultural phenomenon can be preserved in a society without a collective function, as the functionalist approach in anthropology has emphasized (Holmwood 2010). Hence, the claim that a certain phenomenon has been preserved more or less intact according to its formal qualities presupposes that the functions and meanings that this phenomenon has had for the communities in which it was used have adapted to the cultural, social and environmental changes over the course of time. When this period of time expands to centuries and reaches close to the modern era, such changes are presumably significant and hardly leave any cultural field untouched. From a diachronic perspective, oral tradition, which only exists through the repetition of performances, necessarily conforms to the continuous changes in its contexts, even when the oral tradition maintains a relatively stable poetic form, like kalevalaic epics.

The existence of an oral tradition in individual performances means that it can be fixed only to a limited degree, balanced by a flexibility to conform to changing circumstances. A unit of oral tradition, such as a heroic poem, only survives as long as it is performed and passed on to succeeding generations. This means that the unit needs to maintain relevance and meaningfulness in those successive contexts. Fortunately, this does not mean that the context has to remain intact: the relevance and meaningfulness of the poem can spring both from unchanging significations ascribed to the unit even in changing contexts and from changing significations adapted to those contexts. In other words, the formal features of an oral poem can retain relevance in traditional poetics even if the semantic contents of the features have changed, just like words retain relevance in a language even if their meanings change over time. The elements of an oral tradition that are more stable and unvarying are disposed to total disappearance in changing contexts, whereas the elements of the oral tradition that are more flexible have greater potential to conform to the same changing contexts, which also means that they generally retain less information about the remote past. Stable expressions can survive in usage for long periods by gaining new meanings (such as proverbs), or they can survive as fixed constituents of lengthier texts in which their semantic obscurity does not disturb the flow of narration, and in which their obscurity can even be valued as a marker of, for instance, the sacredness or authority of the text.

In connection with diachronic study of oral traditions, Matti Kuusi has observed: "Perceiving disappeared worlds beyond history presupposes a special kind of interaction between factual knowledge, creative fantasy and critical doubt" (Kuusi 1963: 21). This chapter will discuss the theoretical basis and methodological challenges in the interpretation of kalevalaic heroic epic as a historical source. It will begin with a brief overview of the poetic tradition and of earlier research that connected the heroic epic with the Viking Age. Focusing on a few poems and the heroic characters in them, it will continue to open discussion on the challenges and possibilities connected to the use of kalevalaic epic as source material in the study of the historical period defined as the Viking Age in Finland (on which, see Ahola & Frog). This will be done in a way that the results should remain more within the realm of facts and criticism and stray less to fantasy.

Kalevalaic Epic

A large share of kalevalaic epic is arguably archaic both in form and subject matter although it was primarily recorded no earlier than the nineteenth century. The earliest documented pieces of poetry in the Kalevala-meter are from 1544 (*Rucouskiria*, a prayer book by Mikael Agricola). The earliest documented pieces from epics are from the latter part of the eighteenth century (e.g. Kuusi 1963: 12). Kalevalaic poetry had largely disappeared from southern and western Finland by the beginning of the nineteenth century, when the first serious undertakings to collect 'Finnish' oral traditions were undertaken. It was soon discovered that the liveliest epic traditions prevailed on the peripheries of Finno-Karelian cultural area, in the backwoods of Värmland in Central Sweden and especially in the eastern border area.

This was in the time after Finland became a Grand Duchy of the Russian Empire in 1809. The young student of medicine Elias Lönnrot was among the first collectors to cross the border and enter the sparsely populated backwoods of Viena Karelia in the north, near the White Sea. In the 1830s, Elias Lönnrot made several trips into Viena Karelia, on which he collected a significant amount of epic poetry. He arranged and edited the poems into a concise narrative entity which he published in 1835 with the title *Kalevala, taikka vanhoja Karjalan runoja* ['Kalevala, or Old Poems of Karelia']. This work became very influential and inspired further collection of this poetry. After additional journeys in Viena and Eastern Karelia to collect poetry, and with the help of the material collected by numerous colleagues, Lönnrot published a revised and expanded version of *Kalevala* in 1849, known as the national epic of Finland today.

The greater part of the vernacular kalevalaic poetry that was collected has been compiled in the publication series *Suomen Kansan Vanhat Runot* (*SKVR*) ['Old Songs of the Finnish People'], published across the period 1908–1948 in 34 volumes. The 35th volume, representing previously unpublished poems from some collections, was published in 1997. The volumes of this series are arranged according to the geographical areas from which the poems they present have been recorded.

Kalevalaic poetry was a language of tradition applied in numerous different genres in addition to epics, such as in incantations, wedding songs, lullabies, etc. Singing was not exclusive to communal gatherings and feasts but was really a part of daily life, as has been described in numerous travelogues in the nineteenth and early twentieth centuries. Epic was sung both in groups and alone: in fields, in forests, on fishing and hunting expeditions, and so on.[1]

It is noteworthy that the collections of kalevalaic poetry do not necessarily offer an accurate picture of the relative significance of different branches of the poetry within the communities where they were recorded. Within the rich diversity of poetic genres, epic was among the most valued types of poetry from the perspective of the collectors. Especially after the publication of *Kalevala*, a major interest was to find additional and complementing poetic passages related to the published epic. The collectors sought out performers of epic who were renowned for their abilities and knowledge.

It is notable that, in the latter part of the nineteenth century, the epic poetry that was preserved in the remote periphery of the Finno-Karelian language area was already associated with the central and oldest cultural area in Finland, the Southwest (Map 1).

A. A. Borenius (1873) noted that the poems of Viena Karelia included linguistic and other features that seemed to indicate western Finland as their original context. It is indeed peculiar that the only examples of an epic poem

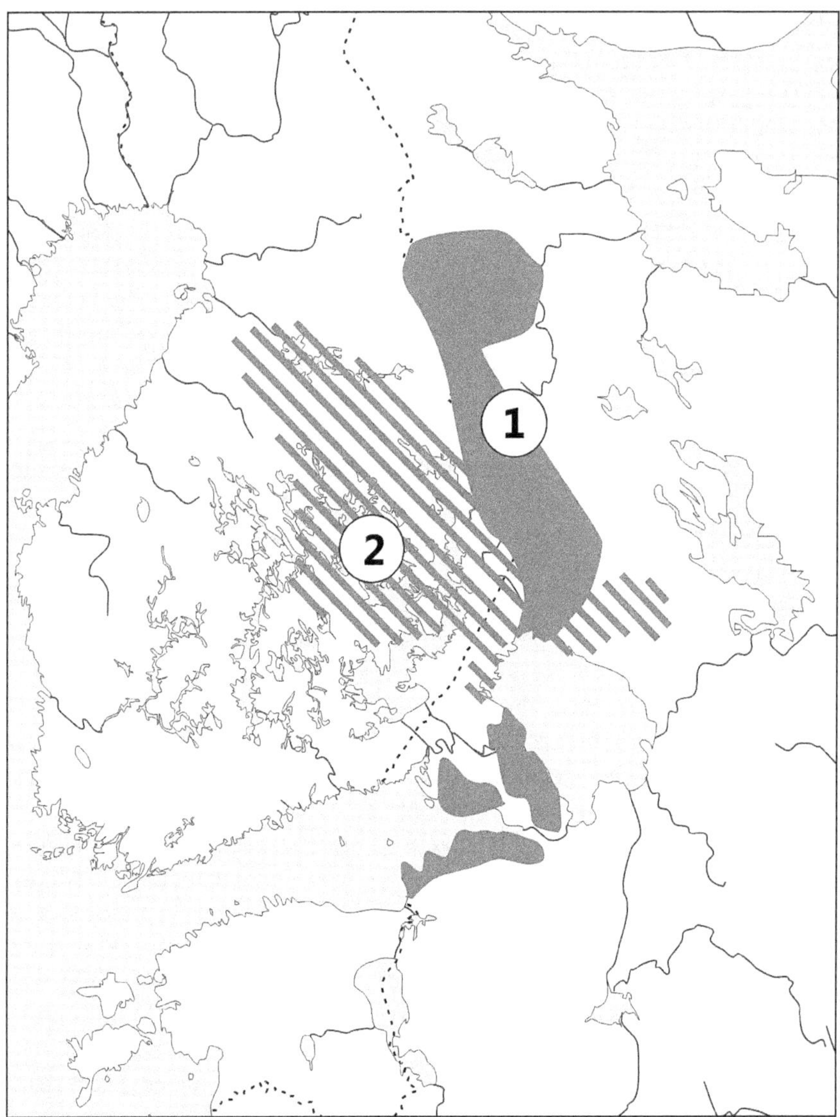

Map 1. The most important areas where kalevalaic epic has been recorded, representing areas where epic was (1) more frequently and (2) less frequently recorded in the nineteenth century. Following Kuusi 1963: 27.

(*The Bond*, described below) that deals with longing for sea raiding voyages in connection with emblematically Germanic phrasing and terms such as *penninki* (cf. Old Norse *penningr* ['coin; money']), were only met in the watershed area which nowadays comprises the border area between Finland and Russia. This area is as remote as possible from the sea or, for that matter, historical Germanic influence.

Kalevalaic Heroic Epic

The epic cycles that are addressed in the following are those most frequently encountered in discussions of kalevalaic heroic epics that derive from the Viking Age. These epics describe heroic war expeditions, often across the sea, with swords, spears and helmets as war gear. Such war gear is among the imagery that has been associated with the Scandinavian Viking Age since the Romantic period (see Aalto). The ethos and even individual elements of narration in these epics have recognizable equivalents in the Scandinavian saga literature and Scandinavian poetry associated with the Viking Age. The normalized contents of individual poems are inevitably constructions of researchers from the range of variation encountered in the tradition, but that does not compromise the identification of certain features, language use or story patterns as traditional. The naming of the poems here follows that in the anthology of kalevalaic epic, *Finnish Folk Poetry: Epic* (Kuusi *et al.* 1977). This naming allows readers, for whom the original language is difficult to access, to easily find examples of the quoted poems together with English translations in that anthology (itself selections from *SKVR*).

Kaukamoinen and Lemminkäinen

The poem of *Kaukamoinen* tells about the title hero who is not invited to a great feast. He decides to attend it anyway, in spite of his mother's warnings, and travels to the feast overcoming fantastic obstacles on the way. In some versions of the poem, he gets into a duel with the master of the feast and, in the different versions of this extended narrative, he is either killed or conquers his opponent, subsequently escaping revenge by fleeing to an island across the sea.

Läksi merta laskomaha	He set off to go to sea
Somerta sirottamaha	to heave ballast overboard,
Melan vaskisen varassa	leaning to a paddle of iron
Kokan kultasen nojassa.	leaning to a prow of gold.
Laski päivän, laski toisen	He sailed for a day, sailed for a second.
Jopa peänä kolmantena	And on the third day
Jo näkyvi Pohjan soari	the island of Pohja appears,
Soari kulta kuumottavi.	the gold island glimmers.
(*SKVR* I_2 790, 20–25.)	

On this island he angers the menfolk by seducing their women and is forced to flee again. The hero Lemminkäinen, often interchangeable with Kaukamoinen in kalevalaic poetry, is differentiated from the latter through shamanistic imagery. Lemminkäinen's death follows the confrontation at the feast, after which his mother makes a more or less successful attempt to resurrect the hero. The material in these poems was intertwined in the nineteenth century to the degree that it is impossible to completely distinguish them from one another (In *SKVR*, both cycles usually appear under the title *Lemminkäisen virsi* ['The Song of Lemminkäinen']).

The Bond

The Bond (or in *SKVR*, *Ahdin ja Kyllikin runo* ['The Poem of Ahti and Kyllikki']) is a poem about a bond between a man (Ahti) and his wife (Kyllikki). In marriage, Ahti had promised not to leave for war and Kyllikki not for other men. However, Kyllikki fails to keep her promise and nothing prevents Ahti from preparing his war-ship. He invites his comrade Teuri, who gladly joins him, in spite of having a newlywed wife. Teuri leaves the marital bed in a hurry and dresses up on the run:

Otti Teuri keihäänsä,	Teuri took his spear,
Ei ole keiho suuren suuri	the spear is not very large
Eikä keiho pienen pieni,	Nor is the spear very small,
Keiho keskikertainen:	the spear is of medium size:
Susi putkessa puhusi,	A wolf spoke on the shaft,
Kasi nauku naglan päässä.	a cat meowed in the head of the nail.
Lykkelöö keihoansa	He puts his spear
Muien keihojen sekaah.	among other spears.
Nuoret souti, airot notkui,	The young rowed, the oars bended,
Vanhat souti, päät vapisi.	the old rowed, their heads trembled.
Airon pyyryt pyynä vinku,	The oar handles whistled like a hazel hen,
Nenä joiku joutsenena,	the oar points sang like a swan,
Perä kratsko kaarnehena,	The aft croaked like a raven,
Hangat hanhina hatsahti.	the oarlocks honked like geese.
(*SKVR* I_2 906, 49–62.)	

The Orphan

The poem about the consequences of the blood feud between the families of Untamo and Kalervo is labeled as *The Orphan* by Kuusi (*SKVR*: *Kalevanpojan kosto* ['The Revenge of Kaleva's Lad']). This poem tells about the survival of Kalervo's young son as the only survivor of the family. It turns out to be impossible to have this son killed, who in many variants appears as a slave of Untamo's family, accomplishing the tasks he is given in ways that cause great damage.

The Sampo

The cycle of poems about the mysterious object called *sampo* (*SKVR*: *Sampo*) include poems about the forging of this mythic source of abundance for the benefit of the people in *Pohjola* ['North(-Place)'], as well as about how the hero Väinämöinen organized its theft on a sea-raid and the pursuit of the thieves by another ship to climax in a battle at sea.

Tuosta Pohjola havatsi,	Then Pohjola noticed,
Pohjan eukko ylös nousi,	the hag of Pohjola got up,
Itse Pohjolan emäntä	the lady of Pohjola herself
Juoksi riista riihen luokse	ran to the game store
Kartanoa katsomahan:	to see the yard:
Riista kaikki pois kadonna.	all game had disappeared.
Katso karjansa katovan,	She saw her cattle disappear,

Alenevan arviohon.	the diminishing of its value.
Pani joukon jousihinsa,	She armed troops with bows,
Laitto miehet miekkohinsa,	she armed men with swords,
Sata miestä soutamahan,	she put a hundred men to row,
Tuhat ilman istumahan;	a thousand just sitting;
Läksi Väinämön jäljestä.	She went after Väinämö.
(*SKVR* VII_1 679, 69–81.)	

These poems also describe the eventual loss of the *sampo* at the outcome of the battle when it falls into the sea. This part of the epic cycle has been connected to the Viking Age, particularly through the motifs of a journey across the sea in a ship full of warriors in order to regain the mill(-like) object and of its loss, which resembles elements in the Old Norse tradition of the stolen mill Grotti, similarly lost at sea (as found e.g. in the eddic poem *Grottasǫngr* ['The Song of Grotti']).

The Courtship

The Courtship (*SKVR*: *Kilpakosinta* ['The Courtship Competition']) is a poem presenting a bridal-quest narrative about the incredible tasks a suitor has to accomplish in order to persuade his prospective mother-in-law to give her daughter in marriage. In some versions, this happens in the presence of a competing suitor.

A Diachronic Approach to Kalevalaic Epic

Poetry in Kalevala-metric form has probably been performed in the Finnic language area already since the beginning of the first millennium (Leino 1986: 140; Korhonen 1994: 86–87). Kalevala-meter is itself a conserving aspect of the tradition that structures language in each line of poetry. This is an unrhymed trochaic tetrameter in which requirements of syllabic quantity in stressed syllables and the preference of alliteration limited word choice and variation in reproduction. Lines, couplets and longer passages in which the expression met the metrical rules in a fluent and esthetically appealing way could become fixed and even used in numerous different poems as epithets and stock phrases found across wide geographical areas (Kuusi 1977: 62–67; Leino 1994). The conventional opening formula of the poem *Kaukamoinen*, for example, *Savu saarella palavi / tuli niemen tutkaimessa* ['Smoke burns on an island / a fire on the tip of a peninsula'] was widespread across the whole area where the poem was performed (Frog 2010: 372–376). As an example of a shorter widespread poetic idiom, the epithet *tinarinta* ['tin (or bronze) chested'] is widespread as a metonymic expression for a young girl[2] – an expression that has been connected to the typically plentiful female bronze jewelry used in the Iron Age (see below). The relative fixedness even of such small constituents of poems prevented the poetry from changing rapidly.

The narrative frame was another aspect of epic that limited variation. Narrative expressions and plot structures were connected to each other, and their key events often were expressed with established stock phrases. On the one hand, this strengthened the solidity of plot structures; on the other hand, it could lead the narration to a track which normally belonged to a wholly different story in a performance through a single changed expression. Generally, however, the fixed key elements had a preserving role, like mooring posts around which variation was stabilized.

The heroic epic poems contained elements that were alien to the immediate context of performance, such as mentions of archaic weaponry or jewelry. According to Väinö Salminen (1934: 171–182), singers sought to perform the epic poems in their conventional form, avoiding variation, because they were considered to narrate historical events (see also Virtanen 1968; Harvilahti 1992; Frog 2010). In other words, heroic and mythic deeds described in the epics were collectively attributed with qualities of an ethnic *mythic history*, as Anna-Leena Siikala (1994b; 1994a: 145) has discussed. This was a status of a sacred history that promoted the maintenance of the narratives and their traditional, conventional constitutive elements intact. Mythic histories are typically performed in the form of a tale or an epic poem and their transmission is done with special care. The protagonists in these narratives are gods, heroic ancestors or otherwise remarkable persons. The historicity of these narratives is in their reception and function for the community in which they are performed and the mythic dimension of the narratives is an acceptance of supernatural elements (Siikala 1994b: 15–16). Fundamentals of this understanding enabled even those elements where significance or meaning had become unclear to be loyally repeated. In other words, the fixed elements could have value for the performers even without a function as a key narrative element.

The fundamental levels of cognition, the indigenous mentality and worldview, which function as the springboard for cultural expressions, are slow to alter and can maintain cultural features even through historical changes. A strong and influential narrative resists change and can remain relevant in changing social and cultural contexts to the degree that it consists of cultural, environmental and psychological elements that are identifiable and recognizable through changing discourses and poetic tastes. Many of the heroic epic poems were met in a recognizably similar form across wide areas. This wide distribution, correlated with local and regional socially stable forms along with the recognizable social resistance to variation combine to indicate their old age and also formal stability. Anna-Leena Siikala's (1994b) research on mythic images and motifs in kalevalaic poetry has demonstrated that, even if the surrounding world changed, the ways it was observed, comprehended and expressed in narrative could remain recognizably similar across long periods of time and through radical religious and social changes, with some of these mythic images and narrative motifs exhibiting continuities even going back long before the Viking Age.

Kalevalaic Heroic Epic and the Viking Age in Scholarship

Already at the dawn of investigations into kalevalaic epic, the pioneering researchers dated the poems' context of origin to the Viking Age and earlier on various, more and less intuitive grounds (see e.g. Porthan 1983 [1766–1778]). For example, Elias Lönnrot believed that the epic poems, as well as the entity which he discerned out of them (*Kalevala*), depicted actual historical events that were connected to the immigration of Karelians to Bjarmaland (Viena Karelia) during the first centuries AD (Kaukonen 1979: 92–94).[3]

The observation that kalevalaic poetry in Karelia bore Western Finnish features together with the notion of the conservatism of Kalevala-meter provided a thrust towards the conception of kalevalaic poems as items of oral literature that had concrete original textual forms. This was the idea that an original textual poem had subsequently dispersed and had been changed and 'corrupted' as it spread from person to person and generation to generation, migrating from region to region until was recorded in many different forms by collectors. The conception of original textual forms was so strong in the nineteenth century that when Elias Lönnrot compiled *Kalevala*, it was received as a 'discovery' of the original epic entity rather than as the compilation or composition by Lönnrot that it was. Only in the latter part of the nineteenth century was the usability of *Kalevala* as a source in the research of kalevalaic poetry questioned. Julius Krohn (1885) stressed that Elias Lönnrot's editorial work affected both the general appearance of epic and also the form of individual poems. *Kalevala*'s authority had, however, grown to such an extent and was also so available that it was still used in some studies well into the twentieth century – and outside of folklore studies, it is even sometimes used still today.

The so-called Historical-Geographic Method was developed around the transition from the nineteenth to the twentieth century by Julius Krohn (esp. 1885) and his son Kaarle Krohn (esp. 1918). This was the first attempt to create a scientific method to reach for the origins of the kalevalaic poems conceived in terms of these 'original forms' based on collected poetry. Julius Krohn first introduced the Historical-Geographic Method in folklore studies in *Suomen kirjallisuus I: Kalevala* ['Finnish Literature I: Kalevala'] (1885). The method was further developed and brought into international recognition by his son Kaarle Krohn, the first professor of folklore studies in Finland (and in the world). The method was based on a theory of the diffusion of traditions. The method was used to determine the history of migration and development (diffusion) of particular poems. It combined linguistic and philological methods. The contents and distribution of different redactions of a poem were studied in order to determine the primary, original features of the poem. These primary features enabled the determination of its chronology of development, of the routes via which the poem spread from the place of origin, as well as enabling a reconstruction of its original form.[4]

According to Kaarle Krohn, the form of epic heroic poetry which was collected in Karelia was the result of development of individual features and the conglomeration of the original poems that were composed in the south-western Finland (Krohn 1903–1910: 819–821) but which had spread to Karelia over a period of centuries. According to Krohn, most of this poetry received its essential form in the Middle Ages, but that there was discernible a group of poems (*The Orphan*, *Kaukamoinen*, *Lemminkäinen* and *The Bond*) that referred to history (as opposed to mythology). In his view, these poems "reflect trade relations with Gotland, raids on the Baltic Sea, and hostile terms between the Finns and the Swedes on the Southwest coast of Finland" (Krohn 1903–1910: 832). Krohn stated that the period that these poems reflected was datable to the last phase of heathenism according to evidence of individual words and features of expression (Krohn 1903–1910: 832–833).[5]

Kaarle Krohn saw the same warrior ethos in these poems that Andreas Heusler had discussed in his attempts to reconstruct the ancient Germanic poems out of later, mainly Scandinavian, heroic poetry (Krohn 1903–1910: 836–838). Krohn maintained a view according to which the heroic poetry was created at a time when Finns were only beginning to gain a superior position within the largely Germanic population of western Finland (700–1100 A.D.),[6] and that similarities between the Scandinavian and Finno-Karelian epic traditions derived from a common Circum-Baltic tradition (Krohn 1914: 102, 175–176). Later, Krohn considered an even larger number of the heroic epic poems historical to the extent of narrating deeds of individual, named heroic chieftains and to reflect a Viking Age western Finnish aristocrat milieu in details of clothing, weaponry, transport, wealth and luxuries (Krohn 1914: 304–334, 341–347; 1918: 216–226). Krohn correctly points out that a poem and its subject can be of different ages, and suggests that the heroic epic poems derive by their subject from the Viking Age although the poems were composed in the thirteenth century.

The text-oriented approach to oral traditions underlying the Historical-Geographic Method was oriented to the reconstruction of the 'original' forms of oral poems. This approach gave little attention to the active use of the oral traditions in the culture that was studied. This method approached oral poetry as objects of oral tradition that could migrate and vary in time in a reconstructible way. The researchers' belief in this philologically based method and its universal applicability was very strong. However, despite appearing sophisticated and systematic, the method required selection between different redactions of the tradition in several phases that could only be based on the intuitive insight of the researcher: the weakness of the method was in dealing with what was variable and varying in the tradition (Honko 2000: 7–8). The central site of this methodological problem was connected to the tendency to neglect the role of the individual in collective tradition.

Despite the weaknesses of the Historical-Geographic Method as it was propagated at that time, Kaarle Krohn is credited with formalizing diachronic research of kalevalaic epic with a solid (as it was regarded at that time) methodological base that remains in the background of research done even today (Frog 2013). His work was careful and learned, yet his conclusions – based on a proposed historical background of the poetry – are occasionally less firmly grounded, and nationalistic tendencies emerge in his interpretations. However, it is notable that many of the basic ideas he had about the connections between the heroic epic and the Viking Age, building on the ideas of his father, have remained relevant to the present discussion.

As the Historical-Geographic Method failed to build reliable reconstructions of 'original' epic poems, the attention in diachronic research of kalevalaic epic was directed to more general levels of expression. Väinö Salminen questioned many of Krohn's views about the migration of poetry and the relations of poems to historical contexts. He stressed that the comparative research of the themes and subject matter of the poems was needed before arguments for their historicity. (Salminen 1934: 238, 242–243, 250–252.) Emil N. Setälä (1932: 34) claimed in his study on the *sampo* that, "In reality, we can only conclude that the general contents of the original poem have been such and such, and that we can in the best case find an ancient detail, but we cannot reconstruct an entire ancient poem."

Martti Haavio maintained that kalevalaic poems are remnants of the historical context from which they derive, but that these are no longer in forms that would reflect any single context. According to Haavio, the poems consist of numerous layers because they have been recomposed over and over again, in different locations. However, the age of a poem is not the age of the subject matter, which can in several cases be considerably older. Haavio nevertheless asserted that it is possible to discern contextual information, such as that concerning the cultural-historical milieu – the historical surroundings, the belief system and contexts – to which the subject matter in poems refers. (Haavio 1935: 11–18.) Haavio divided the epic chronologically into thematic periods of origins: into poems based on aetiological myths, poems based on nature myths, shamanic poetry, the "Sampo saga", and Viking poems (Haavio 1980: 292–293). He counted *Kaukamoinen*, *Lemminkäinen* and *The Bond* among the Viking poems. According to Haavio, these poems emanate a "genuine Viking spirit": longing for war, formidable feasts, erotic adventures and duels; such motifs only had counterparts in the "milieu of this time" (Haavio 1980: 216). Haavio claimed that the subject matter in the heroic poems was created in western Finland in the Viking Age, after the connections with Estonia were diminished, which would have taken place during the Migration Period (Haavio 1935: 11–18). In Haavio's romantically colored discussion, *The Bond* is a poem about how "men longed [to travel] beyond the seas like the brisk Vikings" (Haavio 1935: 23) and that duels, feasts, singing and playing as elements associated with a hero belong to this *Zeitgeist*.

Jalmari Jaakkola was a historian who considered heroic epic to present historical narratives deriving from the Viking Age, and that these were only corrupted by mythical elements to a certain degree (Jaakkola 1935: 446–457, 474–475). Leaning upon reconstructions of the poems made by Kaarle Krohn, he argued that their 'original' (i.e. reconstructed) forms belonged to a definable historical milieu within which they were composed and that this historical milieu was accurately reflected in the poems. Jaakkola divided the epic poetry into three thematic categories, each corresponding to the cultural milieus of regions where the poems were presumed to have originated: sea poetry, originating on the coast of southern Finland and Ingria; farming poetry, originating in a district of active farming in southwestern Finland; and poetry which describes the heroes' journeys to the realm of the mythical 'other', *Pohjola* or *Pohja* (such as *The Sampo*) originating in the southern inland district connected by rivers to both the shore of Southwest Finland (the River Kokemäenjoki) and Gulf of Bothnia (the River Kyröjoki). (Jaakkola 1935: 470.) Jaakkola's treatment is problematic in several respects: *a*) it relies on Krohn's problematic reconstructions of individual poems; *b*) the role of mythic imagination is marginalized and dismissed as superficial interference from folk-fantasy and fictionalization; *c*) these hypothetically reconstructed poems are then elevated to the status of historical texts; and *d*) the reconstruction is used to situate each text geographically with a construal of the socio-economic environs in which it was 'originally composed' as a recounting of actual events. This limits the reliability of Jaakkola's findings, but it reflects well the hopes that were then projected upon kalevalaic epic in connection with historical study.

The relationship of individual passages or images in kalevalaic poetry with the material environments of the past has been discussed in numerous scientific writings, especially as illustrative or contextual evidence for archaeological findings (e.g. Europaeus 1925; Lindqvist 1945–1946; Leppäaho 1949; 1950; also Lehtosalo-Hilander 1987). This type of approach was heavily criticized by Väinö Kaukonen (1987), who stressed the processual and continuously transforming nature of kalevalaic poetry. Kaukonen denied the value of this poetry as a historical source beyond the moment of performance. Although Kaukonen's responses are somewhat exaggerated, there remain valid methodological problems in relating archaeological findings to kalevalaic poems. Central among these problems are tendencies to over-interpret both archaeological and poetic evidence, especially in earlier scholarship (see also Frog), and the corresponding tendency of selective and nominal readings of the poems. This becomes evident for instance in Lehtosalo-Hilander's tracing of the origins of the epithet *tinarinta* ['tin (or bronze) chested'] for a young woman to the Iron Age on the basis of the customariness of showy bronze jewelry in Finland during this period (Lehtosalo-Hilander 1987). This suggestion does not take into account the popularity of such ornamentation still in recent times in closely related cultures, such as among the Seto in southeastern Estonia (where the same epithet was used in the corresponding poetic tradition).[7] Nor does this suggestion consider that the epithet has alternative semantics in the Ingrian kalevalaic tradition as a euphemism for a beautifully singing bird.[8] This does not mean that the suggestion could not hold true, but further delving into material and poetic evidence concerning Finno-Karelian and adjunct cultures may provide such suggestions with depth and firmness.

Matti Kuusi (1949) conducted a fundamental typological analysis of the cycle of poems connected to the creation and theft of the mysterious mythic object called *sampo*. Kuusi's analysis leaned heavily on philological and stylistic analysis situated in relation to settlement history. He suggested that a story about a sea raid was behind the poems, and argued that this story was composed in poetic form in the Viking Age. The core narrative, including the creation of the world, the forging of the *sampo* and the theft of the *sampo*, was expanded with the composition of *The Courtship* as well as a poem about the forging of a golden maiden. (Kuusi 1949: 349–350.) Kuusi suggested that this poetic entity was carried by settlers who migrated to Karelia along different routes, remaining largely in this form in the North whereas in the South its focus was shifted towards the courtship theme (Kuusi 1949: 355–356).

In his later research on the diachronic development of kalevalaic epic, Kuusi not only employed textual comparisons of different versions of a poem in different areas, but he also attempted to construct a general model of the development of poetic styles and narrative strategies in kalevalaic poetry. Kuusi argued that even though the exact original form of the kalevalaic poems was unrecoverable, careful comparative study enabled the identification of the original *thematic content* of poems and allowed the stages of their later development to be unraveled (Kuusi 1977: 40). This was possible owing to connections between the poems as circulating verbal texts and the language, religion, habits, livelihoods etc. of the time of their origins (Kuusi 1963: 16). The original thematic content of a poem can, according to Kuusi, be reached by a comparison of its different redactions to uncover the primary themes, motifs and stylistic features of the poem as a composition (Kuusi 1963: 24–27). Kuusi placed the primary aspects uncovered from different poems in dialogue with his conceptions of how, through history, connections with different neighboring cultures marked the language and mentality of poetic expression (Kuusi 1977: 38). Each poem, each of its episodes, and each individual linguistic, stylistic or structural element of the poem had a place within this model and interfaced with a respective historical context.

According to Kuusi, the origins of the different groups of kalevalaic epic belonged to certain periods of history. *Mythological poetry* (*varhaiskalevalainen runous*) belongs to the oldest stratum of kalevalaic poetry. This poetry reaches back to the emergence of Kalevala-meter and the mythic ideas and images may be rooted in still earlier periods. *Shamanic poetry* and *Adventure poetry* (*sydänkalevalainen runous*) can be argued to have developed in Finland and Karelia during the Migration and Merovingian Periods as well as during the Viking Age. The fact that poetry of this era does not exhibit versions among the Estonians or the Votes was considered evidence that it does not have roots in a common Finnic cultural heritage (on the diversification of Finnic languages, see Kallio). According to Kuusi's model, the emergence of a human dimension and dramatic dialogue in the poems, accompanied by the development of earlier deities into culture heroes and the depiction of the world as a stage for heroic deeds, were characteristic of the Iron Age and especially of the Viking Age as effects of increased Germanic contacts. (Kuusi 1977: 49.) In his view, contacts with travelling Scandinavian traders and warriors led Karelians to conduct similar journeys, inspiring poems such as *Kaukamoinen* and *The Bond*, in which pleasurable journeys and exciting sea adventures are contrasted with the hero's wife and home. Another epic poem that Kuusi attributed to the

Viking Age was *The Courtship*. (Kuusi 1949: 349; 1963: 236.) A characteristic thematic feature in kalevalaic epic that – according to Kuusi – belongs to the Viking Age is the concentration on people and personal relationships. This included psychologically convincing characters and ethnographic realism together with representations of erotic love, heavy use of dialogue and three-time repetition in the series of questions and answers. (Kuusi 1949: 347–349; 1963: 216–230; 1977: 50–51.) The vocabulary and ethnographic depictions in these poems fits with the Viking Age or the period preceding it (Kuusi 1963: 248). Triangulating formal and stylistic features with linguistic characteristics and content, Kuusi considered these features and emphases typical of poetry that derived from the Viking Age in this "jaunty and masculine" (Kuusi 1977: 51) group of kalevalaic epics. Kuusi's vision of the phases of kalevalaic poetry was reconstructed from synchronic material and largely based on inference and interpretations. Nevertheless, the poetry that he connected with the Viking Age was largely in line with the general consensus, which had remained fairly consistent through the history of the discipline since the time of Julius Krohn.

A reorientation of research on kalevalaic poetry and other oral traditions occurred in the wake of Post-Modernism. Changing emphasis highlighted the problematics of earlier diachronic research with a near-complete shift in focus to synchronic contexts in the 1960s–1970s. Anna-Leena Siikala is one of the few scholars to treat diachronic aspects of the epic traditions since that time. Distancing herself from the vision of Matti Kuusi and the long tradition of text-emphasis, Siikala has advanced discussion towards more fundamental levels of expression in the epic poetry. She interprets symbolic expressions of deeper semantic levels, of mental models that derived from ancient eras. As central cultural expressions, epic poems are connected to different levels of the cultural ground from which they spring. They simultaneously reference multiple contexts engaged through the history of their existence on numerous levels, ranging from archaic images rooted in the Finno-Ugric heritage to the symbolism of Iron Age battle and warfare and on through the medieval and more recent Christian cultural environments. Her seminal study in this area culminates in an account of the historically diverse models in the traditions of the spiritual specialist, a shaman-like ritual practitioner or a sage (*tietäjä*) (see Frog). Her discussion of the age of certain elements in the epic poetry relies largely upon parallels in Scandinavian sources. Based on this comparative study, Siikala suggests that the kalevalaic epics about courtship (*The Courtship*) and raiding (*The Sampo*) belong to narrative traditions that were common across cultures in northern Europe in the Viking Age. Much of the imagery that these poems contain is derived from ancient mythic mentality whereas this imagery was intertwined with the conventions of heroic narration. In the course of sociocultural changes that took place in the Middle Ages, these poems transformed and received new meanings, yet in areas where the Church had less influence, especially in Viena Karelia, the poems retained more of their ancient features. (Siikala 1994a: 148–149, 270–271, 272–275, 279–280.) According to Siikala, the parallel features between medieval Scandinavian materials and kalevalaic epic do not necessarily imply direct loans between the Scandinavian and Finno-Karelian narrative traditions but rather a common background of otherworldly imagery relevant to and shared by these cultures (Siikala 1994a: 285–286, 296–297).[9]

Towards Kalevalaic Heroic Epic in Viking Age Finland

The span of time from the Viking Age to the time when the epics were recorded is long – in most cases more than seven centuries. During this intermediate period, there were extreme changes in the contexts within which the poetry was performed. This was recognized already by Elias Lönnrot and expressed in his introduction to the *New Kalevala* (Lönnrot 2005: 7), however convinced he was of the ability of kalevalaic poetry to illuminate aspects of the past.

Expression in kalevalaic epic leans on references to concrete surroundings. The historical preservation of such references requires a certain degree of sensibility in changing contexts. Poetry and individual poems are multilayered both in terms of their content units and their narrative techniques (Kuusi 1977: 40). The meanings of individual narratives were created against the context-bound sphere of the experiences of the performers and their audiences. Individual words or poetic images could be used in numerous connections, and these connections affected their meanings for the cultural community in every period throughout the history of the poems. Individual poems have each had their place and function in the poetic culture. The potential to identify with epic figures as well as the more general value of epic as entertainment played a remarkable role in the continuity of use of the epic poems. Individual expressions of differing length have been available within the poetic culture as elements for constructing many different kinds of poems, and the meanings of the expressions have likewise varied according to different narrative frames, different times and different contexts of performance. The changing meanings eventually altered the texts themselves. Single words, lines, clusters of lines as well as narrative actors and motifs could be exchanged in order to maintain a sense of internal logic of a poem, resulting in the variation evident in the collections of the poetry. (See Harvilahti 1992.) The different diachronic approaches to the kalevalaic poetry discussed above were all attempts:

- to categorize and organize the diverse corpus of kalevalaic poetry
- to discern an original or normalized text out of the diversity of documented forms
- to date categories of poems or their features to particular historical eras
- to discover the significance and meaning through history of these categories for the communities that performed them (and later for researchers who recorded and analyzed them)

There are severe challenges in the use of oral poetry as a source for historical research in each step of the analysis, facing the constant risk of (potentially quite subtle) circularity in argumentation:

1. The corpus of poems collected in the nineteenth century is not fully representative of the traditions that prevailed at the time when they were documented and earlier periods remain beyond the scope of direct evidence. The construction and isolation of categories of nineteenth-century traditions as reflecting a 'Viking Age' milieu raises questions of their representativeness of such an early period when many of the other traditions that were prevailing in the nineteenth century had not reached Finland as early as the Viking Age.
2. Categories developed and described by researchers cannot fully depict the indigenous categorization of the tradition at any individual moment in history. Categorization is dependent on the interpretation and selection of diverse traditional materials, while the structuring of the corpus through categories reciprocally directs the researcher's analysis and thought.
3. The generalizations made in order to discern a normalized form of a poem inevitably do some degree of violence to the documented texts. When the material is diverse or scarce, even minor presuppositions may markedly shape the development of these generalizations and significantly affect the findings or interpretation.

The research material is inevitably decontextualized from the earlier historical environment. Consequently, conclusions that can be drawn directly from the material itself are both limited and conditional, while analysis must proceed through an ongoing negotiation of prejudices and presuppositions on the one hand and through ongoing dialogues with findings and relevant indicators from other fields of research on the other. Dialogues with other fields of research reveal significant changes in technologies, social practices and cultural contacts that can be reasonably postulated to have impacted imagery and themes in the oral tradition. However, connecting a poem in the oral tradition to the Viking Age through its imagery and themes does not reciprocally illuminate the Viking Age as such. Poetic images and expressions that are presumed to have originated in the Viking Age have had a long history of repetition in performances, and even textual environments where they were conventionally applied undoubtedly faced changes across the centuries. Although the Viking Age may have provided essential conditions for certain images and themes through social changes, it does not necessarily follow that these entered the epic tradition at that time as opposed to later. These observations present significant methodological concerns that require care and caution when considering potential relationships between documented epics and the Viking Age.

A Comparative Approach

One way to date the different elements of the poems is to compare them to other traditional texts that were produced closer to the studied period. The comparative study of the traditions of adjacent areas, namely Scandinavia, is an important basis for arguments dating kalevalaic heroic epics to the Viking Age. Such comparisons imply close connections between the cultures within which these traditions were maintained. However, comparative textual analysis produces the points of comparison itself: one finds parallels by looking for them.[10] In an historical approach to a tradition, the relevance of the results of comparative analysis has to be evaluated separately against supporting evidence provided by other fields of research. For instance, similarities in single aspects of cultures that are distant from each other spatially, temporally and/or culturally, can be based on similarities in human experience or in the tradition system of the compared cultures. In this case, such similarities are only of phenomenal value, unless there can be shown historical circumstances that have enabled cultural contacts or common roots behind the studied traditions.

Adventurous narratives and an exemplary character to which they are connected constitute the core elements of a heroic epic. The essence of this heroic character is constituted of the situations with which he is faced, of his reactions to these situations, and of the complementary implications these constituents evoke in the tradition community. The following example of a comparative study proposes a hypothesis that the *heroic character* in kalevalaic epic is a narrative element of a relevant level of abstraction and that it represents one of the slowly changing key elements of an epic poem. The example study will illustrate that a particular, disruptive heroic character in kalevalaic epic has equivalents in the epic traditions of other cultures and, if this reflects a historical relationship, comparison can carry information about cultural connections as far in the past as the Viking Age. In the following, the heroic character will be discussed as a cognitive core or a point of departure for heroic narration.

The heroic character in the kalevalaic poems of *Kaukamoinen* and *Lemminkäinen* exhibits essential similarities with outlaw characters in medieval Icelandic sagas – so-called Family Sagas (*Íslendingasögur*) – and especially in the biographical saga that represents an outlaw as a heroic character, *The Saga of Grettir* (*Grettis saga Ásmundarsonar*), from the early fourteenth century. The Family Sagas were based on historical traditions and presented historical Icelandic personae from the Viking Age. Grettir's character was nevertheless construed largely on the basis of heroic models. Grettir is depicted in the saga as a stubborn, exceptionally strong and heroically ambitious Icelander. He was sentenced to outlawry, and the saga is primarily devoted to Grettir's struggle for survival and his heroic feats while he lives as an outlaw. As a conclusion to Grettir's biography, he withdrew to an island where he could eventually only be overcome and killed with the aid of sorcery. The saga was largely based on oral traditions that depicted the immensely strong outlaw according to traditional models for depicting a warrior hero (Halldórsson 1977; Ahola 2005; 2014: 356–365). The saga is extremely protracted and interwoven with numerous sub-plots, yet Grettir's character and biography are clearly perceived. In a typical medieval fashion, the saga is built around its central events by expanding them and supplementing these with interpolations (Clover 1982).

When outlaw characters are focal characters in Icelandic saga literature, they are presented as superior warriors who are able to overcome even otherworldly opponents. Nevertheless, they are rejected by their own community. The kalevalaic hero Kaukamoinen shares these broad qualities. These qualities are complemented by specific motifs that are more narrowly interfaced with communal activity in society and conceptual models for interpersonal relations, especially between genders and family generations. Both cultures can effectively illustrate hostile relations between the hero and his community in particular narrative motifs such as an intrusion to a communal gathering as an uninvited guest. The hero's relations with the opposite sex are often socially unaccepted and he is forced to rely on his mother for support rather than on the protective institutions of the community, such as a leader, peer group or father and immediate male kin. The heroic figure of Kaukamoinen is directly paralleled by the kalevalaic hero Lemminkäinen. However, rather than threatened with retribution for his disruptive behavior, Lemminkäinen is killed as an outcome of disrupting the feast and the relationship to his mother is manifested through an omen that leads her to recover him from the world of the dead. A number of the essential qualities are also foregrounded in *The Orphan*. In this case, however, significant structural differences affect how motifs are realized, such as the death of the hero's mother preventing her later support and the hero being raised as an unwanted child. This situates the hero in the household that he disrupts as a social environment rather than having him enter the household as an uninvited guest at a central social event. Interestingly, although the hero of *The Orphan* lacks connections to the motifs in the later life of Icelandic saga outlaws that are more prominent with Kaukamoinen and Lemminkäinen, he is characterized by other motifs associated with the youth of these outlaws as indicators of their later heroic quality.[11]

The same heroic type appears in the two narrative traditions. The superiority and arrogance of this type is realized in antisocial behavior and socially disruptive actions, and he is also depicted as a sexually hazardous figure. In the manner of warrior heroes in general, he demonstrates his strength and capability by overcoming supernatural opponents and other dangers, and his antisocial conduct does not inhibit from conceiving him as a heroic character. At the same time, his manly strength and sexual vigor are juxtaposed with his dependence of his mother, who saves her son from an 'honest fight' with his pursuers and thus compromises his heroic quality altogether.

The outlaw character as found in Icelandic saga literature is a product of the cultural and literary environment of the thirteenth and fourteenth century Iceland. This outlaw character is connected to numerous characters in another branch of saga literature, the so-called Legendary Sagas (*fornaldarsögur*), as well as in heroic poetry. In these texts, warrior-heroes raid in hostile environments, overcome superior and supernatural opponents and win the favor of noble ladies. Although the Legendary Sagas are indebted to continental romance literature – especially in superficial descriptions of clothes, character qualities and the splendor of courts visited by the heroes – not unlike Grettir, these heroes and the central events of their fantastic biographies reflect indigenous oral traditions which could already boast of a long history. The fantastic quality of these sagas and associated Germanic epic poetry is far more consistent with the quality of kalevalaic epic than the more naturalistic Family Sagas. The closest parallel to the kalevalaic heroes nevertheless remains a group of characters in the Family Sagas and not heroes of the Legendary Sagas. Although this would suggest a non-generic connection between the traditions, it does not exclude the possibility of a heroic tradition that only entered literary expression in connection with the outlaw characters of the Family Sagas.

This comparison can be complemented by triangulation with a similar heroic character found in North Russian heroic epic traditions of so-called *bylina* poetry. The first records of *bylina* poetry in writing are from the eighteenth century whereas the most important collections postdate the mid-nineteenth century. By this time, the tradition was met only in Northwest Russia and in a few places in Siberia. Generally speaking, these heroic epics narrated about a number of heroes who, at the service of the Prince, successfully fought and overpowered enemies (often Tartars) and supernatural opponents that threatened the Kievan Rus'. There are some heroic characters among the *bylina* poetry that resemble the rejected hero of kalevalaic and Scandinavian traditions. Most of the *bylina* heroes are superior warriors and are told to have achieved superhuman victories over enemy armies or dragons. The hero's role as a superior warrior is not uncommon in the world's heroic epics. However, the superiority of the warrior in *bylina* poetry is connected to the rejection from the hero's own community and manifested at a communal feast to which the hero appears uninvited in a number of cases, clearly characterizing a heroic type or model in this tradition.[12] The hero's mother also emerges as central for these heroes as the only reliable support. As in kalevalaic and Scandinavian traditions, the mother's role highlights the isolation of the hero from the male community.[13] (See e.g. Bailey & Ivanova 1998.)

These heroic traditions of the three different cultures differ from each other in many respects. In spite of this, they exhibit an important similarity in addition to numerous parallels between specific narrative elements not elaborated on here: the rejected and disruptive character appears in a focal role, and this is in a narrative genre where the focal role itself presents the character as a hero – a hero of epic proportions – while the construction of that role is especially accomplished between the hero's disruption of a communal feast where he is an outsider on the one hand and on the other, his relationship with his mother, in isolation from a broader male community. Although broad, these similarities do not seem likely to be accidental and suggest a common background to the heroic traditions. The degree to which they reflect cultural contacts in a given historical period is a more problematic question. For example, the significant common elements of an intrusion at a feast and the importance of the mother to the hero are also central to the heroic character of Odysseus and they may have an incredibly long history in Indo-European cultures, although they may have functioned quite differently in their relationship to the construction of the hero's identity. It is therefore difficult to assess when they may have developed into a constellation for constructing a particular heroic type in the epic traditions of Northern Europe or how and why this constellation would be shared cross-culturally by groups of such different linguistic and cultural backgrounds.

There are several possibilities that could account for the resemblance of the heroic characters in these three traditions, such as:

1. This heroic character type and strategies for constructing this identity were adapted from a Scandinavian tradition (West) into kalevalaic and *bylina* traditions (East), either before the thirteenth century, when the earliest Scandinavian written texts were produced, or later, as a descendant of the heroic character that was represented in saga literature as one trait of the tradition.
2. The heroic character was adapted from the East to the West, whence this adaptation would have taken place prior to written documentation of Scandinavian examples in the thirteenth century.
3. The traditions of a rejected hero in the three cultural spheres derive from a common background in a (broadly) definable historical period.
4. The resemblances are caused by a wider background of the narrative traditions, suggested, for instance, by biographical patterns recognized in Indo-European heroic biographies (e.g. de Vries 1963).
5. There is no historical connection but the heroic characters developed in the respective cultures independently and their resemblance is, if not wholly coincidental, attributable to societal and cultural circumstances that led to the relevance and attractiveness of such a heroic character.
6. There is no historical connection and the resemblance is largely a facade constructed by the selective reading, interpretation and category-construction of the researcher.

When placed in dialogue with the broader corpora of each culture, the possibility of point (6) is tested and breaks down. Point (5) is necessary for consideration and interesting because of the great differences between the social and cultural environments with which the three cultural traditions were associated. It is also necessary to recognize that societal and cultural circumstances are also essential to the heroic model having relevance in cultural contact and exchange for these to become established and esteemed in vernacular epic traditions. Point (4) is also relevant to engage in dialogue: the Indo-European biographical pattern is almost certainly relevant, but as Finnic languages are not Indo-European, the kalevalaic epic traditions cannot belong to that tradition without adapting it through cultural contact (unless this pattern is considered to be depictive of indigenous Finno-Ugric tradition as well). The Scandinavian and kalevalaic patterns also share the marked deviation from this pattern in that the biography does not conclude with the hero's social (re)integration. This makes it relevant to consider the possibility that the three traditions derive from a common background in a (broadly) definable historical period (3) or may have been adapted cross-culturally either from east to west (2) or from west to east (1).

Connections between Finns, Karelians, Scandinavians and Slavs are well attested in historical, linguistic and archaeological evidence. However, Slavic contacts with Finnic groups seem to have become vivid during the Viking Age (see KALLIO), which is also the period in which trade routes were opening between Scandinavia and the East with intensive contacts between Germanic and Slavic groups, even resulting in a Germanic rulership in Novgorod, which then moved to Kiev – the **Ruþs*, the ethnonym from which *Russia* derives and which may be connected to the Finnic ethnonym for Swedes, *Ruotsi* (SCHALIN). The Viking Age thus presents one possible venue when Finns, Karelians, Scandinavians and Slavs were in vivid communication, in which cultural interaction and exchange of folklore would parallel that in language (see HÄKKINEN; KUZMIN; SCHALIN) and material culture (cf. RANINEN & WESSMAN; LAAKSO). The heroic narratives discussed here are not uniform, but this does not mean that they cannot have a connection: the temporal and cultural distance between the recordings of the traditions and the period of contact would necessarily result in differences even if the traditions were local adaptations – *oicotypes* – of a tradition with common origins. The adaptation of a new element to a culture results in an oicotype of this element as its adaptation to an existing cultural system or tradition ecology (see FROG). In comparative research, it is not reasonable to expect to find perfect parallelism between the manifestations of a traditional feature in different cultural contexts. If the heroic traditions discussed above have a common background in the intercommunication between groups of warrior-tradesmen, for instance in the area of Ladoga as Kuusi has suggested, it would mean that this tradition had to adapt to different cultural environments and then to different milieus before being manifested in documented sources centuries later (Icelandic materials from the thirteenth century onwards, collections of Karelian and Russian epic traditions mainly in the nineteenth and early twentieth centuries) in those forms that are accessible to the present day researcher.

The expressions of which these texts consist had meaning primarily in the contexts that they were performed in. Even if the rejected heroic character of the Northern European epic traditions derived from heroic traditions that had emerged centuries earlier, its manifestations in different medieval Icelandic literary genres were adaptations to the current milieu and cultural environment (for theoretical premises, see Honko 1981; 1985). The meanings attested for this heroic character, and hence its use and expressions in different narrative genres, only partially implement in the recorded texts those meanings that this heroic character had had in earlier times. The meanings were newly generated in the new contexts. For instance, in the medieval Icelandic cultural environment and within the genre of the Family Sagas, the role of a rebellious hero rejected by his community was displayed by an outlaw character. This character also acquired meanings against associative elements in other contemporary cultural expressions, such as biographies of Norwegian kings, mythological texts and saints' lives as well as the conceptions about rejection they promoted. In the Family Sagas, all these conceptions and associative meanings affected the use of the heroic character in different connections, which led to the polysemy of the medieval Icelandic concept 'outlaw' (Ahola 2014).

The attachment of similar qualities or motifs to the kalevalaic, Icelandic and Russian heroic epic traditions can be argued to imply mere phenomenological parallelism if there is not a recognizable historical venue for a connection between the traditions. On the basis of internal evidence suggestive of some relation among these narrative traditions, it is only possible to pose hypothetical suggestions about their relationship: it remains impossible to state anything certain. The contributions of other disciplines will gradually, through dialogue with one another, develop a reconstructive image and understanding of the cultural milieu of the Viking Age in Finland. If this milieu appears adaptable to the worldview reflected through kalevalaic heroic epics, and moreover if it appears more convincingly relevant to and consistent with the heroic world and mentalities of these epic models than the worldviews of later eras, then those dialogues may help better situate these epics and their historical backgrounds. If this becomes the case, then the heroic epic can, at least on some level of generalization and in relation with some cultural fields, perhaps reciprocally help to illuminate the Viking Age in Finland with aspects of interests and even ideologies and mentalities – as something more than mere decoration. This kind of study simultaneously opens new questions concerning kalevalaic poetry as a system of textual entities of different orders and new questions concerning the impact of the historical origins of the poems upon their meanings and usage in the time that the poems were recorded. This kind of an approach can elevate the early notions of the discrepancy between poetic expressions and the context in which they were performed, such as the case of maritime adventures narrated in the midst of inland wilderness or the case of wide-spread poetic images that were discussed above, as indicators of the diachronic depth of the poetry in addition to their function on the occasion of singing as traditional narrative elements that a singer utilized in order to lead the audience into the world of fantasy.

Conclusion

Comparative research can give suggestions for the uses and functions – and hence the mode – of heroic epics in the tradition system. The manly functions of heroic epics have, for instance, had relevance in contexts that may reach all the way from the Viking Age to the nineteenth century. These functions can be interpreted in terms of entertainment, the discussion of sensitive matters for the community and the elevation of themes that the poems present through collective means (feasts, fights, courting, etc.). This view highlights the significance of the particular circumstance in connection to which the piece of poetry is performed or actualized, or its employment as a role model or explanation of conventional action. Heroic epic has not, however, been the whole field of tradition even in the notorious Viking Age. The tradition system has consisted of many elements that have not left a recognizable trace. In the ethnography of Viking Age Finland, it is also necessary to take into account the possibility of forms of tradition that have not left traces in the subsequent tradition and that do not conform to the stereotypical image of a manly, warlike period because otherwise the image of the oral tradition becomes rather twisted.

In the interpretation of the preserved epics, it is necessary to notice that the frames for their interpretation are highly limited: the information about the sociocultural circumstances of the period in question only provides a partial model of the reality against which the meanings of the epic poetry were only produced. When there are no detailed texts available, the relation of epics to this model of reality has to be interpreted on the basis of general thematic topics and images. These topics and images were only connected to the actual surroundings to a limited degree and through differing modes of reference. Recent research on combining poetic conventions of different genres of kalevalaic poetry as a means of generating meaning in the synchronic nineteenth century poetic culture (Tarkka 2005) and within an individual's repertoire (Timonen 2004) has effectively questioned the whole concept of a stable kalevalaic 'poem' and the premises of its diachronic depth. These studies and the insights they offer need to be taken into account in the diachronic research of kalevalaic poetry.

When reconstructing a culture in a distant past, a researcher operates within wide margins for error. In order to still be able to talk about research and not politics or fantasy, it is necessary to carefully bring to light not only everything of which there *is* evidence, but also of which there is *no* evidence: an acknowledgement of the limiting frames of interpretation that the discussion must remain within. Active interdisciplinary research can give extensive insight into the diachronic study of epic tradition by providing information on such topics as settlement history, environment and cultural contacts that can be reflected upon in reconstructing the development and history of epic poetry. This study, for its part, can contribute to the general overview of the circumstances in Finland during the Viking Age.

Notes

1 Salminen 1934: 130–151; Virtanen 1968: 17–25; Kuusi 1977: 72–74; Tarkka 2005: 40–43; Frog & Stepanova 2011.

2 See e.g. *SKVR* I2: 1101; I4: 232; VII1: 100; XII2: 5147; XIII4: 12387.

3 See the articles "Suomen synty" (1990b [1836]) ['The Birth of Finland'] and "Muinelmia" (1990a [1836]) ['Ancient Memories'] in Elias Lönnrot's journal *Mehiläinen*.

4 Krohn 1918: 37–51; Hautala 1949: 192–197, 242–245; Kuusi 1977: 40; Kuusi 1980; Frog 2013.
5 Kaarle Krohn seems here to have followed the insight of his father Julius Krohn (1885: 574), who argued that the poems *Kaukamoinen* and *The Orphan* had their historical background in the Viking Age.
6 The idea of a dominating Germanic population in western Finland no longer holds: see Schalin; Raninen & Wessman.
7 I want to thank Frog for bringing this to my attention.
8 E.g. *SKVR* XIII1: 183, 2522; XIII2: 2716; XIII3: 10092.
9 For a more recent approach to this phenomenon in terms of the development of cross-culturally "shared systems of traditional referentiality", see Stepanova 2011.
10 Seppo Knuuttila pointed this out in a private conversation in the winter 2002.
11 These motifs appear as a cluster in connection with the fairytale type Strong John (ATU 650A) known as *kolbítur* in the Icelandic folklore. The cluster of motifs comprise a description of an unpromising youth who accomplishes the tasks he is given in a destructive way. Whereas in the folk tales, Strong John later proves to be able to use his strength constructively as a hero, in *The Orphan*, the destructive behaviour appears as a form of revenge.
12 Especially to the heroes Ilya Muromets, Dobrynya Nikitich, Vasily Kazimirovich, Sadko and Vasily Buslayev.
13 Such as in connection with the bylina heroes Dyuk Stepanovich, Vasily Buslayev, Dobrynya Nikitich and Khoten Bludovich. Especially the Novgorodian *bylina* hero Vasily Buslajev embodies the rejected hero.

References

Sources

Grettis saga Ásmundarsonar. Ed. Guðni Jónsson. Íslenzk fornrit 7. Reykjavík: Hið íslezka fornritafélag, 1964.

Suomen Kansan Vanhat Runot I–XIV. Helsinki: Suomalaisen Kirjallisuuden Seura, 1908–1948.

Suomen Kansan Vanhat Runot XV. Helsinki: Suomalaisen Kirjallisuuden Seura, 1997.

Literature

Ahola, Joonas. 2005. Islantilaissaagan monitasoinen rakenne. Unpublished licentiate thesis. Helsinki: University of Helsinki.

Ahola, Joonas. 2014. *Outlawry in the Icelandic Family Sagas.* PhD thesis. Helsinki: University of Helsinki.

Bailey, James, & Tatjana Ivanova. 1998. *An Anthology of Russian Folk Epics.* Armonk / New York: Sharpe.

Borenius, A. A. 1873. Missä Kalevala on syntynyt? *Suomen Kuvalehti* 1: 269–274.

Clover, Carol. 1982. *The Medieval Saga.* Cornell University Press: Ithaca / London.

Europaeus, Aarne. 1925. Etelä-Pohjanmaan asutuskysymyksiä. *Kalevalaseuran vuosikirja* 5: 144–188.

Frog. 2010. Multiformit kalevalamittaisessa runoudessa. In Seppo Knuuttila, Ulla Piela & Lotte Tarkka (eds.). *Kalevalamittaisen runouden tulkintoja.* Suomalaisen Kirjallisuuden Seura: Helsinki. Pp. 91–113.

Frog. 2013. Revisiting the Historical-Geographic Method(s). In Karina Lukin, Frog

& Sakari Katajamaki (eds.). *Limited Sources, Boundless Possibilities: Textual Scholarship and the Challenges of Oral and Written Texts*. RMN Newsletter 7. Helsinki: Folklore Studies, University of Heslinki. Pp. 18–34.

Frog & Stepanova, Eila. 2011. Alliteration in (Balto-) Finnic Languages. In Jonathan Roper (ed.). *Alliteration in Culture*. Houndmills: Palgrave MacMillan. Pp. 195–218.

Haavio, Martti. 1935. *Suomalaisen muinaisrunouden maailma*. Porvoo - Helsinki: WSOY.

Haavio, Martti. 1980 [1952]. *Kirjokansi: Suomen kansan kertomarunoutta*. Helsinki: WSOY.

Halldórsson, Óskar. 1977. Goðsögnin um Gretti: In Jakob Benediktsson, Einar G. Pétursson & Jónas Kristjánsson (eds.). *Sjötíu ritgerðir helgaðar Jakobi Benediktssyni 20. Júlí 1977*. Reykjavík: Stofnun Árna Magnússonar. Pp. 627–639.

Harvilahti, Lauri. 1992. The Production of Finnish Epic Poetry: Fixed Wholes of Creative Compositions? *Oral Tradition* 7(1): 87–101.

Hautala, Jouko. 1954. *Suomalainen kansanrunoudentutkimus*. Helsinki: Suomalaisen Kirjallisuuden Seura.

Holmwood, John. 2010. Functionalism and Its Critics. In Charles Crothers (ed.). *Historical Developments and Theoretical Approaches in Sociology* II. EOLSS Publishers.

Honko, Lauri. 1981. Four Forms of Adaptation of Tradition. In Lauri Honko & Vilmos Voigt (eds.). *Adaptation, Change, and Decline in Oral Literature*. Helsinki: Suomalaisen Kirjallisuuden Seura. Pp.19–33.

Honko, Lauri. 1985. Rethinking Tradition Ecology. *Temenos: Studies in Comparative Religion 21*. Pp. 55–82.

Honko, Lauri. 2000. Thick Corpus and Organic Variation: An Introduction. In Lauri Honko (ed.). *Thick Corpus, Organic Variation and Textuality in Oral Tradition*. Helsinki: Finnish Literature Society. Pp. 3–28.

Jaakkola, Jalmari. 1935. *Suomen historia II: Suomen varhaishistoria: heimokausi ja "Kalevala-kulttuuri"*. Porvoo / Helsinki: WSOY.

Kaukonen, Väinö. 1979. *Lönnrot ja Kalevala*. Helsinki: Suomalaisen Kirjallisuuden Seura.

Kaukonen, Väinö. 1987. Arkeologia ja esikirjallinen runous. In Martti Linna (ed.). *Muinaisrunot ja todellisuus: Suomen kansan vanhojen runojen historiallinen tausta*. Historian Aitta 20. Jyväskylä: Gummerus. Pp. 20–28.

Korhonen, Mikko. 1994. The Early History of the Kalevala Metre. In Anna-Leena Siikala & Sinikka Vakimo (eds.). *Songs beyond the Kalevala: Transformations of Oral Poetry*. Studia Fennica Folkloristica 2. Helsinki: Suomalaisen Kirjallisuuden Seura. Pp. 75–87.

Krohn, Julius. 1885. *Suomalaisen kirjallisuuden historia I: Kalevala*. Helsinki.

Krohn, Kaarle. 1903–1910. *Kalevalan runojen historia*. Helsinki: Suomalaisen Kirjallisuuden Seura.

Krohn, Kaarle. 1914. *Suomalaisten runojen uskonto*. Helsinki: Suomalaisen Kirjallisuuden Seura / WSOY.

Krohn, Kaarle. 1918. *Kalevalankysymyksiä: Opas Suomen kansan vanhojen runojen tilaajille ja käyttäjille ynnä suomalaisen kansanrunouden opiskelijoille ja harrastajille*. Suomalais-Ugrilaisen Seuran Aikakauskirja 35. Helsinki: Suomalais-Ugrilainen Seura.

Kuusi, Matti. 1949. *Sampo-eepos: Typologinen analyysi*. Helsinki: Suomalais-Ugrilainen Seura.

Kuusi, Matti (ed.). 1963. *Suomen kirjallisuus I: kirjoittamaton kirjallisuus*. Helsinki: Suomalaisen Kirjallisuuden Seura.

Kuusi, Matti. 1977. Introduction. In Matti Kuusi, Keith Bosley & Michael Branch (eds. & trans.). *Finnish Folk Poetry: Epic*. Helsinki: Finnish Literature Society. Pp. 21–79.

Kuusi, Matti. 1980. Suomalainen tutkimusmenetelmä. In Outi Lehtipuro (ed.). *Perinteentutkimuksen perusteita*. Porvoo: WSOY. Pp. 21–73.

Lehtosalo-Hilander, Pirkko-Liisa. 1987. Läntisen Suomen muinaispukujen ja kansanrunojen välisistä yhteyksistä. In Martti Linna (ed.). *Muinaisrunot ja todellisuus: Suomen kansan vanhojen runojen historiallinen tausta:* Historian Aitta 20. Jyväskylä: Gummerus. Pp. 51–65.

Leino, Pentti. 1986. *Language and Metre: Metrics and the Metrical Systems of Finnish*. Studia Fennica 31. Helsinki: Suomalaisen Kirjallisuuden Seura.

Leino, Pentti. 1994. The Kalevala Metre and Its Development. In Anna-Leena Siikala & Sinikka Vakimo (eds.). *Songs beyond the Kalevala: Transformations of Oral Poetry*. Studia Fennica Folkloristica 2. Helsinki: Suomalaisen Kirjallisuuden Seura. Pp. 56–74.

Leppäaho, Jorma. 1949. Kalevala vertailevan muinaistieteen valaisemana. In F. Heporauta & Martti Haavio (eds.). *Kalevala: Kansallinen aarre*. Porvoo: WSOY.

Leppäaho, Jorma. 1950. Tarsilaisen poltto. *Kalevalaseuran vuosikirja* 30: 99–111.

Lindqvist, Sune. 1946–1946. Muinaisruotsalaisia Kalevala-kuvia. *Kalevalaseuran vuosikirja* 25–26: 152–163.

Lönnrot, Elias. 1990a [1836]. Muinelmia. In Elias Lönnrot, *Valitut teokset 2: Mehiläinen*. Raija Majamaa (ed.). Helsinki: Suomalainen Kirjallisuuden Seura. Pp. 9–14, 69–76, 87–93, 97–93.

Lönnrot, Elias. 1990b [1836]. Suomen synty. In Elias Lönnrot, *Valitut teokset 2: Mehiläinen*. Raija Majamaa (ed.). Helsinki: Suomalainen Kirjallisuuden Seura. Pp. 6–9.

Lönnrot, Elias. 2005 [1849]. *Kalevala*. Helsinki: Suomalaisen Kirjallisuuden Seura.

Porthan, Henrik Gabriel. 1983 [1766–1778]. *Suomalaisesta runoudesta*. [*De Poësi Fennica*]. Helsinki: Suomalaisen Kirjallisuuden Seura.

Salminen, Väinö. 1934. *Suomalaisten muinaisrunojen historia I*. Helsinki: Suomalaisen Kirjallisuuden Seura.

Setälä, Emil Nestor. 1932. *Sammon arvoitus*. Helsinki: Otava.

Siikala, Anna-Leena. 1994a. *Suomalainen samanismi: Mielikuvien historiaa*. Helsinki: Suomalaisen Kirjallisuuden Seura.

Siikala, Anna-Leena. 1994b. Kalevalan Pohjola: Itää vai länttä, myyttiä vai historiaa. In Väinö Jääskeläinen & Ilkka Savijärvi (eds.). *Tieten tahtoen*. Studia Carelica Humanistica 3. Joensuu: Joensuun Yliopiston Humanistinen Tiedekunta. Pp. 9–21

Stepanova, Eila. 2011. Reflections of Belief Systems in Karelian and Lithuanian Laments: Shared Systems of Traditional Referentiality? *Archaeologia Baltica* 15: 128–143.

Tarkka, Lotte. 2005. *Rajarahvaan laulu: Tutkimus Vuokkiniemen kalevalamittaisesta runokulttuurista 1821–1921*. Helsinki: Suomalaisen Kirjallisuuden Seura.

Timonen, Senni. 2004. *Minä, tila, tunne: Näkökulmia kalevalamittaiseen lyriikkaan*. Helsinki: Suomalaisen Kirjallisuuden Seura.

Virtanen, Leea. 1968. *Kalevalainen laulutapa Karjalassa*. Helsinki: Suomalaisen Kirjallisuuden Seura.

de Vries, Jan. 1963: *Heroic Song and Heroic Legend*. Frome / London: Oxford University Press.

Kaisa Häkkinen

Finnish Language and Culture of the Viking Age in Finland

Language is a man-made system to enable and facilitate human interaction, and under these circumstances it has always generated lexical designations for referents worth speaking about for some reason or other, and updated the lexical inventory when necessary. Every living language has undergone a long process of development, and stored masses of information over time. Thus every natural language constitutes a multi-layer package of diachronic knowledge of its speakers and their neighbours, environment, culture, objects, relations, habits, contacts and other circumstances the speakers of the language have once been exposed to.

How to Open the Package

There are basically two different approaches at hand when investigating historical changes of the vocabulary of a natural language. Historical studies in a proper sense of the word presuppose availability of written sources. By means of manuscripts and printed items, potential changes of the lexis can be identified and attested when comparing documents of the same language of different ages with each other.

As far as the Finnish language is concerned, the historical method is limited in use to (early) modern times. The first book ever printed in Finnish was a modest *Abc Book* of Michael Agricola, which appeared probably in 1543. In addition, there are some manuscripts, but none of them is significantly earlier. When investigating older strata of the lexis, the standard procedure is linguistic comparison. Cognates, i.e. the 'same' words found with a wide distribution within the same language family, can be assumed to be indigenous and of early origin, provided they do not show any apparent characteristics (e.g. phonotactic or semantic properties) of later innovations or loans. To put it very simply, the wider the distribution of the cognates, the older the word is supposed to be. On the other hand, words with a wide geographical distribution but also showing counterparts in geographically adjacent languages belonging to other language families are assumed to be old borrowings in one direction or the other. Words with

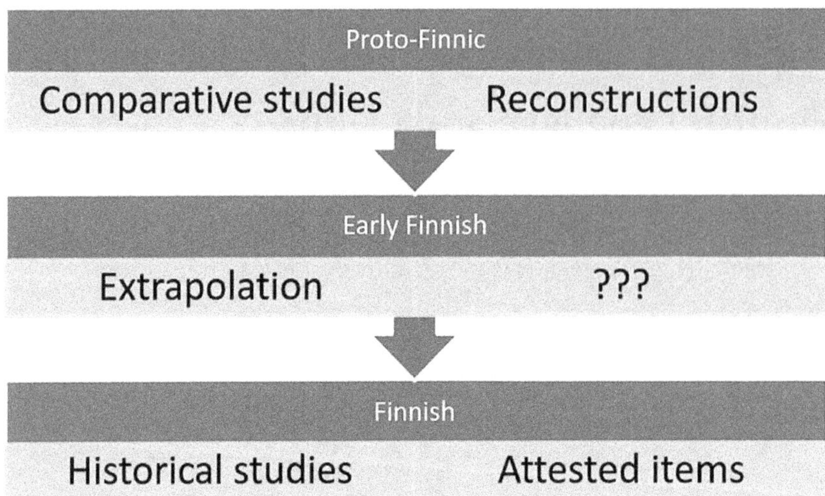

Fig. 1. An Approach to the prehistory and history of Finnish.

a narrow distribution are interpreted as later neologisms, either indigenous or loanwords, depending upon the languages in which they occur.

The prehistory and development of Proto-Finnic, i.e. the common predecessor of all Balto-Finnic languages such as Finnish, Estonian, Vepsian, Votic etc., is relatively well known thanks to intensive research and traditional comparative studies on Finno-Ugric languages. The history of written Finnish since the middle of the sixteenth century is quite well documented too. In contrast, very little attention has been paid to the processes that led to the formation of Finnish as an independent sub-unit after the break-up of Late Proto-Finnic and to the rise of a Finnish ethnicity and nation as they can be defined nowadays. This is understandable for practical reasons: there are no linguistic means to approach the beginnings of this phase directly. The state of the situation is illustrated in Fig. 1. The only way of getting knowledge about this 'black hole' is a kind of linguistic extrapolation. The Viking Age falls in the middle of this linguistically challenging period.

There are so many shared properties and joint historical innovations in the Balto-Finnic languages that the existence of a Proto-Finnic period has not been called into question. Yet there is no undisputed way to date the gradual (?) break-up of Late Proto-Finnic and the beginnings of the independent development of Finnish, or more exactly, of the Northern Finnic dialects that develop later into Finnish (for chronological alternatives see e.g. Kallio 2006 and Kallio). The linguistic period falling between the Late Proto-Finnic and the rise of literary Finnish does not even have an established name, even though the period lasted something like one and a half millennia and masses of revolutionary changes took place, especially during the Middle Ages, as Finland was officially joined with Sweden and Christianity was established through a collaboration of ecclesiastical and secular power.

The first signs of Christianity appeared in Finland towards the end of the first millennium. In Finland this period is called the Late Iron Age rather than the Viking Age (see RANINEN & WESSMAN), but in a Scandinavian context they are equivalent. In the history of the Finnish language, this period has sometimes been called *varhaissuomi*, literally 'Early Finnish' (e.g. Ikola 1968; see also SCHALIN), but the term has not become established. The lack of an established label in linguistic research reveals the fact that the period has been very much overlooked in linguistic research so far. It has been seen as a kind of 'mission impossible'.

Building up a Methodological Framework

All the major changes Finland underwent during the Viking Age and the Middle Ages have left traces in the evolution of the Finnish vocabulary. The lexical development cannot be observed directly, however, as there are virtually no Finnish documents of medieval origin apart from some proper names of places and persons in Latin and Swedish records. Some birch bark letters written in Old Karelian have been found in Novgorod, but they do not throw light upon the status of the Finnish of that time directly. Therefore, innovations and changes of that dark period must be identified and dated in an indirect way, starting with comparisons of well-established strata of the Finnish lexis, both older and younger. If we know through traditional comparative studies which elements and characteristics of Modern Finnish already existed in Late Proto-Finnic, we can be sure that they must have been there between those checkpoints too, even if we cannot prove it with historical documents. Innovations later than those of the Middle Ages can be verified by written material.

Loanwords constitute another useful source of knowledge. The Balto-Finnic languages share a considerable number of old Indo-European loanwords, which in most cases can be classified further as (Proto-)Indo-European, Aryan, Baltic (or Balto-Slavic) and Germanic loans. On the basis of these previously known loanwords, we can say much about the structure and relative chronology of prehistoric forms of Finnish. Several Indo-European languages have been documented in written records earlier than the Finno-Ugric ones. So advantage can be taken of those records when reconstructing older forms of Finnish words. In several cases, knowledge of the changes of source languages may enable dating of lexical innovations in the target language. Fig. 2 shows a parallel description of the historical background of Swedish and Finnish (a more detailed specification is given by SCHALIN). The names of the language periods mentioned there will be used later in this chapter.

Of those loanword strata mentioned above, two layers are especially interesting in terms of the Viking Age. The first one consists of those Scandinavian loanwords which can be dated to the end of the first millennium of the Christian era. In principle, they could be classified as Swedish loanwords, as the individual history of Swedish is usually estimated to start with the Viking Age, but in practice, all the Scandinavian languages were still in the midst of the process of disintegration and thus they were very similar to each other at that time.

From Pre-Germanic to Swedish		From Early Proto-Finnic to Finnish	
(Proto-)Indo-European	→ 2000–1500 BC	Early Proto-Finnic	→ 1500 BC
Pre-Germanic /Early Proto-Germanic	1500–1000 BC	Middle and Late Proto-Finnic	1500–1 BC
Proto-Germanic	1000–200/100 BC		
Northwest Germanic	200/100 BC – AD 200	Early Finnish	AD 1–1540
Proto-Scandinavian (Proto-Norse, Runic Scandinavian) and Old East Scandinavian (Old East Norse)	AD 200–500/800		
Runic Swedish	AD 800–1225		
Old Swedish	AD 1225–1526		
Modern Swedish	AD 1526–1900	Old (Literary) Finnish	AD 1540–1810
		Early Modern Finnish	AD 1810–1880
Contemporary Swedish	AD 1900–	Modern Finnish	AD 1880–

Fig. 2. Chronological stratification of Swedish and Finnish in relation to one another. For dating see e.g. Hofstra 1985: 387; Bergman 1984; Ikola 1968: 36; Häkkinen 1994: 11–16.

The other layer of special interest is a number of Old Russian loanwords. For geographical reasons, direct contacts between ancient Finns and Russians were not possible until the latter half of the first millennium AD, when the settlement area of the speakers of East Slavic reached the Ingrian and Novgorod regions, and it is perfectly plausible that a crucial factor behind the new contacts was northern trade, activated especially by the trade route from Scandinavia to Byzantium via the great rivers of Russia. Among those old loanwords there are some items clearly connected to trade, e.g. *laatu* ['quality'], *määrä* ['quantity'], *tavara* ['goods, merchandise'], and *turku* ['market place']. (For a traditional survey of Old Russian loans see e.g. Kalima 1952; an updated review has been elaborated by Saarikivi in 2009.)

Among the Old Russian loanwords there are also a few items indicating familiarity with Christianity, e.g. *pakana* ['pagan'], *pappi* ['clergyman'], *raamattu* ['scripture(s)', only later more exactly the 'Holy Bible'] (Ikola 1998), and *risti* 'cross'. The age of the borrowings has been determined on phonological evidence, and the dating suggests that the ancient Finns got the first impulses of Christianity from the east, even if the majority of the population of Finland was converted by the missionaries of the Western Church somewhat later.

As useful as the loanwords may be in investigating prehistoric relations between languages and speakers, there are certain problems involved in loanword research too, and this applies to Germanic contacts especially. As the timespan of contacts extends from the last phase of the Stone Age (Indo-European loans with Germanic characteristics) to modern times (Swedish, German, English etc.), it is often hard or simply impossible to say exactly at what time the borrowing process actually took place. In many cases it is possible to conclude on the basis of phonology that a certain word must have been borrowed before or after certain sound changes took place in the languages in contact, provided there is knowledge of the historical phonology of both parts of the loan process. Yet another problem is to fix the relative chronology obtained by comparative studies for absolute years, centuries or even millennia. It is also perfectly possible for many competing explanations to exist for one lexical item and there is no way to rank them on linguistic grounds.

Contextual Setting

As the lexis of a language represents linguistic material consisting of sounds, morphemes and semantic properties, the theories and methods applied within research must be primarily linguistic as well. Nevertheless, if we want to use language as a key to the culture and to find out what the language can tell us about its former speakers and the world they once lived in, mere linguistic analysis is not enough. Words are bi-partite signs consisting of form and sense, and the sense or the meaning comprises a conceptual connection between the linguistic form (phonological and morphological substance) and the referent it denotes in the language-external world. Tangible objects, such as tools and ornaments, are especially easy to transfer from culture to culture. Words often come and go with their referents. In practice this means, for instance, that loanwords are usually taken from the same source as the objects labelled with the word concerned. Simple borrowing does not even imply any deeper knowledge of the source language or culture. Therefore, it is of vital importance to acquire as much knowledge as possible of the contacts and circumstances of the epoch the linguistic analysis is to be focused on.

In the case of the Viking Age, the linguistic approach leaves many questions unanswered, or more exactly, many possible answers are left open by the scanty linguistic evidence. In these instances further tools are needed to estimate the plausibility of different solutions. Indeed, there are several branches of science dealing with the past, e.g. archaeology, history, Church history, ethnology, folkloristic studies, archaeobotanical study, medicinal history, environmental history, socioeconomics and so on. All these branches may contribute to the research of the Viking Age.

What do we actually know about Finland as it was towards the end of the first millennium of the Christian era? A concise survey of the material culture concerned has been given by Laakso. Archaeological evidence based mainly on graveyards has shown that there was permanent settlement in those parts of the land which can be connected with some traditional dialectal areas attested later (Finland Proper in the south-western part of the land, Satakunta, Häme (Tavastia) and Savo inland, and Karelia on the north-western coast of Lake Ladoga; for details see e.g. Huurre 1979: 219). It may not be too daring to suppose that the principal division of the Finnish dialects had already emerged with those settlement areas. On the other hand, as the dwelling sites only covered a small proportion of the land it seems obvious that all the speakers of those ancient dialects could not be in continuous interaction with each other. So there cannot have been any standard language common to all, but only different dialects; and foreign impacts coming from different directions did not reach all the population of Finland at one and the same time. In addition to the permanent settlement, there may have been nomad-type habitation which has not left traces as clearly recognisable as the graveyards of the settled population.

What do we know about the ways of life of the ancient Finns? The traditional sources of livelihood were fishing, hunting and gathering, but in addition to this, agriculture had been well established in the areas which were permanently settled. Archaeological and archaeobotanical studies have shown that all the principal cereals cultivated in the historical period in Finland were already well known during the Viking Age and even earlier. The oldest remains of barley (*Hordeum vulgare*), which is the oldest cereal in Finland, has been dated to 1500 BC (Rousi 1997: 61), then there are rye (*Secale cereale*) and a species of wheat (*Triticum turgidum*), dated to the Pre-Roman Iron Age (Rousi 1997: 67, 79), and common oats (*Avena sativa*) from the fourth century of the Christian era (Rousi 1997: 88). The oldest finds of common wheat (*Triticum aestivum*) are of about the same age (Rousi 1997: 73). In addition to the cereals, there were other cultivated food plants such as a kind of turnip (probably *Brassica rapa*; *nauris* in Finnish), pea (*Pisum sativum*) and bean (*Vicia faba*). The last is especially interesting because the Finnish word for bean is *papu*, which is a well-known Russian loanword of very early origin (for phonological evidence, see Kalima 1952, especially 77).

Virtually all cultivated plants in Finland are of foreign origin. As shown above, several important species were imported before the Viking Age, and there are further examples that could be mentioned. So it is plausible that the ancient Finns of the Viking Age were as interested as their ancestors in learning more about agriculture and new products they could take into cultivation in their own farmlands.

As for clothing, it has been shown that, besides traditional leather and fur materials, wool and linen were used for woven articles of clothing such as shirts, skirts, aprons and gowns. Aprons and gowns might be decorated with bronze spirals. Towards the end of the Viking Age silver chains with pendants made of foreign coins were adopted. Festival dress included a sheath-knife. Luxury items such as swords, metal vessels, glassware, woven fabrics and spices were imported. Among other things a new type of axe, a broad-bladed battle axe, was introduced. This kind of axe is called *tappara* in Finnish, and the word itself is known to be an Old Russian loan. A new kind of sickle was also imported from Novgorod. The Finnish name of the tool is *sirppi*, which is of Old Russian origin too. (For phonological criteria of the Russian loans see Kalima 1952: 38, 62.)

As for foreign contacts, international trade seems to have increased significantly, and especially the contacts with Scandinavia intensified. Silver coins were adopted, and as they were weighed in order to determine their actual value, scales were needed as important tools by merchants. On circumstantial grounds, the Finnish word *vaaka* 'scale' could well date from the Viking Age; there are now linguistically motivated and chronologically variant loan explanations from Proto-Germanic (Hofstra 1985: 313) to Old Swedish (SSA III: 383).

The circumstantial facts mentioned above are not scientific novelties; on the contrary, they are common knowledge presented in ordinary textbooks (see e.g. Huurre 1979: 173–205), and this is the reason they are so important. The basic information which is generally known and accepted creates the (pre)historical framework to be used in sorting and ranking alternative linguistic explanations. It serves no purpose to arrive at linguistic interpretations which are improbable or even totally impossible from the historical point of view.

Even if the chances of linguistic research focused on the Viking Age of Finland are strictly limited, the value of lexical investigations has been noted and acknowledged in some archaeological studies. Pirjo Uino (2003: 268–369), for instance, has stated in her summary chapter on the Viking Age of Karelia that most of the Old Russian or Pre-Russian loanwords are so-called cultural words which mirror innovations and foreign contacts in different domains of life. She also emphasises the fact that a number of items of merchandise are archaeologically invisible, i.e. they consist of or are made of organic materials which do not last, or they are intangible by nature, like new ideas and ways of thinking. In these cases, linguistic evidence is the principal source of knowledge for incoming innovations, vague or ambiguous as it may be.

Some Illustrative Cases of Potential Loanwords of the Viking Age

The first phase of an etymological research process always includes collecting all the necessary lexical base material. For Finnish, this means in practice that cognates in related languages, counterparts in neighbouring languages and variants in Finnish dialects are collected and presented for comparison. In traditional representations, it is not unusual that an etymology of a word does not contain anything else but a list of corresponding words with no explanations whatsoever, and the data comes as such to the reader for interpretation (see e.g. the articles *veli* ['brother'] and *veri* ['blood'] in *Suomen kielen etymologinen sanakirja*). Loans are indicated with an arrow-head, and hypothetical or reconstructed words are marked with an asterisk, but there is no clue of the actual age of a word, unless it is attested in historical sources. As the written records of Finnish are of late origin, and even these sources have still not been thoroughly analysed, information on the chronological relations remains highly inadequate. So the need to support or reject the results of a linguistic analysis with the help of other kinds of information about the item or phenomenon in question is unavoidable.

Case 1: *äyskäri* ['baler']

The Finnish word for 'baler' appears in two principal variants, one with back vowels (*auskari*) and the other with front vowels (*äyskäri*). The back vowel variant is obviously original, even though the front vowel variant is the one which has been established in the standard language. The older variant has counterparts in Estonian (*hauskar* etc.) and in Karelian (*auskari, hauskari*), but not in other Balto-Finnic languages. The Balto-Finnic distribution being significantly restricted, it is not necessary to derive the word from the common proto-language of all Balto-Finnic languages.

In most etymological studies the Finnish *auskari/äyskäri* is judged to be a Scandinavian or a Swedish loan. On phonological grounds it is clear, however, that the standard Swedish alternative is out of the question. The corresponding word in modern Swedish is *öskar*, and in Old Swedish it was *ösekar*. The initial vowel *ö-* of the Swedish word cannot give a diphthong like *au-* or *äy-* in Finnish. Therefore we must look for a more suitable source form in some earlier stage of the Scandinavian languages. In addition, attention must be paid to consonants too. On the basis provided by the attested Germanic counterparts, the oldest form of the word in Proto-Germanic has been reconstructed as something like **aus(t(r)a-kaza-*. In North Germanic there was a significant change as the voiced fricative *-z-* developed into a liquid consonant *-ʀ-* (**aus(t(r)a-kaʀa-*). The phonological changes of North Germanic are not mere hypothetical reconstructions, since they are attested in runic inscriptions. As the Balto-Finnic counterparts show liquids as well, we can conclude that the loan cannot be taken from Proto-Germanic but from a later Scandinavian language form, e.g. Proto-Scandinavian or Old East Scandinavian, but before the word-initial diphthong *au-* had changed into the (Old) Swedish *ö-*. This change took place during the Runic Swedish period (e.g. Bergman 1984: 21). So it is perfectly possible that the loan dates from the Viking Age. (For Germanic forms see further e.g. LÄGL I: 46.)

As for circumstantial evidence, there is nothing against the solution presented above. A baler is a useful implement for seafarers. Archaeological finds allow us to suppose that nautical activities and contacts with Sweden increased during the Viking Age in Finland, and even some Finns seem to have taken part of the journeys to the east (Uino 2003: 354–357). There must, then, have been some expert knowledge of ships and the necessary equipment.

Case 2: *humala* ['hop']

A shared term for hop is present in all Balto-Finnic languages, but not in any of the more distantly related languages. In Estonian it is *humal*, in Livonian *umàl*, in Veps *humau* and so on (see closer e.g. LÄGL I: 120–121). There are very similar words in Mordvin, Mari and Hungarian, but these have been explained as separated loanwords and thus they can be left aside when investigating the Balto-Finnic material.

In a normal case of indigenous lexical material, the conclusion would be that a word like *humala* with a maximal distribution among the Balto-Finnic languages should derive from their common proto-language, i.e. Late Proto-Finnic. Yet there is still lexical and other data to be taken into account, and the totality of facts makes this conclusion implausible.

The first argument against the Proto-Finnic origin of *humala* is the fact that the 'same' word is present in some Indo-European languages, e.g. in Swedish (*humle*) and Latin (*humulus*). In fact, the Finnish word *humala* is a well-known German loanword denoting the plant *Humulus lupulus*. The plant grows wild in certain parts of Finland, but it has no indigenous name in Finnish. Obviously the ancient Finns did not pay any attention to this plant as they could not use it for any purpose. The situation changed dramatically when hops became an important ingredient for beer. This innovation has been dated to the early ninth century, i.e. to the beginning of the Viking Age (Rousi 1997: 337). At first, hops in the wild state were collected, but very soon it became a cultivated plant and an important item of merchandise too.

As for the sound structure, the word *humala* is ambiguous. The reconstructed form for Proto-Germanic is **χumalan-*, and the corresponding form of Old Scandinavian (Proto-Norse) is **humalā*. In Old Swedish it had lost the word-internal vowel *a* and acquired an extra consonant *b* in the cluster in the middle of the word (*humble*), so it must have been borrowed into Finnish before that change. The older forms are equally suitable for loan originals, but the Proto-Germanic alternative can be seen as less probable, as there was obviously no reason for borrowing the word during the Proto-Germanic period.

The oldest remains of hops in Finland have been found in Hämeenlinna, and they have been dated to the eleventh century. Finds of the same age are known from Valamo Island in Lake Ladoga, now belonging to Russia. (Lempiäinen 2007: 105–106.) Hops were needed for flavouring and – what may have been even more important – preservation in the beer-brewing process. In those times, beer was the most used alcoholic drink in the northern parts of Europe, and there was a great demand for hops everywhere.

Case 3: *laukka* ['Allium sp.']

As stated earlier in this chapter, many cultivated plants were imported and cultivated for regular food production in Finland prior to the Viking Age. Now we may ask if there were some edible plants which were typical for or extremely popular among the seafarers of the Viking Age. Indeed, some *Allium* species attained great importance during this period. The use and cultivation of *Allium scodoroprasum*, the sand leek, for instance, was apparently promoted by the trading activities of seafarers. The sand leek is edible, but it is not usually cultivated for food purposes. Instead, it is known as a special indicator plant for sea passages from the Mediterranean to Scandinavia. The seafarers of Gotland in particular distributed the sand leek throughout the Baltic Sea region during the Viking Age, and for a good reason: the plant was known as an effective medicinal product against scurvy, a disease resulting from a deficiency of vitamin C, which was common among long-distance seafarers in the past, as there were no fresh fruits or vegetables aboard to prevent the disease. Even now there is plenty of sand leek vegetation along the so-called Kalanti Passage, a sea route which runs from Sweden to the Åland Islands and farther on to Vakka-Suomi, the south-western corner of Finland. (Hinneri 1997: 65–66.)

The Finnish word *laukka* 'garlic, onion, leek' was recognised as a German loanword as early as in the nineteenth century, yet there are different opinions on the actual date of borrowing. Every piece of linguistic evidence seems to denote a very old loan, as the word is present in all the Balto-Finnic languages except in Vote, and the sound structure harmonises with the reconstructed Proto-Germanic original **laukaz* (LÄGL II: 178–179). Yet it has been assumed that the loan should be dated to the Viking age, as edible plants of the *Allium* genus became a favourite dish in Scandinavia at that time as far as we know. Some unspecified *Allium* plants were mentioned as foodstuffs in the saga literature of the thirteenth century. (KLM X: 85–88.) As the Swedish descendant of the Proto-Germanic **laukaz* is *lök*, it is clear that the borrowing must have taken place prior to the sound change **au* > *ö* (cf. *auskari* above). Anyway, there remain several chronological alternatives for dating from Proto-Germanic to Old East Scandinavian and Runic Swedish.

It is not quite clear when exactly the onion (*Allium cepa*) and garlic (*Allium sativum*) were taken into cultivation in the Nordic countries, but probably they were first distributed by the Romans in Central Europe and among the Germanic tribes there, and came only somewhat later to Scandinavia. This being the case, it is not plausible that the loan could have been transmitted as early as from Proto-Germanic to Late Proto-Finnic. It must be added that there is no archaeobotanical evidence on the cultivation of *Allium* species in the Baltic Sea region prior to the fourteenth century (Latałova *et al.* 2007: 53; Häkkinen & Lempiäinen 2011: 235). Anyway, the Germanic word **laukaz* may be older than the use and cultivation of onion and garlic, as it may have referred first to *Allium* species growing wild, such as chives (*Allium schoenoprasum*) or ransoms (*Allium ursinum*, sometimes called 'wild garlic'). The Germanic/Scandinavian origin of the word nonetheless makes one think that foreign influence has been decisive when making use of these natural resources in Finland.

Benefits of a Multi-Disciplinary Approach

As seen above, there are many aspects of cultural history that linguistic analysis can shed light on. Even more could be done, and indeed much work has already been done. Instead of the examination of individual words, we can identify and collect all the words meeting established linguistic criteria for a certain loanword stratum and group them into semantic spheres to see what kind of historical or cultural inferences could be made on the basis of the totality. Still, there remain relevant questions unanswered. Even if we can determine certain words as loans on linguistic evidence, we cannot know the reasons why and how they were actually borrowed, unless we know something of the needs and intentions of those people adopting new lexical items. The diffusion of words mirrors the diffusion of culture, but we cannot understand a culture through a concise selection of words only. If we want to connect the results of a linguistic historical analysis to reality, we must know much more about the real world as it is and as it was earlier.

For some time, linguistics has tended to be an autonomous branch of science, without any connections to other branches. As far as synchronic grammar is concerned, this may work in some sense. In the case of the lexis, however, relations between words, meanings and referents cannot be ignored. Real understanding of the contents and significance of lexical development requires knowledge of the context where the evolution has taken place. Therefore a kind of lexical archaeology is needed to establish realistic and plausible connections between words and their referents. This task cannot be performed by linguists alone. Of course, we can try to collect all the necessary information of archaeological, historical, theological, medical, botanical facts which are needed for interpretation of words and their meanings, but it is much faster, easier and more reliable to ask those experts who really know those matters from their own research work.

So far, Early Finnish (AD 1–1540) has been viewed as a virtually inaccessible period for the study of the language history of Finnish. Now there seem to be several ways to proceed. The first alternative for a linguist is to look into structural criteria which point directly to the Viking Age. Those criteria may not be available in the language under examination itself, but they may be detected in the source language of loanwords (cf. *auskari* above). We can also start with a maximal inventory of lexical material and exclude all those items which can be proved to be older or younger than those of the Early Finnish period, and then we can estimate whether it is possible to date the rest expressly to the Viking Age on circumstantial criteria (cf. *humala* above). Or, instead of linguistic material, we can start with cultural innovations, and then look into their names and see if they can be interpreted as language innovations of the Viking Age on linguistic grounds (cf. *laukka* above). So there are plenty of good motivations for a linguist to tackle the problems of reconstructing the past in close co-operation with other branches of science aiming at the same goal.

References

Abbreviations

KLM = *Kulturhistorisk leksikon for nordisk middelalder fra vikingetid til reformationstid.* Vol. X.
LÄGL = *Lexikon der älteren germanischen Lehnwörter in den ostseefinnischen Sprachen.*
SKES = *Suomen kielen etymologinen sanakirja.*
SSA = *Suomen sanojen alkuperä.*

Literature

Bergman, Gösta. 1984. *Kortfattad svensk språkhistoria*. Stockholm: Bokförlaget Prisma.

Hinneri, Sakari. 1997. *Viikinkien Kalantiväylä*. Rauma: Sakari Hinneri & Erkki Santamala.

Hofstra, Tette. 1985. *Ostseefinnisch und Germanisch. Frühe Beziehungen im nördlichen Ostseeraum im Lichte der Forschung seit 1961*. Groningen: Drukkerij van Denderen B. V.

Huurre, Matti. 1979. *9000 vuotta Suomen esihistoriaa*. Helsinki: Otava.

Häkkinen, Kaisa. 1994. *Agricolasta nykykieleen. Suomen kirjakielen historia*. Porvoo–Helsinki–Juva: Werner Söderström Osakeyhtiö.

Häkkinen, Kaisa & Lempiäinen, Terttu. 2011. *Aaloesta öljypuuhun. Suomen kielellä mainittuja kasveja Agricolan aikaan*. Helsinki: Teos.

Ikola, Osmo (ed.). 1968. *Suomen kielen käsikirja*. Helsinki: Weilin+Göös.

Ikola, Osmo. 1998. Sana *raamattu* Agricolalla ja uudemmassa kirjasuomessa. *Sananjalka* 40. Pp. 7–23.

Kalima, Jalo. 1956. *Slaavilaisperäinen sanastomme. Tutkimus itämerensuomalaisten kielten slaavilaisperäisistä lainasanoista*. Suomalaisen Kirjallisuuden Seuran toimituksia 243. Helsinki: Suomalaisen Kirjallisuuden Seura.

Kallio, Petri. 2006. Suomen kantakielten absoluuttista kronologiaa. *Virittäjä* 110. Pp. 2–25.

Kulturhistorisk leksikon for nordisk middelalder fra vikingetid til reformationstid. Vol. X. 1965. København; Rosenkilde og Bagger.

Latałova, Małgorzata & Monika Badura & Joanna Jarosińska & Joanna Święta-Musznicka. 2007. Useful plants in medieval and post-medieval archaeobotanical material from the Hanseatic towns of Northern Poland. In Sabine Karg (ed.) *Medieval food traditions in Northern Europe*. Publications from the National Museum. Studies in Arcaheology & History Vol. 12. Copenhagen: The National Museum of Denmark. Pp. 39–72.

Lempiäinen, Terttu. 2007. Archaeobotanical evidence of plants from the medieval period to early modern times in Finland. In Sabine Karg (ed.) *Medieval food traditions in Northern Europe*. Publications from the National Museum. Studies in Arcaheology & History Vol. 12. Copenhagen: The National Museum of Denmark. Pp. 97–118.

Lexikon der älteren germanischen Lehnwörter in den ostseefinnischen Sprachen I: A–J, II: K–O. 1991, 1996. A. D. Kylstra, Sirkka-Liisa Hahmo, Tette Hofstra, Osmo Nikkilä (eds.). Amsterdam–Atlanta, GA.

Rousi, Arne. 1997. *Auringonkukasta viiniköynnökseen. Ravintokasvit*. Porvoo–Helsinki–Juva: Werner Söderström Osakeyhtiö.

Saarikivi, Janne 2009. Itämerensuomalais-slaavilaisten kontaktien tutkimuksen nykytilasta. *The Quasquicentennial of the Finno-Ugrian Society*. Mémoires de la Société Finno-Ougrienne 258. Helsinki: Suomalais-Ugrilainen Seura. Pp. 109–160.

Suomen kielen etymologinen sanakirja. I–VI. 1956–1978. Lexica Societatis Fenno-Ugricae XII. Helsinki: Suomalais-Ugrilainen Seura.

Suomen sanojen alkuperä. Etymologinen sanakirja I: A–K, II: L–P, III: R–Ö. Suomalaisen Kirjallisuuden Seuran toimituksia 556, Kotimaisten kielten tutkimuskeskuksen julkaisuja 62. Helsinki: Suomalaisen Kirjallisuuden Seura.

Uino, Pirjo. 2003. Viikinkiaika n. 800–1100 jKr. In Matti Saarnisto (ed.) *Viipurin läänin historia 1. Karjalan synty*. Lappeenranta: Karjalan kirjapaino. Pp. 313–382.

Johan Schalin

Scandinavian–Finnish Language Contact in the Viking Age in the Light of Borrowed Names

Scandinavian–Finnish language contact in Viking Age Finland is no easy topic to tackle, owing among other things to the scarcity of sources. The issue can be approached from a number of angles, none of which provides a complete picture. For Early Finnish (*Varhaissuomi* = EFi) effectively no written sources are available. Diachronic loan-word research may provide valuable findings, but for the purpose of pinpointing the date of an etymology by this methodology, the 'Viking Age' constitutes a rather short period of time, even within the extended time span (AD 750–1250) applied for the eastern Baltic in this publication (see introduction).

Proper names constitute a valuable, albeit limited, source of information. While historical records mostly date from the fourteenth to fifteenth centuries, some isolated older toponyms are known from Latin, Old Swedish (OSw) and Old Russian sources. Even if most attestations are not quite as old as the Viking Age, these provide a corpus of proper names, some of which may date back that far. If a name was borrowed from one language into another before attestation, phonological criteria may be used to frame the date of the borrowing with a varying margin of uncertainty.

A glimpse of toponyms borrowed from Early Finnish (and/or possibly from early Estonian) into Old Scandinavian is indeed available in the thirteenth century 'Danish Itinerary' contained in the *Liber census Daniæ* by king Valdemar II. Another huge corpus of names consists of medieval borrowings preserved in Swedish dialects up to today. Most of these may be assumed on phonological and/or historical grounds to date back to the thirteenth or fourteenth century, for example *Köklax* (a village in Espoo) < OSw. (dial.) **Köuk(a)laxe* ← EFi. (or Estonian) *Kauk(a)laksi*. Studies of such names in the Åboland archipelago (south of Turku) by Ritva-Liisa Pitkänen have shown that some Finnish terrain names behind these loan etymologies should be dated to "the latter half of the first millennium" or "a few centuries before the settlement" (which started in the twelfth century). The archipelago is full of bays, islands or peninsulas with only a few metres of variation in altitude. For names containing references to such localities,

Pitkänen also relies on estimates for the pace of post-glacial uplift (rebound = glacial isostatic adjustment) of the seabed (Pitkänen 1986: 345–348, although cf. 370).

By analogy, the Finnish loan originals of medieval Swedish names or other Finnish names known to be medieval may partly be from the Viking Age also in other regions where continuity of settlement may be shown to have existed. This especially applies to names of large islands and waters, which are normally known to best resist change. It may also apply to the names of some larger localities, such as those of the oldest parishes, which may preserve names of pre-Christian areal administrative entities (*muinaispitäjät*). Ethnonyms may also be particularly well preserved.

As a scholar primarily occupied with Scandinavian and Finnic Iron Age language change and language contact, I will not attempt to embark on an exhaustive inventory of proper names in Finland datable to the Viking Age based on external and/or later attestations. Instead, I will select some examples relevant to Scandinavian–Finnish language contact, where a linguistic argument may provide added value to their understanding.

In addition to some examples from the Danish Itinerary, I will give special attention to a couple of Viking Age names in Scandinavian sources, particularly the name *Tafstalonti* known from an eleventh-century rune stone, and a name *Herdalar* in the land of the *Finnlendingar* mentioned in a skaldic poem by the eleventh-century poet Sighvatr Þórðarson. This name was recorded by Snorri Sturluson in Iceland a couple of centuries after Sighvatr. As no loan etymology is plausible for the attestation of the name *Finland* on rune stone U582 from Söderby-Karl in Roslagen, I have chosen to mention this attestation only as a contemporary parallel to the attestation of the name *Tafæistaland*.

In addition, I will present two cases where the methodology of diachronic linguistics in its own right may hint at language contact before, during or after the Viking Age. I have chosen the name OFi. *Kiulo* ~ Sw. *Kjulo* corresponding to present day Fi. *Köyliö* and the name OFi. *Ahuen maa* ~ OSw. *Alandh* corresponding to present-day Sw. *Åland*, both of which have been widely discussed between linguistic and onomastic scholars and where I have made a contribution with my own research. For the same reasons, I will also touch upon the name Fi. *Kymi* ~ Sw. *Kymmene*.

Methodological Considerations

As sound change and relative chronologies are largely reconstructible, relative chronologies for neighbouring languages may be synchronised one with the other through the analysis of lexical borrowings. With regard to borrowings between Early Finnish and East Scandinavian, the chronology of the latter is much better known. Profound sound changes during the period AD 500–800 may serve as reliable dating criteria for postdating a borrowing to a period after the beginning of the Viking Age. For the end of the Viking Age, few reliable criteria exist. Indeed, ninth- to eleventh-century Runic Swedish is very similar to the archaic dialects of twelfth- to fourteenth-century settlers. For EFi., only relative chronologies are reliable.

For borrowed proper names, an approach based on sound change alone can produce reliable results only under critical scrutiny and favourable circumstances. The risk of wrong assumptions is much greater than for common nouns for the following reasons:

Firstly, proper names function as designators to the referent with no proper 'meanings' in a strict sense. Whatever meaning might be associated with the lexical elements used as a basis for naming indeed becomes functionally redundant through the genesis of the proper name. Any perception of 'meaning' is of little help when postulating etymologies for proper names because possible reminiscences of the original naming basis are unreliable and often shortlived. In the case of loan etymologies, such reminiscences typically disappear instantly without the support of bilingual populations.

In order to establish a loan etymology, one may also have problems ruling out extinct loan words or human names. If a village is called *Kuninkaala*, it obviously does not mean that the name is Proto-Germanic and the village is prehistoric even if the first element is the PGmc loanword *kuningas* ['king']. Analogous cases are tricky if the appellative is extinct. Such an extinct appellative has been postulated behind the names *Vammala*, *Vammaskoski* and *Vampula*. The appellative would have been borrowed from a Scandinavian original meaning 'stomach', represented today by English *Womb* and Sw. *Våmm*. This etymon, describing the belly-like shape of a river, has also been productive in toponyms in Swedish (SPNK respective entries, cf. Koivulehto 1987: 32). In a similar way, the assumed naming basis for the name *Harjavalta* (old parish/municipality in Western Finland) is an extinct EFi. man's name because the location most certainly appears younger than the etymology. Moreover the man's name is far from hypothetical as it is attested in Germanic. The name was borrowed from a PSc original **Harjawalda-*, with a later representative in the Norse name *Haraldr* (presupposing a Runic **Hariwaldaʀ* cf. engl. *Harold* and *herald*), and referred to in Latin as *Chariovalda* (Janzen 1947: 77ff.; Koivulehto 2007: 76). The original for the now extinct EFi. man's name **Hauho*, reflected in an old parish name in southern Finland, would have cognates in later representatives of Germanic *hauha-* ['high' also meaning 'noble, highly regarded']. Logically, the toponym cannot be older but it must indeed be younger than the genesis of this man's name. The name of the southwestern parish *Perniö* clearly derives from a man's name as well, a name that one way or another has its roots in Scandinavian or West Germanic. The dating is not clear, nor is it clear beyond doubt whether the Swedish name *Bjärnå*, first attested as *in Birnum* (1330), *Bernaa* (1352), *Beerna* (1405), *Birno Sokn* (1442), *Biærna* (1450) and *Byerno* (1457), is an autonomous follower of that man's name, a genuine genetic 'doublet', or a rather early reborrowing from Early Finnish (FSB: s.v. 'Bjärnå'; SPNK s.v. 'Perniö').

In general, the use of human names as naming bases has caused trouble and controversy. In areas of remote colonisation, the use of personal names is manifestly widespread as the names of the colonisers have been more widely known than indigenous terms for local features such as topography (Huldén 2012: 244ff.). From the point of view of linguistic methodology, however, this introduces a further arbitrary complication, as 'meaning' is removed not only from the referent but also from the naming basis itself: practically any toponym will have an element resembling some individual's personal name and is thus opened to potential etymologies in a rather arbitrary fashion. An illustrative example would be the name **Karjas*, discussed below as a possible cognate of the name *Herdalar*. A suggestion that it could have been formed on the name *Makarios* (Huldén 2001: s.v. 'Karis'; NB the suggestion is later withdrawn in FSB: s.v. 'Karis') is notoriously difficult either to verify or refute, given all the uncertainties involved (why not *Ansgarius* or *Zacharias*?). Yet, it is beyond doubt that personal names have been the naming basis for many toponyms and Lars Huldén (2012: 245ff.) maintains that also rivers in Finland, including even rivers of prehistoric significance such as *Kymi* and *Eura*, seldom have primary names, but are named after localities through which they flow, which he in turn often interprets to have received their names after persons.

It is furthermore important to note that proper names are subject to unexpected sound change, to the extent that onomastic scholars without a good understanding of historical linguistics have difficulties in coming to grips with this issue. Keeping in mind varying confused accounts on this issue, it is good to make clear that sound change in proper names is not completely arbitrary, nor are proper names indeed exempt from sound laws operating on common nouns. Yet sound change is often accelerated by wear and tear much as in pronouns and particles, probably as a result of frequent use and the reasons given in the following paragraphs. Hence the Old English name *Eoforwic* has been shortened to *York* and the name *Leicester* is pronounced as if it were spelled *Lester*.

Because proper names are often preserved as compounds, in which different stress patterns would cause some syllables to lose emphasis, syllables are often shortened or lost altogether. As we will see below, elements forming part of a compound thus develops differently from the corresponding common noun. Thus names containing the word *town* as a less emphasised element, such as in *Sutton* (< 'south town'), today end in *-ton* rather than *-town*.

Moreover, the arbitrary relation between form and 'meaning' in proper names also delinks proper names from the mechanism governing the declension of common nouns. Proper names can easily change declension. In Old Swedish, names of lakes are predominantly declined as masculines while rivers are feminines regardless of the declension of the corresponding common noun. Moreover fossilisation may occur in the case of obscure morphemes, which may be preserved and incorporated into the stem after they have disappeared from the paradigms of the common nouns. Thus where an OSw. dative plural ending *-om* was fossilised, as in the name *Sundom*, the ending would at the latest have started to behave like a part of the stem when the use of the corresponding ending disappeared from the common language. Obsolete morphemes are of course just as arbitrary in terms of meaning as the rest of the elements of the name.

Last but not least, a community that passes the proper names on to later generations may very well, based on their form alone, have conflicting or obscure ideas of their original naming bases. Thus any particular name would be prone to undergo so-called folk etymology, where later uninformed assumptions about the naming basis would feed back changes into the form of the name. The name for the municipality *Esbo* (attested as older *Æspa*), is probably such a case: this name is believed to be from a derivative of the name for the tree *asp* ['aspen, *populus tremula*']. After association with the very productive naming element *-bo* (as in *Åbo* ['Turku']), the /p/ has become /b/ by folk etymology. These changes are obviously irregular with regard to sound laws.

Against this background, great caution is called for in attempting to establish loan etymologies for prehistoric proper names on the basis of one sided considerations. Phonological similarity is a necessary precondition, but even if the match is perfect, as in Lauri Kettunen's proposal (discussed below) postulating a verb **tavastaa* as an original for **Tafæistaland* ['Häme'], the argument does not carry weight unless backed up by attestations and/or valid evidence from the other auxiliary disciplines of onomastic research. The competing proposal by Adolf Neovius, relying on a hypothetical Finnish name ***Taustamaa*, and in particular my criticism of it, is an example of the opposite: disregarding or violating phonological history is not uncommon but does not produce uncontested results.[1]

In the best of cases, a credibly obvious genetic 'doublet' exists in the language providing the borrowing, namely a later representative of the loan original. Yet, such doublets are unfortunately too seldom available.

The Periodisation of Scandinavian and Finnish Language History

In order to be able to follow the argumentation on the chronology of loan words and the direction of borrowings, it is necessary to establish a common periodisation of the development of the two language families. Some of the earlier languages in the table below correspond to 'reconstruction levels', used by diachronic linguistics to codify certain theoretical historical stages of development by means of the comparative method.

The reconstructed level called Proto-Germanic (PGmc) is thus a theoretical image of the common ancestral language common to all Germanic languages, including in particular Gothic, which belongs to a separate branch of Germanic, so-called East Germanic. Northwest Germanic is in a similar fashion a theoretical image of the common ancestor of all contemporary Germanic languages, the Scandinavian and the West Germanic ones alike. By the time Northwest Germanic was spoken, a separate branch called East Germanic was already separated, soon to be documented through Gothic.

The next stage was the separation of West Germanic and North Germanic: West Germanic branch developed into Old High German, Old English, Old

Saxon and so forth while North Germanic branch became the languages of Scandinavia, of which the common reconstructed form is called Proto-Scandinavian (or sometimes Proto-Norse). Proto-Scandinavian is already documented in a handful of runic inscriptions, and is thus one of the oldest documented languages of Europe. The carvings are so scarce, however, and so inconsistently spelled, that the knowledge of this 'Runic' language relies heavily on the comparative method as well. The records are just enough to double check and fine tune the theoretical work of scholars. Yet the existence of carvings contributes a lot to the division of Proto-Scandinavian into early, middle and late stages of development.

It is common in the literature to put a divide between Late Proto-Scandinavian (or Late Proto-Norse or 'Common Scandinavian') and subsequent stages portrayed as precursors of the languages of present nation states (Old Swedish, Old Danish, Old Icelandic etc.). A grey zone in this respect is a period of four or five centuries roughly corresponding to the Viking Age. Inscriptions in the later runic *futhark* (runic alphabet) also belong here. On the one hand, there is a tendency to transcribe all these inscriptions in a very Norwegian/Icelandic (Norse) type of orthography and emphasise how close this language was to archaic Old (West) Norse that was documented some centuries later. The concept of *fornnordiska* [literally 'Old Nordic'] is also used and the corresponding Finnish term *muinaisskandinaavi* [literally 'Ancient Scandinavian'] is standard in Finnish language literature. Notwithstanding this, Swedish linguists have traditionally included this period in the history of national language development, calling the dialects then spoken in their country *runsvenska* ['Runic Swedish'].

In this work, I have opted to dispense with both the later nation states and the aspiration for Scandinavian unity. Since the chosen focus of this volume is the Viking Age in the Baltic region, it is justified to use a terminology which adequately describes the dialect map relevant at that time. During the Viking Age, Scandinavian dialects in the Atlantic area formed a western group while dialects in the Baltic Sea area formed two eastern groups. The main divide within the eastern group was between late Runic in Denmark and Sweden on the one hand and in Gotland on the other. These differences have their roots in the last period of Proto-Scandinavian, which I shall call Early East Scandinavian, and it continues to be relevant throughout the period of the later runes.

Using 'Old East Scandinavian' even for the first texts in Latin characters could also be justified because differences were still small. Some place names on the Finnish cost recorded in the Danish Itinerary are for example explicitly called 'Danish'. This is certainly not meant to be distinctive from 'Swedish', as the distinction was not yet perceived as meaningful in the thirteenth century. Nevertheless, I have opted to use mainly 'Old Swedish' (in parallel with 'Old Scandinavian' where the context requires) for the era from 1225 when the language was codified in Latin characters. Here there is enough reason to follow well-established practice as there are large corpuses labeled Old Swedish and Old Danish respectively.

Table 1. An absolute chronology (column 1) of the development from Proto-Germanic to Early New Swedish (column 3) with comparison to the development from Middle Proto-Finnic to Old Finnish (column 5) and accompanied by the abbreviations used in this chapter for the relevant reconstructed stages of language development (columns 2 and 4).

Period	**Abbr.**	**Development stage of Scandinavian**	**Abbr.**	**Development stage of Finnic**
500–100 BC	PGmc	Proto-Germanic	MPF	(early) Middle Proto-Finnic ~ *(varhainen) keskikantasuomi*
100 BC – AD 200	NwG	Northwest Germanic	MPF	(late) Middle Proto-Finnic ~ *(myöhäinen) keskikantasuomi*
AD 200–400	PSc	(Early) Proto-Scandinavian ~ *(tidig) urnordiska*	LPF	Late Proto-Finnic ~ *myöhäiskantasuomi*
AD 400–550	PSc	(Middle) Proto-Scandinavian ~ *(medel-) urnordiska*	CF	Coastal (Gulf of Finland) Finnic
AD 550–750/800	EESc	Early East Scandinavian ~ *sen (östlig) urnordiska*	NF	Northern Finnic
1225/1375 AD	OSw (classic)	Old Swedish ~ *klassisk/äldre fornsvenska*	EFi	Early Finnish ~ *varhaissuomi*
1375–1521/1540 AD	OSw (late)	Old Swedish~*yngre fornsvenska*	EFi	Early Finnish ~ *varhaissuomi*
1521/1540–1732 AD	ENSw	Early New Swedish~*äldre nysvenska*	OFi	Old Finnish ~ *vanha suomi*

The periodisation of Finnic is a more difficult issue. The only uncontroversial reconstruction levels are Proto-Uralic, Proto-Finno-Permic and Late Proto-Finnic. For the purpose of this chapter, only the last is relevant. Late Proto-Finnic is an image of the common ancestral language of the Finnic (or also called Baltic Finnic) languages from South Estonian in the southeast to Meänkieli in the northwest and from Livonian in the south-west to Vepsä in the east. Knowledge of Middle Proto-Finnic, which covers a sequence of older stages of this same language, may be acquired by means of internal reconstruction, comparison with previous reconstruction levels and loan-word studies.

The intermediate stages between Late Proto-Finnic and Old Finnish are all difficult to recover (cf. Häkkinen). Any meaningful reconstruction depends on one's understanding of the branching of the family tree. Any absolute chronology for any of the Finnic languages will be prone to criticism. Yet, for the purpose of presentation in this chapter, it is opportune to establish correspondences to the Germanic chronology, which is absolute, albeit provisionally and with reservations, as shown in Table 1. In that respect, I follow closely the family tree and the chronology for Finnic presented in Petri Kallio's chapter "The Diversification of Proto-Finnic" in this publication.[2]

Suggested Viking Age and Pre-Viking Age Loan Etymologies

It is symptomatic that, because of all the methodological limitations involved, very few suggested pre-historic loan etymologies have been accepted, while only some of them have been conclusively refuted. In the course of the early twentieth century serious scholars like Saxén, Pipping, Karsten and others proposed hundreds of Proto-Scandinavian loan etymologies for Finnish toponyms, but among these, none appear to have been permanently accepted without dissent. On the other hand, far from all of them have been convincingly refuted. This is indeed almost equally difficult because of methodological constraints.

Serious and recently discussed candidates for Early East Scandinavian, Proto-Scandinavian or Pre-Scandinavian etymologies among Finnish toponyms would include at least **Ahve-* (as in *Ahvenanmaa*, from PGmc), *Aura* (NwG or later), *Eura* (PGmc), *Kainuu* (PSc or EESc), *Karjala* (NwG) and *Kymi* (PGmc or older). There is also one example based on, or mixed with, ethnonymic use, namely **hämä-/Häme* (PG). Most of these etymologies are older than the time span chosen for this publication. (Koivulehto 1987: 33–37; Schalin 2008a; 2008b; 2012; cf. also SPNK respective entries.)[3]

With the possible exception of *Ahvenanmaa*, which much like *Vammala* above may in fact reflect an appellative, none of these names has a probable genetic doublet preserved in Swedish which would attest to the existence of the assumed loan original. If we include attestations in the form of other proper names presumably representing a similar etymology, we may mention the *Oder* (in Germany) for *Aura* and *Eura*, *Härjedalen* (in Sweden) for *Karjala* and *Kymmen* (in *Värmland*) for *Kymi*. We have already discussed two examples of borrowed names which were borrowed as men's names from PSc but have passed into toponymic use later, namely *Harjavalta* and *Hauho* (Koivulehto 1987: 31–32; 2007: 76). The date of origin for these two toponyms may not be recovered by linguistic methods but may well be pre-Christian as the names themselves are pre-Christian.

In addition to the overall uncertainties resulting from the nature of the matter, at least three of these etymologies are challenged by Lars Huldén. For *Eura*, Huldén (1997: 184 ff., FSB: s.v. 'Eura') proposes a young origin from some short form of the medieval man's name *Eberhard, Evert* etc. The proposal is rejected by Koivulehto (2007: 77; for the PGmc etymology by Koivulehto see Koivulehto 1987: 33–36 and SPNK: s.v. 'Eura'). The name *Aura* Huldén derives from some short form of the name *Abraham* (FSB: s.v. 'Aura'). Huldén (2012: 245ff.) characterises Koivulehto's argumentation as elegant, but remains unconvinced as he holds the conclusions as "too good to be true", which I take to mean that the postulated antiquity of the names alone renders the hypothesis implausible as hardly any other names are from Proto-Germanic. The alternative etymologies for these rivers cast little light on the Viking Age and there is no reason to pursue the argument any further here.

For the Finnish name of the *Kymi* river, Koivulehto and Huldén uphold competing Pre-Swedish etymologies (Koivulehto 1987: 36–37; Huldén

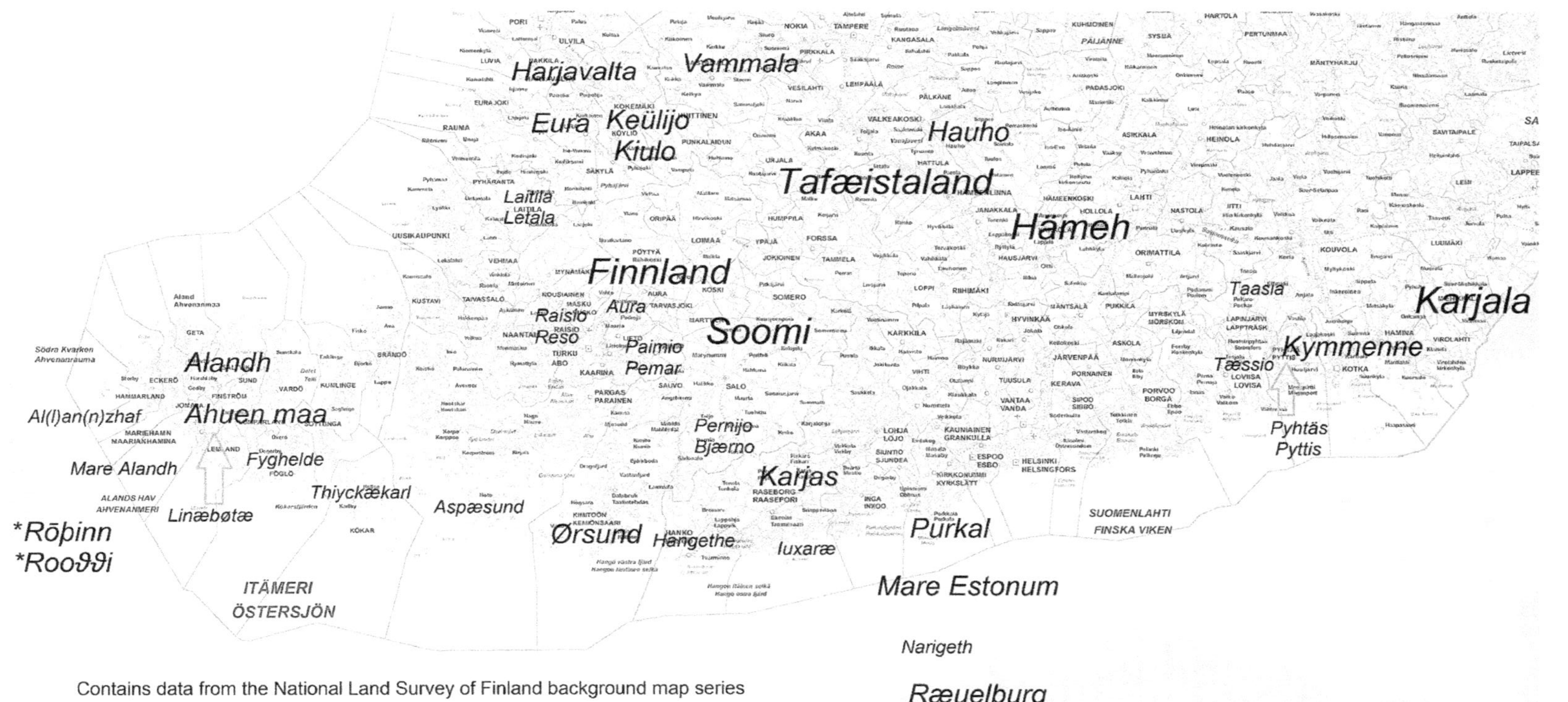

Map 1. Toponyms in and adjacent to Åland, Satakunta, Häme, Finland Proper and Nyland discussed in this chapter (NB: spellings are not uniform).

1997: 184 ff.). Koivulehto's etymology, which elegantly derives the name from a Proto- or Pre-Germanic appellative cognate to the verb *come* and with the meaning 'accessible' or 'navigable', falls outside the time frame of this chapter,[4] while Huldén's etymology would indeed be from the Viking Age. In a recent article on the Swedish name *Kymmene*, I have recapitulated Koivulehto's criticism of Huldén's etymology and added several arguments against it (Schalin 2012). Huldén proposes deriving both EFi. **Kymi* and OSw. *Kym(m)en(n)V* from the same Proto-Scandinavian man's name, *Kunimund-*, supposedly first applied to a locality at the mouth of the river. For such a borrowing and the changes in form, meaning and use involved in it, there is simply not enough time to explain the Finnish data. The data includes an archaic e-stem, which is left unexplained (Koivulehto 2007: 77), and the transferred use as an appellative, which must be rather old, judging from the fact that it has been used as a naming basis for other waters in the region.

The OSw. name *Kym(m)en(n)V* has a peculiar trisyllabic structure heavy in geminates and, as I have argued, is not the expected outcome of the man's name *Kunimund-*. The traditional way of explaining it as a borrowing from Finnish is also flawed. The name can, however, be analysed as the remains of a compound, where the first element is an Early Finnish borrowing **Kymi* and the second is the Old Swedish word *-mynne/-minne* ['mouth of river'] (FSO-LEX: s.v. 'minne'; FSVLDB: s.v. 'amynne'). The borrowing probably predates the Swedish settlement in eastern *Nyland* (Fi. *Uusimaa*) by at least a few generations, being from the twelfth or thirteenth century at the latest (Schalin 2012). There is in fact no purely linguistic reason not do date the borrowing even earlier, to the earlier centuries of the Viking Age.

In this context, it is worth mentioning that, in the area just west of the river Kymi, some well-known attempts have been made on linguistic grounds to find earlier Swedish names than the centuries typically associated with the settlement. The unusual consonant correspondence in Sw. *Pyttis* cf. Fi. *Pyhtää* has been used as one platform of argumentation and the unusual vowel correspondence between Sw. *Tessjö* cf. Fi. *Taasia* as another. Yet, alternative explanations have been favoured in order to avoid the uncomfortable and perhaps unnecessary assumption of eighth century Scandinavian settlement (Granlund 1956:80, 84ff., with references). In recent years, quite ambitious amateur archaeologists have been working in this same region, uncovering findings claimed to date from the Viking Age (Jäppinen & Nygård).

Borrowed Names with Unexpected Doublets, Including Finnish Köyliö ~ Old Finnish Kiulo ~ Swedish Kjulo

In contrast to these presumed few older borrowings there is a plethora of obviously younger Finnish names in south-western Finland which do have genetic doublets in Finnish and Swedish. A majority of them may easily be explained as medieval borrowings. Some datings may, however, deserve closer study. It is noteworthy that all genetic doublets in Finnish-speaking areas do not reflect well the rather regular sound correspondences established by Pitkänen for the Åboland (Turku) archipelago (cf. **Kaitasaari* → *Keitsor*). For example, *Paimio* is not reflected as ***Peimo* in Swedish (but rather *Pēmar*), *Raisio* does not give ***Reiso* but *Rēso* and *Laitila* reads *Lētala* rather than ***Leital*. These reflexes may in my opinion best be explained by dialectal differences within Swedish. From the late Viking Age onwards, the monophthongisation of OESc *-æi-* to standard OSw. *-ē-* was in progress and should have spread first from overseas by urban immigrants to the nearby provincial capital of Turku already during the Viking Age (as defined in the introduction of this publication). Unlike in rural dialects with primary diphthongs spoken in Swedish-speaking archipelago villages, the borrowings could have been adapted to this productive sound change. Therefore, the pronunciation in Turku has prevailed for localities of administrative importance in Finnish-speaking areas.

One name deserves closer study because of the apparent need to backdate its sound correspondences beyond the Swedish settlement. The genetic doublet Sw. *Kjulo* ~ Fi. *Köyliö* is used for a lake, an island in the lake, a creek draining the lake into the River Eura, as well as a settlement/ parish on the shore of that lake. The oldest attestations are recorded in standard handbooks as *Kiulo–Kiulæ* (1392), *Kiwla* (1420), *Kyula* (1458). Stellan Waldenström (2005: 18 with references), who has studied the name thoroughly, also gives *Thiula* (1365), *Kiula* (1368) and *Kyula* (1372). These attestations are all similar to the name in OSw. and testify first and foremost to the form in that language. The first attestation compatible with the modern Finnish language name is *Köylijoki* (1640) for the river. The name of the lake is, however, recorded earlier as Old Finnish *Kiwlo* in "Piispa Henrikin surmavirsi", a poem describing the slaying of the national saint, Bishop Henry, which according to the legend should have occurred in 1156 (regarding the historicity of missionary activities and a first crusade see Ahola & Frog): "Kyllä kierrän Kiwlon järven, ympäri joki koveran" ['I will indeed circumvent Lake *Kiwlo*, [going] around the bending river'].

This attestation is hard to date as it has been passed down for generations in oral tradition but it may have roots in (the last decades of) the thirteenth century (Heikkilä 2009: 161 ff.). All the same, phonologically there is no way EFi. **Kiulo* could have developed into OFi. *Köyliö*. Neither is the reverse development conceivable. These two diphthongs are kept well apart in the Finnish language in all environments. Therefore the most economical solution is to assume that while the form Fi. *KöylV-* (the *V* stands for a vowel of unknown quality and the hyphen for a later suffixation, possibly the remains of the word *joki* ['river'], which is common in names ending in *-io/ -iö*) is hardly a borrowing from Old Swedish, the form OFi. *Kiwlo* indeed is. The substitutions are straightforward. A reverse direction of borrowing (EFi. **Kiulo* → OSw. *Kiulo*) is conceivable in terms of sound substitution but would leave the form *Köyliö* isolated and unexplained. Lars Huldén (FSB: s.v. 'Kjulo') states that the form *Köyliö* probably is a "secondary" formation but he does not reveal how in his view this "secondary" form could have arisen.

Fig. 1. U1040 Fasma – Riksantikvarieämbetet. Photo: Bengt A Lundberg – 2001-04-26.[5]

Ralf Saxén (1905: 170 ff.) first suggests (alongside another theory which he later refutes himself) that the Finnish form may be a borrowing from an older precursor of the Scandinavian name *Kiule*, which is attested on rune stones U1039 and U1040, which are from around the last third of the eleventh century. Five years later Saxén (1910: 81ff.) proposes a derived

PSc/EESc name **Keuliaz* or **Keuliōn* from a common noun **keulaz*, represented later by ON *kjóll* ['(large) ship']. Saxén assumes a sound substitution with Finnic **eü* (front vowel variant of **eu*) regularly resulting in OFi. *öy*.

Waldenström (2005) rightly points out that OSw. *Kiul-* cannot be the outcome of PSc/EESc **Keuliaz* or **Keuliōn* because i-mutation would have resulted in ***Kȳl-*. He also correctly points out that OFi. *Kiwlo*, as in the poem, could well be a later borrowing from Old Swedish. The hypothesis of Waldenström, based on a Proto-Scandinavian appellative describing the shape of the island *Kjuloholm* ~ *Köyliönsaari*, is given favourable consideration by Huldén in the latest edition of FSB (s.v. 'Kjulo').

Unfortunately, Waldenström misrepresents Finnish vowel harmony, assuming that the vowel /i/ in the second syllable is a necessary precondition for the back vowel glide **eu* to mutate into the front vowel glide **eü*. In Finnish, front-vowel words may occasionally arise spontaneously from back-vowel words with only slight or no differentiation in meaning. For all these reasons it seems extraneous to operate with a concept of i-mutation in order to explain the front-vowel form of *Köyliö*. Indeed, in light of parallel borrowings, the sound substitution assumed by Saxén appears to be a very archaic Pre-Scandinavian one. In recent decades it has been argued (Hofstra 1985: 44–47, 177–179; Schalin 2004: 28) that Germanic loans where the Finnish diphthong *-öy-* (< NF **-eü-*) corresponds to Proto-Germanic **-eu-* all seem relatively old on account of other criteria. Examples of the Pre-Scandinavian type include *löytää* ['to find'] < **leütä-* ← **χleutan* and *pöytä* ['table'] < **peütä-* ←**beuđa-*. The name could of course in theory have passed into to a front vocalic form much later: *köyliö* < **keül-* < **keul-* < **kepl-* ← **keul-*.[6] Such an assumption remains rather speculative. In any event a definite *terminus ante quem* for such an unparalleled development would be the EESc sound development *-eu-* > *-iu-* (see Haugen 1976: 154; Holm 1996: 111, 117).

In short, CF **Keül-* could in theory have been borrowed from Germanic **KeulV-*, later represented by OSw. *Kiulo*, but parallels seem in that case to suggest a dating roughly as old as Middle Proto-Finnic (=MPF) ~ PGmc/NwG, or in absolute chronological terms corresponding to the Roman Iron Age. With this chronology, I see no reason to go deeper into discussion on the archaeological evidence used by Waldenström (2005: 29), by which he attempts to demonstrate a continued Scandinavian influence from around AD 550 until the Middle Ages. In my view his starting point falls some 300 years short of the requirement in order to make the necessary sound substitutions of the borrowed name plausible.

Finally, the preservation of a genetic doublet in two languages for centuries for an inland creek like *Köyliöjoki* or a corresponding settlement on the island *Kjuloholm* is hard to argue in light of the fact that so few of the other proposed Pre-Scandinavian etymologies have a valid doublet. The cases of *Taasia* ~ *Tessiö*, *Pyhtää* ~ *Pyttis* and *Perniö* ~ *Bjärnå* remain doubtful, as already stated, whereas the case of Sw. *Åland* ~ Fi. *Ahvenanmaa*, which is not an assured doublet either, is not analogous because it is a major locality in the middle of a language contact area.

As I have pointed out in a previous article (Schalin 2008a: 418), a solution based on a younger chronology is possible by assuming the reverse order of borrowing. EFi. *-eü-* (before its development into Old Finnish *-öy-*) might have rendered *-iu-* in Old East Scandinavian or Old Swedish, namely in the absence of OESc ***-eu-*, which by then had disappeared from the language completely.[7] The only alternative substitution would have been OESc *-øy-*, a diphthong that was about to become a dialect marker and perhaps therefore avoided in the Swedish language community around Turku, just as happened with the OESc diphthong *-æi-* in the names *Pēmar*, *Rēso* and *Lētala*. Still there could have been just enough time for a reborrowing of the Old Swedish name into late-medieval EFi. *Kiulo* of the poem.

In my view, this direction of borrowing is much more plausible. According to Stellan Waldenström (2005), an interpretation of OSw. *Kiul-* as a borrowing from Finnish through sound substitution had already been suggested by Liisa Nuutinen in a *pro gradu* thesis from 1988. According to him Nuutinen does not give any weight to the possibility of a PSc borrowing into Finnish but regards the Finnish element *Köyl-* as original in this respect. Nuutinen reportedly also studies other names in south-western Finland beginning with *Köyl-*, which include one medieval attestation *Köylinkoski* 1469 from Orimattila. The existence of such names adds to the weight of my argument.

In conclusion, I believe that the single Old Finnish attestation *Kiulo* is a reborrowing from Swedish. The Old Swedish name *Kiulo* is in turn a borrowing from Early Finnish **KeülV(j)o(-)*. I am neutral as to the discussion on the etymology of the Finnish name element **Keül-*. I would not *a priori* exclude a Northwest Germanic origin along the lines of Saxén and Waldenström, but other etymologies, such as the one based on a Sámi origin, may be more probable. In any event, the Old Swedish name appears in my view to be secondary, and thus of limited value when discussing the original etymology.

King Valdemar's Itinerary from the Thirteenth Century

The text of the itinerary is in Latin and forms part of a longer document known as Codex ex-Holmensis A 41 or by the better-known inauthentic name *Liber census Daniae* or in Danish *Kong Valdemars jordebog*. The codex is a collection of theological, historical and fiscal literature without a logical order. The historical and fiscal parts reflect significant knowledge of geographical and economic facts. The Codex was compiled around the year 1300 but the genesis of its different parts date back in varying degrees of decades, some as far as the first half of the thirteenth century (for a thorough discussion, see Gallén 1993: 13–19; for a faximile edition and transcriptions of the text Gallén 1993: 50–53; cf. Zilliacus 1994: 49ff.). There are good arguments for an early dating of the itinerary on the substance matter of the text. The route described follows more sheltered waters than medieval navigation is known to have used. The change of routes was due both to the post-glacial uplift of the seabed and the shift to larger carriers of the Hanseatic type (Zilliacus 1994: 50ff.).

Moreover the toponyms referred to in the itinerary reflects a situation where Old Swedish (referred to by the author as 'Danish', noting that a distinction of 'Danish' from 'Swedish' would hardly have been meaningful at that time) names had stabilised in the south-western parts of the Åboland archipelago but only eastward as far as *Aspö*. Names with continuity in today's Swedish are in Åland *Linæbøtæ* (*Lemböte*), *Fyghelde* (*Föglö*), *Thiyckekarl* (*Kökar*) and *Iurima* (*Jurmo*, today annexed to Korpo parish). The name *Aspø* (*Aspö*) in southern Korpo marks the end of continuity with the exception of *Hangethe* (*Hangö by/Kapellhamnen*) and perhaps *Purkal* (*Porkala*) further east.

East of *Aspö* and *Jurmo*, the names have in some cases been replaced before new records appear in late-medieval times. This applies mainly (but not only) to some 'Danish' names. For Scandinavian borrowed names with Finnish loan originals, it is hard to determine whether they show continuity in Old Swedish or rather if they have been preserved in Early Finnish for a longer time and borrowed into Old Swedish thereafter. Only the name *Hangethe*, which designates an important mainland harbour, unambiguously shows continuity in Old Swedish from the itinerary's attestation until late medieval times.

The fact that the eastern names in the text are quite scantily preserved in Swedish may indicate that they reflect a time rather before than after the large scale settlement of the Finnish south coast by Swedish peasants. This would be much more consistent with a dating to the early thirteenth century. By the first decades of the fourteenth century the Swedish settlement had already established itself in a continuous coastal strip, also including the easternmost parts of the Nyland province. A good case has been made for a hypothesis that speakers of Old Swedish had settled in parts of Korpo parish relatively early (Zilliacus 1994: 41–46). This would correlate well with the tendency of preservation for most of the names in Korpo.

The westernmost name that has disappeared from the language is *Aspæsund*. It may have referred to a sound next to *Aspø*, perhaps one that no longer exists due to the post-glacial uplift. Interpreted in this context, it seems equally possible, however, that it referred to a longer navigable stretch through the wider *Aspö/Nötö* archipelago, much like the names *Ämbarsund* in *Föglö* or *Barösund* in *Ingå* today.[8] Other names may have disappeared from the language randomly or due to the change of use in connection with the developing Swedish settlement. These would include *Malmø* (now *Nötö* < ['cattle island'] in southern *Nagu*), *Refholm* (now perhaps *Lökholm* < ['leek island']), *Ørsund* (now *Kyrkosund* < ['church sound'] in *Hitis*), *Cuminpe* (now the tip of *Hangöudd* or *Hankoniemi*), *Lowicsund* (somewhere near *Tvärminne*), *Karienkaskæ* (now *Hästö-Busö* in *Ekenäs*) and *Hæstø* (now *Orslandet*). There is no way of determining how long this more ancient layer of names, to which *Hangethe* and the other preserved names of the itinerary undoubtedly may be added, had existed. As I have stated above regarding the borrowed name *Kymmene*, there is no purely linguistic reason not do date this layer even earlier, to the earlier centuries of the Viking Age.

The location represented by the name *Ørsund* in *Hitis* was pinpointed in 1991. Archaeological excavations there have been conducted by the National Board of Antiquities. Results published so far indicate that a market place existed there during the Viking Age (Edgren 1995; 1996; 1999; Raninen & Wessman). A few Viking Age artefacts have also been found on the northern shores of *Hangö*, next to a sheltered harbour, which corresponds well to the assumed location of *Hangethe*.

As for the name *Iuxaræ*, which in modern local archaic dialect is pronounced [jʉ:sarø:], I believe that the spelling may reveal that it was yet to be borrowed permanently into Old Swedish. I have found no orthographic explanation for the spelling with "x" and hence a phonematic one could be tested. The origin of the name is thought to be EFi. **Juutinsaari* ['the island of the Jutes'] (Zilliacus 1994: 85 and works there cited). If syncope had occurred already early in this Finnish (or Estonian) dialect, the [t] would have appeared adjacent to the [s]. This was all the more likely if the first element was not in genitive but nominative case **Juutt(i)saari*. It is not at all sure that this dialect possessed the sequence [-ts-]. Modern Finnish words with *-ts-* like *katsoa* ['to look'] and *metsä* ['forest'] should in those days have been pronounced with a geminate fricative **kaϑϑo-* and **meϑϑä*. Therefore an underlying form **Juut-saar(i)* may have emerged with a variant surface structure (pronounciation) [jūksār]. The phonetic similarity of *-ts-* and *-ks-* is striking, especially as the Finnish 's' is dorso-postalveolar rather than dental.[9] Later an assimilated form [ju:ssa:ri] would have served as an original for the Old Swedish borrowing, still pronounced with a long vowel [jʉ:sarø:].

An additional argument for a later borrowing is the short central vowel of the second syllable. Further west names like *Bengtsår* in Bromarv, *Högsåra* (< **Hautasaari*) in Hitis and *Åvensor* (< **Ahvensaari*) in Korpo proves that they participated in the late-medieval Old Swedish sound change a: > å:. They are therefore borrowed and nativised before that sound change. The pronunciation [jʉ:sarø:] reflects an unexpected short vowel /a/, without secondary stress. The name could have been permanently borrowed in the fifteenth century, after the abovementioned sound change, when the long vowel /ā/ had became a very peripheral phoneme in the Old Swedish of that region, and occurred exclusively before very few consonant clusters. The literary contemporary Finnish *Jussaari* is most certainly a much later reborrowing from literary Swedish *Jussarö*.

Not much further east from this location the name *Horinsaræ* is obvoiusly not yet nativised as the text itself states that the Danish name was *Hestø*: "Inde horinsaræ quod danice dr hestø ii" ['From *Horinsaræ*, which the Danes call *Hestø* 2 rowing shifts'].[10] This name must later have been borrowed into Old Swedish in time for it to be attested as *Oris* (1451) > Sw. *Oorss* (1534) [u:rs] in the *Ingå* archipelago. The Danish name suggests that the original was **Orihinsaari* or **Orhinsaari* ['Stallion Island'],[11] which is still the preferred interpretation, even if the later pronunciation [u:rs] presents difficulties for

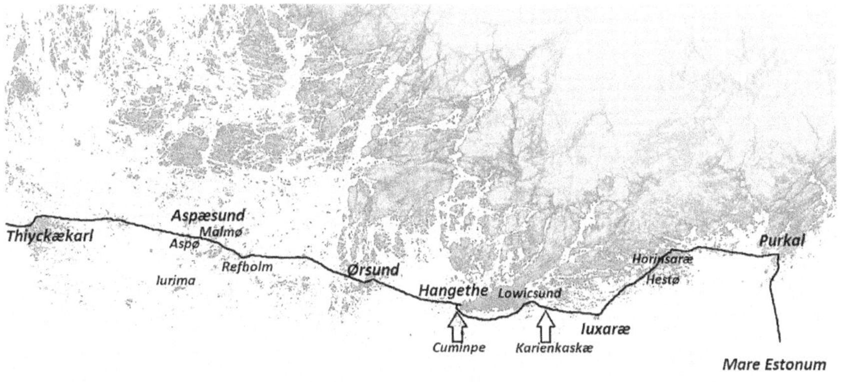

Map 2. Toponyms mentioned in the Danish Itinerary located according to Zilliacus 1994.

the assumed sound development. One would assume [ɔrins] or [ɔrisso:r] or the like with a mid-low vowel. This difficulty has justified an alternative interpretation as an original *Ohδensaari* ['Bear Island']. This etymology cannot, however, explain why the EFi. alveolar spirant *δ would occur as /r/ so much earlier than expected and in a so-called 'l-area', where the preferred OFi. representation of the EFi. *δ. was *-l-* rather than *-r-*.

My suggestion is that the pronunciation [u:rs] could also reflect older **Orn(i)s(ar)* because the cluster *-rn-* is known to lengthen the preceding vowel, which subsequently would have risen. In this case, the attested *Oris bol* (1451) would be a worn down form of an intermediate **Ornis(ar)* representing metathesis of *-in-* > *-ni-* with relation to the primary borrowing **Orins(ar)* (and its loan original). Likewise the day *onsdag* < *ōþinsdagh* ['Wednesday'] is pronounced [u:nisdag] in several East Nyland dialects. The element **-ar* could have been dropped when reanalysed as an obsolete genitive ending.

The root vowel of the last name *Purkal* does not reflect the vowel of the assumed Finnish original *Porkkala*. Unlike in Early Finnish, no phonemic opposition could, in Old Swedish/Danish of the thirteenth century, have been upheld between [o] and [u] in this position. Therefore the spelling could easily have shown random variation. The spelling may in my view not be used to determine whether this name had been nativised in Old Swedish or whether it still occurred as an ad hoc borrowing.

Overall, there is no evidence that a single name of Early Finnish (or Estonian) origin attested in the itinerary appearing east of *Hangethe* was permanently borrowed into Old Swedish in the early thirteenth century. Indeed, I have argued that the name *iuxaræ* corresponding to EFi. **Juutsaari* and Sw. dialect [jʉ:sarø:] may indicate that at least this name was not. This leaves *Hangethe*, a village and harbour just north of the contemporary town, as the easternmost name of the itinerary indisputably nativised in Old East Scandinavian and preserved into modern Swedish, *Aspø* in Korpo being the second-most easterly name of this character. East of this geographic area the name *Kymmenne* should also have been nativised at the latest by the thirteenth century.

In these names mentioned in the itinerary, be they Finnish or Danish names, few features are available that would make them stand out as clearly older than the source text. The second part of the name *Hangethe* is certainly obscure, which makes it a candidate for an old name together with other names containing that element (alongside *Narigeth* ~ *Naissaar* occurring in the itinerary itself and for example also *Dageida* ~ Gutnish *Dagaiþ* ~ Estonian *Hiiumaa*). The first element seems to be a borrowing from Fi. *Hanka* ['bifurcated peninsula' and as an appellative also 'oarlock']. The first element of the name *Iurima*, mentioned above, is equally obscure. If it could be shown that it contains the well-known Baltic word for 'sea', as in Latvian *Jurmala*, this would certainly bear testimony of a lost borrowed noun in a local dialect and would therefore hint at its great age.[12]

The Name Tafæistaland

Two toponyms in present-day Finland, attested as being from the Viking Age, are OESc *Tafæistaland* and an attestation of the name *Finland* on the rune stone U582 (now lost, but documented in the seventeenth and eighteenth centuries) from Söderby-Karl in Roslagen. The latter name appears in a text translated 'Björn and Igulfrid raised the stone in memory of Otrygg, their son. He was killed in Finland.' This is an interesting and contemporary parallel to the attestation of the name *Tafæistaland*. As no proposed loan etymology is involved, however, I have chosen not to discuss this attestation any further.

The Old East Scandinavian name *Tafæistaland* appears in a runic inscription classified as Gs13 from Hämlinge, Söderby, Valbo socken, Gästrikland, Southern Norrland, Sweden. The inscription is dated to the first half of the eleventh century and the line in question reads: **in h-n uarþ tauþr a tafstalonti**, which in normalised OES spelling usually is recorded as *en h[a]nn varð dauðʀ a Taf[æi]stalandi* ['and he died in Tafæistaland']. The name *Tafæistaland* here appears with the ending for the dative singular case. The diphthong that is inserted in normalised spelling is based on the fact that the name also appears in early-fourteenth century Old Icelandic sources in the form of *Tafeistaland* (the vowel correspondence *æi* ~ *ei* is regular) and the simple fact that runic inscriptions often lack runes. The name corresponding to the first element also spells *Tafæist-* in other inscriptions, as we shall see below.

The whole inscription rendered into English reads:

> Brúsi had this stone erected in memory of Egill, his brother. *And he died in Tafæistaland*, when Brúsi brought (= led?) the land's levy(?) (= army) in memory of ……, his brother. He travelled with Freygeirr. May God and God's mother help his soul. Sveinn and Ásmundr, they marked.

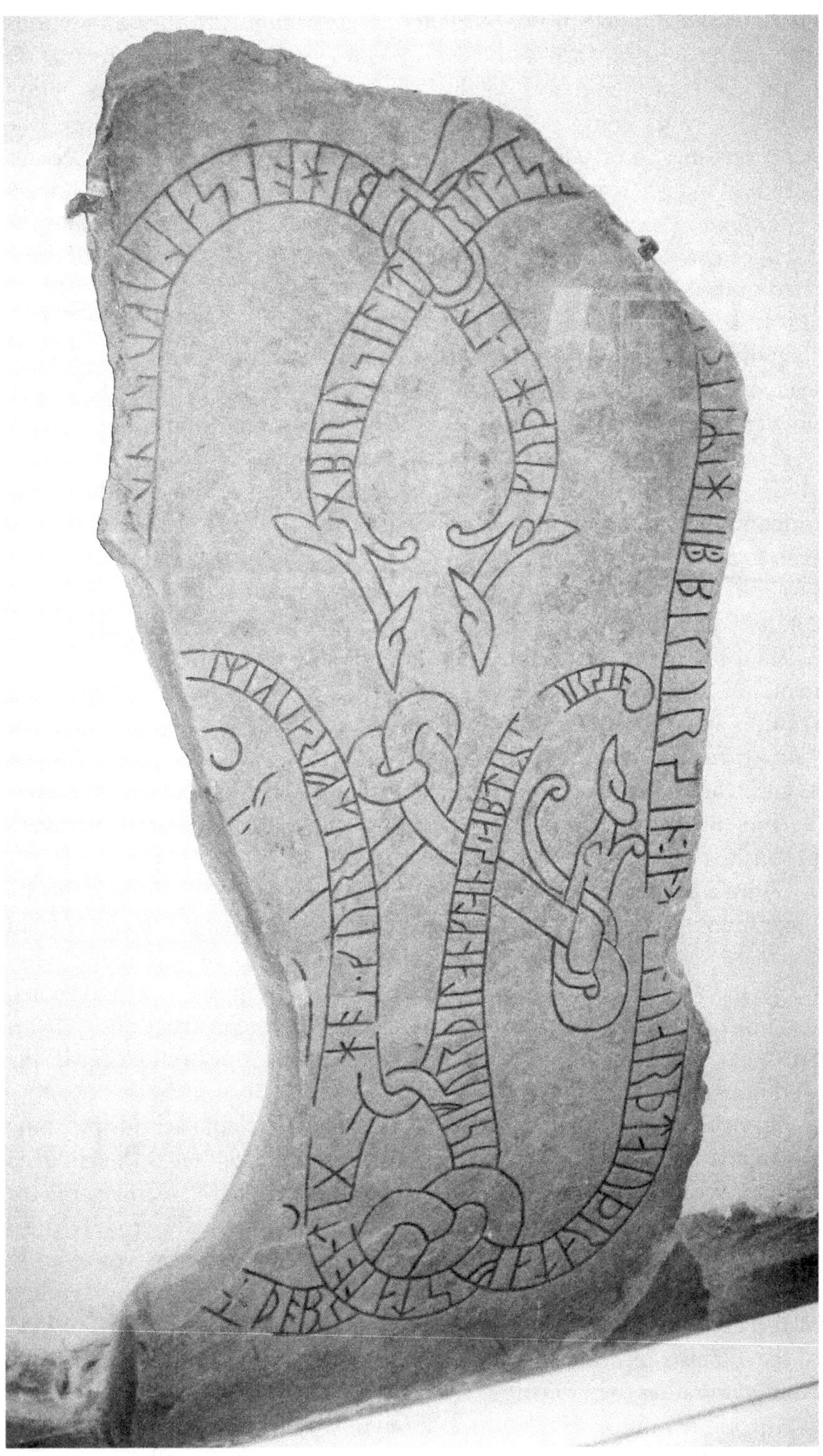

Fig. 2. G13 Gävle. Photo: Berig (Own work 2008-02-28).[13]

From medieval sources we know that the name is synonymous with the name of the Finnish province *Häme* or *Hämeenmaa*. Other attestations include: *de Teuestia* (1237) and *in Tavastia* (1303). They show fluctuation in the vowel of the second syllable but no attestation (with the exception of Gs13 above) completely lacks a vowel/syllable in this position. The name qualifies in this chapter on borrowed names because Adolf Neovius proposed in 1908 that Runic *Tafstaland* was a borrowing from Early Finnish **Taustamaa* ['hinterland', e.g. the land (viewed from the sea) 'behind' the older coastal settlements of Finland proper]. This is the single solution cited in the standard handbook on Swedish toponyms in Finland (FSB: s.v. 'Tavastland') while the new handbook on Finnish toponyms (SPNK: 450) states that the hypothesis is not refuted. Both publications refer to the lack of evidence of a Finnish loan original. The semantics of the hypothesis are also not very convincing. Yet in my view, the hypotheses may indeed be refuted, in particular with regard to the sound correspondences.

The word *tausta* ['background', 'wealth'] is first attested in Juslenius' lexicon of 1745. Another shorter derivative *taus* seems to be the older one with cognates in related languages (cf. Veps *tagus*, Vote *taguz* and Sámi *duogaš* ['wealth, property']). Even if a Finnish word **tausta* existed in the Viking Age, which is highly doubtful in light of this data, it would, as a derivative of *taka*, have been trisyllabic, EFi. **taγusta*, and the purely hypothetical name for *Häme* would have been **Taγustamaa*. Therefore the hypothesis requires a very awkward substitution **Taγusta-maa* → **Tafæista-land* (or **Tafa(i)sta-land*). A sound substitution with /f/ for /γ/ in the original is just as farfetched as *-æista-* (or *–a(i)sta-*) for **-usta-*, even as a folk etymology.

Therefore there are enough problems even in the phonological area alone to consider this hypothesis unfounded.

From a phonological point of view, no similar problems undermine the suggestion of Viljo Nissilä, who reconstructs a man's name **Tapainen* from which he derives a toponym **Tavaistenmaa*. Because of the many other necessary assumptions involved, however, this proposal has not gained much acceptance. The same may be said for the reconstruction by Lauri Kettunen of a hypothetical verb **tavastaa* ['go hunting/wandering in the wilderness']. (SPNK: s.v. 'Tavastland'.)

From here we may conclude that there is not sufficient basis for pursuing a loan etymology for the Swedish name *Tavastland*. Neither is there a need for one. According to one of the alternatives recorded in SPNK the name is a straightforward formation from the ethnonym *Tavast* ['person from Häme']. The structure of the Scandinavian name includes a connecting vowel *-a-* in the middle of the compound. It must be analysed as a genitive plural ending of the first element. *Tafæist-a-land* should therefore be read as 'the land of the Tafæists'. From this it follows that the toponym is derived from the ethnonym rather than the other way around.

As pointed out in SPNK, the ethnonym would in this case contain the element **Aistaz* ['Estonian'] and a preceding element *Taf-* ['laggard']. The compound is plausible under the assumption that the Scandinavians were inclined to perceive that the Finnic communities on both sides of the Gulf of

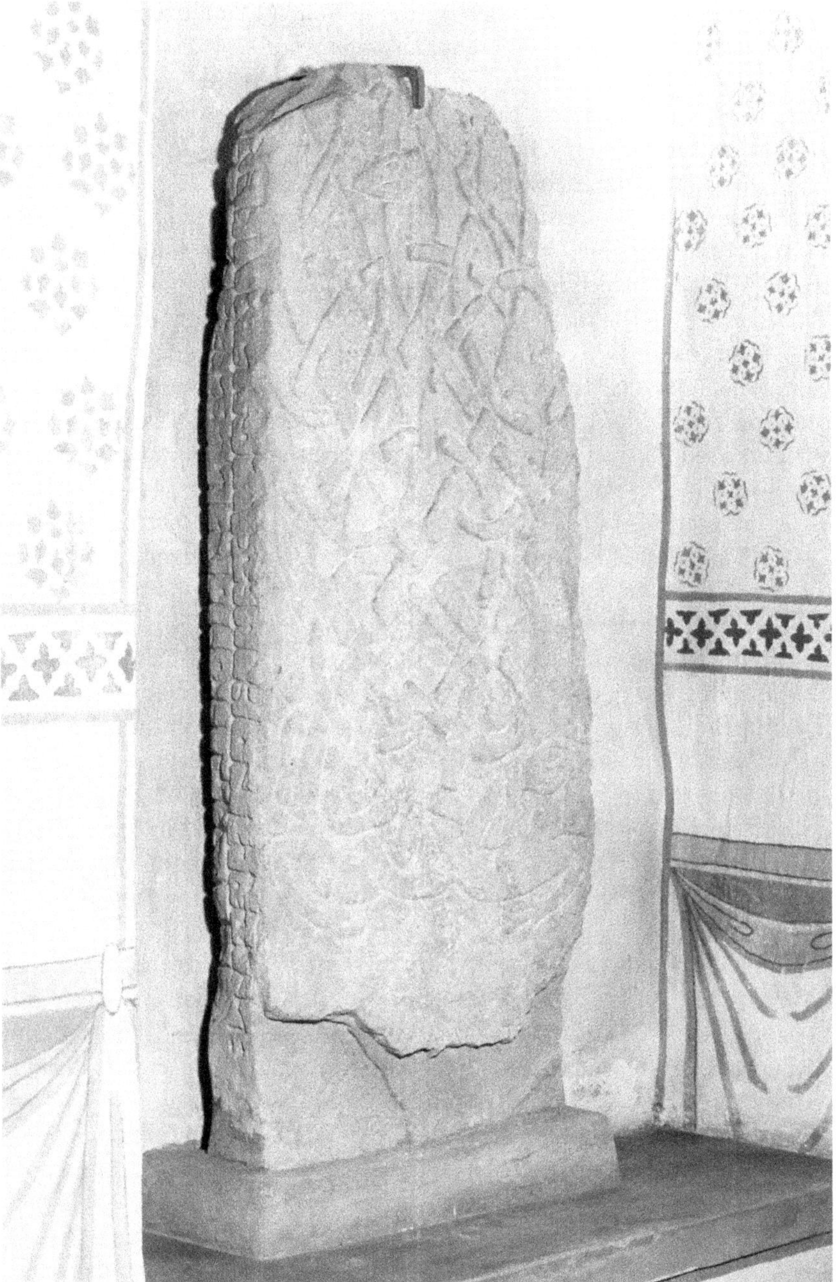

Fig. 3. U722 Löts kyrka - Riksantikvarieämbetet. Photo: Bengt A Lundberg - 1995-09-18.[14]

Finland indeed belonged to similar ethnicities. The ethnic component may have come in handy to distinguish the *Tafæist* communities from the Sámi ones. Both ethnicities would have been present in the vicinity of each other in large parts of today's Southern Finland.

According to this interpretation, the ethnonym would also have been the basis for the formation of the man's name *Tafæistr*, attested on the rune stone classified as U722 from Löts kyrka, Löts sn, Trögds härad, Uppland. The line in question reads: **tafaistr * lit * raisa : stain * at . . .**, which in normalised OES spelling should be recorded as *Tafæistʀ let ræisa stæin at* . . . ['Tafeistr had the stone raised in memory of . . .'].

Another attestation appears on the rune stone classified as U467 Tibble, Vassunda sn, Ärlinghundra hd. The line in question reads: **tafaist-. . . . . .-sa stei(n) * þen. . .**, which in normalised OES spelling should be recorded as *Tafæist*[*ʀ*] . . . [*ræi*]*sa stæin þenn*[*a*] ['Tafeistr . . . this stone raised . . .'].

The first element also exists as a stand-alone man's name *Taf-*. This name would of course not be formed on the basis of the ethnonym. Rather it is indirect evidence for the productivity of the adjective *Tafʀ* ['laggard'] as an attribute used for naming men, be it as a proper name or as an ethnonymic qualifier.

An attestation of this name appears on the rune stone classified as Vs FV 1988; 36 in Jädra, Hubbo socken, Västmanland. The line in question reads: **taf : lit : risa : estn : þina : hitiʀ : kri(m)ut . . .**, which in normalised OES spelling is usually recorded as *Taf let ræisa stæin þenna eftir Grimmund* ['Taf had this stone raised in memory of Grimmundr'].

Returning to the question of the ethnonym discussed above, there are no compelling reasons to take the runic sequence **tafstalonti** to mean that a form with a missing second syllable would be the oldest one. All other attestations cited include a vowel in this position. On the other hand, it is not sure that the original diphthong *-æi-* was pronounced in this position as such in eleventh-century OESc. The fact that the diphthong appears in a less emphasised syllable could explain the unexpected vowel in the medieval name *Tafvast* attested in Latin as *in Tavastia* (1303).

The varying vowel representation may be explained as the remains of different case and/or compound forms, the pronunciation of which had developed conditioned on the variation in stress patterns. The profound changes in the language taking place in and around the eighth century were largely dependent on accent and length. A shortening of *-æi-*, which in length equals a long vowel, gave different results depending on when it happened. For a shortening during Old East Scandinavian times, one would expect /æ/ as in Sw. *hälsa* ['health'] (derived from OESc *hæil-* ['whole']) or *älska* ['to love'] (derived from EESc **æil-* ['fire']; see also VAEO: s.v. 'elske'). A shortening of an older date and/or in a less stressed syllable could give /a/, as in the compounded Norse name *Óláf-* from **Anulaiƀu-*. This name is well known for its many attested variant forms *Ólaf-* ~ *Óláf-* ~ *Áleif-* showing precisely the phenomenon described at the beginning of this paragraph (Janzén 1947: 85, 108–109).

Therefore, some case forms of the ethnonym could have retained the diphthong as in *Tafæistr*, while the regular outcome for some case forms, where the relevant syllable was minimally stressed (*$^{*}Taf^{ai}stumz$*) would have been *Tafast-*. Thus the variations in the vocalism is consistent with Scandinavian origin, especially if we may assume that the ethnonym, if not

Fig. 4. Vs Fv1988;36 Jädra – Photo: Berig (Own work 2007-08-30).[15]

the toponym, is older than or concurrent with the changes taking place in and around the seventh century.

As regards considerations belonging to other disciplines, contacts with the Tavastians would have been likely either in the Kokemäki river region, on the south coast of Finland between the Pikkala creek and the Kymi river or possibly in Halikko Bay, used by Tavastians as a trading point.

The Names Swedish Karis ~ Finnish Karja(h)a- ~ ? Old Norse Herdalar

The first event ever supposed to have occurred in *Finland* is a skirmish attributed in the thirteenth-century *Óláfs saga Helga* ['The Saga of Óláfr the Saint'] of *Heimskringla* (OSH, SOH) to the adolescent Saint Óláfr. According to what is known about Óláfr's youth, the encounter must have taken place in 1008. This portion of the text, describing his 'third battle', contains a poem by Sighvatr Þórðarson (995–1045). The combat, or rather the military debacle, is told in the saga, attributed to the Icelander Snorri Sturluson (1179–1241), to have occurred close to *byggðir nokkurar* ['some inhabited places / settlements'] called *Herdalar* (cf. ON *dalr* ['dale, vale'], archaic West Norse and OSw. pl. *dalar*) in *Finland*, somewhat inland from the *Bálagarðs síða* ['shore/coast of *Bálgarðr*'] (cf. ON *garðr* ['realm, inhabited property, enclosure']) and inhabited by the *Finlendingar*. The place names and ethnonym are attested in Sighvatr's poem, which is otherwise low on informational content:

> Hríð varð stáls í stríðri
> ströng Herdala göngu
> Finnlendinga at fundi
> fylkis niðs hin þriðja.
> En austr við lá leysti
> leið víkinga skeiðar.
> Bálagarðs at barði
> brimskíðum lá síða.
> (Source: OSH Chapter 9 "Orusta þriðja")

> The third fight was at Herdales (or 'Army-Dales'), where
> The men of Finland met in war
> The hero of the royal race,
> With ringing sword-blades face to face.
> Off Bálagarðr's shore the waves
> Ran hollow; but the sea-king saves
> His hard-pressed ship, and gains the lee
> Of the east coast through the wild sea.

Since a suggestion in 1895 the location has often been identified with a village *Hirdal* in the Ingå parish, western Nyland province. The millennium of this event was celebrated in Ingå in 2008 (VNUR). In an article published in that same year, I argued that the identification with the village Hirdal, supported by J. R. Aspelin, Gunvor Kerkkonen, J. M. Granit, Ola Brenner, Jarl Stormbom and Gustaf Sundman, is not sustainable for the following reasons (Schalin 2008a).

The first mention of Ingå's *Hirdal* is from 1540, *Hijrendaall*. The spelling of all the oldest attestations points to a long palatal vowel and a third medial syllable subsequendly lost. The name is thus not phonologically consistent with ON *Herdalar*. Being a minor village, Hirdal is far too small to fit Snorri's description of *Herdalar* as 'some settlements', and it is also too small to have mobilised a successful defence against these Viking ships. According to the history of settlement, Hirdal was founded on the outskirts of the medieval communities of *Finnpada* and *Backaby* (Kerkkonen 1945: 172f). Thus it is also far too young to have existed in 1008. Moreover, if we attach any credibility to the narrative, Hirdal is closer to the shore than *Herdalar*, which was located several hours' walk inland. After the Vikings had fled to the ships and had set sail, according to the story, the *Finnledingar* marching along the shore followed the ships, which tacked their way towards the open sea. If correctly described, this is consistent only with the topography of the western shore of the bay *Pojoviken* (Fi. *Pohjanpitäjänlahti*), equalling the eastern shore of the peninsula *Hangö udd* (Fi. *Hankoniemi*) some 15 miles further west from Hirdal. The south-western coast in any other location is heavily indented by bays and peninsulas.

In many ways, the description of this skirmish would fit the ancient parish of *Karis* (late OSw. *Karis* is a secondary formation from earlier OESc/OSw. **Karjas* ← EFi. **Karjas/ Karjaha-* still preserved in Fi. *Karjaa*). The parish shows some continuity of settlement throughout the Viking Age and could have been the most important community existing at that time on the south coast exposed to a naval raid. This most western region of present day Nyland would definitely in pre-Christian times have qualified as 'Finnish' (extension of Finland Proper) rather than 'Tavastian'. As Unto Salo (2000: 158f., 212 note 21; 2008: 199) points out, there is a striking phonological similarity between the first part of the ON name *Herdalar* and the PGmc/NwG loan original postulated for the Finnish name **Karjas*, notably **χarjaz* ['army, host, crowd, mob'] (for the etymology see SPNK: s.v. 'Karjaa' and Nissilä 1954 & 1962). The same word is preserved in the Icelandic noun *her* and Swedish *här* with the same meaning. A derived weak masculine occurs as a man's name on rune stone SÖ 32 in Skåäng, Vagnhärad parish, Hölebo, Södermanland as well as on the comb DR 207 from Vimose, Fyn island, Denmark, dated to the second century AD. As I have reminded elsewhere (Schalin 2008a), this etymon has also been productive in Swedish as a designator of pre-Christian administrative recruitment areas, as shown by the common nouns Sw. *härad* and *hundare* (< **hunda-harja*), both meaning 'district' (SEO: s.v. 'härad'; Pamp 1988: 79f.; Andersson 2004: 6–8; 2005: 13 f.).

It should be noted that the NwG etymology of the name *Karjaa* is not uncontroversial. Similar names exist elsewhere, including an important settlement south of the Gulf of Finland from where the name could have travelled (perhaps in the Viking Age?).

Apart from the uncertain etymology, a solution based on the assumption that ON *Herdalar* indeed is a reminiscence of this word has at least three weaknesses. Firstly, the unlikely assumption is necessary that the name had been preserved in Scandinavian from the (late) Roman Iron Age, when the substitution **k-* ← **χ-* ceased to be productive (cf. later Fi. *hartia* ← EESc **harđiō-*). A later borrowing should have produced Fi. ***Harjaa* unless of course an exceptionally archaic sound substitution may be assumed under influence of the common noun Fi. *karja*. This noun today means 'cattle' but at that time it is still likely to have carried the meaning of its loan original.

Note that Unto Salo (2000: 158 ff.) assumes a retranslation from Finnish, with an unlikely sound substitution triggered by the consciousness of the meaning of the Finnish name.

A second minor weakness is the topography described above. In order to follow the ships along the shore of *Hangö udd*, the inhabitants of *Karjaa* would have to helicopter themselves across the bay of *Pojoviken*. In order to save the hypothesis, one could of course assume a larger prehistoric parish of *Karjah-*, including the core settlements of present day *Tenala* (Fi. *Tenhola*) west of the bay, implying a larger recruitment area for the defence of these habitations. While continuity of settlement throughout the Viking Age is explicitly assumed for *Karjah-*, including present-day *Snappertuna* (Forsén & Moisanen 1995: 33–38; Haggrén *et al.* 2003: 19ff.; Alenius *et al.* 2004), one could speculate that *Tenala* was also originally an offshoot of this settlement, existing already in 1008. However, this is in any event a minor weakness not least because the saga source was written more than two centuries later in Iceland by someone who likely had no first-hand knowledge of any coasts on the Baltic Sea.

This brings us to the third, rather grave weakness: the reliability of the saga itself. The poem of Sighvatr in itself is more or less contemporary with the event and should have been passed on to the fourteenth century protected by its stringent metrics. The names *Herdalar* and *Bálagarð*, however, are compounds of common nouns of that time, nouns closely associated with the theme of the poem. As pointed out by Clive Tolley in the November 2011 seminar, the words are rather suspicious as compounded names comprised of thematically relevant elements and could thus be ad hoc formulations during the composition of the poem rather than historical toponyms.[16] Productive invention of ad hoc compounds, such as 'kennings', was a common tool for poets to be able to formulate their story without violating the strict metrics. Lars Huldén (2012: 249) has recently suggested that *Bálagarðr* ['the realm/ enclosure of (bon)fires'] is originally a kenning meaning 'hell, inferno, realm of death'. Huldén backs up his argument with half a dozen of other attestations, some of which relate to other geographical areas and others that appear have no geographic connotations at all. Even in Sighvatr's poem, the word occurs in the context of sorcery and severe danger.

The narrative, on the other hand, is clearly secondary to the poem and may include later attempts to elaborate on obscure elements in it. As many poems of the same saga do contain names of real and identifiable places, Snorri might have reinterpreted a kenning into a geographical context.

In the case of Sighvatr's poem, *Balgarðr* carries both alliteration and rhyme and *síða* carries the type of rhyme that requires participation of the vowel in the position requiring this rhyme on a heavy syllable (Frog, p.c). This might favour the interpretation that it indeed did not represent a geographical term before Snorri. However, *Herdalar* carries neither alliteration nor rhyme and merely completes three of the required syllables of the line and requirements of stressed positions, the technicalities of which remain open to debate (Frog, p.c.). This would leave some more space for an interpretation that *Herdalar* represents a geographical name, but in the absence of any other tangible indication to that effect, one must remain very reserved.

On the whole, I am no more inclined to propagate my own suggestion than in 2008, when I concluded that the possibility of etymological coincidence between **Karjas* and *Herdalar* may not be ruled out. Indeed the weaknesses of the hypothesis seem to outweigh its strengths. Of course this would by no means contradict the good arguments for locating the event somewhere in the area where *Finland* meets the open seas of the *Baltic* such as the one discussed above. Neither would this undermine the possible Northwest Germanic etymology of *Karjaa*. One must only caution against using the attestation of the name *Herdalar* as remarkable evidence for either.

The Names Old Finnish Ahuen maa ~ Old Swedish Alandh

It has been long known that both the first element of OSw. *Alandh* and the first element of OFi. *Ahuen maa* could reflect a Germanic (feminine) noun for running water, attested in Gothic *aƕa* and ON *ā*. ~ OSw. *ā*. The Finnish form is easily explained as a borrowing from this word. The correspondence between Gothic and Scandinavian is phonologically regular, remembering that the nominative and accusative of the Early East Scandinavian word is in fact **ah(w)u* rather than ***ahwa*, sometimes wrongly cited.

Semantically, the association with this etymon creates just as many problems as it solves, because the province of *Åland* is certainly not known for its rivers and there is no independent evidence for reconstructing other meanings for the word **ah(w)u*, than indeed 'river', which is attested also in Gothic and therefore reconstructable to Proto-Germanic (Andersson 1964–1965: 281 with references). The phonetic similarity is however so striking that there is scope for improvement of the hypothesis by adding one or two reasonable assumptions. In theory, one can proceed in two different directions.

Several scholars since the 1960s (Ståhl 1964; Andersson 1964–1965; Huldén 1976; cf. FSB: s.v. 'Åland') have interpreted the latter element *-land* as meaning 'large island' rather than 'province'. The arguments for that are quite convincing since the phonological correspondences of the two names requires a borrowing that is older than the emergence of a meaning of 'province' for the word *land*, alongside the established meaning 'large island'. Some large neighbouring islands (*Hammarland*, *Lemland* and *Lumparland*) indeed carry names based on that long established meaning. As regards semantics the argument remains problematic for the first element of the name. The postulated naming basis 'river island' is quite odd. There are no proper rivers on the barren islands of the Baltic Sea and the streams on the *Åland Islands* are rather brooks than creeks. In the Iron Age they would have been even tinier as they drained lesser water sheds. In theory one could speculate that some scarce brooks on a few islands in the Baltic might stand out as a naming basis for those islands. Yet, accepting that logic in one case, rouses the expectation to find another analogous example of the naming basis 'creek island'. Indeed it is disturbing in that regard, that even though there is a myriad of named islands in Sweden and Finland, not a single example exists, where then lexeme *Å-* (or Fi. *Joki-*) as a first element would refer to a watercourse on that island (see further Schalin 2008b: 26). It is noteworthy that of the three scholars, which have defended that hypothesis, each has differed in proposing his favoured Åland rivulet (Ståhl 1964; Andersson 1964–1965: 290ff.; FSB s.v. 'Jomala'). Moreover it is not clear which island, according to an Iron Age shore line, the name would refer to. In his classical monograph on toponyms in *Åland* Lars Hellberg (1987: 233) thus deems "very unlikely" that the name *Åland* is based on any known stream in that province.

A second way to salvage the hypothesis, is to assume a meaning of 'island(s)' for the first element, which is present in at least one derived stem of the same etymon, namely Sw. *ö* traditionally reconstructed OESc. *øy* < (Middle) PSc. **auju* < NwG. **awjō-* < PGmc **ag^{w}jō-*. At first glance that would solve much of the semantic problem because islands are just as abundant and characteristic for the area as rivers are not. Yet, the most obvious naming basis 'island province' has been categorically dismissed as anachronistic for a Proto-Scandinavian name (Ståhl 1964: 12ff.). Hence, unless the last element *-land* can be argued to be a late Viking Age addition, we would have to look for a naming basis involving one single more ancient island, the 'island of islands'. Despite its apparent tautology, the latter is plausible in the Baltic where the post-glacial uplift of the seabed has caused islands in the ever changing archipelago to merge into larger entities over time. A formation *Skärlandet* ['Skerry Island'] or ['the large island characterised by accreting skerries'] or ['the large island of the archipelago/ skärgård'] is found in the *Ekenäs* archipelago. Another possibility would be a naming basis such as the 'island of peninsulas' or the 'island of the watery meadows', based on various other well-known meanings of this particular word for island (SEO: s.v. 'ö'; VAEO: s.v. 'øy').

Phonologically a solution based on this lexical item is very problematic, though, since the expected outcome, prima facie, would be *Öland* rather than *Åland*. Indeed a major island/province in Sweden carries precisely the name *Öland* (SOL: s.v. 'Öland') and the ancient Scandinavian name for *Saaremaa* in Estonia is Icelandic *Eysýsla*, Sw. *Ösel*. The vocalism of these names would effectively constitute counter examples for the vocalism of such a compound, unless they can be shown to be compounded considerably later.[17]

In a previous article I have given preference to postulating, in order to explain the vowel, a borrowing into Early East Scandinavian from Northern Finnic (Schalin 2008b: 23ff), based on an idea first put forward by Lars Huldén (1976), but which he later has set aside in favour of his preferred option. I there explained the Finnic loan original, namely the precursor of the name *Ahveen-maa*, attested in 1833, as an early borrowing into an appellative meaning 'islands, archipelago' from a Proto-Germanic lexeme today represented by Sw. *ö* ['island'] ~ Icl. *ey* ['ibid'], thus developing and modifying ideas by Heikki Ojansuu (1920: 4–5) and Matts Dreijer (1979: 112 ff.). The borrowing would have occurred before the development of

PGmc *g^w > *-w-* in this word. Naming based on this Germanic appellative (or in some cases its synonymous weak stem), which in plural appears to have meant a 'cluster of island', is attested at least in Scandinavian language for many localities, one further north along the Finnish west coast, and several occurrences across Sweden, always appearing in the plural: *Öja*. Also (*Vestmanna*)*eyjar* off the coast of Iceland is colloquially called *Eyjar*.

The Middle Proto-Finnic suffix **-eš* > **-eɧ* > *-eh* may well have been added as a reflex of the plural ending, or spontaneously as in the name *Häme*, resulting in (late) MPF **Aɧveɧ*. The suffix is certainly attested in (1833) *Ahveen-maa* whereas the earlier attestation of *Ahuen maa* is ambiguous as vowel length was not marked in spelling at the time. A reborrowing of early NF **Ahveh-* 'the archipelago region' into EESc. around the sixth century could have resulted in OSw. *Ālandh*, on condition that the substitution of the second syllable (probably **Ahwa-* with accommodation to the most common stem vowel for compounds), would not trigger i-mutation. One challenge for this kind of reasoning, which I have attempted to solve (Schalin 2008b: 25ff.), is to explain the later annexation of the elements *-land* and *-maa* respectively, and separately in the two languages.

Here we face a riddle, after all, which may only be solved through a comprehensive assessment of analogous cases and pursuing a maximum economy of unnecessary assumptions. If we want to maintain that the phonological match is not a coincidence we firstly have to accept that the name is older than just about all the other names in that region. In addition we either have to:

1. Accept and explain the unlikely naming basis 'creek island' (Ståhl 1964; Andersson 1964–1965: 290ff.; FSB s.v. 'Jomala'), as well as an additional assumption of a differential treatment of the first element (sound substitution) in relation to the latter (translation),
2. Accept the assumption of a (re)borrowing from Finnish and explain how and when the Finnish name originated, as well as the later annexation of the elements *-land* and *-maa* respectively (Schalin 2008b),
3. Postulate a hypothetic word, derived with a suffix from the same etymon, which might allow us to dispose of a number of the other necessary assumptions (Greule 2004: 75ff.),[18] or
4. Postulate an even earlier Pre-Roman Iron Age borrowing (cf. endnote 17), with the shorelines of those times, thus reducing the postulated borrowing events from two to one.

The fall-back option would always be there, meaning that the phonological resemblance is more or less coincidental and the name is not necessarily older than most of the other names in Åland (for possible interpretations on that basis see Schalin 2008b: 27n.4). I will return with a comprehensive assessment in the forthcoming publication (Schalin with Frog 2014), also elaborating the analysis of options 3 and 4 above, as well as the fall back option.

*The Name Early Finnish *Rooϑϑi (?< *Roocci) ~ Old Swedish *Rōþ- ~ Old Russian Rus' and Old Swedish Rȳtzer*

The prevailing understanding is that the Russian name *Rus'* is considered a borrowing from Finnic and the Finnic name is considered a borrowing from East Scandinavian (Häkkinen 2005: s.v. 'Ruotsi'; Andersson 2007 and works there cited; but differently Stang 1996: 185ff.).

The Finnic word has representatives in all Finnic languages (although the meaning further east is 'Lutheran Finnish' rather than 'Swedish') and exhibits forms that are regular with regard to sound correspondences (see Kallio). Therefore the word should rather be reconstructed to a distinctively common Finnic stage of development. A certain margin of uncertainty follows from the fact that the word could have entered one Finnic dialect and continued through a dialect continuum undergoing so-called nativisation. Even with this assumption, the dating could be no later than the ultimate break-up of the continuum of dialects north and south of the Gulf of Finland respectively, which puts it at the end of the first millennium at the latest (see Kallio). If the Finnic peoples indeed mediated a term for Swedish seafarers to East Slavic, it would be natural to assume that this happened in the very beginning of or before the Viking Age, before the Ladoga–Volchov trade route had become established. After that, the Slavs would of course have had no reason to borrow an ethnonym from a Finnic language.

The OESc etymology for the Finnic name is problematic. The medial consonants were traditionally explained as a substitution of the sequence -*ðs*- in **rōðs*- as in OSw. *rōþs-land, rōþs-karl, rōþs-mæn* (so still in SSA s.v. 'Ruotsi'; Heide 2006). Severe problems with this etymology have been put forward during past decades, first by Sven Ekbo and Juluis Mägiste in 1958 (for references see Stang 1996: 286f.; Andersson 2007: 8). Most importantly, the word in question would not to begin with have been declined with a plain -*s* in the genitive during the early Viking Age. Relevant data strongly suggest that the genitive would originally have been something like **rōþ(r)aʀ* (from a u-stem) or **rōþrs* (cf. SEO: s.v. 'rodd'). The proposition, which has been forwarded instead (which Andersson accepts), namely that the borrowing would have been based on a syncopated **rōþʀ* or **rōðʀ* from a former u-stem, also presents unparalleled difficulties with regard to morphological substitution practices.

In order to develop a discussion on the strengths and weaknesses of all the arguments involved further research is necessary. It is my intention to return to this problem in another context. In the meantime, attention could be drawn to a promising line of reasoning, overlooked so far, which is to discard the assumption of the sibilant in the loan original. The precise phonetic value of LPF *-*cc*- during its development into EFi. *-*ϑϑ*- is not reconstructable for each intermediate stage. It has been thought to emerge during the genesis of consonant gradation (Lehtinen: 171–172 with references). A substitution for that geminate of Early East Scandinavian -*þ*- could not be completely ruled out, even in the absence of parallels.

A final word may be said about the OSw. ethnonym *Rȳtzer* ['Russian']. There is no easy explanation for the fronted character of the rounded root vowel in this word. No front vowel variants exist in Finnic (nor indeed in Slavonic or Eastern Baltic) languages, serving as a potential loan original. Any genetic development from the EESc original word is also ruled out. A reborrowing from EFi **Ruoϑϑi* (Heikkilä 2014: 189n.167) presents considerable phonological and chronological difficulties, not to mention the semantic ones, and cannot be accepted. The only conceivable origin would be a precursor of the Middle High German form *Riuze*, still reflected in the German duchy of *Reuss* (SEO: s.v. 'Ryss'). In Old East Scandinavian, unlike in Western, the sequence *Riū-* was regularly assimilated to *Rȳ-*.The same could probably occur through a nativising sound substitution some time towards the end of the Old East Scandinavian period. Also this hypothesis requires further study.

Conclusion

As we have seen above, the borrowing of names between East Scandinavian and Early Finnish occurred in prehistoric times but it is hard to date these borrowing events with sufficient precision to say whether a borrowing has occurred precisely during the Viking Age or indeed before or after it. There are a number of Finnish toponyms that may have pre-Scandinavian etymologies. Apart from the possible exception of *Ahvenanmaa* none of these names necessarily has a preserved doublet in Swedish. I have previously proposed that the name *Åland* may be a reborrowing from North Finnic a century or two before the Viking Age but the argument relies heavily on a likely but moot premise that the Finnish and Swedish names are indeed phonologically related. And if the names are phonologically related, an explanation involving a much older common origin may be more elegant.

The name *Tavastland* is no borrowing at all but together with the name *Finland* it testifies to continuing Scandinavian–Finnish contact throughout the Late Iron Age. Borrowing of common nouns bears witness to the same, as seen in KAISA HÄKKINEN's chapter in this publication.

The name Sw. *Kjulo* may well be borrowed from EFi. towards the end of the Viking Age, as periodised in this publication. Probably it belongs to a stratum of eleventh or twelfth century borrowings in south-western Finland, adapted to the Turku pronunciation of Swedish. Other more ancient solutions are possible but not probable. The name *Karis* is certainly, like so many other names in the Swedish-speaking areas (cf. *Ors* and *Jussarö*), a borrowing that would not necessarily predate the Swedish settlement. The name Fi. *Karjaa* may or may not be a borrowing from Northwest Germanic but whether the attestation *Herdalar* in the Icelandic sagas is a correct etymon which increases this probability is highly doubtful. The ethnonym *Ruotsi* ['Swedish'] probably predates the Viking Age, but the etymology will continue to be discussed. The Swedish names *Kymmene* and *Hangethe* ['Hangö Village'] are archaic in the context of medieval names and appears to predate the Swedish settlement by at least a few generations. Together with a number of later forgotten names mentioned in King Valdemar's Itinerary, they seem to a greater or lesser extent earlier than the thirteenth century.

Notes

1 See, for example, the criticisms of Jouko Vahtola's research (in Koivulehto 2007: 67–76) and of Paula Wilson's (in Schalin 2007).
2 For an absolute chronology of Scandinavian see Wessén 1958: 4–24; Nielsen 2000: 286f.; Pettersson 2008: 71–80; cf. Haugen 1976: 8–9; for more on early loan word stratification, see Kallio 2012.
3 On the eve of publishing the volume containing this chapter, the doctoral dissertation of Mikko Heikkilä (2014) was published. This dissertation contains proposals of new etymologies and various detailed claims relevant to this chapter, much of which is supportive of my findings, but it was not possible to critically assess all of these claims or fully integrate them into this chapter in the time available.
4 Mikko Heikkilä has recently attempted to argue that the Swedish name Kymmene may be a later representative of the Germanic loan original of Fi. *Kymi.*, rather than a reborrowing, an idea earlier floated by Juha Janhunen (Heikkilä 2014: 263–265).
5 CC-BY-3.0 (http://creativecommons.org/licenses/by/3.0)], via Wikimedia Commons.
6 In light of parallels, one would expect from a Proto-Scandinavian sequence **keul-* Coastal Finnic **kepl-/kekl-* as in *keula* ['bow'] < *kepla/kekla* ← **skeula* (> NSw. *skjul* ['shelter']) or ← **keula* ['(large) ship'] (LÄGLOS: s.v. 'teuras', 'keula').
7 Still today, the sequence remains unpronounceable, as can be heard when a Swedish speaker pronounces words like *Euro* and *terapeut.*
8 The Hälsinge law states that "If *leþung* goes over the sea or out of *Aspasund*, then they are not obliged to deliver the *leþungslama*." This Aspasund has been identified with several places, including a strait near *Aspö* in Stockholm's southern archipelago, on the border between Uppland and Södermanland, but also *Aspæsund* in Korpo has been mentioned (Gallén 1993: 71).
9 At a completely different stage of Pre-Finnic language development, the sequence *-ts-* was also absent. At that time, Pre-Iranian words containing the sequences *-ts-* or *-dz-* were borrowed into Pre-Finnic with *-ks-* as in *kahdeksan* ['cardinal 8'] (Parpola 1999: 198; Koivulehto 1999: 219–225).
10 The measurement of distances in the text is based on a rowing shift (*ukesio*). Later this terminology was used for an old sea-mile, which is roughly equal to 4 nautical miles (Zilliacus 1994: 54).
11 The loss of word-initial [h-] in pronunciation, followed by random variation in spelling with or without initial 'h-' is an ancient feature in many Uppland dialects, coincidentally preserved well into modern times also in the Ingå dialect. The spelling of EFi. **Orhinsaari* as *Horinsaræ* could be used as evidence of a resident population in Ingå originating in Uppland before the time of the itinerary, but of course the spelling could also come from an informant being a native of that province.
12 Applying the possibility of a man's name here, the medieval Low German form for George, *Jurian*, would fit well
13 Item CC-BY-3.0 (http://creativecommons.org/licenses/by/3.0)] via Wikimedia Commons.
14 CC-BY-2.5 SE (http://creativecommons.org/licenses/by/2.5/se/).
15 CC-BY-3.0 (http://creativecommons.org/licenses/by/3.0)], via Wikimedia Commons.

16 Coincidentally, a valley named *Härdalen* and some adjacent mountains called *Härdalsbergen* are situated at the western fringe of the Saltvik parish in Åland, just north of Ödkarby.

17 For many names even in the oldest stages of Proto-Scandinavian the expected compositional suffix *-ja-* is attested as a simple *-i-*, even after short root syllable (Syrett 1994: 70ff.; Janzén 1947: 77ff). Such a sequence would typically not cause i-mutation. If the word had been compounded early enough (the first element in the compound would probably have come in so-called stem form with a suffix ending in *-ja-* rather than *-jō-*), it is not at all clear how the wear and tear typical for toponyms would have shaped it and thus whether the result would be i-mutation after all.

18 A rather attractive proposition by Albrecht Greule relates the name to the German names *Ehn* and *Ehnheim* (AD 788 *Ehinheim*) based on a word, which he reconstructs as **Ah(w)ina*. A proposition very similar to that of Greule had been made by Hugo Pipping already in 1917 (1964–1965: 280 ff., Huldén 1976: 220), which Greule fails to take note of. This proposition never gained acceptance because its postulated appellative could not be established in Scandinavian vernacular. If such an appellative would have existed, one would contrary to Greules expectation expect it in a form in accordance with Verner's law, such as **Awina-*, which in turn could, however, have become *Å(l)land* rather than *Ö(l)land* anyway (cf. Nielsen 1985: s.v. 'ålam'; VAEO s.v. 'ær').

References

Sources

Codex ex-Holmensis A 41 = Gallén 1993: 49, 50, 53

DR 207 = http://runer.ku.dk/VisGenstand.aspx?Titel=Vimose-kam & http://www.arild-hauge.com/danske_runeinnskrifter1.htm (14.08.2014)

GS13 = *http://luxor.fivebyfive.be/all/3130* & *http://www.christerhamp.se/runor/gamla/gs/gs13.html* (15.7.2014)

GÄSTRIKLAND = Hauge, Arild. Runeinnskrifter fra Gästrikland. *http://www.arild-hauge.com/se-runeinnskrifter-gaestrikland.htm* (15.7.2014)

OSH = Heimskringla eða Sögur Noregs Konunga Snorra Sturlusonar: *Ólafs saga helga* *http://lind.no/nor/index.asp?lang=&emne=asatru&vis=s_i_olav_haraldsson* & *http://www.snerpa.is/net/snorri/heimskri.htm* (15.7.2014)

SSW = Sanan Saattaja Wiipurista 1833, nro 13. *http://agricola.utu.fi/julkaisut/julkaisusarja/kktk/sanansaattaja/SSV1833-13.html* 15.7.2014 The spelling of the word "Ahveen maan" in the source was checked from Kotimaisten kielten tutkimuskeskus by e-mail in 2008.

SÖ 32 = http://www.arild-hauge.com/raa-se/Soe-32-Skaaaeng.htm & http://www.christerhamp.se/runor/gamla/so/so32.html & http://www.arild-hauge.com/se-runeinnskrifter-soedermanland.htm (14.08.2014)

U582 = *http://skaldic.arts.usyd.edu.au/db.php?if=srdb&table=mss&id=17406* (15.7.2014)

U722 = *http://luxor.fivebyfive.be/all/2291* & *http://www.arild-hauge.com/raa-se/U-722-Loets-kyrka.htm* & *http://www.christerhamp.se/runor/gamla/u2/u722.html* (15.7.2014)

U1039 = *http://luxor.fivebyfive.be/all/2608* (15.7.2014)

U1040 = *http://luxor.fivebyfive.be/all/2609* & *http://www.arild-hauge.com/raa-se/U-1040-Fasma.htm* (15.7.2014)

UPPLAND = Hauge, Arild. Runeinnskrifter fra Uppland. *http://www.arild-hauge.com/se-runeinnskrifter-uppland.htm* (15.7.2014)

Vs Fv1988;36 = *http://luxor.fivebyfive.be/all/3069* & *http://www.christerhamp.se/runor/gamla/vs/vsfv1988-36.html* (15.7.2014)

VÄSTMANLAND = Hauge, Arild. Runeinnskrifter fra Västmanland. *http://www.arild-hauge.com/se-runeinnskrifter-vaestmanland.htm* (15.7.2014)

Abbreviations

FSB = Finlandssvenska bebyggelsenamn.
FSVLDB = Fornsvensk lexikalisk databas.
FSO-LEX = Finlands svenska ortnamn -namnledslexikon.
SEO = Hellqvist 1980 [1922]. *Svensk etymologisk ordbok.*
SOH = Snorre Sturluson 1844: *Heimskringla.*
SOL = Wahlberg 2003: *Svenskt ortnamnslexikon.*
LÄGLOS = Kylstra *et al.* 1991–2012: *Lexikon der älteren germanischen Lehnwörter in den ostseefinnischen Sprachen..*
SKAS = Suomen keskiajan arkeologian seura – Sällskapet för medeltidsarkeologi i Finland
SKS = Suomallaisen Kirjallisuuden Seura
SSA = *Suomen sanojen alkuperä* (1992–2000).
SPNK = Paikkala 2007: *Suomalainen paikannimikirja.*
VAEO = Bjorvand & Lindeman 2007 [2000]: *Våre arveord.*
VNUR = Om Snorre och Olav.

Literature

Alenius, Teija, G. Haggrén, H. Jansson, & A. Miettinen. 2004. Ulkosaariston asutuksesta autiokyläksi: Inkoon Ors poikkitieteellisenä tutkimuskohteena. *SKAS* 2004(1): 4–19.

Andersson, Sven. 1964–1965. Landskapsnamnet Åland. *Budkavlen* 43–44: 280–300.

Andersson, Thorsten. 2004. Svethiudh, det svenska rikets kärna. *Namn och bygd: Tidskrift för nordisk ortnamnsforskning* 92: 5–18.

Andersson, Thorsten. 2005. Svethiudh arkeologiskt förankrat. *Namn och bygd: Tidskrift för nordisk ortnamnsforskning* 93: 13–15. Uppsala.

Andersson, Thorsten. 2007. Rus' och Wikinger. *Arkiv för nordisk filologi 122.* Pp. 5–13.

Bjorvand, Harald, & Lindeman, Fredrik Otto. 2007 [2000]. *Våre arveord: Etymologisk ordbok.* Revidert og utvidet utgave. Oslo: Instituttet for sammenlignende kulturforskning.

Dreijer, Matts. 1979. *Det åländska folkets historia I.1: Från stenåldern till Gustaf Vasa.* Mariehamn: Ålands kulturstiftelse.

Edgren, Torsten. 1995. Kyrksundet i Hitis: ett arkeologiskt forskningsprojekt kring en av "det danska itinerariets" hamnar i sydvästra Finlands skärgård. *Budkavlen* 74: 49–66.

Edgren, Torsten. 1996. Arkeologi i Hitis utskär. *Skärgård* 19(3): 15–21.

Edgren, Torsten 1999. *Fornlämningar och fornfynd i Hitis utskär.* Kimito: Sagalundgillet.

Finlands svenska ortnamn -namnledslexikon. Available at: http://kaino.kotus.fi/svenska/ledlex/ (last accessed 12.8.2012).

Finlandssvenska bebyggelsenamn. Available at http://bebyggelsenamn.sls.fi/ (last accessed 28.7.2014). Earlier edition available in hard copy equals Huldén 2001.

Fornsvensk lexikalisk databas. Available at: http://spraakbanken.gu.se/fsvldb/ (last accessed 15.7.2014).

Forsén, Björn & J. Moisanen. 1995. Svartån och bebyggelsen runt denna. *Finskt museum* 100(1993): 26–49.

Gallén, Jarl. 1993. *Franciskansk expansionsstrategi i Östersjön. Redigerad och utgiven av Johan Lind.* Helsingfors: Svenska litteratursällskapet i Finland.

Granlund, Åke. 1956. *Studier över östnyländska ortnamn.* Studier i nordisk filologi 44. Skrifter utgivna av Svenska litteratursällskapet i Finland 358. Helsingfors 1956.

Greule, Albrecht. 2004. Entlehnte 'Wasserwörter' in den ostseefinnischen Sprachen und die frühgermanische Hydronymie. In Irma Hyvärinen, Petri Kallio, Jarmo Korhonen & Leena Kolehmainen (eds.). *Etymologie, Entlehnungen und Entwicklungen: Festschrift für Jorma Koivulehto zum 70. Geburtstag.* Mémoires de la Société néophilologique de Helsinki 43. Helsinki: Société néophilologique. Pp.73–82.

Haggrén, Georg, H. Jansson & A. Pihlman. 2003. Snappertunan Kullåkersbacken: Unohdettu tutkimuskohde unohdetulla paikalla. *Muinaistutkija* 2003(3): 13–23.

Häkkinen, Jaakko. 2010. Jatkuvuusperustelut ja saamelaisen kielen leviäminen II. *Muinaistutkija* 2010(2): 51–64. Available at: http://www.elisanet.fi/alkupera/Jatkuvuus2.pdf (last accessed 15.7.2014).

Häkkinen, Kaisa. 2005. *Nykysuomen etymologinen sanakirja.* 3rd edn. Helsinki, WSOY.

Haugen, Einar. 1976. *The Scandinavian Languages: An Introduction to Their History.* London: Faber and Faber Limited.

Hausen, Greta (ed.). 1920–1924. *Nylands ortnamn: Deras former och förekomst till år 1600* I -III. Skrifter utgivna av Svenska litteratursällskapet i Finland 152, 160, 177. Helsingfors: Svenska litteratursällskapet i Finland.

Heide, Eldar. 2006. Rus 'Eastern Viking' and the *víking* 'Rower Shifting' Etymology. *Arkiv för nordisk filologi* 121. Pp. 75-77. Available at http://eldar-heide.net/Publikasjonar%20til%20heimesida/rus%20viking.pdf (last accessed 9.8.2014).

Heikkilä, Mikko. 2014. *Bidrag till Fennoskandiens språkliga förhistoria i tid och rum.* Helsingfors: Helsingfors Universitet. Available at: https://helda.helsinki.fi/handle/10138/135714.

Heikkilä, Tuomas. 2009. *Sankt Henrikslegenden.* Helsingfors: Svenska litteratursällskapet i Finland / Stockholm: Bokförlaget Atlantis.

Hellberg, Lars. 1987 [1980]. *Ortnamnen och den svenska bosättningen på Åland.* 2nd edn. Studier i nordisk filologi 68. Helsingfors.

Hellqvist, Elof. 1980 [1922]. *Svensk etymologisk ordbok.* 3rd edn. Lund: LiberLäromedel Lund - Bröderna Ekstrands Tryckeri AB.

Holm, Gösta. 1996. Nordiska studier: Femton uppsatser om ord, namn, dialekter, filologi, stilhistoria och syntax. In Christer Platzack & U. Teleman (eds.). *Festskrift till Gösta Holm på 80-årsdagen den 8 juli 1996.* Lund: Lund University Press.

Huldén, Lars. 1976. Namnet Åland. In Christer Platzack & U. Teleman (eds.). *Festskrift tillägnad Gösta Holm på 60-årsdagen den 8 juli 1976.* Nordiska studier i filologi och lingvistik. Lund: Lund University Press. Pp. 218–224

Huldén, Lars. 1997. Younger Names of Old Rivers. In Ritva Liisa Pitkänen & K. Mallat (eds.). *You Name It: Perspectives on Onomastic Research.* Studia Fennica Linguistica 7. Helsinki: SKS. Pp. 178–186.

Huldén, Lars (ed.). 2001. *Finlandssvenska bebyggelsenamn: Namn på landskap, kommuner, byar i Finland av svenskt ursprung eller med särskild svensk form.* Skrifter utgivna av Svenska litteratursällskapet i Finland 635. Helsingfors: Svenska litteratursällskapet i Finland.

Huldén, Lars. 2012. Namn och bygd och Finland. *Namn och bygd: Tidskrift för nordisk ortnamnsforskning* 100: 229–249. Available at http://www.kgaa.nu/upload/tidskrifter/4_2012.pdf (last accessed 11.8.2014).

Janzén, Assar. 1947. De fornvästnordiska personnamnen. In Assar Janzén (publ), Johs. Brøndum-Nielsen, S. Erixon & M. Olsen (eds.). *Personnamn.* Nordisk Kultur 7. Stockholm / Oslo / Köpenhamn. Pp. 22–186

Jäppinen, Jouni & Rune Nygård. *Talonpoikia, seppiä, lohiylimyksiä. Arkeologian harrastajien tutkielma Kymijokilaakson rautakautisesta asutuksesta.* ISBN 978-

952-93-3862-7 (PDF). Available at http://rautakymi.fi/Prologi.html (last accessed 20.7.2014).

Kallio, Petri. 2012. The Prehistoric Germanic Loanword Strata in Finnic. In Riho Grünthal & Petri Kallio (eds.) *Linguistic Map of Prehistoric North Europe.* Mémoires de la Société Finno-Ougrienne 266. Helsinki: Société Finno-Ougrienne.

KARTSÖK = Lantmäteriets KartSök och Ortnamn. Avaliable at: http://www.lantmateriet.se/Kartor-och-geografisk-information/Ortnamn/ (last accessed 15.7.2014).

KARTTAPAIKKA = Kansalaisen karttapaikka – Maanmittauslaitos. Available at: http://kansalaisen.karttapaikka.fi (last accessed 15.7.2014).

Kerkkonen, Gunvor. 1945. *Västnyländsk bebyggelse under medeltiden.* Skrifter utgivna av Svenska Litteratursällskapet i Finland 301. Helsingfors: Svenska Litteratursällskapet i Finland.

Koivulehto, Jorma. 1987. Namn som kan tolkas urgermanskt. In *Klassiska problem inom finlandsvensk ortnamnforskning.* Studier i nordisk filologi 67. Skrifter utgivna av Svenska litteratursällskapet i Finland 539. Helsingfors: Svenska litteratursällskapet i Finland.

Koivulehto, Jorma. 1997. Were the Baltic Finns "Club-Men"? – On the Etymology of Some Ancient Ethnonyms. In Ritva Liisa Pitkänen & K. Mallat (eds.). *You Name It: Perspectives on Onomastic Research.* Studia Fennica Linguistica 7. Helsinki: SKS. Pp. 151–169.

Koivulehto, Jorma. 1999. Varhaiset indoeurooppalaiskontaktit: Aika ja paikka lainasanojen valossa. In Paul Fogelberg (ed.). *Pohjan poluilla: Suomalaisten juuret nykytutkimuksen mukaan.* Bidrag till kännedom av Finlands natur och folk 153. Helsinki: Finska Vetenskaps-Societeten.

Koivulehto, Jorma. 2007. Kriittisiä havaintoja paikannimitutkimuksesta. In *Satakunnan vanhaa paikannimistöä.* Satakunta: Kotiseututututkimuksia 25. Turku: Satakunnan Historiallinen Seura. Pp. 66–81.

Kylstra, A. D., Sirkka-Liisa Hahmo, Tette Hofstra & Osmo Nikkilä. 1991–2012. *Lexikon der älteren germanischen Lehnwörter in den ostseefinnischen Sprachen* I–III. Amsterdam / Atlanta, GA: Rodopi.

Lehtinen, Tapani 2007: *Kielen vuosituhannet.* Suomen kielen kehitys kantauralista varhaissuomeen. SKS. Helsinki.

Nielsen, Niels Åge. 1985. *Dansk etymologisk ordbog: ordenes historie.* 3. reviderede udgave med et tillæg, 4. oplag. Gyldendals røde ordbøger. Gyldendalske Boghandel, Nordisk Forlag A/S, Copenhagen – København.

Nielsen, Hans Frede. 2000. *The Early Runic Language of Scandinavia: Studies in Germanic Dialect Geography.* Indogermanische Bibliotek. Heidelberg: Universitätsverlag C. Winter.

Nissilä, Viljo. 1954. Syntymäpaikkaa ja -yhteisöä ilmaisevia sanoja nimistössämme. *Virittäjä: Kotikielen seuran aikakausilehti* 58: 246–287.

Nissilä, Viljo. 1962. Karjalan nimestä. *Virittäjä: Kotikielen seuran aikakausilehti* 66: 345–367.

Ojansuu, Heikki. 1920. *Suomalaista paikannimitutkimusta.* Turku: Turun Suomalaisen Yliopistoseura.

Om Snorre och Olav. Available at: http://www.vnur.org/vnur/vnurprojekt/projekthirdal/ (last accessed 15.7.2014).

Paikkala, Sirkka (ed.). 2007. *Suomalainen paikannimikirja.* Kotimaisten Kielten Tutkimuskeskuksen Julkaisuja 146. Jyväskylä: Kotimaisten Kielten Tutkimuskeskus ja Affecto Finland Oy.

Pamp, Bengt. 1988. *Ortnamnen i Sverige.* 5th edn. Sverige: Studentlitteratur.

Peterson, Lena 2004: Lexikon över urnordiska personnamn. Available at: http://www.sprakochfolkminnen.se/sprak/namn/personnamn/lexikon-over-urnordiska-personnamn.html (last accessed 13.8.2014).

Pettersson, Gertud 2008 [1996]. *Svenska språket under sjuhundra år: En historia om svenskan och dess utforskande.* Upplaga 2:4. Lund: Studentlitteratur.

Pitkänen, Ritva Liisa. 1986 [1985]. *Turunmaan saariston suomalainen lainanimistö.* 2nd edn. Suomen Kirjallisuuden Seuran Toimituksia 418. Helsinki: Suomen Kirjallisuuden Seura.

Ringe, Donald. 2006 [paperback 2008]. *From Proto-Indo-European to Proto-Germanic. A Linguistic History of English Volume I.* Oxford University Press, New York.

Salo, Unto. 2000. Suomi ja Häme, Häme ja Satakunta. In Jukka Peltovirta (ed.). *Hämeen käräjät* 1. Hämeenlinna: Hämeen Heimoliitto ry. / Harjavalta: Emil Cedercreutzin Säätiö.

Salo, Unto. 2008. *Ajan ammoisen oloista: Satakunnan ja naapurimaakuntien esihistoriaa.* Suomen Kirjallisuuden Seuran Toimituksia 1093. Helsinki: Suomen Kirjallisuuden Seura.

Saxén, Ralf. 1905. *Språkliga bidrag till den svenska bosättningens historia i Finland I: Egentliga Finland, Satakunta och södra Österbotten.* Helsingfors: Finska Litteratur-Sällskapet.

Saxén, Ralf. 1910. *Finländska vattendragsnamn.* Studier i Nordisk Filologi 1. Skrifter utgivna av Svenska Litteratursällskapet i Finland 92. Helsingfors: Svenska Litteratursällskapet i Finland.

Schalin, Johan. 2004. Itämerensuomalaisen *leütä-vartalon lainaperäisyys. *Virittäjä: Kotikielen seuran aikakausilehti* 108(1): 24–33. Available at: http://www.iki.fi/jschalin/?cat=15 (last accessed 15.7.2014).

Schalin, Johan. 2007. Röster från språkstriden: Gamla ortnamn begeistrar. *Språkbruk* 2007(4). Available at: http://www.kotus.fi/index.phtml?l=sv&s=590 (last accessed 15.7.2014).

Schalin, Johan. 2008a. Härdalar, namnet *Karis* och den första nedtecknade händelsen i Finlands historia. *Finsk Tidskrift* 2008(8). Avaliable at http://www.iki.fi/jschalin/?cat=15 (last accessed 15.7.2014).

Schalin, Johan. 2008b. *Ahuen maa* ja *Alandh*. *Sananjalka* 50: 24–37.

Schalin, Johan. 2012. Namnet *Kymmene*. In Tiina Hyytiäinen *et al.* (eds.). *Per Urales ad Orientem: Iter polyphonicum multilingue: Festskrift tillägnad Juha Janhunen på hans sextioårsdag den 12 februari 2012.* Mémoires de la Société Finno-Ougrienne 264. Helsinki: Société Finno-Ougrienne. Pp. 389–398.

Schalin, Johan with Frog. 2014 (in press). Toponymy and Seafaring: Indications and Implications of Navigation along the Åland Islands In *The Viking Age in Åland: Insights into Identity and Remnants of Culture.* Ed. Joonas Ahola, Frog & Jenni Lucenius. Annales Academiae Scientiarum Fennicae Humaniora series. Helsinki: Academia Scientiarum Fennica.

Ståhl, Harry 1964: Saklig ortnamnsforskning. *Namn och bygd. Tidskrift för nordisk ortnamnsforskning* 52, 1–14. Uppsala.

Stang, Håkon. 1996. The Naming of Russia. *Meddelelser Nr. 77 Universitetet i Oslo. Slavisk-baltisk avdeling.* Available at http://idrisi.narod.ru/stang.pdf (last accessed 9.8.2014).

Snorre Sturluson. 1844. *Heimskringla: The Chronicle of the Kings of Norway.* Trans. Samuel Laing. London, Available at: http://lind.no/nor/index.asp?lang=&emne=asatru&vis=s_e_olav_haraldsson (last accessed 15.7.2014).

Suomen sanojen alkuperä: Etymologinen sanakirja I–III (I: A–K; II: L–P; III: R–Ö). 1992–2000. Helsinki: Suomen Kirjallisuuden Seura ja Kotimaisten kielten tutkimuskeskus.

Syrett, Martin. 1994. *The Unaccented Vowels of Proto-Norse.* North-Western European Language Evolution. Supplement vol. 11. Odense University Press. Odense.

Wahlberg, Mats (ed.). 2003: *Svenskt ortnamnslexikon.* Utarbetat inom Språk- och folkminnesinstitutet och Institutionen för nordiska språk vid Uppsala universitet. Uppsala.

Waldenström, Stellan. 2005. Kjulo i Finland och Kjula i Sverige – samma ursprung?. In *Namn och bygd: Tidskrift för nordisk ortnamnsforskning* 93: 17–35.

Wessén, Elias. 1958. *Svensk Språkhistoria I: Ljudlära och ordböjningslära.* 5th edn. Stockholm / Lund: Almqvist & Wiksell.

Widmark, Gun. 2004 [2001]. *Det språk som blev vårt: Ursprung och utveckling i svenskan: Urtid - Runtid - Riddartid.* Acta Academiae regiae Gustavi Adolphi 76. Uppsala: Kungl. Gustav Adolfs Akademien för Svensk Folkkultur.

Zilliacus, Kurt. 1994. *Orter och namn i "Finska skären".* Helsingfors: Konstsamfundet.

Frog

Myth, Mythological Thinking and the Viking Age in Finland

Mythology holds an interest and relevance for many disciplines investigating prehistory. This is because mythology interfaces with numerous aspects of culture and cultural expression. The present chapter is intended to help non-specialists approach mythology and its utility in research on the Viking Age in Finland. It concentrates on folklore materials, limitations of the data and the navigation of problematic areas that arise from common assumptions about mythology or its sources.

The Viking Age has held a special place in research on 'Finnish' mythologies. Referring to 'Finnish' mythology normally means Finno-Karelian or North Finnic mythologies generally. Not surprisingly, research in this area is the offspring of Romanticism, born in the heat of Nationalism. Alongside language, the *longue durée* of mythology established it as an area of research in discourse about cultural origins and heritage. Within this discourse, 'mythology' became a nexus of activity because it was viewed as a key to national ideologies. Modern identities were 'Christian' at that time: Europe had gradually become culturally and ideologically unified through Christianity with its enormous institutional mechanisms. National identity-building required an alternative model for unification, which was provided by turning to ethnic culture. The term *nation*, from the Latin verb *nascor* ['to be born'], originally referred implicitly to common genetic origins. Romanticism took hold of vernacular mythology as a key to nation-building, providing resources from which the common and unifying ideology of the ethnos could be recovered and rebuilt – albeit rebuilt with a hat and tie rather than helmet and sword. Germanic cultures and scholarship provided a primary conduit through which Romantic ideals arrived in an emerging Finland. Along with these influences, the Viking Age became identified as a grand, illustrious era – an era of expansion and empire-building, when men were men, and women wore helmets too – and, indeed, the last era before the ethnos was smothered beneath a blanket of Christianity.

Approaching Mythology

The words *myth* and *mythology* are used in many ways, not all of them consistent. How these terms are used can affect how we think about things, especially when their meanings are taken for granted. Before turning to mythology in the Viking Age, it is worthwhile to preface discussion with an introduction to what this troublesome thing called 'mythology' actually is. A bit of space will be given to opening some problems and terms, and then to briefly outlining a semiotic approach to myth and mythology (semiotics being the science of signs and meanings) that allows these terms, handled loosely in popular discussion, to be defined and used for analytical discussion.

The terms *myth* and *mythology* derive from Classical Greek. In spite of this noble heritage and global use, the terms are surprisingly young in most languages: *myth* is not attested as a word in English, for example, before the nineteenth century (*OED*: *s.v.* 'myth'). The Classical Greek *mythos* ['story'] and *mythologia* ['story, storytelling'] did not mean 'myth' and 'mythology' as understood today. The Greek words were used for any stories or storytelling that was fantastic or for entertainment, and the category of *mythos* was opposed to the categories associated with truth, logic and knowledge (*logos*, *historia*). Modern derivatives of the term 'myth' are a product of Romanticism: 'myth' was taken up and reinvented as a term for *a narrative about a god, gods, and/or otherwise describing the establishment or destruction of the present world order, that others mistakenly believe or once believed to be sacred truth.* (See further e.g. Eliade 1963 [1968]: 1–2; Doty 2000: 4–30.) Put another way, the origin of the term 'myth' is rooted in a distinction between 'us' and 'them', between the authoritative, educated European elite who had Christianity – i.e. Scripture and sacred doctrine – and everyone else who only had 'myths' – untrue stories associated with their false religions. This basic paradigm soon developed a corresponding opposition of Eurocentric science versus 'myth' as the primitive alternative to science and scientific thinking – 'us' versus 'them'. Quite simply, the term 'myth' was invented and constructed through Romanticism in order for Europeans to talk about 'the other'. (See also Csapo 2004.) This is important to recognize because, although use of the term has significantly advanced in research, the 'us'–'them' opposition remains embedded in the semantics of 'myth' in popular culture: 'myth' is used to refer to that which is 'not scientific' or 'not Christian'; it is invariably bound up with a perspective of the user to refer to 'a false belief that needs to be corrected'. This is particularly pronounced in the modern 'myth of mythlessness',[1] which posits that 'we' have no myths today, and whenever 'we' discover myths that we do in fact have, these must be eradicated – a theme which has become the foundation of the popular television program *Myth Busters*.

In research, the term 'myth' evolved in relation to philology and related disciplines of cultural studies. Owing to initial use of the term to refer specifically to 'stories' (Greek *mythoi*), the disciplinary development of ideal text-type categorization systems treated 'myth' as a genre like the fairytale, belief legend, anthem or novel (see e.g. discussions in Bascom 1965; Honko 1989; Briggs & Bauman 1992). This approach was inclined to remove myth from communicative practices and correspondingly isolate or oppose 'story', as an ideal narrative, and 'ritual', as social activity, which together constituted 'religion'. At the same time, the term 'mythology' advanced from variously a synonym for myth or a term for the art of interpreting myths (*mytho-logy* as 'the study of myths') to the term for a coherent collection of myths as texts, which could often also include the supernatural and sacred aspects of the present world order. The Christian versus non-Christian opposition advanced to oppositions of science versus superstition and modern versus primitive, reinterpreting the fundamental 'us'–'them' opposition from different (but still Eurocentric) perspectives. Theories of mythology interpreted 'myths' as pre-scientific speculation, reflections of fundamental psychological tensions in society, and so forth, all in the search to explain it as a phenomenon (see Csapo 2004). This had the consequence that "religion was divested of its autonomy in human life and regarded as a mental illusion or as the product of social conditions" (de Vries 1967 [1977]: 221). It was seen as "essentially a human project to formulate a stable and meaningful dimension behind the accidental, chaotic, and shifting realities of human existence" (Bell 1997: 12).[2] The latter half of the twentieth century brought comprehensive and revolutionary reassessments of these perspectives and approaches.

Discussions on mythologies had started off with an inclination to reconstruct 'myths' as cultural heritage objects from the traces in diverse sources, reconstituting them from the dust of history. Identifying such reconstructions with a genre as an ideal text-type category was only relevant to a small part of any corpus or mythology and it was also focused on texts as objects removed from social realities. This led 'myth' to be used sometimes with reference to unattested stories that were only known through brief comments or allusions and presumed by scholars to have once been narrated. The academic production of a corpus of such myths was complemented by inclinations to see a mythology as a coherent system which included, for example, gods and cosmological images like the world pillar about which narratives were completely lacking. Thus, ideas that a mythology was a system constituted of 'myths' (as stories) helped to reciprocally enable 'myth' to be used for any of a mythology's constituents. Initially, this meant that, if a story was lacking, one could be reconstructed, but rather than simply talking about stories and rituals, increased attention began to be given to social practices and to how people think, perceive and understand. This approach highlighted *mythological thinking*, or how people think *through* a mythology. From this view, to adapt the phrase of Claude Lévi-Strauss (1962: 128), a mythology is constituted of things that are *bonnes à penser* ['good(s) to think with'].

Early approaches to mythological thinking (e.g. Cassirer 1925) have been developed with attention to social processes and semiotics. In this light, mythology has been described as "a mode of signification" (Barthes 1972 [1957]: 109) or "idiom of expression" (Goodman 1993: 53) and "a form of *knowing*" (Doty 2000: 55–56, original emphasis). This corresponds to popular use of 'myth' to refer to beliefs of others that are untrue according to either mainstream thinking (e.g. it is a *myth* that there are honest lawyers) or scientific investigation[3] (e.g. it is a *myth* that you can catch AIDS from a toilet seat). Narratives thus become only one small part of multiple interfaced systems of mythology that are used by people and socially negotiated (which includes e.g. 'myth busting'). Rather than uniform ideal models, there is variation and even contestation in what are described as *mythic discourse* as the broad field of understandings and cultural activity of myths and the images, symbols, cultural practices and behaviours associated with them (Goodman 1993; Frog *et al.* 2012). Approaching mythology through mythological thinking and mythic discourse provides a valuable point of departure for relating mythology to data from different disciplines.

Roland Barthes (1972 [1957]) described mythology in terms of *naturalization* – 'myth' is "overturning culture into nature or, at least, the social, the cultural, the ideological, the historical into the 'natural'," realizing "moral, cultural and aesthetic consequences [...] as being a 'matter of course'" (Barthes 1977 [1971]: 165). The vitality of a myth can be seen as the degree of naturalization, the degree to which the myth is simply an implicit understanding of physical, social and emotional realities (cf. Lakoff & Turner 1989; Doty 2000: 137–140) or "a set of unconsciously held, unexamined premises" (Jewett & Lawrence 1977: 17). Mythological thinking (i.e. thinking through myths) and analytical thinking can be considered extremes on a spectrum, a matter of degree between absolutes that can never be independently realized.[4] This spectrum is connected to the vitality of myths and can be described in terms of a non-reflective apprehension of meaningfulness (i.e. when 'recognizing' something includes a package of valuations, associations, interpretations and possibly an emotional load) as opposed to objectified analysis and interpretation. According to this approach, myth can be broadly defined as *a socially constructed non-reflective model for interacting with the world and interpreting experience* (also used metonymically of those myths which have lost vitality), and 'mythology' can be used as general term for *a dynamic cultural modelling system, constituted at the level of myths, that provides an essential core to cultural competence by infusing cultural practices with meaningfulness.* In this broad sense, mythology can be considered a fundamental or foundational aspect of cultural identity. In other words, although there were continuities of language and culture through the process of conversion to Christianity, this model would suggest that Christian culture and so-called pre-Christian culture were also fundamentally different. This would also be consistent with evidence of diverse archaeological cultures that could simultaneously reflect a common language group (cf. LAAKSO; see also the discussion in Nordberg 2012). This approach has consequences for the use of terms: *myth* will not be used in the narrow sense of story; *mythic* will be used to qualify symbolic elements of the mythology that occur independent of narratives or in narratives and in other traditions that do not themselves belong to the mythology (e.g. legends, tales, rituals); the adjective *mythological* will be reserved for the sphere that exists outside of the present world order (e.g.

the creation of the world) and also for otherworld locations that cannot be accessed without supernatural power or assistance (e.g. the realm of the dead).

This approach to myth avoids the issue of 'belief', which is a personal, subjective interaction with the modelling system and not essential to effectively engaging a mythology nor even to manipulating it.[5] It extends all of the way down to very fundamental levels of cognitive processing (cf. Lotman & Uspenskij 1976; Lakoff & Turner 1989: esp. 66), which can be practically distinguished as *deep mythology*. The inclusion of deep mythology in a coherent approach is important for several reasons. At the most basic, it provides a strong theoretical foundation for approaching the *surface mythology* – gods, stories, mythic images, otherworld topography, etc. A surface mythology can be approached according to the metaphor of a language: mythic images, motifs, figures, beings, locations, and narratives all (to the degree that they are mythically vital) provide a symbolic lexicon that can be used and combined according to rules and in constructions rather like a grammar. Anna-Leena Siikala (2012) has shown that local and regional variation in these symbols, their use and ways they are combined can be productively approached according to 'dialects' of mythology. A deep mythology's conceptual modelling is essential to mythological thinking and interfaces with surface mythology, and yet it is easily marginalized and neglected in discussion – e.g. whether illness is caused by invisible arrows shot by witches, invisible beings called 'viruses' and 'bacteria' invading your body, or the loss of part of your soul. The symbolic 'language' of the surface mythology is both central to the broader mythology as a modelling system and also concretizes it in resources that can be utilized, manipulated and that can also be contested and negotiated. According to this semiotic model, mythological thinking at the level of deep mythology is a largely unconscious process, while mythological thinking through the surface mythology is an imaginal process which can be consciously engaged for a diversity of social, magical and personal purposes (see Doty 2000; Siikala 2002a; Tarkka 2012). The surface mythology constitutes the socially constructed symbolic worlds that inform the meanings of social and phenomenal realities.

Sources

The mythology in the Viking Age in Finland can only be approached in terms of its situation between different periods. This is necessary because there are no vernacular written sources from Finland in the Viking Age. Perspectives on the history of the mythology necessarily develop according to a relative chronology. Diverse data is triangulated in order to situate that relative chronology in relation to a fixed period on an absolute chronology. The diversity of data falls into multiple types which present diverse challenges.

Synchronic evidence of mythology emerges in the archaeological record, which presents outcomes and by-products of cultural practices that engage both surface and deep mythologies. The problem is that, in semiotic terms, we recognize signifiers – images, motifs and so forth – that clearly carried mythic significance, but we lack access to their signifieds – i.e. we have no clear idea what they meant to the people using them or why they were important. For example, the use of pottery animal paws atop cremation remains in Åland (Callmer 1994) or either nailing coffins shut with spear points or casting spears into a grave (Wickholm 2006) were clearly strategic and meaningful acts – they can be reasonably supposed to engage a symbolic world of living surface mythologies (cf. Price 2012). However, without access to these symbolic worlds, the symbols speak in an unfamiliar language: we can recognize the importance of what is 'said', but the 'words' remain incomprehensible.

Ritualized aquatic burials, for example, were likely interfaced with broader aspects of a mythology (Wessman 2009; 2010: 75), but the specific connection imagined between water and the otherworld remains a mystery. Rather than the symbolic world of the surface mythology, some burial practices may only reflect a much more fundamental 'way of thinking' about the individual's identity in life or death at the level of deep mythology. Cremation cemeteries under level ground are characterized by distributing remains and grave goods among a more or less level stone-covered ground: these practices suggest conceptions related to individual identity in death or to the transition of becoming an ancestor (see Wessman 2010: 57–61). It is not always clear where evidence reflects symbols interfaced with the living mythologies of users or other aspects of physical and social realities. Evidence that a boat was used in a cremation burial is therefore not necessarily evidence that the boat was symbolically connected to ritual practice – wood treated with tar burns well and may have simply been a practical choice. Similarly, the symbol of the cross in the Viking Age suggests contacts with Christianity, but crosses may have been considered ornamental when the symbol first arrived or used as a practical attribute related to trade with Christians (cf. Wessman 2010: 80–81; Korpela). In the archaeological record, the Viking Age is marked by the beginning of the transition to inhumation burials. This is a radical change in practices even where there is a continuity in the place of burial – i.e. within a cremation cemetery under level ground. (Wickholm 2008: 91–92; Wessman 2010: 78–80.) Nevertheless, it is difficult to distinguish how changes in cultural practices that gradually advance to norms reflect changes in mythologies, or perhaps changes in emphasis or in the symbols applied within established mythologies (cf. Nordberg 2012). The challenge of such archaeological data is that it can only be interpreted in relation to other material.

Written sources offering additional perspectives begin to appear in the thirteenth century, shortly after the Viking Age. Medieval Church documents generally mention 'pagans' without interest in accounts of mythology or practice, and a statement in 1229 that the Church in Finland may take possession of pagan *lucos et delubra* ['groves and temples'] (FMU 77) may be idiomatic (cf. the same Latin phrase e.g. in Isaiah 17:8) rather than making direct reference to vernacular practices. More detailed written accounts are from the perspectives of other (Christian) cultures. Old Norse saga literature provides numerous accounts relevant to magical and ritual practices of Sámi on the Scandinavian Peninsula. However, their accounts of trading expeditions to territories associated with Finland and Karelia tend to represent these places as either being little different socially and culturally from Norway and Sweden or they tend to blur these territories with Norse imaginings of otherworldly realms inhabited by giants and other supernatural beings. A notable exception is the description of a raid of a temple of the so-called Bjarmians that supposedly took place in *c.* 1025 on or near the White Sea, according to *Óláfs saga Helga* ['The Saga of Saint Óláfr'] (see KOSKELA VASARU).[6] This description mentions that the god of the temple was called *Jómali* and that Bjarmians mixed valuables with earth in the burial mound. *Jómali* is recognizable as a cognate of Finnish and Karelian *jumala* ['god, supernaturally empowered being'] (Tolley 2009 I: 54). The description of a mound mixing earth and grave goods would be consistent with the cremation cemeteries under level ground mentioned above (although these would have been more flat than a mound *per se*). Similarly, the Russian *Primary Chronicle* describes a Christian's encounter with a 'Chud' shaman that includes a description of the shaman's use of an ecstatic trance and subsequent description of his journey in remote otherworld locations (see Tolley 2009 I: 80–81). These accounts offer a number of indicators of familiarity with the mythologies and ritual practices of other cultures. They are simultaneously problematic because they exhibit characteristics suggestive of legend traditions rather than objective ethnographic historical accounts. Although *Óláfs saga* may validly reflect popular knowledge of Finnic mythology and cultural practices, this occurs within a widely encountered narrative pattern about a raid on a heathen temple associated with the mytho-heroic and fantastic sagas (see Power 1985). In the saga, this information is not included with the aim of communicating accurate information about Bjarmian culture: it serves a rhetorical function of increasing the impression of a 'true' story in a historical king's saga. The saga was written in Iceland two centuries after the events, opening the possibility that the cultural information was not originally 'Bjarmian' (cf. Power 1985: 20). The description of the Chud shaman presents still more clearly some sort of Christian legend, in which the shaman describes his own gods through Christian images of demons in Hell and states that his gods fear the symbol of the cross. A legend of this type could be used to describe any culture in which there was something approximating shamanic practices.

The thirteenth century also offers the earliest vernacular written source for mythology. This is found among the Novgorod birch bark inscriptions (in Cyrillic script). The inscription of Novgorod 292 appears to be a magic charm text about 50 letters long (Figure 1). It begins *jumola[n]nuoli* ['God('s) arrow' or 'magically empowered being('s) arrow)'] and interpretation becomes increasingly problematic as the inscription progresses. The text appears to be a charm for healing harm caused by 'magic shot'.[7] The charm has been thought to be linguistically North Finnic, but phonetic evidence of the charm itself remains problematic. (See further Laakso 1999.)

Fig. 1. Novgorod birch bark inscription 292. The transcription can be transliterated:

jumolanuoli·I·nimiži
noulisìh[l?]anoliomobou
h[l?]oumolasoud'nii[p?]ohovi

Photo reproduced courtesy of Prof. V. L. Yanin, Birch Bark Literacy from Medieval Rus: Contents and Contexts http://gramoty.ru/index.php?no=292&act=full&key=bb

Vernacular written evidence does not otherwise begin to appear until the sixteenth century. In 1551, the first Lutheran Archbishop of Finland, Michael Agricola, published two lists of twelve false gods each in the preface to his translation of the *Psalter* (see e.g. Krohn 1932; Anttonen 2010: 48–57; 2012a). In 1553, Archbishop Makari of Novgorod complains that in Karelia children are taken to wielders of magic to be given a name before being taken to a priest for baptism (see Kirkinen 1970: 130–131). Additional, often ambiguous evidence begins gradually to accumulate in seventeenth-century court documents reporting magical practices while a land register from 1618 lists one Mihaila Moisief *wanha wäinämöinen* ['old Väinämöinen'] as living on the northeast coast of Lake Ladoga (Salmi, Manssila Village) (Kirkinen 1970: 129). In the eighteenth century, academic investigations develop an interest in these areas of culture with the rise of Romanticism. This led to the increasingly active and objective documentation of traditions. Epic Kalevala-meter poetry was particularly esteemed (AHOLA), and especially documented in the era of nation-building when Finland was a Grand Duchy of the Russian Empire (1809–1917) – a political circumstance that allowed access to Russian Karelia where these traditions were still vital. There are now astounding quantities of data – *c.* 150,000 items of Kalevala-meter poetry are indexed in the folklore archive of the Finnish Literature Society, in addition to vast numbers of prose accounts, sayings, taboos, belief traditions and enormous quantities of ethnographic data. This same era produced the majority of data on other Finno-Ugric and Uralic cultures. Data on these other populations provides essential contexts for considering earlier periods of language and culture among these groups. Rather than isolated glimpses, these more recent corpora present richly developed perspectives on the mythology and cultural practices *at the time when they were documented*, while the early scholars eagerly active in collection and research were zealously engaged in Romantic (and sometimes fanciful) attempts to reconstruct mythologies, histories and ethnic identities.[8]

Heavy criticisms of this earlier research and its methodologies led the whole direction of inquiry to become highly controversial and devalued across the latter half of the twentieth century. This early research was developed on weak (and sometimes intuitive) foundations of theory, low source-critical standards (NB: according to today's standards), and was easily inclined to the selective handling of materials or allowed ideological ends to lead interpretations of the data (cf. RANINEN & WESSMAN). This research also failed to recognize methodological challenges concerning what the corpora can and cannot inform us about the Viking Age. This early work nevertheless continues to provide some of the most interesting and significant resources for approaching mythology in the Viking Age, and it is therefore useful to have some cautionary foundations and basic strategies for approaching it.

Cultures, Heritage and a Mythology Shift

Mythology, as introduced above, is an essential aspect of culture. The distribution of languages and cultures in territories of Finland and Karelia were quite different in the Viking Age than when the majority of the sources were documented. This is particularly important to recognize because the territories where Finno-Karelian mythologies survived most vitally were in regions of Karelia, and especially those regions that, from the perspective of the Russian Empire, were a remote wilderness comparable to Siberia – they were places where religious and secular authority had long remained fairly superficial for the small, scattered communities (cf. Pentikäinen 1978: 100–104; Siikala 2002a: 329, 339). However, Finno-Karelian languages and cultures did not yet inhabit these territories in the Viking Age. This makes it necessary to address the change in the distribution of languages before turning to chronological gaps between the Viking Age and written sources. A broad outline will therefore be offered here of the changing distribution of linguistic-cultural groups across the Iron Age up to the time when sources were documented. This description nevertheless remains in many respects a fluid relative chronology because it is not possible to make precise and comprehensive correlations between intangible evidence of language and culture on the one hand and the tangible evidence of the archaeological record on the other (see further AHOLA & FROG).

Following PETRI KALLIO's description of the spread and break-up of surviving Finnic languages, Finnic languages were probably spoken in communities along both coasts of the Gulf of Finland already in the Pre-Roman Iron Age (*c.* 500–1 BC). Germanic languages were likely spoken in at least some coastal areas of what is now Finland at when the Finnic populations arrived in the preceding centuries and there is no reason to believe that Germanic languages were not still present at that time. Finnic languages were otherwise concentrated in territories of what is now Estonia and to the east (see also Saarikivi 2006; Rahkonen 2011). Around that time, predecessors of Sámi languages had probably been neighbouring peoples inland of Finnic language groups and spread rapidly through territories of Finland and

Karelia and further onto the Scandinavian Peninsula (Aikio 2006; AHOLA & FROG, Map 2)). This expansion probably did not result in the displacement of all coastal populations on the Baltic Sea (cf. Aikio 2009; cf. Saarikivi 2004b: 173, Map 1). The majority of the territories were at that time probably inhabited by Palaeo-European linguistic-cultural groups that were gradually assimilated to Sámi and it remains uncertain whether any of these Palaeo-European languages may have survived into the Viking Age (Aikio 2006; 2009; Saarikivi 2004a; 2006; cf. Carpelan 2001). The Finnic language groups do not appear to have begun encroaching on inland territories of Finland and Karelia until the Migration Period. By the Viking Age, settlements had withdrawn from the coasts and North Finnic languages were likely established somewhat further inland, especially in Satakunta, Finland Proper (i.e. the south-western tip of Finland) and Häme (Salo 2004; cf. Wessman 2010: 30, map 19). There is no evidence for Germanic language areas in Finland at that time, although this does not mean an absence of multilingualism (SCHALIN). Sámi was the dominant language across the majority of territories of Finland and Karelia (see also KALLIO; KUZMIN). A (probably South) Finnic language population or populations began migrating into the Northern Dvina River basin in this period (Saarikivi 2000; 2006: 295), and although the Chuds have been identified as a Finnic cultural group (e.g. Vepsians), recent toponymic research has presented compelling evidence that a main people called Chuds were not Finnic, but rather a distinct, if closely related Uralic language group (Rahkonen 2011). The Viking Age appears to be the period of a breakup of the North Finnic dialect continuum into distinguished languages (KALLIO). Migrations of Finnic populations from western territories of Finland carried cultural influences into the Ladoga region and presumably cultural practices as well (Uino 1997), suggesting that distinctive cultural differences had already developed between these groups at that time.

Although archaeological data allows the situation of evidence in an absolute chronology, other evidence presents outcomes of social and historical processes, and it is precisely these intermediate processes that remain obscure. Rather than absolute chronologies, only relative chronologies are possible from within that data of intangible culture. These relative chronologies can then be correlated with one another and triangulated with evidence on absolute chronologies in order to assess the most probable historical processes which these reflect. By the eighteenth century, Finnish and Karelian were the main languages up to Lapland, with Slavicization encroaching on Karelian areas in the south, east and northeast. Earlier, Sámi populations in these territories had already undergone a 'language shift' – i.e. people gradually stopped using Sámi and increasingly relied on a Finnish or Karelian (and later also Russian) as a socio-historical process.[9] Moreover, Sámi language(s) of these territories are now extinct and the preceding languages assimilated by Sámi have completely disappeared (cf. KUZMIN). The shift from Sámi in the Viking Age to Finnish and Karelian in the period of ethnographic documentation appears to have been far more comprehensive than simply one of language. The spread of Finnish and Karelian language areas was also a spread of Finno-Karelian mythologies and cultural practices: this was not simply a language shift, but also a mythology shift. Correlating mythology documented in the nineteenth century with Viking Age archaeological cultures must take into consideration not only a historical gap between tangible and intangible evidence, but also the spread of language, mythology and cultural practices.

The Viking Age on a Long-Term Continuum Model

Earlier scholarship tended to assume that Finland and Karelia were 'always' North Finnic language areas. Furthermore, investigations into the history of the mythology tended to be unidirectional, beginning with nineteenth and twentieth century textual sources and attempting to project this back to a pre-Christian cultural environment with a pure and ideal reconstructed mythology. Since that time, incredible advances have been made in understanding how these and other traditions function, vary and develop, leading to many new perspectives on diverse aspects of these traditions and their sources, ranging from the text-criticism of individually recorded textual evidence to different traditions' relationships to Uralic mythologies and linguistic-cultural heritage. Situating these perspectives in dialogue with one another allows multidimensional imaging of synchronic and diachronic processes in the traditions. Addressing synchronic and diachronic variation as social and historical processes will be prefaced here by introducing a rudimentary framework of a historical continuum model for the linguistic-cultural traditions in question.

A valuable tool for developing a continuum model is Lauri Harvilahti's (2003: 90–115) *ethnocultural substrate* or *ethnocultural substratum*. This term describes the broad synchronic system of fundamental elements (language, poetics, images, motifs, figures, narratives, etc.) that are constitutive of cultural competence. It provides a valuable tool in developing historical perspectives by facilitating lateral indexing across a diversity of data and traditions (see Frog 2011c). This is a modelling strategy that presupposes contextualization in a comprehensive cultural milieu. An individual substratum emerges as an ideal hypothetical model negotiated around a 'core' of relevant indicators of changes that distinguish one substratum from those which precede and follow it (see Frog 2011c: 24–25, 32–34). The model produced is abstract, ideal and descriptive. It minimizes variation both within and between substrata in order to construct a frame of reference for analysis and the correlation of further data from different areas or disciplines (see Figure 2). Traditions, whether inherited or borrowed, always emerge in a present filtered through the semiotics and cognitive models of the contemporary culture. Sources from the nineteenth and twentieth century must be approached in this light, assessing meaningful elements and mythological thinking along a historical continuum. Each substratum presents an emergent heritage which adapts and changes in relation to internal developments and to outside influences. Together, these produce and become the next substratum. The emergent process of the historical progression of ethnocultural substrata can be

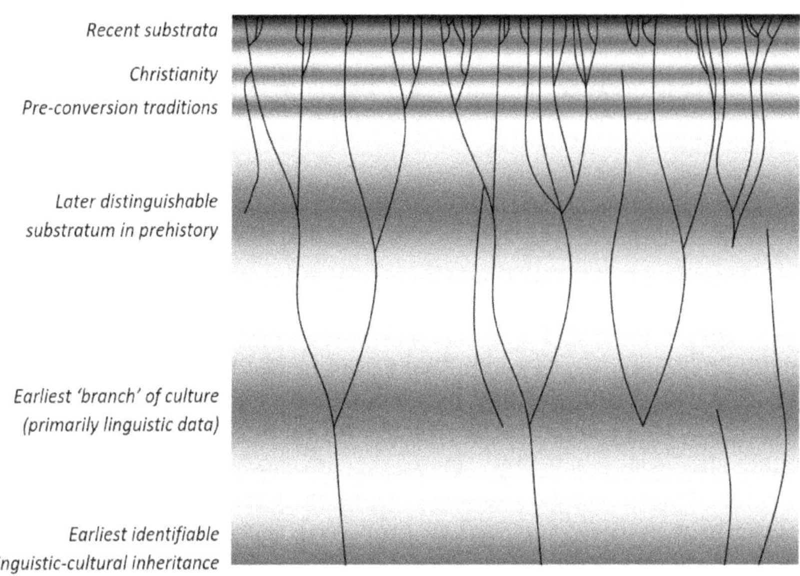

Fig. 2. Simple visual representation of ethnocultural substrata (dark horizontal bands) as lateral indices across multiple continuum models (vertical stemma diagrams). Each ethnocultural substratum emerges around a 'core' of relevant indicators of change differentiating it from earlier and later periods while the transition between substrata remains largely undefined. 'Deeper' strata become increasingly broad and generalized because variation leads to increased abstraction along individual continuum models and the quantity of material relevant for indexing becomes increasingly limited. The decrease of identifiable material in earlier substrata does not reflect fewer traditions, but rather a much smaller percentage of the tradition ecology that can be discerned – normally the most socially and semiotically central. Comparative evidence may present certain otherwise unattested traditions in earlier substrata that were not maintained (e.g. that a certain god or word disappeared or certain practices ceased).

approached on a historical continuum, although the chronology may remain relative (see Frog 2013a). Substratum models then provide a resource for addressing specific cases and discussing characteristics of change that may only gradually (or ambiguously) accumulate in the (potentially fluid) process of historical transition between distinguishable periods. Continuities through historical change are implied in traditions that reflect earlier cultural eras. No less implied are discontinuities owing to adaptations and revaluations by which the tradition could remain current and relevant. The ethnocultural substratum model helps avoid pitfalls of treating cultural and semiotic phenomena atomically or in isolation from one another. It also highlights that mythology is not an eternal and unchanging constant that was knocked out of place by Christianity, and thereby provides a frame for thinking about mythology in terms relevant to the particular period. As a continuum model is developed, it provides a resource in relation to which data can be approached, and specific data can also be approached in dialogue with the model.

When developing a continuum model for surface mythologies in a culture, it is useful to begin from the earliest discernible linguistic-cultural era as a base-line frame of reference – bearing in mind that some mythic images and core motifs of certain mythological narrative plots could have a much, much longer history (see e.g. Meletinskij 1997; Napolskikh 2012; Witzel 2012). For Finnic and Sámic cultures, this base-line is so-called Proto-Uralic, the hypothetical language from which all Uralic languages ultimately derive, and subsequently Proto-Finno-Ugric (following the separation of Samoyedic languages), each of which is correlated with a linguistic-cultural group of speakers. Strategies comparable to those employed in historical linguistics offer some general perspectives on these early periods through the examination of huge quantities of comparative data. What can be said concerning mythologies in these early linguistic-cultural eras remains limited to a fairly narrow set of fields, as well as remaining hypothetical, highly abstract, and sometimes conditional on additional factors.[10] For example, the mythology likely had a central dualist structure of a male sky-god and his antithesis, a dualist bird-diver motif as the narrative core of the world-creation, a vertically structured cosmology connected by a pillar or tree as the *axis mundi* with a water-barrier or hole separating the lower sphere, and a form of Central and Northern Eurasian or 'classic' shamanism.[11] Although the term 'shaman' is now popularly used as an extremely broad and flexible term, classic shamanism is characterized by certain essential features. Among these is the conceptual model (deep mythology) of a separable soul, ecstatic trance-state rituals in which the shaman or his representative spirit-helpers take journeys (imagined in physical terms) as a representative of the human community, and also visit remote otherworld locations on these journeys in order to engage the inhabitants of mythic world.[12] Certain features come into slightly sharper focus in Proto-Finno-Ugric: **Ilma* ['Sky'] was the name of the sky-god and **nojta* was a probable term for a shaman who enters unconscious trace states and goes on soul-journeys.[13] This frame of reference immediately reveals radical discontinuities between the linguistic-cultural heritage and the documented North Finnic traditions: the central dualist structure of sky-god and antithesis is only prominent in legend traditions concerning the thunder-god and his on-going struggles with an adversary (the devil / devils or the demon / demons);[14] the earth-diver myth presents Väinämöinen without an accompanying figure in the role of the sky-god; the ritual specialist tradition was founded on verbal magic with a deep mythology that was fundamentally incompatible with classic shamanism because it rejects conceptual models of a separable soul in both ritual practice and illness diagnostics.[15] This remarkable discontinuity is not paralleled, for example, in Sámi traditions – i.e. something changed.

Of course, change is not surprising on a continuum model of *c.* 4500 years: this is only a point of departure. These processes can be further clarified by distinguishing additional substrata, narrowing in on the Viking Age. Comparative evidence reveals a labyrinth of changes clearly connected to cultural contacts between Proto-Finno-Ugric and the recorded sources.

The role of contacts makes it difficult to situate indicators of developments on a chronology, particularly in earlier periods. Some early influences are only identifiable through the mythological lexicon. For example, loan-words can provide relevant indicators of changes in mythological thinking, such as the Indo-Iranian loan **juma* ['god; sky'] apparently borrowed in a period before Finnic and Volgic branches of Uralic languages separated. This loan suggests a new way of thinking about supernatural beings, or other changes in the lexicon such as **Ilma* ['Sky'] of Proto-Finno-Ugric dividing in Proto-Finnic into the common noun **ilma* ['sky, weather'] and theonym **Ilma-ri* ['Sky-Being'] in parallel with **juma* dividing into **juma* and **juma-la* ['god, supernaturally powerful being']. The latter process is also associated with cultural contacts that, for reasons unknown, spread through both Finno-Ugric and Indo-European cultures, in most cases displacing the theonym meaning 'Sky' with a common noun for 'god' derived from it (i.e. 'one of the sky') rather than distinguishing the term for the god from 'sky' by producing a new derivative as in Finnic languages (**Ilma>*Ilma-ri; *juma>*juma-la*). In this case, the changes are not associated with words or word-forms borrowed from another language. (Summarized from Frog 2012b.) Consequently, it is not possible to tell which language groups this change may have started in.

The same problem is met in the early adaptation of a world-egg motif into the Finno-Ugric earth-diver world-creation, which is found as a broad regional phenomenon in several Finno-Ugric cultures and also in Indo-Iranian.[16] Caution is required in presuming that this is simply the case of one of these two cultures influencing the other. These were not monolithic cultures but rather communities of language speakers in contact. Our ideal perspectives on earlier periods of language minimize the probably fluid variation in dialects across these communities. It is also necessary to consider that additional cultures may have been involved in these processes.[17] There are no doubt numerous strata in these early periods but correlating and ordering them on even a relative chronology is highly problematic and conditional with relatively few exceptions (e.g. **juma* was borrowed before the development > **juma-la*). Mythology is not static: these terms, concepts, figures and narratives have been filtered and adapted through era after era of transformations until it may only be possible to identify continuities rather than the earlier significance and relationships to a mythology in an early ethno-cultural substratum. Nevertheless, developing perspectives on different ethnocultural substrata on a continuum can offer frames of reference for concurrent mythologies that remain beyond the available sources but outside communities undergoing these changes, as will be discussed below.

The closer developments are to the period of documentation, the fewer ethnocultural substrata through which the mythology has been filtered and the fuller the perspective that can be developed. For example, the introduction of iron-working technologies into Finnic cultural areas was "a technological quantum leap" (Salo 2006: 31), and this historical process presents a 'core' around which a broad ethnocultural substratum can be developed. The process appears to have begun in coastal communities (which may have been linguistically Germanic) around 500 BC and spread in the following centuries. Archaeological evidence paralleled by Germanic linguistic loans suggests the technology was learned from Scandinavia (Hofstra 1985: 322–324; Salo 1992: 103–107; cf.: Salo 2006: 30–31). This is a technology which could not be assimilated independent of cultural practices, conceptual models and ideology (Haaland 2004). The technology gradually penetrated almost every area of cultural life. Iron-working technology had a tremendous impact on the semiotics of Finnic cultures and ways of thinking, taking a particularly prominent position in the surface mythology (Hakamies 1999; 2012; Salo 1992; 2006). These technologies both carried new mythological conceptions and narrative material and also provided essential conditions for new mythological conceptions, symbols and narrative material to become established. Comparative evidence reveals that a system of surface mythology (including narrative material and world models) was passed cross-culturally in the Circum-Baltic region with this technology. This mythological material became connected to the dominant sky-god who had authority over thunder (see further Frog 2012a; 2013b). Here it becomes possible to identify a complex 'package' of influences, which may have assimilated and masked earlier material associated with bronze-working. At the same time, several of the mythic images including thunder and lightning as the sound and sparks of a smith hammering iron in heaven are specific to this technology.[18] This 'package' became associated with **Ilmari* in North Finnic cultures, who presumably had a continuity of centrality as a sky-god extending back to Proto-Finno-Ugric **Ilma*.

The discontinuity of conceptual models from classic shamanism noted above also appears to have been associated with the assimilation of a different technology – in this case, a technology of verbal magic that provided a new primary tool and medium for engaging the otherworld. This ethnocultural substratum is associated with another 'package' of developments bound up with the new language-based technology. The development is specific to North Finnic cultures where it is heavily indebted to Germanic models,[19] and it had revolutionary impacts on mythological thinking. The assimilation of this new technology produced a new type of ritual specialist, the *tietäjä* ['knower, one who knows'], who became "the heir to the role played by the shaman in ancient communities" and who "preserved shamanic models of thought" (Siikala 2002a: 42). However, these models of thought were integrated into the ideology imported with the new system (cf. Siikala 2002a: 320–349). The new language-based technology of incantations made it possible for the *tietäjä* to verbally actualize the otherworld directly without 'going there' on a soul-journey. This was rather like the Iron Age equivalent to introducing the cellular phone: wherever a crisis might be, it was no longer necessary to run up and down the world pillar like a shaman – incantations provided a direct line of contact with the sky-god, who could instantly supply mythic weapons, armour and aid. This new technology was comprehensively interfaced with both a surface mythology of images and narrative material and also with a deep mythology of conceptions of unseen forces in both this world and the other world, of the body and of illness and conceptions of how to interact with these. (This is not unlike the way modern medicine functions in relation to ideas of illness, the human body, fundamentals of chemistry and science as understood today.) Rather than complementing the established mythology and being assimilated to it, the assimilation of this new technology is associated with a comprehensive restructuring of the core of the surface mythology. Presumably on the basis of Germanic models, **Ilmari*'s antithesis and adversary **Väinä* became the cultural model for the new ritual specialist Väinämöinen (paralleling Germanic Odin). Whereas **Ilmari* appears to have been the dominant sky-god when the 'package' of mythological material associated with iron-working technology was introduced, a thunder-god simply called 'Old Man' (*Ukko*, *Äijä*, etc.) appears in the later sources as the dominant sky-god and main supporter of the *tietäjä* specialist, while only scattered traces remain of Ilmari's or Ilmarinen's[20] identity as a sky-god and he appears otherwise as a mythic smith subordinate to other figures. (See Frog 2012a; 2013b.) This change appears to have happened subsequent to the introduction of iron-working and identification of **Ilmari* as the smith of heaven. It can be reasonably associated with the restructuring of the mythology with the emergence of the technology of incantations and the associated ritual specialist called a *tietäjä*.

Anna-Leena Siikala (2002a) has offered an exposition of this tradition of ritual specialist and the many strata of images and motifs embedded in the *tietäjä*-mythology. The process of the institution's emergence and especially the development of an essential 'tool box' of conventional poems and poetic resources for the associated language-based technology remains mysterious. This process seems to have taken place in the Iron Age and may have remained localized to a relatively small network of communities for centuries as it developed a socially stable form. The process of its spread is likely associated with the migration of groups from western Finland east to Karelia (mentioned above), when the North Finnic areas were relatively small. This situates the process centrally in the Viking Age. Following the break-up of the North Finnic languages, this language-based technology would have spread across territories of Finland and Karelia with the spread of the languages themselves. The spread and rise to dominance suggests that this technology, mythology and associated ideology interfaced in a practical and/or compelling way with cultural changes at that time. The transition should be considered as nothing short of a conversion process – a conversion to the *tietäjä*-ideology, mythology and associated ritual practices. The kalevalaic mythology is not simply comprised of narratives and images; this was a mythology of very conservative poems – not just 'stories' but very structured texts (that eventually became internationally familiar in a refurbished form through Elias Lönnrot's *Kalevala*). The stories of these poems were only exceptionally narrated outside of that poetic form. This scenario best accounts for the fact that the core repertoire of central texts or poems, the poems at the heart of the mythology, were recorded across the whole broad area where the mythological narrative traditions survived – i.e. they spread not just as 'stories' but as poems, as texts. This also accounts for the fact that the core repertoire is marked by western Finnish language and 'Germanicisms' (e.g. Borenius 1873; Kuusi 1949; Siikala 2002b: 39), and it is consistent with arguments that the *tietäjä*-mythology centrally developed and spread from the Häme region (see Siikala 2012: 441–451 and works there cited; cf. Kuusi 1994a; Frog 2011c: 34–35). Put simply, the specialist's essential tool-box of mythology and incantations spread with the institution itself and (gradually) became the central Finno-Karelian mythology.

The *tietäjä*-tradition exhibits an opposition and even villainization of 'shamanism' – a *noita* ['shaman'] was an outsider, a dangerous and magically empowered 'other' – and the language shift of Sámi populations to Finnish and Karelian also involved a shift in mythology, a transition from shamanism to the *tietäjä*-tradition. Christianity and Christianization processes began penetrating these North Finnic linguistic-cultural areas within centuries of the (probable) initial spread of the *tietäjä*-institution. Thus the spread of Christianity may have interacted with the *tietäjä*-institution while it was becoming established and presumably still competing with vernacular shamanism. Such interaction is manifested in the great enrichment of incantations and their images that appear to have been adapted under or through early Christianity (see Kuusi 1963; Siikala 2002a).[21] More general influences from Christianity may have been, for example, making the thunder-god more of a *deus otiosis*, remote from the world like the Christian God (cf. Frog 2013b), while the Virgin Mary was engaged as a compelling figure, fusing with inherited images of an otherworld female being or goddess (Siikala 2002a: 199–203). Although the specialists may have considered themselves Christian or even representatives of Christianity in their own eyes (see discussion in Frog 2013b: 89–91), from a modern perspective, the Christian mythology remained in many respects complementary and almost secondary in its assimilation and dialogue with the earlier mythology (cf. Siikala 2002a: 342); Christian epics and mythic figures inhabiting them did not commingle with the vernacular figures of the Väinämöinen-centered mythology, which remained dominant.

This rather simple continuum model, represented visually in Figure 3, illustrates the degree of stratification in the mythology and suggests that the Viking Age may have been a major turning-point in the history of North Finnic mythologies. Although there were clearly many potentially quite drastic changes through history, none seem to have brought such a radical restructuring as observed here with the displacement of the inherited sky-god, who had a continuity extending at least as deep as Proto-Finno-Ugric. In addition, as these traditions spread and became dominant, they also displaced other mythologies among other North Finnic groups. In other words, kalevalaic mythology may be considered the outcome of a sort of 'bottleneck' in the history of the mythology. The core of that mythology or of the essential 'tool-box' of the specialist may primarily reflect mythology that developed, was current and transformed in a small system of communities during the establishment of a vernacular form of this language-based technology which had to be adapted from foreign models (see Frog 2013b). The spread of the technology then carried this repertoire of mythological

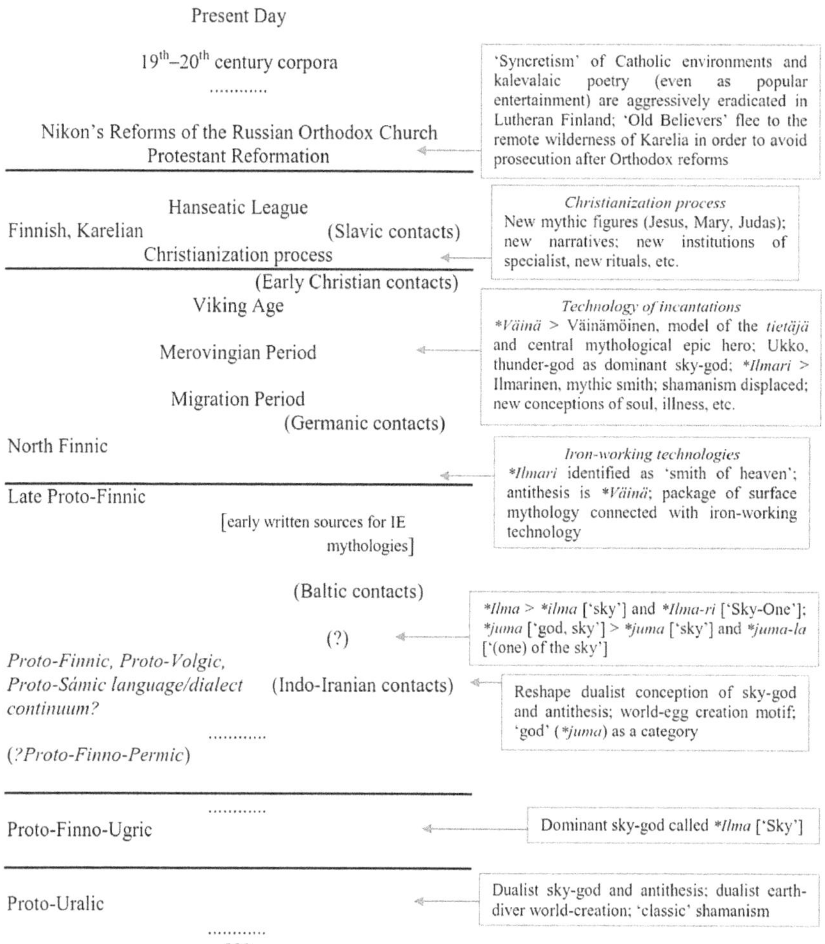

Fig. 3. Continuum of currency through ethnocultural substrata. A continuity of any term, concept or tradition-phenomenon assumes that it maintained value and relevance (with probable adaptation and revision) through periods of cultural change. Periods more remote from corpora of data are therefore veiled behind more ethnocultural substrata through which they have been filtered. The opacity of many developments since Proto-Uralic problematizes assessing more than an abstract image of ethnocultural substrata prior to the Iron Age.

texts and alternative forms were eclipsed in the process. Even if some local mythological traditions were assimilated (producing, for example, the different local or regional narrative accounts of the origin of iron or the origin of vipers), the core of the surface mythology appears to have been quite stable. Thus, Agricola's lists of gods from 1551 acknowledge cultural diversity and may even reflect regional variation, but later evidence does not support that comprehensively different systems of mythological figures were maintained in Häme and Savo, respectively.

Mythologies through Social Practice

A common modern myth about mythology is that it forms a single, coherent and uniform system. Oceans of academic ink have been spilled attempting to create this sort of united vision from a cacophony of sources. Presumptions that Finno-Karelian (a Finno-Ugric) mythology should follow the ideal Classical (Indo-European) model resulted in trying to hammer a round peg through a square hole. For example, basic conceptual categories of 'gods' and 'heroes' were simply inappropriate to the vernacular tradition, which is even apparent in the lexicon: the common noun for 'god' (*jumala*) can also be used to refer to other supernaturally powerful agents, including a living, powerful practitioner of magic or *tietäjä* (*SSA* I: 247; Anttonen 2012b: 174). Attempts to conform the sources to these models resulted in claims that the sky-god Ilmarinen and the sea-god Ahti coincidentally had the same names as a heroic smith and a Viking sea-farer (e.g. Krohn 1932: 62–63, 65–66). The famed Sampo-Cycle provided the essential framework for Lönnrot's construction of *Kalevala* but caused scholars endless headaches because it opens with the creation of the world by a giant demiurge and concludes with the same figure on a Viking-like sea-raid.[22] Approaches especially to Uralic and Finno-Ugric mythologies have gradually changed.[23] Scholars have become increasingly comfortable with the fact that mythologies change and adapt with historical processes and that they may vary between communities and regions within a larger linguistic-cultural group – what Anna-Leena Siikala (2012) describes as 'dialects of mythology'. However, there may be variation in mythology or multiple mythologies within a single community. At the extreme, this might manifest as Christians and non-Christians, but there may also be variation by genre of folklore or cultural practice.

A mythology or mythologies (whichever way it is described) can be systemic in the sense that the diversity of its parts and features may be distributed systematically across all different social practices. This should not be confused with considering the mythology to be uniform as a unified system (cf. Honko 1981a: 26). The structural interrelations and distribution of genres and cultural practices in social life can be approached through the biological metaphor of a 'tradition ecology',[24] in which traditions are not randomly combined and changes within one tradition that is already established in a social environment will impact others. From an objective and analytical perspective, mythology may even appear chaotic and internally contradictory. This requires address because the mythology may appear quite differently from the perspectives of different disciplines according to the sources that are used and how those sources are approached.[25]

Mythology can only exist and be maintained through cultural practices: it is a *social* semiotic phenomenon, and surface mythology in particular can be practically approached in terms of tradition. All traditions only have reality at the subjective level of the individual and the emerging intersubjective spaces of small-group communities.[26] Within that frame, tradition functions as an "enabling referent" (Foley 1995: 213). In other words, each individual handles and manipulates a tradition on the basis of a personal, subjective knowledge and understanding with expectations concerning the knowledge and understandings of others; others interpret expression on the basis of what they subjectively know and understand with expectations about the speaker or performer (hence 'intersubjective'). Those subjective and intersubjective understandings develop through exposure to and participation in cultural practices across a full spectrum of cultural activity – from epic poetry and proverbs to parody and contesting discourse. The subjective reality of a tradition is therefore always bounded by both the space and time that describe the limits of an individual's experience, and the negotiation of that understanding as a social process. This provides an essential frame of reference for both slow and rapid changes in the cultural activity of a tradition as those changes become socially conventional. Participants in the tradition may, of course, only be aware of contemporary conventions – conventions which they help to construct and maintain – with no concept of historical variation (cf. Gills 1996).

Traditions function at the level of small-group communities and networks of those communities in interaction. Every tradition is maintained through social practices and has functions in a community (e.g. magical, ritual, socializing, entertainment; cf. Honko 1981a). Success in those functions does not demand reconciliation across them or even across different narratives on the same subject (cf. Frog 2011b: 11). Participants in a community more frequently accept them without awareness of incongruity or contradiction (see Converse 1964). In other words, most people do not think about them together – to use Barthes' term, each is 'naturalized' to its particular social context. Within a community, a tradition is *socially negotiated* as an intersubjective referent. This is particularly apparent in the maintenance of a narrative as 'mythological' because the ability of a narrative to remain 'mythological' is necessarily in relationship to group identities, the semiotic system and ideological models, all of which adapt and change as a historical process (see also Frog 2013a: 105–106, 109–111; cf. Frog 2010a: 230–237). In mythological narrative traditions, historical variation of its core elements is normally connected to *a*) the emergence or assertion of a new function, interpretation or significance that becomes socially established and advances to the dominant form; or *b*) the loss of social relevance or dislocation from traditional functions. These processes are frequently responses to contacts across communities or cultures that introduce new traditions, models for cultural practices and/or ideologies. Any 'new' tradition is always received in an established semiotic system, cultural environment (complete with ideologies and a full 'ecology' of traditions) and arenas of discourse. This is particularly significant for narratives and practices associated with (surface) mythology because of their interface with semiotic and conceptual modelling systems (deep mythology). Where those modelling systems do not align, that interface will not succeed in the new or emerging cultural environment (e.g. in conversion environments or when adapted from a foreign culture). As a rule, such traditions will not retain status and quality as 'mythic', 'mythological' or even 'magical' when entering a new cultural environment unless *a*) the new cultural environment shares a sufficient common framework of mythology (e.g. Christianity as a common frame of reference); or *b*) the mythological narrative(s) are adapted in conjunction with changes in an ideology and/or understandings of social identity (e.g. as part of a 'package' of cultural material associated with a conversion process). Mythology must either adapt, be displaced or lose its mythic status in the wake of radical changes in concepts of group identity and ideologies. Adaptation into a new system is a social process of finding value and relevance in that context. These processes are normally connected with and propagated through associated cultural practices and ritual specialists.

Mythologies and Social Authorities

The existence and maintenance of surface mythologies through cultural practices is centrally dependent on stable genres as a medium for communication and negotiation. Social institutions tend to be correlated with particular oral genres, such as the *tietäjä*-institution with kalevalaic epic and incantation, the Finnic lamenter with ritual lament or the Christian priest with sermon and Biblical exegesis. An institution (often) maintains specialists in those genres central to cultural practices. Genres present conventionalized constellations of features – ranging from form and aesthetics to specific contents and ideologies. A specialist internalizes and constructs mythologies through genres and cultural practices to the degree of exposure to and interaction with them. In other words, those genres essential to his or her institution's cultural practices may be most central in developing understandings of a mythology and mythologies. A specialist will also develop a much more sophisticated understanding of those mythologies than a non-specialist because of the on-going amount of time and practical considerations of working with them (cf. Converse 1964). Specialization provides these individuals with a particularly authoritative 'voice' in the process of social negotiation, with the possibility to influence social convention (cf. Siikala 1978: 13; Frog 2011d; Stepanova 2012). A non-specialist is more likely to have a simpler understanding building from the most fundamental structures and that is centrally informed by specialists (cf. Wright 1998: esp. 72–73). As such, the institution presents a conduit of authority for the transmission of those genres, with implications for how those genres develop as a historical process. (Frog 2010a: 135–139.)

The mythology propagated by an institution need not be reconciled with the ideologies and functioning of semiotics in genres outside the sphere of the institution (Frog 2011b). Consequently, genres associated with different institutions can reflect very different modelling systems, ranging from poetic features to representations of the otherworld. Thus the central genres for the *tietäjä*, ritual lamenter and Christian priest may all maintain markedly different mythologies even where they coexisted in the same communities. Rather than existing in isolation, specialists in mythology of one institution will frequently develop non-specialist understandings of mythology of other institutions and negotiate with them from that perspective. (This is noteworthy because these are very often precisely the fundamentals of beings, narratives, images and structures that are the most historically enduring in a mythology.) Institutions of ritual specialist (of which there are always many) therefore present authoritative nexuses of negotiation for mythology. The institutions of Christian priest and vernacular healer may individually play a central role in maintaining and systematizing very different networks of myths and mythological narratives. Radical changes in a traditional mythology frequently appear directly connected to an institution of ritual specialist as a *conduit of authority* for that tradition, rather like pillars in the process of social negotiation.[27] (See also Frog 2014a) Conversion processes – whether conversion to Christianity or to the *tietäjä*-institution – occur through these conduits and ritual specialists.

The spread of the kalevalaic mythology was likely a spread and rise to predominance of a particular type of ritual specialist – i.e. the *tietäjä*-institution. In other words, a contest for conversion may both actually and symbolically be a competition between social institutions of ritual specialists and/or social authorities. Rather than 'converting' individuals, the changes in social power structures lead the 'new' ritual specialist to assert authority and responsibility as a representative of the human community in the otherworld and as an otherworld intermediary in public social rituals and crisis situations. The incantation-wielding *tietäjä*-institution constructed an opposition to vernacular shamanism (for which **Ilmari* was presumably still central) and to Sámi shamanism (which was discontinued with the language shift): these different traditions were not only founded on different deep mythologies; social ideologies may have made these *tietäjä* specialists more consciously resistant to assimilating models from the 'other' (cf. also Aikio 2009: 214 on corresponding language ideologies). 'Conversion' of a social or cultural group follows as a consequence of accepting that authority and non-specialist acceptance of the propagated mythology, first at the level of surface mythology (non-Christian gods are 'bad', and thus Jesus and Mary fill their roles in incantations), and progressively penetrating into the deep mythology (incantations are 'bad' or the 'soul' does not separate from a living body). However, no one specialist dominates all spheres of social activity and cultural practice, nor does the assertion of a specialist authority into an established sphere prevent the negotiation of roles within it.

Christianity, for example, carried practices for structuring public social activities and behaviours, yet it did not come equipped with an infrastructure for concerns of personal physical health, personal or family luck, or more or less for anything connected with practicalities of livelihood: these stood outside of its sphere. Tradition ecologies were reshaped, but not completely displaced: local communities maintained specialists, genres and mythologies in those spheres essential to social realities but outside immediate Church authority. Similarly, the Church's prescriptive attention to essential transition rituals (related to birth, marriage and death) generally remained only a few minimal elements. Rather than displacing complex social practices that were long established, Church prescriptions were simply assimilated into them. As a consequence, established mythologies were maintained as complementary or even synthetically integrated in these and other areas of social life. Understandings are inevitably negotiated at the subjective level of individuals, but cultural realities enable the maintenance of dynamic syncretism according to which different mythologies may be engaged complementarily in relation to social practices, bound up with the genres of expression associated with those practices.

Expression is always oriented to a function – someone always uses it to *do* something – and therefore it is never free of the intentions of individuals. The relationship of the ritual specialist to other institutions and ideologies may significantly impact conventions of use and representation in the genres associated with each institution. For example, a parish priest will represent vernacular gods very differently than a *tietäjä*; a *tietäjä* will represent Jesus and Mary very differently than a parish priest; a ritual lamenter may blur Jesus with the ancestral dead. Mythic figures develop and maintain systems of associations and roles as a historical process and they are often rather like the main levers and gears in the negotiation of surface mythologies. These include, for example, roles in particular narratives and associations across narratives, relationships to magical and ritual practices, associations with social identities (e.g. as identity-models) or phenomena in the natural world, etc. On the one hand, these associations and roles simultaneously define and construct the identities of mythic figures: they tend to form constellations around a semantic core or what Jens Peter Schjødt (2009: 17, 20; 2013: 12–13) terms a "semantic center", and they tend to resist significant innovation unless *a*) they have lost their vitality for users and are being adapted to new functions, or *b*) an innovation is more aggressively prompted in the assertion of certain mythic figures over others or to adapt the tradition to changing ideologies.[28] When changes do occur, they will not necessarily extend to every reference or use of a mythic figure in every genre. This is frequently the case where the established uses are somehow dependent on the earlier conception. This appears to be the case in certain incantations which refer to the smith of heaven in riddles or summoning Ilmarinen to manipulate the weather as a sky-god (Harva 1948: 137–151). It also accounts for attributing Ilmarinen with the creation of the vault of heaven using iron-working technologies although only in a summary or reference as his ultimate feat of skill: this act is never 'told' as a developed narrative and has no integrated place in the cosmology.[29] In this way, every ethnocultural substratum carries the marks of a long history, and the mythology may appear very diverse and incongruous across genres and functions rather than coherent and unified.

In the documented era of tradition, Christian and non-Christian mythology were equally valid and relevant, yet Jesus and Mary do not mix with Väinämöinen and Ilmarinen in kalevalaic epics. This separation of mythic figures into groups is historically attributable to their connection to ideologies rooted in different ethnocultural substrata. Within the living tradition, these were simply different epic cycles with different functions but performed by the same singers. (See further Frog 2013b.) The *tietäjä*-institution's role as a conduit of authority in genres of kalevalaic poetry and mythology means that the relevance and functions of the mythology to this institution have shaped these traditions as a historical process – shaping it according to what was used and why (Frog 2010a: 135–139). As a consequence, what we see of Iron Age mythology is primarily through genres for which the *tietäjä* provided the conduit of authority, and this is essentially the mythology that was functionally relevant and interesting to the *tietäjä* as a historically functioning institution. At the same time, it is also necessary to consider functions of genres both for the institution and more generally in society when considering possible long-term continuities and relevance to the mythology. It should also be remembered that the traditions in the Viking Age were certainly no less stratified and multifaceted than when they were documented, although *different* strata would have greater prominence and significance at that time.

The mythology was by no means limited to kalevalaic poetry. The majority of mythic figures actually lack any narration in kalevalaic epic at all. This does not mean that they were less significant to social realities. The thunder-god Ukko has a central position in mythological thinking, ranging from roles in magical and ritual practices to fundamental behavioural patterns (e.g. to avoid being struck by lightning). Nevertheless, there are no kalevalaic epics about Ukko and he does not interact with Väinämöinen and Ilmarinen as an epic hero (Frog 2013b), in spite of the fact that he and Väinämöinen are the two most central vernacular figures for the *tietäjä*-institution (Siikala 2002a). Narratives about Ukko belong to genres of legend and folktale (frequently oriented to entertainment) that both reflect and reinforce mythological thinking about thunder and devils' fear of thunder. This simply indicates that narratives of cosmological proportions maintained through social practices were peripheral to the functions of Ukko. In contrast, Väinämöinen was associated with the creation of the world and provided a mythic model for the institution of the *tietäjä*, the acquisition and use of incantations, and so forth. However, Väinämöinen was not narrated outside of kalevalaic poetry, nor was he an object of ritual activity expected to directly act on the present world. The role of Väinämöinen within the modelling system of the mythology was characterized by narratives about him providing exemplars for identities (*tietäjä*, singer, musician), while the narratives had roles in ritual practices although Väinämöinen did not. (For discussion, see Frog 2013b: 75–83.)

Other figures emerge as little more than names. In some cases, the figure may be archaic and the name has simply persisted in certain functional capacities. This seems to be the case of *Tuoni*, the figure governing the realm of the dead with probable roots in Proto-Finnic and who is mentioned across several genres but never actually described, let alone narrated.[30] The same is possible for the forest-god *Tapio*, who was maintained in hunting incantations and rituals (Harva 1948: 349–354). Others were probably assimilated with function-specific cultural practices and were never associated with narratives or with other narrative figures at all – i.e. they were essential to the systemically integrated cultural mythology in the sense of covering an area of social activities that others did not, but they were not interfaced with other areas of the surface mythology. An example of this may be *Ägräs* (e.g. Harva 1948: 209–220), the god of turnips and possibly of root vegetables more generally who does not appear interconnected with any other aspect of the surface mythology. This emphasizes that within a culture, mythology has always been a dynamic and diversified system bound, maintained and evolving in relation to genres, specialists (including e.g. agriculture, hunting and animal husbandry) and social functions.

Different historical eras are reflected in the corpus, from those which are most central to those which were peripheral or popular and secular. When functions and genres are situated in dialogue with a continuum model, it is apparent that although all of this material may have had a place and even some form of vitality in the cultural mythology at different times, much of it was also secondary, peripheral or supplementary to dominant ideologies and cultural practices: it may have been important, but only within limited spheres and applications. Many figures may have actually been associated exclusively with particular contexts or functions and were no more developed, dynamic and narrated than the modern-day Easter Bunny. Thus the god Ägräs and associated rituals may have been assimilated and developed in conjunction with particular agricultural practices concerned more or less exclusively with root vegetables and never extended beyond that sphere. In other cases, material may reflect much broader and more significant roles in earlier periods which had presumably already significantly narrowed (at least for the *tietäjä*-mythology) before the Viking Age. For example, references to Ilmarinen as the smith of heaven seems to have lost vitality as 'myth' but was maintained for entertainment in secular riddle traditions, and the feat of creating the vault of heaven was maintained functionally as an attribute of the mythic smith Ilmarinen's skill and authority (although unconnected to the cosmology). Similarly, Ilmarinen appears removed from the role of sky-god, except in the function-specific context of certain weather incantations. When considering the mythology in earlier periods, its most socially and cosmologically central elements prove the most historically enduring – i.e. those elements that are interfaced with the most areas of culture on the one hand while being the symbols of the surface mythology most frequently used in reference and manipulation on the other.

The presentation of mythology here may appear to some readers as quite male-dominated. This is in part a function of the fact that the *tietäjä*-institution appears to have had a historical role as the conduit of authority for the mythology that was marked as most socially central to the community. As emphasized above, this was a mythology constructed to reflect especially the interest, needs and identities of the *tietäjä* specialists, in which case, a male-dominated mythology is not surprising. It should also be observed that this socially central mythology is what can be best assessed in long-term perspective, and the farther into history one attempts to gaze, the more basic and central the elements that it is possible to observe. Within the symbolic structuring of kalevalaic epic, Matti Kuusi (1994b) has argued that women are more or less absent as active agents from the most archaic substrata of the mythology and only with the epic poetry linked with Viking themes (on the controversial nature of which, see AHOLA) do women receive roles as active agents and dialogue participants. Women are also found in inhumation burials with swords otherwise thought of as male symbols of power or authority. Kuusi's view remains speculative, but it presents a potential relevant indicator of changing perceptions and valuations of gender roles and gender relations – *or* that the restructuring of the mythology enabled changes that had already been established in the culture to penetrate the poetry as the semiotics of the tradition were restructured (cf. Ahola *et al.* 2015). Kuusi sees Christian poetry and its influences as a later layer of influence, yet this may be connected to the same process with the integration of the Virgin Mary as a central mythic figure in incantations, which is difficult to date. Interesting to observe, however, is that the influence of Christian tradition produced a kalevalaic epic cycle surrounding Mary that in later evidence seems to have belonged to a women's singing tradition rather than being linked predominantly to male singers or the *tietäjä*-institution (Timonen 1994). Although it remains uncertain when this cycle developed, it can be considered to part of the tradition of mythology linked to women's gender. This is more interesting because it raises questions about the role and position of women in the Christianization process, especially as the new religion in Sweden has been thought to have held particular appeal for women there at the end of the Viking Age, not least because it opened and restructured relations between gender roles and social power and authority, allowing women to become potentially significant actors in the public sphere (Gräslund 2001: 65–89). In other words, the alternative mythology and could hold appeal as a resource for changing one's own social position or for restructuring patterns of relation in society more generally.

Within this context, it warrants mentioning lamenters as a category of women ritual specialists with distinct genres and a distinct poetic system in parallel to kalevalaic poetry (Stepanova 2014; cf. Frog & Stepanova 2011). Within this poetic system, lamenters maintained a mythology associated with their own ritual practices which had distinctive differences from the mythology of kalevalaic poetry in the images, mythic topography and even the supernatural beings addressed (Stepanova 2012). Although they did not maintain mythological narratives, the lament tradition functioned through an essential modelling system of mythic images and motifs for actualizing the unseen otherworld, ensuring the transition of the deceased from the living community to the community of dead ancestors, and also for maintaining communication and relationships with that branch of the kin-group in the otherworld. In ritual practice, for example, the lamenter describes the essential features of the deceased individual's journey to the otherworld, how the ancestors prevent the dog from barking, open the gates of the otherworld, meet the deceased with candles, and so forth. Although individual lamenters might have quite detailed understandings of the imaginal otherworld, these events in the unseen world are realized through clusters of images and motifs that do not offer a clear picture of it (nor was offering such a picture the purpose of lamenting *per se*). (See Stepanova 2014.) Some of the key differences between the mythology of laments and of kalevalaic poetry are related to how and why they were used: the realm of the dead was a horrible and dangerous place for the *tietäjä*, who would banish illnesses there to suffer, whereas it was a positive utopian place for lamenters, whose most socially significant ritual role was integrating the deceased into the otherworld community and maintaining open channels of communication with the ancestral dead (Stepanova 2012; 2014). At the same time, the lamenter's genres of practice may have stood outside of the restructuring of the mythology associated with the *tietäjä* tradition (cf. Frog 2014a; Ahola *et al.* 2015). This presents the possibility that certain aspects of the lamenter's mythology may maintain more archaic features, such as conceptualizing the journey to the otherworld in terms of vertical rather than horizontal movement (Stepanova 2012: 262). This tradition has assimilated a significant range of images, motifs and even terminology from Christianity, yet Mary is completely absent from laments in spite of her prominence elsewhere (Stepanova 2012: 276). Differentiating 'men's mythology' from 'women's mythology' is really a question of differentiating the genders of conventional users. The absence of Mary from laments and her presence in incantations is not a question of which gender's mythology Mary belonged to (as the probable women's epic cycle surrounding Mary highlights). Instead, this gives us information about the historical structuring of different genres that may be associated with certain genders and potentially with gendered categories of specialist, and how those categories of individual related to Mary as a symbol.

When looking at any tradition in long-term perspective, it is also essential to consider fields of use within the overall structure of the mythology and the possibility that changes in the mythology may nevertheless leave suspended certain context-specific or function-specific features from earlier substrata. Whether conversion to Christianity or to the *tietäjä*-mythology is in question, these occur at socially central positions in networks of social groups and they interact with and are negotiated in relation to other areas of culture with other specialists. Although they may come with essential 'packages' of mythology, those packages are not comprehensive and do not extend to all areas of culture. Thus the competition between the *tietäjä* and the shaman (*noita*) as specialists can be regarded as a consequence of filling the same social functions within society: their roles were largely overlapping or equivalent within the tradition ecology. Quite simply, you would go to see both of these specialists for more or less the same reasons (illness, theft, sexual issues) although they worked through different technologies and different mythologies. It is almost inevitable that representatives of each institution would try to assert their own institution's authority and mythology over that of the other. Within the social structuring of these institutional roles, the displacement of vernacular shamanism by the *tietäjä*-institution would potentially impact the roles and functions of ritual lamenters – at least insofar as the transition would touch on fields of activity of lamenters, requiring negotiation of each institution's field of activity. The displacement of vernacular shamanism could also have left open areas of social practices in the tradition ecology resulting in ritual lamenters assuming additional roles or functions that would otherwise have been neglected, such as perhaps a role of psychopomp, ensuring that the deceased successfully accomplished the journey to the otherworld and was integrated into the community of ancestral kin (cf. Honko 1974: 158n.137; Stepanova 2012). On the other hand, the spread of North Finnic languages and the language-shift of Sámi populations was not related to only one category of ritual specialist. Language proves fundamental to many ritually-grounded institutions, and thus a change in language may likely require a change in other institutions reliant on verbal art. In other words, a male-dominated *tietäjä*-institution and associated magical technologies were unlikely to be the only institution and package of mythology and practices carried along with the spread of North Finnic languages. The female ritual specialist institution of lamenter was similarly reliant on language-bound genres and the continuity of this verbal art across Finnic cultural areas (Frog & Stepanova 2011: 204–209; Stepanova 2014) indicates that any corresponding Sámi lament tradition was superseded. As these are the two most prominent (and also quite broad) categories of vernacular ritual specialist and each is associated with one of the two predominating vernacular oral-poetic systems, it seems reasonable to suppose that other categories of specialist as well as non-specialist cultural practices followed a corresponding pattern in a broad culture shift.

Approaching Mythology in the Viking Age in Finland

The *tietäjä*-mythology cannot be considered generally representative of most Viking Age cultural environments of Finland and Karelia. The spread of the *tietäjä*-institution very likely involved its co-existence with inherited forms of North Finnic shamanism in the same and/or adjacent communities for some centuries. Most territories of Finland and Karelia were Sámi linguistic-cultural areas and can be assumed to have maintained different mythology and cultural practices. These can be assumed to have been a different reflex of the Finno-Ugric heritage, historically removed from Finnic mythologies. The spread of North Finnic languages through these territories likely augmented the opposition between these competing institutions with contrasts of Finnic and Sámi language, culture, cultural practices and mythologies. Approaching Sámi mythology is highly problematic. Perspectives offered by the conservative textual support of kalevalaic epic are lacking. Although it is possible to develop some general perspectives on Sámi shamanism (see e.g. Bäckman & Hultkrantz 1973), there is significant variation in the mythologies of different Sámi language groups (see Rydving 2010). This problematizes approaching Sámi mythology in most territories of Finland and Karelia which are generally unattested. These mythologies likely developed historically from a common heritage of other Sámi mythologies rather than being identical to them. They presumably developed differently owing to more intensive historical contacts with North Finnic groups and other cultures of these territories than with the uncertain cultures of Lapland in the north and Germanic cultures on the Scandinavian Peninsula.

The differences are more difficult to estimate because the majority of these areas appear to have been inhabited by a branch of Sámi languages that was completely assimilated (Kuzmin) – i.e. their historical relationship to attested Sámi languages would seem to go back to a period before the attested Sámi languages became distinct from one another.[31]

Different mythologies may also have been maintained in the majority of North Finnic cultural areas in the Viking Age. The ethnocultural substratum perceived through later evidence traces back to a localized bottleneck that eventually overlaid and eclipsed the mythologies of other North Finnic (Sámi, and perhaps also other) groups. These other mythologies are now largely irrecoverable, although some perspectives can be gained when approaching them through a continuum model. Additional perspectives may become possible in the future through detailed examination of variation in less central mythological narratives, such as the origin of fire, that could (at least potentially) have persisted in local or regional cultures rather than being displaced by the corresponding narrative carried with the *tietäjä*-mythology. This provides an important area for exploration in future research.[32] Perspectives on these mythologies require projecting back to an ethnocultural substratum prior to the emergence of the *tietäjä*-institution – i.e. approximations of the mythology that preceded its revolutionary restructuring. These perspectives remain very general and hypothetical. They also remain conditional on the degree to which the essential features of the mythology in the cultural environment where the *tietäjä*-institution emerged were generally representative of North Finnic mythologies. This information can be correlated with broader perspectives on cross-cultural patterns relevant to the Circum-Baltic area, such as thunder-god traditions (cf. Frog 2011a), smith of heaven traditions (Laurinkienė 2008; Frog 2012a; 2013b), and so forth. The lament tradition is also significant because this institution of ritual specialist was almost certainly current in the Viking Age. As a common Finnic heritage, the lament tradition likely had an unbroken continuity through the transition linked to the *tietäjä*-institution. It also participates in a broad Circum-Baltic cross-cultural pattern of lament traditions in which Baltic, Slavic and even Germanic cultures seem to have participated (see further Stepanova 2011: esp. 140). These traditions have potential for insights into image systems and structures that may reflect constitutive elements of the mythology in earlier periods, although these will be only some aspects of earlier mythologies rather than offering a comprehensive picture and they should not be considered necessarily equivalent to those of other institutions.[33]

The bottleneck in the history of North Finnic mythologies problematizes approaching different sources, which must be situated in this light. For example, the *jumola*[*n*] *nuoli* of the Novgorod 292 inscription (see Figure 1, above) reflects a technology of verbal magic suggestive of the deep mythology of the *tietäjä*-institution. Moreover, use of the technology of writing with a magical language-based technology is almost certainly rooted in foreign models whether through Christian models or Germanic runemagic. This presents a fair possibility that Novgorod 292 reflects a mythology related to, or at least parallel to, the *tietäjä*-institution. However, this is not a metrical charm nor have verbal or structural formulaic parallels to the charm been identified. This could also reflect a parallel and independent assimilation of the technology that gave rise to the *tietäjä*-institution. In this case, it could be a reflex of the adaptation of the technology which evolved the structured form and repertoire of the *tietäjä*-institution in western North Finnic territories but which may have taken shape differently in its initial spread to other areas. It could also be a unique and local synthesis of charming technologies to a Finnic vernacular on the basis of Slavic of Christian models. The Novgorod 292 inscription is unique, making its broader significance highly ambiguous.

The Old Norse description of a sacred site and naming a god *Jómali* can provide another illustrative example. Use of this term may reflect knowledge of Finnic traditions, but not necessarily of the *tietäjä*-mythology – especially if the theonym was indeed used by Bjarmians on the White Sea. Approached in dialogue with the continuum model, the evidence can be assessed in relation to ethnocultural substrata prior to the *tietäjä*-institution in order to consider whether outcomes of a corresponding linguistic-cultural heritage could produce this theonym through different historical circumstances. In other words, this may reflect the mythology and practices of a *different* Finnic culture that was not yet affected by the spread of the *tietäjä*-institution. This possibility would suggest a different culture in which a local reflex of classic shamanism would presumably be maintained. For the sake of discussion, some (extremely conditional) hypothetical alternatives may be explored. The term *Jómali* suggests a Finnic language because the development **juma* > **juma-la* appears specific to the Finnic language group. The appearance of the noun for 'god, supernaturally empowered being' as a theonym is curious and problematic. Ethnocultural substrata discernible through the evidence of the *tietäjä*-institution indicate that – at least in the environment where the institution developed its essential stable form – **Ilmari* was the dominant sky-god and smith of heaven. There is nothing to suggest that this was not generally established in the networks of language communities that became Finnish and Karelian. This could simply be a confusion resulting during contact or even in later narrations of these 'foreign' cultures by Norsemen. However, if *Jómali* is not a confusion and renders a cognate of *jumala* as a primary theonym, this would suggest Finnic social groups in which the theonym **Ilmari* had been superseded in use by a common noun, or replaced by a deity called 'God'. This parallels the use of *Jumala* under Christianity, which could hypothetically reflect a local or regional vernacularization of Christianity (cf. Frog 2014a). However, this same shift to 'God' as a primary theonym happened as part of a broad (and mysterious) cross-cultural development in a fairly early ethnocultural substratum, potentially already a millennium or more before the Viking Age. The shift can be observed only in the lexicon, where it affected Baltic and Germanic languages, and also in the Volgic branch of Finno-Ugric languages. (Frog 2012b: 29–34.) Through dialogue with the continuum model, the appearance of **Jumala* rather than **Ilmari* could suggest some connection with this process and thus a more distant relation of this mythology to that which was local where the *tietäjä*-institution took shape. This could be consistent with the model that the Finnic populations which migrated to the Northern Dvina River basin were linguistically closer to South Finnic or to KALLIO's Inland Finnic, where the mythology may have developed quite differently – that is, if these were the Bjarmians and the Bjarmians indeed worshiped a god called *Jómali* (~ *Jumala*). However, the picture is more complicated because it cannot be certain that the **juma* > **juma-la* development was *exclusive* to Finnic languages. Developments in Sámi languages have erased evidence of this lexical development or its absence. More significantly, the continuum of Finno-Ugric languages between the Finnic and Volgic linguistic-cultural groups underwent a language shift before being documented. Whereas the **juma* > **juma-la* development is attested for Finnic languages but not the **Ilmari* → **Jumala* development, the **juma* > **juma-la* development is not attested in Volgic languages but the **Ilma* → **Juma* development is. If *Jómali* does indeed accurately represent a primary theonym, then it could potentially derive from one of these languages, such as Meryan, which was geographically adjacent to Volgic languages while linguistically closer to Finnic (on which see Helimski 2006). Meryans were not only prominent in the history of cultural contacts but a very direct and intimate cultural contact and exchange is evinced in the clay paw burial rite found in Meryan territories, where it appears to have been assimilated through contact with populations of the Åland Islands (Callmer 1992; Frog 2014a). When linguistic evidence of the **juma* > **juma-la* development for these other languages is lacking, identifying *Jómali* as a specifically Finnic loan must be recognized as a probability rather than as a certainty.

When approaching mythology in the Viking Age, broad patterns, models, minimal symbolic 'words' of the mythology (images, motifs) and the mythological lexicon can be cautiously approached according to the highest degree of probable relevance. This presents highly abstracted perspectives on the relevant cultural environments (see e.g. the study of Siikala 2002a). The more complex the material, such as a whole narrative, the more caution is required, and this leads into areas in which non-specialists easily become entangled (cf. Figure 4). Part of this problem is related to an inclination to think of a mythology in terms of whole narratives, whether as invariable plots or textual poems, and failure to consider that these may have varied and adapted over time. Consideration of the maintenance of mythology through cultural practices should be taken into account immediately on addressing the sources, with particular attention to the degree of public centrality for the surface mythology and whether it is connected prominently and centrally to an institution of ritual specialist. Although it is possible for prose mythological narratives to maintain very long-term historical continuities (e.g. Frog 2011a), this material is often problematic because prose traditions tend to be more flexible in reproduction and, in Finno-Karelian traditions, to have popular and secular functions that made variation according the situation more acceptable or even required. Kalevalaic narrative poetry is at the other end of the spectrum, characterized by extreme verbal conservatism.

Fig. 4. The mount of Solberga, a bronze buckle from Askeby in Östergötland, eighth century. Sune Lindqvist (1945–1946) interpreted this image as Väinämöinen fishing for Aino in Kalevala (cf. Harva 1948: 367). Insofar as the image can be assumed meaningful and recognizable, the interpretation is not improbable. However, the interpretation is based on Kalevala, in which Lönnrot identified the fish-maiden with Aino as an editorial decision with no foundation in traditional poetry. The episode in Kalevala was based on the epic song Vellamo's Maiden, in which Väinämöinen has replaced an earlier protagonist (Kuusi 1963). However, only a single (ambiguous) motif is represented here, leaving the narrative whole uncertain. The narrative appears to have circulated cross-culturally in the Baltic Sea region (Aarne 1923), and therefore is not assuredly Finnic, nor even assuredly mythological. (Photo © SHM (Swedish History Museum), reproduced with permission.)

The core mythological poems of the *tietäjä*'s repertoire, such as the Sampo-Cycle and adventure of the figure Lemminkäinen, were likely current in some form in the Viking Age (see Ahola). Some mythological poetry suggests still longer continuity although it may have been transformed through the interests and priorities of the *tietäjä*-institution in the restructuring of the mythology. This may have been the case for the creation of a woman through metal-working (associated with the earlier smith of heaven tradition) and the creation of the world (or at least parts of that narrative) (see further Frog 2012a; 2013b). This does not mean that *all* of the narratives of the *tietäjä*'s core mythology were current at that time: this remains only a probability for each individual poem. In general, this probability is greater for mythological epic poems attested across all tradition areas where mythological poetry was maintained. Poems preserved in only a few isolated examples (e.g. *Ahti and Kyllikki*) are very problematic to assess. Use of a mythological poem, episode, image or motif in comparison must consider this. Most challenging, however, is thinking in terms of variation.

Continuity does not mean that these poems did not change and vary over time – especially when Christian models and ideologies had a gradual and increasing impact on the traditions. Nevertheless, as a rule, variation does not occur 'just anywhere' in a poem or story. Generally speaking, semantic, structural and functional cores of tradition tend to be relatively stable in historical transmission while variation tends to occur in semantically and structurally 'light' tissue between these. A general impression of local and regional variation and relative prominence of a particular mythological poem or incantation can be gained by even a superficial survey of examples of in the published critical edition *Suomen Kansan Vanhat Runot* ['Ancient Songs of the Finnish People'] or *SKVR* (1908–1997), organizing more than 86,000 items of kalevalaic poetry first by region, then by genre, and then according to variants of the particular text type. It should be remembered that variation is an essential aspect of living tradition. Most variation has no direct impact on the intersubjective referent of the tradition and the majority of innovations never become established. Among examples of well-attested poems, it is often quite easy to identify certain features or even uses of whole episodes as something localized to a community, network of communities or region. Early research sought to map these in great detail according to a so-called stemma, rather like a family tree of variation (cf. Salmela). However, it often becomes difficult to determine which of two 'deeper' forms may have preceded the other, and the once-popular concrete reconstructions will inevitably produce falsifications: the farther back in time a tradition is projected, the more abstractly and conditionally it should be approached (cf. Figure 5).

Cross-disciplinary uses of folklore material will generally require comparison across different modes of expression and different functions – e.g. in personal names (e.g. Saarikivi 2007), toponymy (Ahlqvist 2012), medieval iconography (Figure 4) or interpreting evidence of cultural practices exhibited in the archaeological record (Wessman 2010). It is therefore important to distinguish what precisely is being compared (see

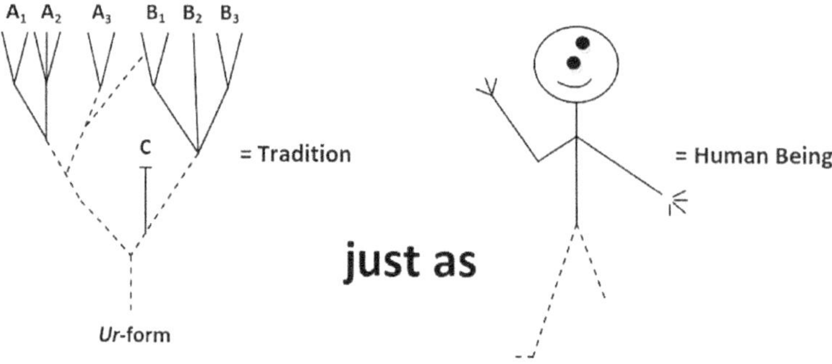

Fig. 5. Stick diagram comparison. A stemma model diagram can provide a valuable tool for visualizing contexts and relationships between materials under comparison, much as a stick figure can be used to indicate a hand, foot or eye in relation to other parts of a human being. It nevertheless remains an interpretation, and a minimal outline which may also be misrepresentative.

Frog 2013a: 111–115). Historical comparison will usually be concerned with continuities in 'content' rather than representation as 'text', and cross-disciplinary comparison will frequently be concerned with a more abstract conceptual model for mythological thinking (cf. Frog 2011a). It is advisable to begin with the smallest meaningful units and structures as a foundation for discussion: the semiotic building-blocks of texts normally exhibit greater historical continuity and stability than narratives or sequences of ritual activity (cf. Siikala 2002a), even if these building-blocks are also the elements which can be most easily adapted to new contexts or transmitted cross-culturally and may have extremely long and rich histories (see e.g. Harvilahti 2009; cf. Krohn 1926). When such building-blocks or small groups of them provide a core for comparison, care should be taken before suggesting that the core elements warrant comparison with a full complex narrative or ritual sequence (cf. Figure 4). These should be approached abstractly, remaining aware that continuities can be most reliably traced in terms compositional elements and their associations with one another and/or with broad conceptual models. (Such a comparison does not exclude a relationship to a whole narrative, it is simply a more cautious strategy for approaching that possibility without over-hasty commitment to it.) The greater the number of elements and the more complex and interdependent their relationships in a parallel, the greater the probability of a relationship.

Special care must be taken to consider whether examples under consideration exhibit socially conventional forms. Often the examples that are most frequently presented and reproduced are selected precisely because they are exceptional in quality, development or detail, or because they are most relevant to a particular argument rather than because they most accurately reflect an average or are representative of norms (Bradley 2012). This sort of selectivity of sources has been problematic within research on kalevalaic mythology: it was only relatively recently that researchers began recognizing that talented performers not infrequently assert their own identities, authority and ideologies through variation (cf. Tarkka 2005: 179–

182), and also that a more richly developed perspective on the tradition and competence in its use actually *increases* the likelihood that an individual will perceive relationships between traditions, attempt to reconcile incongruities or bring vernacular traditions into accord with a changed, predominating (e.g. Christian) worldview (cf. Converse 1964: 214–219). For example, one of the most famous Karelian singers who had great influence on Elias Lönnrot's *Kalevala* omitted the world-egg motif from the world-creation and presented Väinämöinen calling on God to raise the first earth from the primal sea, more in accord with his own Christian worldview (see Frog 2010a: 226–229).

Perspectives

Mythology has a semiotically central position in cultures and cultural practices. It therefore holds great potential as a resource for many disciplines. It is simultaneously elusive and difficult to approach: many of its sources are problematic and still more are neglected or overlooked. The preceding discussion has concentrated on mythology in terms of social practices and institutions of ritual specialist that provide conduits of authority in the maintenance of surface mythology. Recognizing a relationship between mythology and practitioners is essential to any approach to mythology and its sources. In addition, the most promising areas for approaching continuities in mythologies are precisely where these are connected with continuities in practices and specialist institutions: the most extensive evidence of Finno-Karelian mythology relevant to the Viking Age is concentrated precisely in genres connected to institutions of ritual specialists with a continuity of practice extending back into the Iron Age; evidence of mythology is weakest for specialist institutions that did not survive, such as for shamanism. Mythologies in the Viking Age nevertheless remain very much removed and can centrally be approached only through quite abstract and generalized descriptions that offer better perspectives on patterns than on a specific repertoire of concrete narratives. Mythologies in the Viking Age also appear to have been highly diversified across both the same and different linguistic groups. The specialists and their mythologies can be presumed to have differed in North Finnic and in Sámi linguistic groups, while the diversity within each linguistic group remains uncertain. There may also have been additional groups with still other types of specialists, practices and mythologies. This may have been the case for Bjarmians as a possible South Finnic culture. The same questions surround Åland, which not only stood between Germanic and Finnic linguistic-cultural areas but also exhibits ritual practices connected with the remote territories of the Merya. There is even a possibility that in inland regions or in the remote north that there were additional communities of West Uralic speakers of unknown languages or even potentially as-yet unassimilated Palaeo-European groups.

At some point during the Iron Age (i.e. after the sky-god **Ilmari* assimilated the smith of heaven identity and narratives), there was a fundamental restructuring of the socially central North Finnic mythology connected with the emergence of the institution of the *tietäjä*. This institution most likely spread through the relatively small North Finnic dialect continuum in the Viking Age and subsequently spread north with the North Finnic languages, presumably after already assimilating Christian material. There were nevertheless diverse institutions of ritual specialist and these specialists no doubt played an essential role in the maintenance of the surface mythology within each smaller linguistic-cultural group and community. It remains uncertain how long the *tietäjä*-institution existed in parallel with vernacular shamanism. At the same time, the spread of these cultures was not exclusively linked to language or to the *tietäjä*-institution and seems to have been accompanied by other popular genres of expression in Kalevala-meter, lamenters as ritual specialists with their own genres and distinctive form of mythology, and countless other practices. When turning attention to potential interfaces between mythology and the evidence in different sources, such as archaeology or foreign literature, it is necessary to ask *whose* mythology may be reflected, variously in terms of language, culture, and even in terms of the categories of specialist who may be concerned.

Acknowledgements: Research for this chapter has been completed within the framework of the Academy of Finland project "Oral Poetry, Mythic Knowledge, and Vernacular Imagination: Interfaces of Individual Expression and Collective Traditions in Pre-Modern Northeast Europe" of the Department of Folklore Studies, University of Helsinki. Portions of accounts of theory and method have been adapted especially from the extended discussion in "The Parallax Approach" (Frog 2013a, first edition 2012), and see also Frog 2011c, 2012a, 2012b and 2013b as well as advancements of this framework in Frog 2014a and 2014b; illustrative figures and captions appearing here or earlier versions of them have previously appeared in Frog 2013a and its 2012 edition and in Frog 2012b.

Notes

1 This expression was coined by Jewett & Lawrence 1977; see Coupe 1997: 9–13; Doty 2000; Frog 2014b.

2 The human meaning project hypothesis circulated in Christian discourses throughout the Middle Ages and can be traced back still further to Classical Antiquity where it shows up, for example, in Plato's *Phaedrus*.

3 Scientific truths of yesterday can become the myths of today, thus 'erroneous' here is dependent on only ascribing 'myth' to the 'other'. Moreover, the separation of scientific truths and mainstream thinking above is illusory, because the authority of objective science in modern cultures is purely dependent on mainstream thinking.

4 Or at least not be both independently realized and also be analyzable: see Lotman & Uspenskij 1976.

5 The Christian model of conscious subscription to a 'belief' tends to confuse this issue. Most living 'beliefs' are closer to tacit presumptions and intuitions rather

than a conscious subscription – people may not even be aware of them – or they function practically and socially, shaping individual behaviours. In most cases, there is actually no motivation to question or resolve whether one does or does not 'believe' let alone whether or not to consciously subscribe to it – it is simply a thinking process that may engage emotional responses.

6 The passage is the same in both versions of the saga: Johnsen & Jón Helgason 1941: 351; Bjarni Aðalbjarnarson 1941–1951: 294.

7 'Magic shot' is the English term for magic arrows or darts that cause illness (cf. Finnish *pistos*), on which see further Honko 1959.

8 See Hautala 1968; see also discussions in AHOLA; AHOLA & FROG; RANINEN & WESSMAN; AALTO.

9 Documents for White Sea Karelia in the north still show Sámi settlements covering more than half of the area in *c.* 1600, but these populations seem to have gradually adopted the local Karelian dialect (Pöllä 1999: 164, 168). No Sámi are indicated in the region Seesd'ärvi (Fin. Seesjärvi, Rus. Сегозеро; more or less in the center of Karelia) in sixteenth and seventeenth century documents (Mullonen 2001: 14), yet in south-eastern areas of this region, the linguistically Karelian population still refers to themselves as *lappalažet* ['Sámi'] and to their language as *lappi* ['Sámi'] (but call themselves *карелы* ['Karelians'] in Russian). They identify *kajalažet* ['Karelians'] as being further south and refer to their southern neighbours as *vepsä* ['Vepsians']. (Konkka & Konkka 1980: 23–24.) When doing fieldwork in this region, folklore collectors asking for songs in Karelian (*karjalaksi*) would receive songs in Russian, and would have to request songs in Sámi (*lapiksi*) in order to get songs in Karelian. This seems to be an exceptional example of the maintenance of ethnic identity through the historical process of a language shift.

10 See for example Ajkhenvald *et al.* 1989; Napolskikh 1992; Siikala 2002c; Frog 2012a; 2012b; an accessible overview of Proto-Uralic mythology is available in Hoppál 2010: 28–37.

11 On the dualist structure, see Ajkhenvald *et al.* 1989; Frog 2012b; on the narrative core of the world-creation myth, see Napolskikh 1989; 1992; 2012; on the vertically structured cosmology, see e.g. Harva 1923; Hultkrantz 1996; Tátar 1996; Hoppál 2010: 29–31; cf. Eliade 1964; the term "classic shamanism" is taken from Siikala 1978: 14–15; on a form of classic shamanism as part of the heritage of Uralic cultures, see further e.g. Hultkrantz 2001; Siikala 2002a. In the Viking Age in Finland seminars, Clive Tolley emphasized that the identification of shamanism as a part of Finno-Ugric or Uralic heritage is extremely hypothetical because shamanism has been preserved among so few Finno-Ugric cultures and the form preserved in Sámi lacks certain characteristic features (see also Tolley 2009 I: 66–92; for an alternative approach to this problem, see Frog 2012a). A diverse range of evidence nevertheless suggests that a form of classic shamanism, or minimally something close to the shamanism encountered among the Sámi with a corresponding ideology, was established in North Finnic cultures by the beginning of the Iron Age (see e.g. Siikala 2002a). The present discussion is not dependent on that form of shamanism necessarily being rooted in a Proto-Uralic or Proto-Finno-Ugric ethnocultural substratum as opposed to being introduced through cross-cultural contact in an intermediate period prior to the Iron Age. It nevertheless seems probable that a form of classic shamanism was established already in those earliest ethnocultural substrata. It should also be observed that rejecting shamanism as a constituent of those early substrata implicitly presupposes that an otherwise unknown, unattested institution of ritual specialist and ritual practice of 'not-shamanism' was current at that time.

12 See e.g. Vajda 1959; Hultkrantz 1973; Siikala 1978; on the aspect of physicality, cf. also Frog 2013b.

13 On **Ilma* as the name of the sky-god in Proto-Finno-Ugric, see Frog 2012b and works there cited; on **nojta*, see Haavio 1967: 313–314; Rédei *et al.* 1986–1988: 307–308.
14 Cf. Holmberg [Harva] 1927: 313–322. Finnic languages do not have articles (*a* or *the* in English) and consequently, *piru* or *perkele* and other similar terms can be variously interpreted as 'a devil', 'the devil', or even as a personal name 'Devil'.
15 For a fuller discussion, see Frog 2012a; 2013b; for a developed discussion of parallels and differences between these traditions at the level of conceptual modelling and guided imagination, see Frog 2010b.
16 On the Finno-Ugric material, see Napolskikh 1989: 106; on comparison with Indo-Iranian, see Aalto 1975 [1987]: 85–86; see further also Valk 2000: esp. 154; Frog 2012a: esp. 213.
17 For example, the world-egg creation appears to be depicted in Neolithic petroglyphs of an unknown northern culture on the northeast coast of Lake Onega (Lahelma 2008: 155–157; 2010: 142–145), thus the earliest evidence of this mythological material may derive from a culture that is neither Uralic nor Indo-European, as first pointed out by Ülo Valk (2000).
18 On the possible underlying images of bronze-working, see Frog 2011c: 32, 35; on images specific to this technology, see e.g. Salo 2006: 30–31; on bronze-working as more peripheral in overall cultural impacts, see Hakamies 1999: 86–87; 2012.
19 See further Siikala 2002a: *passim*; Frog 2010a: 127–141; Frog 2013b.
20 The forms *Ilmari* and *Ilmari-nen* are equivalent and alternative as are the forms *Väinä*, *Väinö*, *Väinä-mö* and *Väinä-möinen*; the extended forms are especially associated with Kalevala-meter poetry where a four-syllable name like *Ilmari-nen* or *Väinä-möinen* is simply easier to use in a line.
21 Scholars' relative valuation of different genres of folklore was accompanied by a corresponding relative valuation of 'Christian' themes versus the ethnically-based mythology and epic traditions. As a consequence, this Christian material has not been as extensively studied. The general impression of the material is that the Christian substratum was interfaced with these traditions already at an early stage before Finnish and Karelian cultures began to spread significantly inland. If this is the case, the enrichment of the tradition by Christian material seems likely to have taken place when the contact networks between western Finland and Karelia were still vital especially in relation to this institution, whether toward the end of the Finnish Viking Age Proper (750–1050) or in the Later Finnish Viking Age (1050–1250). Following that period, the changing geopolitical situation affected contacts and the alignments of social identities with eastern and western nation-states and eastern and western Churches (Heininen *et al.*), reducing the probability that there would be a rich exchange of cultural practices during that time. On the problems and questions of the possible arrival and assimilation of Christian religion into vernacular culture in western Finland already in the tenth to the twelfth centuries, see Frog 2014a.
22 On this epic and discussions surrounding it, see e.g. Setälä 1932; Harva 1943; Lid 1949; Kuusi 1949; Haavio 1952: 51–63, 208–212; Frog 2012a.
23 For a current collection of works and approaches, see Frog *et al.* 2012.
24 See e.g. Honko 1981b; 1985; for an overview of the concept and history of the term, see Kamppinen 1989: 37–46.
25 For example: a researcher of Kalevala-meter poetry will receive a different impression than a researcher of ritual laments, legends or sermons; ethnographic material on rituals gives a different impression than narrative traditions; a linguist can examine names and terms irrespective of whether these are attached to information about narratives, rituals or popular beliefs.

26 The following is a usage-based model of tradition according to the theory of the Activating Power of Expression presented in Frog 2010a; see also Frog 2013a: 109–111. For a usage-based approach to language, see Tomasello 2003.

27 See further Frog 2010a: 137, 232; 2011c: 32–34; on 'conduits' of transmission of traditions, see von Sydow 1948: 12; Dégh & Vázsonyi 1975.

28 For discussion of such identities in terms of 'tradition dominants', see Eskeröd 1947: 79–81; Honko 1981a: 23–24; 1981b: 35–36.

29 See e.g. Haavio 1967: 136–137; Kuusi *et al.* 1977: 524 and poems #7–8; Hakamies 2012; Frog 2012a.

30 Tuoni is fully integrated into the world of mythological narratives, incantations and laments, but almost nothing is known of Tuoni as a mythic being – even her(?) gender is uncertain (see e.g. Siikala 2002a: 145–153; Stepanova 2012). The etymology of the name has been traced back to an extremely early Germanic contact (*SSE* III: 330) probably meaning 'Death'. Although not cognate with Old Norse *Hel* ['Death'], the female being ruling the realm of the dead, this etymology would present a common semantic and structural basis for both names being rooted in the same culture, but the background nevertheless remains obscure. Although Tuoni does in fact appear in some narrative poems, it should be observed that in these cases Tuoni's name has simply been inserted in a conventional narrative in the place of e.g. Hiisi ['Devil'] and other names. This process seems connected to the increasing use of mythic figures, their names and mythological narratives in secular fantastic tales for entertainment. These cannot be considered necessarily representative of Tuoni's (earlier) identity in the mythology (beyond an identification with an otherworld location) when that identity is in no way distinguishable from other identities which more commonly fill the same role.

31 It may be interesting to note that the geographical scope and rate of the spread of language and culture could be a relevant factor here. Where the linguistic-cultural system has spread over a new area more quickly, its internal variation may be less pronounced. In contrast, long-term habitation in the same local areas may lead to greater diversity within those areas – much as language variation is far greater in a smaller geographical space in southern Estonia, in the area from which Finnic languages are thought to have spread, whereas they are far more uniform across large areas of Finland and Karelia. If the Sámi languages spread from territories of southern Finland and Karelia, Sámi languages (and perhaps mythologies) may have been far more diverse in this area during the Viking Age than in Norway and Sweden.

32 These patterns of variation have been surveyed and discussed (e.g. Krohn 1924; Sarmela 1994), but these discussions have lacked a developed frame of reference regarding the historical spread of the *tietäjä*-institution and the spread of both Finnic and Sámi languages.

33 For example, certain aspects of the lament tradition and its images are dependent on changes in burial practices such as the shift to inhumation from cremation (cf. Stepanova 2011: 137). These developments in the tradition have undoubtedly masked and even completely displaced corresponding mythic images and conceptions associated with cremation burial practices, including descriptions of preparations, the cremation event and the collection and deposition of remains. Nevertheless, some fundamental structures of laments in the imaging of the mythic world, its inhabitants and access to it may be closer to models of the inherited Finnic reflex of classic shamanism rather than to the *tietäjä* traditions, such as emphasis on vertical movement to the otherworld.

References

Sources

FMU = Hausen, R. 1910–1915. *Finlands medeltidsurkunder* I–II. Helsingfors: Kejserliga Senatens Tryckeri.

SKVR = *Suomen Kansan Vanhat Runot* I–XV. 1908–1997. Helsinki: Suomalaisen Kirjallisuuden Seura.

Literature

Aalto, Pentti. 1987 [1975]. Connections between Finnish and Aryan Mythology. In *Studies in Altaic and Comparative Philology: A Collection of Professor Pentti Aalto's Essays in Honour of His 70th Birthday*. Studia Orientalia 59. Helsinki: Finnish Oriental Society. Pp. 80–98.

Aarne, Antti 1923. *Das Lied vom Angeln der Jungfrau Vellamos: Eine vergleichende Untersuchung*. FF Communications 48. Helsinki: Academia Scientiarum Fennica.

Ahlqvist, Arja. 2012. Blue Stones in the Context of Traditions of Worshiping Stones in Former Finno-Ugric Territories of Central Russia. In Frog, Siikala & Stepanova 2012: 434–467.

Ahola, Joonas, Frog & Ville Laakso. 2015 (forthcoming). Raptors in Iron Age and Medieval North Finnic Cultures to c. AD 1500: Perceptions and Practices. Oliver Grimm & Ulrich Schmölcke (eds.). *Premodern Falconry and Bird Symbolism – Interdisciplinary and Practical Considerations: The Global Perspective in Relation to Northern Europe*. Schriften des archäologischen Landesmuseums Ergänzungsreihe. Wachholtz: Neumünster.

Aikio, Ante. 2006. On Germanic–Saami Contacts and Saami Prehistory. *Journal de la Société Finno-Ougrienne* 91: 9–55.

Aikio, Ante. 2009. *The Saami Loanwords in Finnish and Karelian*. Oulu: University of Oulu.

Ajkhenvald, Aleksandra, Eugene Helimski & Vladimir Petrukhin. 1989. On Earliest Finno-Ugrian Mythologic Beliefs: Comparative and Historical Considerations for Reconstruction. In Hoppál & Pentikäinen (eds.). *Uralic Mythology and Folklore*. Ethnologica Uralica 1. Helsinki: Finnish Literature Society. Pp. 155–159.

Anttonen, Veikko. 2010. *Uksontotieteen maastot ja kartat*. Tietolipas 232. Helsinki: SKS.

Anttonen, Veikko. 2012a. Literary Representation of Oral Religion: Organizing Principles in Mikael Agricola's List of Mythological Agents in Late Medieval Finland. In Catherina Raudvere & Jens Peter Schjødt (eds.). *More than Mythology: Narratives, Ritual Practices and Regional Distribution in Pre-Christian Scandinavian Religions*. Lund: Nordic Academic Press. Pp. 185-223.

Anttonen, Veikko. 2012b. The Sampo as a Mental Representation of the Mythic Origin of Growth: Towards a New Comprehensive Theory. In Frog, Siikala & Stepanova 2012: 171–187.

Bäckman, Louise, & Åke Hultkrantz. 1978. *Studies in Lapp Shamanism*. Stockholm Studies in Comparative Religion 16. Stockholm: Almqvist & Wiksell International.

Barthes, Roland. 1972 [1957]. *Mythologies*. New York: Hill & Wang.

Barthes, Roland. 1977 [1971]. Change the Object Itself: Mythology Today. In Roland Barthes. *Image - Music - Text*. London: Fontana Press. Pp. 165–169.

Bascom, William. 1965. The Forms of Folklore: Prose Narratives. *Journal of American Folklore* 78(307): 3–20.

Bell, Catherine. 1997. *Ritual: Perspectives and Dimensions*. Oxford: Oxford University Press.

Bjarni Aðalbjarnarson. 1941–1951. *Heimskringla* I–III. Íslenzka fornrit 26–28. Reykjavík: Hið Íslenzka Fornritafélag.

Borenius, A. A. 1873. Missä Kalevala on syntynyt? *Suomen Kuvalehti* 1: 269–274.

Bradley, Jill. 2012. Building a Visual Vocabulary: The Methodology of 'Reading' Images in Context. In Frog & Pauliina Latvala (eds.). *Approaching Methodology*. RMN Newsletter 4. Helsinki: Folklore Studies, University of Helsinki. Pp. 31–40.

Briggs, Charles L., & Richard Bauman. 1992. Genre, Intertextuality, and Social Power. *Journal of Linguistic Anthropology* 2(2): 131–172.

Callmer, Johan. 1994. The Clay Paw Burial Rite of the Åland Islands and Central Russia: A Symbol in Action. *Current Swedish Archaeology* 2: 13–46.

Carpelan, Christian 2001. Late Palaeolithic and Mesolithic Settlement of the European North: Possible Linguistic Implications. In Christian Carpelan, Asko Parpela & Petteri Koskikallio (eds.). *Early Contacts between Uralic and Indo-European. Linguistic and Archaeological Considerations*. Helsinki: Suomalais-Ugrialainen Seura. Pp. 37–53.

Cassirer, Ernst. 1925. *Sprache und Mythos: Ein Beitrag zum Problem der Götternamen*. Leipzig: B.G. Teubner.

Converse, Philip. 1964. The Nature of Belief Systems in Mass Publics. In D. Apter (ed.). *Ideology and Discontent*. London: Free Press. Pp. 206–261.

Coupe, Laurence. 1997. *Myth*. New Critical Idiom. London: Routledge.

Csapo, Eric. 2004. *Theories of Mythology*. London: Blackwell.

Dégh, Linda, & Andrew Vázsonyi. 1975. The Hypothesis of Multi-Conduit Transmission in Folklore. In D. Ben Amos & K. Goldstein (eds.). *Folklore. Performance and Communication*. Approaches to Semiotics 40. The Hague: Mouton. Pp. 207–254.

Doty, William G. 2000. *Mythography: The Study of Myths and Rituals*. 2nd edn. Tuscaloosa: University of Alabama Press.

Eliade, Mircea. 1964 [2004]. *Shamanism: Archaic Techniques of Ecstasy*. Princeton: Princeton University Press.

Eliade, Mircea. 1968 [1963]. *Myth and Reality*. Harper Torchbooks. New York: Harper & Row.

Eskeröd, Albert. 1947. *Årets äring: Etnologiska Studier i skördens och julens tro och sed*. Nordiska Museets Handlingar 26. Stockholm: Nordiska Museet.

Foley, John Miles. 1995. *The Singer of Tales in Performance*. Bloomington: Indiana University Press.

Frog. 2010a. *Baldr and Lemminkäinen: Approaching the Evolution of Mythological Narrative through the Activating Power of Expression: A Case Study in Germanic and Finno-Karelian Cultural Contact and Exchange*. UCL Eprints. London: University College London.

Frog. 2010b. Narratiiv kui ravi: Riituse-etendus ja narratiivi aktualiseerumine kogemusena. *Mäetagused* 45: 7–38.

Frog. 2011a. Circum-Baltic Mythology? – The Strange Case of the Theft of the Thunder-Instrument (ATU 1148b). In Vaitkevičienė & Vaitkevičius 2011: 78–98.

Frog. 2011b. Distinguishing Continuities: Textual Entities, Extra-Textual Entities and Conceptual Schemas. *RMN Newsletter* 2: 7–15.

Frog. 2011c. Ethnocultural Substratum: Its Potential as a Tool for Lateral Approaches to Tradition History. *RMN Newsletter* 3: 23–37.

Frog. 2011d. Snorri Sturluson *qua* Fulcrum: Perspectives on the Cultural Activity of Myth, Mythological Poetry and Narrative in Medieval Iceland. *Mirator* 12: 1–29.

Frog. 2012a. Confluence, Continuity and Change in the Evolution of Myth: The Case of the Finno-Karelian Sampo-Cycle. In Frog, Siikala & Stepanova 2012: 205–254.

Frog. 2012b. Evolution, Revolution and Ethnocultural Substrata: From Finno-Ugric Sky-God to the God-Smith *Ilmarinen*. In Adriaan van der Hoeven & Cornelius

Hasselblatt (eds.). *Finno-Ugric Folklore, Myth and Cultural Identity*. Studia Fenno-Ugrica Groningana 7. Maastricht: Shaker. Pp. 25–43.

Frog. 2013a. The Parallax Approach: Situating Traditions in Long-Term Perspective. In Frog & Pauliina Latvala with Helen F. Leslie (eds.). *Approaching Methodology*. 2nd rev. edn. Helsinki: Academia Scientiarum Fennica. Pp. 99–129.

Frog. 2013b. Shamans, Christians, and Things in between: From Early Germanic Contacts to the Conversion of Karelia. In Leszek Słupecki & Rudolf Simek (eds.). *Conversions: Looking for Ideological Change in the Early Middle Ages*. Studia Mediaevalia Septentrionalia 23. Vienna: Fassbaender. Pp. 53–98.

Frog. 2014a (in press). From Mythology to Identity and Imaginal Experience: An Exploratory Approach to the Symbolic Matrix in Viking Age Åland. In Joonas Ahola, Frog & Jenni Lucenius (eds.). *The Viking Age in Åland: Insights into Identity and Remnants of Culture*. Helsinki: Academia Scientiarum Fennica.

Frog. 2014b. Mytologia on katsojan silmässä: Miten myytit merkityksellistävät maailmaa. In Seppo Knuuttila & Ulla Piela (eds.). *Ympäristömytologia*. Kalevalaseuran vuosikirja 93. Helsinki: Suomalainen Kirjallisuuden Seura. Pp. 59–73.

Frog, Anna-Leena Siikala & Eila Stepanova. 2012. *Mythic Discourses: Studies in Uralic Traditions*. Studia Fennica Folkloristica 20. Helsinki: Finnish Literature Society.

Gills, John R. 1996. *A World of Their Own Making: Myth, Ritual, and the Quest for Family Values*. Cambridge: Harvard University Press.

Goodman, Lenn E. 1993. Mythic Discourse. In Shlomo Biderman & Ben-Ami Scharfstein (eds.). *Myths and Fictions*. Leiden: Brill. Pp. 51–112.

Gräslund, Anne-Sofie. 2001. *Ideologi och mentalitet: Om religionsskiftet i Skandinavien från en arkeologisk horisont*. Occasional Papers in Archaeology 29. Uppsala: University of Uppsala.

Haaland, Randi. 2004. Technology, Transformation and Symbolism: Ethnographic Perspectives on European Iron Working. *Norwegian Archaeological Review* 37(1): 1–19.

Haavio, Martti. 1952. *Väinämöinen: Eternal Sage*. FF Communications 144. Helsinki: Academia Scientiarum Fennica.

Haavio, Martti. 1967. *Suomalainen mytologia*. Porvoo: Werner Söderström.

Hakamies, Pekka. 1999. Ilmarinen ja kansanomaiset teknoutopiat. In *Kalevalan hyvät ja hävyttömät*. Ed. Ulla Piela, Seppo Knuuttila & Tarja Kupiainen. Helsinki: Suomaliasien Kirjallisuuden Seura. Pp. 79–92.

Hakamies, Pekka. 2012. Ilmarinen and Popular Techno-Utopian Conceptions. In Frog, Siikala & Stepanova 2012: 188–204.

Harva, Uno. 1922. *Der Baum des Lebens*. Helsinki: Suomalainen Tiedeakatemia.

Harva, Uno. 1943. *Sammon ryöstö*. Porvoo: Werner Söderström.

Harva, Uno. 1948. *Suomalaisten muinaisusko*. Porvoo: WSOY.

Harvilahti, Lauri. 2003. *The Holy Mountain: Studies on Upper Altay Oral Poetry*. FF Communications 282. Helsinki: Academia Scientiarum Fennica.

Harvilahti, Lauri. 2009. Keskiaikaiset eepokset ja niiden suullinen perusta. In Marko Lamberg, Anu Lahtinen & Susanna Niiranen (eds.). *Keskiajan avain*. Helsinki: Suomalaisen Kirjallisuuden Seura.

Hautala, Jouko. 1968. *Finnish Folklore Research 1828–1918*. The History of Learning and Science in Finland 1828–1918 12. Helsinki: Tilgmann.

Helimski, Eugene. 2006. The "Northwestern" Group of Finno-Ugric Languages and Its Heritage in Place Names and Substratum Vocabulary of the Russian North. *Slavica Helsingiensia* 27: 109–127.

Hofstra, Tette. 1985. *Ostseefinnisch und Germanisch: Frühe Lehnbeziehungen im nördlichen Ostseeraum im Lichte der Forschung seit 1961*. Groningen: Hofstra.

Holmberg [Harva], Uno. 1927. *Finno-Ugric, Siberian*. The Mythology of All Races 4. Boston: Marshall Jones.

Honko, Lauri. 1959a. *Krankheitsprojektile: Untersuchung über eine urtümliche Krankheitserklärung.* FF Communications 178. Helsinki: Suomalainen Tiedeakatemia.

Honko, Lauri. 1981a. Four Forms of Adaptation of Tradition. In Lauri Honko & Vilmos Voigt (eds.). *Adaptation, Change, and Decline in Oral Literature.* Studia Fennica 26. Helsinki: Suomalaisen Kirjallisuuden Seura. Pp.19–33.

Honko, Lauri. 1981b. Traditionsekologi: En introduktion. In Lauri Honko & Orvar Löfgren (eds.). *Tradition och miljö: Ett kulturekologiskt perspektiv.* NIF Publications 11. Lund: Liber Läromedel. Pp. 9–63.

Honko, Lauri. 1985. Rethinking Tradition Ecology. *Temenos: Studies in Comparative Religion* 21: 55–82.

Honko, Lauri. 1989. Folkloristic Theories of Genre. *Studia Fennica* 33: 13–28.

Honko, Lauri. 2000. Thick Corpus and Organic Variation: An Introduction. In Lauri Honko (ed.). *Thick Corpus, Organic Variation and Textuality in Oral Tradition.* Studia Fennica Folkloristica 7. Helsinki: Finnish Literature Society. Pp. 3–28.

Hoppál, Mihály. 1999 [2007]. Shamanism and the Belief System of the Ancient Hungarians. In *Shamans and Traditions.* Bibliotheca Shamanistica 13. Budapest: Akadémiai Kiadó.

Hoppál, Mihály. 2010. *Uralic Mythologies and Shamans.* Budapest: Hungarian Academy of Sciences.

Hultkrantz, Åke. 1973. A Definition of Shamanism. *Temnos: Studies in Comparative Religion* 9: 25–37.

Hultkrantz, Åke. 1996. A New Look at the World Pillar in Arctic and Sub-Arctic Religions. In J. Pentikäinen (ed.). *Shamanism and Northern Ecology.* Berlin: Mouton de Gruyter. Pp. 31–49.

Hultkrantz, Åke. 2001. Shamanism: Some Recent Findings from a Comparative Perspective. In Juha Pentkäinen, Hanna Sarresalo & Chuner M. Taksami. (eds.). *Shamanhood. Symbolism and Epic.* Budapest: Akadémiai Kiadó. Pp. 1–9.

Jewett, Robert, & John Shelton Lawrence. 1977. *The American Monomyth.* Gardon City: Anchor–Doubleday.

Kamppinen, Matti. 1989. *Cognitive Systems and Cultural Models of Illness: A Study of Two Mestizo Peasant Communities of the Peruvian Amazon.* FF Communications 244. Helsinki; Academia Scientiarum Fennica.

Kirkinen, Heikki. 1970. *Karjala idän ja lännen välissä I: Venäjän Karjala renessanssiajalla (1478-1617).* Helsinki: Kirjayhtymä.

Konkka & Konkka 1980 = Конкка, У. С., & А. П. Конкка (eds.). 1980. *Духовная культура сегозерских карел конца XIX – начала XX в*, Ленинград: "Наука".

Krohn, Kaarle. 1924. *Magische Ursprungsrunen der Finnen.* Trans. Arno Bussenius. FF Communications 52. Helsinki: Academia Scientiarum Fennica.

Krohn, Kaarle. 1926. *Die folkloristische Arbeitsmethode: Begründet von Julius Krohn und weitergeführt von nordischen Forschern.* Oslo: Aschehoug

Krohn, Kaarle. 1932. *Zur finnischen Mythologie.* FF Communications 104. Helsinki: Academia Scientiarum Fennica.

Kuusi, Matti. 1949 *Sampo-eepos: Typologinen analyysi.* Suomalais-Ugrilaisen Seuran Tutkimuksia 96. Helsinki: Suomalais-Ugrilainen Seura.

Kuusi, Matti. 1963. Varhaiskalevalainen Runous. In Matti Kuusi (ed.). *Suomen Kirjallisuus* I. Helsinki: Suomalaisen Kirjallisuuden Seura. Pp. 129–215.

Kuusi, Matti. 1994a. Questions of Kalevala Meter: What exactly did Kalevala Language Signify to Its Users? In A.-L. Siikala & S. Vakimo (eds.). *Songs Beyond the Kalevala: Transformations of Oral Poetry.* Helsinki: Suomalaisen Kirjallisuuden Seura. Pp. 41–55.

Kuusi, Matti 1994b. The Sampo: Farewell Lecture at the University of Helsinki. In Matti Kuusi. *Mind and Form in Folklore: Selected Articles.* Helsinki: Suomalaisen Kirjallisuuden Seura. Pp. 53–65.

Kuusi, Matti, Keith Bosley & Michael Branch (eds. & trans.). 1977. *Finnish Folk Poetry - Epic: An Anthology in Finnish and English*. Helsinki: Finnish Literature Society.
Laakso, Johanna. 1999. Vielä kerran itämerensuomen vanhimmista muistomerkeistä. *Virittäjä* 1999(4): 531–555.
Lahelma, Antti. 2008. *A Touch of Red: Archaeological and Ethnographic Approaches to Interpreting Finnish Rock Paintings*. Iskos 15. Helsinki: Finnish Antiquarian Society.
Lahelma, Antti 2010. Äänisen kalliopiirrokset ja kalevalamittainen runous. In Seppo Knuuttila, Ulla Piela & Lotte Tarkka. *Kalevalamittaisen runon tulkintoja*. Kalevalaseuran vuosikirja 89. Helsinki: Suomalaisen Kirjallisuuden Seura. Pp. 135–153.
Lakoff, George, & Mark Turner. 1989. *More than Cool Reason: A Field Guide to Poetic Metaphor*. Chicago: Chicago University Press.
Laurinkienė, Nijolė 2008. La imagen del cielo y los motivos de la creación del Sol en la mitología báltica. *Culturas Populares* 6: 1–10.
Lévi-Strauss, Claude. 1962. *Le totemisme aujourd'hui*. Paris: PUF.
Lid, Nils. 1949. Kalevalan Pohjola. *Kalevalaseuran vuosikirja* 29: 104–120.
Lindqvist, Sune. 1945–1946. Muinaisruotsalaisia Kalevalakuvia. *Kalevalaseuran vuosikirja* 25–26: 152–163.
Lotman, Iu. M., & B. A. Uspenskii 1976. Myth - Name - Culture. In Henryk Baran (ed.). *Semiotics and Structuralism: Readings from the Soviet Union*. White Planes: International Arts and Sciences Press. Pp. 3–32.
Meletinskij, Eleazar Moiseevich. 1997. *Das paläoasiatische mythologische Epos: Der Zyklus des Raben*. Ethnologische Beiträge zur Circumpolarforschung 2. Berlin: Reinhold Schletzer.
Mullonen 2001 = Муллонен И. И. 2001. История Сегозерья в географических названиях. In В. П. Орфинский (ed.). *Деревня Юккогуба и ее окресности*. Петрозаводск: "Издательство Петрозаводского государственного университета". Pp. 11–35.
Napolskikh, Vladimir. 1989. The Diving-Bird Myth in Northern Eurasia. In Mihály Hoppál & Juha Pentikäinen (eds.). *Uralic Mythology and Folklore*. Ethnologica Uralica 1. Helsinki: Finnish Literature Society. Pp. 105–113.
Napolskikh, Vladimir. 1992. Proto-Uralic World Picture: A Reconstruction. In J. Pentikäinen (ed.). *Shamanism and Northern Ecology*. Berlin: Mouton de Gruyter. Pp. 3–20.
Napolskikh, Vladimir. 2012. The Earth-Diver Myth (A812) in Northern Eurasia and North America. Twenty Years Later. In Frog, Siikala & Stepanova 2012: 120–140.
Nordberg, Andreas. 2012. Continuity, Change and Regional Variation in Old Norse Religion. In Catherina Raudvere & Jens Peter Schjødt (eds.). *More than Mythology: Narratives, Ritual Practices and Regional Distribution in Pre-Christian Scandinavian Religions*. Lund: Nordic Academic Press. Pp. 119–151.
OED - Oxford English Dictionary I–XX. 2nd edn. Oxford: Clarendon Press, 1989.
Pentikäinen, Juha. 1978. *Oral Repertoire and World View: An Anthropological Study of Marina Takalo's Life History*. FF Communications 219. Helsinki: Suomalainen Tiedeakatemia.
Pöllä, Matti. 1999. Migration from Finland to Viena Karelia in 1600–1720 and Preservation of the *Kalevala* Poetry. *Journal de la Société Finno-Ougrienne* 88: 161–172.
Power, Rosemary. 1985. Journeys to the Otherworld in the Icelandic *Fornaldarsögur*. *Folklore* 96(2): 156–175.
Price, Neil. 2012. Mythic Acts: Material Narratives of the Dead in Viking Age Scandinavia. In Catherina Raudvere & Jens Peter Schjødt (eds.). *More than Mythology: Narratives, Ritual Practices and Regional Distribution in Pre-Christian Scandinavian Religions*. Lund: Nordic Academic Press. Pp. 13–46.

Rahkonen, Pauli. 2011. Finno-Ugrian Hydronyms of the River Volkhov and Luga Catchment Areas. *Journal de la Société Finno-Ougrienne* 93: 205–266.

Rédei, Károly, *et al.* 1986–1988. *Uralisches etymologisches Wörterbuch* I–II. Wiesbaden: Harrassowitz.

Rydving, Håkon. 2010. *Tracing Sami Traditions: In Search of the Indigenous Religion among the Western Sami during the 17th and 18th Centuries.* Oslo: Institute for Comparative Research in Human Culture.

Saarikivi, Janne. 2000. Kontaktilähtöinen kielenmuutos, substraatti ja substraattinimistö. *Virittäjä* 104: 393–415.

Saarikivi, Janne. 2004a. Is There Palaeo-European Substratum Interference in Western Branches of Uralic? *Journal de la Société Finno-Ougrienne* 90: 187–214.

Saarikivi, Janne. 2004b. Über die saamischen Substratennamen des Nordrusslands und Finnlands. *Finnisch-Ugrische Forschungen* 58: 162–234.

Saarikivi, Janne. 2006. *Substrata Uralica: Studies on Finno-Ugric Substratein Northern Russian Dialects.* Tartu: Tartu University Press.

Saarikivi, Janne. 2007. Finnic Personal Names on Novgorod Birch Bark Documents. *Slavica Helsingiensia* 32: 196–246.

Salo, Unto. 1992. Raudan synty. *Sananjalka* 34: 103–122.

Salo, Unto. 2004. Suomen ja Hämeen synty. *Suomen Museo* 2003: 5–58.

Salo, Unto. 2006. *Ukko: The God of Thunder of the Ancient Finns and His Indo-European Family.* Washington D.C.: Institute for the Study of Man.

Salo, Unto. 2010. Raudan synty. In Seppo Knuuttila, Ulla Piela & Lotte Tarkka (eds.). *Kalevalamittaisen runon tulkintoja.* Kalevalaseuran vuosikirja 89. Helsinki: Suomalaisen Kirjallisuuden Seura. Pp. 114–131.

Sarmela, Matti. 1994. *Suomen kansankulttuurin kartasto II: Suomen perinneatlas – Atlas of Finnish Ethnic Culture II: Folklore.* Helsinki: Suomalaisen Kirjallisuuden Seura.

Schjødt, Jens Peter. 2009. Diversity and Its Consequences for the Study of Old Norse Religion: What Is It We Are Trying to Reconstruct?. In L. P. Słupecki & J. Morawiec (eds.). *Between Paganism and Christianity in the North.* Rzeszów: Wydawnictwo Uniwersytetu Rzeszowskiego. Pp. 9–22.

Schjødt, Jens Peter. 2013. The Notions of Model, Discourse, and Semantic Center as Tools for the (Re)Construction of Old Norse Religion. *RMN Newsletter* 6: 6–15.

Setälä, E. N. 1932. *Sammon arvoitus.* Helsinki: Otava.

Siikala, Anna-Leena. 1978. *The Rite Technique of the Siberian Shaman.* FF Communications 220. Helsinki: Academia Scientiarum Fennica.

Siikala, Anna-Leena. 1992. *Suomalainen Šamanismi: Mielikuvien Historiaa.* Suomalaisen Kirjallisuuden Seuran Toimituksia 565. Helsinki: Suomalaisen Kirjallisuuden Seura.

Siikala, Anna-Leena. 2002a. *Mythic Images and Shamanism: A Perspective on Kalevala Poetry.* FF Communications 280. Helsinki: Suomalainen Tiedeakatemia.

Siikala, Anna-Leena. 2002b. The Singer Ideal and the Enrichment of Poetic Culture: Why Did the Ingredients for the *Kalevala* Come from Viena Karelia? In Lauri Honko (ed.). *The Kalevala and the World's Traditional Epics.* Studia Fennica Folkloristica 12. Helsinki: Finnish Literature Society. Pp. 26–43.

Siikala, Anna-Leena. 2002c. What Myths Tell about Past Finno-Ugric Modes of Thinking. In A.-L. Siikala (ed.). *Myths and Mentality: Studies in Folklore and Popular Thought.* Studia Fennica Folkloristica 8. Helsinki: Finnish Literature Society. Pp. 15–32.

Siikala, Anna-Leena. 2012. *Itämerensuomalisten mytologia.* Helsinki: SKS.

Stepanova, Eila. 2011. Reflections of Belief Systems in Karelian and Lithuanian Laments: Shared Systems of Traditional Referentiality? *Archaeologia Baltica* 15: 128–143.

Stepanova, Eila. 2012. Mythic Elements of Karelian Laments: The Case of *syndyzet* and *spuassuzet*. In Frog, Siikala & Stepanova 2012: 257–287.
Stepanova, Eila. 2014. *Seesjärveläisten itkijöiden rekisterit: Tutkimus äänellä itkemisen käytänteistä, teemoista ja käsitteistä*. Kultaneiro 14. Joensuu: Suomen Kansantietouden Tutkijain Seura.
von Sydow, C. W. 1948. On the Spread of Traditions. In C. W. von Sydow. *Selected Papers on Folklore Published on the Occasion of his 70th Birthday*. Copenhagen: Rosenkilde & Bagger. Pp. 11–43.
SSA = *Suomen sanojen alkuperä: Etymologinen sanakirja* I–III. Helsinki: Suomalaisen Kirjallisuuden Seura, 1992–2000.
Tarkka, Lotte 2005. *Rajarahvaan laulu: Tutkimus Vuokkiniemen kalevalamittaisesta runokulttuurista 1821–1921*. Helsinki: Suomalaisen Kirjallisuuden Seura.
Tarkka, Lotte. 2012. The Sampo: Myth and Vernacular Imagination. In Frog, Siikala & Stepanova 2012: 17–39.
Timonen, Senni. 1994. The Mary of Women's Epic. In A.-L. Siikala & S. Vakimo (eds.). *Songs Beyond the Kalevala: Transformations of Oral Poetry*. Helsinki: Suomalaisen Kirjallisuuden Seura. Pp. 301–329.
Tolley, Clive. 2009. *Shamanism in Norse Myth and Magic* I–II. FF Communications 296–297. Helsinki: Academia Scientiarum Fennica.
Tomasello, Michael. 2003. *Constructing a Language: A Usage-Based Theory of Language Acquisition*. Cambridge: Harvard University Press.
Uino, Pirjo. 1997. *Ancient Karelia: Archaeological Studies – Muinais-Karjala: Arkeologisia tutkimuksia*. Ed. Torsten Edgren. Trans. Jüri Kokkonen. Suomen Muinaismuistoyhdistyksen Aikakauskirja 104. Helsinki: Suomen Muinaismuistoyhdistys.
Vajda, Lászl6 1959. Zur phaseologischen Stellung des Schamanismus. *Ural-Altaische Jahrbücher* 31: 456–485.
Valk, Ülo. 2000. *Ex Ovo Omnia*: Where Does the Balto-Finnic Cosmogony Originate. *Oral Tradition* 15(1): 145–158.
de Vries, Jan. 1967 [1977]. *Perspectives in the History of Religions*. Trans. Kees W. Bolle. Berkeley: University of California Press.
Wessman, Anna. 2009. Levänluhta: A Place of Punishment, Sacrifice or Just a Common Cemetery? *Fennoscandia Archaeologica* 26: 81–105.
Wessman, Anna. 2010. *Death, Destruction and Commemoration: Tracing Ritual Activities in Finnish Late Iron Age Cemeteries (AD 550–1150)*. Iskos 18. Helsinki: Finnish Antiquarian Society.
Wickholm, Anna. 2006. "Stay Where You Have Been Put!" – The Use of Spears as Coffin Nails in Late Iron Age Finland. In H. Valk (ed.). *Ethnicity and Culture: Studies in Honour of Silvia Laul*. Muinasaja Teadus 18. Tartu. Pp. 193–207.
Wickholm, Anna. 2008. Reuse in Finnish Cremation Cemeteries under Level Ground: Examples of Collective Memory. In Fredrik Fahlander & Terje Oestigaard (eds.). *The Materiality of Death*. Oxford: Archaeopress. Pp. 89–97.
Witzel, E. J. Michael. 2012. *The Origins of the World's Mythologies*. Oxford: Oxford University Press.
Wright, Robin M. 1998. *Cosmos, Self, and History in Baniwa Religion: For Those Unborn*. Austin: University of Texas Press.

Afterword

Joonas Ahola, Frog & Clive Tolley

Vikings in Finland?

Closing Considerations on the Viking Age in Finland

Wrestling with the interconnection of 'Finland' and the 'Viking Age' has not afforded simple and unambiguous answers, but for many readers it may nevertheless have led to new or perhaps even unexpected insights and understandings. The many contributions to the present volume have offered numerous perspectives on a range of topics and materials. These discussions have carried readers along many roads in different directions on a journey of exploration of Finland in the Viking Age and the Viking Age in Finland. Although the volume is now coming to a close, this has been just a single step on that journey, which is far from over. Here, in these final pages, we will take a brief look back at the roads just travelled, considering some of the links between them, and also consider the roads that lie ahead, with thoughts on what can be built on this foundation and what can be done to explore beyond it. This discussion has no pretence of being exhaustive. It is instead developed by bringing forward a few thematic threads that run through the volume that can be considered key issues when addressing the Viking Age in Finland. The purpose of this closing chapter is not to review the preceding discussions but rather to highlight and discuss some of the central topics that unite them, as well as to draw attention to a few points that have remained beyond their scope or for which they may provide the foundations in future research.

Fundamental Terms and Definitions

The most fundamental requirement for discussing history is having a language to talk about it. In other words, it is necessary to have sets of relevant terms and mutual understandings of what those terms mean and how they are used. Such terminology is particularly important for working across disciplines for which the frames of reference may vary considerably.

Choices in terminology become complicated by the fact that every term is entangled with its history of uses. For example, the term 'Finland' cannot be separated from discourses of nationalism and nationhood, which has at times been quite heated. Similarly, the period that is here generally referred to as the Viking Age has been politically charged in Finland since the nineteenth century, especially in connection to the construction of Finnishness and a Finnish nation on the one hand (Ahola & Frog), and with the question of Swedish language and the historical identity of the Swedish-speaking population of Finland on the other (Aalto). This period became linked to right-wing nationalist ideologies that in many respects reached a watershed in Europe during World War II. These struggles in identity politics are in numerous ways at the root of images of 'Vikings' and imaginings of the 'Viking Age' in Finland today (Raninen & Wessman). The terms 'Finland' and 'Viking Age' are thus socially and politically charged no less than their referents. On the other hand, avoiding these terms would be no less marked as a choice and does not resolve the problems so much as produce new terms with different markedness.

A key function of terms is to open a recognizable frame of reference. In one respect, talking about 'Finland' in *c.* AD 1000 is almost nonsensical: Finland is a modern, historically constructed geographical and political space (cf. Kuusela; Tolley); in that respect, there was nothing comparable to it 1000 years ago. Geographical and political spaces would have been regarded quite differently at that time, presumably with a number of 'lands' of varying scope recognized by different populations. However, alternative convenient and recognizable ways of referring to these are lacking. We do not know the vernacular terms of that era and a hypothetically reconstructed place name for 'Finland' (as in Salo 2000) might be interesting as a novelty, but would not itself open a recognizable frame of reference for discussion (and would no doubt develop the same connotations as 'Finland': cf. Emberling 1997: 300). Archaic terms from other languages might be more familiar, but they tend to refer to more specific places that can only be loosely defined at best, or simply to describe a place according to the people who live there. For example, Old Norse *Bjarmaland* literally means 'land of the Bjarmians' and is identified with multiple locations around the White Sea (Koskela Vasaru). Terms like *Bjarmaland* or *Turjanmaa* (Ahola) also merge into imaginal topography, converging with otherworld realms of giants or the dead: names of remote places did not have the same concreteness as we ascribe to them today. Such terms may also be misleading where they correspond to modern place names, such as Old Norse *Finnland* ['Finland'], which may have referred to a localized area on the south-western tip of Finland (Finland Proper; cf. Tolley 2009 I: 40–41), *Kvenland*, which may correspond etymologically to the inland region of Kainuu but seems to have referred to coastal areas on either side of the Gulf of Bothnia (Tolley 2009 I: 41–43), and *Tafæistaland*, which corresponds to the Modern Swedish name for the district of Häme (Tavastia), although it was presumably defined according to where Tafæistians lived at that time (Schalin). It is a practical reality that our own contemporary geography and the spatial divisions familiar from it provide the most rudimentary and widely accessible frame of reference for talking about locations and cultures in history.

Contemporary geography belongs to non-specialist competence whereas the more specialized a term, the fewer the people who can use it easily and without introduction. Of course, the use of a term like 'Finland' (as with 'Denmark', 'Norway' or 'Sweden') is also prescriptive: it defines a space according to current geopolitical borders that have quite different relevance for different disciplines (AHOLA & FROG); this delineation of space also simultaneously groups different areas together that were distinct in the Viking Age while cutting apart others. This term also inevitably links to current national identities and the cultures linked to those identities with implications of reconstructing a shared history of those cultures. Thus the choice of 'Finland' here was centrally concerned with opening as accessible a frame of reference as possible which could then be negotiated. The contributions to this volume have worked quite effectively with this term as a tool for making the past accessible through a commonly recognized reference frame. Doing so has, to varying degrees, involved reconsidering and redefining 'Finland' for the Viking Age, advancing toward a better understanding of both the real and imagined relationships between cultures of that era in different territories and the cultures in Finland and Karelia today. 'Karelia' is often mentioned in these discussions and several alternative terms are introduced (Finno-Karelia, North Finnic cultural areas, etc.) in order to more explicitly flex the geographical arena under discussion. It will be interesting to see if a new, alternative and broader term for territories on this side of the Baltic Sea is developed in the future. For the present, however, 'Finland' is the only one of these terms presently widely recognized in Western scholarship (which is notably not the case for Russian scholarship). Significant change in the shared terminology of international discussions at an interdisciplinary level will likely be dependent on changes in awareness of the relationships of nations and cultures more widely today.

The term 'Viking Age' is no less problematic, and terms such as 'Late Iron Age' have been preferred in recent research (cf. HÄKKINEN; KUUSELA; RANINEN & WESSMAN). Either term functions in periodising the Iron Age (cf. LAAKSO), as have others, such as 'heathen period' (AALTO), but none of the terms are unmarked. Both the terms 'Viking Age' and 'Late Iron Age' construe a contextualizing frame for discussing material. Terms like 'Late Iron Age' are suggestive of an approach based in archaeology that characterizes broad cultural areas in relation to technologies even if, in a number of territories under discussion, Iron Age cultures remained relatively little changed until recent centuries (KORPELA). An advantage of this term is that it does not carry the baggage of controversy that has historically developed around the terms 'Viking' and 'Viking Age' (AALTO; AHOLA & FROG; RANINEN & WESSMAN). At the same time, it is also a more specialist term: it is less likely to carry much significance for non-specialists. Without introduction, non-specialists may not be certain of the precise period referred to, such as whether the 'Late Iron Age' is the same as, overlapping with, or complementary to the 'Viking Age'. Consequently, this term is also less likely to allow them to infer a context without this being introduced, for example linking the period to other contemporaneous cultures or relating it to periods that preceded and followed it. In contrast, the term 'Viking Age' belongs to non-specialist competence that readily connects and contextualizes 'Finland' among the social and historical processes that were fundamental to both the Germanic cultures and polities of Scandinavia on the one hand and to Slavic (and associated) groups in Russia on the other. More significantly, the term 'Viking Age' invites links to be made between discussions of this period in 'Finland' with debates relating to other contemporary areas. The choice of terms is, in a sense, a choice of tools, and different terms are better equipped for different aims. The choice of 'Viking Age' orients discussion toward international discussion, which has been our goal here. Like 'Finland', this term is linked to a number of discourses both historical and current today, but like 'Finland', the choice of 'Viking Age' here was centrally concerned with opening as accessible a frame of reference as possible which could then be negotiated.

Nevertheless, a key concern has been the validity of relating the 'Viking Age' to 'Finland': the periodization also ought to be depictive of culturally specific historical phases in order to be conveniently applicable for discussing threads of development within the particular sphere of culture(s). Many chapters in this collection illustrate that those factors that characterize the Viking Age in Scandinavia not only affected populations and circumstances in Finland and Karelia but in fact apply to the circumstances of North Finnic cultures (especially extended mobility, trade and settlement expansion). Consequently, there are good grounds to apply the label 'Viking Age' to the period in question in Finland. At the same time, the correlation of these phenomena in Finland and Karelia as corresponding to or equivalent to those among Germanic Scandinavian groups as well as among associated Slavic and other groups that formed the Rus' was enabled by coordinating multidisciplinary discussion in relation to the Viking Age as an international frame. These findings reciprocally offer a point of reference for considering the relevance of the Viking Age and its implications for these other cultures.

The dating of this period to AD 800–1050 can find a general correlation in the archaeological evidence as a period distinguishable within the Iron Age in Finland (Laakso), but these dates are based on events that took place in the North Atlantic, in relation to which other phenomena came to be interpreted (cf. Talvio). The determinant dates themselves lack a direct connection to events east of the Baltic Sea. The primary advantage of the Scandinavian dating of the Viking Age is that it forms a more or less uniform periodization within international research (cf. Koskela Vasaru). However, these dates prove rather narrow for the historical circumstances in Finland: some of the processes of mobility and trade seem to have been under way slightly earlier and the transition to Christianity, seen as a key cultural transition concluding the Viking Age in Scandinavia, came significantly later. The artificiality of the customary periodization is highlighted by describing the period following the Viking Age as the 'Crusade Period' (1050–1150/1300), which refers to the European crusades to Jerusalem, at a distant remove from cultures of Finland and Karelia. This term creates confusion because it becomes conflated with the crusades in the Baltic Sea region, beginning east of the Baltic Sea in *c.* 1200 and probably not first launched in Finland until 1249, nearing the end of the period in question. This perception is augmented by the fact that the Viking Age for other cultures is followed by the Christianization and medievalization, whereas these processes reached Finland and Karelia much later, only being annexed by medieval Europe as Sweden and Novgorod expanded their authority through these territories (HEININEN *ET AL.*). (AHOLA & FROG.)

The introduction to this volume discussed the relevance of the Viking Age in the periodization of the history of Finland. This was an era of social and historical developments that were impacted by Scandinavian contacts but also paralleled them (especially with regard to Scandinavian activity directed to the east) in culturally distinct ways. This does not mean that Finns and Karelians were 'Vikings' in the sense of raiders harrying the Northern Seas: there were equivalent processes observable among Finnic cultures which can be fruitfully regarded within the broader frame of corresponding processes in other cultures occurring in the same period. The term 'Viking Age' is thus adapted as a generally accessible term to refer to the period that manifested Norse 'Viking' raiders on the coasts of the British Isles but also manifested corresponding developments in other cultures for which such an accessible terminology is lacking. This approach proposed reassessing the Viking Age not as a period of the Iron Age with a universal chronology of *c.* 800–1050 but rather on a chronology calibrated to the cultural arena concerned, like the Iron Age itself. This proposal led to a calibration of the period in relation to regionally relevant dates of the founding of the trading center of Staraya Ladoga in 753 and the so-called Second Swedish Crusade in 1249, periodizing the Finnish Viking Age to *c.* 750–1250 (which can be practically distinguished as the Viking Age in Finland Proper of 750–1050 and the Later Viking Age in Finland 1050–1250 to facilitate correlation with international chronologies). This broader periodization resolves some aspects of arbitrariness in the earlier periodization scheme, even if this use of 'Viking Age' stretches it from referring to Scandinavian 'Vikings' *per se* to a broader phenomenon in north-eastern Europe that took multiple culture-specific forms of which Scandinavian Vikings were only one – and which thus requires acknowledging that the phenomenon did not necessarily take place in all of these cultures at precisely the same time. Whereas the earlier periodization had been so narrow that it was problematic for some disciplines to address, this broader model presents a more viable frame of reference for multidisciplinary discussion.[1] This broader frame could prove useful especially in research that scrutinizes areally or culturally limited phenomena that are linked to the defining factors of this period and the possibility that certain changes in some phenomena may have advanced in a series of stages across different cultural areas. Of course, periodization is an analytical construct as a research tool, and this adaptation of an existing tool to a new and more flexible application will be tested through future scholarship to determine whether it should be replaced entirely.

Ethnicities

The study of history is the study of people. Identifying who exactly is being studied is therefore crucial. This has proved a key issue in investigations of the Viking Age in Finland, especially when attempting to correlate archaeological evidence with foreign sources on the one hand and with later vernacular evidence of language and culture on the other. A number of names for different groups seem to suggest a variety of ethnic populations – *Finns*, *Lapps*, *Bjarmian*, *Kvens*, *Ves'*, etc. Linguistically based variations in toponymy support this view (Kuzmin), as do patterns in the archaeological record, such as differences in practices between presumed Finnic groups in the region of Satakunta and Finland Proper as opposed to the south and Häme (Tavastia) inland to the east (Salo 2000; cf. Talvio). However, the notion of an 'ethnos' or 'ethnicity' as a distinctive qualifier is not unproblematic. In fact, it is not always clear whether a particular category of people or culture is an 'ethnos' or perhaps something else – such as 'Viking', which today is commonly used like an ethnonym or term for an ethnic group whereas the Old Norse term *víkingr* would mean something more like 'pirate' (Ahola & Frog). The key question is: what features qualify the distinction between ethnicities? For example, Salmela focuses on genetic identities while Tolley and Kallio give attention to language; Frog highlights mythology and mythological thinking while cultural practices evinced in archaeological data are foregrounded in the contributions of Laakso and of Raninen & Wessman. As these authors note, none of these features may alone conclusively define an ethnic group, and thus research is faced with the challenge of considering these different relations. This topic is as problematic as it is central and thus warrants discussion here.

Part of the difficulty of the question is rooted in how we tend to think about ethnicity. Ethnicity is first and foremost a recognition of belongingness with one group of people as opposed to others through a shared, social identity. As observed in the introduction, different types of identities, from social roles to belongingness to an ethnic group, become socially associated with a constellation of features that are seen as belonging together, characterizing one role or group as opposed to others. The features forming such constellations may include, for example, linguistic features, clothing and appearance, body language and behaviours, and any number of traditions. It is widespread throughout the world to correlate this belongingness with some type of kinship relation. We perceive this kinship today through the lens of modern science and thus conceptualize it in terms of genetics, but as Frog points out, the word *nation* etymologically implies an ideology of a common birth. However, this sense of identity is not dependent on genes: the Finns in western Finland are genetically closer to Swedes than to Finns in eastern Finland (Salmela), yet they speak the same language and would hardly be defined as representatives of different ethnic groups. Ethnic identification is a social phenomenon, and thus even where it is viewed as inherited through kinship, the relevant genealogy may be socially constructed or simply inferred without a genetic link *per se*.

The formation of ethnic identities in social interaction essentially means that ethnicities become rooted as individual conceptions about social groups on a larger scope. These conceptions are seldom formed on the basis of any single marker and, today, as undoubtedly in prehistory, an individual may conceive himself as belonging to several social groups simultaneously. This means that the practitioners of a similar livelihood, for example trade, may have identified themselves similarly and expressed this identity by external markers such as clothing even if their mother-tongue was different and they represented distinct kin-groups. (AHOLA & FROG.) In a transitional era characterized by mobility such as the Viking Age, ethnicities may have been continuously negotiated and therefore difficult if not impossible to fully differentiate on the basis of the evidence that has been preserved. This holds true not only of the dynamics between an 'ethnos' of Viking Age Finland that is marked by permanent settlements and cemeteries and an 'ethnos' that occupied the inland areas and lived predominantly on hunting, fishing and gathering. The same holds equally true of the diversity and dynamics *within* and *across* these groups. The groups speaking Finnic languages may appear relatively uniform at the level of material culture in the archaeological record. These groups may have shared certain features linked to common cultural practices related to, for example, agriculture, whereas they could have distinguished themselves from each other quite sharply in other areas for which evidence is lacking, such as clothing, wedding rituals and the gods they addressed. This problem becomes still greater with hunter-gatherers for whom archaeological evidence is more limited – groups which may have been startlingly diverse yet tend all to simply be jumbled together under the label of 'Sámi'.

Ethnicity is commonly linked with language. Within a group, this tends to follow Eduard Sapir's (1986: 16) adage that "'He talks like us' is equivalent to saying 'He is one of us'." When considering individuals outside of the group, there is frequently an observable correlation between the designation for ethnic group and the language that they speak, or '*He talks like them* is equivalent to saying *He is one of them*' – i.e. *Swedish people speak Swedish.* This is important to bear in mind because it can significantly affect how we think and talk about cultures in earlier periods. We designate historical populations and groups with terms that correlate with an ethnic identity often bound up with the language that we presume those people spoke (e.g. 'Finnic'). Moreover, there is a longstanding inclination to imagine these historical cultures through the cultures that are familiar and recognizable today. JARI-MATTI KUUSELA has stressed that in Finnish archaeology this pattern of thinking has led to a polarized dualism – cultures are either Sámi or Finnic – and suggests that it would be best to avoid the use of ethnic terms entirely. When addressing archaeological cultures, we nevertheless tend to presume that its members were characterized by a single language even if we acknowledge uncertainty about which language this was. However, the relationship between language, culture and ethnic identity is not so simple. Correlating any one feature with a particular ethnos, be it a language or making a particular type of ceramics, reduces the constellation of features that socially characterizes the particular ethnos to a metonym – one trait characterizing the whole. However, the same type of pottery may be made in speech communities with different languages and the same language may be spoken by groups making different types of pottery. Archaeology has given extensive attention to considering the potential of different artefacts and practices to be emblematic of certain social identities as opposed to others. The challenge is that, from the constellation of features linked to an ethnic identity, certain sets of features become observable through their outcomes in the archaeological record while others become observable through linguistic and folkloric data (see Ahola & Frog). Works in the present volume introduce these issues, but their advancement through future research will depend on finding ways to correlate these categories of data. Methodologically, this will very likely not be something that can be done directly, but rather through advancing perspectives on potential links between language and archaeological cultures, for example through toponymy, then considering whether, where and to what degree correlations can be made across such diverse data, and thereby only gradually advancing toward a more dynamic (although most probably still very abstract) idea of some of the key features that different ethnic groups perceived as differentiating themselves from one another in different centuries (see Saarikivi & Lavento 2012).

Settlements, Contacts and Migration

Closely linked with the problems of addressing ethnicities are questions of understanding settlements, contacts and migration in Finland and Karelia during the Viking Age. In a sense, perspectives on these topics are complementary to perspectives on ethnicities: rather than 'who' the people were, these are questions of 'where' they were, how groups were connected to one another and when and why they moved. The questions are inevitably connected with 'culture', even if no attempt is made to say anything about that culture *per se*.

The problem of settlements has primarily been a central concern of archaeology. When a 'settlement map' of Finland is found in books discussing the Viking Age, this in fact primarily represents a distribution of cemeteries rather than evidence of buildings or other structures: cemeteries and settlements are simply inferred to have more or less the same distribution. Laakso highlights the problematics of this with an example of a relatively recent discovery of an area of settlement where, quite simply, no-one had looked before – and suddenly an uninhabited area of the map became inhabited. This method of modelling is further problematized by the fact that not all funerary practices produce cemeteries or monuments. Palaeobotanical evidence, such as that discussed by Alenius, offers indications of regular and developing land cultivation in additional areas, which is also a relevant indicator of stable settlement (from which it may, however, be remote), yet sparser and smaller settlements may have left no clear marks of their existence in the landscape (Laakso). Another significant problem here is that the discussion of settlements often leads to an unbalanced impression: it implies an opposition between settlements as 'where people lived' as opposed to 'where people did not live'. In other words, a 'settlement map' normally gives either the impression that most of Finland and Karelia was uninhabited or it suggests a binary opposition between the marked locations where 'Finns' lived and the blank parts of the map that were wilderness areas where 'Laplanders' (if anyone) lived – areas where, owing to differing funerary practices and/or nomadic life-ways, the signs of habitation are difficult or impossible to recognize in the archaeological record (KUUSELA).

Toponymy also provides a valuable source for settlement history. This field has great potential to produce new information because it is only in recent decades that it has emerged as a concentrated area of research in Finland and Karelia (LEIVISKÄ). Place names reveal the language people spoke at the time when those names became connected to the landscape. This can produce information about where speakers of those languages lived in different times and about the language spoken by an earlier population that was displaced or assimilated at some point in history. Toponymy has therefore played a key role in developing an understanding that Sámi was widespread through Finland and Karelia before the Finno-Karelian languages became dominant (LEIVISKÄ; KUZMIN) even if the particular research may not extend to inferences about cultural practices or the distinction of ethnic identities within and across languages. Place names also reveal long-term contacts between groups or their mutual awareness, as in the case of Scandinavian place names from the Viking Age for locations in Finland (SCHALIN). Toponymy can also be used in conjunction with archaeology, not only in attempts to correlate evidence of an archaeological culture with a language group (see Saarikivi & Lavento 2012) but also using place names and associated data from local folklore to determine potential sites for investigation. Most recently, the use of toponymy resulted in the find of Finland's earliest known church in Ristimäki ['Cross Hill'] in Kaarina, Finland Proper, dated to the turn of the thirteenth century (Ruohonen 2013). Toponymy can potentially also be of value in targeting sites for the investigation of cultures that may not have had fixed settlements, such as seasonal sites used by mobile communities (Vilkuna 1971; Salo 2000: 39–44). Comparisons between this kind of toponymical and palaeobotanical evidence would make it possible to ask whether some such mobile communities may have practiced limited forms of agriculture in connection with seasonal mobility or had other impacts on the immediate ecology. This could offer more penetrating perspectives into the constellations of cultural practices in which different cultures of the period engaged.

Perhaps the greatest challenge for developing perspectives on settlements is that archaeology and toponymy by themselves offer only two-dimensional perspectives on cultures, cultural groups and their practices in different historical periods. However, these perspectives can be greatly elaborated through evidence of contacts. This is the central significance of written records relevant to the Viking Age east of the Baltic and to the north and east of the Gulf of Finland. Such sources invariably saw these areas and cultures as peripheral, and as geographically and historically remote, viewing them especially as foreign and pagan 'others'. Such sources tend to either be quite vague (e.g. Church correspondence) or to offer lively descriptions that, however, have the character of popular legends or fictionalized history, leaving their reliability open to question (Frog); yet they nevertheless offer a range of information that can be placed in dialogue with other material. As Kaisa Häkkinen emphasizes, loanword vocabulary reveals the history of language contacts (see also Tolley). Within the linguistic data, loanwords end up on a broad relative chronology, but Häkkinen illustrates how this type of information can be contextualized in relation to information from other disciplines to develop a more three-dimensional picture, even if the actual spread of such loans through the different dialects and even different languages remains obscure (cf. Kallio). Evidence of folklore reveals similar but complementary types of information also on a relative chronology but has great potential to offer insights into, for example, new images of heroic ideals (Ahola) and changes in belief systems and mythology (Frog). The key challenges with these and other types of data from later periods are correlating them with an absolute chronology and distinguishing which archaeological cultures they are potentially relevant to, and which they are not. The contributions of the present volume have illustrated the importance of coordinating information across disciplines in order to make advances in our understandings, yet the majority of the work here remains foundational. For many disciplines, the 'Viking Age' has not been a targeted period of interest (at least not for most of the last century). There now appears to be a pressing need to develop surveys of up-to-date information that will facilitate such comparisons: the correlation of relevant information across disciplines requires the availability of that knowledge to scholars of other fields.

The distinction of the Viking Age in different disciplines has repeatedly emphasized that the Viking Age must be viewed in relation to eras that precede and follow it. It has been stressed that the Viking Age was characterized by contacts and connectivity (Heininen *et al.*). Recognizing the changes in contacts is also a significant factor in the correlation of data across disciplines – most particularly for disciplines such as linguistics and folklore studies when correlating their relative chronologies with absolute chronologies. The Migration Period (AD 400–600) was similarly characterized by mobility, and interestingly seems to have happened at the same time as a general warming trend not unlike that of the Viking Age (cf. Helama). In that period, foreign influence in archeological artefacts of Finland and Karelia is mostly of Baltic origin, but this changes so that the artifacts show an intensification of connections with Sweden especially in the Viking Age (Laakso; Raninen & Wessman). There are also signs of increasing contacts between the hunter-gatherer communities and agriculturally based groups in central inland Finland during this period (Raninen & Wessman). This increase in inland interaction may be connected to outward-oriented fur trade (although cf. Kuusela). Indeed, the land route between Häme and the trade centers in Finland Proper, the so-called Ox Road (*Härkätie*), may have originated as early as the Viking Age (Talvio). Distance is always relative and dependent on perspectives as well as on the available means and possibilities for travel (Korpela). For some, the distance from central Finland to the coast may have seemed longer than for others seemed the distance from Finland overseas, far into alien lands. Finnish and Sámi influence is observable in wide areas across the Baltic Sea and in North Russia in the form of individual artifacts evidently of these origins. It remains unclear to what degree these artefacts are indicators of widely mobile individuals from Finland and Karelia or have been carried via trade (cf. Kuusela). Nevertheless, they remain of sufficient number to suggest that there were Finnic and Sámi individuals who were actively mobile during this period (Raninen & Wessman), whereas people in Åland seem to have grown rich on eastern trade and been extremely active – even spreading their cultural influence to West Uralic cultures along the Volga (Ahola & Frog; Raninen & Wessman; Talvio).

Water routes were fundamental to long-distance mobility, and their significance may have been foregrounded by changes in technologies that enabled the faster and lighter ships with more versatile sails in which the Norsemen sailed the seas (Heininen *et al.*) as well as the smaller boats developed for the inland water routes of Finland and Karelia (Raninen & Wessman). These technologies and the travel that they produced instated a new type of connectivity in contacts and interactions. Sea traffic arrived along longstanding routes via the Gulf of Finland (cf. Schalin) to Lake Ladoga, which became a central junction of water routes in all the cardinal directions, while the climatic warming trend (Helama) allowed the establishment of sailing routes around the northern coast of Norway for encounters with Finnic and Sámi groups on the shores of the White Sea (Koskela Vasaru). At the same time, inland water routes connected territories of Karelia and eastern Finland to Lake Ladoga (Korpela), others also enabled travel from the White Sea to the Gulf of Bothnia across northern Finland (Kuusela), while the lake systems and waterways were an essential factor in the contact networks and spread of inland cultural groups in southern Finland (Salo 2000). The combination of technologies and increased connectivity of water travel would likely have changed the significance of this mode of travel and how it was perceived (cf. Korpela). This mobility was linked to contacts, for which there were a variety of contact zones (Ahola & Frog). Cross-cultural contacts among Finnic, Scandinavian and Slavic groups were most probably concentrated at nexuses of trade such as Staraya Ladoga as targets of long-distance mobility. These interactions involved not only the exchange of products of material culture (Laakso; Raninen & Wessman; Talvio) and vocabulary (Häkkinen; Kallio; Tolley); they also told stories, compared heroes and learned about one another's traditions, with relevant indicators from folklore evidence that these interactions advanced toward shared symbols, frames of reference and to some degree even ideologies, which were then carried back to the respective cultural traditions (Ahola).

Trade increased mobility on a micro level, probably both by individuals travelling abroad on foreign ships (whether voluntarily or forcibly) and by groups that manned their own vessels. At the same time, mobility took place also on a macro level as settlements in southern Finland expanded towards the east and north as well as migration to the Lake Ladoga region, while Karelian culture expanded towards central Finland (Ahola & Frog; Kuusela; Kallio; Kuzmin; Leiviskä). Although it is possible to observe these networks and mobility, it remains challenging to differentiate mobility and contacts from migration. It is clear that Sámi languages and culture spread through Finland and Karelia before Finnic languages (cf. Kuzmin). There is also evidence that Germanic language groups had a significant position in coastal areas east of the Baltic before Finnic languages (Ahola & Frog; Schalin). Petri Kallio offers an overview of the diversification of Finnic languages through the Viking Age with comments on their distribution. His discussion makes it clear that Finnish and Karelian later spread significantly in order to become dominant in the territories where we know them today. Not all contacts involved a balanced exchange and synthesis: the Finno-Karelian expansion involved a displacement of fundamental aspects of Sámi culture and cultural practices (Frog). However, our understanding of *how* these processes occurred remains remarkably vague.

The increase in mobility appears to have had direct significant impact especially on those populations that practiced agriculture and dwelt in permanent settlements. Most of the territory in Finland was however populated by mobile populations, living predominantly on hunting, fishing and gathering. The limited evidence of these populations in the archaeological record coupled with the assimilation of the majority of their languages and cultures makes it impossible to assess how extensively these processes may have affected them. For example, rich loan substrates from Germanic and Finnic languages in documented Sámi languages include names for gods and vocabulary of ritual and cultural practices indicative of such impacts. Similarly, expansions of agricultural practices and fixed-settlement communities would necessarily impact the mobility of such communities and their use of resources in the landscape.

Cultural transitions did not necessitate the unanimous efforts of masses: already relatively small numbers of individuals could have been at a nexus of goods and practices and affect shifts of language and culture in local populations through their networks. Genetic affinity between populations of western Finland and Sweden (Uppsala and Västmanland) could suggest a male-dominated immigration from Sweden to Finland. Although it is impossible to conclude when this took place (Salmela), such a male population would require interactions with local populations – for brides at an absolute minimum. This sort of example raises questions about the processes behind linguistic, archaeological and folkloric data indicative of movements of culture, cultural products and language. As became clear from the discussion of ethnicities above, we presently understand enough to know that earlier ideas of the movement of culture and language by one population displacing another is horribly oversimplified. In order to move beyond this, more sensitive perspectives on the social construction of identities are needed. This requires the cooperation of a range of disciplines which can offer a spectrum of perspectives on the features characteristic of different groups as well as what happens in encounters between groups in these processes of migration and expansion.

Livelihoods, Economy, Ecology and the Environment

A significant topic that is connected to questions of both ethnicities and settlements is livelihoods – what people actually did to survive in the Viking Age. Livelihoods in the territories of Finland and Karelia tend to be approached in terms of two broad categories. This is followed by an inclination to assign them to 'Finns' and 'Sámi' in the binary construction of ethnicities for the period, which is no less of an oversimplification, as stressed above. The first category of livelihood is characterized by animal husbandry and cultivation of land and associated with fixed settlements. The second category is characterized by hunting, fishing and gathering, associated with mobile populations. In practice, all of the cultural groups in Finland and Karelia can be assumed to have maintained different types of mixed-subsistence livelihoods. These would have varied according to the locally and regionally available resources, as well as varying seasonally (RANINEN & WESSMAN). For example, seal hunting is likely to have been of significance in coastal areas (cf. KUUSELA) whereas this would simply not be possible in inland regions. Especially the border areas between zones of culture must have represented various combinations, such as seasonal farming, hunting and fishing.

Trade seems to have become increasingly important for the acquisition of necessities during the course of the Viking Age. This may be connected to the shift in emphasis of livelihoods on the coast of Gulf of Bothnia (KUUSELA). Products acquired by hunting seem to have been especially valued items of trade. Fur trading is considered to have been a characterizing factor in the Finnish Viking Age (e.g. TALVIO; LAAKSO; KORPELA). Trade and exchange is visible especially in Islamic coins (TALVIO) which begin to flow into the Baltic Sea region in conjunction with a change in Islamic regime (*c.* 750) and a new demand for furs in the south (Kovalev 2001). The Lake Ladoga area must have been important for the fur trade for all of northern Finland and Karelia (KORPELA). Trade with merchants from abroad seems to have been heavily based on silver in most regions, but the silver seems to have remained primarily local to the trading posts and with trading the intermediaries, whereas local trade remained based primarily on barter exchange (TALVIO; RANINEN & WESSMAN; HEININEN *ET AL.*). Interestingly, trade is one of the sites where there appears to have been a difference in cultural practices in probable Finnic cultures of south-western Finland. Silver trade became significant for territories of Finland Proper and Häme (not to mention the Åland Islands) and these are the territories linked to the practice of burying hoards. On the other hand, the archaeological record reveals that scales were common among the population of Satakunta just along the coast to the north and a clear indicator of trade – but if these groups bartered in silver, they do not exhibit corresponding tendencies to accumulate it or deposit it in the ground, and presumably had a correspondingly different orientation in trade. In this case, trade seems not only to have been a practice of livelihood, but how that livelihood was practiced offers relevant indicators of regional and perhaps socially recognized ethnic differences.

The environment placed conditions on livelihoods, which in turn placed conditions on settlement areas. As Denis Kuzmin points out, the toponymic data on settlement areas of Vepsians correlates with the landscapes where the form of agriculture that they practiced was viable. The cultivated area in Finland during this period seems to prove larger than has been previously thought and it seems that slash-and-burn cultivation has been conducted in areas relatively distant from settlement sites (cf. Alenius). Paleoclimatic evidence shows that in the beginning of the Viking Age, annual rainfalls were plentiful, much more so than today, whereas they decreased in the course of the Viking Age. Nevertheless, environmental conditions would still place constraints on settlement areas where these livelihoods would be practiced. This is especially important for the viability of agriculture and animal husbandry (which requires the ability to produce and prepare sufficient hay to maintain the livestock through the winter). Consequently, the degree of reliance on these livelihoods was a determinant on how far to the north settlements could advance both coastally and inland (Solantie 2005). Towards the end of the period, the progressively warmer and drier summers probably placed crops at greater risk in those areas where agriculture had been practiced for several generations (Helama), whereas the same changes in conditions may have made crops more viable farther north or in parts of the landscape that had previously been too wet. For some groups, these changes may have prompted, for instance, changes in preferred livelihoods and corresponding shifts in culture.

Livelihoods and cultural practices change through both internal innovations and external contacts. When these change, they affect perceptions of the environment. These perceptions are anthropocentric and ethnocentric. In other words, individuals perceive the world through culturally based (and culturally biased) experience: how we and others interact with the world around us, what we use in it and the relevance of different things to our lives gives meaning to things in the world and features of the environment. Where these do not have bearing on people's lives, they are not distinguished and meaningful, and to that degree remain invisible to people in that culture (Lotman 1990: 58). Consequently, different cultural groups and even different generations within a context of cultural change may perceive the same environment quite differently (Frog 2014). This process produces reflections in the lexicon. For example, Häkkinen points out that 'hops' (Fi. *humala*) seem to have remained undistinguished – hops were not differentiated from weeds – until the Viking Age, when they became valued for their use in making beer. The known settlement sites that were founded in central Finland during the Viking Age are centered along water routes, and especially at junctions in lake systems, as though to ensure accessibility to as wide a range of wilderness areas as possible (Raninen & Wessman). This settlement pattern itself implies that waterways were not only important for the livelihoods of these cultural groups but also that they came to be perceived as meaningful to those groups precisely in relation to this connectivity (and potentially to the control of connectivity in the area). This process would have extended to all areas of the environment, and to the symbolic significance and associations of everything in it – such as the meaningfulness and power of thunder, the way of thinking about the sky, the source of fish or wild game in the forest, and so forth (Frog). Thus later folklore suggests that North Finnic groups conceptualized the forest as clearly separate from space inhabited by 'humans' and that they correlated the forest symbolically with a mythic otherworld such as the realm of the dead (Frog 2014; Anttonen 2011: 159–169; Tarkka 2013: 327–382). Consequently, cultural practices and settlements are not simply conditioned by the environment, they also construct the perception of that environment for the members of the society.

From Culture to Its Constellation of Features

No doubt a multitude of distinct ethnic groups peopled the various parts of Finland and Karelia during the Viking Age. Each of these would probably qualify as a distinct ethnos, and perhaps networks of such ethnic groups saw themselves as belonging to a broader ethnic category – being more like one another than like others – in an identity possibly linked to language. Each of these was certainly characterized by particular constellations of features that made them both distinct and distinguishable. The preceding discussion has addressed this only in the broadest terms of ethnic identities and ways of life. However, it is also possible to turn more concentrated attention to specific factors or aspects of culture, which are sites that will require more concentrated attention to fill out our images of cultures and cultural changes during this period.

The range of features that might be taken into consideration is quite broad. Boat-building technologies, for example, were of fundamental importance to enabling the mobility and connectivity characterizing the Viking Age. Technologies are also key factors for certain livelihoods. For example, it has been suggested that the development of agriculture as a significant element in livelihoods in the environment of Finland was dependent on iron-working technologies (Solantie 2005: 37), which would also mean that adopting the relevant practice of agriculture would become dependent on adopting the relevant technologies, learning about how they work and what to do with them. The development and integration of these techniques took place both locally, as inventions responding to immediate needs, and especially as borrowings in intercultural interaction that intensified remarkably during the Viking Age. Religion is another site of culture that belongs to the constellation of features characterizing different ethnic groups, with its different sides of ritual practice and mythological modelling. These clearly adapted and changed across the Viking Age. This is most apparent in the arrival of Christian-based practices, but also in the probable spread of vernacular religion from western Finland to Karelia (Frog; Uino 1997: 174–179). No doubt indications of relationships between epic traditions of Germanic, Slavic and North Finnic groups (Ahola) had parallels in stories of gods and understandings of mythic worlds, although there is far less evidence of these traditions for comparison. Such considerations extend into other areas of cultural practices such as cultural aesthetics and different arts of expression such as in oral poetics and visual representations in iconography. The diversity of fields of culture each warrant concentrated attention as well as their particular features that can be elements within and across the constellations that characterized distinct ethnic identities. Trade-centered interactions and alliances resulted in the exchange of more than just artifacts, fashion, narratives and technologies. These interactions constructed the meaningfulness and associations of these individual features (Ahola & Frog) and also altered the conception of the surrounding world as well as an individual's possibilities to function in it (Heininen *et al.*; Korpela). Developing a valid image of the changing general world-views of the ethnic groups inhabiting the Viking Age requires an interdisciplinary approach that addresses questions connected to developments occurring in this period in different fields such as material culture, language and aesthetics in its many expressive forms.

The Viking Age was a significant period within Finnish history at the threshold of so-called prehistory and history (as the era when written evidence begins). It was a period of transition in many ways, marking the history that followed as becomes observable in retrospect even if its significance and future consequences could not even be imagined at that time. Moreover, it was during the Viking Age that key cultural areas of Finland, and partially also of adjacent areas, evolved. These cultural areas have, for example, affected how political borders have been drawn in the following centuries. It is the comprehensive image of the Viking Age in Finland that enables positioning the territory and cultures of Finland and adjacent areas within the picture of Europe in this period and may contribute to its understanding. As the preceding chapters of this volume have made clear, the Viking Age stands out as a pivotal era of transition in the history of Finland and Karelia.

Notes

1 Cf. Ahola; cf. also the absolute chronology of language development of Schalin.

References

Anttonen, Veikko. 2011. *Uskontotieteen maastot ja kartat*. Tietolipas 232. Helsinki: Suomalaisen Kirjallisuuden Seura.

Emberling, Geoff. 1997. Ethnicity in Complex Cocieties: Archaeological Perspectives. *Journal of Archaeological Research* 5(4): 295–344.

Frog. 2014 (in press). Mytologia on katsojan silmässä: Miten myytit merkityksellistävät maailmaa. In Seppo Knuuttila & Ulla Piela (eds.). *Ympäristömytologia*. Kalevalaseuran vuosikirja 93. Helsinki: Suomalainen Kirjallisuuden Seura. Pp. 59–73.

Kovalev, R. K. 2001. The Infrastructure of the Northern Part of the 'Fur Road': Between the Middle Volga and the East during the Middle Ages. *Archivum Eurasiae Medii Aevii* 11: 25–64.

Lotman, Yuri M. 1990. *Universe of the Mind: A Semiotic Theory of Culture*. Trans. Ann Shukman. Bloomington: Indiana University Press.

Ruohonen, J. 2013. Kirkollisen kulttuurin alkulähteillä: Kaarinan Ravattulan varhaiskeskiaikainen kirkko ja kirkkomaa. *Historiallinen Aikakauskirja* 2013(4): 433–440.

Saarikivi, Janne, & Mika Lavento. 2012. Linguistics and Archaeology: A Critical View of an Interdisciplinary Approach with Reference to the Prehistory of Northern Scandinavia. In C. Damm & J. Saarikivi (eds.). *Networks, Interaction and Emerging Identities in Fennoscandia and Beyond: Papers from the Conference Held in Tromsø, Norway, October 13–16 2009*. Helsinki: Suomalais-Ugrilainen Seura. Pp. 177–239.

Salo, Unto. 2000. Suomi ja Häme, Häme ja Satakunta. In Jukka Peltovirta (ed.). *Hämeen käräjät I*. Hämeenlinna: Hämeen heimoliitto. Pp. 18–231.

Sapir, Eduard. 1986. *Selected Writings in Language, Culture, and Personality*. Berkeley: University of California Press.

Solantie, Reijo. 2005. Aspects of Some Prehistoric Cultures in Relation to Climate in Southwestern Finland. *Fennoscandia Archaeologica* 22: 28–42.

Tarkka, Lotte. 2013. *Songs of the Border People: Genre, Reflexivity, and Performance in Karelian Oral Poetry*. FF Communications 305. Helsinki: Academia Scientiarum Fennica.

Tolley, Clive. 2009. *Shamanism in Norse Myth and Magic* I–II. FF Communications 296–297. Helsinki: Academia Scientiarum Fennica.

Uino, Pirjo. 1997. *Ancient Karelia: Archaeological Studies*. Suomen muinaismuistoyhdistyksen aikakauskirja 104. Helsinki: Suomen Muinaismuistoyhdistys.

Vilkuna, Kustaa 1971. Mikä oli lapinkylä ja sen funktio. *Kalevalaseuran vuosikirja* 51: 194–230.

List of Contributors

Sirpa Aalto, University of Oulu

Joonas Ahola, University of Helsinki

Teija Alenius, University of Helsinki

Frog, University of Helsinki

Kaisa Häkkinen, University of Turku

Lassi Heininen, University of Lapland

Samuli Helama, Finnish Forest Research Institute

Petri Kallio, University of Helsinki

Jukka Korpela, University of Eastern Finland

Mervi Koskela Vasaru, University of Oulu

Jari-Matti Kuusela, University of Oulu

Denis Kuzmin, University of Helsinki

Ville Laakso, University of Turku

Matti Leiviskä, University of Oulu

Sami Raninen, University of Turku and the Pirkanmaa Provincial Museum

Elina Salmela, University of Helsinki

Johan Schalin, University of Helsinki

Tuukka Talvio, The National Museum of Finland

Clive Tolley, University of Turku

Anna Wessman, University of Helsinki

Abstract

The chapters of *Fibula, Fabula, Fact – The Viking Age in Finland* are intended to provide essential foundations for approaching the important topic of the Viking Age in Finland. These chapters are oriented to provide introductions to the sources, methods and perspectives of diverse disciplines in a way that is accessible to specialists from other fields, specialists from outside Finland, and also to non-specialist readers and students who may be more generally interested in the topic. Rather than detailed case studies, the contributors have sought to negotiate definitions of the Viking Age as a historical period in the cultural areas associated with modern-day Finland, and in areas associated with Finns, Karelians and other North Finnic linguistic-cultural groups more generally. Within the incredible diversity of data and disciplines represented here, the Viking Age tends to be distinguished by differentiating it from earlier and later periods, while the geographical space is quite fluidly defined for this era, which was long before the construction of modern nations with their fenced and guarded borders. Most significantly, the contributions lay emphasis on contextualizing the Viking Age within the complexities of defining cultural identities in the past through traces of cultural, linguistic or genetic features.

The volume opens with a general introduction to the topic that is intended to provide a frame of reference for discussion, paralleled by a closing afterward. The following chapters are organized according to three thematic sections which reflect the three aspects of any discussion of the Viking Age in Finland: *Time*, *Space*, and *People* – because any discussion of the 'Viking Age' in 'Finland' is necessarily concerned with individuals, societies and cultures.

Index of Cross-References between Chapters

Index of Personal Names

Index of Place Names

General Index

Studia Fennica Ethnologica

Memories of My Town
The Identities of Town Dwellers and Their Places in Three Finnish Towns
Edited by Anna-Maria Åström, Pirjo Korkiakangas & Pia Olsson
Studia Fennica Ethnologica 8
2004

Passages Westward
Edited by Maria Lähteenmäki & Hanna Snellman
Studia Fennica Ethnologica 9
2006

Defining Self
Essays on emergent identities in Russia Seventeenth to Nineteenth Centuries
Edited by Michael Branch
Studia Fennica Ethnologica 10
2009

Touching Things
Ethnological Aspects of Modern Material Culture
Edited by Pirjo Korkiakangas, Tiina-Riitta Lappi & Heli Niskanen
Studia Fennica Ethnologica 11
2008

Gendered Rural Spaces
Edited by Pia Olsson & Helena Ruotsala
Studia Fennica Ethnologica 12
2009

Laura Stark
The Limits of Patriarchy
How Female Networks of Pilfering and Gossip Sparked the First Debates on Rural Gender Rights in the 19th-century Finnish-Language Press
Studia Fennica Ethnologica 13
2011

Where is the Field?
The Experience of Migration Viewed through the Prism of Ethnographic Fieldwork
Edited by Laura Hirvi & Hanna Snellman
Studia Fennica Ethnologica 14
2012

Laura Hirvi
Identities in Practice
A Trans-Atlantic Ethnography of Sikh Immigrants in Finland and in California
Studia Fennica Ethnologica 15
2013

Eerika Koskinen-Koivisto
Her Own Worth
Negotiations of Subjectivity in the Life Narrative of a Female Labourer
Studia Fennica Ethnologica 16
2014

Studia Fennica Folkloristica

Pertti J. Anttonen
Tradition through Modernity
Postmodernism and the Nation-State in Folklore Scholarship
Studia Fennica Folkloristica 15
2005

Narrating, Doing, Experiencing
Nordic Folkloristic Perspectives
Edited by Annikki Kaivola-Bregenhøj, Barbro Klein & Ulf Palmenfelt
Studia Fennica Folkloristica 16
2006

Mícheál Briody
The Irish Folklore Commission 1935–1970
History, ideology, methodology
Studia Fennica Folkloristica 17
2008

Venla Sykäri
Words as Events
Cretan Mantinádes in Performance and Composition
Studia Fennica Folkloristica 18
2011

Hidden Rituals and Public Performances
Traditions and Belonging among the Post-Soviet Khanty, Komi and Udmurts
Edited by Anna-Leena Siikala & Oleg Ulyashev
Studia Fennica Folkloristica 19
2011

Mythic Discourses
Studies in Uralic Traditions
Edited by Frog, Anna-Leena Siikala & Eila Stepanova
Studia Fennica Folkloristica 20
2012

Studia Fennica Historica

Medieval History Writing and Crusading Ideology
Edited by Tuomas M. S. Lehtonen & Kurt Villads Jensen with Janne Malkki and Katja Ritari
Studia Fennica Historica 9
2005

Moving in the USSR
Western anomalies and Northern wilderness
Edited by Pekka Hakamies
Studia Fennica Historica 10
2005

Derek Fewster
Visions of Past Glory
Nationalism and the Construction of Early Finnish History
Studia Fennica Historica 11
2006

Modernisation in Russia since 1900
Edited by Markku Kangaspuro & Jeremy Smith
Studia Fennica Historica 12
2006

Seija-Riitta Laakso
Across the Oceans
Development of Overseas Business Information Transmission 1815–1875
Studia Fennica Historica 13
2007

Industry and Modernism
Companies, Architecture and Identity in the Nordic and Baltic Countries during the High-Industrial Period
Edited by Anja Kervanto Nevanlinna
Studia Fennica Historica 14
2007

Charlotta Wolff
Noble conceptions of politics in eighteenth-century Sweden (ca 1740–1790)
Studia Fennica Historica 15
2008

Sport, Recreation and Green Space in the European City
Edited by Peter Clark, Marjaana Niemi & Jari Niemelä
Studia Fennica Historica 16
2009

Rhetorics of Nordic Democracy
Edited by Jussi Kurunmäki & Johan Strang
Studia Fennica Historica 17
2010

Fibula, Fabula, Fact
The Viking Age in Finland
Edited by Joonas Ahola & Frog with Clive Tolley
Studia Fennica Historica 18
2014

Studia Fennica Anthropologica

On Foreign Ground
Moving between Countries and Categories
Edited by Marie-Louise Karttunen & Minna Ruckenstein
Studia Fennica Anthropologica 1
2007

Beyond the Horizon
Essays on Myth, History, Travel and Society
Edited by Clifford Sather & Timo Kaartinen
Studia Fennica Anthropologica 2
2008

Studia Fennica Linguistica

Minimal reference
The use of pronouns in Finnish and Estonian discourse
Edited by Ritva Laury
Studia Fennica Linguistica 12
2005

Antti Leino
On Toponymic Constructions as an Alternative to Naming Patterns in Describing Finnish Lake Names
Studia Fennica Linguistica 13
2007

Talk in interaction
Comparative dimensions
Edited by Markku Haakana, Minna Laakso & Jan Lindström
Studia Fennica Linguistica 14
2009

Planning a new standard language
Finnic minority languages meet the new millennium
Edited by Helena Sulkala & Harri Mantila
Studia Fennica Linguistica 15
2010

Lotta Weckström
Representations of Finnishness in Sweden
Studia Fennica Linguistica 16
2011

Terhi Ainiala, Minna Saarelma & Paula Sjöblom
Names in Focus
An Introduction to Finnish Onomastics
Studia Fennica Linguistica 17
2012

Studia Fennica Litteraria

Changing Scenes
Encounters between European and Finnish Fin de Siècle
Edited by Pirjo Lyytikäinen
Studia Fennica Litteraria 1
2003

Women's Voices
Female Authors and Feminist Criticism in the Finnish Literary Tradition
Edited by Päivi Lappalainen & Lea Rojola
Studia Fennica Litteraria 2
2007

Metaliterary Layers in Finnish Literature
Edited by Samuli Hägg, Erkki Sevänen & Risto Turunen
Studia Fennica Litteraria 3
2008

Aino Kallas
Negotiations with Modernity
Edited by Leena Kurvet-Käosaar & Lea Rojola
Studia Fennica Litteraria 4
2011

The Emergence of Finnish Book and Reading Culture in the 1700s
Edited by Cecilia af Forselles & Tuija Laine
Studia Fennica Litteraria 5
2011

Nodes of Contemporary Finnish Literature
Edited by Leena Kirstinä
Studia Fennica Litteraria 6
2012

White Field, Black Seeds
Nordic Literacy Practices in the Long Nineteenth Century
Edited by Anna Kuismin & M. J. Driscoll
Studia Fennica Litteraria 7
2013

Lieven Ameel
Helsinki in Early Twentieth-Century Literature
Urban Experiences in Finnish Prose Fiction 1890–1940
Studia Fennica Litteraria 8
2014

www.ingramcontent.com/pod-product-compliance
Lightning Source LLC
Chambersburg PA
CBHW080752300426
44114CB00020B/2704